Hotel Management and Operations

Hotel Management and Operations

Edited by

Denney G. Rutherford, Ph.D.

Associate Professor
Washington State University

 VAN NOSTRAND REINHOLD
New York

Library of Congress Catalog Card Number 88-34343
ISBN 0-442-20534-1

Printed in the United States of America

Cover: Photo courtesy of H.O.K. Architects.

Van Nostrand Reinhold
115 Fifth Avenue
New York, New York 10003

Van Nostrand Reinhold International Company Limited
11 New Fetter Lane
London EC4P 4EE, England

Van Nostrand Reinhold
480 La Trobe Street
Melbourne, Victoria 3000, Australia

Nelson Canada
1120 Birchmount Road
Scarborough, Ontario M1K 5G4, Canada

16 15 14 13 12 11 10 9 8 7 6 5 4 3 2 1

Libary of Congress Cataloging-in-Publication Data

Hotel management and operations: [readings / compiled by]
    Denney G. Rutherford.
        p.   cm.
    Includes bibliographies and index.
    ISBN 0-442-20534-1
    1. Hotel management.   I. Rutherford, Denney G.,
1942– .
    TX911.3.M27H663   1989
      647'.94'068—dc19   88-34343
                                                  CIP

This book on hotel department operations is proudly dedicated to those graduates of ours who are now departmental managers and above. Like every educator's successful students, they make us look good. Here's to you guys: Denise, Jeff, John L., Stephanie, Kim, Janet, Nina, Steve, Bruce, Sandra, Patti, Walt, Rob, Tatiana, Frank, Fred, Janet J., Loren, Rick U., Ann Marie, Harley, and all the rest of you out there. Keep up the good work!

Contents

Preface

This textbook project was born out of a range of frustrations. While there are many outstanding textbooks in the hotel management field that deal with significant portions of operations—particularly housekeeping, front office, and food and beverage—there are very few, if any, up-to-date books that try to treat in a balanced and in-depth way each department in the hotel. One frustration was that some texts that dealt with these departments spent an inordinate amount of time focused on one aspect of hotel operations—usually either front of the house or food and beverage. Other departments, for better or worse, were treated as minor players. Consequently, students and readers of such texts were given only a cursory introduction to the intricacies of that department, its management, its people, and its interactive function in the overall hotel organization.

Another frustration I encountered was using currently available material to promote the idea of critical thinking among students of hotel administration. By critical thinking I refer to that process whereby the student is exposed to a number of different viewpoints within a theoretical structure. From analysis of those viewpoints, he or she becomes better able to synthesize a viewpoint about hotel operations that will enable him or her to approach intelligently whatever practical situations may confront them in the "real world."

There is a conventional wisdom that goes "something may be okay in theory but it doesn't work in practice." Like economist Milton Friedman, I reject that statement. If theory doesn't work in practice, it is lousy theory. What professors need to guide students in understanding is that theory (in the words of Friedman) explains, predicts, or controls, and it does this in different ways given different variables in different organizations. This is another issue or frustration that this book is designed to address; by gaining an appreciation for what a *variety* of observers, thinkers, researchers, and commentators think about a topic, a student can feel better prepared to find ways to apply theory in a practical setting or situation.

BOOK ORGANIZATION

The book is divided into a number of sections, each section dealing with a specific department or hotel organizational activity. At the outset of the book is an introduction and overview with appropriate editorial comments, some basic organizational theory, and a section on general managers. General managers are included as a separate section here in order that students may gain some insights into that job which is at the apex of every hotel organization.

Each succeeding section deals with a separate department. The suggested readings relative to these departments have been chosen to illustrate the mission of the department; the personnel of the department; issues of management in the department; and (in some cases) interdepartmental relations and issues.

Each section is preceded by introductory material written by the author. These segments are meant to be used by the instructor as readings for the students. These represent a synthesis and overview of my observations, study, and research about hotel organizations. In some cases you will find my editorial comments to be controversial. In some cases you will find areas with which you may disagree. It is so intended. This is a dynamic and rapidly changing industry. In many ways hotel organizations are adapting to meet new market and operational realities. To do this effectively and successfully, hotels are going to be experimenting with a lot of new ideas. My purpose in these introductory comments, in addition to providing the overview, is to float some "trial balloons" of potential new ideas.

HOW TO USE THIS BOOK

Readings from the various sections of the book should be chosen in such a manner that the instructor will best present the material according to his or her course plan. In most cases, not all of the readings will be valuable or pertinent to every instructor's course outline. Additionally, at the end of each section I have compiled Suggested Readings, which serve to enhance either in breadth or depth, and in some cases both, a student's knowledge and understanding about the material in that section. Typically, I will assign some of the Suggested Readings for the single purpose of getting students into the library and looking through industry-related research, trade journals, and books.

Another specific technique in this regard is to add readings of your own choosing, especially topical, popular, or business literature. These can be stories that compare or contrast the way "theory" plays out in the real world. It also gives the instructor the opportunity to "customize" these sections to his or her specific requirements.

CASE STUDIES

The reader will note that each section does not have a case study. This is deliberate, for a couple of reasons. First, typical students at this level are not fully versed in the "case method," and this is a course and a book that does not necessarily lend itself to the form of case analysis as practiced in upper-division and graduate school classes. The other reason is that most issues that face any given department manager in a hotel organization are significantly interrelated to other departments.

The cases presented here are designed to be most successfully attacked in a multidimensional way. In other words, the student who does the best job of "solving" these cases will be the one who thinks critically about the issues involved, not only how they relate to the primary character in the case, but how that central character may have to utilize the other resources of the hotel and its departments to address his or her problem.

A simple analytical framework for cases such as these follows the model that normally goes:

- What are the problems?
- What are the facts?
- Who are the important players?
- What are the potential solutions?
- Based on analysis of the above, the student is asked to take a stand and from among the list of potential solutions, choose one that is most likely to result in a useful solution.

Using this model, there is no "right" answer. The instructor is free to judge the quality of the student's work based on variables such as analytic ability; use of resources; demonstration of understanding of departmental and managerial roles; and so forth.

GUEST SPEAKERS

I generally use two or three guest speakers per term in my class. I have some tried-and-true "designated hitters" who will always respond, and I know from experience that they are outstanding lecturers who bring to classes such as this an excitement and affection for the industry that is truly inspiring to students. I also have sought out and used on a special basis people with very narrowly defined roles who serve to illustrate one emerging topic or issue. The cautions here are to avoid overloading the class with guest speakers because in the final analysis, most of these people are not pedagogically trained in instructional processes. As a result, they can sometimes have difficulty getting their points across. I should add, however, that at no time in my experience in the classroom has a guest speaker ever significantly contradicted what I have been asking the students to learn. It has never been an issue. One hotel may run a front office a little bit differently than another hotel, but from the standpoint of adhering to a "theoretical structure," there has never been a problem.

One technique that we have used with success is to encourage the students (as part of what may be an extra-credit process) to assemble a panel of managers from among their friends or employers. These people will be charged with addressing one specific issue of interest to the entire class. This gives the students some experience in, first of all, talking with managers; second, coordinating and defining a specific event; and third, leading a discussion toward some agreed-upon goal. This has been a very popular event in our educational term, and every year we look forward to those times when the students can effectively take over a class period and actively participate and contribute to the learning process.

PEDAGOGICAL TECHNIQUES

The use of a resource book such as this lends itself to creating a classroom environment built around a very simple outline:

- *Mission of the department.* How does this department fit in the big picture of the hotel's organization?
- *People.* Who are the personnel? What are the jobs? What are the opportunities? What are the good and bad points of work in this department? What are the practical realities in this department?
- *Interactions.* How does this department connect to other departments in the hotel? Which are the departments that it is closest to? Which departments does it not interact with on a regular basis?
- *Management.* Who are the managers of this department? What is the career track for these people? Where do they go from here? What are the major issues they face in managing this department?

Utilizing a book of readings as a resource for a classroom structure such as this allows the instructor to ask a lot of "compare and contrast" questions and explore an issue in some depth. An example would be a discussion about policies of overbooking in the front office or reservations departments. There may be a number of critical issues that are involved here in playing off the various authors' and researchers' ideas. Involving the students in this sort of dialogue allows them to debate the issue in a way that enhances the learning process rather than simply memorizing a list of facts and figures and regurgitating it back on an objective exam.

This sort of material also lends itself to essay-type test questions. However, those who prefer objective examinations can construct numerous test items from each reading assigned.

CONCLUSION

This book has been designed and assembled to provide a broad range of thinking, research, and commentary about contemporary issues in the management of modern hotel departments. If you have suggestions that may improve future editions of this book, please feel free to contact me directly.

Personally, I am looking forward to the day when I check into your hotel, and when you as general manager are perusing recent check-ins, see my name and say, "That's the guy who wrote that book." I hope we can find the time to talk about hospitality careers and dreams. Best of luck wherever your futures take you in this dynamic, exciting, and rewarding industry.

Acknowledgments

No project of this scope is ever completed successfully by one individual. I would very much like to acknowledge and thank those who have assisted, advised, and consulted with me on this book.

First of all, recognition should go to the authors of the various articles included here who have contributed their thoughts, research, ideas, opinions, and expertise to this exercise in critical thinking about hotel departmental operations. Without the rich mixture of interest and talent extant in the hospitality profession and its educational establishment today, this collection of readings would not have been possible.

Our departmental secretary, Diane Iverson, labored mightily with my dictation, deadlines, and editorial style. She always did it with good cheer and in a very helpful fashion.

Helen Stevens and her crew in the Word Processing Center, John Porter, Lorie Mochel, and Ann Nelson, had the task of transcribing the various articles from their journal formats to a standard form suitable for publication in this book. They did an outstanding job of this and also of presenting tables and figures and organizing references and citations in an easily accessible form.

My mother, Thelma Rutherford, did great work in the tedious process of editing and proofing the typed articles. Similarly, Katherine Ault, my sophomore high school English teacher, demonstrated how far a teacher's influence can extend by still being willing and available to double-check my grammar, punctuation, spelling, and style.

The support of Terry Umbreit, David Whitney, and Rom Markin needs also to be acknowledged, as does the editorial assistance of Judy Joseph and her staff at Van Nostrand Reinhold.

Without the assistance of the professionals listed above, this book would still be an unrealized collection of thoughts and articles. I hope everyone who embarks on similar activities has the great good fortune to be assisted as I have been in this regard.

Contributors

James Abbey, University of Nevada

Roy Alvarez, School of Hotel Administration, Cornell University

Mario J. Arnaldo, Philippine Airlines

Rick Bechtel, Cole and Weber

Florence Berger, Cornell University

William J. Corney, University of Nevada

Jacques C. Cossé, Hilton Hotels Corporation

David Dann, Hong Kong Polytechnic

Stanley W. Davis, Cornell University

Jerry Dunn, Freelance Writer

Robert W. Eder, Washington State University

Dennis H. Ferguson, School of Hotel Administration, Cornell University

Myrle Finn

A. Neal Geller, Cornell University

W. Gerald Glover, Michigan State University

Wayne C. Guyette, University of New Orleans

Bjorn Hanson, Laventhol & Horwath

Timothy Hornsey, South Devon College of Arts and Technology

Richard M. Howey, Pennsylvania State University

Allen W. Hubsch, Hotel Corporation of America

Holly Hughes, Managing Editor, *Successful Meetings*

John G. Kaiser, Summa Four, Manchester, New Hampshire

Samad Karkouti, Georgia State University

William E. Kent, Georgia State University

Lothar A. Kreck, Washington State University

Inge Krieg, Los Angeles Bonaventure

Daniel R. Lee, Drexel Burnham Lambert

Robert C. Lewis, University of Massachusetts

David A. Ley, University of New Hampshire

Robert J. Martin, University of Nevada

Jon P. McConnell, Washington State University

Susan V. Morris, Marriott Hotel in Toronto

Geoffrey A. Parker, Georgia State University

James R. Pickworth, University of Guelph

Robert L. Plunkett, Cornell University

Leo M. Renaghan, Pennsylvania State University

Louis B. Richmond, Seattle Sheraton Hotel and Towers

Denney G. Rutherford, Washington State University

Jeffrey D. Schaffer, Virginia Polytechnic Institute and State University

William J. Schill, University of Washington

Raymond S. Schmidgall, Michigan State University

Affiliations correspond to the time of publication of individual articles.

Hans J. Schnitzler, Registry Hotel Corporation
Patti J. Shock, Georgia State University
Rex S. Toh, Seattle University
David A. Troy, TIMA Corporation
Leigh Tunney
Denise Turk

W. Terry Umbreit, Washington State University
William J. Wasmuth, Cornell University
David L. Whitney, Washington State University
Jane Wiegenstein, Washington State University
Glenn Withiam, *Cornell H.R.A. Quarterly*

SECTION 1

Overview

INTRODUCTION

The vast majority of research articles and essays in this book deal with one or more aspects of what has been called the "art and science" of modern hotel management. It should be noted that the word *modern* can signal an expression that is loaded with the potential of much misunderstanding. Hotels are changing and will continue to change. As a result, the techniques of management of modern hotels have to adapt to changing circumstances. When modern hotel organizations are discussed in a later section, we will confront some of the issues that dictate and influence this change.

INFLUENCES

Like many other American businesses, hotels have been affected by shifts in emphasis among the country's *living patterns*. People and industry have moved from the so-called Rust Belt to the Sun Belt. There has been a concentration of hotel activities in reborn and reconstructed central cities. This can be contrasted with the boom in suburban and interstate highway interchange hotel and motel construction of the 1950s and 1960s.

Demographics also play a role in this regard and will continue to do so in the foreseeable future. As the "baby boom" generation and its children mature, the population of the country will for many years be older, healthier, and more well educated than previous generations. These facts will present new challenges and opportunities to all business managers.

Technology, in the form of computers and labor-saving mechanical equipment, has had and will have a major effect on the way in which hotels are managed and operated.

The concept of *market segmentation*—ever-increasingly finely tuned market definitions—will dictate hotel structures, organizations, and management tactics that are designed to pay particular attention to those market segments.

The well-documented change in the complexion of the *national economy*—from one that emphasizes goods to one that emphasizes services—has kindled a number of new ideas about the way in which we manage the design and delivery of these services. Hotels, restaurants, and travel services are now seen as unique entities that dictate special kinds of managerial techniques and strategies.

Changes in people's *travel patterns* have also altered the way in which we manage our hotel properties. Deregulation of the airlines, with the "hub/

spoke" design of airline services, has changed the way millions of people travel each year. Many hotel companies are now locating major hotel properties adjacent to hub air-transport facilities, taking advantage of the fact that business travelers may not need to travel to a central business district (CBD) to accomplish their purposes in a given area. Meetings and conferences can now be scheduled within a five-minute limousine ride from the air terminal, and the business traveler can be back on the plane for his or her next destination before the day is over, without having had to stay overnight in a CBD hotel.

New *patterns of investment* in hotel facilities have emerged in the last two decades, and more attention is now paid to achieving optimum return on investment. Because people from outside the hotel industry are now participating in the financial structuring of the hotel industry, hotel operations are no longer dependent on the vision of a single entrepreneur. Managements now have to design tactics and strategies to achieve heretofore unanticipated financial goals. This has also altered the complexion of management of the modern hotel.

Changes in the way hotels were structured and organized were originally prompted by the visions of the people (usually men) who led the companies. Due to the reasons cited above, hotel structure and organization is now a product of careful analysis and consideration by a broader range of people than in the past.

Lee's article on the growth of four hotel giants provides some insights into the processes and progression of four very familiar names in the hotel industry. There are other stories, to be sure, but these illustrate in a broad sense typical developments of hotel and other lodging companies and their organizations from their founding in the heyday of the entrepreneur to their emergence in the modern era.

How They Started: The Growth of Four Hotel Giants

Daniel R. Lee

This is the story of four hotel chains—Hilton, Holiday Inns, Marriott, and Ramada. As with any story, though, more is involved than just four persons or four single companies. The Hilton we know today is the end product of a merger between the old Hilton and Statler chains, and the spinoff of Hilton International. The Holiday Inns company of today is the result of a series of acquisitions and divestitures. Marriott is a diverse company that branched out from food and lodging to cruise lines and amusement parks. Ramada, too, has branched out from its early position as a group of roadside hotels to a company encompassing upscale operations and gaming.

But these descriptions are the *end* of the stories. Treating the chains in alphabetical order, let us *start* with Conrad Hilton's purchase of a small hotel in Texas, early in this century.

HILTON: BUSINESSMAN DELUXE

In 1919, Conrad Hilton traveled to Cisco, Texas (east of Abilene), to buy a bank and cash in on the profits of the oil boom then under way. As it turned out, the bank operators wanted too much for their business to suit Hilton. But Cisco was a small town with a great many oil workers, and Hilton noted with great interest that the local rooming houses were prospering. Hilton changed his plans and convinced his partners to buy a hotel, the Mobley, which Hilton described as "a cross between a flophouse and a gold mine" (Hilton 1957, 109). Hilton's assessment of the hotel's financial promise was correct, and he was able to rent rooms to local workers in eight-hour shifts. (Ironically, the banking business turned sour when the price of oil dropped

This article was originally published in the May 1985 issue of *The Cornell Hotel and Restaurant Administration Quarterly*, and is reprinted here with the permission of the Cornell University School of Hotel Administration. © 1985.

from $3.00 to $1.00 a barrel, diminishing the collateral for many banks' loans.)

At the Hotel Mobley, Hilton instituted many of the policies that would make him successful in later years. Among these was the imaginative use of all the space in the hotel to produce revenue. For instance, Hilton converted a banquet room to more sleeping rooms. (Later, he tucked restaurants and rental stores into little-used nooks and crannies of the Plaza, Palmer House, and Waldorf-Astoria.)

Hilton's greatest strengths were his financial ability and his negotiating savvy. In the beginning, he knew little about food preparation and did not concern himself with the niceties of first-class service. The profits from the Mobley were plowed into acquisition of other hotels; Hilton owned or controlled eight by 1930, most of them in Texas, although he had bought and sold several other operations along the way.

The Great Bust

Hilton's hotels were generally financed with medium-term balloon notes, often for 100 percent of the purchase price, a common practice in the 1920s. The theory at the time was similar to that applied to farmland in the 1870s—the real estate would appreciate sufficiently to secure later payments. When the economy collapsed, however, travel almost ceased, and real estate prices plunged. Like many others, Hilton defaulted on his payments and his hotels were repossessed.

But Hilton's largest creditor had apparently gained respect for Hilton's ability to run a hotel and hired him to operate the foreclosed hotels. By 1939, Hilton had managed to reassume control or ownership of five of his eight hotels, and he was ready to expand again. Armed with financing, Hilton was able to bid for large, luxurious properties at Depression-era prices.

The Drake

In 1937, Hilton bought the $4-million Sir Francis Drake in San Francisco for $275,000 cash plus the assumption of a reduced first mortgage of $1.5 million. Next he purchased and rebuilt the Breakers at Long Beach, a resort that had been closed when an earthquake cracked its foundation. It had cost $1.5 million to build; Hilton paid $171,000 for it and spent a similar amount to repair the facility. He also started to acquire mortgage bonds for the Stevens in Chicago, then the world's largest hotel (2,600 rooms). He sold the Sir Francis Drake in 1940 at a profit of $500,000, which he used to buy the Town House in Los Angeles.

Hilton had to wait for the Stevens, because the military took it over during World War II, paying off the mortgage bonds at par. With some of his profits on the bonds, Hilton in 1943 purchased two New York City properties, the Roosevelt (then a fashionable hotel adjacent to Grand Central Station) and the Plaza. Hilton was not yet satisfied, though; he wanted to own the greatest hotel of its day, the Waldorf-Astoria.

During the early 1940s, Hilton gradually purchased the mortgage bonds of the Waldorf at depressed prices (as low as a nickel on the dollar). The hotel business was difficult during the war. Although hotel rooms were filled, the competition of scarce materials and labor had driven up costs, and price controls limited profits. Still, Hilton was convinced that the economy would boom after the war.

But Hilton had to wait for the Waldorf, too. The war ended, and the military released the Stevens. Trying to buy the property, Hilton was outbid by a Chicago contractor, and his own offers were refused. As a negotiating tactic, he turned his attention to bidding for the Palmer House, Chicago's "Waldorf." The ploy was successful—too successful; Hilton left Chicago owning both the Palmer House and the Stevens (later renamed the Conrad Hilton).

New York Stock Exchange

In 1946, the Hilton chain was still a group of individual businesses owned by different partnerships. Hilton wanted to capitalize on the name and reputation of these first-class hotels, so he reorganized most of them into a public corporation. In 1947, Hilton Hotels Corporation became the first hotel company to be listed on the New York Stock Exchange.

Ironically, the switch to a publicly held company nearly cost Hilton his dream of owning the Waldorf-Astoria. In 1949, when he made his move, the Waldorf had been a steady money-loser, and the board of directors to which he was now accountable considered the purchase too risky. So Hilton formed a separate partnership (the corporation was one of the partners) to purchase the Waldorf's equity for $4.5 million. By 1952, the hotel was in the black, and the partnership had sold the hotel back to the corporation. The Waldorf has since been one of Hilton's consistent success stories.

As the economy boomed in the early 1950s, Hilton prospered. He purchased the Hotel New Yorker (then the world's third largest) and leased the Deshler-Hilton in Columbus, Ohio. He sold the Plaza and the Town House. He purchased the Shamrock Hotel in Houston and unexpectedly found oil on the property.

Competitors

Hilton was not the only company to assemble a hotel chain, however. In the 1940s, it faced a number of competitors. Archrival Sheraton operated 16 hotels in the U.S. and five in Canada. (In 1982, Sheraton still had more rooms than Hilton.) The Pick Hotels Corporation (now a part of Americana) owned 21 hotels in 19 cities. Knott Hotels was a strong presence in New York City, operating 11 hotels there and 11 in other cities. (The firm had dwindled to six hotels by 1975, when it was purchased by Trusthouse Forte.) Milner Hotels had more than

200 small hotels throughout the country, and still operates ten of those aging hotels today. Hilton's biggest competitor, however, was Statler Hotels Corporation, which had been built by the country's premier hotel operator, Ellsworth Statler. The accompanying box tells the story of how Statler built his hotel chain, and how his widow, Alice Statler, continued its operation for nearly 30 years after his death.

Merger

By 1954, Alice Statler was ready to relinquish the operation of her late husband's hotel chain; no heir-apparent was in sight. When Hilton heard rumors that the company might be for sale, he was ready to try for it, but real estate developer William Zeckendorf was first in the door with an offer of $111 million. The Statler company announced tentative acceptance of the Zeckendorf offer.

The word "tentative" meant that the door was still open a crack, and Hilton stuck his foot in that crack. He flew to New York to meet with Alice Statler, praising her operations of the hotel chain, assuring her that he would maintain both its standards and its name if he were to acquire it, and matching Zeckendorf's $111 million offer. She finally

---

Statler: America's First Hotelier

Ellsworth M. Statler differed in many ways from the man who eventually owned his hotel chain. Hilton was a successful banker who entered the hotel business at 31 almost by accident; Statler was carrying bags in the Hotel McLure (in Wheeling, West Virginia) at the age of 13. Hilton acquired his chain through negotiation and the purchase of financially distressed properties; Statler built his hotels from scratch. Hilton's hotels encompassed a hodgepodge of styles and quality levels; Statler's hotels were boringly similar in name, style, and size. Hilton tried to finish his business day at 6:00 P.M. and loved to dance into the evening; Statler was undeniably a workaholic.

Statler's first hotel was a large, temporary structure built for the 1901 Pan American Exposition in Buffalo, New York. The exposition, colored by the assassination of President William McKinley, was a commercial failure, but Statler was able to turn a small profit on his venture. He used this money to build another temporary hotel—this time for St. Louis's Louisiana Purchase Exposition of 1904, a more successful fair. Statler liquidated this hotel with a profit of $361,000 (enormous for its day).

Modern convenience. A keystone of Statler's success was his attention to contemporary amenities. His first permanent hotel, built in Buffalo in 1908, featured a bathroom in every guest room, running ice water, telephones, electric light switches by the door, and other innovations. The private bathrooms alone revolutionized the industry, leaving most existing hotels outmoded.*

A major innovation credited to Statler is the plumbing chase (now a commonplace of high-rise construction), a vertical corridor for pipes and other utilities. The plumbing chase allowed Statler to offer a room with a bath at a competitive rate ($1.50). By 1927, Statler had hotels in Cleveland, Detroit, St. Louis, and New York City, where he built the 2,200-room Pennsylvania Hotel (across from Penn Station, now the New York Penta), the largest hotel of its day.

Carrying on. Statler died unexpectedly in 1928, but his widow, Alice Seidler Statler, continued the expansion of his hotel chain. Through tight cost controls and conservative financing, she was able to keep the hotel company solvent during the Depression (making it virtually the only major hotel company to avoid default).

Alice Statler operated the hotel chain until 1954, when she sold the chain to Conrad Hilton.

*Floyd Miller, *Statler: America's Extraordinary Hotelman* (New York: Statler Foundation, 1968).

agreed to tender to Hilton the 42 percent of the company's stock she controlled, and Zeckendorf was out the door before he even knew he had competition.

Expansion Abroad

Hilton's acquisition of the Statler chain was at the time the largest private real estate transaction in history. Statler's 10,400 rooms were merged with Hilton's 16,200; the company's operating earnings rose from $4.8 million in 1954 to $9.6 million in 1956. But this was not the only expansion opportunity Hilton pursued. He had long operated, under a management contract, a small hotel in Chihuahua, Mexico (the Palacio Hilton). The boom that followed the war witnessed a strong U.S. dollar, American travelers ready to venture overseas, and greatly improved air travel. At the same time, many of Europe's hotels had been destroyed, giving U.S. hotel companies an opening for expansion. Hilton did not want to own real estate overseas, however. He decided to expand internationally by providing his company's design, name, and management expertise to local owners—giving the company a significant growth vehicle with virtually no investment.

The arrangement was popular. Hilton International opened its first hotel in San Juan, Puerto Rico, in 1949. Its great success encouraged similar hotel arrangements in Madrid, Istanbul, and Mexico City, among others. By 1964, Hilton International operated 29 hotels in 22 countries.

Despite his business acumen, Hilton was late to take advantage of one of this century's great lodging opportunities, the one wrought by changes in travel modes. Heavily involved in overseas operation and the acquisition of the Statler chain, Hilton failed to jump into the new marketplace of roadside, airport, and suburban hotels created by the rise of the interstate highway system and of air travel in the mid-1950s. Almost all of Hilton's hotels were in center-city locations, often near train stations. People were traveling less by train and more by air, however; as a result, business trips could often be accomplished in one day. Hotels near train stations found business dropping off, as fewer travelers took an overnight room near the train station. The adage of "location, location, location" found new meaning, as the ideal hotel locations shifted dramatically.

Hilton eventually did start opening roadside and airport hotels, but rather than abandon the center-city hotels, he embraced the growing market for meetings and conventions as a replacement for individual business travelers.

Carte Blanche

Another disappointment was created by Hilton's foray into the credit card business. Prior to 1958, hotel companies issued their own credit cards to their patrons (as department stores still do today), but Hilton tried to capitalize on its nearly 1,000,000 card holders by selling 66 percent of its credit subsidiary to the public and seeking agreements with car rental firms and other vendors to accept the card. The logic of this move may have been sound, but the competition (American Express and Diners Club) was strong, and other hotel chains would not honor the card. Hilton eventually sold the card (now known as Carte Blanche) to Citibank, which in turn sold it to Avco Corporation. Hilton received Avco shares for this transaction (and a $20 million profit when Textron recently acquired Avco). Although the credit card business was not successful for Hilton, the financial results of its credit card transaction have been favorable.

New Generation

By the late 1950s, Barron Hilton, Conrad's second son, had become vice-president of Hilton Hotels (although he reportedly once turned down an offer of employment from his father because the pay was too little). Nick Hilton, Barron's elder brother, was chairman of the executive committee of Hilton International. The presence of the two brothers in one company, together with the fear that Hilton might be taken over by a conglomerate, may have been a factor in one of Conrad Hilton's more questionable business decisions—one that eventually created a new domestic competitor and has hindered Hilton's overseas operations for 20 years.

Spinoff

The Hilton International subsidiary was spun off in 1964 (and was indeed acquired—by TWA—in 1967). Nick Hilton became an officer of Hilton International, while Barron Hilton remained with the domestic company. Hilton domestic was forever banned from using the Hilton name overseas, while Hilton International agreed to choose a new name for any hotels it might build in the U.S. The company chose "Vista International" as its new name, and several U.S. hotels are now operating under that title.

Hilton Hotels continued growing in the U.S., and has recently returned to overseas operation, under the "Conrad International" name.

New Stance

Under Barron Hilton, the company shifted its emphasis from hotel ownership to management contracts and franchise agreements. The company retained the "family jewels," the now priceless downtown hotels, such as the Waldorf and the Palmer House. By 1970, Hilton owned or leased more than 25,000 rooms, managed another 10,000, and franchised nearly 8,000 rooms in the U.S.

Flamingo

In 1970, Barron Hilton made a deal that was as important to Hilton Hotels as his father's acquisition of the Statler chain. Hilton once sat on the board of directors of MGM, a company that was controlled by Kirk Kerkorian. Kerkorian operated the Flamingo, the oldest of the gambling casinos on the Las Vegas strip, and was building the new International Hotel in Las Vegas. Hilton quickly saw the revenue potential of gaming. When Kerkorian found his finances strained, Hilton resigned from the MGM board so he could buy part of the casino subsidiary

(International Leisure). Hilton Hotels ran the hotel portion of the business for a year, while learning the gaming business from its new partners. Shortly after, Hilton purchased the remaining interest in the casinos (Lee 1984). The investment has been a good one; the two casinos accounted for more than 35 percent of Hilton's operating income almost every year since their acquisition.

HOLIDAY INNS: REALIZING EXPECTATIONS

A long-time entrepreneur (popcorn, moviehouses, airplane rides, Wurlitzer distribution), Kemmons Wilson developed the idea for Holiday Inns as the result of what he called "the most miserable vacation trip of my life." Largely a cottage industry in the early 1950s, roadside lodges were of unpredictable quality and price. Wilson believed he had seen a great untouched opportunity. In 1952, near Memphis, Tennessee, he opened the first Holiday Inn, which featured large rooms, two double beds, a restaurant, and a swimming pool. It was an instant success, and continued operating at over 80 percent occupancy for more than 15 years (Lundberg 1969).

By 1954, Wilson had built three more inns in Memphis. These inns were distinguished from their competitors by more than a restaurant and large rooms. From the start, they were intended to appeal to families traveling by car. They were much larger than the typical operation (which usually had fewer than 30 rooms), and they were of consistent quality. Though some motels offered free TV at the time, Wilson went one better by promising free TV, free ice, and a telephone in every room. As a result, the Holiday Inns concept spread rapidly, outstripping Wilson's ability to raise capital. Holiday Inns began selling franchises in 1955, and the company went public in 1957.

Franchises were not a new idea, by any measure. Feudal nobility franchised its farmland; the oil, beverage, and automotive industries had long franchised distributorships. But Holiday Inns was one of the first companies to franchise motels, and it improved on the franchise idea by applying stricter operating standards than had previously been common among franchise companies.

Highways

The growth of Holiday Inns closely paralleled the growth of the interstate highway system, which often bypassed existing hotels, and created new lodging locations. From 1955 to 1974, the lodging firm and the highway system grew rapidly. Holiday Inns cannily sold its franchises for specific locations, rather than for geographical areas. When a new highway was built, therefore, a new franchise location was created, even in areas that had previously been considered saturated.

The company supplied its franchisees with almost everything but the land, and some clients even sought help with site selection. For a fee, Holiday Inns allowed the franchisee to choose among several designs, then built the building, and manufactured and delivered the furniture. Once the inn was open, Holiday Inns supplied soap, towels, and paper products from its centralized purchasing network. The company also supplied processed foods for the restaurants, and its large printing operation sold collateral material throughout the system.

Holidex

The company also benefited from its early use of marketing and reservation networks, which helped book new inns even before they were constructed. (Holidex II, the company's reservation system, accounted for as much as 30 percent of room-nights sold in 1982.)

Diversification

As the interstate highway system neared completion, and as the economic boom slowed in the 1970s, the company found itself with few motels waiting to be built. To maintain further growth, Holiday Inns attempted to diversify by purchasing Continental Trailways and Delta Steamships. Delta turned out to be profitable for the company until 1982, when international economic conditions and changes in U.S. subsidies threatened the steamship business. Holiday sold Delta to Crowley Maritime. The company had hoped the Trailways buses would provide additional customers for its inns. But in the face of deregulation and rising energy prices, Trailways was sold in 1979.

In 1969, Wilson made a decision that ultimately changed the company's direction, although not in the manner he might have anticipated. So that the company would own more of the hotels that bore its name, Wilson purchased 60 inns from two of its largest franchisees. In both transactions, however, the franchisees retained management contracts. As a result of these purchases, one of the franchise holders, Roy Winegardner, became the company's second-largest stockholder, after Wilson himself.

Changeover

Shortly after this transaction, the losses from Trailways and the reduced travel resulting from gasoline-price increases caused a 90-percent drop in the value of Holiday Inns stock. Wilson, who had been hoping to reduce his responsibilities, turned to Winegardner, who was willing to become chief executive officer to recoup his capital loss.

At this time, the integrated development system that had once been so profitable became a burden, largely because fewer new hotels were being constructed, and also because court rulings had released franchisees from the obligation of purchasing all supplies from the parent company. So Holiday Inns disposed of its furniture manufacturing, food-processing and printing businesses. Subsequently, franchisees were assisted with design only, not construction.

Instead of a diversified and vertically integrated motel-production company, Winegardner envisioned Holiday Inns as a hospitality company that would provide food, beverage, lodging, and related entertainment and communications services. The company began selling some hotels, updating others, and cutting off franchisees that could not meet upgraded standards. The mix of hotels was improved to balance roadside, airport, and downtown hotel locations. Holiday Inns purchased the Perkins restaurant chain and merged with Harrah's, the Nevada casino operator. It was at this point, in 1979, that Kemmons Wilson retired from the company, leaving Winegardner in charge.

Today, there are some 1,500 Holiday Inns in the U.S. and 215 overseas. The bulk of the firm's revenues (57 percent) still stem from its lodging system, but gaming interests in Nevada and New Jersey supplied 39 percent of operating income in 1982.

MARRIOTT: PERSONAL TOUCHES

In 1927, J. Willard Marriott arrived in Washington, D.C., to open one of the first A&W root-beer stands in the eastern U.S. Business was good that summer, but as the days shortened, Marriott realized that the root-beer business might not be so good in the colder months. To make up for the seasonal lag, Marriott decided to sell food, a violation of his A&W franchise agreement. First he won agreement from A&W to allow him, as a special case, to sell food (O'Brien 1977, 127). Then he chose to sell Mexican food—chile con carne and tamales, which were popular in the west and southwest—and changed the name of his stand to "Hot Shoppe." Despite its popularity in the west, Mexican food was little known in the east. Marriott enlisted the cooperative chef at the nearby Mexican embassy as a menu consultant, and the ingredients were ordered from a supplier in San Antonio, Texas.

Curb Cuts

The stock market crashed shortly afterward, but Marriott's location was a good one, and he and his wife Allie worked 16-hour days to make the Hot Shoppe succeed. As the New Deal started, Washington was prosperous in relation to the rest of the country. Soon there were six Hot Shoppes in Washington, and Marriott was expanding into Baltimore and Philadelphia. As an additional attraction to customers, he was among the first to offer drive-

up service (convincing reluctant zoning officials that his shop was little different from a gas station). To maintain his profits, he implemented strict financial controls, centralized food production with standard menus, and supplied his restaurants from a central commissary.

The Hot Shoppe near Hoover Field (relocated and renamed National Airport) provided Marriott with a chance to expand his business. In 1937, he had noticed that many travelers were stopping off at his stand before boarding airplanes. He proposed to Eastern Air Transport (now Eastern Airlines) that he prepare box lunches for its passengers. In so doing, he essentially invented the airline catering business.

While World War II slowed the company's growth, Marriott continued expanding through the 1950s, operating more than 90 Hot Shoppes by the end of the decade. In 1953, Hot Shoppes became a publicly held company.

Ice Cream

The Hot Shoppe adjacent to National Airport provided Marriott with another chance for diversification. In 1957, he attached 360 guest rooms to the restaurant. Now known as the Twin Bridges Marriott, it was noteworthy for its drive-up check-in window, where Marriott registered guests while Allie dished out ice-cream cones for children.

As coffeeshops gradually lost popularity, Marriott was able to expand his lodging business, while at the same time adapting the Hot Shoppe to other food concepts, Hot Shoppe Jr.'s (fast food) and Hot Shoppe Cafeterias. The importance of the lodging business grew, however, as that of the Hot Shoppes declined.

Expansion

In 1964, J.W. Marriott, Sr., curtailed his daily role in the company by appointing his son, J.W. (Bill) Marriott, Jr., to the presidency. The father retained his position as chairman of the board. Bill Marriott's expansion philosophy was less conservative than his father's, and the company began a rapid expansion of its restaurant business. In 1967, Marriott acquired the Big Boy chain and Farrell's ice-cream parlors. The company developed the Roy Rogers fast-food chain, expanding the Hot Shoppe Jr., and built dinner-houses under a number of names. The most recent restaurant expansion was in 1982, when Marriott purchased the Gino's fast-food chain and converted most of the restaurants to the Roy Rogers brand.

The company's expansion in the lodging business was even more pronounced. In 1970, Marriott operated 11 hotels, with 4,770 guest rooms. By the end of the decade, the company operated more than 100 hotels with 45,000 guest rooms.

Coasters and Cruisers

Marriott's expansion carried it into other businesses; the company purchased Sun Line cruiseships and opened two Great America amusement parks. The high cost of park development ($160 million) and strong competition slowed Marriott's opening of other parks, and the company ultimately spun off the Great America parks. Marriott views the cruiseships essentially as floating hotels and includes the Sun Line in its hotel division.

Ideals

Marriott is one of the few companies that does not operate hotels in Las Vegas or Atlantic City. Marriott company philosophies reflect the attitudes of its founding family. Devout Mormons, the Marriotts believe in hard work, honesty, and the value of the family unit. Gambling casinos seem to make a poor fit with that philosophy.

Marriott's 1982 operations embraced the hotel division, some 200 Big Boy restaurants, 365 Roy Rogers units, flight kitchens at 51 domestic airports and 22 international airports (the company served some 160,000 air meals in 1982), and contract food facilities at 140 corporate sites, 100 hospitals or nursing homes, and 20 colleges.

Singular

Although he differed with his father on the speed of expansion, Bill Marriott did not abandon his father's principle of central control of operations. As a result, virtually every operating detail is specified in large manuals, and decision-making is centralized at the regional or corporate level.

This adherence to standard operating procedures may sometimes represent a constraint to the unit manager, but it helps explain Marriott's reputation for consistency. If the food and beverage manager at an individual Hilton property, for instance, wants to change a menu, he or she might need only the approval of the property's general manager to do so. At Marriott, the impetus for a change would most likely come from the regional level. The regional food and beverage manager would ask Marriott headquarters to design a new menu using highly standardized recipes.

Marriott differs from other chains in three other ways. Its hotels are generally not unionized, the company deals with very few franchisees, and the company is a vertically integrated hotel-design and construction company (much as Holiday Inns and Ramada Inns were during their growth periods). Marriott has essentially been in the real estate development business; its specialists travel the country analyzing markets and locations for new hotels, rather than waiting for proposals by potential franchisees.

RAMADA: RETIREMENT OASIS

The Ramada chain constituted the second career of Marion Isbell, a Chicago restaurateur who sold his food service businesses in the 1950s. Still in his forties, Isbell retired to Arizona, but he was not content to remain idle. Soon he was building roadside motels around Phoenix and Flagstaff, using the name Ramada, which is Spanish for resting place or oasis.

By 1959, Isbell and his partners owned 14 motels and recognized the potential that was shown so clearly by the expansion of Holiday Inns. In 1962, the partners incorporated and started competing head-on with Holiday Inns, both chains growing with the interstate highway system. Like Holiday, Ramada established design, construction, and purchasing divisions, so that the company was essentially a one-stop shopping center for hotel developers and operators. Ramada would help potential franchisees find a site, propose designs for the building, and provide everything needed for operation from soap to a reservations network.

Ramada was also building inns on its own as fast as the highway system expanded and sites became available. By 1969, however, new sites were harder to find as the interstate system neared completion.

In the 1970s, Ramada expanded through the purchasing of existing hotels and resorts. The company attempted without great success to diversify into campground operation and car rental. For the first time, it moved out of the U.S. into Europe, where it now operates 11 inns. It also entered the field of hospital management in California by pooling its interests with Howard E. Johnson (no connection with orange roofs). With this transaction, Johnson became the vice-president of Ramada's hospital group.

When the rise in energy prices froze the tourism business in 1974, Marion Isbell's son, Bill Isbell, was just taking over company operations. Earnings fell from $15.3 million in 1973 to $1 million in 1975. Rather than continue attempts at expansion or diversification, the younger Isbell began streamlining the company, concentrating on the basic lodging and franchising business. The company refurbished its inns, and franchisees were encouraged to do the same. This improvement was well-timed; as the tourist business recovered, Ramada's sales outpaced the industry and earnings rebounded, reaching $17.5 million in 1980.

Gaming

Although his business was hospital management, Johnson was also familiar with the casino business. Apparently through Johnson's interest, Ramada became interested in operating a casino. Its first overture was to the Del Webb company, which operated the Mint and the Sahara in Las Vegas, as well as casinos in Reno, Lake Tahoe, and Laughlin (a small gambling area in southern Nevada), and had purchased a casino site in Atlantic City. Although Ramada purchased nearly 7 percent of Del Webb's stock, it was never given an expected seat on the company's board of directors. Consequently, it sold the stock (at a substantial profit).

Determined to become a gaming operator, Ramada purchased Atlantic City's defunct Ambassador Hotel, with the intention of renovating it. Unfortunately, Ramada's timing was poor. New Jersey officials had just decided to start encouraging new construction and discouraging renovation projects. Ramada was eventually able to refurbish the Ambassador, but between local government regulation and the corrosive effects of ocean air, the job entailed far more new construction and expense than originally anticipated.

While waiting for approval on the Ambassador, Ramada was encouraged by Nevada gaming officials to purchase the Tropicana, an elegant casino on the Las Vegas strip. Nevada regulators apparently hoped that Ramada's ownership would steady the fortunes of the Tropicana, which has had a checkered past.

Churning

Between 1976 and 1982, Ramada's lodging chain shrank by 35 percent. Some of the sales were prompted by the need for cash to enter the gaming business; other properties were spun off because they were not profitable. The investment in Atlantic City began to pay off in 1982, as the Tropicana-East (the erstwhile Ambassador) participated in the continuing boom there. Revenues from the New Jersey operation were greater than those of the entire hotel division in 1982. Ramada plans to continue updating its system by selling older hotels and building new properties.

MANAGEMENT CONTRACTS

Although these four hotel chains once pursued the ownership of hotels, recent figures show that all four have been moving away from property ownership in favor of managed hotel operations. The percentage of Hilton rooms owned by the company, for instance, dropped from about 33 percent in 1974 to less than 20 percent in 1983 (Provident National Bank 1985). Marriott's drop in ownership was even steeper; the company owned more than 50 percent of the rooms that bore its name in 1974, but by 1983, that figure was closer to 15 percent. During the same period, Ramada went from 20 percent room ownership to 10 percent, and Holiday Inns dropped from about 22 percent to just under 20 percent.

By far, Holiday still owned the most rooms in 1983, about 310,000, while Ramada, Hilton, and Marriott each owned fewer than 100,000.

References

Hilton, Conrad. 1957. *Be My Guest*. Englewood Cliffs, NJ: Prentice Hall.

Lee, Daniel R. 1984. Hotel casinos: Strong odds for growth. *Cornell Hotel and Restaurant Administration Quarterly* 25(3): 20–29.

Lundberg, Donald E. 1969. Kemmons Wilson. *Cornell Hotel and Restaurant Administration Quarterly* 9(4): 100–103.

O'Brien, Robert. 1977. *Marriott*. Salt Lake City: Deseret, 127.

Provident National Bank, Philadelphia. 1985. *Hotel and Motel Management* 200(2): 1.

Suggested Readings

Books

Gomes, Albert J. *Hospitality in Transition*. Houston: Pannell, Kerr, Forster Company, 1985.

Hilton, Conrad. *Be My Guest*. Englewood Cliffs, NJ: Prentice Hall, 1957.

Jarman, Rufus. *A Bed for the Night: The Story of the Wheeling Bell Boy, E. M. Statler, and His Remarkable Hotels*. New York: Harper & Row, 1952.

Article

Page, Gary S. "Pioneers and Leaders of the Hospitality Industry." In *Introduction to Hotel and Restaurant Management*, edited by Robert A. Brymer, 21–29. Dubuque, IA: Kendall/Hunt, 1984.

SECTION 2

Organization

INTRODUCTION

CLASSIC ORGANIZATION

In the organization of hotels in the United States at the turn of the twentieth century, the European classic hotel organization model was predominant. This structure was built around two major hotel managerial personalities: the chef and the maître d'hôtel. The chef was the chief or "king" of the kitchen. In many ways he represented a feudal lord on his estate who held sway over everything that had to do with preparation of food in the hotel. This structure recognized the importance of the role that food and its preparation played in the hotels of the time.

Similarly, the maître d'hôtel was the "master" of all service in the hotel and it was his responsibility to make sure that the interaction of the hotel's staff organization and the guest was managed in a way to ensure that the guest was always served promptly and properly and in line with the hotel's policy.

For many of the same reasons cited earlier as to why management of hotels has changed, hotel organization structures also have changed. As our knowledge of our guests and the markets they rep-

resent enlarged and became more precise, specializations within the hotel organizational structure grew to help the organization most effectively manage and deliver its services.

Stoner and Wankel (1986, 233–34) have said that the organizing process involves balancing a company's need for both stability and change. They go on to outline organizing as a multistep process based on that proposed by Dale (1967).

- Organizing details all of the work that must be done to attain the organization's goals.
- Organizing provides for dividing the total work performed into a group of activities that can be performed by one person or a group of people.
- Organizing combines the work of an organization's members in some logical and efficient manner.
- Organizing sets up a mechanism to coordinate the work of the organization members into a unified, harmonious whole.
- Organizing sets up a mechanism to monitor the effectiveness of how well the organization is achieving its goals.

In the modern hotel organization, a complex line and staff structure has emerged to reflect this theoretical organizing process.

Figure 1 depicts a typical organization chart for a large hotel. Note that with the exception of top managers, the other departments are identified by function rather than title. This is to indicate that in most modern hotel organizations we find job titles and their inherent duties varying from company to company. Looking at an organizational chart by function rather than by job title allows us to look at the organization from an industry-wide perspective.

Note also that in this chart the two major operating divisions have been identified as Rooms Division and Food and Beverage Division. Again, on a company-by-company basis individual functions may find homes in various divisions but basically hotel organizations are set up to deliver these two basic services to their guests, through either the sales of rooms and/or food and beverage.

What may differ in a given hotel company's organization are the placements of the other departments. The departments on this organization chart should not be considered exclusive or exhaustive but typical and illustrative of a hotel organization chart.

For purposes of illustration, the aforementioned "line" and "staff" functions are defined as follows:

Line Functions

These typically are hotel employees in organizational components who have regular or semiregular contact with the organization's guests. The line operations in a hotel organization are the Rooms Division and Food and Beverage Division. Obviously, some departmental functions within each line division will have more or less guest contact than others, depending on the nature of their jobs.

For instance, under most circumstances security people will not have much regular guest contact; housekeeping staff may have somewhat more guest contact, but in the Rooms Division, obviously the front office staff will have the vast majority of guest face-to-face contact.

Similarly, in the Food and Beverage Division, as a line division, the employees of the restaurant, bars, room service, and banquet departments will have a tremendous amount of face-to-face guest interaction, however only under special circumstances will the food-production staff under the hotel chef interact on anything but an irregular basis with the guests.

Staff Functions

These are generally those "behind-the-scenes" sorts of activities that support the line functions and under most circumstances have little or no guest contact, although major components of their jobs are to influence the quality of a guest's stay.

In the chart shown, for instance, engineering has been included as a staff function for those reasons. The success of the engineering function heavily influences the quality of the guest's stay and at the same time the other functions of the Engineering Department support the activities of almost every other department in the hotel.

For instance, the Engineering Department maintains and repairs equipment that is crucial to all of the hotel's line functions—from the food-production equipment in the kitchen, to the tables and chairs in the dining room, to the accounting machines, the furniture in the lobby, and the carts that the bellhops use to transport guests' luggage. Viewed from those perspectives, the Engineering Department can be considered a true staff department that serves and supports at any given time any or all of the other departments in the hotel.

Other typical hotel organization charts will place the Engineering Department in the Rooms Division. This may be because that is where engineering works best in that hotel's organization, or it may be only tradition.

This situation may also be true for other departments that in the past have been traditionally thought of as "rooms division" functions. Security is one example. In some organizations, housekeeping has been changed to a staff function rather than strictly rooms, for housekeeping by definition "keeps" the entire house.

FIGURE 1
Typical hotel organization chart

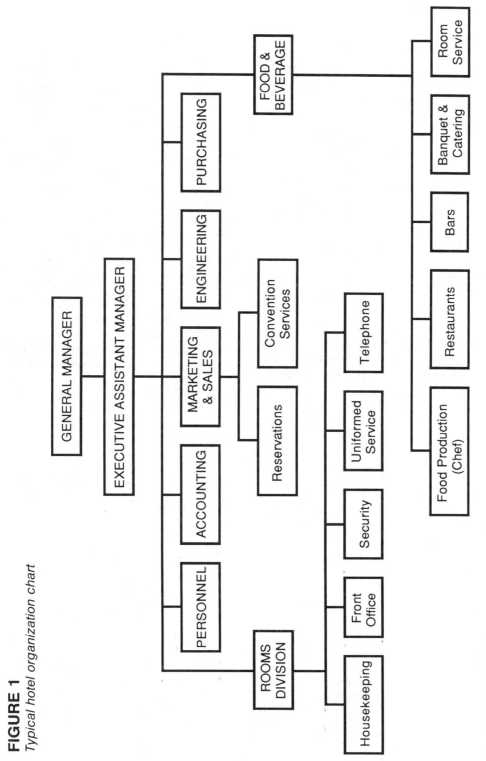

(graphics by P. & J. Mason)

Organizations for the Modern Era

Organizations, however, are more than just boxes and charts. The most modern business organization structures have not changed much in form since the Roman Catholic Church first designed the pyramidic structure as a visual depiction of organizational relationships with which we are so familiar today.

What does affect organizations, not so much in their pictorial view, but in the way in which the organization responds to external and internal stimuli, can be seen by analyzing several of the articles included here and the readings that are suggested at the end for further study.

Jeffrey Schaffer's article addresses the relationship of competitive strategy and organizational structure based on forces that exist within the market that particular hotel is designed to serve. These findings are based on empirical research with more than 100 lodging firms and support the theory of a strategic-choice model and the relationship among competitive strategy, structure, and the subsequent performance of the organization in serving its market.

Other views of the peculiar dynamics of hotel organizations involve the Dann and Hornsey analysis of the processes of conflict within a hotel organizational structure. Their discussion highlights the areas in which interdepartmental conflict can and does occur and offers a cogent and provocative explanation of the dynamics of such conflict.

Finally, the Glover article treats one of the pathologies of organizational life with a discussion of an inventory of organizational ineffectiveness characteristics.

While there exists no dearth of literature on hotel organizations, these three articles serve to highlight some of the current thought and research about the relationship between organizational structure, marketing strategy, and organizational problems and the organization's people. Additional insights can be gained from parts of the suggested readings.

Structure and Strategy: Two Sides of Success

Jeffrey D. Schaffer

The lodging industry can be thought of as a hostile marketing environment, a fragmented market characterized by low shares and many operators. Lodging chains have been in existence for more than 50 years, yet the industry is not dominated by just a few companies; there are almost 400 operators listed in the 1984 AH&MA *Directory of Hotel and Motel Systems.* The top 25 hotel chains still account for only 47 percent of the total U.S. lodging supply. The largest single operator in the industry, Holiday Corporation, owned just 2 percent of the total room supply in 1984, and even with its franchised inns represented only 11 percent of the U.S. lodging supply (Lee 1984). Occupancy rates have not risen in recent years, but most lodging organizations have continued to develop new hotels at a steady pace (*Wall Street Journal,* 26 November 1984).

In such a competitive environment, it is essential that lodging companies carefully pick an appropriate market strategy and match that strategy with an organizational structure that allows the company to fulfill its goals. In this article, the author will use examples from several hotel companies to show the importance of matching organizational structure, competitive strategy, and marketing environment.

STRATEGIC CHOICES

This process of matching structure, strategy, and environment is the basis of the "strategic choice" model of organizations. In essence, the model states that organizational performance is largely the outcome of a series of choices made by the creators or top echelon of the organization. The top managers must assess the market environment of the organization's chosen product and choose the ap-

propriate competitive strategy. Then they must create an organizational structure that properly supports that strategy (Galbraith and Nathanson 1978).

If tight control is the organization's market strategy, then the top managers should limit the exercise of discretion by subordinates (perhaps by creating strict job specifications) and hold most of the decision-making authority in their hands (by requiring unit managers to refer all but the most routine matters to higher levels). On the other hand, an organization that seeks to exploit new markets might assign lower managers "fuzzy" responsibilities and give them wide decision-making scope so that they quickly take advantage of market changes.

The choice of strategy and structure is not a onetime event, because the market environment is dynamic. Therefore, lodging organizations must continuously engage in matching their competitive strategies and organizational structures to the product and market environment. What results is a cycle of adaptation (see Exhibit 1). As the market changes, management must review the question of exactly how to serve the market. Then management must adjust its competitive strategy to the new market situation and make sure its organizational structure and processes fit the strategy.

Competitive Strategy

Think of an organization's competitive strategy as the means by which it attempts to link with, respond to, integrate with, or exploit its environment. The organization's "patterns of decisions" reflect its strategy and the position of the firm in its environment. The strategy determines the coherence and internal consistency of the company in its environment, gives the firm identity, and allows it to mobilize its strengths. It also determines whether the firm will be successful. The strategy addresses the

This article was originally published in the February 1986 issue of *The Cornell Hotel and Restaurant Administration Quarterly,* and is reprinted here with the permission of the Cornell University School of Hotel Administration. © 1986.

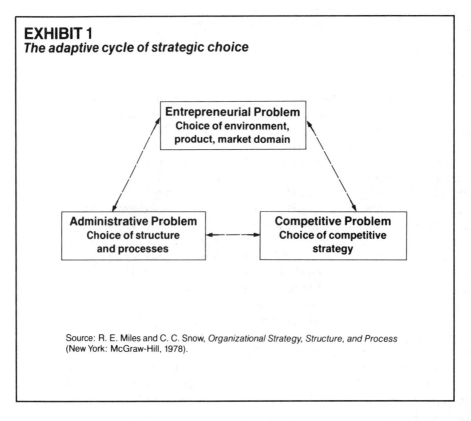

EXHIBIT 1
The adaptive cycle of strategic choice

Entrepreneurial Problem
Choice of environment,
product, market domain

Administrative Problem
Choice of structure
and processes

Competitive Problem
Choice of competitive
strategy

Source: R. E. Miles and C. C. Snow, *Organizational Strategy, Structure, and Process*
(New York: McGraw-Hill, 1978).

organization's environment as a set of problems and opportunities that the organization can seize upon and solve (Andrews 1980).

CHOICES

In theory, the universe of potential strategies and organizational structures is unlimited. But researchers have suggested that only three strategic postures constitute stable decision patterns (Miles and Snow 1978; Hall 1980). These strategies are the alternatives for an organization to apply in adapting to its environment, and they reflect the interaction between the firm's target market and its approach to attaining an advantage in that market (Porter 1980).

In the remainder of this article, the author will discuss these strategies as they are employed today in the hospitality industry. The stable strategies are presented in Exhibit 2, along with researcher's descriptions of the typical competitive methods and strategic characteristics associated with each.

HOLDING THE FORT

Organizations that pursue a *defender* strategy concentrate on improving the efficiency of their existing operations. Efficiency becomes a major determinant of successful performance.

Functional policies (in operations, marketing, research and development, and finance) are aimed at a cost-leadership objective. Attaining this objective requires the company to strive for cost reductions based on past experience, tight cost and overhead controls, and aggressive efforts to minimize costs in all aspects of the firm's operations. Quality, ser-

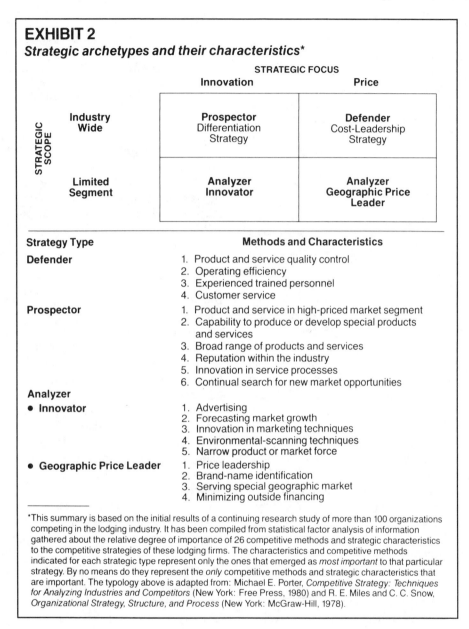

EXHIBIT 2

*Strategic archetypes and their characteristics**

| | | STRATEGIC FOCUS | |
		Innovation	Price
STRATEGIC SCOPE	**Industry Wide**	**Prospector** Differentiation Strategy	**Defender** Cost-Leadership Strategy
	Limited Segment	**Analyzer Innovator**	**Analyzer Geographic Price Leader**

Strategy Type	Methods and Characteristics
Defender	1. Product and service quality control 2. Operating efficiency 3. Experienced trained personnel 4. Customer service
Prospector	1. Product and service in high-priced market segment 2. Capability to produce or develop special products and services 3. Broad range of products and services 4. Reputation within the industry 5. Innovation in service processes 6. Continual search for new market opportunities
Analyzer • **Innovator**	1. Advertising 2. Forecasting market growth 3. Innovation in marketing techniques 4. Environmental-scanning techniques 5. Narrow product or market force
• **Geographic Price Leader**	1. Price leadership 2. Brand-name identification 3. Serving special geographic market 4. Minimizing outside financing

*This summary is based on the initial results of a continuing research study of more than 100 organizations competing in the lodging industry. It has been compiled from statistical factor analysis of information gathered about the relative degree of importance of 26 competitive methods and strategic characteristics to the competitive strategies of these lodging firms. The characteristics and competitive methods indicated for each strategic type represent only the ones that emerged as *most important* to that particular strategy. By no means do they represent the *only* competitive methods and strategic characteristics that are important. The typology above is adapted from: Michael E. Porter, *Competitive Strategy: Techniques for Analyzing Industries and Competitors* (New York: Free Press, 1980) and R. E. Miles and C. C. Snow, *Organizational Strategy, Structure, and Process* (New York: McGraw-Hill, 1978).

vice, and innovation are certainly not ignored in a defender strategy, but maintaining lower costs than competitors is the theme of the strategy. To implement this strategy effectively, the organization must specify the behavior and actions of its members in a way that ensures the use of efficient methods and procedures throughout the organization.

When cost-effective methods have been established, an organization that pursues a defender strategy seeks to avoid deviations from its specified policies and procedures. To do so, management must centralize control of operations, specify behavior, and limit individual discretion. Responsibilities and desired actions are specified in detailed, formal policies and procedures; decision-making at lower organizational levels is limited. When managers encounter situations that require deviations from predetermined policies and procedures, they must refer the decision to the top hierarchy, where decision-making authority is concentrated.

Marriott for the Defense

Marriott Hotels is one successful lodging firm that appears to use a defender-like strategy. Marriott's mission statement says, in part, "The primary mission of this corporation is one of providing efficient, productive, profitable, friendly, and controlled service within various product lines" (*Standard and Poor's* 1983). The terms "efficient," "productive," and "controlled" seem to reflect Marriott's basic competitive posture and philosophy.

Marriott apparently tries to attain a leadership position as a low-cost, high-efficiency operator in its market segment. A Marriott manager said, "One of our primary objectives is to provide high-quality food and service to the customer at the lowest possible price" (*Standard and Poor's* 1983). The idea of providing high quality at the lowest possible price reflects a defender-like competitive strategy. Furthermore, Marriott's integration, which allows it to handle every aspect of hotel development internally—from feasibility studies and design to construction and operation—is one of its greatest competitive advantages.

Marriott's organizational structure appears to fit its strategic orientation. The firm's operations are very systematic. All aspects of its operations are standardized, and operating managers' individual discretion is apparently kept to a minimum.

Further evidence of a defender-type philosophy and organizational structure can be adduced from the comments of a vice-president of operations, who said:

Our primary purpose is to offer *deluxe accommodations at a reasonable price*. Although we may *not be quite as willing to offer new innovations* as is our prime competitor, Hyatt, we can provide customers with a comparable and consistent product, generally at an advantageous price. We accomplish this by utilizing a *highly systematic approach* to our business both in terms of quality and cost control [emphasis added] (Washko 1984).

The vice-president of Marriott franchise organization echoed these ideas when he said, "The reason that Marriott has only a few franchises is the company's *control focus*. Franchisees must meet Marriott's high standards relative to *quality and cost control*" [emphasis added] (Carter 1984).

New Worlds to Conquer

The primary focus of *prospector* organizations is the search for innovative market opportunities. These organizations regularly experiment and attempt to respond to emerging environmental trends. Prospectors create change and thrive on uncertainty. They focus on product and market innovation, and efficiency is not an overriding concern. The primary capability of prospector-type organizations is finding and exploiting new product and market opportunities. They systematically add new products or markets, so they must develop and maintain the capacity to monitor a wide range of environmental conditions.

Prospectors strive for flexibility, so they can move quickly in new directions. Employees in these companies are usually generalists who are given broad authority to decide how to deal with a given situation. Seldom routine or mechanical, operations are not constrained by excessive written job descriptions or procedures. The prospector's push for flexibility results in more reliance on personnel and less emphasis on standardization. To facilitate rapid response to environmental changes, this kind of company decentralizes authority, control, and decision-making; the organization is informal to encourage innovation. As a result, the prospector's hierarchy is usually short, and information is spread among individuals and units rather than held at higher levels.

Unusual and Unique

Hyatt Hotels is a successful lodging company that seems to be an example of a prospector pursuing a differentiation strategy. In contrast to Marriott, Hyatt exploits market opportunities by providing *"unique* physical facilities, *unusual* food and beverage themes, and *special* service styles" [emphasis added] (Garbedian 1980). The following comments of a top Hyatt manager expand on this point: "Each [Hyatt] hotel manager has percentage goals [that] we expect him or her to reach. To meet [these] goals, we expect the property's management to be aggressive and *implement different policies*" [emphasis added] (Garbedian 1980).

In a recent seminar, the general manager of one of Hyatt's Regency Hotels made the following comments about Hyatt's competitive strategy:

Each [Hyatt] general manager is *totally responsible* for his hotel. There are *not* a lot of standard operating procedures. We are expected to succeed through ingenuity and creativity.

Our marketing plan involves positioning our product as *unique in the marketplace.* . . . An example is our chef's table, where community leaders are invited to have lunch with our chef right in the middle of our kitchen. A special table is set in the midst of the hustle and bustle, and the chef prepares a special menu for our guests [emphasis added] (Douglas Forseth 1984).

The manager's comment about the absence of standard operating procedures reinforces the perception of Hyatt as a prospector, with a decentralized organizational structure that matches its competitive strategy.

THE NARROW WAY

Analyzers

Analyzers come in two varieties. The *geographic price leader* has a competitive strategy that involves operating in very narrow segments of the industry's environment. The other type, the *innovator,* operates simultaneously in two types of product or market domains—one relatively stable, and the other in flux.

Analyzers aim for a particular buying group, segment of a product line, or geographic market. Their strategy is built entirely around serving a particular target market very well. Unlike prospectors and defenders, these organizations do not try an industry-wide approach.

The premise of the analyzer strategy is that the firm should be able to serve its narrow target more effectively or efficiently than its more broadly positioned competitors. Analyzers work to achieve differentiation, cost advantages, or both within their chosen market segment. But this strategy implies some limitation on the overall market share that can be attained, because there must be a tradeoff between profits and volume.

In a stable market situation, analyzers act much the same as defenders. As price leaders, they attempt to make their operations routine and standard and to focus on efficiency. In more turbulent markets, analyzers watch competitors closely for new ideas. When they see promising ideas, innovative analyzers attempt to adapt them for their own operations. The analyzer classification, then, includes companies that are price leaders (defenders), companies that innovate (prospectors), and those that mix the two strategies. The distinguishing feature of analyzers is that they operate in a narrow market niche or geographic area, while defenders' and prospectors' operations are usually more widespread.

La Quinta and American Motor Inns (AMI) are successful firms that appear to be applying an analyzer-type competitive strategy. Although AMI no longer exists under that name, the company's founders are operating some of the former AMI inns under the name of Krish Hotels. The remainder of the AMI properties are now under the control of Prime Motor Inns. The analysis of the AMI strategy still applies to Krish's operations.

Southwestern Price Leader

La Quinta aims for one market segment and limits its geographic dispersion. The pleasure traveler is of little concern to La Quinta. The company's focus is on the sales and business traveler. "La Quinta

Motels provide business people with comfortable, *inexpensive* lodging and quick access to their business destination," said one manager (*Dun's Review* 1980).

Simplicity is the key to La Quinta's operating strategy. Its basic idea is to avoid many of the complexities other motel companies face by trying to serve a broader market (Gorden 1976). La Quinta's management points out that the extra features complicate motel operations. Instead of the large buildings, extensive public space, restaurants, conference halls, and banquet rooms that most companies build to appeal to a broader market, La Quinta's strategy is to build no lobbies, run no restaurants, and cater no banquets, while it courts the business traveler.

Primarily located in the sunbelt, most La Quinta inns have between 100 and 130 rooms. Almost all the motels are situated on major highways, close to airports, and within three miles of commercial centers. Despite their relatively small size, the inns feature a swimming pool, 24-hour telephone service, and same-day laundry service. The company makes certain that food service is available by building a freestanding restaurant on the property and leasing it to an independent operator. The unit managers are usually a retired couple who live on the premises. They are highly trained in how to run a rooms-only operation with a *low cost, no-frills* approach (Pickering 1984).

From the above description, one can conclude that La Quinta's competitive strategy involves a narrow market and a limited geographic focus, coupled with a cost-leadership approach.

Dual Markets

AMI's strategy contrasted with that of La Quinta, because La Quinta limits its expansion geographically, while AMI limited its system by type of location. An AMI senior vice-president explicitly pointed to the company's "expense consciousness" as a prime factor in achieving desired operating results. Also stressing the importance of cost control, AMI's senior vice-president for development at-

tributed the company's success primarily to three factors: (1) a focus on secondary markets that larger, more powerful competitors would probably leave alone, (2) aggressive cost control (unit managers are compensated based on their ability to achieve operating objectives through cost control), and (3) central corporate control of all aspects of unit operations (a congruent structure) (Krish 1984).

TROUBLE

A fourth category, that of *reactors,* could be added to the typology presented in Exhibit 2, but reactor organizations fail to develop a viable strategic focus or a leadership position. These organizations are dominated by a perception of great environmental change and uncertainty to which they are unable to respond effectively. They lack a consistent strategic pattern for adjusting to their environment.

Lacking consistent response mechanisms, reactor organizations are unstable. Either their managements fail to articulate a viable organizational strategy, or the strategy is well-articulated but the organization's design is not consistent with the strategy.

Imperial 400 might be classified as a strategic reactor. This company's strategy is to situate competitively priced motels (averaging 40 to 50 rooms) in downtown areas (*Imperial "400" National, Inc., Annual Report* 1982). The company believed that this locational strategy would provide the best opportunity for a maximum year-round occupancy, and the downtown area would provide customers with a choice of freestanding restaurants and other amenities, obviating the need for expensive in-house food and beverage facilities.

The company hoped its unusual *co-owner management* would permit it to maintain uniform standards, and the company also planned to develop a nationwide advertising and referral system. Imperial 400 has encountered problems implementing its owner-manager strategy, however. Its primary difficulty has been maintaining corporate operating standards for efficiency and cost (Ishael 1982). The decentralized co-ownership structure required *closer corporate supervision* to achieve cost objectives than the company originally anticipated. The absence of a match between the organization's structure and its (apparently) cost-focused defender (or analyzer) strategy may have resulted in an inconsistent set of response mechanisms, which, in turn, probably have contributed to this firm's performance difficulties.

CONGRUENCE

Successful implementation of each strategy type (prospector, defender, or analyzer) requires a sustained commitment to a single strategic approach. A firm that does not or cannot develop a leadership position in accordance with one of these three strategic types is likely to find itself in a very poor position. But the mere choice of an appropriate competitive strategy will not ensure high performance levels, unless the organizational structure is also appropriate and fits the strategy.

Steadfastness

A study of 64 firms in eight different industries found that the top performers share strong common strategic characteristics, regardless of the nature of their industry (Hall 1980). This study found that high performers generally moved purposefully toward and vigorously defended a winning strategic position, whether it be lowest-cost (defenders), differentiation (prospectors), or a focused approach combining parts of the first two (analyzers). The results of the study left little doubt that consistency and clarity of purpose help to mobilize and coordinate internal resources in gaining and defending a leadership position.

Preliminary research findings from more than 100 lodging firms support the strategic-choice model and the relationship between competitive strategy, structure, and subsequent performance. Additional research will be required to evaluate and validate these emerging organizational perspectives as they relate to the lodging industry. But here is a useful framework for lodging practitioners and researchers to understand and evaluate organizational performance in the lodging industry—namely, that strategic choices, though dynamic, must be limited to a few workable competitive strategies, and, further, that these strategies must be implemented through appropriately matched organizational structures.

Towards A Theory of Interdepartmental Conflict in Hotels

David Dann
Timothy Hornsey

Interdepartmental conflict is an area of research which has been somewhat neglected not only in the hospitality industry but throughout management research (Hunt 1979). Whereas conflict between employer and employee (vertical conflict) has been

Reprinted with permission of Pergamon Press from Dann, David, and Timothy Hornsey. "Towards a Theory of Interdepartmental Conflict in Hotels." *International Journal of Hospitality Management,* vol. 4, no. 1, 1986, pp. 23–28.

the subject of considerable study and analysis, that between employees operating at the same hierarchical level (horizontal conflict) has been largely ignored (Elliott and Elliott 1974). Despite this, the prevalence of interdepartmental conflict in hotels seems to be one of the distinctive features of their operation. The frequency with which hotel and catering operations appear to experience interdepartmental conflicts cannot be adequately explained by concepts of interpersonal differences or merely through a greater understanding of the external environment in which the actors behave. Horizontal conflicts within hospitality seem to occur irrespective of the external environment of the unit. Hence, there would appear to be something in the nature of the operation or its social environment which causes or heightens intergroup differences within the hospitality industry. Interdepartmental conflict within the hospitality industry has tended to be explained within a unitary frame of reference and has placed undue emphasis on ideas of personal difference, with the result that solutions have largely revolved around the establishment of superordinate goals (Venison 1983). The pluralist approach is seemingly more realistic in accepting that the organization is made up of a multitude of different groupings who may well have different interests and goals (Fox 1974). Only by the adoption of such a stance can any real understanding of interdepartmental conflict in hotels be attained.

This article outlines 4 reasons which may heighten interdepartmental conflicts in the hospitality industry, either in isolation or collectively: (1) Interdependence—the relationship that exists between departments; (2) Environment—the framework within which activities occur; (3) Rewards—the nature of the total payment package; (4) Status and stigma—the perceptions of workers within the industry about themselves and others.

INTERDEPENDENCE

The level of interdependence between departments in many situations is necessarily high if the customer is to receive a satisfactory service. There have been a number of studies which have indicated that where there are high perceived levels of interdependence between departments then interdepartmental conflict tends to increase (March and Simon 1958; Sofer 1972; Filley 1975; Bowey 1976). Interdependence in hospitality situations is caused by the nature of work flows; the product or service that the customer receives is the outcome of close and often immediate co-operation between two or more departments. Coupled with this the time requirements

for coordination are very short compared with other industries in that they can often be measured in minutes or seconds (Whyte and Hamilton 1965). The reasons why interdependence causes conflict between departments can be considered in a fourfold manner: autonomy, reciprocity, role conflict, and goal differentiation.

It has been suggested that there is a struggle for autonomy in the workplace and that there is a fundamental conflict between the desire for independence and the necessity of interdependence (Pondy 1967; Snow 1981). Where this struggle for autonomy is frustrated then conflict will arise between the parties who are directly concerned. This could be the situation between the kitchen and the restaurant where the waiting staff cannot feel in control of their work due to their dependence on chefs for their raw materials. Snow (1978) further develops this concept in relation to the hospitality industry by suggesting that staff have a desire to be in direct control of their own work, yet in positions of interdependence this is clearly not possible, so they try to exert pressure on those with whom they are interdependent, the result of which is conflict.

Perceived reciprocity may also be a cause of conflict due to interdependence between the parties. Where it is perceived by one of the sides that the other has acted unfairly or without due concern or a favor has been done but not returned then there appears the potential basis for a conflict situation. Where levels of interdependence are particularly high, as between the kitchen and the restaurant, then the opportunities for this type of conflict tend to increase. One party may often have to ask "favors" of the other in order to satisfy the guest or meet the internal requirements of the situation.

Goal differentiation between the parties is probably the most important reason, that has been cited in the literature to date, for interdepartmental conflict in hotels. Bowey (1976), Nailon (1978), and Mars and Nicod (1984) all considered interdependence to be a determinant of interdepartmental conflict in restaurants and hotels, as the two parties, while being interdependent, placed different de-

FIGURE 1

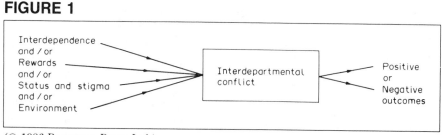

mands upon the situation. The chef's concern was primarily with quality and that of service staff primarily with speed. In other situations this might be reversed but it would appear that the different objectives of the staff may heighten the problems caused by interdependence. Clearly the degree of interdependental conflict caused by interdependence will vary with the nature of the situation. Mars and Nicod (1984) suggested that there were likely to be higher levels of conflict in lower classes of establishment where there is a greater differentiation between the desire for speed from the waiter and any aspirations that the chef may have concerning quality; in better classes of establishment both parties have a greater concern for quality thereby lessening the potential for conflict.

ENVIRONMENT

The social environment may also be a cause of conflict (Berger and Luckman 1967). The environment of the hospitality industry has a number of distinctive features which may add to the development of conflict situations; these include the triadic relationship that exists between management, staff, and the customer; the speed of operation, causing stress and pressure for the operatives; the styles of leadership used and the territorial perspectives of the participants.

Mars and Mitchell (1976) have pointed out that a characteristic feature of the hospitality environ-ment is the triadic relationship which exists between the staff, the customer, and the management.

Many members of staff are faced with conflicting situations between the demands placed upon them by the customer and those by the situation and their working colleagues. This type of role conflict certainly adds to the stress factors inherent in the task and adds to the pressure that exists between those departments which have direct contact with the customer and those that do not. Staff who occupy positions which are at the interface between the organization and the customer (boundary roles) have been identified as adapting their attitudes and work behavior to cope with this situation and thereby emphasizing their differences from colleagues in other departments (Parkington and Schneider 1979; Shamir 1983).

The perspective taken by Homans (1951) of considering groups in terms of their internal and external environments may be of assistance in the understanding of the effects of the triadic relationship. The external environment and the predominant features of the triadic relationship are dictated by the nature of the tasks which staff undertake. The task is clearly very different for staff, such as restaurant service staff and receptionists, who come into direct contact with guests than it is for those who have limited guest contact, such as chambermaids and chefs. Staff who face the customer have very different pressures from those who do not; the outcome of this might be a lack of understanding of the roles of those in other departments and this may facilitate increased levels of conflict between them. The internal environment of the group may well be dictated by the external environment in which it operates and this provides the answer as to why, for instance, chefs and waiters may perceive themselves to be very different types of people. Studies on waiting staff have shown them to be highly individualistic in their perspective (Mars and Nicod 1984), yet kitchen staff have the reputation of stronger collectivism. Such differences in group solidarity and the different value systems which emerge (Sayles 1958; Elliott and Elliott 1974) may aggravate the conflicts which exist between the parties. Hence the real source of the conflict may lie in the external environment which the participants face, especially their role in interacting with the customer, rather than any form of direct relationship between the two groups.

The environment in which staff conduct their activities may be one of stress and pressure (Whyte 1948; Bowey 1976; Snow 1978, 1981). If the working relationship presents a source of stress, rather than reward or satisfaction, then this could lead to the staff looking for an outlet for this pressure, the most immediate outlet being those people from other departments with whom they come into contact for resources. Whyte (1948) noted how waiters and waitresses "let off steam" at the hot plate due to the pressure exerted upon them by guests. Although the recipients of these outbursts were the chefs they were not the direct cause of the problem, they were merely the people with whom the service staff had the most immediate contact and were the most obvious target for their frustrations.

The nature of the hospitality environment at unit level tends to require a multitude of quick decisions to cope with the large number of unplanned and unpredicted situations which arise. Shamir (1978) suggests that the industry is characterized by a desire for rigidity in operations at corporate level and flexibility in the units. Whereas this would appear to call for an organic form of organization, the industry has been typified by more authoritarian leadership styles (White 1973) and more formalized organization and communication patterns. This style of leadership and organization, in a situation which appears to call for a different approach, may add to the conflicts which are faced by the parties (Filley 1975).

Staff also develop territories for themselves and may start to perceive themselves as entities which act independently from other parts of the firm. Any intrusion directly or indirectly into their territory may be treated as an invasion and resisted as such (Ardrey 1967). The kitchen and the front office desk have very clear physical barriers which divide them from other departments and chefs have a reputation of building a strong territorial perspective about their place of work. Yet, in the restaurant/kitchen relationship the waiter must come directly to the interface between the two territories, the hot plate, many times within his normal processes of work, making him resistant to the potential "intruder to his territory" and increasing the conflict between the parties.

Certainly the nature of the environment in which tasks are performed and the tasks themselves would seem a key factor in determining the reasons for interdepartmental conflict in hospitality organizations.

REWARDS

Rewards may cause conflict between departments through perceived differences in individual rewards or perceived differences in the distribution of scarce resources. Feelings of deprivation, with regard to rewards, tend to emerge from a basis of comparison (Sofer 1972). Whenever one party believes that they are less well off than those in other departments, a basis for conflict is established. One would expect rewards to be of primary concern to workers in the industry as it is often viewed as one of low pay. This has not always been found to be the case; Snow (1981) and Shamir (1977) both speak of the social orientations of workers within the industry. However, recent research by Kung in Hong Kong into job satisfaction and labor turnover among food service personnel in chain hotel operations suggests that there may be a cultural element which should be considered (Kung 1984).

The presence of tips as a feature of the industry is likely to lead to distorted perceptions with regard to the earnings of other staff. In a non-service organizational setting the reward system is directly responsible for linking the individual with the organization and its goals; in situations where a substantial proportion of the individual's income is not received through the organization then there is no mechanism to link the individual to the organization and its goals. If this is the case for only one set of dependents within a highly interdependent situation then the basis for potential conflict is formed (March and Simon 1958).

The most typical conflicts occur between departments, one of which is a direct recipient of tips whereas the other is not. Waiters are recipients; chefs non-recipients; chambermaids recipients; receptionists non-recipients (Nailon 1978). The reason for this could be that tip recipients develop different attitudes from non-recipients. For instance, recent research by Shamir (1983) found that tip recipients had a more favorable attitude towards the customers and the management than non-recipients. Although Shamir does not indicate their relative perceptions towards each other, it is clear from his work that the perception of the job by tip recipients and non-recipients differs. Snow (1981) also noted that perks such as fiddling and tips had the effect of dividing staff within the organization with the result that common interests were not realized.

Differences in perceived rewards may be further distorted by the perceived opportunity for fiddles between the various departments. Certainly, as Mars (1982) and Mars and Mitchell (1976) have pointed out, fiddles are an important part of the total reward package and where one party perceives the opportunity for fiddles as being higher within another department this may be a source of conflict between the two departments.

Lastly, scarce resources are quoted by a number of authors as a reason for interdepartmental conflict (March and Simon 1958; Sofer 1972; Elliott and El-

liott 1974; Filley 1975; Wilmot and Wilmot 1978). In hospitality situations scarce resources could be considered in terms of personal rewards or departmental resources. Where there is a struggle for scarce resources between departments and where it is perceived by one of the parties that the distribution of resources has not been equitable, then the likelihood of interdepartmental conflict increases.

If workers do perceive themselves as being within a low pay industry, then perceived differences in reward may be strongly felt and add to conflict which occurs between departments. Rewards may well be seen as a major source of conflict between staff in the hospitality industry.

STATUS AND STIGMA

The rigid organizational hierarchies of the hospitality industry and the traditions under which they have grown have led to a very highly differentiated and established status system in hospitality organizations. This status system is developed around the job title that the individual carries. Some positions carry a particular status within the organization whereas others, such as that of the kitchen porter, carry a distinct stigma (Saunders 1981). This is clearly an issue of perception; how the member of the staff perceives him- or herself and others within the work situation. If he/she perceives his/her position as being of low status or others of high status then this may be a cause of conflict between the parties (Stagner and Rosen 1966). As Sofer (1972) points out, man behaves in the workplace according to his perception of reality and in industrial conflicts a crucial factor is the reality of opposed interests as perceived by the parties.

The status system is established through tradition and myth and reinforced through group pressure. Where staff are grouped together around a similar task they tend to develop ideologies which emphasize their distinctive contribution to the organization and which differentiate them from other groups with whom they have contact (Sofer 1972). Hence each group may develop its own subculture and values which may involve negative or indifferent attitudes towards other organizational groups. Certainly conflict occurs in hospitality situations where there are differences in belief between the parties and although the occupational hierarchies which develop may differ somewhat between establishments (Whyte 1948; Sprott 1958) there does seem some uniformity in the way in which waiters/chefs and housekeeping staff/receptionists perceive each other. These perceptions appear to be based upon traditionally negative preconceptions and may form a basis for conflict between the departments.

Negative perceptions of perceived status and stigma in hospitality are reinforced by the high percentage of overseas workers and, in some situations, of female workers employed in the industry. Snow (1981) has noted that some groups face more barriers than others in their desire to enter into higher paid or more prestigious occupations; in particular this seems to apply to female and immigrant labor. Members of these groups find themselves limited in their range of occupational choice to the lowest paid, least skilled work which would not be considered acceptable to those people who are able to work elsewhere. In many cases these types of workers may be reluctant entrants who are forced into the industry through a lack of opportunity elsewhere in the labor market (Dronfield and Soto 1980). They will probably enter the industry with a perceived sense of stigma which may then be reinforced by colleagues, management, and customers. They will be particularly receptive to the opportunity for conflict with other departments as their involvement with the organizations is likely to be low.

There does appear to be a tendency amongst immigrant groups within the industry to work together and form very cohesive groups based upon nationality, religion, or values/beliefs (Venison 1983). This may well be a primary source of conflict where perhaps the waiters are predominantly Spanish and the chefs West Indian. Whyte (1948) also noted that the conflict across the hot plate was in part a sexual

conflict as chefs were male and the waitresses female and the males tended to believe themselves superior.

Service staff are in a subordinate position to the needs of the customer and it is a part of the adjustment process to accept that role (Mars and Nicod 1984). Where this position is partially refuted then there may be a feeling of role incongruence on the part of the staff member. Also, service staff are often required to "act out" two differing roles, one with the customer and one with fellow group members or with staff from other departments (Hughes 1958). It has been noted that due to the duality of the roles they play, service staff tend to be very sensitive to threats to their self-image, whether those threats come from customers or fellow workers. This sensitivity is likely to enhance the opportunities for conflict situations between departments.

Status and stigma perceived by one set of workers with regard to another and reinforced by tradition may well be a contributory factor in ascertaining the reasons for high levels of conflict between departments in the hospitality industry.

SUMMARY

In order that the discipline of hospitality management is adequately understood, researched, and taught, the development of theory must underpin practice and experience. Interdepartmental conflict seems to be a common feature of the hospitality industry and its prevalence appears to be little understood. Conflict, it is suggested, emerges because of factors connected with interdependence, environment, rewards, or status and stigma, or a combination of these factors. We have made no attempt to apply value judgments as to whether these conflicts are desirable or undesirable, or to attach any relative importance to any of the factors. There is now a need for further research into the phenomenon of interdepartmental conflict in hospitality to establish its frequency, the reasons for its occurrence, and its value.

The Cult of Ineffectiveness

W. Gerald Glover, Ph. D.

A company's culture is the basis for how things are done in the firm. The culture can be one of cold precision, warm excellence, or sincere bumbling. Culture usually results both from organizational characteristics and from top management's ability to formulate goals and transmit them to the rest of the company's managers and employees. Properly developed, a corporate culture can be a tool management uses to build product quality and staff productivity.

When management misunderstands the effects of corporate culture and allows a "cult of ineffectiveness" to develop, the quality of products and services may suffer. In this article, I will describe some of the organizational characteristics that commonly give rise to a cult of ineffectiveness.

MISSING STANDARDS

Lack of Agreement on Expectations

A lack of consensus on standards generally gives rise to an ineffective corporate culture. No one agrees on what work is to be performed, let alone how well it should be done and what methods are appropriate. Each employee may do it his or her way. One supervisor will apply different standards than others do, and those standards may even change from day to day. Because top management has not set up a method for achieving consensus on what should be happening in operations and service delivery, a multitude of standards may exist for each job. As a result, the product is inconsistent, guests are confused (or displeased), managers and employees are dissatisfied.

This article was originally published in the February 1987 issue of *The Cornell Hotel and Restaurant Administration Quarterly,* and is reprinted here with the permission of the Cornell University School of Hotel Administration. © 1987.

Inconsistent delivery of products and services. Inconsistency is probably the most frequent cause of problems in assuring service quality. When an entree is prepared differently by each cook, when one room has enough towels while the next one doesn't, when one front-desk clerk is warm and the next is abrupt, the guest will be dissatisfied. The hotel or restaurant will seem like an entirely different one on each visit, depending on which set of standards the guest experiences. When guests don't know what to expect from a hotel or restaurant, they often just stay away.

Measuring and managing quality. If there is no consensus on standards, it follows that there can be no measurement of standards. Yet measuring employees' conformity to standards is a critical management task. This function typically involves coaching, discipline, team-building, and documenting and evaluating performance. Departments concerned with personnel and service management are generally those where measurement is particularly lacking. This is a result of the low priority senior management often assigns to measurement in these areas, the absence of clearly developed goals, and inability to delegate responsibilities. In particular, many managers dismiss the idea of measuring quality by reporting the commonly shared idea that "you can't measure service because it's intangible." Service is a real social event between the employee and the guest. Its quality can be observed and documented through guest focus groups and guest feedback.

Evaluation based on activity, not results. How often are employees rewarded for looking busy, regardless of what results they achieve with all their activity? In both the management suite and the front desk, performance is often evaluated in terms of "sweat on the brow," "bean counting," or simple appearance. In such cases, the quality of the work performed is not as important an evaluation criterion as the number of hours worked or the number of crises encountered.

The goal of guest service is obscured when promotions, recognition, and compensation are not the result of meeting agreed-upon standards. Instead, corporate games and a good appearance—down to the right color tie—can be more important to getting ahead than, say, achieving a low turnover rate among employees or having high guest satisfaction.

UNBALANCED ACCOUNTABILITY

Accounting procedures for some parts of a hospitality operation are more sophisticated than others. For good reason, financial accounting is highly developed, while the accounting procedures for measuring the effectiveness of managers and supervisors in overseeing employees and the services they deliver are less precise. Without effective controls, however, the "people" area can become ineffective. If management does not place a priority on maintaining some kind of human-resources and social-quality accounting system, the likely results are employee turnover, inconsistent product quality, damage to equipment, and lower productivity.

INEFFECTIVE COMMUNICATIONS

Broken or misunderstood communications causes problems wherever it occurs, but the problem of faulty communication is more subtle than mere misunderstanding. Many organizations suffer from a one-way channel of communications—namely, from the top down. Ideas and responses from the employees are seldom sought, and comments from guests are not appreciated. Neither group's comments are considered in management decision-making. Such top-down communication engenders a cult of ineffectiveness, just as surely as misunderstood communications or poor communication skills.

SYMPTOMS, NOT CAUSES

The cult of ineffectiveness places great emphasis on remedies for symptoms, rather than delving for underlying problems. On superficial inspection, many operational and guest-service problems seem simple. If a waiter is rude, he must be told to be pleasant. This is like treating a fracture with a Band-Aid; the solution does not get at the underlying cause of the problem. In fact, the waiter's rudeness may have less to do with the waiter, and more to do with inappropriate selection and training or poor management practices. In problem-solving, symptoms must be used as clues for discovering the real problem.

LACK OF RECOGNITION

Praise is an important part of managerial feedback. It costs nothing, and it does wonders for employee morale. Yet many employees never hear from their manager unless there is a problem. Indeed, most managers must honestly admit that they rarely bother to let employees know when a job has been done well. Employees should not automatically have a sinking feeling when the manager wants to talk to them.

ABSENCE OF TEAMWORK

Many corporate cultures reward competition among company employees. Some businesses actually encourage conflict and one-upmanship. When employees are rewarded for taking individual action, the development of teams can be thwarted. Yet a busy front desk, a crowded dining room, or a drive-up window at lunchtime demands that employees work as a team to deliver prompt and satisfactory guest service.

The development of a team of employees also prevents a department or unit from collapsing when a talented manager or supervisor is promoted or leaves. If the cult of ineffectiveness has allowed the supervisor to set all standards, then the departure of that supervisor could leave the unit with no bearings. A successful company would have a management system of standards that would not change as supervisors come and go.

TRAILING, NOT TRAINING

Trailing is the most common means used by managers for training new staff members. In this method, a new hire trails an experienced employee to learn how the job is done. This practice transfers one of the most important managerial responsibilities to a line employee. The new hire learns the operation's policies as they are understood by the experienced employee, who may not have a clear view of the company's objectives. Any time a manager might save this way is soon lost in correcting problems created by the practice.

Moreover, even when training is handled by managers, it is seldom based on clearly stated job standards or founded on basic competency. To do the job right the first time, employees must be given the skills and knowledge necessary to meet a company's performance standards.

Sink-or-Swim Management

Management trainees are also victimized by a form of on-the-job training—but they often don't have even the luxury of another manager to observe. Managers and supervisors are often expected to sink or swim as they are introduced to new responsibilities. Line employees particularly face this situation when their outstanding performance wins them a promotion. They are often moved up without being given any training in the distinctive responsibilities of a supervisor. The newly minted supervisor is left to draw on the existing corporate culture and to learn the job by trial and error.

RECRIMINATIONS

Rather than treat a guest complaint or other product problem as an opportunity to improve the operation, complaints are often occasions for blame, defensiveness, and finger-pointing. Part of the problem is that people don't like to admit direct responsibility for making a mess of a job, preferring instead to sweep problems under the rug. But management also has a duty to limit problems in the first place by establishing a complete understanding of how each job should be done. When management has laid this foundation, problems can be identified and solutions found, without unnecessary recriminations.

EFFECTIVENESS

Many hospitality managers fail to recognize the difference between effectiveness and efficiency. Merely completing a job ahead of a deadline is not sufficient to ensure excellence. The work must be done on time, of course, but the effort must result in achievement of established standards. The definition of "getting the job done" should include delivering the product or service right on the first try.

NOT JUST SIMPLE ARITHMETIC

An organization is more than the sum of all its operations and departments. It also includes a culture that influences much of what occurs in the business. This culture is shaped—intentionally or accidentally—by the actions of the company's top managers. This informal social organization affects all levels of the company, and it strongly influences the company's ability to deliver its products and services to the customer.

Rather than allow a cult of ineffectiveness to grow, top managers should consciously promote a culture emphasizing consistency, productivity, and a participation at all levels in problem-solving and achieving consensus on standards. Only a "proactive" management stance can lead to true excellence.

References

Andrews, K.R. 1980. *The concept of corporate strategy.* Homewood, IL: Richard D. Irwin.

Ardrey, R. 1967. *The territorial imperative.* London: Collins.

Berger, P.L., and T. Luckman. 1967. *The social construction of reality.* London: Allen Lane.

Bowey, A. 1976. *The sociology of organisations.* London: Hodder and Stoughton.

Carter, Gerald. 1984. Lodging management. Paper presented at seminar, 8 February 1984, Virginia Polytechnic Institute and State University.

Dale, Ernest. 1967. *Organization.* New York: American Management Association, p. 9.

Dronfield, L., and P. Soto. 1980. *Hardship hotel.* London: CIS.

Elliott, D., and R. Elliott. 1974. *Goals and goal conflict.* Milton Keynes, Great Britian: Open University Press.

Filley, A.C. 1975. *Interpersonal conflict resolution.* Glenview, IL: Scott, Foresman.

Forseth, Douglas. 1984. Lodging management. Paper presented at seminar, 20 February 1984, Virginia Polytechnic Institute and State University.

Fox, A. 1974. *Man mismanagement.* London: Hutchinson.

Galbraith, J.R., and D.A. Nathanson. 1978. *Strategy implementatin: The role of structure and process.* New York: West.

Garbedian, D.M. 1980. Hyatt hits new heights. *Restaurant Business,* 1 October.

Gorden, Mitchell. 1976. La Quinta Motor Inns carves out growing trade in economy field. *Barron's* 56 (31 May): 26–27.

HCITB. 1981. *The image of hotel and catering work.* London.

Hall, W.K. 1980. Survival strategies in a hostile environment. *Harvard Business Review* 58 (September-October): 75–85.

Homans, G.C. 1951. *The human group.* London: Routledge and Kegan Paul.

Hornsey, T., and D. Dann. 1984. *Manpower management in the hotel and catering industry.* London: Batsford.

Hughes, E.C. 1958. *Men and their work.* Glencoe, IL: Free Press.

Hunt, J. 1979. *Managing people at work.* New York: McGraw-Hill.

Imperial "400" National, Inc., Annual Report, 1982.

Ishael, Julia. 1982. *Imperial "400" Inc.: An administrative profile.*

Krish, Sam. 1984. Corporate strategies in the hospitality industry. Paper presented at seminar, 30 May 1984, Virginia Polytechnic Institute and State University.

Kung, C. 1984. Assessment of job satisfaction and its relationship to turnover of food service personnel in high tariff chain hotels in Hong Kong. Unpublished thesis, Iowa State University.

La Quinta: How to woo the business traveler. 1980. *Dun's Review* 115 (April): 146–48.

Lee, Daniel R. 1984. A forecast of lodging supply and demand. *Cornell Hotel and Restaurant Administration Quarterly* 25(2): 27–40.

March, J.G., and H.A. Simon. 1958. *Organizations.* New York: John Wiley.

Mars, G. 1982. *Cheats at work.* London: Allen and Unwin.

Mars, G., and P. Mitchell. 1976. *Room for reform.* London: Milton Keynes, Open University Press.

Mars, G., and M. Nicod. 1984. *The world of waiters.* London: Allen and Unwin.

Miles, R.E., and C.C. Snow. 1978. *Organizational strategy, structure, and process.* New York: McGraw-Hill.

Nailon, P. 1978. Tipping: A behavioral review. *HCIMA Review* 2:231–41.

Parkington, J.J., and B. Schneider. 1979. Some correlates of experienced job stress: A boundary role study. *Academy of Management Journal* 22:270–81.

Pickering, Laurie. 1984. La Quinta Motor Inns, Inc.: A strategic history and case analysis. Unpublished report, Virginia Polytechnic Institute and State University.

Pondy, L.R. 1967. Organizational conflict. Concepts and models. *Administrative Science Quarterly* 12:296–320.

Porter, Michael E. 1980. *Competitive Strategy: Techniques for Analyzing Industries and Competitors.* New York: Free Press.

Saunders, K. 1981. *Social stigma of occupations.* Farnborough, U.K.: Gower.

Sayles, L.R. 1958. *The behavior of industrial work groups.* New York: John Wiley.

Shamir, B. 1977. *A study of managers' and staff attitudes to living-in and other aspects of hotel employment.* London: Cornewell, Greene, Bertram, Smith.

Shamir, B. 1978. Between bureaucracy and hospitality. *Journal of Management Studies* 15:285–307.

Shamir, B. 1983. A note on tipping and employee perceptions and attitudes. *Journal of Occupational Psychology* 56:255–59.

Snow, G. 1978. Unionisation in the hotel and catering industry. Unpublished thesis, University of Bath, U.K.

Snow, G. 1981. Industrial relations in hotels. Unpublished thesis, University of Bath, U.K.

Sofer, C. 1972. *Organisations in theory and practice.* London: Heinemann.

Sprott, W.J. 1958. *Human groups.* London: Penguin.

Stagner, R., and H. Rosen. 1966. *Psychology of union-management relations.* London: Tavistock.

Stoner, James A., and Charles Wankel. 1986. *Management.* Englewood Cliffs, NJ: Prentice-Hall, pp. 233–34.

U.S. lodging industry is staggered by room glut and building boom. 1984. *Wall Street Journal* 26 November.

Venison, P. 1983. *Managing hotels.* London: Heinemann.

Washko, George. 1984. Corporate strategies in the hospitality industry. Paper presented at seminar, 25 May 1984, Virginia Polytechnic Institute and State University.

White, M. 1973. Management styles in hotels. *HCIMA Journal* October.

Whyte, W.F. 1948. *Human relations in the restaurant industry.* New York: McGraw-Hill.

Whyte, W.F., and E.L. Hamilton. 1965. *Action research for management.* Homewood, IL: Richard D. Irwin.

Wilmot, J.H., and W.W. Wilmot. 1978. *Interpersonal conflict.* Dubuque, IA: Wm. C. Brown.

Suggested Readings

Articles

Schaffer, Jeffrey D. "Strategy, Organization Structure and Success in the Lodging Industry." *International Journal of Hospitality Management* 3 (1984): 159–65.

Schaffer, Jeffrey D. "A Dynamic Model of Organizational Performance in the Lodging Industry: The Role of Competitive Strategy and Organization Structure." *Proceedings,* CHRIE Conference, Seattle, WA, 1985, 168–73.

SECTION 3

General Managers

INTRODUCTION

In most companies, someone who has attained the title of general manager (GM), or something similar, heads the organization. It is generally considered the acme of one's career for most of us in the hotel field. In many hotel companies the job of general manager is one that serves as the springboard to corporate jobs for some, and larger and more prestigious properties for others.

Surprisingly, very little has been written about hotel general managers. Only recently has very much attention been paid to how these people's careers have developed and what sorts of skills and strengths they bring to their jobs.

In his 1981 article, Mario Arnaldo presents a statistical profile of hotel general managers. He draws a demographic picture of his sample and goes on to comment about aspects of job satisfaction. He also provides an analytical framework for reporting how these GMs allocated time and importance to a number of classic managerial roles.

Arnaldo's findings on managerial roles may be compared or contrasted to the issues raised by David Ley in his analysis of whether the most effective GM displays leadership skills or entrepreneurial skills.

Another aspect of career development of general managers is explored in the Rutherford and Wiegenstein article, which looks in depth at the role of mentoring as it could be measured to affect the success and satisfaction of a hotel general manager's career. These authors conclude that seeking out and maximizing mentoring relationships can have a number of positive effects on the careers of managers.

In the suggested readings for this section, Swanljung and Pickworth both explore additional career-related aspects of hotel executives and how managerial careers are developed in chain organizations.

Hotel general managers have jobs that provide rewards and incentives not found in many other industries. The Rutherford and Wiegenstein article outlines a number of common executive "perks" and also comments on others that may be unique to the hotel business. Students and industry professionals who aspire to reach this point in a career progression are well advised to structure a mechanism of inquiry that allows them to answer the question: What elements contribute to the success of people who are general managers in my company? The research and commentary presented here is a start in building that particular structure of inquiry.

Hotel General Managers: A Profile

Mario J. Arnaldo

What sort of people find their way to this important position, and what do they do once they get there?

Hotel general managers occupy a crucial role in the midst of hotel operations, where they are in close contact with employees and guests, as well as top management. The decisions they make in this strategic position play a large part in determining the effectiveness of the hotel staff and the satisfaction of the hotel guest. Whether the properties they manage provide superior service and realize their profit potential is largely a function of the general managers' expertise.

Surprisingly, however, very little research has been performed concerning this central management function in the hospitality industry (Ley 1980; Nailon 1968). The present study was conducted with the aim of filling this gap by providing a profile of the hotel general manager (GM) that would identify (1) the personal characteristics of the GM, and (2) the GM's allocation of time and importance to ten managerial roles. The author hopes that this profile will provide a better understanding of the type of person who occupies the position of general manager and what this position entails. Such information should give decision-makers in the hospitality industry a more precise understanding of this critical management function and allow them to develop and evaluate general managers more effectively.

SAMPLE AND METHODOLOGY

Questionnaires were sent to hotel GMs employed by 15 of the 50 largest hotel chains in the United States. Eighteen GMs were randomly chosen from each of these companies for the survey. Of the 270

GMs who received questionnaires, 194 sent usable responses, for a response rate of 71.9 percent. These GMs managed a diverse range of properties, as indicated in Exhibit 1.

The general managers were asked to provide information about their educational backgrounds, their age and sex, their level of job satisfaction, their feelings about various methods of evaluating GM performance, and their views concerning preparation for a career as a hotel GM. In addition, they were asked to classify their managerial activities in terms of ten managerial roles identified by Mintzberg (1973) and to rate the amount of time and importance they assigned to each of these roles.

THE RESULTS

The average GM was a 30-year-old male who had completed four years of college; notably, for every GM with only a high-school education (11 percent), two had completed graduate school. Nearly half of the GMs attended four-year college programs. Of the 171 GMs who attended college at either the graduate or undergraduate level, approximately equal numbers were enrolled in hospitality and nonhospitality programs (see Exhibit 2).

Roughly one-third of the GMs surveyed reached their present positions after 11 to 15 years in the hospitality industry. A high degree of job transfer was implicit in the number of GMs—a full 44 percent—who had held their current jobs for only one to two years. Likewise, approximately 45 percent of the GMs had worked for their present companies for only one to five years (see Exhibit 3).

THE SATISFIED GM

Although they changed jobs fairly frequently, the GMs surveyed in this study indicated a relatively high degree of satisfaction with their jobs. One-third

This article was originally published in the November 1981 issue of *The Cornell Hotel and Restaurant Administration Quarterly,* and is reprinted here with the permission of the Cornell University School of Hotel Administration. © 1981.

EXHIBIT 1
Property profile of surveyed GMs

Geographical location of property

New England	31	(16%)
North Central	33	(17%)
South Atlantic	42	(22%)
South Central	51	(26%)
Mountain & Pacific	37	(19%)

Annual room sales*

Under $1 million	51	(31%)
$1–3 million	81	(49%)
Over $3 million	32	(20%)

Physical setting of property

Center-city	70	(36%)
Highway	45	(23%)
Resort	26	(13%)
Airport	26	(13%)
Suburban	27	(14%)

Average room rate*

Under $28	52	(30%)
$28–$37	68	(40%)
$38–$47	24	(14%)
Over $47	28	(16%)

Number of employees

Under 61 employees	49	(26%)
61–80	18	(9%)
81–100	16	(8%)
101–150	31	(16%)
151–250	18	(9%)
251–350	13	(7%)
351–450	14	(7%)
451–600	9	(5%)
Over 600 employees	23	(12%)

*Dollar figures reflect 1980 price levels.

EXHIBIT 2
GM personal and educational profile

Sex

Male	186	(96%)
Female	8	(4%)

Age

Under 25	6	(3%)
25–35	81	(44%)
36–45	57	(31%)
46–55	29	(15%)
Over 55	13	(7%)

Education
(highest level achieved)

High School	22	(11%)
College:		
Hospitality		
2-year	14	(7%)
4-year	53	(28%)
Grad	18	(9%)
	85	(total)
Nonhospitality		
2-year	24	(12%)
4-year	39	(20%)
Grad	23	(12%)
	86	(total)

EXHIBIT 3
GM professional profile

Years in the hospitality industry

1–5 years	19	(10%)
6–10	42	(22%)
11–15	66	(34%)
16–20	29	(15%)
Over 20 years	36	(19%)

Years with present company

1–5 years	85	(45%)
6–10	50	(26%)
11–15	37	(19%)
16–20	7	(4%)
Over 20 years	11	(6%)

Years in present position

1–2 years	84	(44%)
3–4	52	(27%)
5–6	23	(12%)
Over 6 years	31	(16%)

of the GMs termed the overall working conditions of their jobs very satisfactory and another 40 percent found the conditions satisfactory. Only 5 percent found the working conditions of their jobs unsatisfactory, and another 22 percent said they were "neutral" about their jobs.

Hotel general managers found nearly all of six job components identified by the researcher appealing. Guest relations was the component that received the highest ranking; 87 percent of the GMs gave it a rating of 1, 2, or 3 on a scale of 1 (most appealing) to 5 (least appealing). Guest relations was followed closely by employee relations, marketing and sales, property maintenance, and finance. The least appealing aspect of the general-manager position was found to be paperwork; only 58 percent of the GMs gave it a rating of 1, 2, or 3.

MANAGERIAL ROLES

As shown in Exhibit 4, the GMs were asked to indicate the amount of time and importance they assigned to each of ten managerial roles. These roles fell into three basic categories: interpersonal, informational, and decisional. The study did not assess the relationship between these categories; rather, the GMs were asked to provide a relative ranking of their allocation of time and importance to the various functions within each category.

The role of leader clearly absorbed more time than any other interpersonal role, and was also thought to be most important. Of the informational roles, both monitoring and disseminating were said to be relatively time-absorbing and important, while the role of spokesman consumed less time and was considered correspondingly less important. With the exception of the negotiator role, all of the decisional roles absorbed roughly equal amounts of time, according to respondents. The entrepreneurial role was judged to be the most important of the decisional roles, although a significant discrepancy was evident between the amount of time (35.6 percent) devoted to this role and the degree of importance (55.2 percent) it was judged to have.

EXHIBIT 4
GMs' allocation of time and importance to 10 managerial roles

Managerial Role	Time (Most) 1	2	3	(Least) 4	Importance (Most) 1	2	3	(Least) 4
Interpersonal								
Figurehead	6.7%	33.0%	60.3%	—	10.3%	27.8%	61.9%	—
Leader	71.7	23.7	4.6	—	86.1	12.4	1.5	—
Liaison	18.5	56.2	25.3	—	11.3	61.9	26.8	—
Informational								
Monitor	40.2	47.0	12.8	—	49.5	42.8	7.7	—
Disseminator	48.0	46.9	5.1	—	46.9	49.0	4.1	—
Spokesman	9.3	17.0	73.7	—	9.3	17.5	73.2	—
Decisional								
Entrepreneur	35.6	27.8	20.6	16.0	55.2	22.7	14.4	7.7
Disturbance Handler	23.7	40.7	25.3	10.3	21.1	38.2	27.3	13.4
Resource Allocator	32.0	33.5	26.8	7.7	27.8	33.5	29.9	8.8
Negotiator	6.2	14.4	28.4	51.0	8.8	18.0	23.7	49.5

JOB PERFORMANCE

Exhibit 5 shows the GMs' assessment of the appropriateness of seven criteria for evaluating their job performance. The GMs were asked to rate these criteria on a scale of 1 (not appropriate) to 5 (very appropriate). Responses of 1, 2, or 3 were designated as signifying "not appropriate." A response of 4 or 5 signified that the criterion provided an appropriate measure of job performance.

The ratio of payroll to room sales received the most endorsement as an indicator of successful job performance. The average annual room rate was also judged to be a relatively appropriate indicator, as was the ratio of payroll to food and beverage sales. The ratio of payroll to the number of rooms was judged least appropriate of the seven indicators mentioned.

It is interesting that none of the performance indicators proposed by the researcher was judged to be appropriate by more than 75 percent of the GMs. When asked what other factors would be used in evaluating their performance, the GMs emphasized such people-related criteria as personnel management, guest satisfaction, and their own personal qualities (creativity, planning ability, etc.), as opposed to the operation-related criteria proposed by the author. Of the numerous suggestions of appropriate performance-evaluation criteria, 75 percent fell under the broad category of people management and 25 percent under the category of operations management (e.g., control and financial procedures, property maintenance, compliance with company policy).

CONCLUSIONS AND RECOMMENDATIONS

Ninety-three percent of GMs maintained that their jobs were more complex today than they were five years ago. If the hospitality industry is to keep pace with the growing complexity of hotel operations as seen from a GM's perspective, it will be necessary to develop more sophisticated and effective methods of training and evaluating GMs and of understanding their managerial activities. The present study offers a number of ideas as to how the industry should proceed with this project.

Training

When asked to identify the four most important topics out of a field of seven areas of study that should be covered in a course for newly appointed general managers, 42 percent of the GMs gave precedence to personnel management (see Exhibit 6).

Accounting and finance followed, with 21 percent of the GMs citing it as the most important area of study. The GMs apparently believed that their effectiveness and the success of their properties rested on their ability to motivate and direct the hotel staff members directly responsible for the execution of hotel operations. As one of the GMs remarked, "A manager must obtain the best performance possible from his staff—continually evaluating their results—and act accordingly." The GM's training should reflect the fact that he achieves his results through the activities of other people.

EXHIBIT 5
GM's evaluation of selected job-performance criteria

Criterion	Appro- priate	Not appro- priate
Payroll/Room sales	74.9%	25.1%
Room rate	68.8%	31.2%
Payroll/Food & beverage sales	66.9%	33.1%
Occupancy	61.9%	38.1%
Room sales/Rooms	55.0%	45.0%
Payroll/Rooms	46.8%	53.2%
Room sales/Em- ployees	41.5%	58.5%

EXHIBIT 6
Most important topics of study for novice GMs

Topic	Number of times mentioned:			
	1st	2nd	3rd	4th
Personnel	67 (42%)	56 (33%)	43 (27%)	31 (23%)
Accounting & finance	33 (21%)	47 (27%)	33 (20%)	27 (20%)
Marketing	21 (13%)	24 (14%)	32 (20%)	27 (20%)
Management	26 (16%)	20 (12%)	22 (14%)	11 (8%)
Properties management	3 (2%)	7 (4%)	13 (8%)	20 (15%)
Food & beverage	4 (3%)	8 (5%)	14 (8%)	11 (8%)
Rooms & housekeeping	4 (3%)	8 (5%)	5 (3%)	5 (4%)

Evaluation

While the bottom line has undeniable importance in the evaluation of general managers' performance, the participating GMs believed other, more qualitative (as opposed to quantitative) considerations should also be addressed in the evaluation of their performance. Such factors would include the GM's ability to plan creatively, to relate to guests successfully, and to manage employees effectively. Evaluation procedures that take these factors into account should be developed.

Managerial Roles

This study identified a number of managerial roles—those of leader, monitor, disseminator, and entrepreneur—that GMs judged to be very important and that absorbed large amounts of their time. This information might be applied in the development of training programs emphasizing these crucial functions. In addition, further research might attempt to make correlations between GMs' effectiveness and their allocation of time and importance to various managerial roles.[1]

The Effective GM: Leader or Entrepreneur?

David A. Ley

Although the general manager is critical to a hotel's performance, top management's ability to identify the characteristics of successful general managers is an often-overlooked area of research.

If a hotel's occupancy and revenues meet budget projections while costs and labor turnover are controlled, the property's general manager can be fairly confident of receiving a favorable performance evaluation from his superior. Management and researchers, however, know very little about what effective managers actually do on a day-to-day basis to produce these desired results. To address at least one aspect of this issue, the research reported below attempted to establish whether effective managers allocated their work time differently from counterparts rated less effective.

This article was originally published in the November 1980 issue of *The Cornell Hotel and Restaurant Administration Quarterly*, and is reprinted here with the permission of the Cornell University School of Hotel Administration. © 1980.

METHODOLOGY

The researcher examined the daily activities of general managers at seven comparable hotel properties to determine how they allocated their time to various managerial roles. The study's participants held management positions in company-owned, 140- to 170-room properties (each offering dining room, cocktail lounge, banquet, and swimming-pool facilities) serving a clientele of families and business travelers. The seven participants had held their management positions at these hotels for six months or more.

The researcher first observed the management activities of each participant in detail and recorded the time allocated to each activity for three representative work days during the peak business months of July and August. The activities were later classified on the basis of the ten work roles defined by Mintzberg (1975): figurehead, leader, liaison, monitor, disseminator, spokesman, entrepreneur, disturbance handler, resource allocator, and negotiator. Second, the researcher asked for a corporate-office rating of each manager's effectiveness: two managers were rated highly effective, three effective, and two less effective. It was therefore possible to compare a manager's day-to-day activities to his effectiveness rating.

Because of the small sample size and the relatively brief observation period, the researcher could not draw specific inferences from the data or develop a representative profile of the general managers' allocations of time for each of Mintzberg's ten work roles. Particularly suggestive results regarding the leadership and entrepreneurial roles surfaced, however, and are reported here because of their interest to both practicing managers and academic researchers.

RESULTS

When the leadership and entrepreneurial activities of the managers surveyed are examined, it appears that *highly effective managers allocate time to these two roles differently from less effective managers* of similar hotels.

Leadership role. Mintzberg describes the manager in the role of leader as "responsible for the motivation and activation of subordinates: respon-

sible for staffing, training, and associate duties" (Mintzberg 1973, 92). Since lodging chains frequently emphasize these leadership responsibilities, the researcher anticipated that highly effective managers would spend more time in the leadership role—interacting more with their staff and delegating to others as much of the daily routine work as possible.

Instead, the two innkeepers who were judged highly effective spent *less* time in the leader role than the two less effective managers (Exhibit 1). None of the managers devoted more than one-fourth of his work day to leadership activities.

Entrepreneurial role. The study suggests that highly effective managers spend more time on entrepreneurial activities than do managers with lower effectiveness ratings; the results indicate further that a hierarchical relationship may exist between the amount of time managers allocate to entrepreneurship and judged effectiveness (Exhibit 1).

The highly effective innkeepers were those observed initiating the most activities to expand the hotel's business potential, to improve the property, to supervise changes, and to suggest ideas for fur-

EXHIBIT 1
Relationship between managerial effectiveness and time allocated to leadership and entrepreneurship

Innkeeper	Judged Effectiveness	% of Working Time Allocated to: Leadership	Entrepreneur- ship
1	HE	2.6	17.1
2	HE	9.4	9.8
3	E	22.5	7.1
4	E	5.2	5.0
5	E	11.6	4.3
6	LE	12.2	4.2
7	LE	21.8	1.8

HE = Highly effective. E = Effective. LE = Less effective.

ther improvement to top management. The researcher found these entrepreneurial efforts to be an important part of the highly effective innkeepers' management styles.

Time on the job. The higher-rated innkeepers in the study spent more time on the job than the inn-

keepers rated less effective, substantiating the anxieties expressed by several innkeepers. Some managers believed the length of their work day influenced the district or corporate office's evaluation of their effectiveness. General managers rated more effective tended, it was found, to work later "in case a call came in from the head office."

The Mentoring Process in Hotel General Managers' Careers

Denney G. Rutherford
Jane Wiegenstein

A pilot study of mentoring in the hospitality industry found surprisingly little evidence of mentoring among general managers and other supervisors. But the results of a follow-up study, presented below, support the supposition that mentoring exists and has helped many managers.

Mentoring is generally thought of as a relationship between a guide, teacher, or sponsor and a younger, less-experienced colleague, whom the mentor assists in making his or her way in a career or through the organization (Moore 1982). During the past five years, the contribution of mentoring to career development has received increasing attention in both scholarly and popular publications. As an attribute of careers, mentoring has been investigated by a number of researchers who have highlighted the importance of a mentor to a protégé's success in an organization (Dalton, Thompson, and Price 1977; Levinson 1978; Kanter 1977; Schein 1978).

Because a pilot examination of mentoring in the hotel industry found the mentoring relationship did not predominate among any of the various groups surveyed (front-office managers, directors of housekeeping, food and beverage managers, and general manager), and because this finding seemed

to contradict much of what has been written about mentors, the authors undertook a larger study of hotel general managers (Rutherford 1984). The authors sent a survey questionnaire to 200 GMs selected from a list of 600. Seventy-six (40 percent) responded. This article discusses the GMs' responses to the following questions raised in the pilot study and by previous researchers (Roche 1979; Schmidt 1961).

- What is the true incidence of mentoring among hotel GMs?
- Are mentored GMs more highly paid?
- Do mentored GMs operate more profitable hotels?
- Do mentored GMs' careers advance faster?
- Are mentored GMs more satisfied with their jobs?
- What do mentored GMs think of their experience? and
- What are the forms and dynamics of the mentoring relationship?

The forms and dynamics of the mentoring relationship are of particular interest. While it is not clear that everyone needs a mentor, James Clawson (1980) points out,

> Young adults beginning their careers and more-experienced managers alike would have greater insight into the real developmental processes of their own careers if they understood better the nature of the mentor-protégé relationship in general, and how to manage the developmental aspects of their immediate superior-subordinate relationships in particular.

THE MENTORED MAJORITY

About two-thirds of the respondents reported having had a mentoring relationship. Those reporting mentors tended to be college graduates and many of these held hotel-restaurant degrees (see Exhibit 1). The percentage of GMs reporting a mentoring relationship is remarkably similar to that found in previous studies, indicating a high degree of conformity between the GMs and the general business population (Roche 1979). The result indicates the current study is probably a more accurate representation of the career experiences of hotel GMs than was the pilot study.

Success Measures

For working (or aspiring) GMs, the most interesting findings of this study probably deal with "success measures" of mentored careers—namely, that sponsored or mentored managers rise faster in their careers and manage more profitable hotels than those without mentors (Schmidt 1961, 92, 148–49, 159–60). In addition, the authors investigated the proposition growing out of other studies that those with mentors are more highly paid than those who rose through the ranks on their own. Another potential measure of success is the level of fringe benefits or perquisites (perks), which can represent lucrative components of executive-compensation packages. That job satisfaction is enhanced by mentoring relationships has also been suggested by a number of researchers.

As shown in Exhibit 2, there are indeed differences between those GMs with mentors and those without. Though none of the differences is statistically significant, their collective implications are interesting. Mentored managers reported salary levels nearly $6,000 greater than the salaries of mentorless managers. To be sure, an average salary in a population whose reported salaries range from $26,000 to $180,000 is a tenuous figure, and it is impossible to state that mentoring has given these GMs a higher average salary, but the results are consistent with those of earlier studies.

Schmidt (1961) found the mentoring process influenced another measure of managerial effectiveness, operational profits. Profits among managers reporting a mentoring relationship averaged about

EXHIBIT 1
Incidence of mentoring among surveyed hotel general managers

	Mentor	No mentor	Population total (n)
	67.1% (n = 51)	32.9% (25)	76
Among men	69.4% (50)	30.6% (22)	72 (96% of sample)
Among women	33.3% (1)	66.7% (2)	3 (4% of sample)
Among college graduates	64.4% (38)	35.6% (21)	59 (86.8% of sample)
Among hotel-school graduates	65.2% (15)	34.8% (8)	23 (42.6% of sample)
Mean age	42.5	44.5	43.2
Mean years in industry	20	19.4	19.9

EXHIBIT 2
Success and effectiveness measures among hotel general managers

Measure (average):	Mentor	No mentor	Population mean
Salary	$68,395	$62,625	$66,498
Profit	$4.35 million	$3.84 million	$4.22 million
Per-room profit (among those reporting profit)	$6,891	$6,361	$6,758
Years from entry to first managerial assignment	3.93	4.40	4.08
Years from first managerial assignment to general manager	5.98	5.02	5.66
Number of hotels worked in as general manager	3.58	2.80	3.32

one-half million dollars greater than those reported by GMs without mentors. Caution in interpretation is again necessary, however, because the surveyed GMs managed hotels ranging in size from fewer than 400 rooms to more than 1,000 rooms. A better comparison was made possible by calculating per-room profit or loss, and this figure also showed slightly more profitable operation among mentored GMs, though not at a statistically significant level.

While the mean profit shown in Exhibit 2 tends to support the idea that mentored managers make more money, the mean profit figure does not include losses, which were reported by three mentored managers and one without a mentor. The worst of these losses, a staggering $14 million, was reported by a mentored manager, but his estimate was based in part on the structure of the hotel's mortgage and ownership arrangements and was not necessarily attributable to operations. In any event, previous studies reported profits only (no losses), so this study has followed that pattern.

While tests of statistical significance do not show differentiation between the two groups, the body of evidence tends to support previous findings about the connection of mentoring and profitability of hotels.

Career Movement

Mentored GMs reported spending less time in sub-managerial or training positions than their mentor-less colleagues. On the other hand, once those without mentors were out of the training ranks, they tended to rise more swiftly from their first managerial assignment to GM. (Once promoted to GM, however, the managers without mentors reported slightly less career mobility.) This finding is surprising, for most persons who praise the positive aspects of the mentoring process suggest that mentored managers would rise more swiftly, especially since career success is generally equated with mobility.

Again, the differences between those with mentors and those without are not great, so it is not possible to conclude that the mentoring process plays a substantial role in career movement. Furthermore, reports of career movement should be interpreted with a grain of salt, because (like some other items in this survey) they are subject to bias arising from selective recollection.

Perks

Many common fringe benefits are not available to hotel GMs. Indeed, physical exams, parking, company cars, and liability insurance were the only benefits reported by more than half of the GMs surveyed. Many hotel GMs, however, have benefits that are not generally available to managers in other industries. These may range from regular dining to laundry services and on-premise living quarters. As a result, such perks as admission to an executive dining room or country-club membership may in effect be supplanted by common hospitality-industry practices. Exhibit 3 sets forth the distribution of common executive perks among the responding GMs. With the exception of deferred compensation, there was no substantial difference between the availability of perks for those with mentors and those without.

Satisfaction

Considering the discussions over the implications of the mentoring process, one might intuitively conclude that job satisfaction constitutes a point of demarcation between those with mentors and those on their own. This prediction has not always been borne out in other studies. School teachers with a single mentor, for instance, reported more job satisfaction than those who had more than one mentor,

and those with one or more mentors reported a surprising degree of job burnout (Fagan and Walter 1982). Another study found only a mild relationship between mentoring and career satisfaction (Campion and Goldfinch 1983).

GMs in this study generally reported high levels of satisfaction with various aspects of their careers and jobs (as shown in Exhibit 4). The only differences between the two groups of respondents lay in the mentored group's more positive assessment of the fairness of its salaries and economic position compared to those of other hotel professionals, and in the greater willingness to consider leaving the hotel profession shown by some in the mentored group.

One possible reason for the mentored group's reporting economic treatment might be that the mentored GM has a more intimate view of organizational complexities and therefore is better able to judge the fairness of his or her recompense (Schein 1978). A simpler explanation is that mentored GMs are economically better off than their counterparts without mentors.

The other divergence, on reported willingness to leave the industry, is mystifying. If the mentored group is well paid, has good benefits, is highly sat-

EXHIBIT 3
Fringe benefits granted to hotel general managers

Benefits	Mentor (n = 51)	No mentor (n = 25)	Total (% of sample)
Physical exam	51% (26)	48% (12)	50%
Special parking	73% (37)	80% (20)	75%
Stock options	27% (14)	16% (4)	24%
Assigned company car	61% (31)	76% (19)	66%
Liability insurance	55% (28)	52% (13)	54%
Country-club membership	33% (17)	36% (9)	34%
Luncheon-club membership	31% (16)	32% (8)	32%
Special vacation policy	37% (19)	36% (9)	37%
Financial counseling	16% (8)	12% (3)	14%
Deferred compensation	39% (20)	20% (5)	33%
Assigned chauffeur	4% (2)	4% (1)	4%
Executive dining room	33% (17)	44% (11)	37%

EXHIBIT 4

Comparison of personal feelings of career satisfaction among hotel general managers with mentors and those without

Statement	Percentage agreeing	
	Mentor	No mentor
I am successful compared to others of my age.	85.9%	88.0%
Top management listens to my judgment.	94	96
I don't have the chance to use all my abilities.	29.5	40
I am fairly paid.	90.2	70.8
My economic position has improved in the last two years relative to that of other hotel professionals.	70	56
My economic position has improved in the last two years relative to that of those outside the profession.	64	60
I am satisfied with my present position.	84.3	80
I have considered leaving the hotel profession in the last two years.	25.5	8
I would be less satisfied with life outside the hotel industry.	60	68

isfied, and has profitable operations, why do so many respondents contemplate a career change? One corporate hotel officer suggested that those who have enjoyed mentoring relationships have greater confidence, allowing these individuals to consider themselves capable of succeeding at an array of challenges. This particular phenomenon might be a topic for further research, for such a situation has not been suggested by other researchers (although the mentored GMs who would consider a career change represent only 17 percent of the total sample).

In general, these hotel GMs are a happy group of executives. They are more satisfied than those responding to a previous survey about mentoring (Roche 1979).

The Managers Speak

Although no statistically significant association was found between mentoring and most measures of a manager's career success, the mentoring process has ardent supporters among those who have had mentors. Their testimony, shown in the accompanying box, indicates the psychological impact of mentoring. These statements made in support of mentoring take on more meaning when viewed against the total lack of comments received from the mentorless GMs. That this group was unmoved to comment (even negatively) underscores the importance mentored GMs attach to their experiences.

Getting Started. An overwhelming majority of the respondents (85 percent) cited their own performance as the initial impetus for the mentoring relationship. Fewer than 20 percent ascribed the relationship to chance, similar interests, or a recommendation from another person. Only one respondent reported a company-sponsored program as the origin of the mentoring relationship.

The tendency of most GMs to feel that their performance attracted the mentor's interest helps to explain the lukewarm response of most respondents to the idea of formal mentoring programs. One GM commented, "Perhaps because it involves so much in the way of compatibility between mentor and 'mentee'—it *cannot* be an assigned task." Another warned, "The fastest way to kill such a potentially powerful tool would be to make it corporate policy."

Views on Having a Mentor	**Views on Being a Mentor**
• "As our organization is a family-owned and family-operated hotel chain, the mentoring process has brought me into the family in a semi-official way."	• "I believe in mentoring as one of the most powerful management-education tools available."
• "My mentors never gave me answers; they gave me the right questions."	• "[I] take pride in helping them help our industry, as well as themselves."
• "[I learned] ethics, allegiance, personal dynamics, and standards of appearance, [and also to] develop a sense of humor."	• "I enjoy seeing young people progress."
• "My mentor probably taught me more about the hotel business than four or five years of college could have done."	• "I believe mentoring is vastly underplayed in importance and use in the industry."

Formalized programs, though they may enhance performance and career development, undercut what these GMs say is the prime motivator of the relationship: individual merit and worth, as embodied in performance.

Dynamics. Only 10 percent of the respondents reported that they did not look up to their mentor. Forty-one percent of those surveyed characterized the relationship with their mentor as friendly, while the remainder said the relationship was either not close or strictly professional.

Despite evident tensions in some of the relationships as time went on, none of the respondents reported that a relationship had disintegrated into unfriendliness. Twenty percent indicated that they had felt a need to break away from their mentor at some point. For almost one-fourth of the protégés, the mentoring relationship evolved into a peer relationship.

Interaction

The most important functions performed by the mentor appeared to be helping the protégé gain confidence and providing counseling on career moves. The confidence factor was mentioned prominently by the GMs, regardless of the length of their relationship. For established managers,

then, a boost in confidence was as important as it was to those just starting out.

About half the protégés cited political advice, help in understanding the organization, and the sharing of technical expertise as important contributions made by their mentors. About a third of the respondents said their mentor helped with cutting through red tape and teaching the protégé how to work with people. Thus, what the mentor did for the protégé on a personal level apparently had a more resounding impact than anything the mentor might have been able to convey in the way of organizational savvy or expertise.

Most of the protégés adopted some of the characteristics of their mentors over the course of the relationship. The mentor's dedication influenced the largest number of respondents (63 percent). Frankness, persistence, and honesty on the part of the mentor were also admired and emulated by about 40 percent of the protégés.

Repeating the Cycle

Almost all of the protégés went on to serve as mentors to others. When asked what prompted them to do so, 82 percent answered that mentoring was part of any manager's role, 71 percent mentored others for the emotional paybacks (mentoring made them feel good), and 59 percent indicated that their own positive experiences as a protégé had prompted them to become mentors. While relatively few (16 percent) cited power as a reason for mentoring, 43 percent did believe they benefited from having a protégé.

That mentoring was overwhelmingly seen by those surveyed as one of the manager's roles suggests that it may be somewhat easier in the future for young managers to find mentors than it has been in the past. This could be good news for women and minorities, who might benefit from mentoring relationships even more than white males. On the other hand, to say mentoring "is part of any manager's role" may be a stock response, checked almost as a matter of convention. Even if this were the case, the fact that 82 percent of the respondents agreed with the proposition attests to mentoring's growing acceptance.

Except in a few instances, no connection was found between the cordiality or length of the mentoring relationship and the responses to questions regarding the functions performed by the mentor, reasons for becoming a mentor, or views on mentoring and its relationship to career development and job satisfaction. This suggests that the mentoring relationship need not be an intimate or lengthy one to be important and useful to the protégé.

Duration. Most of the relationships lasted from one to five years (52 percent), while a smaller group (35 percent) extended for more than ten years. The mean duration was three years. Relationships lasting one to three years were without exception characterized as not close or strictly professional. The longer the relationship endured, the more likely it was to be characterized as friendly. Length did not inevitably connote intimacy, however. About one-third of the protégés whose relationships with their mentors lasted ten years or more still reported the connection to be strictly professional. Protégés with longer-standing relationships were more likely to report looking up to their mentors. Three years appeared to be a cutoff point: those whose relationship lasted one to three years tended to be more ambivalent about their mentors (slightly over half reported looking up to their mentors somewhat).

Protégés whose mentoring relationships lasted from one to five years did benefit from them, however. Like those with longer relationships, many of these respondents reported that their positive experiences as a protégé led them to mentor others. This group was also somewhat more likely to cite benefits accruing from the protégés as figuring in the decision to become a mentor. Those with briefer relationships were more likely to feel that their mentors had benefited more from the relationship than they had. Few of those having relationships of longer than five years indicated such a position. This finding suggests that protégés with briefer relationships may have seen the relationship in utilitarian terms, and would mentor others with the same expectation.

Intimacy. The degree of intimacy had surprisingly little effect on the survey responses. Those who described their relationship as friendly were more likely to cite the mentor's listening to ideas and career counseling as important dimensions of the relationship, but still, degree of intimacy made no difference in the reported perception of whether the mentor's interest was crucial to the protégé or whether the respondent cited positive experiences as a protégé as a reason for becoming a mentor. Those who characterized their relationship as strictly professional, however, were less likely to agree that everyone who succeeds has a mentor and were more likely to oppose the establishment of formal mentoring programs. Respondents in this group were also more likely to deny that the mentor had promoted their careers.

New Patterns

Although many of the managers sampled felt that their performance on the job was responsible for attracting the interest of their mentor, young managers do not need to wait for their superiors to appreciate their level of performance. Actively seeking a mentor can more quickly produce positive results, as one manager recalled:

> I found that almost anyone will be a mentor if he or she is appealed to. In other words, I would ask a senior vice-president a question, and he would answer. I would then research the issue for hours and draft a report and submit it, asking for comments. When they realized I was interested enough to put 10 to 20 hours of my time into a 20-minute discussion, then they were interested in giving me 20 minutes once in a while.

This young manager's enterprise could not have gone unnoticed by his superiors; those 20-minute episodes "once in a while" surely had a cumulative benefit for his career.

This experience shows that mentoring relationships do not have to match the classical stereotype, based on the long-term, intimate relationship Telemachus enjoyed with his tutor, Mentor. As just discussed, mentoring relationships do not have to be intimate or last for years to have positive effects. These two conclusions—the importance of actively seeking mentoring relationships and the effectiveness of short-term contacts—have important implications for those who have had difficulty establishing a mentoring relationship.

A Leg Up

Mentoring apparently has had a positive influence on the careers of hotel GMs. Although the presence or absence of a mentor did not absolutely distinguish the managers on the basis of success, effectiveness, or job satisfaction, the general pattern of responses and the statements made by many of the GMs make it clear that mentoring has contributed decisively to their careers. Mentoring appears to have played a particularly important role in encouraging many of these managers, as one said, "to make the right move at the right time." This supports prior studies' conclusions that managers who make the right contacts eventually find themselves at more profitable properties.

If a vote were taken among hotel GMs, it is safe to say there would be overwhelmingly positive support for mentoring. While this support may not extend to formal mentoring programs, some hotels and other organizations have experimented with assigning people as sponsors in a narrowly defined sense—with positive results. Further research is needed on the extent to which such programs exist in the hotel and restaurant industry.

Another topic of interest is the incidence and effect of mentoring among women and minorities. The authors' study shed little light on this matter, because of the sparse representation of women and minorities in the sample.

A mentoring relationship does not necessarily have to result in statistically measurable difference in success, effectiveness, or job satisfaction to have a positive influence on managerial careers. The significance of mentoring is ultimately a matter of individual perception. The respondents in this study repeatedly echoed the words of one GM: "Mentoring is an absolute must. Without it, you do not move into the great jobs."

CASE STUDY—"A Model Career"

As vice-president of personnel for the Crimson Cougar Hotel Company, you have been approached by Sue Hadley, front-office manager of the Pittsburgh property, and James Harris, food and beverage manager of the Washington, D.C., property. They each seek your advice as to how best to prepare themselves and structure their careers to give them the best chance to advance to general manager of a Cougar property.

From your readings, suggest career tactics and strategies with rationales to both Sue and James. Be sure to treat realistically the potential positives and negatives inherent in any analysis of this sort.

Endnotes

[1]This was the approach taken by Ley (see References). The small size of Ley's sample (seven GMs) makes further research in this area desirable.

References

Campion, Michael A., and John R. Goldfinch. 1983. Mentoring among hospital administrators. *Hospital and Health Services Administration* 28(6):89.

Clawson, James G. 1980. Mentoring in careers. In *Work, family, and career,* ed. C.B. Derr, p. 144. New York: Praeger, p. 144.

Dalton, G.W., P.H. Thompson, and R.L. Price. 1977. The four stages of professional careers. *Organizational Dynamics* Summer:19–42.

Fagan, M. Michael, and Glen Walter. 1982. Mentoring among teachers. *Journal of Educational Research* November–December:116.

Kanter, Rosabeth M. 1977. *Men and women of the corporation.* New York: Basic Books.

Levinson, D.J. 1978. *The seasons of a man's life.* New York: Alfred A. Knopf.

Ley, David. 1980. The effective GM: Leader or entrepreneur? *Cornell Hotel and Restaurant Administration Quarterly* 21(3):66–67.

Mintzberg, Henry. 1973. *The nature of managerial work.* New York: Harper & Row, p. 92.

Mintzberg, Henry. 1975. The manager's job: Folklore and fact. *Harvard Business Review* 53(4):49–61.

Moore, Kathryn M. 1982. The role of mentors in developing leaders for academe. *Educational Record* (Winter):23–28.

Nailon, Philip W. 1968. A study of management activity in units of a hotel group. Master's thesis, University of Surrey, U.K.

Roche, Gerald R. 1979. Much ado about mentors. *Harvard Business Review* 57(1):14–27.

Rutherford, Denney G. 1984. Mentoring and the hospitality manager. *Cornell Hotel and Restaurant Administration Quarterly* 25(1):16–19.

Schein, Edgar H. 1978. *Career dynamics: Matching individual and organizational needs.* Reading, MA: Addison-Wesley.

Schmidt, Wesley I. 1961. The study of the origins, education and occupational definition of hotel managers as related to career patterns of security and success. Doctoral dissertation, Michigan State University.

Suggested Readings

Books

Mintzberg, Henry. *The Nature of Managerial Work,* New York: Harper & Row, 1973.

Schmidt, Wesley I. "The Study of the Origins, Education and Occupational Definition of Hotel Managers as Related to Career Patterns of Security and Success." Doctoral dissertation, Michigan State University, 1961.

Articles

Pickworth, James R. "Managerial Jobs in Chain Organizations." *Cornell Hotel and Restaurant Administration Quarterly* (February 1982):30–33.

Swanljung, Mikael. "How Hotel Executives Made the Climb to the Top." *Cornell Hotel and Restaurant Administration Quarterly* (May 1981):30–34.

SECTION 4

Front Office Management

INTRODUCTION

Among other things, the student of hotel administration will find the front office referred to as the "hub," the "nerve center," the "brain," or some other name suggesting centrality in the modern hotel. As H. E. Heldenbrand stated in his now-classic 1944 book *Front Office Psychology,* ". . . To the guest, the manager is largely represented by the front office, and the unseen head will be judged favorably or otherwise by the guest treatment there" (Introduction). The observations, opinions, and research presented in this section are chosen to illustrate the centrality of the front office in the modern hotel.

Rick Bechtel's article on becoming a temporary front office clerk at a major hotel gives a perspective from outside the industry as to some of the complexities of operating a hotel front desk. Rutherford's research on the front office manager suggests, among other things, that the job of the front office manager (FOM) is changing in the modern era and presents a model by which the job of the FOM may be analyzed.

Being the "hub" or "nerve center" of a modern hotel has as one of its positive aspects the fact that front office staff is keenly aware of what is happening at virtually every level of the hotel's organizational structure. One of the negative aspects is that the front office also serves as a lightning rod for guest complaints. This can be one of the most difficult things for the front office staff to learn to deal with—especially the frequency and sometimes the intensity of guest complaints. The two articles contributed by Robert Lewis and Lewis and Morris analyze major elements of this issue and suggest some ways to look at it in a more constructive and analytical way.

One of the major sources of complaints related to the front office are those having to do with the accuracy of guest reservations and the details attendant thereto. Corney and Toh both treat the sometimes-vexing managerial problem of coping with reservations, no-shows, late cancellations, overbooking, and optimization of rooms inventory management.

Everyone who learned as a new desk clerk the meaning of the phrase "rack rate" also learned shortly thereafter that very few hotels ever achieve the ideal of renting rooms at "rack rate" on anything approaching a regular basis. The practice of discounting room rates is, therefore, nearly universally pervasive in the hotel industry. James Abbey tackles aspects of this question with regard to the applicability of discounting as a strategy to address declining occupancy rates.

Two other issues conclude this section. While several preceding selections predicate aspects of their analyses on sophisticated automated equipment, computers are not always necessarily the complete answer to any given problem. Alvarez, Ferguson, and Dunn talk about the danger in assuming that equipment will solve all service problems in a front office, particularly in a large hotel.

Automation and, to a certain extent, deregulation of the communications industry, has focused intense interest upon yet another issue—call accounting. Kaiser's article discusses how hotels can use call accounting to turn what previously has been an unprofitable service into a profit center. While it is not discussed in Kaiser's article, it should be noted that the practice of call accounting has become somewhat controversial, particularly in those instances where hotels have added too much profit to their call-accounting systems. They have generated significant negative publicity and customer animosity. Issues such as this hark back to Lewis's articles about guest complaints.

The articles presented here for consideration represent only a suggestion of the range of issues attendant to any modern hotel front office department. Duties, obligations, and responsibilities of front office personnel will change from hotel company to hotel company based on such variables as market segmentation, organizational structure, corporate philosophy, and individual leadership. It is not suggested that these articles are either exclusive or exhaustive, but at this time they represent the direction of current thought and commentary relative to front office management.

OVERVIEW OF FRONT OFFICE PERSONNEL

While front offices may be organized in a number of different ways that depend on market segment, organizational or corporate philosophy, and practical or physical realities, the job functions described below are normally expected to be found within the front office. This may vary, of course, from company to company.

These descriptions are the editor's synthesis of personal experience, industry standards, and the writings of the authors listed in the suggested readings at the end of this section. The books included there are outstanding, in-depth treatments of the intricacies of modern front office management and are widely used as textbooks and training aids.

Reservations

The clerical staff that performs the reservation function handles a number of tasks that are important to the orderly accumulation and dissemination of reservation information to the appropriate departments.

Generally speaking, the reservations staff handles guest communication and correspondence regarding reservations at the hotel. These contacts with potential guests can be through correspondence in the form of mail, telephone, telegraph, or through a centralized computer reservation system. On the basis of this information, the staff creates and maintains reservation records for all advance reservations in the hotel. Once the information has been collected, staff members produce and mail or otherwise communicate the appropriate confirmations and/or guarantees to the requester.

As a part of reservations responsibilities, they track future room availability and may initiate forecast of rooms sales and occupancy.

Finally, on the day the guest is expected, the reservation staff will "bring forward" reservations to the front office. This may be in the form of a physical reservation card or document or simply the release of temporal information in the hotel's data processing system.

It should be noted that in some hotel companies, the functions of reservations may be shifting to the marketing or sales department. This recognizes the importance of the sales department in producing group business and the close relationship that the sales staff and the reservations people must attain. By the same token, in other hotel organizations, the reservations staff may remain in the front office, which has historically been its focus.

Cashier

As the name implies, cashiers deal with the maintenance and settling of guest accounts in the front office. Specifically, they are responsible for posting vouchers or charges that arrive during the day and evening shifts to guest accounts or the city ledger.

Generally speaking, cashiers are responsible for maintaining timely and accurate guest account folio balances. In most hotels the cashiers are the members of the front office staff who handle all cash transactions and checkouts of hotel guests at the front desk. They are responsible for settling of guest accounts in whatever form payment is tendered: charge card, cash, check, or transfer to some master account.

It should be noted that in some hotels the function of cashier is combined with that of room and or reservations clerk because the size of the hotel demands it. In larger hotels, cashier is likely a separate function, and several individuals may fill that role.

Night Auditor

While the night auditor typically works at the front desk, in an increasing number of hotels the night auditors are the responsibility of the hotel controllers (see Howey, "Evolution of the Night Audit," in Section 11 of this book). The fundamental role of the night auditor is to assure the hotel that departmental accounts and guest accounts are in balance at the close of the business day. To that end the night auditor posts charges and vouchers to guest accounts that are not posted by the day or evening cashiers; participates in routines that verify the accuracy and completeness of all guest accounts; and balances guest folio entries and departmental records. A major portion of the night auditor's function is to post room and tax charges to guest accounts. Finally, the night auditors balance all accounts for the next day's business.

A significant portion of the night auditor's task may involve tracking errors and discrepancies in room and departmental accounts; hence the term *auditor.*

Room Clerks

The task of the room clerk is one that varies greatly from company to company and hotel to hotel. The size of the hotel, the market of the hotel, and the ambiance of the hotel are all elements that may have an effect on the design of the room clerk's job. Suffice it to say, the room clerk is one of those positions whose focus at the front desk is very important to guest relations.

Among the major responsibilities of the room clerk are helping the guest determine what particular room rate is most appropriate to that guest's wants and needs. This will vary, of course, with the type of accommodation the guest desires, the length of stay, and other requirements that are needed to register the guest. The room clerk will then assist in the performance of the registration procedure, assign a room, help the guest determine the method of payment, and initiate the rooming process by dispensing and controlling keys and dispatching bell staff to assist the guest to the room.

The room clerk will report as necessary to front office management and is generally trained and expected by that management to recognize and evaluate special situations and arrange for their attention. In many ways the room clerk is the eyes and ears of management regarding the operation of the hotel and its interface with the guest. To this extent, it is an extraordinarily important position.

Front Office Assistant Manager

Generally, the front office assistant manager supervises on a day-to-day basis all of the operations and personnel of the front office. The front office assistant manager performs duties under the guidance and direction of the front office manager. He or she is responsible for the smooth functioning of front office activities and processes and may work specifically with tour groups and/or corporate clients to ease their access to the hotels and its services.

The front office assistant manager will assist the front office manager in hiring, staffing, scheduling, and training other front office personnel. A particular responsibility of the front office assistant manager is to monitor the status of guest accounts, and perhaps participate in the authorization of check cashing and credit terms within policy guidelines. A major expectation of the front office assistant manager is that he or she be able to fill in at all front office positions in an emergency.

Other Functions

Other traditional functions within the front office may or may not be the province of a particular individual, but nonetheless are performed by front office personnel at some level.

Mail, Messages, and Telephones. Historically, when people traveled by train and boat, hotel stays were much longer than the average stay today. The management of mail in those days before ubiquitous high-quality telecommunications was very important. With the advent of personalized travel by automobile and swift long-distance travel by air, hotel stays became shorter and telephone messages assumed greater importance.

Now, however, with the advent of "overnight" mail and package service, Fax-type document transmission, and sophisticated telephone communications, the management of mail, document, package, and message service for hotel guests is more important than ever. Today's business traveler relies on modern communications to an extent never before imagined, and a hotel's failure in this context can be costly to both parties.

Hotels whose clientele demands high-quality communications service are wise to consider carefully the design and control of the mail, message, and telephone function in the front office.

Guest Service. The bell staff, door greeters, garage and parking attendants, and other uniformed service staff are now seen by most hotel companies as an integral part of the whole service delivery system, as opposed to the personal "fiefdom" of the old-style bell captain. Guest service may also include the specialized duties performed by the concierge (see "Keepers of the Keys" in Section 6).

Supervision of these services may or may not be the responsibility of the front office manager, but since these personnel participate in many crucial guest-hotel activities, they probably are. Consider, for example, initiating the guests' experience (door staff, garage, parking); assisting the guest in transition to the front desk (bell staff); participating in the rooming process (bell staff, luggage); and answering special questions or making extraordinary arrangements (concierge). As these examples attest, guest service is now much more than simply carrying suitcases, and as such should be treated as a professional and integral part of a hotel's service design.

Front Desk Success at the Westin Seattle

Rick Bechtel

Hotel managers have always been confronted with a peculiar irony where front desk operations are concerned. Unquestionably, desk personnel have more impact on guests than any other single group of employees. They are the first to say hello and the last to say good-bye. In between, it is usually the desk clerk to whom guests turn for information, assistance, or resolution of a complaint.

However, front desk work is often tedious and stressful. The pay is traditionally low, and rarely is there much opportunity for advancement. As a result, front office managers have difficulty finding well-qualified people. Morale tends to run low, turnover is high, and performance is less than optimal. And that in turn shows up as guest complaints, errors in the audit, and recurring problems of all kinds.

A notable exception can be found at The Westin Hotel, Seattle, operated by Westin Hotels (formerly Western International). Casual observation quickly reveals a front desk operation that is both efficient and accurate. Satisfaction among guests is unusually high, and this year the hotel (formerly called the Washington Plaza) was again granted a Mobil 4-star award for excellence.

As a former front desk manager at a small resort hotel, I was intrigued and wanted to learn more. I called on James Treadway, the hotel's general manager, with the idea of developing a story around the hotel's record of success. He suggested that I actually go through the hiring process and experience a first day on the job. It was a terrific idea, and arrangements were made that same day.

It's a standing joke among Westin Hotel employees these days that any job applicant who can

find the way to the personnel office has demonstrated sufficient aptitude to be hired. The reason is that, while construction is underway on the hotel's new twin-tower, Personnel has been temporarily relocated in the basement of the existing tower. Once the new tower is completed, the department will occupy a handsome new suite of offices there.

Fortunately, I was guided by an employee, sparing me the embarrassment of becoming lost and ensuring that I was on time for my interview with Assistant Director of Personnel Dotty Heberling.

I fully expected the interview to last no longer than 20 or 30 minutes. I was in for a few surprises. In reality, I was there for more than an hour. Dotty was interested not only in my related experience and aptitude for dealing with the public, but also in my career goals and perceptions of how working at the hotel's front desk would serve them. She posed a variety of hypothetical situations and asked how I would cope with each. And though she knew of my familiarity with front desk operations, she took special care to portray the job as completely and honestly as possible.

There were, as Dotty explained them, two distinct but related reasons for her thoroughness. First, these days the hotel has a higher caliber of employee than ever before. Turnover is low, and competition for jobs is keen. Employees and applicants alike know that when the twin-tower is completed in summer 1982, opportunities for advancement will grow. That fact, together with the hotel's current Mobil 4-star rating, makes it a highly desirable place to work.

But a second reason, which accounts in part for the first, lies in the Westin's strict policy of "promotion from within," a policy shared by all Westin hotels. "When we hire a room clerk," explained Dotty, "we have to consider that we may also be hiring a future general manager." And Dotty should

Reprinted with permission from Bechtel, Rick. "Front Desk Success at the Westin Seattle." *Lodging Hospitality* (June 1982), pp. 34, 36, 43.

know—in just five years she progressed from cashier to room clerk, night auditor, front office supervisor, relief assistant manager, and employment manager before assuming her present position.

Such examples provide more-than-ample incentives for employees occupying even traditionally low-paying jobs. Some 50 to 60 percent of front desk personnel are members of the hotel's management training program, while another 20 percent aim to join the program when the opportunity occurs.

Having passed Dotty's scrutiny, my interview with Front Office Manager Taylor Terao was the last step in the hiring process. Like Dotty, Taylor's rapid advancement with the hotel is inspiring. After managing restaurants for 13 years, he joined the then-Plaza as a room clerk, progressing in just a year and a half to auditor, cashier, assistant front office manager, manager of the newly opened Planter's Lounge, lobby restaurant manager, and front office manager, a post he has held since October 1980.

I gathered from the tone of our conversation that Taylor was probing to determine how well I would mesh with other front desk employees. We talked about different directions for career growth and about front office policies. Then Taylor gave me a behind-the-scenes glimpse of the front desk operation and introduced me to some of the staff. Finally, he announced that I was accepted on the front desk crew and added, to my surprise, "We've given you a great deal to consider. Before you make your decision, take some time to think things through. Then, if you're still interested, call me before 10 a.m. tomorrow." This, of course, would allow a graceful exit, should I get cold feet, and would also provide Taylor with extra proof of my motivation. In a real situation, I'd have called back that afternoon.

After completing a brief two-hour orientation, I was fitted for my uniform, awarded a training badge, and deemed ready for action. I was to begin working from 11 a.m. to 7 p.m. Although at odds with the normal 7 a.m. to 3 p.m./3 p.m. to 11 p.m. routine, these hours would allow me to observe both check-in and check-out. As is generally the case, the Westin was gearing up for a 95 percent occupancy rate. It would provide an excellent opportunity to watch the crew at work.

When I arrived, I was immediately greeted by Taylor, who informed me that he would be spending extra time with me that day. This is customary and is done for two reasons. It allows the new employee to ease into the job and to become familiar with hotel and desk operations. It also permits Taylor to establish a working relationship and lasting rapport with the new employee.

We began with another tour of the hotel, only this time I was introduced to key personnel in all departments, and their functions were explained in greater detail. The tour also included an examination of various sizes and styles of accommodations. Virtually all rooms at the Westin offer an impressive view, either of Puget Sound or the Cascade mountain range. Having previously worked in a very old resort hotel where no two rooms were alike, I quickly recognized the value in this.

As with most hotels, the Westin's front desk operation performs three basic functions—room clerk, cashier, and auditor. Previously, there had been a fourth role known as the "mail and information" clerk, whose responsibilities paralleled those of the room clerk, with the exception of check-ins and complaint handling. More recently, however, mail and information functions have been incorporated into the room clerk's duties, with employees rotating between the two. Eventually, Taylor hopes to extend the rotation to include cashier duties. This, he believes, will result in more knowledgeable employees, less fatigue, and a smoother operation.

Working at each day shift are two room clerks, two cashiers, a supervisor, and an assistant manager. My presence would be additional until I had become proficient with mail-and-information functions.

The training schedule remains rather basic for the first one to five weeks, depending on how quickly the employee catches on, what particular role is planned, and so forth. After that, it generally takes considerably longer—as much as a year—to fully know the hotel and its front office. During that period, the employee rotates through all three basic positions and in all likelihood is given supervisory responsibilities.

We returned to the front desk, and Taylor turned me over to Assistant Manager Chuck Abbott for a more thorough indoctrination. Morning rush had just subsided, and Chuck was eager to take advantage of the lull.

While Chuck spent a moment with Taylor, I had my first moment alone as a room clerk, so I wasted no time. I strolled up to the desk, absorbing the friendly, relaxed atmosphere, and exuding confidence. Suddenly, a man darted from behind a pillar and sent a small envelope sailing across the desk at me. "Here!" he blurted, "I don't know what to do with this." "I'll take care of it for you," I replied. Quick thinking on my part. Fortunately, another clerk had witnessed the episode and showed me where to drop the envelope, containing the man's key.

I ventured even closer to the action, sliding behind the "rack" for protection. Another man approached with a determined look on his face. Locking his gaze into mine, he announced, "Lowry. L-O-W-R-Y." Not knowing whether to congratulate him on his spelling, check him in, or find "Lowry" for him, I said, "Just a moment, please," and grabbed another employee for assistance who promptly checked Mr. Lowry in.

Having thus "handled" my first two situations, I returned to Chuck. Desk personnel around me seemed relaxed and confident, despite a brief surge in activity. I observed one room clerk handle check-ins for four guests simultaneously, carefully dividing his attention among them and accomplishing the task without a hitch.

The Westin has a spacious, comfortable lobby. Subdued, yet elegant, its richly paneled walls and thick carpeting provide an air of Old World elegance. The more typical lobby sounds were occasionally punctuated by conversation in foreign languages. I was told that about 20 percent of the hotel's guests are from other countries. Although most speak some English, when communication problems do

arise, the guest is escorted to the concierge station adjacent to the front desk. Each concierge speaks at least one other language and is experienced in working with foreign guests. In addition, the personnel department keeps a current file on foreign language proficiencies among its 500 + employees.

The concierge department, a relatively recent addition to the Westin's services, performs a variety of guest services that previously befell front desk employees. For example, in addition to giving directions and other routine assistance, the concierge staff has an impressive network of local contacts, enabling them to secure last-minute reservations at even the most sought-after restaurants, theaters, and attractions. And should a guest forget his tie, the concierge can, with a phone call, send a local department store representative scurrying over with a selection to choose from.

All of this has served to reduce congestion and streamline services at the front desk. "The program still is in its infancy," Chuck explained, "but already we're beginning to see results. Everything that increases our efficiency shows up in terms of guest response—more compliments and fewer problems."

There also is some talk of placing VIP check-ins under the concierge umbrella to provide more specialized service. The Westin keeps track of its preferred visitors—those who stay more than three times annually. Folios prepared in advance, prior extension of credit, and other conveniences help speed the check-in process and convey a feeling of special attention, which guests remember.

The reservation system itself contributes mightily to the operation. In my own past experience, reservations were handled by desk personnel, along with everything else. Moreover, the process was all done by hand, resulting in incredible confusion, frequent errors, and inordinate stress. At the Westin Seattle, in contrast, a separate department handles reservations. A key ingredient of the operation is a huge facility in Omaha, where reservation requests pour in on Westin's toll-free number. These, together with daily updates from individual properties, are keyed into Westin's computer-based

Westron reservation system, which maintains information on room availability and bookings for a full 52 weeks.

Each day, the hotel's reservation staff receives from the computer a variety of pertinent information on each incoming guest. The information is recorded on reservation slips, which are then placed in racks and delivered to the front desk that evening. The morning desk crew arrives to find the day's reservations arranged alphabetically and identified as to guest status, special requests, and so on. Moreover, since the computer already has taken the hotel's accommodations profile into account, room assignments can be made as guests arrive, eliminating a pesky source of confusion.

The smooth proficiency of the front desk operation became increasingly evident as the afternoon wore on. By 4 p.m., the anticipated heavy check-in was in full swing. Without any conscious effort to organize the operation, desk personnel seemed to anticipate needs automatically. In fact, I was surprised when one clerk turned to me during a free moment and said, "Whew! That was quite a rush." I hadn't even noticed a bulge at the desk. But that is, after all, one measure of an efficient front desk operation. The more smoothly it runs, the less noticeable it is.

Regardless of the standards employed, however, the Westin Seattle scored high marks. Far-sighted policies on promotion, thorough hiring practices, people-oriented management, and an efficient, well-organized system combine to overcome the traditional problems of front desk operations.

My day behind the desk wound to a close, and with it, my brief career at the Westin Seattle. Reflecting on my earlier experience with front desk management, I kept thinking, "If only I had known then what I've learned today."

As I prepared to depart, Cheryl Dowling, the evening supervisor, complimented me on my performance, adding, "You've got a job here if you ever want one."

Thanks, Cheryl. If I can ever find my way to Personnel again, I just might take you up on that.

The Front Office Manager: Key to Hotel Communications

Denney G. Rutherford

Since the front office manager is usually viewed as the key to the efficient and orderly operation of a hotel, the author has researched the job and activities of this individual in an attempt to provide data about an area which he says was "intuitively known" but never "empirically explored."

Current literature implies that the activities of the front office are so important to the daily operations of the hotel that it occupies a preeminent position among other departments. Gray and Liguori (1980, 99) call it "the nerve center of the hotel," echoing an early work by Heldenbrand (1944, 7) indicating

that it "becomes a sort of listening post for management." Kasavana (1981, 20) says that the "front office is responsible for carrying out all the front-of-the-house functions and serves as a liaison between management and guests. Regardless of how the hotel is constructed or organized, the front office is always an essential focal point." Renner (1981, 17) notes that the area "is always at the center of the guest-service activities . . . [and] from within the hotel, the front office is viewed as a key de-

Reprinted with permission from Rutherford, Denney G. "The Front Office Manager: Key to Hotel Communications." *FIU Hospitality Review*, vol. 3, no. 2 (Fall 1985), pp. 38–48.

partment that coordinates and sets the pace for most guest services. . . ."

It is curious, therefore, that there exists no published research on the individual who is given the daily task of directing the activities of the front office—the front office manager (FOM).

In the works quoted above, only Renner (1981, 14) and Gray and Liguori (1980, 53) give the job of front office manager the merest of notices. Each of the authors treats the operations of the desk in comprehensive fashion, but there exists no systematic discussion of the dimensions of the position of FOM nor the type of individual who fills it. Kent's article (1975, 190) points to this window in the research, but is concerned in the main with providing motivation for the front office staff.

This project was designed to address this lack of research: Who are these folks and what are the important dimensions of their jobs? The FOM position takes a highly motivated, trained, and competent individual, one who utilizes a special mix of skills, one who can, in the words of one former FOM, handle the "hotel's shortest job description: 'Fill the hotel; don't walk any guests!'" (Christianson 1981). Thus the job of the FOM is an important and crucial step in a hotel's organization and, similarly, a hotelier's career.

DATA SOUGHT VIA QUESTIONNAIRE

A seven-page, two-part questionnaire was used to collect the data. Part I asked FOMs to provide information regarding their personal demographic variables (see Table 1) and items relating to career progress and satisfaction (see Table 2). Part II asked managers to provide input on the relative value of 105 "theoretical" knowledge constructs on the operation of the front office.

One survey package was returned due to a bad address. Of the 99 distributed, 61 usable, completed questionnaires were returned, for a response rate of 61.6 percent. Responses were coded and analyzed using published statistical routines (Nie et al. 1975, 22–33).

Each of the "theoretical" knowledge constructs

TABLE 1
Demographic variables for the front office manager

Variable	Front Office Managers n = 61
Percentage Male	61.0%
Mean Age	30.4
Percentage Caucasian	80.3%
Percentage Single	58.9%
Percentage College Graduate	55.0%
Percentage HRA Degree	33.0%
Reported Years in Industry	6–10
Reported Years in Present Position	2–3

derived from the literature (Vallen 1982) was rated by the FOMs on a 1-to-5 Likert-type scale, with 1 being "of no importance" and 5 indicating "vital importance" to the practice of front office management. This list of constructs should not be considered all-inclusive, but since the text used is one in common usage in educational institutions and industry training programs, the knowledge range represented by this list of 105 can be considered typical.

Mean ratings for each of the constructs were generated and rank-ordered from high to low as seen in Tables 3, 4, and 5. Partitioning the constructs into three groups based on the rank of their

TABLE 2
Salaries of the front office managers

Salary Range	Percentage n = 61
$12,000–14,999	11.5%
15,000–18,999	24.6%
19,000–22,999	18.0%
23,000–24,999	18.0%
25,000 or over	24.6%
Not reported	3.3%

TABLE 3
Front office manager as communicator

Rank Order	Specific Activity	Knowledge Construct General Category	LRS 1–5
1	Communications with Guests	|communications|	4.869
2	Front Office Functions	|front office|	4.820
3	Greeting the Guest	|rooming procedures|	4.787
4	Fire in Hotel	|emergency procedures|	4.787
5	Listening	|communications|	4.770
6	Handling Complaints	|communications|	4.754
7	Emergency Communications	|communications|	4.738
8	Problem Referral	|communications|	4.721
9	Front Office Manager (Asst. Manager—Rooms Div.)	|knowledge of hotel organization|	4.712
10	Interdepartmental Cooperation	|knowledge of hotel organization|	4.712
11	Job of Desk Clerk	|front office|	4.705
12	Communications with Other Personnel	|communications|	4.689
13	Registration	|rooming procedures|	4.689
14	Communications on Telephone	|communications|	4.672
15	VIPs	|rooming procedures|	4.656
16	Increasing Professionalism	|communications|	4.639
17	Full House Management	|reservation procedures|	4.590
18	Accident Procedures	|emergency procedures|	4.557
19	Staffing	|front office|	4.541
20	Room Rates	|rooming procedures|	4.541
21	Behavior Description for Desk Clerk	|communications|	4.508
22	Percentage of Occupancy	|statistics|	4.500
23	Average Room Rate	|statistics|	4.500

TABLE 4
Office manager as facilitator

Rank Order	Specific Activity	Knowledge Construct General Category	LRS 1–5
24	Room Assignment	|rooming procedures|	4.492
25	Medical Emergency	|emergency procedures|	4.492
26	Selling Up/Selling Sister Properties	|rooming procedures|	4.483
27	Front Office Accounting Elements	|front office accounting|	4.467
28	Power Failure Procedures	|emergency procedures|	4.459
29	Day of Arrival Procedures	|reservation procedures|	4.410
30	Paid in Advance	|rooming procedures|	4.410
31	Head Housekeeper (Exec Housekeeper)	|knowledge of hotel organization|	4.407

TABLE 4 *(continued)*

Rank Order	Specific Activity	Knowledge Construct General Category	LRS 1–5
32	Accepting/Denying Reservation Requests	|reservation procedures|	4.393
33	First Aid	|emergency procedures|	4.393
34	Handling Unwanted Guests	|rooming procedures|	4.377
35	Cash Register/CRT	|front office equipment|	4.361
36	Reservation Request	|reservation procedures|	4.361
37	Overbooking/"Walking"	|reservation procedures|	4.361
38	Reservations for Group Bookings	|reservation procedures|	4.361
39	Room Status System	|using hotel racks to accommodate|	4.361
40	Death in Hotel	|emergency procedures|	4.328
41	Cash, Charges, & Credit	|cash & credit|	4.328
42	Handling Credit Cards	|cash & credit|	4.328
43	Housekeeping Report	|using hotel racks to accommodate|	4.311
44	Meaning & Use of Statistics	|statistics|	4.305
45	Reservation Forecasting	|reservation procedures|	4.295
46	Operation of Front Office Computer System	|front office computer systems|	4.283
47	Burglary & Theft Procedures	|emergency procedures|	4.279
48	Handling Checks	|cash & credit|	4.267
49	Cashier's Report	|cash & credit|	4.246
50	Floor Plan	|constructing the room rack|	4.230
51	Management Information from Computer System	|front office computer systems|	4.217
52	Charting Reservation Data	|reservation procedures|	4.213
53	Machine Posting of Guest Accounts	|front office accounting|	4.197
54	Guest Charges	|cash & credit|	4.167
55	Rate Symbols	|constructing the room rack|	4.164
56	Unusual Emergencies	|emergency procedures|	4.158
57	Computerized Room Rack	|constructing the room rack|	4.148
58	General Manager	|knowledge of hotel organization|	4.136
59	Problem of No-Shows	|reservation procedures|	4.115
60	Employee Cash Drop	|cash & credit|	4.100
61	Registered Guests	|city ledger|	4.100
62	Sequence of Rooms	|constructing the room rack|	4.098
63	Design of Computer System for Front Office	|front office computer systems|	4.083
64	Accountant or Controller	|knowledge of hotel organization|	4.068
65	Accounting Source Documents	|front office accounting|	4.033
66	Resident Manager (Exec Ass't or Hotel Manager)	|knowledge of hotel organization|	4.017
67	Paid-Outs/Cash Advances	|cash & credit|	4.017
68	Organization of Room	|constructing the room rack|	4.016

TABLE 5

Front office manager as organizational interface and arbiter of technical minutia

Rank Order	Specific Activity	Knowledge Construct General Category	LRS 1–5
69	Transfers	|cash & credit|	3.983
70	Advance Deposits	|city ledger|	3.917
71	Organization Chart	|knowledge of hotel organization|	3.883
72	Travel Agencies	|city ledger|	3.883
73	Other Symbols	|constructing the room rack|	3.850
74	Symbols for Beds	|constructing the room rack|	3.836
75	Locating Problems	|night audit|	3.833
76	Structure of City Ledger	|city ledger|	3.833
77	Director of Marketing	|knowledge of hotel organization|	3.814
78	Uniform System of Accounts for Hotels	|statistics|	3.780
79	Mail & Key Racks	|using hotel racks to accommodate|	3.754
80	Posting Room Charges	|night audit|	3.667
81	Room Rack Slip	|using hotel racks to accommodate|	3.623
82	Information Racks	|using hotel racks to accommodate|	3.623
83	Trial Balance of Receivables	|night audit|	3.617
84	Physical Ledger	|city ledger|	3.617
85	Categories of City Ledger	|city ledger|	3.617
86	Proving Charges	|night audit|	3.600
87	Non-Registered Guests	|city ledger|	3.576
88	PBX	|front office equipment|	3.574
89	Manual Room Rack	|constructing the room rack|	3.541
90	Audit Procedure-Credits	|night audit|	3.508
91	Folio Trays	|front office equipment|	3.467
92	Distributing Charges	|night audit|	3.450
93	Manual Posting of Guest Accounts	|front office accounting|	3.393
94	Engineer	|knowledge of hotel organization|	3.390
95	Symbols for Baths	|constructing the room rack|	3.377
96	Due Bills	|city ledger|	3.350
97	Programming Front Office Computer	|front office computer systems|	3.300
98	Food & Beverage Manager	|knowledge of hotel organization|	3.271
99	Switchboard	|front office equipment|	3.267
100	Safe Deposit Boxes	|front office equipment|	3.246
101	Other Work of the Auditor	|night audit|	3.217
102	Catering Manager	|knowledge of hotel organization|	3.153
103	Teletype	|front office equipment|	2.933
104	Executive Chef	|knowledge of hotel organization|	2.932
105	Stock Cards	|constructing the room rack|	2.483

Likert Rating Scales (LRS) means from high (4.5 and up, n = 23), medium (4.0–4.49, n = 45), and low (2.483–3.983, n = 37) allows macro-views of the FOM's job from the perspective of the collective opinion of the sample. These macro-views can be characterized by labeling the groups (admittedly arbitrarily) as "Communications" (Table 3), "Facilitation" (Table 4), and "Organizational Interface and [Arbiter of] Technical Minutia" (Table 5).

Other recent research has suggested that the skills of effective communication are among the most vital a manager at any level can bring to his/ her endeavors in the service industries (Rutherford and Schill 1984; Plunkett and Berger 1984; Nyquist, Bitner, and Booms 1985, 195–212). The service being delivered in many ways has no voice with which to speak for itself, and relies to a great extent upon the manager and employees to assist in the transition of service delivery from the firm to the customer or guest. The process is the product in service industries and the intangible nature of the service process renders communication and inter-personal skills much more important than in a man-ufacturing setting.

Nyquist, Bitner, and Booms (1985, 195–212) re-ported research that suggests most communication difficulties in service firms involved a misperception on the part of the customer regarding the firm's ability to deliver the firm's service. With specific reference to hotels, they found that guests making unreasonable demands and/or demands that con-travened policy represented the "dominant source of communication difficulties." Assuming a well-de-signed system to deliver the service and technically competent and trained personnel, it would seem the communications ability of the FOM become central to the traditional managerial tasks of plan-ning, organizing, directing, and controlling.

COMMUNICATIONS IS IMPORTANT TO FRONT OFFICE

Front office communications can be considered to occur singly and/or simultaneously within three dif-ferent contexts illustrated in Figure 1. The first communication context occurs between the front office personnel and the guest or other persons seeking hotel services or information.

Previously published research on front office communications by Farrell (1973) suggests that guest satisfaction, good relations with guests, and good relations with peers and colleagues were all closely linked to good communications.

From the FOMs' rankings in Table 3, nowhere is this more clearly validated than in the pre-eminent position accorded "Communications with Guests." Indeed, all of the choices under the general rubric "Communications" found their way into the top-rated group. While most managers in modern hotel organizations will probably agree that communica-tion with guests and among personnel is important, what is impressive about the numbers reported here is the surprising amount of agreement on the im-portance of the various specific communication ac-tivities. These nine specific references account for nearly 40 percent of the top-rated constructs.

Of the remaining constructs that received high ratings by the FOMs, the elements of the rooming and reservations processes can clearly be consid-ered a form of communication, for it is these ac-tivities that are central to the majority of the face-to-face contact between hotel, front office staff, and guests during the service encounter.

A case can be made for communications-related activities accounting for nearly 60 percent of those deemed most important by the FOMs. A quick pe-rusal of the more highly rated constructs in the second group (Table 4) lends support to this anal-ysis, for the vast majority of those rank-ordered 24 through 38 also pertain to rooming and reser-vations procedures.

The remainder of the constructs highly rated in Table 1 can be related to the broader managerial duties of the FOM. The importance of knowledge of front office functions is highlighted here by a ranking of 2 overall, and ranks 9, 10, 11, and 19 suggest other crucial elements of the front office that are important to the job of FOM. Many of these may be considered the "umbrella" constructs under which the facilitation, organizational, and technical constructs reported in Tables 4 and 5 fall.

The fact that emergency procedures (ranks 4 and

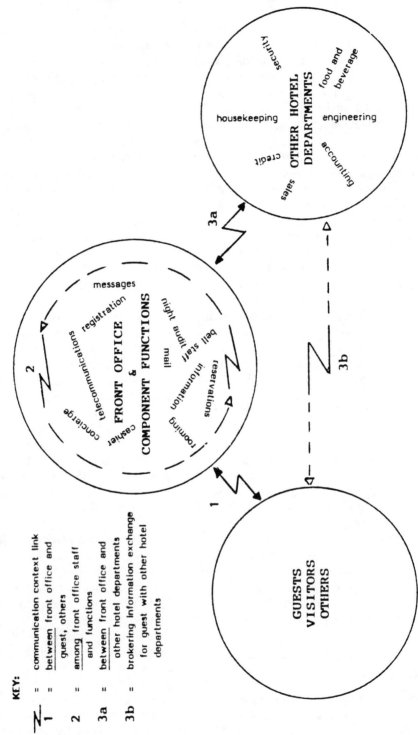

FIGURE 1
Front office communications model

KEY:

⚡ = communication context link

1 = between front office and guest, others

2 = among front office staff and functions

3a = between front office and other hotel departments

3b = brokering information exchange for guest with other hotel departments

OTHER HOTEL DEPARTMENTS

security
food and beverage
engineering
accounting
sales
credit
housekeeping

FRONT OFFICE & COMPONENT FUNCTIONS

messages
registration
telecommunications
concierge
cashier
rooming
information
reservations
bell staff
mail
night audit

GUESTS VISITORS OTHERS

18; and Table 4, numbers 25, 28, 33, and 40) assumed important ranking can be interpreted as a reference to the FOM's role as communicator, for possibly at no other time than during an emergency is the value of clear, accurate, precise, and effective communication more important. The ability to analyze emergencies and resolve them swiftly rests heavily on managers' abilities to communicate effectively in a fashion that does not exacerbate the situation.

This analysis of Table 3 allows the conclusion that the FOMs clearly consider communication in its various forms central to their daily managerial roles. These roles are also closely linked to the first context of the Front Office Communications Model depicting the functional aspects of this area as they relate to the guest within the full service encounter. And, while not predominating as it does in the first group, the communications theme carries over in numerous ways in the analysis of Tables 4 and 5 in light of the Front Office Communications Model.

MANAGER FUNCTIONS AS FACILITATOR

The second context of the Communications Model (Figure 1) occurs among the people representing the various components of the front office itself (rooming, reservations, mail/messages, cashiering, statistics, and the like). These are the daily activities for which the FOMs and their assistants serve as "facilitators" (Table 4). Represented here are the families of procedures and specialized tasks that facilitate the daily duties of the front office personnel, but not necessarily those duties that are always specific to the service encounter. They represent, however, those activities that "oil the wheels" of the encounter or account for many of those "behind the scenes" activities that serve to smooth the delivery of hotel services and provide support for the "encounter activities" of the hotel and the front office. Representative of these are record-keeping in the reservation process, taking and maintaining mail/message files, posting charges and credits to guest accounts, and compiling data and reports from daily routines.

This is not meant to dismiss these activities as a minor portion of the FOM's job. In relative terms, however, the FOMs themselves chose to rank more highly those constructs reported in Table 3. Analysis of the constructs included in Table 4 suggests that those relating to such activities and procedures as accounting, credit, room racks, and equipment might logically be considered to be among those delegated to assistant managers and supervisors for their day-to-day attention.

A curiosity in this context is what initially appears to be the relatively low and scattered importance assigned to computer-related topics (ranks 46, 51, 63, and Table 5, number 97). Particularly with reference to the second context of the model and its associated knowledge constructs, it would seem the current emphasis on switching to fully automated front office systems would be reflected in higher rankings than the mean rank of 64.25 exhibited by the four constructs offered for ranking in this study. Construct 97 probably does deserve its low rank, however, for it is extremely unlikely the FOMs would be doing their own computer programming.

When the computer constructs are compared with those related to "Constructing the Room Rack" (which can be equated with an information-gathering and reporting system of a nonautomated age and whose mean rank is 72.8), it can be seen as an indication that automated systems are emerging in importance. This may also be heralding the demise of the old, inefficient room rack.

MANAGER FUNCTIONS AS INFORMATION BROKER

The third communication context of the model encompasses those regular and typical (or irregular and atypical) sorts of contacts that must occur among and between the front office and other line and staff functions within the hotel organization. These may range from regular daily contacts with housekeeping regarding room status to exchanges of information with sales about reservations horizons and blocking of rooms. Atypical communications in this context may encompass the emergency procedures discussed earlier, special problems dealing with policy or legal questions, or ad hoc requests for front office assistance by other managerial levels.

Knowledge constructs in this communication context relating to hotel organization may be among the most intriguing in this table. While others relating to this category are also spread among the top two groupings of constructs, one-half (n = 6) of those chores appear in this third list, giving it an overall "flavor" that suggests organizational interdependence. It is in this dimension that the FOM acts as a broker in the exchange of information between other departments of the hotel, the front office, and in many ways, the guests.

Guests, typically, have only an ill-formed conception of the complex systems that comprise the delivery of services in a hotel. On a regular basis, the FOM finds that his/her duties must include a number of information exchanges that help the guests better understand their relationships to such hotel departments as security, credit/accounting, and engineering.

High-order guest demands regarding room comfort, spending limits, and understandable concerns about security represent obvious attention-getters in this context. The high visibility of the front office as a representative of top management to the guest makes the FOM and/or designees focal points for these sorts of guest interactions.

The success the FOM has in brokering these exchanges—when required—will have a significant impact on the smooth delivery of the hotel's services. Similarly, the concerns raised by Nyquist et al. (1985), concerning misperceptions on the part of the customer regarding the firm's ability to deliver services, may be alleviated in this instance. If the front office, through the efforts and leadership of the FOM, is able to ameliorate unreasonable demands and minimize demands against policy, this major source of hotel-guest communication difficulties, if not eliminated as a roadblock in the service delivery system, can be, at the very least, managed effectively. The key, of course, according to this analysis of the FOM's job, is the vigor with which

the FOM pursues his/her role as organizational interface.

The remaining knowledge constructs in Table 5 represent the FOMs' lower rankings of individual items from families of constructs accorded higher rankings in the other tables. This is not to suggest that individually or in any combination any of these constructs are useless or inconsequential. In any given hotel these may be appropriate and important to a variety of specific front office tasks. The data do suggest, however, that such formerly technical dimensions of traditional front office systems as symbols (ranks 73, 74, and 95), the various other rack-related items (ranks 79, 82, 89, and 105), and recently outmoded telecommunications equipment (ranks 88, 89, and 103) are less central to the FOMs' job than in the past.

These families of front office knowledge constructs have mean ranks, respectively, of 80.7, 88.8, and 93.3. When compared to the mean rank of computer-related constructs (64.25) reported above, it may be at least speculated that automation has diminished the importance of these latter constructs or pushed them into the background of the FOMs' analysis of operations. More research is needed on this subject.

COMMUNICATION EMERGES AS CENTRAL ISSUE

The most powerful message derived from analysis of the data on the FOM's job is that communication in its various forms is clearly central to the successful mission of the front office. Conventional wisdom that accepts the implications of the opening quotes is in many ways validated by the data analyzed here. It is in making the leap from validated implications to operational reality that the importance of these data may be most usefully implemented by hotel managers.

In order to avoid or minimize the service delivery problems documented earlier and to ease the other tasks of the front office, the major conclusion of this study is that hotel firms should consider communications skills to be an important criterion in considering candidates for the position of front office manager.

Successful FOM candidates will ideally possess demonstrated competencies in both oral and written communications to competently deal with the complexities that exist among and between three contexts of the Front Office Communications Model. Furthermore, since the mission of the front office involves delegation and training by the manager across numerous (and often simultaneous) service-related activities, it is also very important that the FOM exhibits a predilection to help others among the staff learn these skills and appreciate their importance. In short, the FOM must be a communicator in yet another way: as teacher and trainer.

Front office managers themselves and those who expect to fill that position as a logical career step will also be well advised to compare their training, skills, and talents to these data. Increased competitive emphasis on quality of service, combined with escalating room rates and more sophisticated travelers, suggest the successful individuals and firms will be those who minimize the opportunities for miscommunication during all aspects of the service encounter.

The FOMs ranked "Communications with Guests" as the most important activity on the list of 105. This analysis also documents a powerful statement supporting the importance of communication in most other contexts of the FOM's job. Hotel firms wishing to implement specific activities to make the leap from conventional wisdom to operational reality will design those activities around the communications expertise of the FOM and, by extension, of the front office staff.

When Guests Complain

Robert C. Lewis

Resolving the complaints of existing customers is generally far less expensive than winning new customers. Yet many hotels fail to consider the far-reaching impact of the steps they take to resolve complaints. In some cases, a hotel's response to a complaint may actually prevent the customer from returning—and may lead to further business losses via negative word-of-mouth.

The hotel industry is frequently said to be backward in comparison to other industries, but hotels have been pioneers in at least one area: that of soliciting information on whether their customers are satisfied or dissatisfied with their services. Long before such companies as General Electric and Whirlpool offered toll-free telephone numbers to handle consumer complaints, hotels had routinely placed comment cards in guest rooms, and most do so today.

There is a sound basis for providing guests with a formal vehicle for voicing complaints. The negative word-of-mouth spread by a dissatisfied customer has a considerably greater impact on prospective customers than does positive word-of-mouth (Arndt 1967). Yet research has shown that most dissatisfied customers do not complain to the company with which they are displeased (Landon 1977; Warland, Hermann, and Willits 1975; Day, Grabicke, Schaetzle, and Staubach 1981)—for one reason, because they often lack a direct means of doing so. As a result, it may be prudent actually to encourage the voicing of complaints so that the business has an opportunity to resolve the problem and forestall the ripple effect of negative word-of-mouth (Day et al. 1981; Warland, Hermann, and Willits 1975; Gronhaug 1977). Hotels apparently take this view, generally providing easy-to-use, postage-paid cards and often also soliciting oral comments about a guest's stay (e.g., at check-out).

In addition to enjoying a direct means of registering complaints, dissatisfied hotel customers have two other advantages over consumers who are displeased with other types of services or with manufactured goods. First, depending on the cause of the complaint, when hotel customers complain, they can often expect corrective action on the spot. Second, whereas dissatisfied customers sometimes feel that any complaint they make will fall on deaf ears (Landon 1977; Day 1978; Andreason and Best 1977), many hotel companies pride themselves on responding to every complaint they receive and consumers presumably recognize that their hotel complaints are likely to be acknowledged.

For these reasons, hotels theoretically should not have too many dissatisfied customers—provided, of course, that they are successful in the final step of the complaint cycle: complaint resolution. Recent research involving a group of adults who had complained to various companies about a product or service, however, indicates that this final step is not as straightforward as one might suppose (Consumer Dimensions, Inc. 1982). Of the dissatisfied customers sampled in that study, fully 53 percent were disappointed or actually annoyed by the company's response to their complaint. More than a third of those reporting disappointment with the company's response said they would definitely not purchase the product or service in the future; of the consumers who were angry or annoyed with the response, 70 percent said *they no longer used the product or service.* Other research has similarly suggested that responses to complaints may not only fail to resolve a customer's concern but may actually aggravate it (Thomas and Shuptrine [nd]).

Despite the dangers of exacerbating customer dissatisfaction, it is clear that, by resolving complaints effectively, a business can turn a negative situation into a marketing opportunity. Dissatisfied customers who do not complain may simply switch brands; those who *do* complain have been shown to be more brand-loyal than customers who remain silent (Technical Assistance Research Programs 1979; Etzel and Silverman 1981; Lewis and Pizam 1981), so their complaints represent a particularly ripe opportunity to solidify existing loyalty to the business.

For example, a study of customers who had complained to Coca-Cola indicated that the customers who were satisfied with the firm's response told just as many people about their complaint as they told about how well the response was handled. Customers who felt that their complaint had not been resolved, however, told twice as many people about the incident—and in those cases, the word-of-mouth was strictly negative. The study indicated that brand loyalty was reinforced when the company's response was considered satisfactory; when it was not, brand loyalty was severely eroded (Technical Assistance Research Programs, Inc. [nd]).

To investigate the effects of hotels' complaint-handling systems, the author undertook a study analyzing the use of comment cards, the types of complaints received, hotel response to the complaints, and customer reactions to those responses. The results suggest that, if complaint behavior can indeed be turned into a positive marketing tool, hotels may not be taking full advantage of this opportunity to develop brand loyalty.

METHODOLOGY

The study was based upon guest communications to a 175-room hotel, a franchisee of a well-known national chain. Located in the downtown center of a popular summer destination with a population of 60,000, the hotel is not representative of a major city hotel, but rather more typical of franchisee hotels and motor inns in smaller cities throughout the country. Its business mix is somewhat atypical. Nevertheless, there was no reason to believe that the consumers surveyed would differ from any others in similar complaints.

The hotel had received 241 written communications from previous guests during the 18-month period studied. All of the communications had been responded to by management.

A questionnaire and cover letter were mailed to the total population of correspondents, and yielded 120 completed and usable questionnaires (54 percent of the deliverable mailing).[1] These respondents were representative of the total population of the hotel's guests in terms of type and number of complaints and compliments, and sex.[2]

All questionnaire responses were compared to the contents of the original correspondence for verification. Understandably, some differences existed between the two as to the exact complaint or compliment, but the context of the correspondence was generally verified.

Respondents completed a number of five-point Likert-type scales regarding their complaints or compliments, their attitudes and behavior, the hotel's response to their correspondence, and their communication with others. All respondents also completed open-ended questions regarding their likes and dislikes of hotels in general and of this hotel in particular.

FINDINGS

For hoteliers who rely on comment cards to assess their performance, or who routinely react to customer complaints with polite form letters, the survey findings may prove an eye-opener. Both internal and external responses to complaints may warrant conscious re-evaluation by hotel managers, based on the information presented below.

Use of Comment Cards

Of all 241 communications sent by guests to the hotel, only 69 (29 percent) were on comment cards. Among guests who sent *complaints,* 46 percent had used comment cards, half wrote letters to the hotel,

and 25 percent wrote letters to the franchisor. (As these percentages indicate, 20 percent of these respondents had used some combination of the three methods of corresponding.)

The relative rarity of using comment cards as a sole means of registering dissatisfaction or satisfaction was underscored by responses to the survey. Respondents said they used complaints a mean of 29 percent of the time (median—10 percent), to voice compliments 32 percent of the time (median—15 percent), and to make routine comments 22 percent of the time (median—3 percent).

These findings have significant implications. For example, half of the respondents would use a comment card in less than 10 percent of the instances in which they had a complaint. If these figures may be considered representative of the industry overall, it is obvious that, despite the availability of a consumer-complaint procedure, hotels do not hear via the comment card from the vast majority of those who have complaints. Further, 90 percent of the comment-card complaints received come from only half of those who are dissatisfied.

Because the respondents said they were somewhat more likely to use the comment card to compliment than to complain, hotel properties and companies are apparently ill-advised to rely on the ratio of compliments to complaints in evaluating customer satisfaction. The survey suggests that, for every 100 compliments received, there are 213 others that exist but are not expressed; for every 100 complaints received, there are an additional 245 that are not expressed. Consider the major hotel chain that boasts that 51 percent of its guest comments are positive. This chain's 51/49 favorable ratio would translate into an *un*favorable ratio of satisfied to dissatisfied guests (48/52), with 71 percent of dissatisfied customers not even heard from.

Who are the guests who do not use the comment card to complain? First, because the survey respondents generally indicated that they would use a comment card only when quite dissatisfied with the hotel, it is reasonable to assume that among the ranks of the silently dissatisfied are many customers who are only mildly displeased. As discussed below, many of the complaints received from highly dissatisfied customers may be irreconcilable (i.e., the negative attitude manifested is not easily overcome, regardless of any steps the hotel might take). This is not to suggest that hotels should not attempt to resolve these complaints. However, it appears that efforts to resolve complaints are expended on a minority of difficult-to-satisfy complainers, while no effort is geared toward the vast majority of relatively easy-to-satisfy complainers.

A variety of factors appear to affect a consumer's proclivity toward using comment cards, as shown in Exhibit 1 and summarized here:

• Respondents of middle income are considerably more likely to use a comment card, both to complain and to compliment. Those of higher income

EXHIBIT 1
Characteristics affecting use of comment cards

	Would Use a Comment Card to:		
	Complain (mean %)	Compliment (%)	Make Routine Comment (%)
CHARACTERISTICS			
Income			
<$25,000	22.2	33.8	29.1
$25,000 – 40,000	39.9	47.1	29.5
>$40,000	26.1	23.6	14.9
Use of Chain's Other Hotels			
Infrequent	24.6	30.1	23.9
Frequent	36.4	36.4	19.6
Times Stayed at Hotel			
This time only	32.5	43.5	27.4
Repeat stay	24.9	22.2	18.5
Residence			
<125 mi. of hotel	30.3	34.7	23.6
>125 mi. of hotel	24.4	24.5	19.2
Age			
Up to 44 yrs.	30.0	33.4	22.8
45 yrs. and older	27.0	30.1	22.0
Travel Purpose			
Business	29.9	29.2	15.7
Pleasure	28.5	33.8	25.5
Sex			
Male	24.8	27.6	17.2
Female	33.2	37.2	28.0
CONTENT OF THIS COMMUNICATION			
Complaint	23.1	24.4	18.9
Compliment	33.7	45.1	26.9
Both	44.0	38.2	35.4

are less likely to compliment or make routine comments via comment cards.

- Frequent users of a franchisor's other hotels are more likely to complain or compliment, but repeat customers of a particular hotel are less likely to do either.
- Those who live closer to the hotel are more likely to use the card for all purposes.
- Age and travel purpose appear not to affect the likelihood of comment-card usage.
- Females are apparently more inclined to use the comment card for any purpose.[3]

The last figures in Exhibit 1 are of particular interest. Those who had written compliments to the hotel were significantly more likely to complain when dissatisfied (as well as to write compliments or routine comments) than were those who had written complaints. This supports an unproved thesis: Those who are prone to complain will also compliment when warranted; those who are not as prone to complain or compliment do so only when their feelings are quite strong either way.

Nature of Complaints and Compliments

The complaints and compliments received at the hotel under study can be broken down into four broad categories, as shown in Exhibit 2. As would be expected, these categories are correlated with the factors respondents said they liked and disliked about this hotel and the attributes they considered important in any hotel.

The categories shown in Exhibit 2 represent

EXHIBIT 2
Categories of hotel attributes related to complaints and compliments

	Physical Environment	Physical Goods	Service & Personnel	Expectations	
	(Percent of Mentions)				(Total)
Complaints	17%	31%	32%	20%	(100%)
Compliments	49	40	9	2	(100%)
Dislike about this hotel	15	24	49	21	(100%)
Like about this hotel	38	34	18	10	(100%)
Important in any hotel	33	37	21	9	(100%)
	152%*	166%*	119%*	62%*	

Physical environment = Noise, decor, parking, view, atmosphere, ambience, accommodations, room location, etc.
Physical goods = Food and beverage quality, climate control, temperature of pool, elevator service, cleanliness, furniture condition, pool, etc.
Service & personnel = Reservation handling, management attitude, service speed, employee attitude, level of service, etc.
Expectations = Relation to advertising, available facilities, package plan delivery, price-value, etc.

*Totals exceed 100% due to multiple responses.

clues to the management of the hotel as to where it should expend effort. Short of a major renovation, which may not be warranted, changes in the *physical environment* may be largely beyond the control of management. In any event, it was in this category that the lowest number of complaints and the highest number of compliments were received. Given the importance accorded this category by the respondents, management can make use of this information in its marketing efforts.

The attributes constituting the *physical-goods* category are under management's control; they largely involve operation of the plant, and definite steps can be taken to correct problems in this category. Ranked as most important by the respondents, the category drew a high number of complaints but also a high number of compliments suggesting that the hotel is doing reasonably well in these areas but not well enough. Given the possibility of additional unvoiced complaints, management should not draw undue attention to this category of attributes in its marketing efforts until it investigates the problems cited and corrects them.

In the *service and personnel* category, the hotel is obviously in trouble. Although, surprisingly, this category was not ranked high in importance, service and personnel elicited the largest number of complaints and only a minimum of compliments. The mandate to management is clear.

While complaints are relatively high and compliments low in the fourth category—*expectations*—this ratio is predictable. A considerable body of research indicates that dissatisfaction often results from unconfirmed expectations (Gilly 1980; Swan and Trawick 1981). Consumers complain when they don't find the expected, but seldom compliment when the reality matches their expectations. This category is further complicated by the fact that it is difficult to know what customers' expectations are—and, in fact, to meet them if they are known. In this study, however, specific factors were identified that engendered complaints—for example, some hotel facilities (pool, sauna, dining room) that had been advertised were closed or otherwise unavailable to customer when desired. This is not atypical in hotels where operating efficiencies sometimes supersede consumer needs and wants.

Likelihood of Repeat Purchase

The participants were asked how likely they were to "choose to stay" at the same hotel again. Fifty percent indicated they probably would, 30 percent said they probably would not, and 20 percent were unsure. Those who had sent complaints were asked to rate the importance of various factors in their decision to return or not to return. The mean responses (on a five-point scale) were as follows:

Substance of complaint	4.10
Level of disturbance about complaint	3.60
Way complaint was handled	3.00
Overall attitude toward the hotel	2.56

Looking only at the mean scores of the complainers (univariate analysis), therefore, would suggest that the substance of the complaint itself was the primary factor in a respondent's negative decision to return. This makes intuitive sense and is probably the way that most hotel managers perceive and react to customer complaints. (Indeed, this hotel's responses to the complainants were almost totally concerned with the substance of the complaints.) Bivariate and multivariate analysis, however, yielded somewhat different insights.

Respondents who had been indecisive in stating whether they would choose to stay at the hotel again were excluded, and a discriminant analysis was performed to determine which factors most heavily influenced customers who stated they would "likely choose" the hotel again and those who said they would "not likely choose" it again.

This analysis indicated that, among those customers who *would* choose to stay at the hotel again, *the way the complaint was handled* was the major factor in the decision. Highly correlated with "the way it was handled" was the belief that management had investigated the problem and corrected it. By contrast, among those who would *not* patronize the hotel again, the major factor was the substance of the complaint—which was highly correlated with the belief that management did not take corrective action.

Regression analysis using the likelihood of repeat patronage as the dependent variable yielded findings contrary to those of the univariate analysis. The most significant independent variable in this case for those not likely to return was a negative overall attitude toward the hotel, followed by unsatisfactory handling of the complaint.

Regression analysis using satisfaction with the handling of the complaint as the dependent variable showed that a belief that management had not taken corrective action was most significant in explaining high dissatisfaction, followed by attitude toward the hotel.

The discriminant and regression analyses indicated that management must not only eliminate the cause of complaints, but also do a better job of complaint handling. The two tasks are highly correlated, yet separate. Once the cause of a complaint has occurred, the level of disturbance becomes a function of the handling and defusing of the situation. A hotel can reduce the disturbance level by creating a belief in management that in turn will create a change in the customer's attitude. Better yet, if the belief in management is created *before* the customer's attitude becomes negative, the chance of a heightened disturbance decreases and the irritation effect is minimized when problems do occur. After the problem precipitating the complaint has occurred, management's efforts should be directed toward creating an attitude that will minimize the negative effect of the complaint.

The way a complaint is handled is crucial to those who are primarily disturbed over the substance of the complaint. These people want to believe in management's attempts to rectify the situation. They want to believe in management's sincerity, and if this belief is supported, they will probably choose the same hotel again. Complainants have a fairly low level of belief, however, as shown in Exhibit 3.

What can management do about those complainers who are likely never to return? In this study,

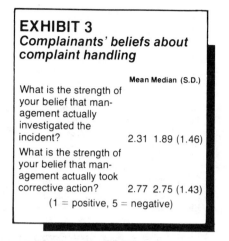

EXHIBIT 3
Complainants' beliefs about complaint handling

	Mean	Median	(S.D.)
What is the strength of your belief that management actually investigated the incident?	2.31	1.89	(1.46)
What is the strength of your belief that management actually took corrective action?	2.77	2.75	(1.43)

(1 = positive, 5 = negative)

such customers appeared to have had a somewhat negative attitude already toward the hotel, for whatever reason. The substance of their complaint increased their level of disturbance, they were not going to be easily satisfied with the resolution, and they had little faith in management's sincerity. Worse, such customers generally passed on negative word-of-mouth almost regardless of how the complaint was resolved, as discussed next.

Word-of-Mouth

Complainants were asked about the extent to which they were likely to tell others about their complaint and its handling, with the results shown in Exhibit 4. The likelihood of making a point to tell others of the incident was initially high *and remained high* if the complaint was not handled to the customer's satisfaction. The likelihood decreased considerably, however, if the complaint was handled well. Equally important for hotel operators was the high likelihood of telling others of the satisfactory handling of the complaint. (Indeed, all of the respondents rated the likelihood of making a point to tell others of a *satisfactory* hotel experience as very high—4.5 on the five-point scale.)

Exhibit 5 has even greater possible implications for managers. At issue was whether complainers would make a specific recommendation to others

EXHIBIT 4
Likelihood of word-of-mouth

		Likelihood of Making a Point to Tell Others:		
	Of the Complaint	Of the Complaint, if handled to your reasonable satisfaction	Of the Complaint Handling, if to your reasonable satisfaction	Of the Complaint Handling, if not to your reasonable satisfaction
Low	15.5%	**34.4%**	15.1%	17.2%
Med.	21.1	23.0	15.1	17.2
High	**63.4**	**42.6**	**69.8**	**65.6**
Mean	3.94	3.21	4.02	3.97
Median	4.57	3.18	4.55	4.62
(S.D)	(1.32)	(1.46)	(1.26)	(1.38)

not to stay at the hotel. As shown, poor handling of the complaint greatly increased the likelihood of a negative recommendation, while satisfactory handling reduced it.

In a further analysis, the likelihood of telling others about the complaint was regressed with 16 other variables. (Fourteen of these accounted for 73 percent of the variance at $p < .001$.) Exhibit 6 shows that disturbance and substance were more important in the likelihood of negative word-of-mouth than they were in the intention not to return to the hotel.

Exhibit 7 depicts the results of a regression analysis in which the likelihood of advising others not to use the hotel was the dependent variable. We may infer from the related variables leading to disinclination toward the product and negative word-of-mouth that "those who will talk, will talk," unless there is a fundamental change in attitude. (Eighty-six percent of the variance was explained by 14 variables in this regression at $< .0001$ significance.)

These analyses support the previous findings. To put it succinctly: When you're mad, you're mad, and you're going to tell everyone about it.

Responses to Complaints

The complainants had received the following responses to their complaints: 25 percent received a single form letter from the hotel; 60 percent received, in their opinion, personal letters from the hotel; 10.5 percent received letters from the franchiser; and the others received some combination of the above. The content of these responses is summarized in Exhibit 8.

The question of what type of response would create a satisfactory resolution in the view of the complainant is always moot. As several writers have pointed out, complaint behavior is often tied to expectations, and those expectations may not even be reasonable to the complainant: "Consumers may complain if they feel they can get something out of it, whether they have a legitimate concern about product performance or not" (Landon 1977, 31). In this study, respondents who were not satisfied with the resolution of their complaint were asked to indicate what it would have taken to satisfy them. Almost half said that a refund would have been a reasonable resolution. A quarter would have liked complimentary rooms and/or meals. And a full 29 percent said they would have been satisfied with a proper response from management, better communication, or a more pleasant relationship. *This was especially true of those who were most disturbed.* As might be expected, those who received responses characterized by trite phrases were prone to be more negative in their word-of-mouth when

EXHIBIT 5
Likelihood of negative recommendation

Likelihood of Advising Others Not to Use the Hotel:

	Based on Complaint Alone	Based on Complaint, if satisfied	Based on Complaint Handling, if satisfied	Based on Complaint Handling, if not satisfied
Low	41.2%	70.7%	72.0%	34.5%
Med.	11.8	12.1	14.0	10.3
High	47.0	17.2	14.0	55.2
Mean	3.12	2.07	1.92	3.45
Median	3.25	1.50	1.36	4.00
(S.D.)	(1.72)	(1.36)	(1.31)	(1.65)

Scale for Exhibits 4 and 5
Low = 1 or 2 on 5-point scale (low likelihood); **Med.** = 3 (uncertain); **High** = 4 or 5 (high likelihood).

EXHIBIT 6
Regression results—likelihood to tell others of complaint as dependent variable

	Sig.	Beta	R²
Level of disturbance	<.0001	.08	.36
Unsatisfactory handling	.004	.24	.13
Likely to tell others of complaint if reasonably satisfied	.004	.34	.11
Substance of complaint	.084	.32	.03
Likely to tell others if not handled satisfactorily	.095	.26	.03

not satisfied, and were disinclined to believe in management's sincerity and corrective action.

SUMMARY

The study summarized in the preceding pages is, of course, an initial effort focusing on the patrons of a single hotel. Nonetheless, in light of the consistency of these findings with those of earlier research concerning other industries, hotel managers should clearly give serious consideration to the cost of customer complaints and the cost of unsatisfactory complaint handling.

Failure to determine customer complaints and resolve them results not only in a direct loss of patronage from affected guests but also in negative word-of-mouth. Satisfactory resolution of guest complaints reduces negative word-of-mouth and increases positive comments. This is not news, but while such statements have often been made, they have seldom been empirically supported. The crucial issue for management, assuming some complaints will always occur, is how to attack the problem.

Six out of ten respondents to this survey had voiced their complaint to management at the time of the incident. Taking the time to send a complaint to the same management personnel one has already informed of the problem would seem to indicate a high level of aggravation (and hence a great barrier for management to overcome if it wishes to resolve the problem).

How do hotels currently respond to complaints?

EXHIBIT 7
Regression results—likelihood to advise others not to use the hotel as dependent variable

	Sig.	Beta	R²
Not likely to choose hotel again	<.0001	.43	.52
Likely to tell others of complaint	<.001	.14	.20
Likely to tell others if not handled satisfactorily	.011	.29	.05
Negative belief that management investigated	.05	.08	.03

EXHIBIT 8
Hotel's responses to complaints (as reported by respondents)

EXHIBIT 9
Further findings

The independent variables of sex and hotel response were found to affect the likelihood of negative word-of-mouth.

Female complainers were more likely than male complainers:
• to tell others about the complaint *if satisfied* with its handling
• to tell others not to use the hotel *if satisfied* with the handling
• to tell others about the handling, whether satisfied or dissatisfied.

Complainers who had received vague or trite responses to their complaints were more likely:
• to tell others about the complaint
• to tell others about the complaint handling
• to tell others not to use the hotel
• not to believe that management investigated the complaint
• not to believe that management took corrective action.

The form of the response varies according to management style, the importance or wrath of the customer, the cost of the resolution, and other factors. But, in whatever form, the process typically includes an apology, an explanation, possibly a promise of corrective action, and a "thank you for telling us so that we can improve our service." When all "reasonable" efforts fail, the tendency is often to categorize the customer as *un*reasonable. Analysis of the data in this study indicates that effective solutions go considerably beyond these perfunctory surface gestures.

Despite the advantages of the complaint mechanism in hotels (enumerated at the beginning of this article), resolution of complaints is easier in many other industries. Inadequate goods can be fixed or replaced; some services can be repeated and corrected. What constitutes a satisfactory resolution when a reservation has been lost or a wake-up call forgotten is less clear. An hour's wait for room service cannot be restored. (Moreover, an unclean room, even though it can still be cleaned, leaves a lasting impression on the consumer.)

Thus, hotels do not have the options that many manufacturers and other businesses have in complaint resolution. They can, of course, refund money, but the damage has already been done; they can offer a complimentary room or meal on the customer's next trip, but this may not be of much help to the distant traveler. Further, although this remains to be proven empirically, it seems safe to say that there are few products that receive as much word-of-mouth treatment as do a hotel's or restaurant's services. Hotels thus have a special problem in complaint resolution.

Interestingly enough, 29 percent of the still-unsatisfied complainants in this study indicated they would have been satisfied simply with a proper response from management. The empirical analysis lends considerable credence to this contention. For some complainers, loyalty will apparently derive largely from good management communications and credibility. For other complainers, even money refunds and complimentary rooms will not suffice to bring them back or to stop them from spreading negative word-of-mouth. Only a change in attitude—to which proper communication, again, is vital—will do that.

The problem is that "complaining customers are often looked on by business as being 'the enemy.' Those who deal with complaints may technically take care of the particular problem but still leave the customer angry: *the 'enemy' mentality begins with the assumption that the customer is wrong*" (Andreason and Best 1977, 101). Word-of-mouth is too powerful a force in the hotel business for any management to make that assumption. Hotel managers must clearly shift their emphasis from making token gestures to changing customer attitudes.

The Positive Side of Guest Complaints

Robert C. Lewis
Susan V. Morris

Several research studies have shown that hotel managers should do everything possible to encourage guest complaints. The reasons for this are obvious. First, receiving and settling a complaint soothes an unhappy guest and forestalls the effects of negative word-of-mouth. Second, complaints show management where the hotel's problems are, so the operation can be improved.

An early study that indicated the importance of encouraging and resolving complaints was reported in a 1983 *Quarterly* article (Lewis 1983a). A later study showed that up to 80 percent of customers whose complaints were resolved satisfactorily were willing to buy other products from the same company, compared with as few as 10 percent of noncomplainers. Satisfactory settlement of a complaint appeared to engender greater customer loyalty than if a problem had never arisen (Zweig 1986).

The 1983 report was based on the responses of 120 former guests at a single hotel. To check whether the complaint behavior of these guests was similar to that of guests at other hotels, we analyzed complaints from two larger studies. This article reports on the findings of those studies and, based on those findings, makes some suggestions for encouraging and handling hotel guests' complaints.

COMPLAINTS AT SIX HOTELS

We asked 1,314 hotel guests to report on complaints from their stays at six hotels in a large eastern city (Lewis 1983b). The guests were to report their complaints in two categories: those that related either to physical or tangible factors in the

This article was originally published in the February 1987 issue of *The Cornell Hotel and Restaurant Administration Quarterly,* and is reprinted here with the permission of the Cornell University School of Hotel Administration and of Robert C. Lewis. © 1987.

hotel, and those that involved intangible or environment factors. The results, shown in Exhibit 1, are clear. When a guest complaint was registered and resolved, the guest was far more likely to return to the hotel than when no complaint was made but not resolved. It is also noteworthy that guests were slightly more likely to complain in person about tangible factors than about intangible problems, which were a little more likely to be mentioned on written cards.

WORD-OF-MOUTH

A subsequent study of nine hotels in a 21-hotel chain showed the strong effects of botched complaint handling and subsequent likelihood of negative word-of-mouth. One of the authors surveyed 479 guests who had written complaints to hotel managers over a one-year period (Morris 1985). Nearly two-thirds of the letter writers had already complained in person at the time of the incident, and a whopping 88 percent of those who had complained reported that hotel employees were unsuccessful in reducing their dissatisfaction. Even more discouraging was the finding that in just over half the cases the employee's handling of the situation actually *aggravated* the complaint.

Half the respondents said it was highly unlikely that they would ever stay at the same hotel again. This finding was backed up by actual behavior. Of those who had stayed at an area hotel since their complaint, 75 percent had purposely avoided staying at other hotels in the chain.

What Happened?

Travelers always enjoy telling others about their travels, but they particularly concentrate on events that spoil their trips. This is shown in Exhibit 2.

EXHIBIT 1
Reported complaint behavior of 1,314 hotel guests

	Tangible Factors	Intangible Factors
Likely to complain immediately to management in person	59%	41%
Likely to complain using guest comment card	50%	48%
Likely to complain later by mail or phone	19%	17%
Likely to return to same hotel when:		
Complaint was not registered	5%	8%
Complaint was resolved	62%	57%
Complaint was not resolved	4%	3%

Survey data were gathered from guests at six hotels in a major city in the eastern U.S.

When they registered a complaint, less than two-thirds of the travelers would tell others about it, but when the complaint was not resolved, nearly three-quarters of the travelers would repeat their story. Even more important, when a complaint was not resolved, 71 percent of the travelers would tell other people to stay away from the hotel, compared to just 43 percent of all those writing to complain.

EXHIBIT 2
Reported complaint behavior of 479 hotel guests

Likely to tell others outside family about complaint, regardless of resolution	62%
Number of people told (average)	12
Likely to tell others when complaint was not resolved	73%
Likely to tell others not to use hotel, regardless of resolution	43%
Number of people told (average)	8%
Likely to tell others when complaint was not resolved	71%

Survey data were gathered from guests at nine hotels in a 21-hotel chain.

In many cases, hotel managements had several opportunities (if they had only known about them) to mollify guests, because 58 percent of the respondents indicated that their complaints were motivated not by one problem, but by a *series* of problems or incidents. Moreover, after the complaints were received, hotel managers generally failed to take advantage of additional opportunities to soothe the guests. Sixty-one percent of the respondents said their complaints could have been handled better, and 34 percent said subsequent complaints could have been forestalled if the situation was handled better when the incident occurred.

Resolving complaints does not have to be expensive. Just 19 percent of the respondents thought they should receive rebates or complimentary rooms or meals. Nearly half would have been satisfied with a better response from management in the form of more detailed or speedier communication and a more pleasant tone to the response.

Higher-Ups

When asked about the method they preferred to use in expressing complaints, just 5 percent of the respondents chose complaining in person at the time of the incident. The most popular choice (24 percent of respondents) was using a toll-free telephone number to reach someone who would handle their complaint directly. Another 22 percent preferred to write a personal letter to the general manager, and 21 percent wanted an in-room card addressed to the president of the hotel chain. An in-room card to the general manager and a personal letter to the president of the chain were each the choice of another 14 percent of the respondents. These results reinforce the observation that people do not like to complain in person and are not likely to do so.

Marketing Opportunity

The results of these studies show that hotels could do a better job of dealing with consumer complaints. Although these studies do not involve food service, we presume that guest-complaint behavior is not substantially different in restaurants. While it is true that a simple complaint can be easily remedied (e.g., a poorly done steak can quickly be replaced with another steak), customer feedback on other problems is probably far less than that received by hotels.

The appropriate handling of complaints may be person-to-person marketing at its finest. Certainly, the satisfactory resolution of a complaint is a tremendous marketing opportunity. This is why marketing-oriented managers should actually seek out complaints. In the rest of this article, we will discuss how to make complaint resolution pay off.

Taking Steps

There are several specific steps that hotel managements can take to encourage and resolve complaints, thereby increasing customer goodwill and loyalty. These steps chiefly involve training managers and employees to deal with guest complaints, opening channels of communication if a complaint is not resolved, and following up on complaints.

Training. Managers and employees should be trained to recognize guest dissatisfaction and en-

couraged to take the necessary action to resolve problems on the spot. Most employees, including managers, seem to try escaping from a complainant, and when they can't run away, their behavior often makes matters worse. We recommend using video and role-playing to familiarize managers and employees with the various ways guests show dissatisfaction and the best way to deal with typical complaints.

The first task, however, is to educate employees in the importance of catching complaints at their origins. This should be a top priority of senior managers, who should show by their own actions that the company is willing to put the time, effort, and money into ensuring guest satisfaction.

The next step is to show guests that the company is prepared to take guest complaints seriously. It is difficult for employees to deal firsthand with dissatisfied guests when they hear the same complaints every day and nothing is being done to correct the causes. Management can take advantage of an opportunity to improve the operation when it listens to *employee* comments.

Hot lines. Hot lines are the hottest concept in marketing today, but very few hotel companies are using them, usually on the grounds that they "can't afford" them. Here is the epitome of shortsighted marketing. If our research results are correct, hotels could take away pillow mints, extra soaps, fancy shampoos, and other management-designed amenities and put the money into a consumer-based feature—a hot line—with the result of increasing guest satisfaction and, therefore, return business.

This conclusion rests on the idea that complaints called into a hot line would be resolved quickly and satisfactorily. It would be essential to give hot-line operators the authority to deal with each situation as they see fit, *on the spot*. Nothing is more aggravating than to be "passed around" from one person to another by telephone. It should be policy not to ask complainants to put problems in writing, since that would negate the purpose of the hot line: namely, speedy resolution.

Moreover, the hot line would have to be staffed

sufficiently to overcome the great disadvantage of centralized telephone numbers—insufficient incoming lines. Repeated busy signals do nothing to improve consumer attitudes.

Hot-line logbooks should be maintained and reviewed daily by duty managers and executive managers. If a guest is still on the premises, managers could provide a follow-up before the guest leaves.

Comment cards. For lack of a better tool, and given management's reluctance to conduct serious ongoing consumer research, comment cards remain the most common instrument for receiving consumer comments. As discussed elsewhere, most such hotel form cards are archaic and uninformative (Trice and Layman 1984).

The card should be postage-paid and addressed either to the general manager or a guest-relations officer, by whatever title that person is known. We don't think it should be turned in at the front desk, because it could be discarded, and we don't recommend sending it to corporate officers, either, because that delays any possibility of a response.

Complaints on guest cards must be answered immediately—preferably by phone, and at least by return mail. The message should be that the guest will receive a letter of resolution from the hotel within the week. The person charged with resolving the complaint should examine the problem firsthand, either in person or by phone, rather than by inter-office memo.

The final letter offering a solution should omit all the trite phrases about how happy the manager is to hear complaints and how the complaint will be forwarded to the appropriate department. Instead, the letter should state in simple language what went wrong and what the hotel will do both to atone for it and to make it right on the guest's next visit. The letter should assume there will be another visit and show that the hotel cares about the guest sufficiently to take care of his or her complaint.

If the complaint is half serious, the hotel should give something away. Now is not the time for pen-

ury. Airlines usually offer a trip anywhere in their system to passengers who will accept being bumped due to overbooking. There's no reason that hotels could not do something similar.

Rewards. The burden for receiving and correcting complaints should rest on the person who is responsible for the operation—the general manager. A creative policy would be to pay this person bonuses for receiving and resolving complaints, and fixing the sources of the complaints (instead of paying bonuses for cutting down on complaints). If he or she is paid for finding complaints, the first thing a GM will do is go out *hunting* for complaints and more satisfied customers will be coming back.

A manager who is rewarded for uncovering and fixing problems can do the same for every department head or supervisor. The GM can keep a log of supposedly cured problems, and when the same complaint shows up again, the GM has a solid basis for evaluating that department head.

Guest-relations director. The time has come in the hotel industry for having a staff member designated as responsible for guest relations or handling complaints. The concept is so rich that we can't believe no one has seriously tried it. The list of tasks this person would have is too lengthy to cover here, but the essential point about this position is that it should carry a relatively high level of authority. This is not the place for a recent college graduate. This position should require substantial experience and should carry a concomitantly high level of pay—somewhere above $25,000. This person should have a cool head and a good, customer-oriented manner. Above all, this person should have the authority to make decisions on behalf of the customer.

Does this sound expensive? On a per-day basis, it would probably amount to the cost of only one room-night. Considering that current customers are the best customers, that's a small price for keeping them happy—and coming back.

The Use of Computer Spreadsheets for Overbooking Optimization and Analysis

William J. Corney

Taking a reservation for service benefits both the supplier and the consumer of the service. The supplier can better schedule resources to match known reserved demand, and overall demand peaks can be flattened by spreading demand across future supply availabilities; the consumer benefits through a guarantee of service and a reduction in waiting time. A major problem arises, however, when reserved service is not used owing to consumer "no-shows."

No-shows arise because the consumer has a change of plans for which the supplier of service is not notified, or because the strategy of "hedging" is used through the reservation of much more service space than is needed in order to guarantee a range of service options. The former is a common occurrence in the hotel industry, while the latter is a daily feature among airlines.

No-shows can have a significant impact on an organization's profitability. The cost structure of many service firms is characterized by a fixed cost that is large relative to the variable component of individual service cost. The no-show represents a loss of revenue against which only a small variable cost applies. Managing the no-show problem in a proper manner, therefore, should be a major objective of all organizations that reserve service.

POSSIBLE SOLUTIONS

A number of solutions to the no-show problem have been proposed. One common approach is to dismiss no-shows as just another cost of doing business.

Reprinted with permission of Pergamon Press from Corney, William J. "The Use of Computer Spreadsheets for Overbooking Optimization and Analysis." *International Journal of Hospitality Management,* vol. 3, no. 4 (1984), pp. 153–157.

Another is to charge consumers that do not show up for reserved service. The airline industry, which experiences no-show rates of up to 30 percent, uses (or is considering using) a wide variety of techniques for discouraging no-shows (Anon. 1981). Methods include: requiring passengers to prepay for tickets at the time reservations are made; providing a discount for the purchase of non-refundable tickets; requiring a credit card number for telephone reservations; pooling data among carriers to cross-check multiple bookings; requiring the reconfirmation of reservations; and overbooking to cover expected no-shows. The overbooking approach, if done in a scientific manner, provides an effective and efficient method to minimize both total service cost and overall impact on the consumer. It also has wide applicability throughout the hospitality industry. Unfortunately, determining an optimal overbooking strategy can be an extremely difficult task. The use of a standard spreadsheet program and knowledge of the overbooking cost structure, however, can lead to a rapid and straightforward resolution to the problem (Kleinfeld 1984).

OVERBOOKING COSTS

There are two major costs associated with an overbooking policy: a long cost of having space available for which there are no consumers (service supply exceeding demand) and a short cost of having too many consumers for the space available (demand for service exceeding supply).

Long costs are typically straightforward in their estimation since they represent the opportunity loss from the absence of consumed service. Because of the domination of fixed costs in service systems, long costs can often be approximated by the lost revenue minus a small variable cost for one unit of service.

Short costs are more difficult to estimate because they contain numerous components, some of which are subjective in nature. If more consumers arrive with reservations than space is available, it is often necessary to provide substitute service at the server's expense in place of the service guarantee (reservation) that cannot be honored. In some cases, the substitute service is required by law, as in the airline industry. For others, the maintenance of consumer goodwill demands that alternative services be granted.

Costs associated with handling this situation can include: (1) labor costs required to find or schedule alternate service for the consumer; (2) transportation costs to move the consumer to the alternate site of service; (3) cost of the alternate service itself; (4) monetary penalties imposed on the server for overbooking; (5) loss of future business by the consumer affected; (6) loss of future business by others not directly affected but who have learned of the failure to honor the reserved service; (7) costs of preparing goodwill letters of apology; (8) costs of any premiums given to the consumer to atone for the inconvenience; and (9) personnel training costs to ensure that employees know how to handle the delicate overbooking situation with minimum negative impact.

COMPUTER SPREADSHEETS

One method of overbooking is to use a rule of thumb that seems to give good results, e.g., reserve an extra 10 percent over capacity. A more rational approach is to develop an overbooking strategy that minimizes total system cost. The spreadsheet achieves this objective easily and inexpensively. A microcomputer and standard spreadsheet software are all that are required. This approach requires specifications of system long and short costs and no-show probabilities, and provides expected costs of alternative overbooking policies. The user can easily choose that alternative which yields lowest overall cost.

No-show probabilities can be found in one of two ways: from an assessment of past data on no-shows or through a subjective assessment procedure. Records of past no-show experiences can provide frequency data that is easily converted to statements of probability, as shown in Table 1. Subjective assessments are "educated guesses" that quantify the chances of the non-arrival of reserved demand. Huber (1974) provides a good discussion of a num-

TABLE 1
Overbooking spreadsheet structure

Number of no-shows, probabilities and long costs

		P_0	P_1	P_2	P_3	•	•	P_n	
		0	1	2	3			n	
		C_L	C_L	C_L	C_L			C_L	
C_S	0	0	C_{L1}	C_{L2}	C_{L3} •	•	•	C_{Ln}	C_{T0}
C_S	1	C_{S1}	0	C_{L1}	C_{L2} •	•	•	C_{Ln-1}	C_{T1}
C_S	2	C_{S2}	C_{S1}	0	C_{L1} •	•	•	C_{Ln-2}	C_{T2}
C_S	3	C_{S3}	C_{S2}	C_{S1}	0 •	•	•	C_{Ln-3}	C_{T3}
•	•	•	•	•	• •	•	•	•	•
•	•	•	•	•	• •	•	•	•	•
•	•	•	•	•	• •	•	•	•	•
C_S	n	C_{Sn}	C_{Sn-1}	C_{Sn-2}	C_{Sn-3}	•	•	0	C_{Tn}

ber of organized procedures for making subjective assessments.

The spreadsheet accepts the probabilities, along with long and short costs in a form shown in Table 1.

The spreadsheet matrix can be illustrated by choosing selected elements and explaining them.

C_{L2} Represents the cost of being long by two service units (i.e., having two service spaces for which there are no consumers). It is found by multiplying C_L by 2.

C_{S3} Represents the cost of being short by three service units (i.e., having three consumers demand reserved service for which there is no supply). It is found by multiplying C_S by 3.

R_2 Represents the probability that there will be two no-shows.

C_S Represents the cost of being short one unit.

C_L Represents the cost of being long one unit.

C_{T2} Represents the total expected cost per day from using the strategy of overbooking two each day.
Zeros on the matrix diagonal indicate a perfect balance of supply and demand, yielding zero overbooking cost.

The value of each of the overbooking possibilities shown on the right side of the matrix is found by determining its respective expected cost. The expected cost of overbooking by two units (C_{T2}), for example, is:

$$P_0(C_{S2}) + P_1(C_{S1}) + P_2(0) + P_3(C_{L1}) + \ldots$$
$$P_n(C_{Ln-2}).$$

The best overbooking strategy is the one with minimum cost. The standard computer spreadsheet software is used by entering probabilities, numbers of possible no-shows and overbooks, long and short costs, and cost relationships into the spreadsheet matrix. The following example will illustrate this approach.

HOTEL EXAMPLE

A popular tourist hotel in a resort area has no trouble reserving all its rooms during the tourist season, but the number of no-shows has kept its occupancy rate below the 100 percent level. Management has decided on developing an overbooking policy. Past records on the tourist season no-show experience yields the information given in Table 2.

The opportunity cost of maintaining an empty room (long cost) is estimated to be $85.00 per night. Costs associated with overbooking for this hotel (short costs) are thought to have the following major components: (1) cost to transport the guest to another hotel; (2) payment of the hotel room for the guest; (3) possible loss of future business. It is estimated that the total of these costs is $134.00 per room.

The spreadsheet is shown in Table 3. The spreadsheet used was Logicalc, run on a Morrow MD3 computer.

Construction of the spreadsheet is straightforward. The first row represents probabilities, his-

TABLE 2
Historical no-show data and probabilities

Number of no-shows	Number of times this occurred	Probability (*number*) (total)
0	2	0.019
1	10	0.094
2	14	0.132
3	33	0.312
4	19	0.179
5	16	0.151
6	8	0.075
7	4	0.038

TABLE 3
Overbooking spreadsheet for hotel example

		0.019	0.094	0.132	0.312	0.179	0.151	0.075	0.038	
		85.00	85.00	85.00	85.00	85.00	85.00	85.00	85.00	Expected
		0	1	2	3	4	5	6	7	loss
134.00	0	0.00	85.00	170.00	255.00	340.00	425.00	510.00	595.00	295.88
134.00	1	134.00	0.00	85.00	170.00	255.00	340.00	425.00	510.00	215.04
134.00	2	268.00	134.00	0.00	85.00	170.00	255.00	340.00	425.00	154.79
134.00	3	402.00	268.00	134.00	0.00	85.00	170.00	255.00	255.00	120.21
134.00	4	536.00	402.00	268.00	134.00	0.00	85.00	170.00	255.00	160.43
134.00	5	670.00	536.00	402.00	268.00	134.00	0.00	85.00	170.00	236.61
134.00	6	804.00	670.00	536.00	402.00	268.00	134.00	0.00	85.00	345.86
134.00	7	938.00	804.00	670.00	536.00	402.00	268.00	134.00	0.00	471.54

torical or assessed for numbers of no-show ranging from zero to seven. The second row is the cost of being left with a room that is not filled. The third row gives alternative possible numbers of no-shows to a situation; for this example, 0–7. The first column provides the cost of having someone with a reservation arrive and not have a room available. The second column provides the range of over-booking strategies available for the manager's use. For this example, it would be the reservation of 0–7 rooms over capacity. For the matrix of costs, the zero diagonal (perfect balance of overbookings and no-shows) separates the shortage of room supply (below the diagonal) and excess of room supply (above the diagonal). Each cost cell below the zero diagonal is calculated by multiplying the short cost ($134.00) by the respective number of rooms short. Each cost cell above the diagonal is calculated by multiplying the long cost ($85.00) by the respective number of unfilled rooms. The expected losses (last column) are found from the expected cost formula presented previously.

Although there are differences among spreadsheet programs, the model described here can easily be handled by any major software product, and with a minimum of training on the user's part.

For the example shown, the expected loss column indicates the smallest expected cost ($120.21) to occur with an overbooking strategy of three rooms.

MODEL EXTENSIONS AND SPREADSHEET ANALYSIS

Complications sometimes exist that require a modification to the spreadsheet model.

Probabilities of no-shows are often not fixed in value but are related to conditions that can be expected to change. The airline industry, for example, experiences different no-show rates for different transportation routes and times of the year (Anon. 1981). Departures from Las Vegas on New Year's Day, as one might suspect, have a different no-show rate than departures from Davenport, Iowa, in the summer. Hotel no-show rates also vary seasonally and in terms of the number of new reservations made on a given day. For these and similar situations, it is necessary to develop unique sets of probabilities for each condition of importance that influences the no-show rate.

Costs may also vary. The season, type of service required, characteristics of the serving unit or of the consumer itself can all affect the cost structure (Williams 1977).

TABLE 4
Overbooking spreadsheet for changed conditions

		0.017	0.051	0.085	0.169	0.237	0.288	0.118	0.034	
		85.00	85.00	85.00	85.00	85.00	85.00	85.00	85.00	Expected
		0	1	2	3	4	5	6	7	loss
155.00	0	0.00	85.00	170.00	255.00	340.00	425.00	510.00	595.00	345.27
155.00	1	155.00	0.00	85.00	170.00	255.00	340.00	425.00	510.00	264.43
155.00	2	310.00	155.00	0.00	85.00	170.00	255.00	340.00	425.00	195.84
155.00	3	465.00	310.00	155.00	0.00	85.00	170.00	255.00	255.00	144.75
155.00	4	620.00	465.00	310.00	155.00	0.00	85.00	170.00	255.00	140.01
155.00	5	775.00	620.00	465.00	310.00	155.00	0.00	85.00	170.00	189.25
155.00	6	930.00	775.00	620.00	465.00	310.00	155.00	0.00	85.00	307.62
155.00	7	1085.00	930.00	775.00	620.00	465.00	310.00	155.00	0.00	454.30

The existence of non-reserved demand to cover no-shows will also affect system cost. Walk-ins or holdovers will reduce the cost of no-shows by assuming the unused capacity. Historical data can provide probabilities of expecting 0, 1, 2, 3, . . . , n units of unreserved demand. The expected value of each possibility can be subtracted from the corresponding long cost in the spreadsheet, reducing this cost. The overall expected loss of each overbooking alternative will then reflect the possibility of non-reserved demand.

For changes of the type described, it is not necessary to create a new spreadsheet; the new data are entered in the old spreadsheet and a recalculate command is given. Expected losses for the new situation will automatically and rapidly be found and displayed.

This feature makes the spreadsheet extremely valuable to the hotel manager faced with uncertain and changing conditions. The manager can easily make "what-if" analyses to see how the optimal strategy would change if costs and probabilities changed.

For example, if short costs in our hypothetical hotel rose from $134.00 to $155.00 and there was also a change in no-show probabilities, what effect would this have on the optimal overbooking strat-

egy? The spreadsheet shown in Table 4 illustrates this situation. The optimal strategy has shifted from overbooking by three rooms to overbooking by four rooms.

A typical manager could find answers of this type in no more than five minutes for each new set of costs and probabilities. All that is involved is entering the changed cost and probability data in the old spreadsheet. The computer makes all recalculations within seconds.

In this manner, a manager can easily make numerous changes in an effort to see how sensitive the best strategy is to possible changes in future conditions.

CONCLUDING REMARKS

Overbooking provides a rational approach to the problem of no-shows. The computer spreadsheet is an easy-to-understand-and-use mechanism for finding the number of reservations to overbook in order to minimize overall long-run system costs. The software is inexpensive and widely available. Not only can it find an optimal solution for a given situation, but its rapid power of recalculation makes "what-if" analyses easy and rapid.

Coping with No-Shows, Late Cancellations, and Oversales: American Hotels Out-do the Airlines

Rex S. Toh

Giving a new twist to an old saying, "There's no business like the no-show business!" for the hotel and airline industries, the problem of no-shows arises when guests and travelers, having decided not to show up, fail to inform the affected parties of their change in plans. If the hotels and airlines were fully booked and have been turning away paying customers, then the no-shows are really depriving these businesses of potential revenues. This creates an unusually tricky problem for hotels and airlines because they are selling highly perishable commodities (unoccupied rooms and empty seats) that cannot be inventoried for future sales. Hence revenues once lost cannot be regained.

NO-SHOW RATES

In a fairly recent study, Gould et al. (1980) reported that in the American hotel industry, the no-show rate is anywhere between 5 and 15 percent in most markets. It is known to be especially high during holidays, peak seasons, and in tourist-oriented cities like Las Vegas, Miami, and Honolulu, where the sheer number of hotels in close proximity makes multiple/speculative bookings possible. American airlines have fared no better. James (1982) has reported that the no-show rate may have gone up to 20 percent recently and is known to be especially high in markets with many duplicated services. During peak demand periods like holidays, and especially during Thanksgiving, it has been said that "No-shows are as traditional as turkey." The problem is particularly acute in Las Vegas where Lady Luck, more than any other factor, has contributed to an unbelievable 70 to 80 percent no-show rate during the holidays.

Late cancellations, to a lesser extent, also create the same problems as no-shows. Together, they cause completely booked hotels to end up with empty rooms and fully reserved flights to depart with many empty seats. The bottom line is this: No-shows and late cancellations reduce hotel occupancy rates and lower airline passenger load factors. In additions, they both cause unnecessary inconvenience to guests and travelers who are turned away because the hotels or flights were supposedly fully booked.

PROTECTIVE OVERBOOKING

The incidence of no-shows and late cancellations has forced hotels and airlines to engage in protective overbooking so that reservations are taken in excess of capacity during periods of heavy demand. They rightfully contend that the effect of unused reservations on their occupancy rates is so deleterious that the practice has been forced upon them by sheer economic necessity. Indeed, in many instances, overbooking to overcome the problem of no-shows and late cancellations may produce advantages by way of operating efficiencies that far outweigh the occasional inconveniences to guests and travelers.

The American courts seem to agree. They have held hotel overbooking to be a customary and justifiable practice for offsetting the losses from no-shows. Writing in February 1980, Gould et al. could find no direct statutory or administrative law governing hotel overbooking, with the exception of one Florida regulation. The now-defunct Civil Aeronautics Board (C.A.B.) held the same view. Despite the 1976 Supreme Court decision in *Nader v. Allegheny Airlines* condemning overbooking as de-

Reprinted with permission of Pergamon Press from Toh, Rex S. "Coping with No-Shows, Late Cancellations and Oversales: American Hotels Out-do the Airlines." *International Journal of Hospitality Management,* vol. 5, no. 3 (1986), pp. 121–125.

ceptive, it declined to outlaw the practice of over-booking, believing that it helps to increase load factors, keeps fares down, and enables more travelers to get seats on flights of their choice.

BUMPS AND WALKS

Unfortunately, whenever flights or hotels are over-booked, it is inevitable that on some occasions more passengers or guests may turn up than can be accommodated. According to past C.A.B. figures, the number of airline passengers with confirmed reservations that have been denied boarding has been between five and nine per 10,000 enplaned. This translates to about one-quarter of a million American passengers bumped each year, of which about half are off-loaded involuntarily. Unlike the previously regulated airline industry, which had to report bumpings to authorities, no one knows the true extent of oversales in the American hotel industry. Evidence to date, however, indicates that the problem is considerable, judging by the amount of literature it has generated.

We have seen that the problem of no-shows and late cancellations forces the airlines and hotels to overbook. This in turn sometimes leads to oversales and the resulting problems of bumps (airlines) and walks (hotels). The problem of no-shows, over-booking, and oversales is therefore a triumvirate of related issues. It follows, therefore, that if over-booking is to be regarded as a necessary evil brought about by the capricious behavior of airline travelers and hotel guests, the problem of oversales can be attacked either by reducing the incidence of no-shows and late cancellations or by directly minimizing oversales or alleviating the adverse effects thereof. In pursuing these worthy objectives, we shall see that the hotels have done a much better job than the airlines.

NO-SHOWS AND LATE CANCELLATIONS

In the American hotel industry, reservations are guaranteed after the customary 6 P.M. deadline for ordinary reservations, but only if the guest prepays for the first night's expenses or gives his credit card number on the understanding that if he fails to cancel the reservation by 6 P.M. of the day of his anticipated arrival, he will be billed for the first night's rent in the event of a no-show. A survey of six of the largest hotels in the Seattle, Washington, area revealed that, among hotel guests with ordinary reservations not committed to a no-show penalty, the no-show rate was around 10 percent. As expected, among hotel guests requesting guaranteed reservations after 6 p.m. and committed to a no-show and late cancellation penalty, the no-show rate dramatically dropped to 2 percent.

It is noteworthy that the no-show rate for the hotels compares very favorably with the airlines' figure of nearly 20 percent. According to hotel industry sources interviewed, many of their guests are repeat customers who are well known to front office personnel and, to avoid future embarrassment, feel compelled to cancel their reservations when they change their plans. An airline passenger, on the other hand, deals with a travel agent who really does not care how or when you fly as long as you do not ask for a refund.

However, the no-show rate for hotels is lower than that of the airlines mainly because the former have done a much better job than the latter of collectively enforcing and collecting no-show penalties. The hotels' record on collections of no-shows and late cancellation penalties is rather impressive. American Express guarantees payment for the first night's rent and is the preferred credit reference. Overall, the collection ratio is about half, the other half being successfully challenged by guests delayed by extenuating circumstances, one of which is, ironically, being bumped by an airline that failed to pass the message on to the hotel. On the other hand, American airlines have had a dismal experience with the collection of no-show penalties. In their earliest experiment, they mailed a total of 16,916 no-show bills totaling $338,047 but succeeded in collecting only $9,428.

Clearly, the success of the hotel industry in dealing with the no-show problem holds many lessons for the airlines. It is manifestly clear that the airlines must start enforcing and collecting the no-show and late cancellation penalties. Taking a cue from the hotels, New York Air has begun taking down credit card numbers and is enforcing a $20 penalty for no-shows and late cancellations. However, despite the individual efforts of the smaller airlines like Frontier and Air Florida, which is offering discounted, non-refundable tickets, it is widely believed that the no-show problem cannot be solved unless, like the hotels, the entire industry adopts and uniformly enforces no-show penalties, given the fiercely competitive nature of the business.

Finally, the hotels have done a much better job of cancelling down-line space when a no-show materializes. Admittedly, this is because, for the hotels, all the guest's activities are internal to the firm. In contrast, an airline traveler on a multisector flight may be traveling on different carriers. The airline industry has yet to come up with a coordinated multi-carrier reservation system that is capable of carrying out immediate post-departure checks to identify the no-shows so that down-line spaces can be released for subsequent sales.

In spite of all the proposed measures and penalties to cut down on no-shows and late cancellations, the problem will never completely disappear. Therefore, *all* airlines and *all* hotels overbook. If a hotelier claims that he does not overbook, he is either lying or simply not doing his job.

DEMAND AND SUPPLY OF HOTEL ROOMS

In order to judiciously overbook and minimize oversales, the components of demand and supply must be understood. The demand for hotel rooms on any particular date comes from four sources listed in decreasing order of allocation priority:

1. *Stayovers* are guests who are already occupying rooms and have new reservations to extend their stay. Naturally, they have first priority in room allocation.
2. *Holders* are guests who, without prior permission from the hotel, extend their stays beyond their scheduled duration. For all practical purposes, legalities aside, a holdover cannot be ejected and has a prior claim over incoming guests.
3. *Ordinary* and *guaranteed* reservations.
4. *Walk-ins* are prospective guests who arrive without reservations. Yesawich (1977) reported that they constitute about 15 percent of a hotel's business. About two-thirds of them arrive after the 6 P.M. cut-off time for ordinary reservations. Walk-ins have the lowest priority and are treated very much like standbys in the airline industry in that they are accommodated only on a space-available basis.

The supply of hotel rooms is obviously fixed in the short run. Typically, a hotel has several rates, each corresponding to a type of room distinguished by size, number of beds, location, view, or any combination of the above. Generally, hotels keep separate inventories of the different rooms for reservation purposes. Therefore, not only is the total supply of rooms fixed, the designated types of rooms are not generally interchangeable unless upgrading is necessary to accommodate an otherwise displaced guest (a walk) because of an oversale.

MINIMIZING OVERSALES AND UNDERSALES

Given the above demand and supply conditions in the hotel industry, Toh (1985) has documented that the room inventory situation will always conform to the following equation: stayovers + holdovers + reservations + walk-ins − no-shows − cancellations − unexpected departures = rooms occupied + upgrades + walks. When the booking situation is tight because of heavy booking, excessive stayovers and holdovers and a smaller-than-anticipated number of unexpected departures, no-shows, and cancellations, the hotel's front office will not accept walk-ins in order to minimize the chances of an oversale.

The airlines face a more or less similar situation.

When a flight is overbooked and the percentage of no-shows/late cancellations appears to be lower than expected, then last-minute sales at the airport will be curtailed and standbys ignored.

It is interesting to note here that the hotels are at a tremendous advantage in avoiding oversales (and undersales) compared to the airlines. First, hotel check-outs occur mostly between 7:45 A.M. and 9:00 A.M. This means that the number of stay-overs and unexpected departures can be determined early in the morning (by the customary noon check-out time at the latest) so that the hotels can determine the acceptable number of walk-ins (who conveniently arrive in the evening) according to the tightness of demand. Second, after the 6 P.M. deadline, the hotels are free to sell unclaimed rooms not covered by guaranteed reservations to the sizeable number of walk-ins.

The airlines, on the other hand, are not so fortunate. They will not know what their final no-show rate will be until about 10 minutes before flight departure, when they can legally start denying seats to late arrivals with confirmed reservations. And even if they could anticipate the number of empty seats on a flight before departure time, the number of last-minute airport ticket sales and standbys does not come close to the number of walk-ins that hotels enjoy.

MONITORING RESERVATION PROFILES

American hotels have also out-done the airlines in monitoring reservation profiles over time. Major hotels make it a point to contact large tour groups 90, 60, and then 30 days before their scheduled arrival date to confirm reservations with non-returnable deposits. The parallel activity in the airline industry is called pre-flighting. Tour groups are contacted well in advance of departure time to confirm reservations and individual passengers are called up a day or two before flight departure to inquire about their latest travel plans. Unfortunately, pre-flighting is practiced only by foreign airlines, mostly in the Orient. As American airlines

do not engage in pre-flight activities, intending no-shows cannot be detected early, which leads either to excessive protective overbooking and oversales or underbooking and empty seats.

Furthermore, the major American hotels have done an excellent job of keeping historical records detailing the no-show, late arrival, and early check-out profiles of large recurrent convention groups. Thus, if the historical records suggest high show-up rates for a particular convention group, then the overbooking levels for the convention period are lowered to avoid oversales. There is no evidence that the airlines in the U.S.A. have made any serious attempt to monitor the past performance of tour organizers.

UPGRADING

When oversales do occur, a practical way of minimizing oversales is to engage in upgrading. Faced with the prospect of turning away a guest with reservations, a hotel will willingly offer the prospective turnaway a more expensive room at the original lower rate. Similarly, the airlines often avoid off-loading passengers by upgrading them to the first class section at no extra charge. Here again, the hotels are more fortunate than the airlines. A guest who is upgraded to a better room normally does not know that the hotel has oversold. However, an airline passenger who has been upgraded may come away with the less-than-confidence-inspiring feeling that he could have been bumped.

BUMPING PROTOCOL

The fact that sometimes oversales cannot be avoided begs the question, "Who gets left out in this game of musical chairs?" The hotel industry has adopted a uniform policy of first-come-first-served. However, the airlines face a rather different situation. When a flight is oversold, all the possible candidates for off-loading are assembled at the same place and time. The rules of the game then allow the airlines to seek volunteers, negotiating with them for mutually acceptable sums below the statutory compensation levels. The airlines will accept the lowest bids, going up just enough to clear the oversale. This way, most passengers would be making the flights they had contracted for or receive the monetary alternatives they considered preferable. Approximately half of all off-loads are volunteers.

Unfortunately, sometimes there are not enough volunteers. More unfortunately, in the U.S.A. there is no uniform policy for bumping. Each airline files its own denied-boarding priority plan with the authorities. Some airlines protect unaccompanied minors and invalids, some favor those already seated on the plane on a first-come-first-served basis, and other airlines simply bump those with the cheapest discount tickets. This lack of uniformity within the industry can be quite confusing to the traveling public.

COMPENSATION

When a passenger is involuntarily bumped, American airlines are required to compensate him by an amount equal to the dollar value of the first remaining flight coupon subject to a $200 maximum. The amount of compensation doubles if the airline cannot arrange another flight to reach the destination within two hours (four hours on international flights) of the original arrival time. To qualify, the passenger must have a prepaid ticket in hand. This means that airlines do not honor oral confirmations by telephone without subsequent ticket purchase. A further exemption discharges the airlines from paying any denied-boarding compensation if an alternative flight can be found that gets the bumped passenger to his destination within one hour of his original arrival time.

In contrast, when a hotel guest with a reservation is turned away, the compensation is very generous and the inconvenience minimal. Recognizing that the displaced guest needs an immediate on-site remedy, rather than monetary damages, he is walked or provided with free transportation to another nearby hotel. The defaulting hotel pays for his accommodation until a room becomes available at the first hotel, or up to the length of the originally anticipated stay. It is to the credit of the hotel industry that all major hotels cooperate to minimize the cost and inconvenience of an oversale, even to the extent of offering room discounts to the defaulting hotels. Furthermore, it is the custom of the trade (although not legally binding) for hotels to compensate oversold guests even if their reservations were not guaranteed, provided they arrive before the 6 P.M. deadline. Thus, unlike the airlines, hotels do honor oral confirmations even when no prepayments have been made.

CONCLUDING REMARKS

It would appear that collectively, American hotels have out-done airlines in coping with no-shows, late cancellations, and oversales. First, a concerted effort by the hotels to enforce a uniform policy of no-show/late cancellation penalties has curtailed the no-show rate to levels much below that of the airlines, which have yet to come up with a similar, uniform and workable plan. Also, although the airlines, unlike the hotels, have an industry-wide computerized reservations system, they have not pressed their advantage by cross-checking reservations to detect multiple/speculative bookings, thereby reducing the number of empty seats flown. Second, given the nature of the industries, the hotels have also done a better job of using their reservation computers to cancel down-line space when a person fails to show up. Third, the hotels have also outperformed the airlines in monitoring demand by advanced contacts with large tour groups and by keeping the historical profiles of the past performance of recurrent convention groups. Tritsch (1977) reports that it is to the credit of the American hotel industry that even competitors exchange information about convention groups and their meeting patterns. It is unfortunate that the American airlines have not adopted the practice of pre-flighting that has been so successfully used by other airlines to confirm reservations and identify intending no-shows. Fourth, when an oversale occurs, the hotels have a uniform first-come-first-served policy in dealing with displaced guests, whereas each airline is allowed to file its own denied-boarding priority plan; this gives rise to unnecessary confusion on the part of the traveling public. Fifth, when an oversale occurs, American hotels have been more generous in their compensation package and, unlike the airlines, they do honor oral confirmations.

The success of the hotels in coping with the related problem of no-shows, overbooking, and oversales, and the admirably uniform and cooperative way in which this success has been brought about, are even more impressive when one realizes that the American hospitality industry has never been regulated by any specialized board or commission. The American airline industry, on the other hand, has been regulated for about half a century but still cannot get its collective act together!

Is Discounting the Answer to Declining Occupancies?

James Abbey

Lodging room rates are occupying the minds of hotel persons throughout the United States today. The selection of proper room rates is a serious source of concern for property owners, managers, and operators in the light of our present economic downturn.

Prior to the 1980s, the lodging industry and the economy as a whole experienced a near-continuous period of expansion. During this time, wages and operating costs increased, but not as rapidly as room rates. Most lodging chains and independents prospered in this boom period. Income outpaced expenses, and profits for most were reasonable, if not good.

In the last two years, this growth has slowed considerably, and consumer demand has decreased. Most would admit the boom has ended and that the economy and lodging industry are now in for a period of adjustment.

Operators throughout the nation are greatly troubled over the slackening demand and the prevailing high level of wages and operating costs.

Their concern is for profits, and rightly so. Flagging sales and diminishing profits have caused a number of chains to look closely at their present pricing policies. A number of large firms have now resorted to discounting of one sort or another to stimulate business. When this type of room rate activity takes place by the industry leaders, others cannot stand idly on the sidelines. Properties become deeply concerned when competition is moving room rates around. Given the present business conditions, coupled with the pricing action of the industry leaders, lodging operators are critically concerned over the vulnerability of their price structure and the problem of establishing a sound rate policy.

HISTORY OF ROOM RATES

The lodging industry has experienced many changes over the last few years. These years have been a period of growth for many hotel companies, but with that growth have come changes in the general philosophy of hotel management. Due to economic factors, we have seen a downturn in business volume, causing hotel companies to become more cost conscious. The market has become a strongly competitive one. Times have changed, and hoteliers are changing, too. Yesawich (1980) states that success in the 1980s will require a lodging property to

Reprinted with permission of Pergamon Press from Abbey, James. "Is Discounting the Answer to Declining Occupancies?" *International Journal of Hospitality Management,* vol. 2, no. 2 (1983), pp. 77–82.

be not only customer oriented, but also competitor oriented.

Before considering the soundness of hotel rates today, the history of room rates should be reviewed. As an indication of what has been happening, we can study trends to draw some valuable conclusions.

Table 1 shows the six-year trend of selected revenue and expense items for 325 transient hotels as reported by Pannell, Kerr, and Forster (1981). The table measures five areas: average room rate; percentage of occupancy; total operating costs and expenses per available room; income after taxes; and the Consumer Price Index. By studying the table, several conclusions become apparent.

Rates Spiral Upwards . . .

Average room rates have increased considerably. In fact, the average room rates at the end of 1981 were 88.3 percent higher than they were in 1976; during the same period, the Consumer Price Index rose only 59.7 percent.

As Occupancy Remains Relatively Stable . . .

Occupancy, despite the rise in average room rates, has remained fairly constant over this period. This can be interpreted as support for the theory that raising room rates has little effect on occupancy. And it might also indicate that the supply of rooms has generally increased at the same rate as demand for lodging has increased (Clark 1982).

Operating Costs Parallel Inflation . . .

Operating costs have spiraled from 1976 to 1981 at an average rate of 10.3 percent. While this seems extremely high, statistics show the increase closely parallels the inflationary rate. Operating costs rose 63.8 percent from 1976 to 1981, while the Consumer Price Index increased 59.7 percent, a difference of only 4.1 percent.

But Are Outpaced by Room Rates . . .

The relationship between operating costs and room rates is not nearly as parallel. The trend has been to increase the room rate at a progressively faster rate than operating costs and expenses. Robert Lewis, in discussing the impact of inflation, explains: "The industry's response to inflation to date has been to raise room rates even faster than costs have risen, allowing most operators to keep expenses as a percentage of sales at a better-than-even level" (Lewis and Beggs 1980).

And Operating Profit Increases

The operating profit per dollar of sale has increased. During the six years under study, the rate of increase amounted to 22.3 percent. However, this is not indicative of the owner's return on investment. It should be remembered that there are other charges below the operating profit line. Income after property taxes and insurance is before deducting rent, depreciation, interest, amortization, and income taxes. Certainly, these costs have increased significantly in light of the high interest rates and the additional depreciation write-off for properties who have invested in improvement and modernization.

In summary, the data suggest the rise in room rates are generally due to two factors:

1. inflation in the over-all economy, and
2. increased operating costs.

A further explanation, not supported by statistical data but nevertheless probably accurate, is the improvements in the product-service offering of hotels.

In general, room rates have been kept within a proper range; however, there are exceptions. In certain areas of heavy demand, rates have climbed too rapidly and are in need of some readjustment. Shapiro (1981) suggests that in some areas price may have outstripped value and because expense-account travelers are cutting back, hotels should

TABLE 1
325 transient hotels, selected revenue and expense items, six-year trend

Year	Average room rate		Percentage of occupancy		Total operating costs and expenses per available room		Income after property taxes and insurance		Consumer price index	
	Amount	% change from prior yr	%	% change from prior yr	Cost	% change from prior yr	%	% change from prior yr	Index	% change from prior yr
1976	29.85	8.4	66.5	5.4	10,520	9.7	19.7	10.7	170.5	5.8
1977	32.50	8.9	68.3	2.7	11,432	8.7	20.3	3.0	181.5	6.5
1978	36.65	12.8	71.5	4.9	12,826	12.2	22.7	11.8	195.3	7.6
1979	42.00	14.6	72.8	1.8	14,166	10.5	25.3	11.5	217.7	11.5
1980	49.62	18.1	69.7	-4.3	15,729	11.0	25.0	-1.2	247.0	13.5
1981	56.21	13.3	66.9	-4.0	17,238	9.6	24.1	-3.6	272.3	10.2
1976–1981		88.3	1976–1981	0.6	1976–1981	63.9	1976–1981	22.3	1976–1981	56.7

Source: Pannell, Kerr, and Foster (1981) Trends in the Hotel Industry, New York.

look closely at the price-value relationship of what they offer.

THE (OVER?) EMPHASIS ON OCCUPANCY PERCENT

One of the most frequently used measures of success in the lodging industry has for years been the occupancy rate. The first question posed when discussing the hotel business is, "What is your occupancy percent?" Understandably, some of the most traumatic periods in the life of a hotel person are when occupancy levels drop. Sales volume is vital, but sales volume is a product of both the number of rooms sold (occupancy) and the price or room rate at which the units are sold.

Most operators recognize the relatively high profit margins possible in the rooms area when contrasted to other profit centers. When occupancy falters, as it has for many today, the first, often illogical, action is to play with room rates to stimulate business. The reasoning goes as follows: Nothing is more perishable than an unused guest room. Rooms must be sold. A rate reduction will build occupancy.

An additional factor that tends to keep the eyes of hotel people turned toward occupancy is the reliance of other departments on guest count. The higher the occupancy, the greater the food and beverage volume. While the lodging property's financial position depends on maximum utilization, it is unwise to consider occupancy alone. It is only good business to sell guest rooms at fair and equitable rates—not less than they are worth.

ELASTICITY OF DEMAND

The belief that a reduction in room rates will generate an increase in occupancy is widespread in the lodging industry today. The economics of this reasoning is the inverse relationship between price and quantity sold. Simply stated—the number of rooms purchased will increase as the price for these rooms declines.

In assessing the relationship between occupancy and room rates, it is worthwhile to consider the demand elasticity for guest rooms. The elasticity concept measures the sensitivity of the number of rooms sold to price changes. In practice, elasticity can be classified in two ways:

1. When the demand is *elastic,* a percentage change in price brings about a greater percentage change in the quantity sold.
2. When the demand is *inelastic,* a percentage change in price brings about a lesser percentage change in the quantity sold.

In regard to room rates, elasticity may be expressed as:

$$\text{Elasticity of demand} = \frac{\%\ \text{change in number of rooms sold}}{\%\ \text{change in price}}$$

In situations of elastic demand, the market is sensitive to changes in price. When this is the case, price reductions are met by a greater percentage increase in number of rooms sold.

In situations of inelastic demand, the change in price will result in a less-than-proportionate change in volume. Thus, the total room revenue actually decreases as the price per room falls. This is because customers do not purchase enough guest rooms at the lower price to make up for the revenue lost through the price reduction. Even though greater sales volume results from the lower room rates (as is expected with the inverse relationship between price and quantity), the increase in sales is not enough to raise or maintain total revenue.

Knowledge of the demand elasticity for particular markets and market segments is important. For example, if it is determined that demand is relatively elastic, prices may be lowered with confidence that room sales will show significant increases. Such a situation normally occurs when there is a great deal of competition and a strong demand for guest rooms in the market.

Is this the case in the lodging market today? That is, is demand elastic? Certainly there is no simple answer to this question.

In the past, it has been reported that pleasure-trip room demand was elastic demand; that is, pleasure travelers would shop for rooms and, within limits, select the lowest price or best-priced room. Business-trip room demand is inelastic; that is, the price of the room is immaterial, as the cost of lodging represents a small percentage of the total cost of the business trip. Borsenic (1966), in studying the elasticity of the lodging industry, also indicated that total room demand was inelastic; that is, a certain number of rooms will be sold each and every night in the industry regardless of the price; travelers must have a room.

However, it is important to note that elasticity is not fixed. It changes over time and is influenced by a number of factors. For example, a recent study by American Express (1982) tends to refute the suggested inelastic demand of the business traveler. Since this is the first survey of the business traveler by American Express, no comparisons can be made with previous years. However, a question with which 71 percent of the 1,300 participating financial and executive officers disagreed was: "Employee travel is part of doing business; we tend to take travel and entertainment expenses in stride and not be overly concerned about how much we are spending on it."

In summary, while knowledge of the degree of elasticity is important information for price setting, it is extremely difficult to determine. The types of customer, the intensity of competition, the local market, and the customer's perception of the availability of substitutes are all factors that alter the demand elasticity for a property. Historically, however, for the industry as a whole, there is little evidence that a change in room rates has any considerable direct effect on occupancy.

THE COST OF DISCOUNTING IN THE SHORT TERM

Operators, before employing discounting to improve sales volume, should be aware that an extra strain is placed on the occupancy factor to increase dollar sales. A commonly held assumption is that a 10 percent increase in occupancy is needed to make up for a 10 percent reduction in rates. Such is false reasoning.

The extra servicing expense for the additional occupied rooms must be taken into consideration. For example, it is reasonable to estimate that the operating costs for renting and taking care of an additional room are 25 percent of the room rate. Therefore, a 10 percent rate reduction would not require a 10 percent, but a 15 percent increase in occupancy to produce the same contribution. Let us briefly review the mathematics.

Assume a 100-room property, an average room rate of $40, and an average occupancy of 70 percent. A variable or operating expense of 25 percent of average room rates equates to a $10 operating cost per room rented and a contribution to fixed costs and profits of $30.

If the $40 rate is discounted by 10 percent to $36, the contribution after subtracting the $10 direct cost is $26.

Using the formula below, we determined an equivalent occupancy of 80.8 percent is required to make up for the loss of sales revenue and for the cost of taking care of the additional rooms.

The lodging operator who reacts to others' price-cutting schemes without understanding the economics of rating rooms may find himself worse off than before. He has doctored his occupancy problems perhaps, but because operating costs have increased, his profits are lower. Now, less money is available for maintenance and he soon ends up with a second-rate property where the lower rate he is charging is justified.

Existing room rate

Average room rate	$40
Operating cost	$10
Existing contribution	$30

Room rate discount of 10%

(continues)

Average room rate $36

Operating cost $10

Discount contribution $26

$$\text{equivalent occupancy} =$$

$$\text{existing occupancy} \times \frac{\text{existing contribution}}{\text{discount contribution}}$$

$$= 70\% \times \frac{\$30}{\$26}$$

$$= 80.8\%$$

$$\text{percentage increase in occupancy} =$$
$$\frac{10.8\%}{70\%} = 15\%$$

THE LONG-TERM EFFECTS OF RATE CUTTING

Not only is rate cutting difficult to justify in the short run, several industry leaders are concerned that its long-term effects may prove detrimental to the health of the lodging industry as a whole (Anon. 1982a, 1982b).

Rate cutting tends to have a snowballing effect. When one large chain announces a blanket discounting plan, it will probably divert customers at the expense of others. But the competitive advantage is short-lived. The word spreads rapidly. Others, sensing a portion of their business lost, work out a pricing scheme of their own to attract business. Snowballing takes place as operators are forced to fight for their market shares by lowering rates. Eventually, the average rates of lodging facilities are driven lower than they should be, and in all probability, the total size of the lodging market is not significantly enlarged.

Further, once rates are cut, a great deal of difficulty could be experienced in trying to restore them to their pre-sale level. In the long term, the public may become accustomed to sale rates. When discounting becomes all-pervasive—when all chains "are holding a sale"—it loses its effectiveness.

Customers who are attracted by discounts are generally the first to seek out new bargains when the rates are increased.

Robert Hazard, Jr., president of Quality Inns International, states:

> When fall comes and the discount program ends, Holiday Inn may find that its guests resent paying the higher prices. It's hard to start a discount program, but harder still to stop it (Hazard 1982).

Thus, the long-term effects of the "discounting parade" could prove disastrous for the lodging industry. Rate cutting cannot be considered as the solution to the lodging industry's slumping occupancies. Rate-reduction plans that divert business from other properties until they are forced to reduce rates should not be employed. It is unsound business—generally in the short run and certainly when considering the long-term consequences. The industry's strength is dependent upon its ability to keep room rates at general price levels.

RATE CUTTING DISTINGUISHED FROM PROMOTIONAL PRICING

It should be made clear that not all reductions in rates constitute rate cutting. Generally, seasonal rates and segment rates are promotional plans that are constructive and legitimate in developing new sources of business. For example, the practice of offering a lower rate during the off-season (or value-period rates, as is the common terminology) generally is not rate cutting, providing the in-season rates are not negatively affected.

Similarly, special rates given to specific market segments do not generally constitute rate cutting, but giving blanket discounts to all guests is self-defeating. Offering discounts to customers you already have, who would have paid the rack rate, makes little sense. Group rates are not damaging to the price structure as long as management makes certain group business does not displace its regular guests. Likewise, package tours are a constructive device, where properly used to promote new business.

Unfortunately, some of the rate-variation schemes we are witnessing today will not create new sales for the lodging industry. The real test of any rate-quoting plan is whether it will bring new guests to hotels or whether it is a form of rate cutting, which diverts existing business from other hotels with benefit occurring only to the bargain-hunting guest (Walker 1968).

Therefore, all rate variations should be judged as to their ability to tap new business. Pricing strategies that do not attract new users and only draw business from competitive properties until they, too, are forced to lower rates should be shelved.

The industry's present infatuation with discounting is often no more than disguised rate cutting. Conceding that demand is off and room rates in many areas are due for some readjustment, rate cutting is not the solution to the industry's difficulties. Cutthroat competition will only compound the problem and is counter-productive. Rate cutting is not an ethical problem as much as it is an unsound business practice and seems a detriment to the entire lodging industry.

ESTABLISHING A SOUND RATE POLICY

There is generally agreement that today's lodging customer is value conscious. There is, however, a mistaken belief by many that value equals price. That is, unless the customer is receiving a low price, he or she is not receiving value.

Value and price are not necessarily equal. An important component of value is quality. A more accurate mathematical representation of value is:

$$\text{value} = \frac{\text{quality}}{\text{price}}$$

This formula suggests that, while value may be increased by a reduction in price, it may also be enhanced by an increase in quality.

Certainly the lodging guest of today is greatly concerned with price. The sight of Mercedeses, Cadillacs, and Lincolns parked at budget properties is evidence of this. However, the most common complaint of hotel guests is not the rate. More often, it would seem, guests are not as concerned with what they pay as what they receive for their money. Efforts to improve services and facilities will go a long way to establish guest satisfaction, and satisfied guests are repeat customers.

In order to determine proper room rates, hotels must consider the quality of their facilities and services as well as what competition offers in the way of accommodation and rates. Further, the lodging operator must assess the cost structure to insure the adequacy of rates to cover costs and provide a fair and reasonable profit. Rates should be evaluated throughout the house to determine if rooms are priced in proper relationship to one another. Thus, a comprehensive study of a number of factors is required in determining a sound rate structure. But once completed, this review could well lead to improved sales for the property.

CONCLUSION

In summary, rate changes should be viewed with an eye toward the future. Certainly, the room rates of many properties may need to be re-evaluated, considering the piecemeal treatment received during their rapid rise prior to the present recession. However, rate cutting has been shown to be counter-productive. Every lodging operator must assess his own rates to determine if his is a sound rate structure. Rather than intuitive judgments of what the market will bear, the operator should base the pricing decision on sound market research and a thorough understanding of the economics of price changes.

How *Not* to Automate Your Front Office

Roy Alvarez
Dennis H. Ferguson
Jerry Dunn

With a gala ball that drew movie stars and royalty, the New York Hilton in 1963 opened what was then the nation's largest hotel. The celebration marked a bold, pioneering step—not just because of the hotel's size, but also because the Hilton had become the first hotel using computer technology to control its front-office operations. The hotel's automated property-management system (PMS) handled such guest-cycle functions as check-in, check-out, and the posting of charges to guests' folios.

And yet by late 1964, the corporation decided to abandon its first front-office computer installation, because the system had failed to meet Hilton's expectations. During breakdowns, it actually *reduced* guest services, and its cost proved unreasonable.

Now, 20 years later, after using various computer systems in the interim, Hilton has developed its own sophisticated property-management system. In the authors' opinion, this system will be successful—providing a healthy return on the corporation's investment and improving service to the hotel's guests.

The experience of the New York Hilton raises several interesting questions:

1. What advantages did the New York Hilton expect from computerizing its front-office operations that induced the property to become a pioneer in hotel automation—as well as a "repeat customer"?
2. What problems arise in automating a hotel?
3. How did the first installation fail to meet the hotel's expectations?

4. Why is the hotel's new PMS expected to be successful?

By answering these questions, this article will provide information that will be helpful to hotels considering the use of a computerized property-management system.

WHY AUTOMATE?

To justify its costs, a property-management system must offer substantial benefits to the hotel and its guests. When the New York Hilton opened its doors with over 2,100 rooms, its size rendered the front-office tasks enormously complex. Many of these tasks are of the kind that people hate but that computers "love"—repetitive, clerical jobs that require a tremendous amount of "number crunching" and other data manipulations, and jobs that demand structured, logical procedures. They include handling reservations, registering guests, updating room status, posting guests' charges, settling folios, and generating reports for use by management.

The computer helps bring order from this chaos of information. (In French, the computer is an *ordinateur*.) It works with great speed and accuracy—solving problems with capabilities that are, literally, superhuman—if its instructions have been well designed and well written.

Hotels can gain five benefits by computerizing their front-office operations:

1. Improved service to guests;
2. Streamlined handling of paperwork and data;
3. Improved control over operations;
4. Generation of complete, timely reports; and
5. Reduced costs and increased revenues.

This article was originally published in the November 1983 issue of *The Cornell Hotel and Restaurant Administration Quarterly*, and is reprinted here with the permission of the Cornell University School of Hotel Administration. © 1983.

An example of each of these benefits will illustrate the advantages a hotel enjoys from a computerized property-management system.

Improved Guest Service

Computers can bring greater accuracy to many transactions; for example, a PMS usually handles reservations more accurately because the system will accept them only when rooms are available. (The New York Hilton's PMS receives reservations directly from Hilton's wide-based reservations system, updating the information every 15 minutes.) Greater accuracy reduces the likelihood of problems that frustrate guests, such as lost reservations (especially those made on little slips of paper), and of overbooking the hotel.

The computer also improves service by giving management accurate, timely information on the hotel's room inventory, lowering the odds that a guest will be given the key to a dirty or occupied room.

Reducing the Paper Chase

Today's computer systems easily streamline the handling of paperwork and data. The computer automatically prints out individual registration forms—eliminating the old manual methods; stores the "rack" electronically—no longer must employees maintain a room rack or tally sheets to keep track of the house manually; and allows different hotel departments to communicate via terminals and phone codes—so that, for example, room-status information need not be carried by hand between the housekeeping department and the front desk.

Guests' folios no longer pass through human hands and minds (both of which make mistakes), and folios do not stack up in a "pit" or "well." Instead, charges are posted directly to electronic folios, so a guest's folio, which under a manual system can become a ragged mess by the end of the week, is now cleanly printed when the guest checks out.

Soon the New York Hilton plans to link the computer systems in its front and back offices. Even

now, a record that comes in as a reservation automatically becomes a registration record and then a cashiering record. In the future, it will automatically be filed as an accounts-receivable record.

Improved Control of Operations

A property-management system usually includes a security program that limits access to its files. Management can therefore set limits on employees' activities within each function, such as reservations or check-in. For instance, the system might not allow the reservation clerk to overbook a particular date or add room-nights to a group reservation without management's approval.

Some systems select a room for an arriving guest in an order predetermined by the hotel's management (within certain limits, such as room type), and may also prevent the clerk from modifying the room rate.

Generation of Reports

A well-designed PMS can generate tremendous amounts of information (or a small amount of tremendous information). The hotel's decision-makers receive valuable reports daily—in multiple copies, if needed—on expected arrivals, rate variance, and revenues. With this information, to cite one example, a general manager can measure the performance of the hotel by comparing the daily revenue report against expected performance as shown by the hotel's operating budget.

Besides scheduled reports, the PMS produces demand reports, such as house tallies. On a screen, the manager can call up a list of the expected checkouts who have remained in the hotel, the number of guaranteed and nonguaranteed arrivals expected, the number of stayovers, the number of rooms committed, the number of rooms available for sale to walk-ins, and so on. With this up-to-the-second information, which is available as often as desired, the hotel gains better control over its merchandise—the room inventory. Using demand reports, a manager can make decisions in response to the flow of guest traffic into and out of the hotel, and thereby maximize the hotel's occupancy rate.

Increased Revenues and Reduced Costs

Each of the previous four benefits gained by using a computerized PMS at least indirectly increases a hotel's revenues or reduces its costs. A computer can cut some hotel costs directly—particularly labor costs—by automating tasks that are clerical and often repeated. With simple instructions to the system, one night auditor can post the room charges and tax for an entire hotel in 10 or 15 minutes. This saves labor costs, and in large hotels, the night-audit staff is likely to be reduced.

The PMS can increase a hotel's revenues through connections, or "interfaces," with other automated systems on the property. Electronic cash registers in food and beverage outlets send charges directly to the PMS, which posts them to guests' folios. No longer can a guest charge a last-minute breakfast and check out before that bill can be posted to the folio. An interface with a telephone call-accounting system increases revenues in the same way, since calls made before check-out always appear instantly on the guest's folio for prompt payment.

The computer's files themselves can be secured with the same "locking mechanism" that limits employees' activities. Passwords or security cards are required to open specific programs and files, so only employees with the proper codes can get into the files.

These examples only begin to show the benefits of a good property-management system. But before the reader puts in an order for one, it is important to look at the built-in problems of hotel automation.

INHERENT PROBLEMS

The complexity of hotel operations, which makes them ideal candidates for computerization, also makes them difficult to automate. Unlike a bank or insurance company, a hotel operates 24 hours a day. It is a complex environment; a huge volume of transactions (many in cash) are handled by a large work force that experiences a good deal of customer interaction and exposure.

This complexity means that the system must be well designed. Its hardware and software must be reliable almost 100 percent of the time, because when the system is "down"—out of commission—the hotel loses touch with its guests and loses control over its business. During such a disaster, the hotel becomes deaf, dumb, and blind.

Computer programs for the back office of the hotel need not be nearly as complex as those for the front office. While back-office tasks can be run on a schedule, the front office is an unstructured environment that never stops moving and keeps no schedule. Back-office processing of such tasks as payroll and accounting is done in "batch" mode, which means that transactions are collected over a period of time and then processed by the computer all at once, in a batch. A power outage or computer "glitch" in the back office may simply mean that bills cannot be sent on a Monday afternoon; delaying them till Tuesday morning is generally not catastrophic to the hotel's operation.

In contrast, the front-office computer system operates in "real-time" or "online" mode, which means that transactions are processed as they occur. Furthermore, almost every transaction possible in the hotel may occur at any time—or all at once. In case of a computer failure in the front office, a clerk cannot just say to a guest, "Do you mind coming back and checking out tomorrow when the system is working?"

Front-office tasks are rarely the orderly kinds that computers are best suited to performing; instead, there are myriad exceptions, such as special room rates, multiple folios per guest, and changed reservations, all of which make automation difficult.

The computer's response time is also critical in a front office, since most of its transactions involve face-to-face contact with the guest. When the guest is waiting, "good service" implies speed. In the back office, without guest contact, the computer's response time is not as important.

In the back office, only a few people use the system, rarely concurrently. But in the front office of all but the smallest hotels, many employees make demands on the system at once—a host of managers, telephone operators, housekeepers, cashiers, and food and beverage clerks. Demand on the system further multiplies during the hotel's rush periods, the morning check-out and the afternoon check-in.

Because of these factors, front-office computer requirements are complex. They are also more sophisticated in larger hotels, where there are more terminals, more users, and more data to process. And the gymnastics that a larger hotel's PMS must perform with its data base are tougher, because people are constantly updating records by creating, modifying, and deleting information. This produces a lot of hard work for the computer—not only in making changes, but also in coordinating all this activity. As a result, the PMS program must have a "lockout" function to ensure that when two employees gain access to the same records, their transactions are processed in sequence. Otherwise, two clerks might check different guests into the same room simultaneously.

In a hotel, a single data base must serve all of the system's functions at once. At the New York Hilton, having 2,100 rooms entails producing 2,100 pieces of information on room status; guests might number 4,000; and there may be three or four folios per room, with charges emanating from a dozen revenue centers. Depending on whether the computer is looking for an available room or handling a guest's folio, it must use the same body of information in a number of different ways. Programming all of this is not easy.

Unfortunately, hotels' special needs were not apparent to those people outside the hotel industry who designed the first property-management systems. During the early "romance," when hoteliers and computer people tried to kiss, they often missed each other's lips. This caused serious faults in both the design of the systems and the choice of hardware.

WHY THE 1963 SYSTEM "FAILED"

The New York Hilton's installation of a property-management system was the first courtship between the hotel and the computer industry. Their lips missed. Not understanding hotels, the computer professionals treated the Hilton like a bank—an inappropriate back-office approach—and the hoteliers did not know the limitations of these apparently magical machines.

Here are some specific reasons that the system failed to meet Hilton's expectations. As the first computerized hotel, the New York Hilton had no experience with real-time data processing, and so the hotel accepted a system whose hardware and software were more appropriate to "batch-mode" processing tasks. Since this was a new hotel, the department heads had not worked as a team before, and because employees moved onto the property only the day before it opened, initial training was minimal.

The computer technology of 1963 did not include the television-like screen and typewriter-like keyboard that are common today. Instead, the system was made up of a *central processing unit,* where all the programs were executed; *auxiliary memory* on magnetic hard disks, where the data base and programs were stored; a *printer* to print folios and reports; and *keypunch machines* and *readers,* where information entered the system. These last two devices proved to be the fatal flaws in the system.

A keypunch machine allows the user to code an 80-column paper card by typing information on a keyboard; the punched card is fed into a reader that enters the data into the system for storage or processing. Without screens and keyboards for the Hilton's clerks to use, getting information into or out of the system depended entirely on the keypunch operators. An unreasonable amount of time was needed to gather information, keypunch it onto cards, and then collect and process the cards. During rush periods, the keypunch operator fell behind, creating long lines in the lobby. Eventually these delays overcame the guests' excitement about staying in a modern hotel with the latest computer wizardry.

The problems were aggravated by the fact that this early system had only one printer. Guests stood in one line while the single printer generated their folios, then in a second line to pay their bills. (Today, each cashier at the New York Hilton has a printer that produces folios at a speed of 300 characters per second.)

Another difficulty was the system's sole central processor and memory. If any part failed, the whole system shut down. Clerks rapidly fell behind in manually registering guests, charges were never posted to folios, and much revenue and goodwill were lost.

Even when it was working properly, the system still did not justify its operating expense of $10,000 per month (in 1963 dollars). And there was the added expense of paying ten full-time data processors, as well as night auditors, clerks, and cashiers. Ultimately, the decision to abandon the system was based on financial considerations.

Despite these problems, the corporation never lost its conviction that computers could tackle the tasks attendant upon running a large hotel's front office. After abandoning the first system, the New York Hilton used an automated room-status system in concert with a manual reservations system and electromechanical cash registers. It has taken two decades, however, for technology to match corporate chairman Barron Hilton's dream by providing an integrated property-management system that is cost-justified and capable of handling a hotel as large as the New York Hilton.

THE INDUSTRY IN THE INTERIM

In the last 20 years, many hotels have automated their operations to some degree. There have been perhaps 50 efforts by vendors to develop property-management systems, often by buying existing systems and redesigning them to meet hotel specifications. Some have been one-time developments, including systems for Caesar's Palace, the Broadmoor, and Disney World. Some large computer companies created hotel systems only to leave the field; Motorola's InnScan system was one example. In that case, computer companies entering the hotel market urged buyers to bypass the Motorola system and wait until their own products were available; most of the newcomers made promises they never kept, but buyers were not as skeptical then as they are today, so they bought the promises. Other large and small companies so underestimated the difficulty of the hotel-automation task that they either went out of business or spent millions of development dollars that they never recovered.

Although automation is becoming more prevalent in the hotel industry, fewer than 1,000 of the more than 4,000 hotels in America have automated their *front offices* to any extent. Of the numerous computer companies and entrepreneurs that have attempted to fill this vacuum, only a handful of vendors have been able to give the hoteliers products that meet their needs—among them, EECO Computers, Inc. (ECI), Hotel Information Systems (HIS), and International Hospitality Systems (IHS), which have all installed over 100 systems. We expect that the larger hotel companies, with their sophisticated in-house data-processing departments and knowledge of hotel operations, will lead the way in the technological development of property-management systems.

THE NEW YORK HILTON'S PMS

In 1972, Hilton Hotel's top financial manager, John Giovenco, saw a unique computer system operating the front office at Caesar's Palace in Las Vegas. Its designers had created "distributive processing," an innovation that multiplies a PMS's speed, capacity, and reliability. The software company owned by Hilton and Transamerica bought the system from Caesar's, named it Compass East, and installed it in the Flamingo Hilton and the 3,200-room Las Vegas Hilton.

Again, technology lagged behind the corporation's dream. Although the system was effective when it worked, the disk drives that stored the data and programs frequently broke down. Finally, Hilton had to stop using the system, and Compass, its subsidiary, wrote off the investment. But with time, as disk-drive technology improved, the Compass East system was resurrected in a highly efficient form. Hilton installed it in Las Vegas and at three more properties: Chicago's Palmer House, the San Francisco Hilton, and the Waldorf-Astoria.

In distributive processing, each terminal is "intelligent," with its own processor inside. The terminal functions as a full-fledged microcomputer, loading programs from the central system's disks into its own memory to perform such tasks as registration or check-out. In contrast, most PMS terminals are "dumb" peripherals with no processing power or memory of their own. They are used simply to get information into and out of the system, while all processing takes place in one central processing unit. As a result, when many employees use the same central processor simultaneously, response time becomes a problem. The more people using the system, the more slowly the system responds.

In the Compass East system, distributive processing "farms out" the work so it is shared among all the terminals; it never reaches a bottleneck at a central processor. The terminals communicate with the central system at a rate of 6,200 words per second, and processing is performed in microseconds. So the response time of the Compass East system is consistent and extraordinarily fast.

Although Compass East's central processing units are not as powerful as some being used, the system may be the only one capable of supporting hotels as large as the Las Vegas and New York Hiltons with an acceptable response time.

Compass East's designers also tackled the crucial problem of "downtime," knowing that a computer failure cripples a hotel. *Problem:* There is no system that will never break down. *Solution:* Design a system that is "redundant," meaning that the PMS has two complete central systems, each separately storing and processing the same data. If either breaks down, the other takes over and the hotel's operations continue without a pause. And since the system's *terminals* replace each other like standardized parts, the failure of a terminal causes no more delay for guests than the time it takes to plug in a new unit. This redundancy, while not as critical in smaller hotels, becomes a major consideration in a larger hotel, where "downtime" can result in either much lost revenue or very complex and costly manual backup procedures.

THE HILTON AUTOMATION LESSON

In two decades, the New York Hilton learned valuable lessons for any hotel or chain considering automation of the guest cycle. As an introduction, here are some basic rules that should be followed unless a hotelier has enough financial resources and data-processing experience to be a pioneer.

Moore's Laws

Today, few hotel companies want to pioneer new products, finding it wiser to learn from the experience of others. In this spirit, Professor Richard G. Moore, of Cornell's School of Hotel Administration, offers these rules to follow when selecting a PMS:

1. Never be the first user.
2. Never be the largest user.
3. Always observe someone else using a similar system.

Here is an explanation of these rules. First, the first user of a system always accepts high risks, as the New York Hilton did in 1963. The explorer enters the unknown without the assurance of success.

Second, a hotelier should be aware that the system whose hardware and software work perfectly in hotels with a given quantity of rooms or transactions may be unable to match that performance in a larger or busier house. Although the system will still work, response time may slow to a crawl in a larger property.

If a hotel cannot find an equally large hotel with a particular system installed, it may try to build specified standards of performance into the sales contract to limit its risk as much as possible—although the risk of breaking the second rule remains.

Third, potential buyers should observe a computer system at work in a *similar* hotel. A system meant for resort properties, for example, may not work well for transient properties—a resort system may handle group reservations and check-ins well, while a transient system is designed to handle tier pricing more effectively.

In observing a system at work, potential buyers should measure the system's response time with a stopwatch, observe its uses in each department, and simply ask the clerks and managers whether it is easy to operate. These investigations help buyers look past the vendor's glossy photographs and the staged demonstrations to test the system under fire.

SMALLER AND SMALLER

A larger segment of the hotel industry can now afford to automate its front offices, because costs have fallen and performance continues to climb. Large hotels can better afford to buy the large amount of hardware they require; medium-size hotels can afford property-management systems whose cost could previously be justified only by large hotels; and even the smallest hotels may soon have inexpensive front-office automation made possible by personal computers as vendors develop microcomputer software. The chances of successful automation are better than ever today.

The computer is not magic; it is only a tool. It is the abacus of 1,000 years ago, the slide rule of 50 years past. It works only as well as the people who design and operate the system. In fact, at a hotel with clumsy, ineffective manual procedures, a computer can exacerbate existing problems, rather than solve them. Finally, a PMS cannot do management's work; managers must still make the judgments. But a computer does free men and women to think, and to make those judgments.

Call Accounting Profits Through Telephone Resale

John G. Kaiser

Hotels and motels use telephone call accounting to keep track of the telephone service that a guest uses. It provides a means to bill the guest for service used and also keeps track of the cost and profit realized from the sale of telephone services.

Since 1981, it has been legal for hotels and motels (or anyone else) to purchase and resell telephone service to their guests. When properly implemented, the process is no more complicated than selling rooms or food and beverage. In fact, telephone service should be treated the same as these other traditional hotel/motel services. Guest telephone usage revenues can quickly become one of your highest profit guest services.

Before 1981, hotels and motels provided telephone service to their guests using the HOBIC system. This stands for Hotel Billing Information Center. HOBIC is a service supplied by the telephone company that provided a means to get "time and charges" on each call made by a guest. Under this system, guest calls were placed on special telephone lines known as HOBIC lines. When the guest dialed a call over these lines, the telephone company operator came on the line and asked the guest for his room number. After receiving the room number from the guest, the operator allowed the call to go through.

Reprinted with permission from Kaiser, John G. "Call Accounting: Profits through Telephone Resale." *Lodging* (October 1985), pp. 32–34, 63.

Upon completion of the call, the "time and charges" were given to the hotel either by telephone (voice quote) or via a teletype machine located on the hotel premises (auto quote).

If all went well, the hotel collected the charges from the guest and paid the telephone company when the bill arrived at the end of the month. Prior to January 1983, the hotel received a commission from the telephone company for collecting the charges from the guest. This commission was in the form of a 15 percent discount on the hotel's telephone bill.

HOBIC is still available, but this system has several inherent problems. The first is that the "time and charges" information often takes 40 minutes or longer to reach the hotel. This results in a loss for the hotel when the charges arrive after the guest has checked out.

Second, there is no way for the HOBIC operator to verify the room number that the guest gives. This results in further loss to the property and guest dissatisfaction when calls are charged to the wrong room.

The third and perhaps most important problem with HOBIC is that, without the commission, the best that a hotel can hope to do is break even. Considering the first and second problems, it is nearly impossible to break even. If you add in the cost of telephone systems themselves and the operating costs, most hotels lose money on telephone service under HOBIC. The special HOBIC trunks and teletype service also carry a monthly fee that can range from $75 to $375, depending on location.

Some properties have sought to make up these losses by inflating the HOBIC "time and charges" by 15 percent or 20 percent. While this does offset some of the losses, it can cost room sales when guests feel that the hotel is overcharging them for telephone service.

All of this changed January 1, 1983: Hotels and motels no longer receive the 15 percent commission for collecting guest telephone charges.

There is a better way. Using a call accounting system, a hotel or motel cannot only provide guests with properly charged telephone services, they can earn substantial profits. These profits can be used to finance new telephone systems to provide still better service to guests or simply to improve house profit.

Unlike the HOBIC service, call accounting systems do not rely on the telephone company for "time and charges" information. The call accounting system connects directly to the hotel's telephone system. This immediately eliminates two of HOBIC's major problems. Since the system is directly connected to the telephone system, it automatically knows which room the call was made from. Second, the time and charges information is available immediately. No additional charges arrive after guests have checked out.

The connection to the telephone system can be made in either of two ways. When the telephone system is a newer, electronic one, the connection is made to the telephone system's Station Message Detail Recording (SMDR) data port. On older telephone systems that do not have this feature, the connection is made to the actual wires extending to the telephones. This is done in the telephone room where all the wires come together. These two methods insure that any hotel or motel, *regardless of the type of telephone system,* can enjoy the benefits of a call accounting system.

The call accounting system receives information from the telephone system about who called where, when they called, and how long the call lasted. The call accounting system is programmed with the rates and tariffs used by the telephone company to price telephone calls. Using this information, the call accounting system calculates the price of the call and then adds in a markup or surcharge as desired by the hotelier. Once the call is priced by the call accounting system, this information is sent either to the front-desk printer for immediate posting or to the call accounting system's memory to be printed later for posting.

When the storage method is used, the charges are usually printed at midnight or some other time convenient for the night-audit process. (For resort or other long-term properties, the information can usually be saved and printed when the guest checks out.)

WHERE DO THE PROFITS COME FROM?

The profits come from the oldest business principle known to man: "Buy low, sell high." Under the old HOBIC system, every long distance call placed over the HOBIC line was billed at operator-assisted rates. On average, these rates are $1.55 per call higher than the standard Direct Distance Dial (DDD) rates that you are used to paying. The $1.55 is referred to as the operator surcharge. The $1.55 surcharge applies to calls over 23 miles. (Other surcharges apply to shorter-distance calls: 1-10 miles = $.75; 11-22 miles = $1.10.) Standard DDD rates are charged by the local phone company when a call accounting system is in place.

When a call accounting system is installed, the hotel can continue to charge its guests the operator-assisted rates and use the $1.55 surcharge as the hotel profit on each call. This method makes the transition from HOBIC to call accounting transparent to the guest. He continues to pay the same rates as before, but the hotel gets the profits. Figure 1 illustrates this through a typical 2-minute call.

This profit margin can be increased even further if special calling facilities such as WATS or other bulk-priced long distance services are used. The margin can also be increased by increasing the guest's charges. Caution should be observed here so as not to sacrifice room sales by charging too much for telephone calls.

Once a call accounting system is installed, a property has the ability to adjust the markup at will. It is usually a simple programming change that can be done on site by the service company or by the hotelier. This also allows the rates to be adjusted for competitive reasons or for marketing reasons. For example, the hotel's weekend specials could include discounted telephone service.

In addition, the call accounting system allows the property to have a great deal of flexibility in the way that they charge for local and other types of calls. These can be priced at per-call flat rates, per-minute charges, or combinations of both. Also, the call accounting system allows the property to charge for credit card or third-party calls. While these call charges are billed to the caller's credit card or to a third party, many hotels charge a service fee of 50 or 75 cents. This is justified, since the caller is using your telephone facilities. It is even possible to set your rates so that it is actually *cheaper* for a caller to direct dial through your facilities than to use a credit card (credit card calls carry a $1.05 operator surcharge).

FIGURE 1
The profit picture:
A sample 2-minute long distance call

	Without Call Accounting	With Call Accounting
First Minute	$ .58	$ .58
One additional minute	.39	.39
HOBIC charge for operator assistance	1.55	-0-
Telephone company charges hotel	2.52	.97
Hotel charges guest	2.52	2.52
Hotel's profit	-0-	1.55

Many call accounting systems have the ability to track administrative telephone usage. This helps to reduce unnecessary telephone expenses and increases profits even further.

More and more properties are acquiring Property Management Systems (PMS). Many PMS systems are capable of automatically posting call charges when a call accounting system is directly connected to the PMS. With this method, the call accounting system sends the charges directly to the PMS, where they are posted to the guest folio.

How large must a property be before call accounting becomes profitable? The answer to this question is based not so much on number of rooms, but on the size of the monthly telephone bill. If the long distance portion of the property's telephone bill is $500 or more, then a call accounting system will have an acceptable return on investment. The chart in Figure 4 will help you to determine the ROI for your property.

Once a call accounting system is installed in a property, the amount of operating expense is small. Depending upon the purchase method chosen, there is usually a monthly or yearly maintenance fee in the form of a service contract. It is quite common for the first year's maintenance to be included in the purchase price. The maintenance fee should include the cost of periodic updates to the pricing information that is programmed into the system.

With most call accounting systems, minimal staff training is needed. In fact, there is one method of implementation that requires no training whatsoever. This method calls for all call time and charges to be printed at the front desk immediately as they occur. Front-desk personnel remove the charge slip from the printer and post it to the guest's folio. If not immediately posted, they are at least placed in the folio for later posting, much the same as restaurant or gift-shop charges might be. This allows a property to operate exactly as it did with HOBIC prior to installing call accounting—but more profitably.

This "no-training" method is offered by call accounting systems that print the call records exactly as they would appear on a HOBIC system. Most front desk personnel are familiar with the format and will handle the call slips just as they did before.

As noted earlier, there is usually a monthly or yearly charge for a service contract and rate updates. Quite often, the call accounting system is provided by the same organization as the property's telephone system. In this case, the call accounting system's maintenance charges may be bundled with the telephone system charges.

This arrangement is becoming more and more prevalent as hoteliers are using the profits earned through the use of a call accounting system to pay for a new telephone system and a call accounting system.

How can a hotel or motel keep track of actual revenue and profits from telephone resale?

Most call accounting systems provide the operator with various types of profit and revenue reports. These typically are in the form of daily profit reports and month-to-date profit reports, and usually divide the calls by type (interstate, intrastate, local, etc.). This type of reporting permits the hotelier to maximize his revenues and profits by making any necessary adjustments in the pricing scheme. (See Figure 3.)

When purchasing a system, check the credibility and reputation of a potential call accounting system vendor and manufacturer. Treat this as you would any other systems purchase. Keep in mind that you will be counting on this system to produce revenues for your property.

Ask your vendor how the telephone rates will be kept up to date and at what cost to you. Some provide a yearly subscription with unlimited updates and others require a payment per update. (The frequency with which this is required is, of course, dictated by the telephone companies and the FCC.)

Find out if the system being considered has remote maintenance capabilities. This allows the vendor to access the system remotely for maintenance and diagnostic purposes. It is also an excellent method of updating the rates.

In sum, the resale of telephone service through telephone call accounting is an excellent source of revenue. It is an ideal way to finance the purchase of a new telephone system or to simply improve your house profit.

FIGURE 2

All call accounting systems provide the basic information required to charge guests for their calls. Systems vary, however, in their specific formats and other operational details. Several reports are shown here.

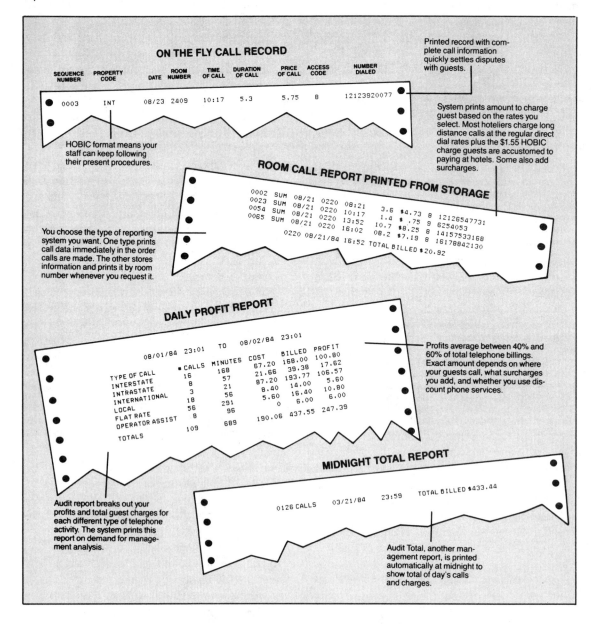

FIGURE 3

Various types of reports are supplied by call accounting systems, including daily and month-to-month revenue breakdowns. Calls are divided by type.

Daily Profit Report
03/20/85 23.59 to 03/21/85 23.59

Type of Call	# Calls	Minutes	Cost	Billed	Profit
Interstate	31	168	67.20	166.00	100.80
Intrastate	8	57	21.66	39.28	17.62
International	3	21	87.20	193.77	106.57
Local	18	56	8.40	13.50	5.10
Flat Rate	56	211	15.60	36.40	20.80
Operator Assist	8	96	0.00	12.40	12.40
Totals	124	609	200.06	463.35	263.29

Month-to-Date Profit Report
03/03/85 23.59 to 03/30/85 23.59

Type of Call	# Calls	Minutes	Cost	Billed	Profit
Interstate	682	3696	1478.40	3696.00	2217.60
Intrastate	176	1254	476.52	864.16	387.64
International	66	462	1918.40	4262.94	2344.54
Local	396	1232	184.80	297.00	112.20
Flat Rate	1232	4642	343.20	800.80	457.60
Operator Assist	176	2112	0.00	272.80	272.80
Totals	2728	13398	4401.32	10193.70	5792.38

FIGURE 4

Monthly telephone bill rather than number of rooms is key factor in determining potential profitability of call accounting system. If long distance portion of property's phone bill is $500 or more, a call accounting system is then considered to provide an acceptable return on investment. This chart will help determine ROI for your property.

Type of Call	Number of Calls		Surcharge Per Call		Profit
Interstate calls	_____	×	$ ___1.55___	=	$ _____
Intrastate calls	_____	×	$ _____	=	$ _____
Local calls	_____	×	$ _____	=	$ _____
Operator-assisted calls	_____	×	$ _____	=	$ _____
			Monthly Profit	=	$ _____
			Monthly call accounting investment	=	$ _____

CASE STUDY—"FRONT OFFICE PATHOLOGIES"

After being transferred and promoted to front office manager of a 600-room hotel in New Orleans from a smaller property of the same chain, you have spent the first five or six months familiarizing yourself with the hotel, its markets, the city, its people and culture. You have also spent a significant amount of time learning the job of front office manager and have concluded that it is significantly different from that of assistant front office manager in a smaller property.

Your front office staff consists of young, mostly college-educated persons and current students. For the most part, they are enthusiastic employees, but lack the innate professionalism that comes from a solid core of knowledge and training. Among the matters that concern you as manager are the following:

- An average of 12–15 guests per week are "walked" to other hotels.
- Several times a week, guests who have checked in are escorted to rooms that are out of order, not clean, or already occupied.
- Guest complaints, either in person or by letter about the hotel, its services, and staff have more than doubled over previous years and are outpacing complimentary letters and comments by about two to one.

Your managerial relations with your staff seem pretty good to you. Your relationships with other managers in the hotel, however, have become strained, particularly with housekeeping and sales.

Calling on your experience in a training program, your stint as a front office assistant manager, and your research and knowledge from your university education, formulate a plan that will allow you to identify and analyze the underlying root causes of the problems outlined above. Be sure to include rationales for the solutions and a plan that will allow you to demonstrate to top management that your analysis and solutions are likely to result in resolutions of these difficulties.

Endnotes

[1] Twenty letters were returned as nondeliverable, and 13 of the replies were unusable. Examples of these replies included comments such as, "Can't remember what I complained about"; two respondents contended they had never stayed at the hotel.

[2] Of the respondents, 27 percent were at the hotel for business reasons, 73 percent for pleasure or personal reasons; 48 percent were male and 52 percent female; they spent an average of 19 nights a year in hotels on business and 15 nights on pleasure; average annual household income was about $40,000; and 81.5 percent lived within 125 miles of the hotel.

[3] Caution should be applied in interpreting this finding. It is possible that when a couple travels and the woman takes the time to complete the card, the man with her was an impetus in her doing so, and vice versa.

References

American Express. 1982. Businessmen looking for cheap rooms: Study. *Hotel and Motel Management* August:1.

Andreason, Alan R., and Arthur Best. 1977. Consumers complain—Does business respond? *Harvard Business Review* July–August:93–101.

Anon. 1981. Airlines move to deter phantom passenger. *Business Week* December:42–43.

Anon. 1982a. Couponing: Tool or threat? *Lodging Hospitality* September:6.

Anon. 1982b. Rate wars underway. *Motel/Hotel Insider* 14:1.

Arndt, Johan. 1967. Role of product-related conversations in the diffusion of a new product. *Journal of Marketing Research* 4:291–95.

Borsenic, F.D. 1966. The lodging market . . . phase I. *Hotel Bulletin* November:12–16.

Christianson, Fred. 1981. Senior assistant manager, Westin-St. Francis, San Francisco. Personal interview.

Clark, J.J. 1982. From the publisher: Sounding a cautionary note. *Cornell Hotel and Restaurant Administration Quarterly* 23:1.

Consumer Dimensions, Inc. 1982. Consumers who complain irked by firm's response. *Marketing News* XV, 21(16 April):3

Day, G.S. 1978. Are consumers satisfied? In *Consumerism: Search for the consumer interest,* eds. D. Asker and G. Day. New York: Free Press, pp. 406–17.

Day, R.I., K. Grabicke, T. Schaetzle, and F. Staubach. 1981. The hidden agenda of consumers' complaining. *Journal of Retailing* 57(3).

Etzel, J., and B.I. Silverman. 1981. A managerial perspective on directions for retail customer dissatisfaction research. *Journal of Retailing* 57(3):124–36.

Farrell, Thomas. 1973. Front office communications: Old and new. *Cornell Hotel and Restaurant Administration Quarterly* 14(1):49–63.

Gilly, Mary C. 1980. Complaining consumers and the concept of expectations. In *Refining concepts and measures of consumer satisfaction and complaining behavior,* eds. Keith Hunt and R.I. Day. Bloomington: Indiana University Press, pp. 44–48.

Gould, R.W., T.J. Ramsey, and J.E.H. Sherry. 1980. The hotelkeeper's contract and the international traveler. *Cornell Hotel and Restaurant Administration Quarterly* 20:67–74.

Gray, William S., and Salvatore C. Liguori. 1980. *Hotel and motel management and operations.* Englewood Cliffs, NJ: Prentice Hall.

Gronhaug, Kjell. 1977. Exploring consumer complaining behavior: A model and some empirical results. In *Advances in consumer research* IV, ed. W.D. Perreault, Jr., pp. 159–63.

Hazard, R. 1982. Discounting hotel rooms: Counterproductive effort. *Canadian Hotel and Restaurant* August:16.

Heldenbrand, H.V. 1944. *Front office psychology.* Chicago: American Hotel Register Company.

Huber, George P. 1974. Methods for quantifying subjective probabilities and multi-attribute utilities. *Journal for the American Institute for Decision Sciences* September–October:430–58.

James, G. 1982. The coming decade in commercial aviation. In *Airline Economics,* ed. G. James. Lexington, MA: Lexington Books, p. 205.

Kasavana, Michael L. 1981. *Effective front office operations.* Boston: CBI Publishing.

Kent, William E. 1975. The life, loves and limits of the lowly desk clerk (or how to fan the flames under the fellows in just four simple phrases). *Hotel and Motel Management* August.

Kleinfeld, Ira H. 1984. General-purpose software adapted for I.E. applications. *Industrial Engineering* February:18–20.

Landon, F. Laird, Jr. 1977. A model of consumers' complaint behavior. In *Consumer satisfaction, dissatisfaction, and complaining behavior,* ed. R.L. Day. Bloomington: Indiana University Press, pp. 31–35.

Lewis, Robert C. 1983a. When guests complain. *Cornell Hotel and Restaurant Administration Quarterly* 24(2):23–32.

Lewis, Robert C. 1983b. Getting the most from marketing research. *Cornell Hotel and Restaurant Administration Quarterly* 24(3):81–85.

Lewis, R.C., and T.J. Beggs. 1980. Inflation: How will the industry cope? *Cornell Hotel and Restaurant Administration Quarterly* 22:12–18.

Lewis, R., and A. Pizam. 1981. Guest surveys: A missed opportunity. *Cornell Hotel and Restaurant Administration Quarterly* 22(3)37–44.

Lyle, Christopher. 1970. A statistical analysis of the variability in aircraft occupancy. *Proceedings of the Tenth AGIFORS Symposium,* American Airlines, New York.

Morris, Susan. 1985. The relationship between company complaint handling and consumer behavior. Master's thesis, University of Massachusetts, Amherst.

Nie, N.H., C.H. Hull, J.G. Jenkins, K. Steinbrenner, and D.H. Bent. 1975. *Statistical packages for the social sciences,* 2d ed. New York: McGraw-Hill.

Nyquist, Jody D., Mary J. Bitner, and Bernard H. Booms. 1985. Identifying communications difficulties in the service encounter: A critical incident approach. In *The service encounter: Managing employee customer interaction in service businesses,* eds. John A. Czepiel, Michael R. Solomon, and Carol F. Suprenant. Lexington, MA: D.C. Heath.

Plunkett, Robert L., and Florence Berger. 1984. Sales skills in the hospitality industry. *International Journal of Hospitality Management* 3(3):114.

Renner, Peter Franz. 1981. *Basic hotel front office procedures.* Boston: CBI Publishing.

Rutherford, Denney G., and William J. Schill. 1984. Theoretical constructs in practice: Managers rate their importance. *International Journal of Hospitality Management* 3(3):101–6.

Shapiro, E.L. 1981. On hotel rates: A matter of opinion. *Cornell Hotel and Restaurant Administration Quarterly* 22:6–7.

Swan, John, and I. Frederick Trawick. 1981. Disconfirmation of expectations and satisfaction with a retail service. *Journal of Retailing* 57(3):49–67.

Technical Assistance Research Programs, Inc. 1979. *Consumer complaint handling in America—Final re-*

port. Washington, DC: White House Office of Consumer Affairs.

Technical Assistance Research Programs, Inc. [nd]. *Measuring the grapevine—Consumer response and word-of-mouth.* Monograph. Atlanta: Coca-Cola Company Consumers Information Center.

Thomas, W.R., and F.K. Shuptrine. [nd]. The consumer complaint process: Communication and resolution. *Business and Economic Review* 21 (June): 13–22.

Toh, R.S. 1985. An inventory depletion overbooking model for the hotel industry. *Journal of Travel Research* 23:26.

Trice, Ashton D., and Walter H. Layman. 1984. Improving guest surveys. *Cornell Hotel and Restaurant Administration Quarterly* 25(3):10–13.

Tritsch, C. 1977. An inside look at how hotels operate. *Successful Meetings* May.

Vallen, Jerome J. 1982. *Check in—Check out,* 2d ed. Dubuque, IA: Wm. C. Brown.

Walker, G.M. 1968. The cost of cutting rates. *Transcript* 25:5.

Warland, Rex H., R.O. Hermann, and J. Willits. 1975. Dissatisfied customers: Who gets upset and who takes action. *Journal of Consumer Affairs* 9(Winter): 148–63.

Williams, Fred E. 1977. Decision theory and the innkeeper: An approach for setting hotel reservation policy. *Interfaces* August:25.

Yesawich, P. 1977. Know your prime prospects: Marketing research for the lodging industry. *Cornell Hotel and Restaurant Administration Quarterly* 17:12.

Yesawich, P.C. 1980. Marketing in the 1980s. *Cornell Hotel and Restaurant Administration Quarterly* 20:35–38.

Zweig, Philip L. 1986. Banks stress resolving complaints to win small customers' favor. *Wall Street Journal* 8 December:29

Suggested Readings

Books

Kasavana, Michael L. *Effective Front Office Operations.* Boston: CBI Publishing, 1981.

Renner, Peter Franz. *Basic Hotel Front Office Procedures.* Boston: CBI Publishing, 1981.

Vallen, Jerome J. Check In—Check Out. 2d ed. Dubuque, IA: Wm. C. Brown, 1982.

Articles

Andrew, William P., and Carolyn U. Lambert. "A Comparison of Quantitative Techniques for Setting Hotel Reservation Policy." *Proceedings of the 1986 C.H.R.I.E. Conference,* Boston, 1986.

Gamble, Paul, and Graham Smith. "Expert Front Office Management by Computer." *International Journal of Hospitality Management* 5(3), 1986: 109–14.

Lambert, Carolyn U., and Thomas P. Cullen. "Balancing Service and Costs through Queueing Analysis." *Cornell Hotel and Restaurant Administration Quarterly* 28(2), 1987: 69–72.

Trice, Ashton D., and Walter H. Layman. "Improving Guest Surveys." *Cornell Hotel and Restaurant Administration Quarterly* 25(3), 1984: 10–13.

SECTION 5

Housekeeping

INTRODUCTION

At a recent gathering of the directors of house-keeping of most of the major metropolitan hotels in a large northeastern city, the following question was posed: How many of you as part of your career plan initially considered housekeeping as a managerial role that had any attraction? The answer, not surprisingly, was not one!

This points up a major dilemma facing modern hotel management structures. One of the most important labor-intensive and largest cost centers in the hotel is neither universally understood nor respected by the bulk of the hotel's department managers, their employees, and (to a large extent) the hotel's guests and clients. There are some encouraging signs, however, that this situation is changing swiftly. Some hotel companies are experimenting with taking housekeeping out of the rooms division and making it a staff function, with the director of housekeeping reporting directly to the general manager. Others are combining house-keeping and other property management functions along with maintenance and engineering. One recent survey found that more than 60 percent of the housekeepers who responded (Rutherford and Schill 1985) were college graduates and 40 percent of the

housekeepers were male, which tends to refute the traditional stereotype of the director of housekeeping as a female who has worked her way up through the ranks of the housekeeping hierarchy.

Inge Krieg's 1977 essay on why the executive housekeeper can no longer be thought of in traditional stereotypical terms outlines a number of the unique managerial challenges facing the executive housekeeper in a large, modern, and technically sophisticated hotel plant.

Professor Robert Martin, writing on how house-keeping departments are organized and staffed, provides an overview and organizational perspective of the department, with attention paid to the responsibilities of the various personnel within the modern housekeeping department.

The article by Rutherford and Schill applies an analytical framework to traditional wisdom about the management of housekeeping departments and suggests a revised model for looking at the way housekeeping managers need to think about allocating their time and resources.

Finally, Professor Martin again addresses an issue that at one time or another faces all hotel and house-keeping managements: the on-premise laundry. Most executive housekeepers under normal circumstances would prefer that they have control over

over their major item of inventory—linen. To provide this complete control, an on-premise laundry is a must. It is an unfortunate circumstance, however, that this was not a consideration in many hotels at the time of their construction, and if an on-premise laundry has been added, it quite often was in space that was neither originally intended nor currently appropriate for laundry activities. Martin outlines the criteria for establishing an on-premise laundry and explores in depth the issues, both technical and managerial, connected with planning and constructing an efficient laundry facility.

In the suggested readings are two other issues central to the management of modern housekeeping departments. The array of "amenities" that hotels can now offer guests to contribute to their creature comforts and cleanliness has grown to be absolutely mindboggling. In the old days, the only thing man-agements and guests expected room attendants to place in rooms other than linen was a bar of soap. Now, a typical situation may include two or three kinds of soap, plus shampoo, hair conditioner, assorted grooming and personal care products, food and beverage items, bathrobes and slippers, and informational packets. This mandates significant attention from the housekeeping manager. These products need to be purchased, inventoried, stored, distributed, and controlled. They contribute in no small part to the complexity of the modern housekeeping manager's job.

Another problem that has been around since hotel guests stopped bringing their own sleeping linens is the control of hotel linen. Judy Rosenberg's article (listed in the Suggested Readings) sets forth one proposed structure for establishing managerial control over hotel linen.

Housekeeping Organizations: Their History, Purpose, Structures, and Personnel

Robert J. Martin

ORIGINS OF HOSPITALITY AND HOUSEKEEPING

By definition, hospitality is the cordial and generous reception and entertainment of guests or strangers, either socially or commercially. From this definition one has the feeling of the open house; the host with open arms; and a place in which people can be cared for. Regardless of the reasons people go to a home-away-from-home, there is the presumption that they will need to be cared for. They will need a clean and comfortable place to rest or sleep, foodservice, an area for socializing and meeting other people, access to stores and shops, and a secure surrounding.

Americans have often been described as a people on the move, a mobile society. As the country expanded, travelers required bed and board. In the early 1700s people found a hospitality structure similar to that in countries of their origin, even though these new accommodations might have been in road houses, missions, or private homes, and the housekeeping might have included no more than a bed of straw that was changed weekly.

Facilities in all parts of young America were commensurate with the demand of the traveling public, and early records indicate that a choice was usually available, based on where you might find the best food, overnight protection, and clean facilities. Even though the inns were crude, they were gathering places where you could learn the news of the day, socialize, learn the business of the area, and rest.

This early business of innkeeping has graduated to become the hotel industry of today, but the main

Reprinted with permission of John Wiley & Sons from Martin, Robert J. *Professional Management of Housekeeping Operations.* New York: John Wiley & Sons, 1986, pp. 3–4, 32, 45–46, 97.

tenets remain: a clean, comfortable room, access to food and entertainment facilities, and a courteous and concerned staff who mean it when they say, "May we be of service?"

Housekeeping departments play a vital role in today's lodging industry. People involved in housekeeping operations service guestrooms, maintain and service public and special areas, and in many instances, operate laundries, recreational, and health facilities. In addition, the people of housekeeping are also a part of the overall team of hosts and hostesses who add their own welcome to our hotel guests. They show concern and care when something goes wrong with the guest's visit, and they are quick to initiate action that will make things right again.

Major hotel companies have been quick to recognize the value of housekeeping and other service-industry workers. Good hotel management does not see housekeeping work as demeaning or menial. To the contrary, all quality hotel operational management personnel have at one time or another performed housekeeping functions and as a result, understand the worth and value of those people who perform such functions regularly.

Those who study the service industry should periodically remember the statement made proud by one of America's most prestigious resorts: "The Greenbrier" of White Sulphur Springs, West Virginia. This statement appears on a sign that is visible as one enters the resort: "Ladies and Gentlemen Being Served by Ladies and Gentlemen."

THE ROOMS DEPARTMENT

Front Desk and Housekeeping

The Rooms Department of a lodging establishment is considered to be that department which is directly and solely involved with all aspects of the sale, occupancy, and servicing of guestrooms. In many companies the department is managed by a person called the Resident Manager. Although the title is somewhat misleading in that it presupposes the idea that the resident manager lives on the premises, most do not. Other titles synonymous with resident manager are: rooms manager, rooms director, director of rooms operations, or simply, hotel manager (not to be confused with the general manager).

The rooms department is usually thought of as a combination of two principal line operating departments: the front office and the housekeeping department. The manager in charge of the front office oversees several subdepartments: reservations, front desk, bell staff, PBX, transportation, possibly concierge, and any other form of guest reception function.

The manager in charge of all housekeeping functions is most commonly known as the Executive Housekeeper. Depending on the size of the hotel, other subdepartments within the housekeeping sphere of operations may include an in-house laundry, or a recreation department. In some cases, by corporate policy, the person in charge of housekeeping may have any one of a number of different titles, all considered synonymous with executive housekeeper. A few such titles are:

Housekeeper
Housekeeping Manager
Director of Services
Director of Internal Services
Director of Housekeeping Operations

For the purposes of this article, all such responsibilities will be directed at the manager known as the Executive Housekeeper.

There was a time when most housekeepers worked under the direction of the front office manager. They were, in fact, not executives but people who had worked their way up from a maid's position, and had little or no training as a manager. Today, however, the size, cost, and complexity of housekeeping operations have put the executive housekeeper on an equal footing with other department managers. As a result, they are now seen to share equally in responsibility under the resident manager for the operation of the rooms department.

The hotel industry is a highly labor-intensive hospitality service business. There may be more total employees involved in foodservice and beverage operations than in any other department, but because of the diversity of such operations (restaurants, lounges, banquet services, and kitchen), there are usually more managers to control the total operation. In housekeeping there is one department head (the Executive Housekeeper) who is responsible for the largest single staff, operating cost center, and physical area of the property.

Today's modern Executive Housekeeper must be a trained manager skilled in planning, organizing, staffing, directing, and controlling operations. He or she must also be skilled in employee and human relations, have a superior knowledge in cost controls, and have a strong technical background in purchasing, decorating, and renovation. Last but not least, the Executive Housekeeper must be an able delegator. Without a strong expertise and inclination to create or pass tasks to others, convey the necessary power to act, and, finally, hold others accountable for their actions, the Executive Housekeeper must personally perform all working functions. And this writer has never found the person yet who could make 3,000 beds in one day.

ORGANIZATION

Housekeeping organizations are as varied as there are types and sizes of hotels. Except for the very small "Bed and Breakfast" operations, the trend today is away from the small eighty-room "mom and pop" hotel. For the purpose of discussing housekeeping organizations, it would, therefore, be appropriate to discuss a size of hotel that might be considered a model appropriate to the greatest variation. The organization to be discussed would fit *any* hotel of two hundred or more rooms. In most cases there would be identical functions, but size would dictate that one person might perform several functions in a small hotel. Obviously, the larger the facility, the greater the need for a larger staff with more individuals to fill each unique function. Consider, then, the following hotel:

A modern suburban corporate transient hotel
Three hundred fifty rooms
Two restaurants (one 24-hour, and one dinner house)
Banquet area with 15,000 square feet of meeting space
Room service
Kitchen to support all food services
Main lounge with nightly entertainment
Banquet beverage service, and service bar outlets for both restaurants and room service
Outdoor pool, and winter indoor pool with health club facilities, sauna, and steam room
Game room (video games, pool, and table tennis)
In-house laundry for rooms department and banquet linen
Two company-owned gift shops

Also consider that the front desk is fully computerized with a property management system.

Hotel Organization

Prior to investigating the housekeeping department organization, it is appropriate to visualize an organization for the entire hotel. The organization diagram in Figure 1 could easily be appropriate for the model hotel just described.

Note the position of the Executive Housekeeper within the organization. Executive housekeepers may occupy greater or lesser positions in any organization. Some executive housekeepers might report directly to the General Manager, others might even hold corporate executive positions. Others might even report to the chief of maintenance. In this case, however, our Executive Housekeeper occupies the position of a middle manager, a full department head equal to the front office manager and other principal department heads on the staff. There are two junior managers who will report to the Executive Housekeeper, the house-

keeping manager and the laundry manager. Both the executive housekeeper and front office manager report to the resident manager, who is a member of the property executive committee. This committee is the top policymaking body for the property under the general manager.

The Housekeeping Organization

Figure 2 describes a reasonable housekeeping department organization for the model hotel.

Note the utilization of the two principal assistants. The housekeeping manager is the first assistant to the Executive Housekeeper and has been placed in direct charge of all guestrooms in the hotel. This emphasizes the delegation that has taken place in that the housekeeping manager is not just an assistant to the executive housekeeper, but a junior manager with a functional responsibility. There are several ways in which this part of the organization can be managed. Each individual room attendant can be scheduled independently from one another or they may be grouped into teams wherein they work as a team and are off together as a team. In this illustration, team staffing and scheduling will be presented because it provides for a more efficient technique of daily scheduling.

The laundry provides another specific function for the assignment of a junior manager. In this case, the technical expertise required is more specific. Such expertise would include knowledge of commercial laundry machinery and equipment, knowledge of piecework production, the utilization of chemicals, and their resultant effects on an expensive inventory of linen. Both junior managers and the Executive Housekeeper have line supervisors that report directly to them. (Below the management level we recognize a structure for employees who are paid by the hour at a given wage rate as opposed to being on salary.) Each supervisor in turn would have one or more hourly workers who work for them to round out the department organization.

Note that the organization shown in Figure 2 under the housekeeping manager is incomplete. The number of floor supervisors or team leaders with

FIGURE 1
Hotel organization (through department head)

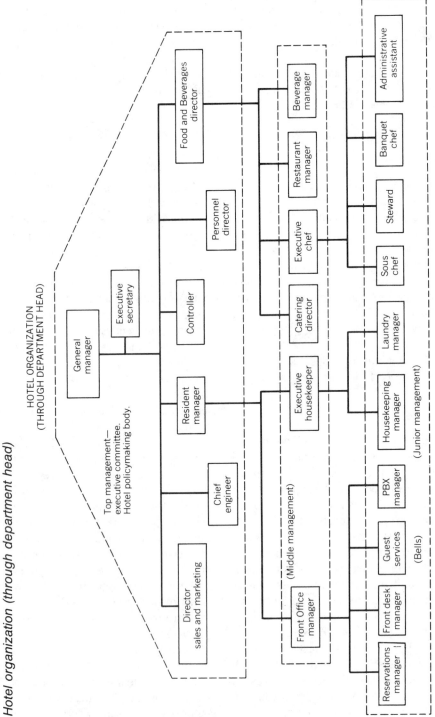

HOTEL ORGANIZATION
(THROUGH DEPARTMENT HEAD)

FIGURE 2
Housekeeping department organization

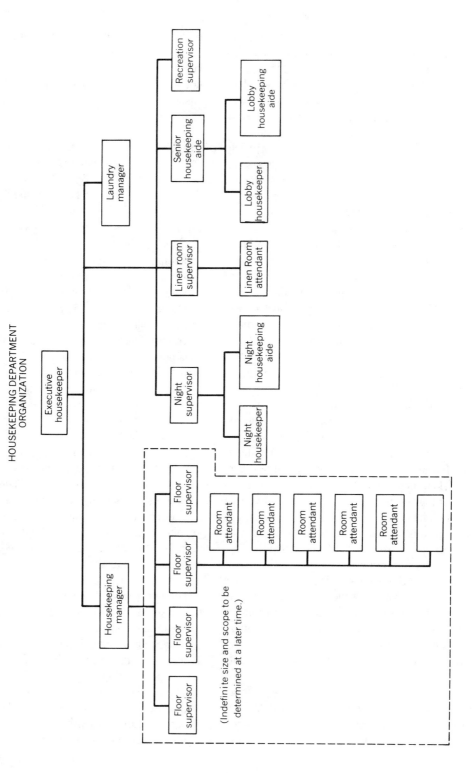

HOUSEKEEPING DEPARTMENT
ORGANIZATION

their teams of room attendants, and other team members, is dependent upon the number of rooms each room attendant might be expected to clean in a given eight-hour period. The national standard for rooms cleaned by one room attendant in one eight-hour period varies from thirteen to twenty rooms per day depending on the market mix of the hotel and its physical structure. Hotels occupied primarily by traveling or group business transient guests are more efficient to clean since occupancy is primarily single occupancy, and such guests are up and out of their rooms early each day. Also, they are inclined to leave their rooms in a lesser state of disarray. In such cases, room attendants can clean from eighteen to twenty rooms per day. When there is more double occupancy with families on vacation, access to rooms for cleaning is more difficult and will cut into the efficiency of staffing. In such cases, room attendants will not be able to clean as many rooms in the same eight-hour period.

Staffing and Scheduling Concerns

In the case of our model hotel of 350 rooms, assume an eighteen-room workload per day. On any 100 percent occupancy day we would need approximately twenty room attendants to clean all guestrooms. Placing these room attendants in teams of five, working under one floor supervisor, creates a need for four such supervisors. Also assume that one section housekeeping aide will be assigned to each team to handle corridor cleaning, to provide certain services to room attendants during the day, and to care for other public areas within the guestroom portion of the hotel. Finally, assume that five laundry workers will be needed in the laundry regularly, and that persons hired to relieve room attendants on days off can also relieve in the laundry for the same purpose.

The complete organization should now come into focus, except for one remaining concern. Hourly personnel cannot work seven days a week but are usually confined to a five-workday schedule. The following formula can serve to establish the rooms' entire cleaning, laundry, and relief staff require-

ment. It allows the manager to increase the staff to allow for days off for regular room attendants, laundry workers, floor supervisors, and section housekeeping aids. (See staffing guide to be discussed later.)

At 100 percent occupancy on a continuous basis:

$$\text{regular staff} \times \text{seven days} = \text{total staff} \times \text{five-day maximum}$$
$$S1 \times 7 = S2 \times 5$$
$$Sx + S1 \times 7 - 5$$

For the model, $S2 = 25 \times 7 - 5 = 35$ total working staff, all limited to a five-day workweek. The additional ten employees can be organized into two teams identical in composition to the regular teams and the laundry workforce. Identifying these two additional teams as swing teams, they will swing in to relieve all regular and laundry personnel teams twice each week and have two days off themselves. This portion of the organization can now be scheduled to work by team units rather than as individual workers, which greatly simplifies personnel scheduling. (For further information on scheduling techniques, the reader is encouraged to read the basic text from which this article is drawn.)

The balance of the housekeeping organization is noted in the functions to be performed, and for purposes of illustration must be scheduled individually. Specifically, personnel required for the second shift, persons required to staff the linen room (housekeeping communications central), and personnel organized under the senior housekeeping aide for public-area cleaning and maintenance round out the total department staff.

The entire housekeeping department staff might then take on the appearance provided in the Staffing Guide outlined in Table 1.

The Staffing Guide is a document that is created to accurately document the need for total personnel. Every position within the department is listed and can be used to fill vacancies when they occur. Note teams are identified by color in Table 1. This identification system shows which teams are regular teams, which ones work in the laundry, and which

TABLE 1
Department staffing guide

Position No.	Title	Name Assigned
	Management Team	
1	Executive housekeeper	_____
2	Housekeeping manager	_____
3	Laundry manager	
	Fixed Team	
4	Linen room supervisor	_____
5	Linen room attendant	_____
6	Senior housekeeping aide (public area supervisor)	_____
7	Public area housekeeper 1 (male)	_____
8	Public area housekeeper 2 (female)	_____
9	Public area housekeeper (relief)	_____
	Evening Team	
10	Night supervisor	_____
11	Night section housekeeper	_____
12	Night housekeeping aide	_____
13	Night (public area) housekeeper 1 (male)	_____
14	Night (public area) housekeeper 2 (female)	_____
15	Night (public area) housekeeper (relief)	_____
	Regular Rooms Cleaning Teams:	
	Red Team	
16	Senior housekeeper (supervisor)	_____
17	Section housekeeping aide	_____
18	Section housekeeper 1	_____
19	Section housekeeper 2	_____
20	Section housekeeper 3	_____
21	Section housekeeper 4	_____
22	Section housekeeper 5	_____
	Yellow Team	
23	Senior housekeeper (supervisor)	_____
24	Section housekeeping aide	_____
25	Section housekeeper 6	_____
26	Section housekeeper 7	_____
27	Section housekeeper 8	_____
28	Section housekeeper 9	_____
29	Section housekeeper 10	
	Brown Team	
30	Senior housekeeper (supervisor)	_____
31	Section housekeeping aide	_____
32	Section housekeeper 11	_____
33	Section housekeeper 12	_____
34	Section housekeeper 13	_____
35	Section housekeeper 14	_____
36	Section housekeeper 15	_____

(continued)

TABLE 1 (continued)

Position No.	Title	Name Assigned
	Green Team	
37	Senior housekeeper (supervisor)	_____
38	Section housekeeping aide	_____
39	Section housekeeper 16	_____
40	Section housekeeper 17	_____
41	Section housekeeper 18	_____
42	Section housekeeper 19	_____
43	Section housekeeper 20	_____
	Laundry	
44	Laundry supervisor (washman)	_____
45	Laundry helper/sorter	_____
46	Laundry attendant (ironer)	_____
47	Laundry attendant (ironer)	_____
48	Laundry attendant (folder/stacker)	_____
49	Laundry attendant (folder/stacker)	_____
50	Laundry attendant (folder/stacker)	_____
	Swing Team 1	
51	Senior housekeeper (swing supervisor)	_____
52	Section housekeeping aide (ST-A)	_____
53	Section housekeeper A-1	_____
54	Section housekeeper A-2	_____
55	Section housekeeper A-3	_____
56	Section housekeeper A-4	_____
57	Section housekeeper A-5	_____
	Swing Team 2	
58	Senior housekeeper (swing supervisor)	_____
59	Section housekeeping aide (ST-B)	_____
60	Section housekeeper B-1	_____
61	Section housekeeper B-2	_____
62	Section housekeeper B-3	_____
63	Section housekeeper B-4	_____
64	Section housekeeper B-5	_____

ones are considered swing teams. This particular staffing guide presumes that a 100 percent staff has been hired to support an occupancy averaging 85 percent or more for an extended period of time. Should occupancies be forecast at a lesser rate, a 100 percent staff need not be hired, and staff vacancies can be distributed over the entire team network. Fluctuations in daily occupancy should be dealt with by scheduling down within each team on a fair and equitable basis. This need to schedule down because of daily occupancy can be delegated to the floor supervisor, but controls must be in place that will guarantee fairness to all who must be cut out of a day's work due to low occupancy.

PERSONNEL AND JOBS IN THE HOUSEKEEPING DEPARTMENT

What follows is a discussion of the various jobs one might find in a hotel housekeeping department. The basic function and scope of responsibility will be indicated for managers' positions; and for hourly jobs, titles and responsibilities will be listed. Where several different names or titles apply to the same function in the hourly structure, each name will be noted.

The Executive Housekeeper

The Executive Housekeeper usually assumes complete direction, operational control, and supervision of the housekeeping, laundry, and recreation departments.

The scope of responsibility is normally broad to insure that the incumbent is given the freedom necessary to do the job. This position is now recognized as a career-enhancing step to future growth. The Executive Housekeeper is to operate the departments under his or her control in the most efficient manner possible through effective application and enforcement of company policies, the use of methods described in standard operating procedures, and the use of sound management principles. The incumbent is primarily responsible for the cleanliness of guestrooms and public areas assigned to the housekeeping department. The incumbent will accomplish tasks through proper training, motivation, and supervision of all personnel assigned to the housekeeping, laundry, and recreation departments.

The Housekeeping Manager

In the model organization, the Housekeeping Manager assumes primary responsibility for guestroom cleaning and servicing and acts as the primary assistant to the Executive Housekeeper. Under the direction of the Executive Housekeeper, the incumbent is responsible for the efficient and orderly management of guestroom cleaning, servicing, and the reporting of rooms status. He or she represents those employees directly involved in rooms cleaning, and should be directly involved in their work schedules. He or she must react to occupancy in scheduling in order that costs be kept under control.

The Laundry Manager

The Laundry Manager normally assumes primary responsibility for operation of the hotel's in-house commercial laundry. He or she will also act as second assistant to the Executive Housekeeper. Under the direction of the Executive Housekeeper, the incumbent is responsible for the efficient and orderly management and operation of the hotel laundry. Through the proper use of personnel assigned, the laundry manager will provide clean linen to the house and to the banquet department according to plans and budgets.

HOURLY EMPLOYEES

The Room Attendant (also known as maid, or section housekeeper)

The incumbent to this position is primarily responsible for guestroom cleaning and servicing. He or she is usually assigned a section of rooms each day, constituting a workload of a designated number of rooms to be cleaned. In general, the room attendant performs the same functions in each room assigned. The room attendant will also conduct certain room checks at set times to assist in determining the reporting condition of the house. These checks will determine rooms occupied, rooms ready (vacant and ready to rent), and rooms on-change (vacant but not yet serviced—also known as check-outs). The room attendant will also participate in general cleaning one or more rooms each day in order to keep quality standards high.

Most room attendants work in compliance with Standard Operating Procedures (SOPs), which may specify as many as 60 items that must meet a given standard in each guestroom. This is not as foreboding as it may sound, but the SOP system guarantees coverage where necessary.

Finally, the room attendant should re-load his or her own linen cart at the end of each workday.

If so organized, the room attendant will be one of several members of a housekeeping team under a floor supervisor.

The Section Housekeeping Aide (previously Section Houseman)

The incumbent to this position works in the guestroom portion of the hotel, attending to the regular and daily cleaning of corridors, elevator cabs and landings, stairwells, service areas, floor linen rooms, vending areas, and other special or unique public spaces in the vicinity of guestrooms. The section housekeeping aide also provides help to room attendants when associated with a general cleaning, if necessary. He or she will also remove soiled linen and rubbish from room attendants' carts on a regular schedule, and will bring supplies from storerooms to floor linen rooms when needed. The section housekeeping aide works at the direction of the floor supervisor, and when so organized, also works as a member of a housekeeping team.

Floor Supervisor (also sometimes known as Senior Housekeeper or Inspector)

Floor supervisors are team leaders, having several room attendants and a section housekeeping aide reporting to them. They are assigned to specific divisions of the rooms section of a property and are responsible for the quality of work performed in the several rooms sections to which their room attendants are assigned. They are also responsible for the public sectors that are assigned to their section housekeeping aides. They make inspections and reports, and are in all respects supervisors of the persons assigned to their teams. They also assist in the personnel administration of the people assigned to them.

Sometimes called inspectress, this may be a misnomer. Many floor supervisors are inspectresses by virtue of the fact that they inspect rooms. Other inspectresses do nothing but inspect rooms, reporting directly to the manager on what they observe, but have no responsibility to correct discrepancies where found because no other staff is assigned to them for work purposes. (This writer is of the opinion that persons who do nothing but inspect guestrooms, then have no employees or authority with which to take corrective action, are a superfluous use of manpower.)

The Senior Housekeeping Aide (in the past known as Head Houseman)

The Senior Housekeeping Aide is a major supervisor in the housekeeping department. He or she is usually placed in charge of all public areas not directly associated with guestrooms. Lobbies, major public corridors, public restrooms, offices, and other areas specifically negotiated as part of the overall housekeeping responsibility are the domain of the senior housekeeping aide. He or she is usually responsible for basic training of section housekeeping aides, and supervision of utility housekeeping aides who might perform specific tasks such as shampooing carpets, washing windows, or performing project work. The senior housekeeping aide is usually responsible for the storage and accountability of cleaning and guest supply inventories. He or she normally works as a supervisory assistant to the executive housekeeper and performs such other tasks as the executive housekeeper might direct.

The Night Supervisor

The night supervisor presumes a second shift that has no management regularly assigned to it. This, of course, can vary depending on the size and complexity of night operations. Other than as intermittently visited by housekeeping management, the night supervisor assumes total control of the department after the major rooms and hotel cleaning evolution for each day has been concluded. Overseeing one or two night room attendants, a night section housekeeping aide, and several night lobby or public area personnel, the night supervisor is accountable for the balance of services to be performed by the housekeeping department for that day. The night supervisor insures that *all* rooms are left cleaned and ready to rent, that guest requests for service or equipment such as cribs, bedboards, extra linen, and the like, are fulfilled. The night supervisor works closely with the hotel night manager, is usually on beeper and capable of making routine inspections throughout the hotel, until the department is secured each evening at the designated time. The night supervisor, like the senior housekeeping aide, is a major supervisor within the department.

The Linen Room Supervisor

Called the main linen room, this physical service area of the hotel is actually the hub of housekeeping communication and activity. As a result, it might be better described as housekeeping central. The linen room supervisor under the Executive Housekeeper is the supervisor in charge of main linen room operations. Maintaining and operating the communication link to the front desk, engineering, and to each guest in need of housekeeping attention is the prime responsibility associated with the job of the linen room supervisor. In addition, the linen room supervisor is sometimes referred to as the chief status operator for housekeeping. Keeping up with, changing as necessary, and reporting the status of each guestroom throughout the day is another major function of the linen room supervisor. He or she is the prime guest contact representative. Also, he or she would oversee the activities of one or more linen room attendants who perform supply and distribution functions for items such as bedspreads, blankets, bed pads, curtains, etc. On the second shift, the night supervisor assumes the responsibilities of the linen room supervisor.

The Laundry Supervisor

Working as a principal supervisor for the laundry manager, the laundry supervisor would supervise

the activities of a laundry attendant. Normally the laundry supervisor would work as the head washperson and would be in charge of the use of all major wash equipment and chemicals. The incumbent to this position would also supervise the workload process and production. In our model hotel, when the laundry supervisor and team of laundry attendants is scheduled off, a swing team supervisor would assume the responsibilities of the laundry supervisor and would bring his or her swing team into the laundry. Since there are two swing teams, each swing team working in the laundry one day each week provides the entire department with maximum flexibility and training.

The Recreation Supervisor

In our model hotel, the recreation supervisor, under the direct supervision of the Executive Housekeeper, would assume responsibility for all recreation areas of the hotel. All swimming pool attendants would work for the recreation supervisor and would be fully Red Cross or water safety instructor qualified. (Swimming pools would be properly "signed" to indicate, "No lifeguard on duty. Swimmers do so at their own risk." This prevents the guests from abdicating responsibility for their own and their children's safety. However, all "pool attendants" would be fully qualified to save a life.) Pool attendants, under the direction of the recreation supervisor, would also service the health club, sauna, and game room for service to guests, cleanliness, and maintenance of order.

Other Employees

There are other employees that might be found in the department and their titles indicate their activity and who they might work for. All positions have titles appropriate to either male or female employees and are therefore non-sexist. Such positions are as follows:

Utility Housekeeping Aide
Linen Room Attendant

Lobby Housekeeping Aide

Laundry Attendant

Housekeeping Trainer (a secondary job sometimes carried by a room attendant to insure
standardization of training)

CONCLUSION

Being involved with housekeeping operations is no
longer the exclusive territory of the female, nor is
it considered menial or less important than any other
function in the hospitality organization. Should anyone think to the contrary, they should try to imagine
hotel operations without housekeeping and they
might find general managers and presidents cleaning
rooms.

Because of the large staffs involved, housekeeping operations provide junior managers outstanding
opportunities to develop leadership potential and
supervisory skills, an opportunity not always available in other departments.

This writer recalls a moment of truth several
years ago when a general manager was overhead
commenting to a utility houseman who at the time
happened to be mopping a men's room at 1:00 in
the morning. The general manager said, "You know,
what you are doing is just as vital and necessary
as what I do every day. We just do different things
and work at different skill levels. When the company
thinks they can do without either one of us, they'll
abolish our jobs. I don't think they will, so until they
do, don't forget your job is just as important around
here as mine is!"

The Executive Housekeeper: No Longer a Glorified Maid

Inge Krieg

While a computer still can't make beds or mop
floors, technological advances provide today's
lodging industry executive housekeepers with a
wide range of equipment to get the job done.

In developing the housekeeping program for
Western International's newest hotel, the 1,500-
room, 35-story Bonaventure in downtown Los Angeles, there were special challenges to meet, beginning with a one-acre lake set in the middle of
30,000 square feet of tiled floor lobby.

The lake collects coins from the guests and dirt
and leaves from surrounding ivy, ficus, and mums.
To clean the lake, housekeeping uses a specially

made water-filtering vacuum to pick up debris, including money, and to filter the clear water back
into the lake. To avoid circulation problems caused
by falling leaves, the lake surface is occasionally skimmed on an emergency basis. To insure
that someone is always on hand to do the job, the
property's housekeeping department, rather
than an outside contractor, is responsible for the
lake.

Today's executive housekeepers need managerial
skills never required before. As administrators of
mammoth departments in multi-million-dollar, pub-
lic-oriented facilities, housekeepers must be flexible,
diplomatic, quick thinking, and have a lot of common
sense. They must be skilled managers of people
and things, as well as teachers, accountants, buyers, and more.

All cleaning and maintenance at the Bonaventure

Reprinted with permission from Krieg, Inge. "The Executive Housekeeper: No Longer a Glorified Maid." *Lodging Hospitality* (October 1977),
pp. 74–75.

is handled in house by the property's 280-person housekeeping staff. Management finds this arrangement more efficient and economical than hiring contract cleaners. An in-house staff also provides flexibility to rearrange schedules to coordinate with the needs of other departments and to save labor costs.

The Bonaventure learned from the Peachtree Plaza, Western's mega-hotel in Atlanta, that dining rooms and lounges can be cleaned *before* they open rather than *after* they close, thus nearly eliminating the need for an expensive, often inefficient, night cleaning shift. At the Bonaventure only nine people clean at night, and shift schedules are arranged so the bulk of the housekeeping work is accomplished between 6 A.M. and 11 P.M., when supervision is built-in.

In addition to caring for the property's 1,500 guestrooms, the housekeeping department must clean and maintain (including wall washing, chandelier cleaning, rug shampooing, and carpet and upholstery repair) three restaurants, an entertainment club, the largest ballroom on the West Coast, two smaller ballrooms, a 24,000-square-foot exhibition hall, 24 small meeting rooms, 24 elevators, miles of corridors, ceilings, service and lobby areas, and all light bulbs and windows.

The director of housekeeping has two assistant directors—one for guestrooms and one for public areas. They each in turn have assistant housekeepers, 16 floor or shift supervisors, 130 room attendants, 95 to 110 house attendants, and linen and uniform personnel.

In addition to standard vacuums and scrubbing machines, special equipment is required for unusual tasks. The lake vacuum is one. Another is an automatic scrubber that both scrubs and strips floors, saving at least 50 percent in time and labor. The Bonaventure floors are 50 percent carpeted and 50 percent hard surface, so combination shampoo-scrubbers, one 19-inch and two 17-inch machines, are used.

Today's housekeepers must also cope with sociological changes that require knowledge of and compliance with a variety of government regulations and policies.

Energy conservation is a company-wide program at Western International. Consequently, the Bonaventure housekeeping crew constantly looks for ways to save energy. Lamp wattages are reduced from 150 to 75 watts wherever possible throughout the hotel.

To comply with equal opportunity programs, the Bonaventure reaches out to minority community organizations, such as the Urban League, Chinatown Service Center, the Charro Career center, and the Minority Women Employment program, to hire workers. It also works with other agencies to employ mentally and physically handicapped people when possible.

Providing leadership for the training and development of housekeepers to meet today's added responsibilities is the task of the National Executive Housekeepers Association. The nearly 50-year-old association is the only professional organization in housekeeping. It works with colleges and universities to develop educational training for young people. It sponsors meetings and publications to give present and prospective housekeepers the opportunity to exchange ideas and techniques. NEHA's efforts have done much to make today's executive housekeeper a true executive and no longer just a glorified maid.

Theoretical Constructs in Practice: Managers Rate Their Importance

Denney G. Rutherford
William J. Schill

It may be postulated that there exists a tripartite audience for an empirically based analysis of topics relating to the importance and functions of hotel housekeeping. That audience consists of: (a) students and faculties of hotel administration in universities and community colleges; (b) housekeeping directors designing and implementing training programs for housekeeping managerial trainees; and (c) corporate housekeepers or housekeeping planners designing systemic housekeeping policy and philosophy.

Because students and faculties in Hotel and Restaurant Administration (HRA) curricula have at best a one-term exposure to the concepts and constructs of housekeeping administration, it is important that fundamentals and essentials be easily grasped and retained.

Housekeeping directors involved in training their managerial staffs also have the aforementioned requirement. Concomitantly, they need to inculcate that vast body of workaday knowledge that administratively accomplishes the goals and objectives of the department. Further than that, however, the director needs to be aware of what families of knowledge can be distinguished as contributing to effort that in one sense separates adequate from superb management and in another sense substantially contributes to the development of future housekeeping directors. These families of knowledge can be represented as existing on a "bulged continuum" from "need-to-know" to "nice-to-know," with the vast majority of the knowledge constructs falling

Reprinted with permission of Pergamon Press from Rutherford, Denney G., and William J. Schill. "Theoretical Constructs in Practice: Managers Rate Their Importance." *International Journal of Hospitality Management*, vol. 31, no. 31 (1984), pp. 101–106.

under the "bulged" portion of the continuum (see Figure 1).

Corporate housekeepers and housekeeping planners need an empirically analyzed structure that can be used to guide participation in personnel recruitment, operations planning, company-wide policy development, and strategic planning within the competitive marketing environment.

EMPIRICAL BASIS FOR THIS PRESENTATION

Traditionally, information on housekeeping administration for hotels has been organized around models set forth in a number of textbooks that date back to the 1951 treatment of hospital housekeeping by LaBelle and Barton. Brigham (1955) focused her analysis of the structure of the housekeeping functions and responsibilities on the small hotel. Tucker and Schneider (1982) have done the most comprehensive job of discussing and presenting the theoretical constructs, responsibilities, relationships, and techniques important to the modern housekeeper in a range of operational situations.

Generally speaking, these works present information in a structure similar to that used in Holiday Inn University's housekeeping curriculum, which says the housekeeper administrates "four major areas of responsibility":

1. Management of people, equipment, and supplies
2. Preservation of building finishes, fabrics, and furnishings
3. Controlling costs
4. Keeping records (quoted by Tucker and Schneider 1982, 38)

FIGURE 1

Continuum array of constructs

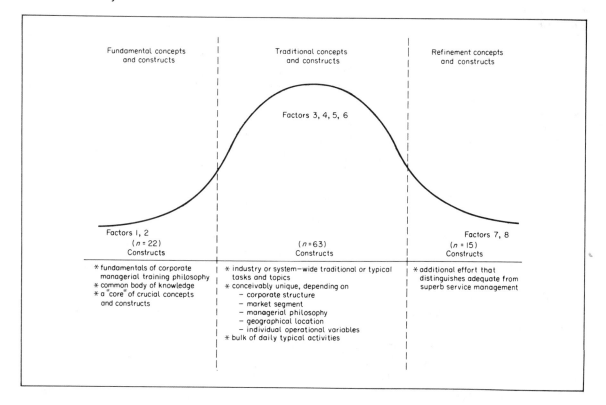

In analyzing the differences between the "folklore and fact" of the manager's job, Mintzberg (1975) came to the conclusion that there were substantial differences between what the popular or academic notion of managers' jobs entailed and what managers actually did. While no attempt is made in the present research to replicate Mintzberg's study among hotel housekeepers, the fundamental question prompting this research grew out of similar curiosities. This article explores the results of research that was designed to compare the relative importance and groupings of all that has been written about housekeeping with what housekeeping directors themselves deem important.

METHODOLOGY

An eight-page, two-part questionnaire was sent to a national sample of housekeeping directors, using 400-room properties as a minimum size criterion. Response rate was 56 percent. Part One sought demographic and career data, which are displayed in Table 1. Part Two asked the housekeeping directors to rate 100 knowledge constructs on a 5-point Likert scale from "Not at All Important" to "Of Vital Importance" as they relate to the study and practice of housekeeping. The knowledge constructs were derived from the housekeeping texts mentioned earlier, with emphasis on Tucker and

TABLE 1
Distribution of demographic data among directors of housekeeping

Variable	Directors of housekeeping (n = 56)
Percentage male	44%
Mean age	36.5
Percentage single	66%
Percentage college graduates	60%
Percentage HRA degree	34%
Reported years in the industry	5–10
Reported years in current position	2–3

Schneider (1982).[1] This list of knowledge constructs should be considered neither exhaustive nor exclusive, but rather, representative of those areas of information important to the management and operation of the housekeeping department in the modern hotel.

Each construct was treated as a separate variable and a *Statistical Package for the Social Sciences* (Nie et al. 1975) frequencies routine generated mean ratings of each on the University of Washington's Cyber 170-750 computer. An additional set of routines[2] was then used to rank-order the means of the constructs (see Table 2).

A factor analysis routine was then applied to the data to permit the identification of groups within the array of responses across the 100 items on the questionnaire. Factors were identified based on loadings on items that were larger than 0.35. This analysis routine resulted in eight empirical factor groupings.

The value the respondents attached to each factor grouping was determined by computing the mean rank for the items (knowledge constructs) in each factor. This served to indicate which constructs need to be presented first when teaching or training individuals on the relative importance of operational and managerial responsibilities within housekeeping departments. The factors were given names to

convey their general content and the results of this analysis are presented in Table 3.

SUMMARY AND DISCUSSION

It is not suggested that the traditional emphasis placed on purchasing (factor 8) is less important to individual managers than resource management (factor 1), nor even that they are totally independent, since elements of the purchasing function are nested in factor 1. Rather, it is suggested that in the light of this analysis, before the housekeeper can effectively control the purchasing function, he or she must be well grounded in the factor groups of knowledge constructs that precede this factor in the schema presented here.

Factor groupings 1 and 2 suggest that the most important or crucial constructs that are fundamental to housekeeping management are those generally related to broad organizational talents, relations with the key departments of sales, security, and front office, and the department's primary mission of cleaning functions.

It should be noted that the knowledge construct of communication (rank order 1, X = 4.911) assumes a position within the first two factors. This rank and grouping is consistent with most contemporary management research commentary and analysis. A recent empirical analysis of critical incidents between service employees and guests (Nyquist et al. 1984) treated communication as the most important variable in managing the service encounter. Mintzberg (1975, 52) found that communication activities, particularly verbal communication in the form of telephone conversations and meetings, are important or in many cases predominant components of the manager's day. A housekeeping manager who must daily communicate among arguably the broadest range of employee classifications and organizational hierarchies is well advised to develop above-average skills related to this knowledge construct.

The constructs related to computer application in the housekeeping department are distributed across three factors (2, 6, and 7) and their factor

TABLE 2
Rank order of Likert Rating Scale (LRS) means

Rank order	Knowledge construct		LRS 1–5
1 Communication	[housekeeper responsibilities]	4.911
2 Leadership	[housekeeper responsibilities]	4.875
3 Training	[personnel functions]	4.839
4 Front office	[relations with other dept's]	4.818
5 Motivation	[housekeeper responsibilities]	4.804
6 Control of	[linen]	4.768
7 Staffing	[personnel functions]	4.768
8 Employee input	[motivation]	4.768
9 Budgeting	[housekeeper responsibilities]	4.732
10 Engineering	[relations with other depts]	4.714
11 Scheduling	[personnel functions]	4.714
12 Organizational ability	[housekeeper responsibilities]	4.696
13 Employee counseling	[personnel functions]	4.696
14 Constructive criticism	[motivation]	4.679
15 Par stock	[linen]	4.625
16 Cleaning supplies	[knowledge of supplies]	4.625
17 Job enrichment	[motivation]	4.618
18 Guest room cleaning procedures	[cleaning procedures]	4.607
19 Guest room supplies	[knowledge of supplies]	4.607
20 Evaluation/promotion	[personnel functions]	4.600
21 Public area cleaning procedures	[cleaning procedures]	4.589
22 Inventory	[knowledge of supplies]	4.589
23 Job enhancement	[motivation]	4.589
24 Use of/training	[knowledge of equipment]	4.571
25 Use of/training	[knowledge of supplies]	4.554
26 Operational inspection	[cleaning procedures]	4.536
27 Job specifications	[personnel functions]	4.536
28 Firing	[personnel functions]	4.482
29 Incentives	[motivation]	4.482
30 Control of all housekeeping functions	[housekeeper responsibilities]	4.464
31 Safety	[housekeeper responsibilities]	4.464
32 Control	[uniforms]	4.454
33 Personnel	[relations with other depts]	4.446
34 Issuing	[knowledge of supplies]	4.423
35 Recordkeeping	[housekeeper responsibilities]	4.418
36 Purchasing	[relations with other depts]	4.411
37 Misuse/mishandling	[linen]	4.393
38 Purchasing	[knowledge of supplies]	4.375
39 Inventory	[knowledge of equipment]	4.339
40 Back of the house cleaning procedures	[cleaning procedures]	4.339
41 Amenities	[knowledge of supplies]	4.321
42 Purchasing	[linen]	4.309
43 Security	[housekeeper responsibilities]	4.304
44 Evaluating	[knowledge of equipment]	4.304
45 Cost	[uniforms]	4.304
46 Housekeeping trends	[general knowledge]	4.286
47 Employee area	[cleaning procedures]	4.286

(continued)

TABLE 2 (continued)

Rank order	Knowledge construct		LRS 1–5
48	Revision/update procedures	[cleaning procedures]	4.286
49	Evaluation	[knowledge of supplies]	4.286
50	Quality control inspection procedure	[laundry]	4.273
51	Purchasing process	[purchasing]	4.268
52	Care of linen(s)	[linen]	4.268
53	Knowledge of area	[housekeeper responsibilities]	4.255
54	Forecasting	[purchasing]	4.238
55	Types	[knowledge of equipment]	4.218
56	Issuing	[knowledge of equipment]	4.214
57	Capital improvements	[purchasing]	4.214
58	Rooms status use	[computer]	4.204
59	Purchasing	[knowledge of equipment]	4.179
60	Function	[uniforms]	4.164
61	Hotel organization	[general knowledge]	4.161
62	Chemicals/detergents/soaps	[laundry]	4.143
63	Importance of use in dept	[computer]	4.132
64	Replacement of	[knowledge of equipment]	4.127
65	Linen care process	[laundry]	4.127
66	Are there housekeeping applications?	[computer]	4.113
67	Comfort	[uniforms]	4.093
68	Maintenance	[knowledge of equipment]	4.071
69	Operational cleaning manuals	[cleaning procedures]	4.071
70	Recordkeeping for repair and replacement costs	[purchasing]	4.018
71	Lobby/arcade shops	[cleaning procedures]	4.018
72	Re-evaluating products	[purchasing]	4.000
73	Purchasing specifications	[purchasing]	4.000
74	Repair/maintenance	[linen]	4.000
75	Security	[relations with other depts]	3.982
76	Maintenance/repair	[uniforms]	3.982
77	Laundry care	[uniforms]	3.981
78	Recruiting	[personnel functions]	3.929
79	F & B cleaning procedures	[cleaning procedures]	3.911
80	Emerging trends/research	[knowledge of supplies]	3.893
81	Energy conservation	[laundry]	3.891
82	Contracted cleaning	[cleaning procedures]	3.875
83	Emerging trends in equipment	[knowledge of equipment]	3.873
84	Accounting	[relations with other depts]	3.857
85	Research	[purchasing]	3.857
86	Fabrics	[uniforms]	3.839
87	Fabric knowledge	[linen]	3.786
88	Uniform care process	[laundry]	3.778
89	(Maid) control use	[computer]	3.755
90	Inventory use	[computer]	3.736
91	Knowledge of governmental regulations	[general knowledge]	3.691
92	Management of other departments	[general knowledge]	3.607
93	Recordkeeping/office management	[computer]	3.604

TABLE 2 (continued)

Rank order	Knowledge construct		LRS 1–5
94	Industry trends	[general knowledge]	3.571
95	Sales	[relations with other depts]	3.482
96	Dry cleaning process	[laundry]	3.463
97	Knowledge of current events	[general knowledge]	3.375
98	Design trends	[uniforms]	3.357
99	Food & Beverage/restaurants	[relations with other depts]	3.321
100	Catering/banquets	[relations with other depts]	3.214

loadings were generally relegated to the latter part of each factor.

In the first analysis, the generally low rank order of computer-related constructs may be an artifact of the current cohort's lack of knowledge about the capabilities of computers and the attendant threatening aura that attaches to many new concepts, but one particularly related to computers. Mintzberg (1975, 52) concludes that managers pay little attention to formal management information systems (MIS) and formulate their decisions from models constructed of "tidbits" of data from informal sources and channels. Mintzberg's study, however, was based on data gathered prior to 1973, and the prolif-

TABLE 3
Factor groupings of constructs

Rank of factor	Name of factor	Mean rank order of constructs in factor	Identification No. of constructs in factor
1	Resource management	43.50	9,95,83,42,37,19,38,25
2	Department managerial responsibilities	45.78	12,1,43,61,4,91,75 18,21,47,71,66,63,89
3	Periodic check points	49.83	31,68,24,87,15,74
4	Hotel organizational, personnel, and departmental concerns	53.37	92,97,36,33,99,84,55,70,72,79 82,48,69,26,16,49,34,7,3,78 20,27,13,8,98,86,32,67,45,76
5	Within department leadership	56.55	35,5,2,59,44,64,40,6,81 88,96,50,22,28,29,23,17,14
6	Strategic planning, current events and technology	56.78	53,30,94,46,10,39,56,90,93
7	Improving task performance	60.45	100,85,54,52,65 62,41,58,11,77,60
8	Purchasing	65.25	73,57,51,80

eration of computer applications specifically designed for all aspects of business, and more recently hotels, has eased the gathering and manipulation of MIS data.

While managers may still build decision models based on "tidbits" of information, this current research suggests that these data may be generated by or channeled through a computer-based MIS designed for housekeeping knowledge constructs related to computers. Based on the distribution of the computer constructs among the factor groupings, housekeeping management should be trained in the applications of computers to the management of their departments prior to or during installation of an MIS rather than after.

The majority of the remaining constructs lumped under the bulge of the continuum represent industry or system-wide traditional tasks or topics that represent the bulk of "workaday" activities for many or most housekeeping departments. These may be unique or may vary widely, depending on corporate structure, market segment, location, or philosophy. As a guide, however, this model offers an alternative to the textbook models for viewing and utilizing the juxtaposition of these knowledge constructs and activities.

COMMENTARY AND CONCLUSIONS

It should be noted that the information presented here is not prescriptive in nature and is presented as a suggested interpretive model. The various audiences for data of these types discussed at the onset will vary according to structure, intent, strategy, and philosophy and should consider new ways to structure and present traditional topics to be more relevant in the modern era.

As early as 1955, Brigham was stating that the "head cleaner" type of housekeeper was no longer adequate to meet the demands of the modern hotel market and that "the person in charge of housekeeping must be intelligent, well-educated and also have the amount of executive ability to fill the position" (p. 10). More recently, Tucker and Schneider (1982, vii) quote Harry Mullikin, chairman and CEO of Westin Hotels as saying that the "keystone" of value demanded by the traveling public revolves around the cleanliness of the accommodations. The cognitive imperative that can be derived from typical comments such as these is that for the housekeeping audiences to most effectively utilize the information available to them, new arrangements of knowledge may be useful.

New arrangements of traditional knowledge, constructs, and tactics such as those explored in the model presented here may present the audiences with windows of operational, educational, or marketing opportunity that improve competitive position or streamline the transfer of knowledge. The dissemination of this knowledge in the most efficient and effective manner is also important, for, as Mintzberg (1975, 60) points out, "The manager is challenged to find systematic ways to share his privileged knowledge." Coupled with the pressures of nonessential or compelling essential distractions, it becomes all the more important for managers to order this dissemination in the most useful fashion.

To date no analytical empirical research has been done on operational aspects of housekeeping and other labor-intensive hotel departments. It is hoped that through suggested models such as that presented herein hotels and others can contribute in a positive way to the advancement of the profession.

The On-Premise Laundry in the United States: Basic Engineering and Operational Considerations Prior to Installation

Robert J. Martin

Jack E. Scott, president of Baker Linen Company of California (1976), believes that one should strongly consider installing an on-premise laundry if monthly laundry costs are in excess of $900. The latest research report by the American Hotel and Motel Association (AHMA), cited and updated by Scott, indicates the following comparisons for a typical 120-room unit:

Weekly in-house laundry costs	$ 324.00
Allowance for weekly linen depreciation	133.91
Total in-house laundry costs	$ 457.91
Weekly outside service costs (using owned linens—8,806 lb. ca. 10 cents/lb.)	$ 880.60
Allowance for weekly linen depreciation	133.91
Total outside laundry costs	$1014.51
Weekly linen rental service	$1782.17

Linen quality has always been a deterrent to in-house laundries, but the primary problem (50/50 polyester blends used in no-iron sheets and pillowcases), has been solved. Modern no-iron linens now undergo a dual finish process, which improves the molecular structure of the polyester fiber, resulting in a linen that retains its no-iron properties throughout its normal life expectancy. Refined blend sheets, therefore, last three times as long as their cotton predecessors. In fact, the polyester fiber in new-generation no-iron linens tends to relax and actually increases in elasticity with use.

The no-iron linen industry has also perfected the equipment components that process new-generation linens. The timing of wash and rinse cycles, temperature control, and the automatic addition of detergents, bleaches, and softeners have eliminated the problems of human error, extensive employee training, and operator inattention. In summary, the reasons for having economical in-house operations outweigh the need to abdicate this important operation to the province of others.

Planning and Pre-Engineering

Some architects of small laundry facilities suggest that an on-premise laundry is nothing more than the purchase of a few washers and dryers and locating them in some remote space in the facility. Such inadequate planning usually results in laundries that must be re-engineered by qualified designers and laundry equipment contractors, with costly modifications occurring.

Schweid (1976) describes one of Canada's newest hotels as a magnificent creation. Location was inspiring, architectural design impressive, accommodations were outstanding, and quality and comfort standards were exemplary. It was perceived as exceptional in every respect save one. In spite of detailed planning, the laundry was poorly engineered. As a result, it had less than half the space required to be efficient. What area it did have was poorly designed. The problem was more than mere engineering and design; machinery was not of the industrial caliber demanded by millions of pounds of laundry each year. In an attempt to keep up with volume, eleven shifts per week were required.

Large laundries are not the only ones that receive

Reprinted with permission of Pergamon Press from Martin, Robert J. "The On-Premise Laundry in the United States: Basic Engineering and Operational Considerations Prior to Installation." *International Journal of Hospitality Management*, vol. 20, no. 40 (1983), pp. 179–185.

improper planning and initial engineering attention. More often it is the owners of small properties who, after having made the decision to have an on-premise laundry, fail to give the consideration and planning that laundry operations warrant.

Small properties may not require the detailed planning needed in larger properties (300 to 2,500 rooms). However, planning variables should apply equally to small as well as large hotel laundries. The AHMA can supply the names of reputable and knowledgeable laundry consultants, engineers, and equipment manufacturers in the U.S., most of whom will engineer laundries and also specify equipment within certain budgetary constraints. In addition, they oversee installation and provide management and worker training during start-up operations. One of the many companies that provide this type of service is Baring Industries of Miami, Florida. Baring (consultant to the laundry industry) has coined the phrase "Systemeering" to represent ten specific services it provides in all of its contracts.

The first five of these steps are defined as follows:

1. Determination of needs. This step involves a meeting with owners, architects, interior designers, engineers, and other project consultants to obtain all the data pertinent to the Laundry/Valet/Housekeeping systems. Data will include the number of rooms, beds, expected occupancy, variety of services, areas of services, and budgetary restrictions. From such data can be composed an overall program containing information about size, type, and location of facilities. Such a report would describe the basic integration and development of the laundry in the overall hotel concept and design.
2. System definition and space allocation. Once needs are defined, specialists concentrate on selecting systems and components most able to handle the project requirements. Interrelationships of those allocated spaces are analyzed from a human engineering standpoint to eliminate costly extra steps, or crossed traffic patterns. Many different approaches are considered in designing a system that optimizes efficiency and therefore economy of operations.
3. Equipment layouts. Labor-saving ideas are meshed with the most efficient work-flow patterns that can be designed within the given space. Alternative system components and layouts are investigated to ensure selection of the best possible system.
4. Equipment selection, specifications, and budgets. The selection of quality options for equipment are presented. Costs are studied, including the basic cost of equipment, escalation costs, and the costs of rigging equipment. Follow-up maintenance considerations are included, along with the expected life of the equipment. Budgets are finalized using standard specifications that can allow for fast tracking to early completion.
5. Detailed drawings and specifications. Equipment connection schedules, mechanical, electrical, and ventilation details are defined showing exact locations of all rough-in points. Such drawings enable the contractor to properly rough-in utilities before equipment arrives. These steps expedite connection and installation of equipment. Detailed specifications for each piece of equipment are provided, reflecting every option selected. All mechanical/electrical requirements must be coordinated with architects, engineers, and contractors throughout this phase.

The other five steps included in Baring's service are:

6. Equipment procurement and shipment, coordination
7. Installation scheduling and supervision
8. Start-up, test, and demonstration
9. Operator training, maintenance
10. After-sale service

Regardless of the size of the laundry facility, all portions of the above "Systemeering" plan are appropriate to the study and preplanning for laundry facilities of any size.

BASIC KNOWLEDGE FOR THE OWNER

Some small properties might not be economically advantaged in such a way as to allow for the services of a laundry consultant. If such is the case, what should be the basic consideration in the development of small in-house laundry operations? The most commonly used and technically correct way of deciding the size and composition of equipment is determined by analyzing linen poundage requirements. It is normal, therefore, to see a laundry equipment manufacturer's design and specify equipment in a similar manner. For example, washers and/or dryers are available with load capabilities ranging from 25 to 600 pounds, allowing for the selection of the most reasonably sized equipment for a given set of requirements. Most washers extract their own wash and rinse water; therefore, separate extractors are not necessary. Recognizing that labor costs will normally be the most severe of all operating costs, it is desirable to specify the optimum size of equipment that will minimize these costs.

In addition, either washing capacity, drying capacity, or handling capacity can provide the primary constraint for the laundry. These three constraints should be balanced. For example, a laundry with 400 pounds of washing capacity operating on a 30-minute cycle, 150 pounds of drying capacity operating on a 50-minute cycle, with adequate space for handling, storing, and folding linen, would be "dryer limited." Whereas, a laundry with one 50-pound washing machine operating on a 30-minute cycle, and one 100-pound dryer operating on a 1-hour cycle, with adequate handling capacity, would be properly sized.

In small operations, the number of dryers are normally related to the number of washers in a 2-to-1 ratio. (For example: two 50-pound dryers with one 50-pound washer.) This rule is based on the fact that a standard drying cycle is more than likely twice as long as a wash cycle. (Exceptions arise when electric dryers are used since they operate more slowly than gas or steam dryers, and different types of loads may require slightly different wash formula times.)

Those laundries equipped with ironers will not require that sheets or pillowcases pass through dryers. Such an operation requires that dryers be used only for terry linen. All of the above factors enter into the planning of how much and what type of equipment needs to be installed.

MAJOR EQUIPMENT REQUIREMENTS

Washers

Consider a typical hotel with 100 guest rooms and linen requirements as shown in Table 1. Table 1 illustrates the approximate poundage (1,000 pounds) of daily laundered linen that will be used as a guide for determining equipment requirements. (Other items such as food and beverage napery and uniforms are excluded from this example for the purpose of simplicity.) *Washer/extractor* selection should be the best balance of machine capability and labor requirements, the best balance being the least machinery that allows for the smallest labor force (one person working an 8-hour shift is optimum). After setting a constraint that requires the production of 1 PAR linen (the total amount of linen required to cover every bed and supply every bathroom once) in one shift, one now selects a "mix" of washing machine capacity that is most practical. One 500-pound washer, washing two loads, which can be completed in about 1 hour washing time, can handle the 1,000-pound requirement, but then the washer would be idle for 7 hours. The opposite extreme, one 50-pound washer working slightly less than a half-hour cycle, can produce the same amount of linen in 10 hours of operation. Practically speaking, two 50-pound washers can produce the 1,000-pound requirement in about 5 hours, and two 50-pound machines cost considerably less than one 500-pound machine and require less energy and mechanical support. Also, there is the added consideration that all linen will not be washed using the same "wash formula." (Linen must be separated by linen types and degree of soiling. Formula refers to the automatic combination of wash timing, rinse timing, temperature control, and automatic addition of chemical detergents, bleaches, and softeners.) In addition, linen must be weighed for proper washing. Apply the weights of each type of linen as noted in Table 1; the practical loading for a 50-pound washer is illustrated in Table 2.

Table 2 shows that two 50-pound washers working one cycle of approximately 30 minutes can complete all wash operations in about 5 1/2 hours.

Dryers

Assuming that a "no-iron" laundry is to be built, as previously stated, the number of dryers related to the number of washers is a ratio of 2 to 1. At 100 percent occupancy, the production of up to 1,000 pounds of washed linen (21 loads of wash) can be accommodated by three 100-pound dryers in a 6 1/2-hour period.

TABLE 1
Linen PAR and weight determination

Assume a 100-room hotel constituted as indicated in the table.

Sheet count:

# Rooms	Type	# Beds per room	Total beds	Total sheets	Weight per unit item in lb	Total wt in lb
10	King Sgl.	1	10	20	2.20	44.0
70	Queen Dbl.	2	140	280	1.45	406.0
20	Queen	1	20	40	1.45	58.0
100			170	340		508.0 lb

Pillow cases:
Generated at the rate of 2 for each queen bed, and 3 for each king bed
$(2 \times 160) + (3 \times 10) = 350$ cases *ca.* 0.25 lb = 87.5 lb

Terry linen:
For bath towels (BT), hand towels (HT), wash cloths (WC) and bath mats (BM), assume 1-BT, 1-HT, 1-WC per pillow, and 1-BM per room.

Item	Quantity	Wt/item (lb)	Total weight (lb)
BT	350	0.714	249.9
HT	350	0.231	80.85
WC	350	0.053	18.55
BM	100	0.437	43.7
Totals	1150 Items		393.0

One PAR total weight:	Sheets	508.00 lb
	Pillow cases	87.5
	Terry linen	393.0
	Total	988.5 lb
	(Approximates	1000.0 lb)

TABLE 2
Load schedules for 1–50 lb washer

Item	Quantity	Total weight	Items/load	Total loads
Sheets (K)	20	44	20	1
Sheets (Q)	320	464	32	10
PC	350	88	175	2
BT	350	250	70	5
HT	350	81	175	2
WC	350	19	350	1
BM	100	44	100	1

Less than 100 Percent Occupancy

By equating washer capacity to 100 percent occupancy on a linear basis, the graph in Figure 1 indicates the number of hours the laundry must operate for any given occupancy.

Figure 1 shows that two 50-pound washers can generate more linen required for 100 percent occupancy in slightly more than 5 1/2 hours; lesser occupancies would require lower wash hour requirements.

FIGURE 1
The on-premise laundry in the U.S.

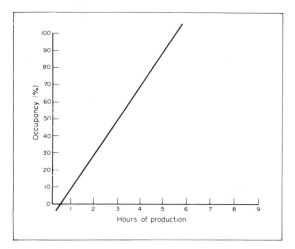

ADDITIONAL EQUIPMENT

Having specified two *washer/extractors* and three *dryers* as basic machinery required for the example property, what other equipment may be considered essential? Chew[3] recommends the following ancillary equipment.

1 soak sink (double basin, plastic formed) for use in soaking stained linens in special wash formulas for spot and stain removal.

5 laundry hampers (either vinyl-coated canvas or plastic molded hamper). This provides two hampers for soiled separated linen, one to receive "washed-wet linen" and two for "washed-dry linen." These hampers should not be used "outside" the laundry.

In addition to Chew's recommendations, the following equipment is also recommended:

6 convertible/mobile linen shelves. Three convertible/mobile storage carts should be positioned in the laundry, receiving clean linen throughout the day. These carts may then be moved to satellite linen rooms for the next day's operation. As linen is removed from the mobile carts to prepare maids' carts, the shelving may be "repositioned" in such a way as to create soiled linen hampers for the next day's housekeeping.

An equal number of mobile linen carts should be

positioned in the satellite linen rooms to accommodate soiled linen during the day. At the day's end they would now be ready to be moved to the laundry for washing the following day. After soiled linen has been removed and sorted, shelving on the convertible/mobile carts is repositioned to accept clean linen. The cycle will then be repeated. (AHMA can provide references on several manufacturers of this type of mobile, convertible shelving.) Such mobile shelving does not preclude the need for some permanent shelving but does remove the requirement for most, and does provide for movement of linen. The total need for most mobile shelving is determined by the number of satellite linen rooms (two for each linen storage area of which one would be positioned in the laundry each day).

1 sheet/spread folders. There are several ways to fold sheets. The sheet-folding alternative is usually dependent on hotel occupancy. Should occupancies be low, in the 40 to 60 percent range, capital expenditures for sheet folders would not usually be warranted or recommended since two attendants working together can fold about 90 to 100 sheets per hour. A 50 percent occupancy in the example hotel yields a workload of about 150 sheets. In such a case two laundry employees are required. Should the workload increase, then it becomes appropriate to consider the capability of one employee folding up to about 300 sheets in a reasonable period of time. In such cases, a sheet folder becomes a reasonable investment.

The folder gives one employee the same production capability as two employees folding sheets by hand.

GENERAL NON-EQUIPMENT FACTORS AND REQUIREMENTS

Linen Supply

About 3 1/2 PAR of linen is required to provide for efficient housekeeping operations. One PAR of linen would be found on the beds and in bathrooms of all guestrooms; one additional PAR would be clean either on maids' carts or on shelves for tomorrow's cleaning operations, and a third PAR would be soiled, awaiting the next day's laundry operations. The half PAR remaining would be related to new linen in storage. (If linen were owned and had to be sent off the property to a commercial laundry each day, then add one additional PAR to total requirements because of the time required to transport linen back and forth to a commercial laundry.)

Floorplan Layout and Size

About four square feet of space for each guestroom will be required for the laundry facility itself, and an additional four square feet per guest room is needed for linen handling and storage throughout the property. Figure 2 shows a typical floorplan layout for a small laundry where soiled linen is first moved to a sorting and wash area.

After washing and drying, linen can be moved to the folding area. Both sheet folding and folded terry can be then moved to convertible/mobile shelving for passage out of the laundry.

A third washer could be added to accommodate expansion. Dryers should be installed as shown and are part of the original equipment. (Note the venting capability.)

If a hot water system is not sufficient to accommodate two washers, a fast-generating hot water heater will be necessary. Gas hot water heaters must be properly vented when installed.

Two *soak sinks* provide the capability of soaking stained and spotted linen rather than using valuable washing time.

A 3-foot × 6-foot *folding table* positioned as indicated is recommended and can be manufactured locally.

Staffing Considerations

The staffing for the example laundry (no food and beverage linen or uniforms considered) is:

1 Washperson
1 Laundry attendant

FIGURE 2

Laundry floor-plan layout, 64 to 98 rooms

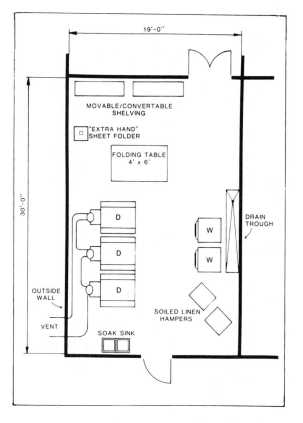

The *washperson* would handle the loading and unloading of washers, and the loading of dryers. The *laundry attendant* unloads the dryers, folds sheets, and stacks terry linen and pillowcases in flat stacks counted as appropriate. Folding rates for the sheet folder are in excess of 100 sheets per hour. A full PAR of sheets (242) can therefore be folded in slightly more than 2 hours by the *laundry attendant*.

The *laundry attendant* would spend the balance of the shift stacking terry linen and pillowcases in counted stacks to be passed to the satellite linen rooms at the end of the day via the mobile line carts.

Laundry Floors

Even with proper drainage, washer spills and overflows will occur. It is therefore essential that the laundry floor be waterproofed. Soiled sorted linen and even clean linen may be found trailing on the floor occasionally, and as a result, the laundry floor must be damp-mopped daily. Linen on the floor is of no consequence provided the floor has been sealed and is kept clean.

Mechanical Engineering Requirements

Small facility equipment, when combined with inadequate engineering considerations such as inadequate electrical, mechanical, plumbing (both water supply and drainage), and ventilation, can create a shut-down. The greatest of these "unrecognized problems" is inadequate water disposal drainage caused by extraction cycles of several washing machines draining simultaneously. For example, can a four-inch floor drain accommodate the drainage from three washers each with a three-inch discharge line? According to most specifications, the answer is no. A drain trough or holding basin that can hold 100 gallons of water can allow for the overload of effluent water under pressure, and will allow time for the drain water to pass into the four-inch floor drain over a period of several minutes. (Refer to Figure 2 and note the specified drain trough associated with the two washers. There is also a provision for drainage of a third washer.)

Ventilation

Of equal importance is the requirement to exhaust moisture-laden air from the three dryers out of the laundry room. Small properties usually have laundries with low ceilings, which compound the problem of dryer effluent exhaust. Most 100-pound dryers exhaust about 800 cfm each. Operating three dryers together results in 2400 cfm of this moist hot air. Also, note that the laundry room will require adequate space through regular doors to "intake or supply an equal amount of air." Without ample intake through regular doors, or a separate forced dry air supply, *dryers* will not operate at specified efficiencies. Some modern dryers now provide for "heat recovery" equipment, which will reduce laundry energy requirements *if* provision is made for this type of accessory in advance.

Provision for Lint Removal

It is absolutely essential that the laundry room and adjacent areas be kept clean and free of lint. Lint is a major fire hazard in laundry operations and must be dealt with accordingly. Not only must lint be removed from dryer air ventilation, but lint must be kept dusted from overhead pipes and hard-to-reach areas. A regular campaign must be maintained to keep lint accumulation to a minimum.

CONCLUSION

Whereas a preponderance of evidence now rests with the positive attributes of having an on-premise laundry, the decision to have a facility does not end the planning equation; it begins the need for accurate planning in earnest. Decisions must be made concerning the proper sizing of equipment, facility layout, ancillary equipment, staffing considerations, work-flow patterns, and floor treatment. A critical factor in preliminary planning is a necessary concern for mechanical, electrical, plumbing, and airflow engineering to insure proper equipment operation after construction and installation. Frequently, once the decision is made to have an on-premise laundry, facility architects unfamiliar with hotel operational design and the need to trim capital costs, overpower the necessity to seek and obtain professional laundry facility advice. Shortcuts in this area create problems that haunt operators during start-up operations and for some time thereafter until they are identified and corrected. The decision to have an on-premise laundry facility begins with the first planning step. Small operators should not become overconcerned about the costs of consulting services. The payback in months and in future years of trouble-free op-

erations far outweighs the initial cost of proper planning and foresight.

CASE STUDY—Progress or Change? Housekeeping in Transition

You are a consultant who has been hired by a medium-sized (450 rooms), full-service hotel in Minneapolis. You are to assist the Executive Housekeeper and his staff in redesigning the housekeeping organization to become more "proactive" relative to modern operational realities and logically foreseeable events affecting the housekeeping function in the hotel.

The hotel has enjoyed high annual occupancy ratings, in the medium to high seventies, with seasonal swings close to 100 percent in the summer and dipping into the low sixties during the winter months. Because of a stable employment picture in the area, high turnover is not a big problem. In fact, the housekeeping department has enjoyed turnover rates in the neighborhood of 15 to 20 percent on an annual basis, which would be the envy of most of the hotel industry in the United States.

Currently, management requires room housekeepers to clean seventeen rooms per day in an eight-hour shift. The linen room is located so that the housekeepers have to check out their entire day's stock of clean linens and carry it on their carts for their entire shift. There are no provisions for significant linen storage on each floor.

According to the engineering department, the above practice has resulted in an increase in service and maintenance calls relative to housekeepers' equipment. Engineering projects that the useful life of housekeepers' carts has been shortened by about 30 percent.

These operational frustrations have not yet manifested themselves in increase in turnover statistics, but the executive housekeeper and the director of human resources have both reported that sick leave, on-the-job injuries, and leave-without-pay requests are up over prior years for the room housekeepers.

Top management has announced a significant program of redecoration, remodeling, upgrading of amenities packages in rooms, and increasing service levels throughout the hotel in order to attract a more sophisticated and upscale clientele. Your job as consultant to the housekeeping department is to make operational, organizational, and structural suggestions that will allow the housekeeping department to participate fully in restructuring the hotel's image and market.

Endnotes

[1] A copy of the instrument is available from the authors.
[2] Available from the authors.
[3] This reference was not cited in the original article [the editor].

References

Brigham, G.H. 1955. *Housekeeping for hotels, motels, hospitals, clubs, Schools.* New York: Ahrens.

LaBelle, A.M., and J. Barton. 1951. *Administrative housekeeping.* New York: G.P. Putnam's Sons.

Mintzberg, H. 1975. The manager's job: Folklore and fact. *Harvard Business Review* July-August:49–61.

Nie, N.H., C.H. Hull, J.G. Jenkins, K. Steinbrenner, and D.H. Bent. 1975. *Statistical package for the social sciences,* 2d ed. New York: McGraw-Hill.

Nyquist, J.D., M.J. Bitner, and B.H. Booms. 1985. Identifying communications difficulties in the service encounter: A critical incident approach. In *The Service Encounter: Managing employee/customer interaction in service business,* ed. J. Czepile, M. Solomon, and C. Suprenant. Lexington, MA: D.C. Heath.

Schneider, M., and G. Tucker. 1989. *The professional housekeeper,* 3d ed. New York: Van Nostrand Reinhold.

Schweid, P. 1976. A laundry in your plants: don't underestimate its importance. *Cornell Hotel and Restaurant Administration Quarterly* 17:40–46.

Scott, J.E. 1976. Why you should install your own laundry. *Lodging,* November:38–139.

Suggested Readings

Books

Martin, Robert J. *Professional Management of Housekeeping Operations.* New York: John Wiley, 1986.

Schneider, Madelin, and Georgina Tucker. *The Professional Housekeeper,* 3d ed. New York: Van Nostrand Reinhold, 1989.

Articles

Anon. "Amenities: Building Goodwill." *Lodging* (March 1985):25–27, 31.

McNamee, Tom. "Which Computer System Should I Choose (Or Should I Even Have a Computer?)." *Executive Housekeeping Today* 8/7 (July 1987):18ff.

Rosenberg, Judy. "Linen Control: From Purchase to Discard." *Lodging* (June 1981):27–29, 62.

SECTION **6**

Engineering, Security, and Guest Services

INTRODUCTION

In a way, engineering, security, and guest services could all be considered "guest services." In most hotels guest services is a very visible component that can include concierge, uniformed service, garage, and specialized recreational and leisure activities. Security for the hotel and its guests and the maintenance of the hotel's engineering system under the best of circumstances are behind the scenes and not generally noticed or experienced by the guest in any but an abstract sense. They are nonetheless services that are critical to a safe, comfortable, and by extrapolation, successful guest stay at your hotel.

As stated in the first of the two articles included here on the engineering function, in the past the chief engineer and his or her department usually have been metaphorically relegated to roughly the same position in the hotel's organization that it physically occupies: in the basement or at the bottom and out of sight. As explored in these two articles, there are numerous indications that the importance of the engineering function can no longer be ignored or treated with any less respect than any other department.

Among the suggested readings are two articles on technical aspects of the engineer's job that indicate the sophistication required by the modern engineer and at the same time focus on the significant contribution the engineering department can make to the hotel's profit picture by saving and or cutting costs. Also strongly recommended is the new textbook by Redlin and Stipanuk for a comprehensive study of the engineering department and its personnel and mission in modern times.

It is an unfortunate fact of modern hotel management that the days of simply providing guest comfort, quality food, beverage and lodging services, and a "home away from home" atmosphere are severely affected by the inventory of problems presented by the predatory elements of modern society. Through the analysis of a typical case involving guest security, Rutherford and McConnell present an exemplar of this threat to modern hotel managements by third parties. This case represents one aspect of new security realities relative to guest safety. In the suggested readings list, the reader will find additional analysis and commentary relative to this critical issue that overlays virtually every aspect of modern hotel security management.

Finally, Withiam's in-depth article on the hotel

concierge explores the emerging and expanding role that guest services play in assisting hotel managements to design and deliver an ever-increasing inventory of services to their guests. The concept of the concierge as it has been traditionally practiced in Europe is being adapted to many hotel managerial frameworks in the United States. This should be indicative of the length to which hotel managements go to provide services to the guest and to meet competition.

The Hotel Engineering Function: Organization, People, and Issues in the Modern Era

Denney G. Rutherford

INTRODUCTION TO THE ENGINEERING DEPARTMENT

History of Department

Historically, the functions and duties of the Chief Engineer, his staff, and the Engineering Department have been relegated to the subconscious of hotel management and certainly to the hotel guests. Their place in the organization was roughly analogous to their place in the building structure: toward the bottom and basically out of sight. The only time the functions of the Engineering Department became noticeable was on those unhappy occasions when something went wrong with one of the building systems and guests and/or management was inconvenienced.

Consequently, in the past, "out of sight, out of mind" treatment evolved for the Engineering Department and as a result the relative importance of that department assumed a diminished role. Also, the personnel of the Engineering Department were craftspeople and semi-skilled workers, usually managed by one of their number who through longevity and perseverance worked his way up through the ranks to supervisory status.

Evolutionary Stimuli

There is now clear evidence that this department is changing in many of the same ways that other departments of a modern hotel have had to change. The reasons for these evolutionary changes are many, but four can be highlighted here. Several of them, of course, are closely interconnected.

Competition. As more and more hotel organizations seek the business of ever more carefully segmented markets, many of the mechanisms of competition manifest themselves first in features of the physical plant. These can range from building design, landscaping, elevators, in-room amenities and facilities, to the latest in traditional fixtures and building systems such as plumbing, kitchen equipment, elevators, heating, ventilating, and air conditioning (HVAC), and the other "behind the scenes" paraphernalia that make up the domain of the Chief Engineer.

Sophistication. Many of these building systems in today's hotels are interconnected and managed in conjunction with other departmental systems and monitored by computerized facilities. This increased sophistication has mandated more sophisticated and knowledgeable management in all departments, but perhaps the most drastic and substantive changes will be (and are) occurring in engineering.

Return on investment. Many modern hotel plants are the result of plans and investments by a wide range of participants, including (but not necessarily always) the management firm that operates the hotel. These investors have the expectation of a certain return on their investment, and subsequently expect that the hotel company will not only keep the hotel filled with guests but keep the property in such a state that the guests will continue to want to come there. This also mandates new dimensions to the engineer's job. The combination of increased competition and sophisticated systems makes for more than a traditional "repair and maintenance" approach to providing the engineering support in all areas of the hotel. To keep the hotel positively contributing to the investors' return on their money, the engineering staff has to be considered a major role player in the financial health of the organization.

This reading is original to this book.

Impact of OPEC oil embargo, 1973–74. The cost, use, management, and conservation of energy have added a new and singular dimension to the job of the Chief Engineer—one that did not exist in pre-1973 operations, simply because energy was so cheap. Buildings were not engineered or managed specifically to save energy.

Since the mid-70s, most hotels and most modern hotel companies have come to recognize energy as one building expense in which significant savings can be made. If accomplished with care, engineering can provide delivery of hotel services without adverse or negative effects on the guest.

This suggests further complications to the engineer's job. Specifically, the engineer (as opposed to the role relegated to the bottom of the organization chart and the back of the house as earlier stated) now needs to have an active presence as a full member of the management staff and needs to become adept at interacting with other department managers.

PERSONNEL

Manager of Engineering Function

Variously referred to as the Chief Engineer, Director of Building Operations, Building Superin-

tendent, or some other combination of those terms, this is the individual who is responsible for the management of the building's systems, its maintenance, repair, and upkeep.

As stated earlier, in the past the Chief Engineers typically were people who worked their way up through the ranks from one of the crafts or as an engineering employee specializing in one of the building systems. They may have been in hotels all of their professional careers, or may have come to a hotel company from engineering positions in organizations as diverse as shipping lines or manufacturing companies, or building engineers in office buildings, university settings, or hospitals.

New evidence, however, exists that suggests this trend may be changing (Rutherford 1987). Chief Engineers responding to this survey describe themselves collectively according to the data set forth in Figure 2. Over 25 percent of those responding to this nationwide survey indicated they have a university degree. Of those, three-quarters were in some area of engineering. This suggests that the sophistication of modern hotel building operations may be mandating management by those whose formal education is more extensive than that required in the past.

In this study, the typical engineer was 44-1/2 years old and had been in the hospitality business

---

FIGURE 1
Engineering department organization

ENGINEERING
MANAGEMENT

|

ASSISTANT

ADMINISTRATION FUNCTIONS	BUILDING SYSTEM FUNCTIONS	CRAFTS
Secretarial	HVAC	Carpenter
Clerical	Plumbing	Cabinetmaker
Purchasing	Electricity	Upholsterer
Inventory	Refrigeration	Painters
Preventive Maintenance	Food Protection Equipment	Groundskeepers
Contracted Services	Computer Systems	
Scheduling	Elevators	
Records		

FIGURE 2
Chief Engineer demographics
(74 respondents)

		(Raw Number if Applicable)
Average Age	44.5	
Percent Male	100.0%	
Percent Caucasian	92.9%	
Median Salary	$35,000	
Percent University Degree	27.0%	(20)
Percent of Degrees in Engineering	75.0%	(15)
Percent of Degrees in Hotel/Business	25.0%	(5)
Average Years in Hospitality Industry	10.9	
Average Years at Present Hotel	6.3	
Average Years in Present Position	6.15	

about 11 years. This suggests that this "typical engineer" has probably had significant on-the-job experience or training in his field in other industries and only recently came into the hospitality industry. After entering the hospitality industry, however, it appears that the Chief Engineers moved rapidly into management and have been fairly stable in their careers, as evidenced by the congruence of average years in present position and average years at present hotel.

Commenting on these data, one Chief Engineer said that in his experience more and more industry engineering managers in the larger or international hotel firms are being recruited from among those people who have had at least some college education, if not actually holding a college or university degree in engineering. He suggested that in his company this does not necessarily reflect a preference for academic training over practical experience but recognizes the realities of doing business in today's competitive environment. It also suggests understanding and being able to manage the sophisticated building systems that the company anticipates installing and being developed for new hotels into the next century.

In that comment lies one key to understanding the future of the Chief Engineer's job. The most successful engineers of the future will very likely be those whose training and education prepare them to think strategically, to recognize trends, and to do their part to help the hotel and its owners meet and deal with the evolutionary issues discussed earlier.

Other Departmental Management Staff

Referring again to Figure 1, depending of course on the size of the hotel and the extent and sophistication of the engineering functions in the hotel, the Chief Engineer may enjoy the services of a staff of administrative people, including assistant managers. These people help carry out the administrative details of operating an increasingly complicated hotel department. Included in these would be secretarial support, which may be combined with a clerical function.

Among the most important administrative functions for the Engineering Department are:

- Helping other department heads make purchasing decisions
- Keeping an inventory of spare parts and building equipment
- Arranging for the performance of preventive maintenance on all building systems
- Administering contract services such as pest control, window washing, landscaping, swimming pool maintenance, groundskeeping, and various construction projects

As the department grows in size and scope, a major administrative function involves scheduling of equipment and personnel to accomplish the tasks of the department. That is another major series of daily tasks that face administration of an Engineering Department. While scheduling may benefit greatly from technological advances such as micro-computers or the hotel's mainframe computer system, in a building whose systems are as complicated and interrelated as a hotel, part of the engineering function has to be prepared to react to non-scheduled events ranging from overflowing toilets to stuck elevators to gas leaks, and so forth.

A final administrative function involves setting the groundwork and maintaining the basis for managerial and administrative decisions that affect the long-term operation of the Engineering Department and by extrapolation the hotel itself. That is the keeping of accurate and up-to-date records regarding the various building systems and installation of capital equipment for which the engineer is responsible.

These are the sorts of administrative details that complicate the job of any manager but may be particularly troubling to the engineer. One of the main reasons for this is that while the Engineering Department is responsible for the maintenance and repair of sophisticated and complicated building systems, under most circumstances these systems or component parts of these systems are often operated by (and perhaps misused by) a wide range of people ranging from employees to guests. Particularly in the case of guests, we have little or no control over the way in which they treat guestroom equipment and fixtures for which the engineer is responsible. Those engineers who have the luxury of a well-developed administrative staff find their job in managing the building and its systems and the attendant problems much easier if complete, accurate, and up-to-date records are available to formulate the basis for planning, purchasing, budgeting, and control.

Technical Specialists

Typical building functions that are the responsibility of the Engineering Department are listed in Figure 1. Each has its own place in providing for the comfort of the guest and participating in the delivery of the hotel's services to the guests. Each has attendant complications that provide challenges for the management and staff of the Engineering Department.

Heating, ventilating, and air conditioning (collectively known as HVAC) is concerned with supplying the various production, public, and guestroom areas of the hotel with a clean, controlled, and comfortable indoor environment. Modern building HVAC systems provide for heating or cooling the air; adding or deleting moisture from the air to adjust for optimum relative humidity; filtering or cleaning the air; and moving the air from place to place within the hotel, providing for a number of complete changes of air in a room per hour dependent upon local codes and activities within that particular area of the hotel.

Among the complicating factors here that challenge the Engineering Department are that various areas of the hotel have various requirements for air. For instance, there is a different requirement in the guestroom areas than there is in the kitchen area. There is a different requirement in public areas such as the lobby and areas such as bars, restaurants, or housekeeping laundry facilities. The engineers call this "providing the system with balance" and it is a major function of the individuals who are in charge of the HVAC of the hotel and adjust the HVAC system to deliver the optimum environment to each of those various areas.

The plumbing system in a modern hotel has to perform a number of balancing functions also. First and foremost in the minds of management of course is the delivery of quality water service to guestroom areas. Guests want high-quality water that is free from visual defects such as dirt or rust, does not carry any odors, and tastes clean and fresh. Guests also want water that is hot enough to shave, bathe, and wash without the danger of scalding themselves; and they also want that water in generous supply. Nothing is more frustrating to a hotel guest who is paying over $100 a night for a room to find that the hotel has run out of hot water in the middle of a morning shave or shower. At the same time the Engineering Department is expected to deliver "production" hot and cold water to the kitchen areas, the housekeeping and laundry areas, and the various food service areas. Providing for the delivery of high-quality water service to the various user groups in the hotel is a major part of the engineering function, one which, of course, is only noticed when there is some obvious defect in the delivery of that particular service.

A similar case may be made for the delivery of electricity to the various areas within the hotel. As in providing high-quality plumbing services, the electrical systems of the hotel also have to be designed and maintained to serve various user groups. Again, like plumbing, there is no substitute for the lack of electricity. The engineering staff must provide the hotel with electrical service designed to meet the needs of individual departments and the needs of guests.

Refrigeration, food production equipment, and computer systems are examples of other building system functions that may be the responsibility of the Engineering Department to repair, maintain, replace, and/or manage. While the maintenance of many of these systems may be contracted with outside agencies such as the supplier, the Engineering Department nonetheless is the first line of defense in keeping the systems operating efficiently.

In most modern hotels the installation and service of elevator systems are generally the province of the elevator manufacturer, and hotels will typically have extended maintenance agreements for the elevators. Most Engineering Departments will, however, closely monitor the operation of the elevator systems. In modern high-rise hotels with high-speed elevator service, the slightest problem with that service should be quickly and easily identified and reported to the contractors. It is generally the responsibility of the Engineering Department to monitor these services and their contracts closely and carefully.

The various crafts represented in Figure 1 are included to be illustrative of the sorts of specialized skills required in varying ways by most hotel Engineering Departments. Depending upon the size of the hotel and complexity of a hotel's services, an Engineering Department may employ on a full-time basis one or more carpenters and cabinetmakers to maintain, repair, and build fixtures and furniture for the hotel's guests and staff. Similarly, if not contracted out, hotels may employ an upholsterer whose major task is to maintain a high-quality appearance of the vast collection of furniture in a typical hotel.

Painting and upkeep of the hotel's grounds and landscaping also represent ongoing functions that require constant attention. These represent services that may be contracted to outside agencies or suppliers but are included here to suggest the range of functions for which the Engineering Department is responsible.

ISSUES

In the previously mentioned study (Rutherford 1987), the engineers surveyed were asked to judge the relative importance of each of a list of 58 statements relating to the operation of a modern hotel Engineering Department. A statistical procedure was applied to rank-order the statements in terms of their rated importance. The 10 most important facets of an engineer's job derived from this list are reproduced in Figure 3 and serve as the basis for suggesting the most pressing issues facing hotel engineering managers at this time.

Departmental Management

Items 4, 6, 7, and 8 suggest that the modern hotel engineers deem activities relating to management of their departments of high importance to success—communicating with employees; providing for a safe environment; being able to organize the various tasks, activities, and personnel in the department; and providing leadership—Each of these suggests that one of the foremost issues facing the Chief Engineer today that involves people-oriented managerial skills rather than the traditional view, which held the Chief Engineer to be more concerned with the technical aspects of his job.

Energy

The fact that three energy-related items were rated in the top 10 by all responding engineers suggests that the entire realm of issues relating to energy has not yet been addressed satisfactorily by the majority of these professionals. It also suggests that energy will continue to be an issue in the foreseeable future.

Relations with Top Management

Another major dimension of the engineer's job can be seen by the importance attached to this issue. Of the other departments that the engineers were asked to rank their relationships with, only two, housekeeping and purchasing, ranked within the top 50 percent of these 58 items. Many of the Chief Engineers contacted for comment agreed with this

FIGURE 3
Importance of this item to operation of my department

Rank	Item	Mean	SD	N
1.	Knowledge of maintenance of equipment	4.760	.633	75
2.	Energy conservation	4.655	.804	74
3.	Energy management	4.589	.761	73
4.	Responsibility for communication with employees	4.587	.680	75
5.	Relations with top management	4.520	.811	73
6.	Responsibility for leadership	4.514	.726	74
7.	Responsibility for safety	4.486	.904	72
8.	Responsibilities of an effective organizational ability	4.453	.810	75
9.	Energy costs	4.444	.854	72
10.	Knowledge of the types of equipment	4.370	.791	73

Scale: 1 = not at all important;
        5 = of vital importance

ranking with top management. They said on a regular basis it is becoming an increasingly important part of their job to not only report to top management but to educate top management as to the importance of the engineering function.

Equipment

It should be noted that the more technical aspects of the Chief Engineer's job are not in any way totally ignored by the collective rankings assigned to these operational statements. That knowledge of maintenance of equipment ranked clearly first among the other statements and knowledge of types of equipment made it into the top 10 suggests that while the job of the Chief Engineer may in fact be evolving toward one of a more managerial nature, some of the traditional technical aspects of the job still play a major role in the daily discharge of an engineer's responsibility.

FUTURE AND CONCLUSION

Data from Empirical Research

Interpretation of the data gathered in survey from a broad cross-section of Chief Engineers and subsequent follow-up conversations with selected engineers suggest that the job of the Chief Engineer

is in fact evolving as suggested at the outset of this chapter.

The engineers themselves describe many incidents of having to deal more with issues and problems related to people and departmental action and interaction than in the past, when most of the issues and problems they had to face on a regular basis involved equipment and systems.

It also appears that in the future Chief Engineers are going to have to be more adept at inter- and intradepartmental organizational politics. To provide the hotel and its guests with high-quality services relative to the physical and environmental systems of the building, the Chief Engineer is going to have to compete with other department heads for scarce resources related to personnel, technology, and "operating elbow room."

Summing up, the Engineering Department, its management, and to a certain extent its staff and technical experts, represent an organizational function of the modern hotel that is in the process of evolutionary change. As stated at the outset, this change is driven by a number of factors. The future of successful hotel organizations will hinge to a great extent on the ability of hotel managements to recognize the importance of the contributions of the Engineering Department to the delivery of guest services and maintaining a high order of return on investments for the owners of the property.

The Evolution of the Hotel Engineer's Job

Denney G. Rutherford

Considering the many substantial changes that have recently affected the hotel engineering department, it is not surprising that the chief engineer's position

is not always clearly understood by others in the hotel. At one end of the spectrum is the perception of the chief engineer (CE) as an irascible curmudgeon who knows the meaning of every clank in every pipe and who knows where to kick the ice machine, how to relight the boiler, and how to make a pool table, a craps table, or a dining-room table (or maybe all three at once) on the same day the

This article was originally published in the February 1987 issue of *The Cornell Hotel and Restaurant Administration Quarterly,* and is reprinted here with the permission of the Cornell University School of Hotel Administration. © 1987.

request comes in. On the other end is the picture of the CE as a manager dressed in coat and tie, who is equally comfortable in the executive suite and the boiler room and who commands an array of modern technology only slightly less complicated than the flight deck of the starship *Enterprise*.

The energy upheaval of the 1970s was a primary impetus for development of the "new" chief engineer's position. Borsenik (1979, 4) points out that during the prior era of stable utility prices, limited hotel services, and low labor costs, maintenance and engineering functions were related to the minor status of a "necessary evil." In the 1970s, a period of rising energy prices and accelerating technical advances, hotel managements started to recognize the critical role that the CE could play. The problem was that many CEs did not have the management skills to balance their excellent technical abilities.

Most written discussions of the CE's role state that the position now embraces more management-oriented functions, but they do not always specify what those functions involve. In his text on hotel engineering, Aulbach states:

> The need for effectively managing the engineering and maintenance department is just as important as it is for any other department. In addition to specialized technical knowledge, the chief engineer must possess managerial abilities if the department is to attain its goals (Aulbach 1984, 53).

Aulbach adds that the role of the engineering and maintenance department has changed over the years from one of "just keeping things running" to one of management (Aulbach 1984, 54). The CE must also stay abreast of rapid technological developments and meet guest demands that involve changes in the physical plant. In this article, I will review the events that have forged a new identity for chief engineers and present the results of a survey of how 74 CEs view their jobs.

FORCES FOR CHANGE

A variety of new challenges have arisen for the hotel chief engineer. Most of these have not come

through sudden revolutions, but rather have developed from a combination of related evolutionary factors. Foremost among these factors is competition. As more hotel organizations have sought the business of ever more carefully segmented markets, many have added technical improvements to their physical plants that must be maintained by the engineering department. These features can range from general building design to specific in-room facilities (e.g., refrigerators) and the latest in traditional fixtures and building systems. The management of these physical assets is fundamental to the CE's job.

Sophistication

Many features and systems in today's hotels are interconnected and managed in conjunction with other departmental systems and monitored by computerized facilities (Marko and Moore 1980a; Marko and Moore 1980b; Saidel 1981). This increased equipment sophistication means all managers must be more knowledgeable, but the most drastic and substantive changes have been occurring in engineering.

As a result, the CE must not only be broadly knowledgeable in the latest equipment and systems, but must also be able to recruit, train, and manage a staff that can meet the challenges of maintaining technologically advanced equipment.

The combination of increased market competition and sophisticated systems has greatly expanded the engineer's job. Instead of the traditional "repair and maintenance" position, the job now involves providing engineering support to all areas of the hotel.

Energy: A New Factor

The cost, use, and conservation of energy have added a new dimension to the job of the chief engineer—one that essentially did not exist before 1973. Because energy was previously so cheap, buildings were neither engineered nor managed specifically to save energy.

Since the restructuring of the energy industry in

the mid-70s, most hotels and hotel companies have recognized energy as one area in which significant savings could be achieved. Most energy-conservation programs provide for delivery of hotel services without adverse effects on the guest. Hotel managements want to avoid, for instance, the extreme case of a guest being requested to take a short shower in a room that costs upward of $100 per night.

The residual effects of the oil embargo of 1973 are two-fold. Hotels that were built prior to 1973 were not constructed to be particularly energy-efficient. Engineers working in those hotels have a difficult job with respect to managing energy. On the other hand, many hotels designed and built after this time contain sophisticated systems that conserve energy without affecting guest comfort. The first instance presents the CE with a managerial problem of "making do"; the second requires continual expansion of the chief's technical knowledge.

Moreover, a mechanical or electronic system can never be the only answer to energy conservation in a business as complex as a hotel. A tremendous amount of attention must be given to training personnel to overcome wasteful habits. Here is a further complication for the CE, because the chief's responsibility for energy conservation extends in this case beyond engineering to all hotel departments.

Theory

From the foregoing discussion, it seems clear that successful CEs should exhibit a blend of technical knowledge and managerial expertise. The discussion further suggests that CEs will be spending a greater percentage of their time on managerial matters and that these have assumed levels of importance at least as great as the technical aspects of the CE's job.

To find out whether these assumptions were true, I sent a survey to a stratified random sample of chief engineers in 200 hotels, representing all regions of the country and balanced equally between large chain operations and small independent operators. Seventy-four usable surveys were returned (a 39 percent response). In addition to soliciting demographic information, I asked the engineers to respond to 58 statements about the operation of the engineering department. The respondents were to judge each statement in two contexts: (1) how important the activity or function was to their department's operation, and (2) how much time they spent on that activity or function annually. These responses were scored on a Likert-type scale.

WHO ARE THE ENGINEERS?

Like many departments in hotels, engineering is dominated by white males (see Exhibit 1). In part, this phenomenon reflects the traditional difficulty that minorities and women encounter in moving into the upper management of any hotel department. But the preponderance of white men is more glaring in engineering than in other fields, presumably because the trades, skills, and backgrounds of workers and managers in this department are historically not those widely open to minorities and women.

The respondents' salaries ranged widely, from below $25,000 to over $55,000. One engineer who reviewed the data was somewhat surprised that half of the reported salaries were below $35,000, because in his experience, someone rising to the level of chief engineer (at least in a chain hotel) would generally command more than $35,000.

This CE also reported that an increasing number of people with college backgrounds and degrees were joining the engineering department, to the exclusion of those who have followed the more traditional "up-through-the-ranks" path. Since there are no comparative data from other studies of chief engineers, it is difficult to determine whether the trend toward college-educated engineers is growing. Other CEs I contacted agreed that chief engineers with college backgrounds are certainly no longer uncommon and may be the wave of the future.

Nearly all the respondents considered their careers to be successful. This assessment was supported by other measures: The CEs said they were

EXHIBIT 1
Characteristics of surveyed chief engineers and hotels

Engineers' demographics and career data

Average age.	44.5
Average years in hospitality industry.	10.9
Average years at present hotel	6.3
Average years in present position	6.1
Median salary	$35,000
Number holding college degree	20 (27%)
Number holding degree in engineering.	15
Number holding degree in business or hotel administration.	5

Engineers' career attitudes

Consider career successful.	98.5%
Feel personal economic position has improved in past five years	70.1%
Seriously considered leaving hotel business in last two years	24.6%
Seriously recruited for another position in last two years	87.1%
Plan to remain in engineering (at unit or corporate level).	83.8%

Hotel data

	Range	Average
Number of guest rooms	124 to 1,865	609
Average room rate	$42 to $450	$97
Total engineering staff.	1 to 130	25.6
Number of engineering managers.	0 to 9	2.6

These figures are based on a survey of 74 chief engineers. All of them were men, and all but six were Caucasian. Seventy percent of the hotels were affiliated with major chains.

---

continually being recruited for other jobs, and they strongly felt their economic position had improved within the previous five years. That the vast majority of respondents intended to remain in engineering also signals confidence in their ability to contribute to the field. These career-satisfaction data compared favorably with the results of a similar survey of hotel general managers (Rutherford and Wiegenstein 1985).

Second careers. A comparison of the average number of years the CEs had spent in the hospitality industry with the ages indicated that many of them come to the hotel business from other industries. This was apparently true, however, only of the old-er CEs. The younger engineers had been in hotel administration for the bulk of their careers.

While the hotels represented in the sample ranged from fairly small (124 rooms) to megahotels (1,800-plus rooms), there was a slight bias toward larger hotels. Seventy percent of the respondents were from chain hotels (the mailing list for the survey comprised 55 percent large chain hotels and 45 independents or regional chains), and the average engineering staff size of nearly 26 would indicate a stronger response from larger operations.[1]

It is possible that one cause for the uneven return is that many chain hotels' engineering departments are organized and managed to be more receptive to research projects such as this one. One international chain, for instance, has requested permission to replicate this study in its own hotels. A corporate officer at another chain said that his firm's changing "corporate culture" increasingly reflects the potential contributions of the chief engineer, so individuals in the engineering department may be more inclined to participate in such research.

TESTING THEORIES

After the engineers judged the relative importance of and time devoted to each of the 58 items in the survey, the statements were ranked according to the importance and time ratings. The 20 most important factors of the chief engineer's job are shown in Exhibit 2. These facets are probably the most pressing issues now facing hotel engineering managers.

Departmental Management

Eight of the top 20 items involved management. The respondents' high ranking of such matters as communicating with employees, organizing and providing training, maintaining a safe environment, and providing motivational leadership suggests the importance of managerial skills, rather than mere technical knowledge.

EXHIBIT 2
Importance ratings for various engineering duties

Rank	Duty	Mean rating
1.	Knowledge of maintenance of equipment	4.76
2.	Energy conservation	4.66
3.	Energy maintenance	4.59
4.	Responsibility for communicating with employees	4.59
5.	Relations with top management	4.52
6.	Responsibility for leadership	4.51
7.	Responsibility for safety	4.49
8.	Responsibility for effective organizational ability	4.45
9.	Energy costs	4.44
10.	Knowledge of types of equipment	4.37
11.	Use of computers for control in monitoring energy costs	4.36
12.	Responsibility for budgeting	4.31
13.	Knowledge of the use of and training on equipment	4.31
14.	Relations with housekeeping department	4.27
15.	Responsibility for effective record-keeping	4.27
16.	Knowledge of the energy requirements of equipment	4.23
17.	Responsibility for motivation	4.22
18.	Computer use in the department	4.19
19.	The personnel function of training and continuing education	4.12
20.	Use of computers for control in preventive maintenance	4.09

Seventy-four chief engineers were asked to rate the importance of 58 job duties or factors on a scale of 1 (not at all important) to 5 (vitally important). These 20 factors were rated most important on average.

Energy

Energy remained a top priority. The fact that five energy-related items were in the top 20 (e.g., number 2: energy conservation; number 3: energy management) indicates that energy is still a problem for most engineers, and that it will continue to be a priority in the foreseeable future.

Management Relationships

Another major dimension of the CE's job was relationships with other managers. This was the number 5 item, and it was ranked far above relationships with individual departments. Commenting on this finding, many chief engineers said regular interaction with top management had become a large part of their job. They not only reported to top management, but were also responsible for educating top managers about the engineering function.

Housekeeping was the most significant department for the engineers, outside of their own. Housekeeping personnel working in all areas of the hotel have become the "eyes and ears" of the engineering manager in monitoring the condition and efficiency of the building's systems and physical assets.

Equipment

Keeping the equipment operating was still the number 1 consideration for the chief engineers. Three other equipment-related items were also in the top 20, and it seems clear that no matter how managerial the CE's position becomes, the technical aspects of the job will still be a concern.

Computers

Most CEs did not rate the items relating to computers, because most don't use computers. Yet computer-related items were very important to the CEs who *did* use automated systems. (Computers are being used to support such responsibilities as energy management and maintenance.)

TIME CONSTRAINTS

The amount of time spent on various aspects of the chief engineer's job corresponded closely to the 20 most important aspects of the job. With only one exception, the 20 items rated most important were also on the list of the most time-consuming duties. Equipment maintenance, for instance, was number 1 on both lists. In this respect, there was a remarkable amount of agreement on the part of the 74 respondents. The congruence of the two lists indicates that these managers have their priorities in order: They are devoting time to the duties they believe are most critical to their departments' operations.

There was a consistent relationship between the importance of the duties and the time available to perform them. In every instance, for all 58 factors, the CEs gave a significantly higher rating to the importance of each factor than to the time devoted to it.[2] Looking again at the number 1 item on both lists, the mean important rating for knowledge of maintenance of equipment was 4.7, while the mean rating of the time devoted to this item was 4.2. One might argue that most managers find they don't have enough time to devote to all their responsibilities, but the CE's job is exceptionally broad and complex. The responsibility for overseeing a diverse collection of personnel and a similarly diverse inventory of complex systems and equipment undoubtedly engenders an unusual managerial strain for the chief engineers. For example, one engineer said his ability to devote time to administrative and managerial duties suffered from the need to dispatch numerous immediate problems involving personnel and systems.

CHANGES

Returning to the question posed at the beginning of this article, the extent to which the role of the chief engineer has changed in recent years, the survey data clearly supported the notion that the chief engineer must keep pace with the rapid development of technology, remain sensitive to the role played by equipment, and be aware of the per-

---

EXHIBIT 3

Time devoted to various engineering duties

Rank	Duty	Mean rating
1.	Knowledge of maintenance of equipment	4.22
2.	Responsibility for leadership	4.08
3.	Responsibility for communicating with employees	4.04
4.	Responsibility for effective organizational ability	3.91
5.	Relations with housekeeping department	3.85
6.	Responsibility for safety	3.78
7.	Relations with top management	3.76
8.	Energy conservation	3.65
9.	Knowledge of types of equipment	3.64
10.	Responsibility for motivation	3.60
11.	Energy management	3.60
12.	Use of computers for control in monitoring energy costs	3.46
13.	Knowledge of the energy requirements of equipment	3.40
14.	Energy costs	3.38
15.	Knowledge of the use of and training on equipment	3.36
16.	Computer use in the department	3.35
17.	Relations with food and beverage department	3.29
18.	Responsibility for budgeting	3.25
19.	Responsibility for effective record-keeping	3.25
20.	The personnel function of training and continuing education	3.23

Seventy-four chief engineers were asked to rate the time devoted to 58 job duties or factors on a scale of 1 (virtually no time) to 5 (substantial time). These 20 factors were rated most time-consuming on average.

---

sonnel-management functions necessary to keep the department functioning.

With their greater involvement in hotel management, chief engineers will have to be more adept at inter- and intradepartmental organizational policies. The CE will have to compete with other department heads for budget resources related to personnel and technology, so that guest services can be maintained.

One CE's View

Energy management emerged as a high-priority issue. Ron Parker, chief engineer of the Four Seasons Hotel in Newport Beach, California, said the energy crises of the '70s "raised consciousness." He added that the greatest prospects for energy conservation in most hotels are still system-related, rather than people-related. In his view, the long-term solution to a hotel's energy needs will require instilling an energy-conservation and management ethic throughout the managerial structure. That ethic will have to filter down to every employee in the hotel, he said.

Parker echoed the collective sentiments of his fellow CEs when he stated that safety is another major issue. A hotel's insurance rates are based on the frequency of accidents, and the chief engineer in most hotels has a significant responsibility for detecting and correcting unsafe conditions.

The data also showed that the engineering department is no longer a minor player in the management of a hotel. Each chief engineer I contacted reported increased visibility among his management peers in the hotel. A study by Wasmuth and Davis (1983) found top management support was particularly vital for reducing turnover in the engineering department. If engineering failed to achieve authorization for needed budget items, morale was damaged. The present study confirmed the importance that CEs attach to their relationship with top management and the time spent on that relationship.

Moreover, the survey results supported the idea that chief engineers are spending more of their time on managerial matters and relatively less on the technical aspects of the job. The engineers themselves described many incidents in which they dealt more with issues and problems related to people and departmental action than in the past. While issues of equipment and systems still played a major role in the engineering manager's day, people problems also demanded a large share of time.

MOVING TOWARD MANAGEMENT

This study sought to document the current role of the hotel chief engineer. Because this is the first study of its kind, there are no comparative data, and other researchers may be interested in testing other aspects of this topic.

Hotel operators can use this information in establishing management structure. Companies may wish to use these data as the basis for comparisons within their own organizations. And engineers may find particular value in comparing operational aspects of their departments and careers to those presented here. If the role and function of the engineering department are indeed changing substantially, hotel companies should document those changes and adjust their policies, personnel, and procedures to take competitive advantage of them.

Understanding and Managing Your Liability for Guest Safety

Denney G. Rutherford
Jon P. McConnell

One day four years ago, Dr. Robert Banks and a friend were walking back to their rooms at the Hyatt Hotel in New Orleans, after having eaten dinner in the city's French Quarter. Just as the men arrived at the hotel's front entrance on Loyola Avenue, two robbers accosted them, and one assailant shot and killed Dr. Banks, who died just four feet away from the entryway to the hotel. Dr. Banks's widow and children brought a lawsuit in U.S. District Court against Hyatt for the man's death.[3]

Could a hotel be liable for a guest's death or injury in such circumstances? Although he was near the door, Dr. Banks was not on the hotel's property at the time of the robbery and shooting. Yet the court found that the hotel was indeed liable for his death. In this article, we will explain the court's reasoning in its decision, and then propose a management policy for limiting your hotel's risk in future cases of this type.

REASONABLE PRECAUTIONS

The essential issue before the court was to determine what would constitute "reasonable" precautions on the part of the hotel for the protection of its guests. The Banks family argued that the hotel

This article was originally published in the February 1987 issue of *The Cornell Hotel and Restaurant Administration Quarterly,* and is reprinted here with the permission of the Cornell University School of Hotel Administration. © 1987.

failed to take reasonable precautions for the safety of the deceased, and that the hotel management owed Dr. Banks a duty to do so. The hotel argued, on the contrary, that it had no duty to protect guests who were off the premises, and that in any event, it had taken reasonable precautions to protect guests who were in the immediate area of the hotel. Furthermore, the hotel argued that Dr. Banks was guilty of contributory negligence or had at least assumed the risk by going out.[4]

The federal-court jury agreed with the Banks family and awarded them $975,000.[5] Hyatt appealed this decision to the U.S. Court of Appeals, Fifth Circuit. Since there was no dispute over the facts of the case, the circuit court's job was to review the inferences of law to be drawn by the unique situation presented by the death of Dr. Banks. The court examined the trial judge's charge to the jury (explanation of relevant law) and found it adequate. In sum, the trial judge stated in his charge that while the hotel was not an insurer of a guest's safety, it did have a duty to protect a guest from foreseeable harm. This is the lesson for hoteliers from this case.[6]

ROUGH NEIGHBORHOOD

To portray the situation involved here, it is necessary to describe the physical setting. The Poydras Plaza Mall is a rectangular structure, the long side of which runs along Loyola Avenue. The Hyatt Hotel is behind the Poydras Plaza Mall, and access to the hotel is through corridors running through the mall. The hotel building overhangs these corridors, which are not, however, part of the hotel property. The legal owner of the entryway near where Dr. Banks was killed was Refco, which owned both the mall and the hotel building. Hyatt's lease for the hotel included the use of the entryway to Loyola Avenue and the passageways through the mall for guests' access. In legal parlance, this made Hyatt an occupier of the entryway and the passageways to the hotel, and Hyatt undoubtedly owed a duty to guests to take reasonable steps for their safety in these areas. The question was whether this duty extended to the area beyond the entryway.

To answer this question required defining what would constitute reasonable protection of a guest. This, in turn, required determining whether there was a known risk of criminal danger to guests and what Hyatt had done to protect guests from any such danger.

The trial court heard evidence that during the three-month period before the Banks killing, there were 16 robberies, 11 of them at gunpoint, in the immediate area of the hotel and one other shooting at the hotel entrance on Loyola Avenue. Moreover, in the three years preceding Dr. Banks's death, there had been five other armed robberies at the spot, as well as 21 incidents reported at or near the entrance—12 of them involving weapons. Hyatt security logs further revealed another 50 incidents, 14 involving weapons, in other areas around the hotel.

Based on this record, Hyatt had agreed with Refco that the latter would pay for security personnel hired by Hyatt to provide security in the area from Loyola Avenue through the mall. (There is no indication in the trial record of whether any security personnel were on duty at the time of the Banks shooting.) Hyatt, Refco, and three other property owners had also asked the New Orleans police to provide additional protection in the area. Upon being refused, the five owners had hired an off-duty policeman to patrol the perimeter of their properties. (The officer was at the opposite end of this large complex at the time of the Banks killing.)

Evidently the jury found that, considering the prevalence of criminal activity in the neighborhood, the hotel's security precautions were not sufficient to meet the standard of reasonable protection.

ASSUMING RISK

In examining the issues of law, the circuit court first considered the hotel's defense of contributory negligence and assumption of risk. The one argument that could support this defense was that Dr.

Banks might have engaged in a struggle with his assailant. The only evidence of this was the unsubstantiated opinion of the investigating detective, who could not begin to assess who might have initiated a struggle, if one occurred. The circuit court agreed with the trial judge's refusal to allow the jury even to consider this defense.

This left the central legal issue: whether there was a duty by the hotel to take reasonable care to protect a guest, even though that guest was not within the confines of the hotel. In its decision, the circuit court found that reasonable care was too low a standard under Louisiana law. In fact, the court found, hoteliers owe their guests a *high* degree of care.

To reach this conclusion, the judges first considered the opinion of the Louisiana Supreme Court in a recent case:

> An innkeeper does not insure his guests against the risk of injury or property loss resulting from violent crime. The innkeeper's position vis-a-vis his guests is similar to that of a common carrier toward its passengers. Thus, a guest is entitled to a high degree of care and protection. The innkeeper has a duty to take reasonable precautions against criminals.[7]

Commenting upon the Supreme Court finding, the circuit-court judges wrote:

> The distinction is no doubt rooted in the belief that business patrons of innkeepers, like those of common carriers and unlike those of other businesses, have entrusted their personal security to the innkeeper.[8]

High Degree

The circuit court found, therefore, that the district court had erred in instructing the jury that the innkeeper owed his guests a duty of reasonable care, rather than a high degree of care. Even under the lesser standard of reasonable care, however, the jury had found in favor of the dead man's family.

A more difficult issue to resolve was whether the hotel's responsibilities extended beyond the confines of the hotel property. There were no court cases from Louisiana bearing on this issue, and few from outside the state. Accordingly, the circuit court began its consideration with the tort law itself. Although Louisiana is the only state whose laws are based on the Code Napoleon, its tort law is not substantially different from that prevailing in the other 49 states. One authority on tort law commented on the extent of the innkeeper's invitation (and duty) to a guest:

> This area of invitation will, of course, vary with the circumstances of the case. It extends to the *entrance of the property* and to a safe exit after the purpose [of the visit] is concluded [emphasis added].[9]

From this research, the circuit court determined that general tort law did not prevent the Banks family from suing the hotel for something that happened outside its door. In the absence of relevant Louisiana laws or court cases, the circuit court turned to four seemingly similar cases from other jurisdictions. In one, a woman walking through a vacant lot on the way to a refrigerator-supply store was injured, and the court found that the store had a duty to maintain a safe walkway.[10] In another, a court said that a grocery store was responsible for an injury occurring in the entranceway to the store's parking lot.[11] In a third case, a hotel was found to have a duty to warn its guests of dangerous waves in the ocean along its beach frontage.[12] In a final case, the plaintiff fell on an unlighted ramp that was not part of the defendant grocery store's premises. An appeals court affirmed the verdict for the customer, stating:

> It was, of course, unimportant that the concealed ramp, into which the plaintiff fell, was not in the occupation and control of the defendant as lessee.[13]

While none of these cases involves the precise situation found in the *Banks* case, each provides a reasonable analogy. The circuit court concluded that holding the hotel liable for an injury outside its front door was sensible, because:

. . . the innkeeper is able to identify and carry out cost-justified (reasonable) preventive measures on the premises. . . . As between innkeeper and guest, the innkeeper is the only one in a position to take the reasonable necessary acts to guard against the predictable risk of assaults. He is not an insurer, but he is obligated to take reasonable steps to minimize the risk to his guests within his sphere of control.[14]

In summary, the court found that a hotel has a duty to take reasonable care for the safety of its guests, and that the duty extends to adjacent areas where guests are likely to go and where the hotel could effectively maintain control of safety.

This case does not, however, stand for the proposition that hotels are made responsible for guests injured while miles away from their hotel, as some have speculated. Dr. Banks, after all, was just four feet from the hotel's entryway. Exactly how far the hotel's responsibility does extend has not been determined. The measure in most negligence cases is what is reasonable under the circumstances.

MANAGERIAL APPROACHES

The court in this case has clearly stated that hotels have a duty to protect their guests, even when the guests are not within the building. This creates a new dimension in managerial responsibilities. For the Hyatt in New Orleans, the determination of what was reasonable hinged on the hotel's response to indications of danger. The hotel management's responsibilities for protecting a guest seem to revolve around the "foreseeable harm" to guests in areas adjacent to the hotel, and the hotel's ability to manage and control that harm.

The courts noted that the hotel's security arrangements for its guests need extend only to the hotel entrance and the immediate surrounding area. Hotels, however, are notorious and obvious targets for legal action under the doctrine that the hotel must take an extra degree of care for its guests. Courts have historically absolved or limited hotels' responsibilities when the hotel has maintained reasonable policies and procedures to cover most contingencies.

If you can predict where your guests will travel in your immediate area, you can adjust your service, training, and policy routines to ensure guest safety and maximize guest utilization of your facilities. Attorneys who represent plaintiffs in liability cases will tell you (off the record) that it is difficult to represent a client who has been hurt because he did something stupid, *if* the hotel had a well–developed policy that included good personnel processes, adequate supervision, regular inspection, and complete documentation.[15]

In this instance, the need to establish "foreseeable harm" is the foundation of the hotel's policy. Your management should assess the question of danger to guests from criminals in your vicinity, and, from that assessment, develop operational activities designed to protect guests from that danger.

UNDER SIEGE

Guests generally do not want to stay in a hotel that seems to be operating under "siege conditions," and they don't want to feel incarcerated in a hotel. Moreover, there are vast numbers of attractions for guests in an urban hotel's immediate vicinity. As a manager, you can predict with fair accuracy which of these attractions will draw most of your guests.

One way to think about which areas are most attractive is through a "gravity model," which states that most of your guests will go to areas that offer sufficient fun or entertainment to overcome the inconvenience or danger of going to those areas. The gravity model has been widely applied in transportation planning, but it has not yet been used for the purpose of developing a hotel's management policy.

You can gather specific information on criminal activity in various areas of your city at various times of the day. It may be that certain neighborhoods adjacent to your hotel are perfectly safe in the daylight, but are troublesome at night. It is up to you to determine which of these areas might threaten "foreseeable harm" and which areas are "attractors." Certainly if police statistics indicated incidences of violent crime in any of the blocks adjacent to your hotel, that information should be made available to your guests.

It may be that defining all potential areas of foreseeable harm is not necessary from the standpoint of liability, but for the purposes of guest service, you may want to cover all neighborhoods in your vicinity.

PERSONNEL POLICIES

Because of the high duty placed on hotels in the *Banks* case, you will need employees who are able to carry out your security policies. To begin with, if there is an identified risk in your immediate area, the obvious presence of hotel security employees at the perimeter of the hotel property is probably a minimum element of high care.

In this context, carefully designed recruiting and hiring policies are essential. The people to whom you are entrusting the protection of your guests must be able to pass background checks involving careful scrutiny. You can be held liable if you have overlooked an item in an employee's background because of overly cursory reference checks (Marshall and Bellucci 1985). Needless to say, you want to hire people who can help you improve guest security, not those who would contribute to the problem.

The standard of a high degree of care also argues for a strong training program. Security employees, for instance, need to be trained in what the potential hazards are, how far they can exercise their authority and responsibility, when to call the police, and what to do in the meantime. Your employees must also understand how they are to interact with guests, when the latter must be warned, for instance, that they are entering a hazardous area.

KEEPING TRACK

Establishing a program of "high care" supervision requires setting policies, keeping records, and seeing to it that prescribed procedures are actually being followed. You should keep training records on your employees and adhere to a system of reg-

ular performance reviews. You should also inspect your security arrangements periodically to ensure that they are up to the hotel's quality standards.

PAPER CHASE

Documentation creates a "paper trail" that demonstrates your hotel's provision of a high degree of care to hotel guests. This paper trail, which can be extensive, should contain the following:

- A written policy outlining procedures, activities, actions, and personnel to implement the policy
- A record of recruiting practices, applications, background checks, and training materials
- Documentation of supervision and inspection
- Reports of inspections of personnel, grounds, and environments and
- Reports of specific incidents related to criminal activity, potential criminal activity, or unusual events in the immediate area surrounding the hotel

This trail of documentation provides the groundwork for a solid defense should something go wrong. In enterprises that deliver a wide range of social services, this is called "covering yourself in paper." In any situation that is fraught with some element of risk, professionals in these endeavors document, as completely as possible, preventive measures taken and facts attendant to the issue at hand. Attention to these details will put you in the enviable position—in the words of one attorney—of having your insurance agent send a limousine for you and buy you lunch when it's time to negotiate insurance premiums.

TWO VIEWS

Hotel managers can choose to view the outcome of the *Banks v. Hyatt* case in two ways. The narrow view is that this decision applies only to Louisiana hotels and holds little interest in a larger context. But this view ignores the fact that, in making its decision, the circuit court looked at cases in other jurisdictions. Eventually, a similar case will be filed in another district or circuit, and the judges there will look at the *Banks* case for guidance. Moreover, the *Banks* decision may even encourage other people to bring suit, if they have experienced a situation that is somehow similar.

We suggest taking a broader view—specifically, that the legal climate in which we manage our businesses is an essentially hostile environment. Legal statutes, administrative codes, and case law limit our managerial freedom. A policy like the one we propose here will go a long way toward making your operation and your guests secure in this environment.

Keepers of the Keys: Concierges in American Hotels

Glenn Withiam

Nearly unknown in the U.S. just a decade ago, concierge service has expanded rapidly to many hotels—either for the hotel as a whole or for exclusive executive-level floors—and concierge service is planned for many new properties, especially those in large cities. The concierge has long been a hallmark of European hotels, and the services offered by the concierge are limited only by human ability. For this article, *The Quarterly* wanted to discover who the American concierges are, what they do, and why the service is offered.

Although concierge service has been established in Europe for more than a century, the date of importation to the United States is not certain. Hilton dates its concierge concept to the acquisition in 1949 of the Waldorf-Astoria, which had a concierge in the Waldorf Towers starting in the late 1930s. Another long-running concierge service is that at the St. Moritz in New York, which had a concierge when real-estate developer Harry Helmsley purchased it in the early 1960s.

BY ANY OTHER NAME

The exact number of hotels with concierges is difficult to determine, partly because large hotel chains

This article was originally published in the November 1983 issue of *The Cornell Hotel and Restaurant Administration Quarterly,* and is reprinted here with the permission of the Cornell University School of Hotel Administration. © 1983.

cannot say which of their franchises have a concierge. Further complicating the effort to tally concierges in the U.S. is a confusion of titles and duties. Sheraton counts at least 21, mostly at its larger properties; 20 of the 21 Four Seasons properties have concierges; Dunfey's six "classic" hotels have concierges, while other Dunfey hotels use the title "guest-service staff." Fifteen of the 24 Westin hotels in the U.S. have concierges, while the remaining nine have a "guest-service director."

Hyatt hotels with "Regency Clubs" usually have concierges in the main lobby, but also have a person designated as concierge specifically for the upper level. The two jobs can be quite different. Hilton representative Louise Harris explained that the chain has ten properties with "Hilton Towers" featuring concierge service, but there are also many Hilton hotels whose bell captain also holds the concierge title. At the Boca Raton Hotel and Club, the concierge is an integral part of the management and is director of transportation service. At many Harley properties, an "ambassador's aide" functions much like a concierge. Certainly most of the larger luxury hotels have concierge service; smaller properties located outside of metropolitan or resort areas tend not to have concierges.

Although luxury-class hotels are practically forced by strong competition to provide a concierge, the need for the service seems clearly established. Lorraine Abelow, a spokesman for Helmsley Hotels, said simply, "The concierge service is implemented to cater to the business traveler." Westin representative Greg Koller pointed out that concierge service can be a competitive advantage. "If one hotel has a concierge, the word gets around; so another hotel says, 'We have to get that.'" Hilton's Harris added, "Hoteliers have come to realize that the frequent business traveler is a steady market—that's where it's at for marketing." She said that the other group attracted by concierge service is foreign travelers. Even at properties without a tower concierge, Hilton operates "international desks" to serve those from overseas.

More than a marketing technique, the concierge is viewed as a necessary "extra" for the service-oriented hotels. "It's what we strive for—better service," said Leona Helmsley, president of the Harley and Helmsley chains. Helmut Horn, manager of the Ambassador East in Chicago, said, "Hotel operators are realizing how important individual guest service is. The concierge is very necessary; to me the concierge should be the anchor person of the hotel, the nerve center of the hotel." Jack Nargil, chief concierge of the Washington Four Seasons, expanded on that idea: "The true concierge is the orchestrator who maintains control of the lobby, sets the tone of the hotel, and monitors the mannerisms and habits of the individual employees. The concierge sees to it that the hotel etiquette is maintained," he said.

On the other hand, the Greenbrier of West Virginia has no concierge, nor does it need one, according to Ted Kleisner, director of operations. He explained that all guests' needs and requests are handled by persons in the more traditional American positions; an executive assistant manager oversees all guest services. "The assistant managers are the pivot persons for guests' requests," he said. Unlike patrons of urban hotels, guests at the Greenbrier resort rarely need help with reservations or scheduling off the premises. "We'd just as soon leave the concierge title in Europe," Kleisner added. "With our 6,500-acre property, we do it all for our guests."

EDUCATING GUESTS

Although frequent travelers have become more accustomed to using concierge service, many hotel guests still need to learn about the function. "Many guests don't know what we do, so we get phone calls," said Virginia Santana, concierge at the Grand Hyatt in New York. "They are concerned that they will have to pay extra for our service, so they are hesitant. Once they discover that there is absolutely no charge, they come to our desk sometimes four or five times." Madeleine Berman, concierge at the Meridien Hotel in Boston, also finds herself educating her guests: "Sometimes the guests just call to ask the telephone number of an airline, and I volunteer to help them by making the call and reservation myself. In effect I'm doing what a travel agent would be doing."

The Parker House's solution to the education problem is a policy of calling guests with a welcome shortly after they arrive in their rooms. "This opens a relationship with the guest, and encourages continuing communication," said manager Philip Georgas. John Neath, concierge at Houston's Inn on the Park, said that he doesn't serve as many people as he'd like to, because guests are still learning about the service, but he added that this is improving because Inn on the Park now also welcomes guests with a call after they first check in. Nargil sees another educational responsibility—teaching management to structure the job correctly. "The amazing thing is that people get the job of concierge, but they don't know what to do. That's absolutely unbelievable. It's a case of management failing to give proper support and training, because they are not committed to the concierge idea."

As a result of the many efforts to promote the concierge and educate the public about the service, travelers are increasingly responding to the service. "Awareness is growing," says Koller. "More and more travelers know what the concierge can do to serve them." At the Grand Hyatt, for example, Santana feels the guests' response firsthand. She commented that by 4:00 in the afternoon guests are lined up several deep at her desk in the main lobby. "It's possible that concierge service is offered because everybody else is doing it, but I think that the truth is that hotels have started to recognize the need travelers have for this service," she said. Santana is convinced that frequent visitors to the Grand Hyatt return partly because of her service.

"Absolutely," concurred Neath. "Three-fourths of our return guests come back because of the extra service. Any hotel can have amenities, but the luxury hotel must offer extra to the guest."

Marjorie Silverman, chief concierge at the Westin Hotel in Chicago, agreed that travelers need concierge service. "As the traveling public has become more sophisticated, hotel services have become more sophisticated," she says. "We minister to the needs of the traveler."

Although she believes European guests look for the service, Anni Hauth, chief concierge at the Ambassador East, added, "Americans who have traveled to Europe have discovered the concierge and discovered how valuable the service is."

The presence of concierge service alone may not necessarily attract guests to a hotel, but as part of a total package of services it is important, commented Robert Dirks, director of marketing for the Waldorf-Astoria. "If we didn't have one, we would feel the effects," he added.

Once they are acquainted with the idea of concierge service, many guests come to expect it. "We have many businessmen here," Berman said, "and since they travel extensively, they are accustomed to using our service." Silverman sees the demand for the service growing. "Much of what we do now involves information, but it will eventually be more and more direct services," she said.

MANY PATHS

Unlike the European tradition of apprenticeship and long attachment to a hotel, the American concierges have a wide variety of job histories and backgrounds. Natalie Moss, who has been concierge at Halloran House for just over a year and a half, said,

"I just fell into it. I had been doing customer service for Ingersoll-Rand, but wanted to try the hotel business." A native New Yorker, she credits her knowledge of the city for her success as a concierge.

The Waldorf's concierge, Herbert Tepper, has been in the hotel business all his life, having held management posts at some hotels. He has been in his current position for five years.

Brian Weider, chief concierge at the St. Francis in San Francisco, once ran a bed-and-breakfast inn, but spent most of his time with the guests instead of overseeing the physical plant. "The owners said, 'Brian, be a concierge.' My first reaction was, 'What's that?' but when I found out, I developed a proposal for Westin."

Nargil comes from a hotel family, although he spent much of his career before becoming a concierge as a political organizer. He has been the chief concierge at the Washington Four Seasons since it opened four years ago.

Silverman has been concierge at the Chicago Westin for three and a half years. "I was returning to work after raising my family," she said, "and I was interested in the hotel. I looked at different areas, but the concierge office was just opening. Since I speak two languages and know the city well, I wrote up a presentation on why I would be a good concierge." Silverman believes knowledge of a city is important, but points out that some concierges are itinerant, traveling to new hotels to set up the service. Although it is difficult at first to "learn" the city, she considers the basic resourcefulness characteristic of most concierges the crucial talent in establishing concierge service.

Although she has been with Hyatt for three years, Santana has been concierge at the Grand Hyatt for just over a year. As a management trainee, she helped Hyatt open the hotel, setting up maintenance and cleaning service contracts. A 20-year resident of New York who holds a marketing degree from Pace University, she prefers to hire staff who are "Hyatt-ized" (those who understand the Hyatt system) and to train them to be concierges.

After 15 years in Boston, Berman, a native of France, is well acquainted with her city. She has been a concierge at the Meridien for two years, having begun by walking in the door at the Copley Plaza when it was launching its concierge service. "Previously, I did an internship with the Tourist Bureau in Boston," she recalled, "and that allowed me to meet many people and learn a great deal about the city." She moved from the Copley to the Meridien to open its concierge service because of the latter hotel's French origin.

The German-born Hauth became familiar with concierges from her time in Europe. Previously a social worker, she wanted to continue in a service-oriented business. An overseas origin is not unusual for concierges; Liloo Alim, concierge at the Four Seasons Hotel in Ottawa, for example, was born in Bombay.

Neath, on the other hand, is a third-generation resident of Houston who has opened three restaurants, operated a Caribbean resort, and lived in Mexico. Once the thrill of opening the restaurants deteriorated into the routine of daily operations, Neath found he became restless. By contrast, of his two years as concierge at Inn on the Park, he said, "Every day is different."

The ability to speak at least one language other than English seems to be crucial to the successful metropolitan concierge. Moss said that most concierge departments hire staffers who have complementary language skills so that a variety of languages are understood. She, for instance, speaks Italian, while Silverman speaks two languages, and Berman is a native French speaker. One of the concierges at the Ambassador East speaks five languages; Hauth said it is important to make international travelers feel at home.

SETTING A TONE

The size and structure of concierge staffs vary somewhat from property to property, while the hours of the service range from about 14 hours per day to 24-hour coverage. The chart in Exhibit 1 compares the hours and staff sizes of a variety of properties. Berman, Silverman, and Neath are all

EXHIBIT 1
A comparison of concierge staffs at some hotels

Hotel	Number of Rooms	Concierge Staff Size	Coverage Hours
Ambassador East, Chicago (Dunley)	282	4	7 AM–1 AM
Boston Meridien	328	3	7 AM–12 AM
Chicago Westin	750	3	7 AM–9 PM
Four Seasons, Washington	218	6	7 AM–1 AM
Grand Hyatt, New York	1,350	6	7 AM–11:30 PM
Greenbrier, White Sulphur Springs (WV)*	700	3	7 AM–1 AM
Halloran House, New York	700	2	8 AM–11 PM
Inn on the Park, Houston (Four Seasons)	384	3	7 AM–11 PM
Parker House, Boston (Dunfey)	545	3	6:30 AM–12 AM
Park Lane, New York (Helmsley)	640	5	24-hour
St. Francis, San Francisco (Westin)	1,167	6	7 AM–10 PM
Sheraton Grande, Los Angeles	470	3	6 AM–12 AM

*Does not use concierge title.

responsible for the bell staff, as is Weider. The Boca Raton Hotel and Club's concierge, Chauncey Cottrell, supervises the bell staff, the door staff, the baggage room, and drivers. The assistant managers at the Greenbrier also handle bell and door staff, porters, valets, and escort services. Nargil is responsible not only for the door and bell staff, but also all telephone contacts, mail, and keys.

Santana's department, on the other hand, is separate from the bell staff, but is part of the rooms division. The Grand Hyatt will soon be adding more staff to run a separate concierge desk for its "Regency Club." While Santana's staff will continue to serve the entire hotel, the special desk will be reserved for the executive-level guests. This new plan at the Grand Hyatt is similar to that existing already at the Helmsley Palace, which has two concierge desks, one for general hotel service and one for its tower level.

For Georgas, the concierge is integral to the rest of the hotel operation. "Our logging system makes it foolproof," he said. "The concierge sees to it that in every operating function of the hotel our standards are maintained. In addition, the concierge makes certain that the guest is not lost from sight after checking in. The concierge calls the guest to make certain that all is well and to find out if the guest has any requests." The concierge's log is more than a record of the concierge's actions; it is a summary of activities in the hotel. In this way, the concierge has become part of the management structure of the hotel.

"This desk is as expansive as imagination and human creativity allow, but your creativity is stifled if management does not understand what the concierge is," Weider said. "American concierges deal with the hotel on an American level by alleviating problems for staff members. We don't have the intimidating European attitude; we have an attitude suggestive of helpfulness. My job doesn't end when the guest checks out."

Horn considers the concierge to be more than adjunct management. "To me the concierge service determines the character of the hotel you are staying in. The concierge responds to more than just the requests of the guests by instead providing structural services."

Nargil agrees that the personality of the concierge greatly influences the way the hotel presents itself to the guest. He explained, "The internal operation of this hotel is based on my knowledge of the city. Our guests, even when they are out on the town, can say, 'This is my hotel in Washington.'"

SPLIT HOTELS

On the other hand, restriction of concierge services is not uncommon, depending on the market orientation of a given property or chain. Marriott, for instance, now has eight properties with a "Concierge Level," similar in concept to Hyatt's "Regency Club" and Hilton's "Tower Level," all of which offer amenities in addition to the concierge—such as an honor bar, turndown service, and express check-out—to those staying on the special floor. Marriott representative Leslie Schlags explained that the decision to include a concierge level depends on the "customer profile and the extent of market demand" in the area surrounding the proposed property. Marriott also has 20 properties with an "executive-level" service that includes the same amenities without the concierge.

For hoteliers coming from the European hotel tradition, restricting the concierge to specified areas of a hotel is unthinkable. "Terrible! Terrible!" said Horn. "It's an absolute violation of the hospitality industry; we're not just a business." Helmsley succinctly commented, "It's nonsensical, I'm sorry to have to say." She likened restricted service to giving the guests on one floor a large towel, but refusing the same to those on another floor. Nargil said, "We believe strongly that the concierge should be accessible to all the guests. This is a perfect example of how the word 'concierge' is used to describe many different services. In my judgment, they don't have a concierge if they restrict it to specialized customers."

Far from restricting its service, the Ambassador East has offered its concierge to the surrounding neighborhood. "The hotel is in the midst of a high-class residential neighborhood. To be a good neighbor, we invited the residents to call when they needed help," said Horn. Hauth reports that the neighbors have responded to the offer. Once she was asked by a neighbor to find a genuine Sacher torte, and ended up calling a business in Vienna to find one.

Sheraton is upping the ante in its newly opened Sheraton Grande in Los Angeles. Not only does the hotel have a concierge, but it will have butler service on every floor. Hotel spokesman Joseph Giudice said that the butlers extend the services of the concierge. "It's like having a floor concierge," he said. In addition to working directly with the hotel's concierges, the butlers supervise the room service on each floor. Giudice added that Sheraton installed the service in its new flagship because "the high-end traveler will spend the money for a perceived return value." Sheraton representative Ellen Thomas said the decision on whether to have a concierge is left to each property.

THE GOLDEN KEYS

The question of membership in the American branch of Les Clefs d'Or, the international society for concierges, is greeted with a mixed reaction by American concierges, particularly those who have been on the job for a relatively short time. Membership in the European-dominated Les Clefs d'Or is by nomination and is restricted to those who have been concierges at least three years. Silverman, an officer, resists the notion that American concierges are somehow diluting the impact of the international society. "There are only some 60 members of Les Clefs d'Or in the U.S.," she said, "but the Italian chapter alone includes 1,000 people." Also an officer, Nargil said that membership in the society encourages American concierges to maintain standards. "The Europeans are beginning to understand that there is a future for the American chapter of Les Clefs d'Or. The key is to find long-term concierges, those who are willing to work in the job for five or ten years," he said. Hauth explained that a major point of joining Les Clefs d'Or is to gain added contacts. "It's a professional network," she said. "We do favors for one another. Wearing the insignia—the golden keys—makes me more noticeable and instantly recognizable." Membership in Les Clefs d'Or means the American concierge has more standing when calling a European concierge with a request.

Weider said that membership in Les Clefs d'Or is open only to concierges who are available to the entire hotel. So, for example, concierges in the lobby of a Hyatt hotel are eligible for membership, while those with the same title—but restricted duties—on the upper level are not considered true concierges. "I don't mean to be disrespectful to these people. They do a good job, but their main function tends to be food-oriented. They don't deal with doctors in the middle of the night, broken glasses, broken legs, and the like," Weider said.

"We are asking for the concierge to be a designated profession, with a patent on the key insignia and the concierge sign," he continued. He said this will reinforce the service-related image of the concierge, and prevent a confusion of titles and duties.

PERSONALIZED SERVICE

The work of the concierge has many common threads from city to city and hotel to hotel. Mail, safe-deposit boxes, tours, showing rooms, room keys, airline and other common-carrier reservations, and many requests for information form the daily web of the concierge's work. Since most concierge stations are located in the main lobby, concierges easily pick up problems referred to them from the front desk. Increasingly, however, patrons seek out the concierges first. Santana's desk is separated from the front desk by only a partition. "We have peak and slack times that complement those of the front desk. Often we can get a key or mail a check so that a guest doesn't have to wait in line for all the people checking in or out at the front desk."

The Washington Four Seasons has no front desk as such, just two reception desks. The concierge there performs much more as the traditional American front-desk staff does. Although Tepper's desk is located in the Waldorf Towers, his service is available to all guests at the Waldorf-Astoria as well.

Despite the common duties, the Parker House's Georgas sees many differences between the function from one city to another. "I opened the Berkshire in New York City," he recalled, "and I found great differences between the work of the New York concierges and those in Boston. In New York, much of the work involves getting theater tickets that are not available, or getting guests into exclusive restaurants where reservations are impossible. This is not the issue in Boston, although there are other needs." Santana echoed that perception, finding travelers in New York more assertive in their requests. "I don't know what the hotel would do without this desk," she said. "It's difficult to keep people content. Most of the travelers in this city are in a hurry to get things done." Dirks added, "For a concierge at a hotel that is not like the Waldorf, the duties would be completely different."

Most concierges attempt to take care of internal problems on their own, or with the cooperation of other department heads, rather than involving hotel management. Some are allowed more discretion than others in solving problems. Moss said, "I try to head off problems by going to the department head when a guest has a problem. I have a little leeway, and I prefer to handle things here. If a TV is broken, I'll call an engineer to fix it. No need to pass the buck." Moss says she has a good relationship with the department heads.

At the Parker House, the concierge has "all the leeway in the world," Georgas asserted. "They have the authority to advise the department of a problem and get action. The logs that are forwarded to me allow me to concentrate on corrections, and they open the top management's eyes to what is happening in the hotel. Sometimes we can lose track of what we are in this business for."

The mandate for the concierge is even stronger at the Ambassador East. "Even if it involves money, the concierge has authority to solve problems, with no question," Horn said.

Silverman finds that she sometimes is a "sort of ombudsman between the guest and the hotel. I get them to cut red tape and do things that they don't ordinarily do," she said. Silverman recalled that a French guest arrived with wrinkled clothes too late for regular valet service. She was able to find a room attendant to iron the clothes. "This is an example of the good cooperation we get," she said. On larger questions, her recommendation carries some weight with management.

For all the responsibility that the concierge holds, pay levels are relatively modest. House contributions can range from $12,000 to over $20,000. Many concierges are able to build their incomes through gratuities, although their services are complimentary. One estimate of tip levels was $7,000 or more per year, depending on the type of hotel and nature of the clientele.

The number of women at concierge desks in America represents a significant difference from the European tradition, where men dominate. Neath suggested that equal-employment standards contribute to this disparity. Horn, on the other hand, believes there are personality differences. "In women, we find a talent for helping people," he said. "Men are generally less impressed by that ethic." Hauth added, "Women are more mentally adjusted to the attitude of pleasing the guest." She believes the rise of women concierges in America has been an education for the male-oriented concierge establishment in Europe, which is finding that women can be just as powerful and as talented in the position as men.

Weider is vexed by guests who refuse to accept women as concierges. "It all started with the Hyatt Hostess program, which employed only women and perpetuated an image of cuteness and fluff. The positive result of this policy is that the field was opened for women, who now can show how effective they can be," he said. He recalled an incident in which one guest waited several minutes for Weider to finish a telephone call so the guest could ask him the location of a specific room. All the time another concierge—a woman—was available to help. "It's aggravating, sometimes it makes you go overboard to protect your staff," he said. "But no staff should be one sex or nationality. You need a mix."

ANYTHING AND EVERYTHING

Each concierge has a recollection of unusual or difficult requests that stand out above the everyday problems. Santana, for example, produced an entire wedding for guests who were coming to the hotel. "I received a call saying that guests who were coming next week wanted to be married. I found a hall, a minister, and flowers, and arranged for the blood test and marriage license." She also arranged to send the frame of a waterbed purchased in New York to Saudi Arabia. A more poignant story Santana tells is of an 80-year-old man who had become disoriented in the city, forgetting which hotel he was staying at. He came into the Grand Hyatt, and Santana phoned around the city to locate the man's hotel.

Silverman once had only 30 minutes to arrange a helicopter ride for a person going from O'Hare airport to a convention. Frequently, she must locate a pharmacist after hours for people with special medical needs. A larger job appeared at 4:00 one Friday afternoon, when she was asked to produce a houseware show the following day. She had to find a printer for party invitations, bartenders, and transportation, all within a 24-hour period.

Moss has found coats for ladies at a bargain by advising them which stores to go to and has hired private jets. "There's always a way," she says. The most unusual request she had was to get a birthday card, put a shoelace in it, and leave it in a guest's room. The shoelace was a birthday greeting from one friend to another, but the latter did not realize his friend was also in New York. Moss enjoyed participating in the surprise.

Neath created a VIP tour of the NASA space center during a recent space-shuttle mission, when the center was closed to the public. He was able to arrange a helicopter flight only by agreeing that the pilot would not know the final approach path to the area until just five minutes before he landed. "It required quite a lot of telephone time," Neath

recalls. "I practically live on the telephone. This is an example of how important is the knack for detail and follow-through for the concierge. It's just bulldoggedness; you never accept a 'no' when you're filling a request by a guest."

The telephone is an important tool for concierges. Weider logs 10,000 outgoing calls in a typical month, and racks up long-distance tolls of $4,000. The incoming calls, he says, are uncountable.

Horn told of the businessman from Iceland who called ahead with a list of things he needed when he arrived at Chicago: documents copied, translations of legal papers made and verified, airline reservations, ground transportation from the airport for himself, his wife, and his daughter, a separate car rental and a shopping trip for the latter two, dinner reservations, laundry (off-hours), and a typewriter in the hotel room. "This one person might have driven a normal hotel crazy, but the concierge should be able to handle all this, as ours did," he said.

Here are some other anecdotes collected from Dunfey's files: An Arab sheik wanted, within 90 minutes, five ballerina costumes and all of John Denver's recordings on eight-track tapes as gifts for his children; Herschel Bernardi didn't like his pillows, so the hotel purchased three goose-down pillows for him; one hotel patron called from out of town when he wanted to propose to his girlfriend, and asked Hauth to arrange a silver limousine complete with roses and a stocked bar, also requesting her to purchase a pair of gloves for his intended and to put a diamond ring on the fourth finger as a part of the proposal; when a departing guest left her full-length mink coat on a chair in the lobby of the Parker House, the concierge chased after her in a taxi, catching her only a few moments before she embarked on a plane.

Regardless of the request, Tepper pointed out, the network of contacts is the key to success. "Availability is also important; I tell the guests to contact me at home if they need something, say, on Saturday," he said.

The concierges agreed that they enjoy working with people and helping to solve problems. Berman said, "I think you have to be of a certain temperament, but you also have to know your way around." She believes a desire to be with people and to be open and friendly motivates most concierges. "One big aspect of the job is that you are the one person that the guests know by name," Silverman said. "They come to the concierge for all their problems." Moss relishes the job partly because of the chance to help people, but also because, as she put it, "The job doesn't require a lot of paperwork."

Weider believes concierges have a need to be of assistance and to help. "It's an instinct that must be fulfilled," he explained. "The opportunity to solve anyone's problems—it's all in your hands." Horn said, "It can't be a structured job. The individual must be creative, imaginative, and have a broad perspective." Helmsley believes an ineffective concierge is worse than none at all. "Have the right person or don't have one at all," she commented.

With the growing sophistication of travelers and the increasing efforts of hotels to differentiate themselves in a crowded market, the services offered by a concierge have become important to the hotel's position in its market. Travelers are now able to choose the level of service they desire based on the extent of concierge service—or lack of it. Some hotels are service-oriented—giving the guest anything that is needed. Some hotels may have the concierge title without the service; others will have the service without the title. "Some operations are trying to change, but we've been the same for 203 years," commented Kleisner. "If you're not going to do concierge service, don't pretend you're doing it." There is no question, however, that concierge service is well established in the United States and Canada and that any hotel that aspires to the luxury market must employ a "keeper of the keys."

Endnotes

[1]The average of 25.6 engineers per hotel is based on 73 hotels. The 74th survey reported an engineering staff of 365—undoubtedly an erroneous number. It's not clear whether this response was a misprint or a facetious response for a hotel of 496 rooms. The figure might be a tally of the total hotel staff. In any event, it was best to discard this particular response.

[2]A t-test of means found every difference to be statistically significant at $p < .05$.

[3]*Banks v. Hyatt Corp.*, 722 F.2d 214 (1984). The suit was brought in federal court on the basis of diversity of citizenship. When two parties in a suit come from different states, the plaintiff may bring the suit in federal court. In this case, the Banks family resided in Louisiana and the Hyatt Corporation was incorporated outside of the state.

[4]At the time of this case, Louisiana recognized the defense of contributory negligence. The law has since been changed to comparative negligence, but many states still permit the contributory-negligence defense. The essence of this concept is that the plaintiff's negligence was in part the cause of his injury, and the defendant should therefore not have to pay for the injury. The assumption of risk is based on the notion that the plaintiff (in this case, Dr. Banks) recognized a danger and accepted it.

[5]A suit was also brought against the property owner, Refco, but the trial court exonerated Refco from liability.

[6]In part, the judge said in his charge to the jury that an innkeeper "is liable for injuries to guests or patrons caused by intentionally harmful acts of third persons, if, by exercise of reasonable diligence, he could have discovered that such acts were being done or were about to be done and could have protected his guests or patrons by controlling the conduct of the [wrongdoer] or by giving adequate warning to enable the guest to avoid him."

[7]*Kraaz v. La Quinta Motor Inns, Inc.*, La. 1982, 410 So.2d 1048, 1053.

[8]*Banks*, p. 221.

[9]W. Prosser, *Law of Torts* 61, at 392 (4th ed., 1975).

[10]*Lowe v. Thermal Supply, Inc.*, La. App. 2 Cir. 1970, 242 So.2d 351.

[11]*Shields v. Food Fair Stores*, Fla. App. 1958, 106 So.2d 90.

[12]*Tahshis v. Lahaina Investment Corp.*, 9 Cir. 1973, 480 F.2d 1019.

[13]*Great Atlantic and Pacific Tea Company, v. Pederson*, 1 Cir. 1957, 247 F.2d 4.

[14]*Banks*, p. 226.

[15]For a discussion of the elements of a policy, see Denney G. Rutherford, "Managing Guest Intoxication: A Policy to Limit Third-Party Liability," *Cornell Hotel and Restaurant Administration Quarterly* 26 (November 1985): 64–69; and D.H. Kerr, *Educational Policy: Analysis, Structure, and Justification* (New York: McKay Publishing, 1976).

References

Aulbach, Robert E. 1984. *Energy management.* East Lansing, MI: Educational Institute of the American Hotel and Motel Association.

Borsenik, Frank D. 1979. *The management of maintenance and engineering systems in hospitality industries.* New York: John Wiley.

Marko, Joseph A., and Richard G. Moore. 1980a. How to select a computing system. *Cornell Hotel and Restaurant Administration Quarterly* 21(1):60–71.

Marko, Joseph A., and Richard G. Moore. 1980b. How to select a computing system. *Cornell Hotel and Restaurant Administration Quarterly* 21(2):8–18.

Marshall, A.G., and E.C. Bellucci. 1985. The high cost of hasty hiring. *Florida International University Hospitality Review* 3(1):5–14.

Rutherford, D.G. 1987. The evolution of the hotel engineer's job. *Cornell Hotel and Restaurant Administration Quarterly* 27(4):72–78.

Rutherford, D.G., and Jane Wiegenstein. 1985. The mentoring process in hotel general managers' careers. *Cornell Hotel and Restaurant Administration Quarterly* 25(4):16–23.

Saidel, David. 1981. A hotelier's guide to energy management. *Cornell Hotel and Restaurant Administration Quarterly* 22(2):57–62.

Wasmuth, William J., and Stanley W. Davis. 1983. Strategies for managing employee turnover. *Cornell Hotel and Restaurant Administration Quarterly* 24(2):68.

Suggested Readings

Books

Aulbach, Robert E. (with George R. Conrade). *Energy Management.* East Lansing, MI: Educational Institute of the American Hotel and Motel Association, 1984.

Borsenik, Frank D. *The Management of Maintenance and Engineering Systems in Hospitality Industries.* New York: John Wiley, 1979.

Burstein, Harvey. *Hotel Security Management.* New York: Praeger, 1975.

Ellis, Raymond C. (Jr.), et al. *Security and Loss Prevention Management.* East Lansing, MI: Educational Institute of the American Hotel and Motel Association, 1986.

Redlin, Michael H., and David M. Stipanuk. *Managing Hospitality Engineering Systems.* East Lansing, MI: Educational Institute of the American Hotel and Motel Association, 1987.

Articles

Anon. "Security: What Courts and Juries Demand." *Lodging* (January 1982):49.

Becker, Herbert P. "14 New Concepts of Energy Management." *Lodging* (October 1982):32, 35.

"Crime in Service Industries: Lodging Services." Reprinted with permission from *Crime in Service Industries,* Department of Commerce, Domestic and International Business Administration, Washington, DC, September 1977. Chapter 5: "Lodging Services." (Courtesy of the U.S. Department of Commerce.)

Haywood, K. Michael. "Managing Risk: Identifying and Controlling Losses and Assuming Risks from Perils." *Florida International University Hospitality Review* (Spring 1985):73–80.

Redlin, Michael H., and Lawrence M. Goland. "Submetering of Hotel Utilities." *Cornell Hotel and Restaurant Administration Quarterly* (February 1984):45–50.

Stipanuk, David M., and Thomas G. Denlea. "Cogeneration: A Way to Cut Hotel Energy Costs." *Cornell Hotel and Restaurant Administration Quarterly* (November 1986):51–61.

SECTION 7

Food and Beverage Division

INTRODUCTION

In an earlier section, in discussing the ways that hotel organizations have changed, it was pointed out that food played a significant role in the organizational structure and product/service mix of hotels in earlier times. It has been speculated that the pre-eminent role played by hotel foodservice in society became significantly diminished with the onset of Prohibition and during the 1920s. People stopped going to foodservice establishments where they couldn't "get a drink." Prohibition gave rise to competition from street restaurants that operated sub rosa as "speakeasies." These restaurants were not constricted by the very visible public nature of hotel dining rooms. This diminished role was compounded in many ways by the Depression years of the 1930s and the war years of the 1940s.

In general, it was very difficult for most hotels' foodservice to recover from the effects of recognition lost during Prohibition. It also proved extremely difficult during the years of economic downturn during the Depression and the uncertainty and reordered national priorities during World War II.

Well-documented major shifts in population and economic emphases began to occur at the conclu-

sion of World War II. Freestanding restaurants continued to compete very effectively with hotel foodservice. There was movement away from downtown or central-business-district hotels. Motels and motor hotels were built on highway and freeway interchanges to take advantage of the mobility of the American family. Fast-food restaurants also made a major impact on the away-from-home eating habits of the American family. Consequently, the cost of providing high-quality competition in the face of these forces was seen by many hotel companies as too great. The net effect of these factors was to lead many hotel guests and operators to believe that hotel foodservice was little more than a "necessary evil." For many operations this became a self-fulfilling prophecy, and hotel foodservice floundered for many years.

It should be noted that this trend appears to have been reversed in recent years. Of the many factors mentioned earlier that mandated organizational change (market segmentation, return on investment, demographic shifts, and so forth), it would seem that return on investment has played a dominant role in this turnaround. The "double whammy" issues of construction cost and return on investment expectations by people from outside the hospitality world strongly suggest that space devoted to foodservice should contribute at least its share to the profit structure of the modern hotel service system.

The articles chosen to be included in this section will touch on these and other issues that are important to the food and beverage function in the modern hotel organization.

FOOD

While operational management of food and beverage functions is well treated by many authors (see the Suggested Readings at the end of this section), the literature on food and beverage *managers* is fairly sparse. Carole Hackett's article on the "Woman Food and Beverage Manager," which is included as a suggested reading, provides some insights into this lack of research. The same can be said for Shock, Kent, and Karkouti's article on catering managers in this section.

Unpublished research by the editor suggests a demographic picture of the hotel food and beverage manager that can be characterized as a white male, between thirty and thirty-nine years of age, married, U.S. citizen, with a bachelor's degree in hotel administration, making more than $35,000 a year. Most of the forty-nine people responding to this survey had not held a job outside of the hospitality industry, and had held about four different managerial jobs in their five- to ten-year hotel careers. These people tended to be very happy with their financial and managerial positions and uniformly looked forward to continuing their careers in the hotel and restaurant business.

Data such as these strongly suggest a true element of professionalism among the managers of the hotel food and beverage function. While more research in this area is definitely needed, it should be noted that some major hotel firms now specifically recruit people who seek to start their careers in the food and beverage area of hotel service operations.

In 1966 Allen Hubsch suggested a number of prescriptions to revitalize hotel food and beverage service. His article is included here in order for the reader to judge how accurately these predictions

may or may not have been realized in the ensuing years. Hanson's article on food and beverage profit echoes some of the concerns raised by Hubsch and may or may not be seen as providing counterpoint.

At many hotels the operation of room service has been treated like the proverbial illegitimate child. Room service has been neither planned for nor designed for in new hotel construction. When providing close to full-service, in-room food and beverage delivery twenty-four hours a day as a competitive amenity became the fashion in recent years, hotels have had to scramble for ways to implement effectively in-room food and beverage service as a competitive comparison point. The articles contributed by Finn and Turk explore the dimensions of this issue.

Few would argue that a first-class executive chef should be anything but the norm to allow a hotel organization to compete effectively for food and beverage business in today's market. It is, however, fairly clear that the chef does not today have the dominant role that chefs had at the turn of the century. Given the importance of the food and beverage function, the question then becomes, Is the chef purely a technician or does this individual need to have developed a significant range of managerial skills to complement the technical and artistic training that we have come to expect from an executive chef? Guyette's research explores this question and suggests a framework for further analysis.

Finally, highlighting the increased importance of the role of all foodservice in hotels is the Shock, Kent, and Karkouti profile of the job of the catering manager. With the increased national attention and focus on the importance of conferences, conventions, and meetings of all kinds, those foodservice professionals who make it their specialty to plan and serve meals and beverages to large groups of people become increasingly important. It is these affairs that represent a significant contribution to the profit picture of hotel food and beverage service. The efficacy of a hotel's efforts in serving the group business market may very well be the difference between profitability of the food and beverage function and some less desirable outcome.

These articles represent only the range of issues that can be considered of potential interest to hotel managerial staffs. The reader is strongly urged to consider these issues, along with those raised in the Suggested Readings and other resources, to develop a clear picture of the complexities of managing the food and beverage functions within the context of a hotel's organization.

BEVERAGE

In any hotel that has more than one formal bar, there is usually a separate function within the food and beverage department called bar or beverage management. Ideally, all matters that concern spirituous liquors, wines, and beers will be coordinated by that office. The beverage manager will have responsibility for purchasing, receiving, storage, issuing liquor, wine and beer inventory, and, quite obviously, will have the managerial responsibility for controlling that inventory.

Additionally, the beverage manager:

- hires, trains, schedules, and controls all beverage and bar personnel;
- promotes the various beverage department services;
- coordinates the requests of other departments that require beverage services—for instance, banquet and catering, room service, chefs, management;
- assures that his or her department is in compliance with federal, state, and local laws and regulations.

The beverage manager administers or manages up to four different types of bars.

The front or public bar is that in which the guest can, if he or she so desires, interact with the bartender and other service personnel. There are provisions for guest seating at the bar itself, which may be part of a restaurant or a separate room or area. There may also be separate tables and stand-up areas available for beverage service. A front bar may or may not include provision for entertainment.

A *service bar* is a "hidden" bar that is designed to be used by the hotel's food and beverage service staff only. It may serve one or more foodservice areas and/or room service and it is designed specifically for efficiency and economy of service. In most cases, speed is considered to be the essential ingredient in service bars, over decorative ambiance. Service bars are typically centrally located in the back of the house out of guest view.

Portable bars are those that are designed for maximum flexibility and can be used in conjunction with beverage sales associated with guest activities anywhere in the hotel or on its grounds. This may be extended in resort areas to include recreational areas.

A new facility popular among many hotels is that of the *in-room bar, mini-bar, or honor bar.* While sometimes the responsibility for inventory of these bars rests with room service, the beverage manager in most cases is also deeply involved in their design, marketing, and control.

In many ways the beverage manager's job can be compared in terms of historical stereotype to that of the housekeeper. Often the beverage manager is one who has worked his or her way up through the ranks of beverage server and preparer, and through experience, longevity, and interest has become the beverage or bar manager. There is reason to believe that in many ways this may be changing. Like many other areas of management within the hotel, the beverage management function is now faced with a range of issues that are more sophisticated and complicated than those traditional beverage management problems of the past. It may very well be that the beverage managers of the future will have to be able to bring to their job a managerial, organizational, and administrative level of sophistication that heretofore has been unnecessary.

The articles selected for this section reflect some of these issues. Parker and Kent, for instance, explore some of the criteria that are important to understand and the problems that are attendant to the issue of utilizing live entertainment in hotels, restaurants, and clubs.

McConnell's article on the danger of requiring scanty costumes on female cocktail servers should be considered instructive. A number of recent lawsuits have been lost by hospitality firms based on this issue alone. If the hotel or restaurant cannot prove that a particular type of costume is not a bona fide occupational requirement, the employees are not required to wear them. Traditional wisdom about what customers want to see in terms of employee costumes is in the process of change.

Leigh Tunney's forceful essay on the trials and tribulations of the modern cocktail server is insightful. Part of the problem is, like it or not, that cocktail and bar personnel are generally stigmatized by guests and other employees as slightly immoral. This is a problem that managers must face and resolve. If you refer back to Dann and Hornsey's article on organizational conflict in Section 1, one of the reasons suggested for this sort of conflict is that employees may carry with them a stigma relative to the elements of their job. It requires sophisticated managerial tactics and strategies to manage and overcome problems of this nature. Very little has been written in the academic literature about the problems and issues of bar management. The articles and essays presented here serve to highlight current problems.

Hotel Food and Beverage Management

Allen W. Hubsch

Dramatic changes have taken place in the hotel industry's attitude toward food and beverage operations in the last ten years. The most significant change in attitude has been that food and beverage has become *important* as a potential source of new profits.

What caused this change in viewpoint? To some extent, necessity dictated it. With hotel occupancies sliding from the 1946 high of 95.5 percent to today's 65 percent, it was obvious that new sources of profit had to be found for survival. The greatest potential supplement to rooms profits lay in food and beverage where gross revenue almost equals revenue from room sales.

How could food and beverage facilities be made more profitable? In the hotel's immediate area, street restaurants and clubs were thriving. Could the hotel compete in this market? Studies revealed that people were eating out more and more. What was needed to attract the patronage of these local citizens? From the necessity for profits and from a hard study of both the competition and the market, there has evolved a new perspective of hotel food and beverage management:

- Profitable food and beverage operations became vital for cash generation.
- Well-merchandised food and beverage operations became necessary for the "image" of a hotel.
- New and exciting food and beverage facilities became important in giving an old hotel a "new look."

These considerations and others have resulted in six significant new developments in hotel food and beverage management:

This article was originally published in the November 1966 issue of *The Cornell Hotel and Restaurant Administration Quarterly*, and is reprinted here with the permission of the Cornell University School of Hotel Administration. © 1966.

1. Food and beverage facilities have become new profit centers.
2. A new food and beverage management style and operating technique have developed.
3. Food and beverage facilities have become drawing cards for guest room sales.
4. Hotel food and beverage operations have utilized street restaurant philosophies.
5. Spaces in hotels have been used more profitably.
6. Investments in new food and beverage facilities have shown profit leverage.

The purpose of this article is to review each of these six developments in greater detail.

FOOD AND BEVERAGE FACILITIES HAVE BECOME NEW PROFIT CENTERS

No longer can food and beverage operations be regarded as necessary evils. Each facility must prove its profitability—each must be a profit center. Emphasis, moreover, must be placed upon the most profitable areas of food and beverage activity. Hotel Corporation of America has found that the most profitable areas and their departmental profit percentages are:

- Banquet Sales (including beverages), which yield 25–35 percent profit.
- Beverage Sales in bars and cocktail lounges, which yield 40–50 percent profit.
- Specialty Restaurants (including beverages), which yield 20–30 percent profit.

Simplified menus, offering an appealing variety of foods, combined with standardized operating procedures, permit us to concentrate on our costs and selling prices so that we can maximize our profit margins.

A NEW FOOD AND BEVERAGE MANAGEMENT OPERATING STYLE HAS DEVELOPED

One new development in successful food and beverage operation has been the creation of the Food and Beverage Manager to supersede the old-style co-management role of Executive Chef and Maître d'Hôtel. In future years, I feel that the Food and Beverage Manager will become even more important in hotel management. Not only will he be well versed technically, but he will require superior management skills, as he must:

- Lead by motivating others under his supervision.
- Provide examples of what is to be done.
- Develop a team spirit and attitude.
- Analyze, organize, create, and develop.
- Uncover and tap the potentials of his market, merchandise his products, tighten his controls, and maximize his profit.

The new operating techniques involve forecasting, budgeting, and cost control systems based upon the sales potential of food and beverages served.

FOOD AND BEVERAGE OPERATIONS HAVE BECOME DRAWING CARDS FOR HOTEL GUEST ROOMS

A hotel's food and beverage facilities can have a significant effect upon guest room occupancy. The trend is for the traveler, whether businessman or tourist, to prefer a hotel or motel with a good specialty restaurant, a swimming pool, and other amenities that make for an enjoyable stay. Attractive restaurant, convention, and banquet facilities help weekend business because conventioneers and their families often come a day or so earlier or stay later in order to combine pleasure with a business trip.

A hotel's image as a good place to dine or hold a banquet makes for guest room referrals when local residents are asked, "What's a good place to stay in your town?" One of the leading restaurants in Hartford, Connecticut, is the Rib Room in H.C.A.'s Hotel America. Our experience has shown that residents of the "Insurance Capital" patronize the Rib Room and recommend the hotel to Hartford's many visitors.

The progressive hotel manager can usually be distinguished from the mediocre operator by his emphasis upon food and beverage management. In popular hotels, food and beverage activity tends to set the pace for the entire hotel operation.

UTILIZATION OF STREET RESTAURANT PHILOSOPHIES

New merchandising ideas and new management policies were needed to make hotel food and beverage facilities competitive with street restaurants—not only to attract local business but to keep hotel guests dining on premises.

Large, formal dining rooms opening off the main lobby were losing money and needed to be replaced with intimate, "atmosphere" rooms with direct access from the street. Menus needed revamping to emphasize food specialties that could be priced to fit the competitive market. Above all, hotel food and beverage facilities needed to be managed and promoted in the same manner as successful street restaurants if they were to capture their share of the restaurant market.

The result has been the hotel specialty restaurant—often several small specialty restaurants—with direct access from the street or parking area. These new specialty rooms are separately merchandised and advertised.

There is an old saying, "If you can't beat them, join them." Hotels, of course, have little prospect of putting street restaurants wholly out of business, but they can benefit by following some of their basic philosophies. Hotels can:

- Establish an easily identifiable image for a specialty restaurant.

EXHIBIT 1

*20-year trend of income and expense—400
hotels*

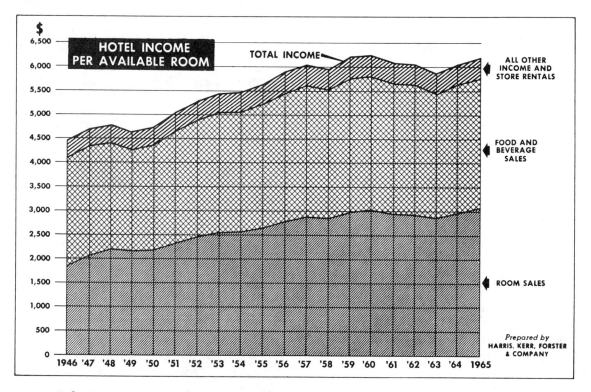

Sales Income & Rentals per Available Room

Year	Rooms	Food	Beverages	Telephone	Other Profits & Income	Store Rentals	Total
1946	$1,834	$1,471	$762	$177	$120	$ 67	$4,431
1947	2,045	1,559	707	169	131	70	4,681
1948	2,191	1,578	631	177	134	72	4,783
1949	2,163	1,499	599	172	134	74	4,641
1950	2,179	1,545	619	180	132	71	4,726
1951	2,321	1,663	648	181	136	75	5,024
1952	2,462	1,753	678	185	138	79	5,295
1953	2,542	1,807	686	185	141	82	5,443
1954	2,565	1,819	680	186	148	82	5,480
1955	2,652	1,868	705	186	147	85	5,643
1956	2,791	1,929	749	189	153	89	5,900
1957	2,891	1,962	754	187	157	85	6,036
1958	2,860	1,925	745	185	155	89	5,959
1959	2,993	1,999	776	193	149	99	6,209
1960	3,024	2,006	781	181	150	106	6,248
1961	2,950	1,945	768	177	152	104	6,096
1962	2,934	1,940	764	170	152	103	6,063
1963	2,866	1,868	734	159	147	100	5,874
1964	2,983	1,902	748	156	146	98	6,033
1965	3,078	1,944	763	158	149	102	6,194

(Source: Harris, Kerr, Forster & Co.)

This 20-year trend of income and expense for 400 hotels across the U.S. shows the importance of food and beverage revenue in total hotel income. Average 1965 income was $3,078 per room. Combined food and beverage revenue averaged $2,707 per room. In some hotels, food and beverage sales averaged higher, in others they were lower, in relation to room sales.

- Create an atmosphere that appeals to customers' "escapist" desire—period rooms, nationality rooms, steak houses, South Sea Isle rooms, garden rooms, hearthside rooms, and so on.

SPACES IN HOTELS ARE USED MORE PROFITABLY

Hotel operators have begun to realize that revenue from stores and offices in ground-level space cannot equal the profits that can be derived from a food and beverage facility, provided, of course, that there is a market for the business. Rental spaces, storage spaces, and little-used areas can often be imaginatively developed into bars, restaurants, private dining clubs, discotheques, or other types of facilities that can yield substantial profits.

Hotel Corporation of America analyzes the profit per square foot of all hotel property in order to determine ways in which to maximize profits. For example, the Royal Orleans Hotel in New Orleans had a seldom-used driveway at the basement level. This driveway, with its rough stone and brick walls, was converted into a 56-seat piano bar and lounge that now has beverage sales of $135,000 per year. The estimated departmental profit is 40 percent of revenue.

The Plaza in New York had 11,000 square feet of non-revenue-producing space on its lower lobby level. This was converted into a new 368-seat Trader Vic's restaurant, one of New York's most popular places to dine.

Many more examples could be cited. Look about your hotel for areas strategically located near well-traversed walkways—is there a place for another food and beverage facility? Can an unused storeroom be revamped into a private dining club? Can a "fast-drink" bar be built into the street corner of your hotel to replace a small rental store?

INVESTMENTS IN NEW FOOD AND BEVERAGE FACILITIES HAVE SHOWN PROFIT LEVERAGE

When a new food or beverage outlet is added to make expanded use of existing kitchen, dishroom, service bar, storage, and other essential space, the fixed costs of the existing facilities are spread over

FOOD AND BEVERAGE SALES (in millions)

1961	$26.8
1962	28.9
1963	27.8
1964	29.5
1965	31.2
1966 est.	33.8

During this period, Hotel Corporation of America opened two new hotels—Hotel America in Houston in 1963 and Hotel America in Hartford in 1964. The company terminated operations at the Edgewater Beach in Chicago in 1962 and at the Roosevelt in New York in 1964.

FOOD AND BEVERAGE DEPARTMENTAL PROFIT
Leverage Obtained by Incremental Sales

	Standard Food and Beverage Profit-and-Loss Statement	Incremental Sales Dollar
Sales	100%	100%
Cost of Goods Sold	35	35
Gross Profit	65%	65%
Payroll	30%	15%
Payroll Burden	6	3
Other Expenses	9	9
Total Expenses	45%	27%
Departmental Profit	20%	38%

a broadened new sales base. Normally, these new outlets can utilize existing staff, with a minimum of new employees, thus increasing staff productivity.

Leverage is provided by the increase in productivity of labor and the subsequent utilization of fixed cost factors over an increased sales base.

The figures on page 186 compare a standard food and beverage departmental profit-and-loss distri-bution with that of an incremental sales dollar whose variable expenses increase percentage-wise but whose payroll expense does not increase propor-tionately because of more productive use of labor dollars.

Clearly, incremental sales dollars can bring in profits at a rate that is greater than that from stan-dard operations.

Hotel Food Service: Where's the Profit?

Bjorn Hanson

Food and beverage (F&B) operations are generally considered an essential feature of hotels. But hotel restaurants' profitability has been in question at least since the development of the Uniform System of Accounts for Hotels (USAH) provided tools for measuring profits. In our firm's experience, de-partment profits from hotel food and beverage range from 10 percent to 35 percent of departmental rev-enue, depending on type of hotel and the sales mix (i.e., the extent of banquet versus restaurant busi-ness, and the ratio of food sales to beverage sales).[1] Such income figures are misleading, however, be-cause they do not reflect all relevant expenses (e.g., administrative and general, marketing, energy).

Depending on one's approach to allocation of these undistributed and fixed charges, the hotel F&B department is generally either unprofitable or, at best, less profitable than a comparable free-standing restaurant. Many factors affect the prof-itability of hotel F&B departments, and this article enumerates some of these factors and compares hotel food-service expenses to those of freestanding restaurants. The factors affecting hotel profitability can be grouped into the following three categories:

role and purpose, location and design, and staffing and organization.

WHY SHOULD HOTELS RUN RESTAURANTS?

The primary purpose of a freestanding restaurant is to generate profit for the owner, whereas the hotel's F&B operation is primarily a service to hotel guests. As a consequence, hotel food-service op-erations usually have different service standards and longer hours of operation when compared to free-standing restaurants, and the multiple food outlets in a hotel often engender diseconomies and dupli-cation.

Standards of Service

Often conceived as an amenity to reinforce the im-age and enhance the service level of a hotel, the hotel restaurant generally has a larger and more stable staff than a freestanding restaurant, so payroll costs are higher. The hotel restaurant usually has greater expenses for development and maintenance for the decorations and operating equipment, be-cause the restaurant must fit with the design of the rest of the hotel.

Another consequence of providing food service as an amenity is that hotel F&B outlets must offer

This article was originally published in the August 1984 issue of *The Cornell Hotel and Restaurant Administration Quarterly,* and is reprinted here with the permission of the Cornell University School of Hotel Adminis-tration. © 1984.

meals at breakfast, lunch, and dinner, seven days a week, and service levels must be up to the standards of the hotel at all times. In contrast, an individual restaurateur can select only the meals and days of operation that are most profitable.

Multiple Outlets

Larger hotels choose to meet guests' various needs by offering coffeeshops, medium-price restaurants, fine-dining sites, and specialty-theme outlets. Operation of multiple outlets, however, usually requires duplicate staffing, extra equipment, and expanded managerial controls. Multiple outlets also increase costs related to the distribution and movement of dishes, utensils, and supplies (e.g., breakage caused by extra handling, and pilferage arising from decentralization).

Room Service

Room service *is* an expected hotel amenity, but it is expensive to operate. Considering the setup, distribution, and collection of room-service trays and the cost of maintaining a staff to respond promptly to room-service orders, room service is by definition an inefficient operation that adversely affects productivity.

Employee Meals

It has become a tradition (and is sometimes a necessity) that hotels and restaurants provide meals to many or all employees. While the USAH requires that the direct cost of an employee meal be allocated to the employee-benefit account of the employee's own department, there is no recognition of the payroll and nonfood supply costs incurred by the restaurant in preparing and serving employee meals. Accordingly, the F&B department bears the major portion of the cost of providing meals to employees in *all* departments of the hotel, not just its own.

Location and Design

The intent of a hotel's design is to create an image for the operation—an appealing structure that is recognizable as a hotel. The hotel's location, likewise, is meant to attract persons in need of lodging (and not necessarily those in need of food). The hotel's design and location, therefore, may cut into the profitability of the hotel's food-service operation.

Location

A hotel site that provides excellent accessibility, visibility, and proximity to generators of hotel demand may not provide the same characteristics for restaurant demand. For example, proximity to a research park (usually a major generator of hotel demand) will likely provide a strong luncheon trade on weekdays, but little or no demand for breakfast, dinner, or weekend food service.

Visibility

Some part of the freestanding restaurant's volume results from prospective patrons' being able to see the restaurant and its menu. The image, price, style of service, and theme of restaurants in hotels, however, are generally not seen from the exterior of the building, so one of the primary avenues for marketing hotel F&B facilities is narrowed.

Size

Another outgrowth of hotel F&B operations' being provided as an amenity is the size of the facilities. Hotel restaurants are usually designed to accommodate peak occupancy, although the peak may occur only once or twice a week. A freestanding restaurant, on the other hand, is generally designed to promote high average seat utilization, and is accordingly smaller. In fact, many restaurateurs believe that it is good for their image to be busy, even to the point of turning away patrons. Because it is more costly to manage and operate a larger facility during low-volume periods, the larger hotel F&B outlets necessarily bear higher operating costs.

MANAGEMENT AND ORGANIZATION

While the owner is personally involved in the operation of most freestanding restaurants, this is seldom the situation in hotel F&B outlets. There may be owner involvement in motor inns and small hotels, but the owner of larger hotels is frequently an investment entity (e.g., a limited partnership), a development organization, or an institution (e.g., an insurance company). The consequence of corporate ownership is a more formal organization with more management, more detailed control procedures, and more participation by organized labor.

Management

The proprietary dedication of the individual restaurant owner who works long and irregular hours to cut costs and boost income is generally absent in hotel restaurants. In contrast to the heroic efforts of the individual entrepreneur, the hotel's F&B department typically has a food and beverage manager, a dining-room manager for each outlet, and a shift manager for each shift not covered by the dining-room manager. There is also more job segregation in a hotel (e.g., stewards, receiving clerks, food and beverage accountants), and substitutes are generally hired to fill in for absent employees (in contrast to the practice common to most restaurants of "stretching" existing staff). This extensive personnel structure means a higher payroll, higher related payroll taxes, and higher employee-benefit costs for the hotel.

Controls

The operation of multiple outlets and the complex organizational structure of the F&B department in a hotel require more income and management controls than are required in a freestanding restaurant. Control procedures in hotels are generally more detailed than in restaurants, requiring more forms, record-keeping, and reconciliations in monitoring sales, purchasing, receiving, and so on. Also, job segregation, the most basic form of internal control, requires more employees. In midsize and large hotels, another layer of control will be provided by yet another position, that of food and beverage controller or auditor.

Labor Costs

In many cities, either restaurants are less unionized than hotels or separate unions represent restaurant and hotel employees. In almost all cases, the benefits and wages are higher for F&B employees in hotels than they are for persons in similar positions in freestanding restaurants. In some cities, for example, hotels determine wage rates for employees who normally receive gratuities without allowing for a tip credit, contrary to the wage calculation for such employees in freestanding restaurants.

Even in nonunion hotels, employee-benefit packages are usually more extensive (and therefore more expensive) than those of restaurants. Nationally, hotels' payroll taxes and employee benefits average 28 percent of direct payroll, compared to 10 percent in freestanding restaurants.

Training

In many hotels, especially hotels operated under management agreements by medium-sized firms, there is a program to train personnel for immediate or future transfer to the firm's other locations. During the periods that employees are working in the F&B department, their salary and benefits may be charged to the department, thereby increasing food and beverage costs. It is true that some chains do not charge these employees' expenses to the F&B department (instead charging administrative and general expense or chain-wide training account), but even in these situations, some of the *other* employees in the food and beverage department will be spending their time training the new employees and not in serving guests.

RED INK

Because of the differences between the USAH and its restaurant equivalent, the USAR, a direct comparison of the profitability of hotels' food and beverage departments to that of freestanding restaurants is difficult. Part of the problem is the imprecision of attempting to allocate undistributed operating expenses and fixed charges on some arbitrary basis (e.g., square footage, ratio of sales, number of guests served). Instead of trying to allocate what the USAH considers undistributed ex-

penses and fixed charges, the table in Exhibit 1 presents a financial comparison of hotel F&B departments with freestanding restaurants by reformating the *restaurant* income statement to be more like that of the hotel F&B department.

Based on the comparison shown in Exhibit 1 (which reflects industry averages), freestanding restaurants' income on sales is 8.5 percent greater than that of food and beverage departments in hotels. The net profit or loss of hotel F&B operations can be estimated with a calculation based on the following two assumptions: first, that the undistributed operating and fixed charges applicable to the food and beverage departments of hotels are the same as those of freestanding restaurants (a con-

EXHIBIT 1
Theoretical income comparison of restaurants with hotel F&B departments

	Hotel F&B	Restaurants
Sales:		
Food	70.0%	74.0%
Beverage	30.0	26.0
Total	100	100
Cost of sales:		
Food	36.6	39.4
Beverage	21.7	27.9
Total	30.9	36.7
Gross profit	69.1	63.3
Other income	3.1	1.9
Total	72.2	65.2
Departmental expenses		
Payroll and related	41.9	31.0
Direct operating	8.7	6.2
Music and entertainment	2.9	0.8
Total	53.5	38.0
Departmental income	18.7	27.2
Difference		8.5%

Note: All figures based on Laventhol & Horwath data. Cost of sales is derived from a weighted average based on dollar sales per seat; therefore, the percentages do not add up.

servative assumption, since most operators would agree that hotel F&B departments' costs are higher than restaurants'), and second, that restaurants average profit of 3.5 percent of sales.

Here is the calculation based on these assumptions:

Freestanding restaurant profit	3.5%
Less: Differential in profitability	
(from Exhibit 1)	8.5%
Theoretical hotel F&B loss	(5.0%)

The reader should realize that this approach is simplistic (it uses data from different sources and understates the undistributed and fixed charges of a hotel F&B department), but it does tell us that hotel food and beverage departments in general operate at a loss of at least 5 percent of sales. Undoubtedly,

the loss is greater, because the above calculation minimizes the expenses of the hotel operation.

Mitigation

This discussion of a hotel F&B department's profitability has not emphasized the incalculable value of that department's contribution to the hotel's image, reputation, and ability to deliver guest services. Certainly F&B service allows the hotel to charge higher room rates, attract more guests, and gain a better market position. Most of the factors negatively affecting hotel F&B profitability cannot be eliminated, but the hotel manager who understands them can work to minimize their impact. At the same time, hoteliers should acknowledge the nonpecuniary benefits of hotel food and beverage departments.

The Executive Chef: Manager or Culinarian?

Wayne C. Guyette

In speaking of his vocation, the great French chef Paul Bocuse often compares cooking to music. For example, in Bocuse's opinion, both a finished dish and a musical performance depend on an element of improvisation that goes beyond the recipe or score. When this improvisation proceeds properly, the results are magical. It is the magic that matters to Bocuse. "For that reason," he says, "I would never use electricity in cooking. It has no magic. I have gas and the spit because a flame is alive. How could you be a blacksmith with no flame? Think what a poor fellow the Devil would be if all he had was electricity . . ." (Blake 1978).

This article was originally published in the November 1981 issue of *The Cornell Hotel and Restaurant Administration Quarterly,* and is reprinted here with the permission of the Cornell University School of Hotel Administration. © 1981.

Hotel general managers at American hotels, faced with the escalating costs of operating their food-service departments—rising prices for food, energy, and labor, and apparent waste in all these areas—are generally not so concerned with the magic of cooking. They are business people intent on turning a profit, and while their executive chefs may think of themselves as artists, the chefs clearly must operate as businessmen as well. This divergence in the roles and responsibilities of the executive chef, who is on one hand a culinary artist and on the other a business manager, represents a significant, if often overlooked, problem in the hospitality industry. The present study was conducted with the aim of clarifying the managerial functions of the executive chef, and of comparing how general managers and executive chefs perceive the chefs' responsibilities.

CULINARY ORGANIZATION

Most first-class American hotels use a modified version of the classic European organizational design for their culinary departments. The primary modification has been the addition of a food and beverage manager, who is responsible for all food and beverage activities. As shown in Exhibit 1, however, the chef retains extensive responsibilities. He is in charge of quantity food production, food preparation for catering and banquet activities, and preparation of food in satellite centers such as coffee shops, specialty restaurants, and room service. The executive chef thus has extensive dealings with the departments of purchasing, stewarding, and catering, and with the maître d'. As a department head, the chef is involved in the traditional management functions of planning, organizing, directing, and controlling, as well as the subfunctions depicted in Exhibit 2.

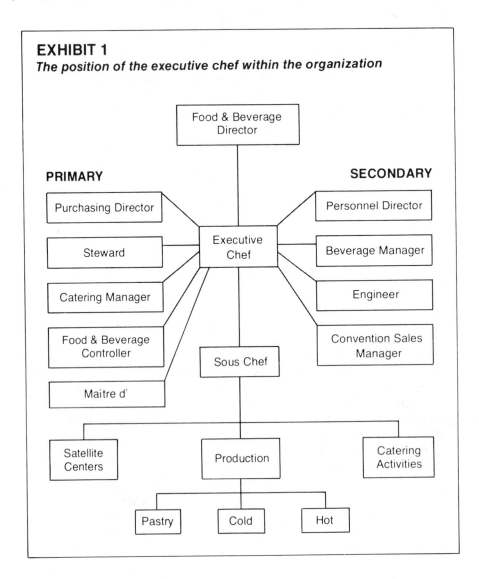

EXHIBIT 1
The position of the executive chef within the organization

The chef's most visible contributions to the operating performance of a property are in the areas of quality food preparation, timely service, and attractive presentation. Less visible, but just as important, is his potentially pivotal contribution to profitability through cost containment and reduction. As shown in Exhibit 3, the chef is in a controlling position to reduce costs in the broad areas of materials handling, food production, and human resources.

THE STUDY

In an attempt to determine how effectively chefs fulfill their various responsibilities, the author conducted two research studies during 1980.[2] Questionnaires were sent to 425 hotel general managers and to 425 executive chefs at the same properties.[3] The questionnaires were designed to determine each group's perception of how well the chefs were fulfilling their managerial functions as businessmen

---

EXHIBIT 2
The executive chef's responsibilities

Planning:	Organizing:	Directing:	Controlling:
• Budgeting	• Recruiting	• Initiating	• Auditing
• Forecasting	• Staffing	• Leading	• Reporting
• Decision-Making	• Hiring	• Motivating	• Observing
• Innovating	• Indoctrinating	• Supervising	• Comparing
• Dept. Policy-Making	• Training	• Communicating	• Evaluating
• Interpreting	• Assigning Resources	• Providing Stimulus	• Adjusting
• Analyzing			

EXHIBIT 3
The executive chef's contribution to profitability

Material Control	Production Control	Labor Control
• Preprocessed Foods	• Work Simplification	• Absenteeism
• Pilferage	• Equipment-Intensive Recipes	• Overtime
• Seasonal Recipes	• Assembly-Line Techniques	• Turnover
• Cyclical Menus	• Preproduction Procedures	• Grievances
• Requisitions	• Nonduplication	• Promotions
• Inventorying	• Equipment Scheduling	• Termination
• Spoilage	• Standardized Recipes	• Transfer
• Storing	• Portion Control	• Performance
• Verification	• Yield Analysis	• Scheduling
• Overordering	• Leftovers	• Sanitation
	• Overproduction	• Safety
	• Underproduction	• Training
	• Equipment Location	• Productivity
	• Preventive Maintenance	
	• Production Procedures	
	• Energy Usage	

and their operational functions as culinarians. Of the 425 questionnaires sent to hotel managers, 129 (30.4 percent) were returned, of which 60.5 percent were found usable (i.e., complete). The executive chefs returned 142 (33.4 percent) of the 425 mailed questionnaires, of which 60.6 percent were found usable. Participants were widely scattered geographically, with most of the 50 states represented.

Both surveys had four sections. The *demographic* section obtained data concerning the age and training of the executive chef, the number of employees he supervised, and the gross food sales of the property for which he worked. The *managerial-* and *operational-skill* sections presented a series of statements referring to managerial and operational skills that the executive chef might be expected to possess. Two six-point scales accompanied these lists of statements; the first focused on the desirability of the listed skills, the second on the degree to which the skills were currently being practiced. The last section of the surveys asked the chefs and the general managers to indicate their agreement or disagreement with a number of general statements regarding the role and status of the executive chef.

THE RESULTS

As shown in Exhibit 4, the typical chef was between 30 and 39 years of age, European-trained, employed by either a convention or metropolitan hotel with gross food sales of at least $2,000,000, and charged with supervising 20 to 59 culinarians.

It was found that general managers and executive chefs generally agreed as to what constituted desirable managerial and operational skills. However, the two groups disagreed significantly concerning the degree to which these skills were currently being practiced by the executive chefs.

Planning Skills

Approximately 90 percent of the chefs judged themselves to be good or very good planners. In contrast, only 63.3 percent of the general managers rated their chefs' planning skills as good or very good (see Exhibit 5).

The chefs perceived themselves to be interpreting their organizations' policies and procedures correctly and instituting those policies and procedures effectively through both short- and long-range planning. The general managers, on the other hand, gave their chefs significantly lower ratings as long-range planners and realistic goal setters. The general managers seemed to feel that their chefs had a good command of *reactive* planning skills—listening and understanding directions, developing short-range plans, and making firm decisions—but judged them to be less successful in the more sophisticated and demanding areas of *proactive* planning—developing long-range plans, generating realistic department budgets, and setting realistic goals.

Organizing Skills

The chefs also judged themselves to be better organizers than did their general managers (see Exhibit 6). Over 87 percent of the chefs rated their organizing skills as good or very good, while only 61 percent of the general managers thought their chefs were good or very good organizers. As in their assessment of the chefs' planning skills, the general managers were most dissatisfied with their chefs' performance in the more difficult and complex areas of interviewing, initiation of work simplification, supervisory training, and prevention of employee grievances.

Directing Skills

The chefs also rated themselves significantly higher in directing skills than did their general managers. Approximately 87 percent of the chefs rated their directing skills as good or very good, as compared to 58.3 percent of the general managers (see Exhibit 7). The general managers' ratings of their chefs exceeded their chefs' self-ratings in the areas of promoting employee morale, resolving conflict, dealing with customers, communicating with upper

EXHIBIT 4

Profile of the executive chef

	General Manager* Respondents (N=78)	Executive Chef‡ Respondents (N=86)
(a) Age of Executive Chef		
21 to 29	13.1%	19.5%
30 to 39	43.5	52.9
40 to 49	25.0	17.3
50 to 59	17.1	10.3
60+	1.3	—
(b) Executive Chefs' Formal Culinary Training		
American culinary apprenticeship program	20.0%	10.2%
European culinary apprenticeship program	52.2	43.0
Vocational-technical program	11.0	15.9
Two-year junior college	4.5	9.1
Four-year college	7.5	10.2
Other	3.0	12.5
(c) Type of Property		
Resort	18.4%	17.4%
Convention	42.1	43.0
Metropolitan	34.2	32.6
Other	5.3	7.0
(d) Gross Food Sales		
$300,000 to $599,999	2.7%	2.4%
$600,000 to $999,999	5.3	6.0
$1,000,000 to $1,499,999	12.0	12.0
$1,500,000 to $1,999,999	9.3	16.9
$2,000,000 or more	70.7	62.7
(e) Full-time Culinary Employees		
19 or fewer	14.8%	2.3%
20 to 39	28.4	41.4
40 to 59	23.0	29.9
60 to 79	5.4	11.5
80 to 99	5.4	8.0
100 or more	23.0	6.9

*Profile of the executive chefs as reported by their general managers.
‡Self-profile of the responding executive chefs.

management, and dealing with their own stress. The chefs rated themselves higher than their general managers did in the areas of portion control, sanitation, motivating employees, handling employee complaints, enforcing safe work habits, and developing teamwork. Both groups found the chefs to be most deficient in the areas of conducting productive staff meetings, counseling employees on problems unrelated to work, and using different leadership styles.

These findings add to the picture of the chef as an unsophisticated manager, beset with difficulties

EXHIBIT 5
Planning skills: Executive chefs' current skill levels

As rated by:	Very Poor	Poor	Fair	Good	Very Good
General Managers	1.5%	8.1%	27.1%	46.4%	16.9%
Executive Chefs		.5%	8.9%	44.9%	45.6%

Rating of individual planning skills*

	Ranking by General Manager	Ranking by Executive Chef	Difference
Make firm decisions	1	8	+7
Develop workable short-range plans	2	2	—
Listen to and understand directions	3	1	−2
Correctly interpret the organization's policies and procedures	4	3	−1
Write marketable menus	5	9	+4
Correctly identify and successfully solve operational problems	6	7	+1
Develop workable long-range plans	7	4	−3
Set realistic (attainable) goals	8	5	−3
Generate realistic department budgets	9	6	−3

*Column 1 shows the general managers' ranking of the chefs' mastery of each skill (1 = a high degree of mastery, 9 = a low degree of mastery).
Column 2 shows the chefs' ranking of their mastery of each skill.
Column 3 shows the difference between the general managers' and the chefs' rankings.

in accomplishing his managerial objectives. In addition, the wide and repeated discrepancies between the ratings of the chefs and those of the general managers highlight the pervasive and problematic isolation of the chef in the organizational structure of the hotel.

Controlling Skills

The category of controlling skills elicited the most agreement between the two groups (see Exhibit 8). However, the chefs continued to rate their overall performance as controllers significantly higher than their general managers rated it; 87.5 percent of the chefs rated their controlling skills as good or very good, while only 60.8 percent of the general managers gave their chefs comparable ratings.

Both groups gave the chefs relatively low ratings in the areas of controlling utility expenses, controlling labor costs, and reducing employee absenteeism and turnover. The general managers rated their chefs somewhat higher in appraising supervisor performance and reducing employee turnover than the chefs rated themselves, but lower in controlling labor costs.

EXHIBIT 6

Organizing skills: Executive chefs' current skill levels

As rated by:	Very Poor	Poor	Fair	Good	Very Good
General Managers	1.4%	8.6%	29.0%	42.5%	18.5%
Executive Chefs	.1%	1.1%	11.7%	41.2%	45.9%

Ranking of individual organizing skills*

	Ranking by General Manager	Ranking by Executive Chef	Difference
Promote positive attitude toward property	1	5	+4
Schedule work assignments	2	1	−1
Generate cost-efficient recipes	3	13	+10
Generate cost-efficient menus	4	8	+4
Delegate responsibility to subordinates	5	12	+7
Recruit an effective culinary staff	6	17	+11
Generate proper purchasing procedures	7	11	+4
Train culinary workers	8	6	−2
Promote food conservation	9	4	−5
Promote positive employee morale	10	7	−3
Alleviate employee grievances	11	16	+5
Delegate authority to subordinates	12	15	+3
Organize an efficient catering department	13	2	−11
Generate proper inventory procedures	14	10	−4
Generate standardized recipes	15	14	−1
Train supervisors	16	9	−7
Initiate work-simplification methods	17	3	−14
Successfully select new employees through effective interviewing techniques	18	18	—

*Column 1 shows the general managers' ranking of the chefs' mastery of each skill (1 = a high degree of mastery, 18 = a low degree of mastery).
Column 2 shows the chefs' ranking of their mastery of each skill.
Column 3 shows the difference between the general managers' and the chefs' rankings.

THE FINDINGS

Taken together, these findings show the executive chef to be a troubled and troubling manager, consistently evaluating his performance in the crucial managerial functions of planning, organizing, directing, and controlling more favorably than his superiors. While chefs and general managers generally agreed as to what constituted desirable managerial skills for the executive chef, there was significantly less agreement as to how well these skills were being practiced.

To explain these dramatic differences, it might be tempting simply to invoke the old saw that poor managers often overrate themselves. While appealing in its simplicity, such an explanation does little to solve the problems evident in the findings. A more constructive explanation of these data lies

EXHIBIT 7

Directing skills: Executive chefs' current skill levels

As rated by:	Very Poor	Poor	Fair	Good	Very Good
General Managers	2.1%	8.2%	31.4%	43.1%	15.2%
Executive Chefs	.6%	1.6%	10.5%	40.6%	46.7%

Rating of individual directing skills*

	Ranking by General Manager	Ranking by Executive Chef	Difference
Supervise minority workers	1	2	+1
Supervise female culinary workers	2	6	+4
Supervise young culinary workers	3	5	+2
Effectively deal with own job-related stress	4	12	+8
Promote positive employee morale	5	21	+16
Maintain effective employee discipline	6	1	−5
Effectively resolve conflict between culinary workers	7	20	+13
Effectively communicate with upper-level management	8	17	+9
Successfully deal with customers on a one-to-one basis	9	21	+12
Develop teamwork	10	3	−7
Enforce safe work habits of employees	11	4	−7
Communicate effectively through the spoken word	12	15	+3
Communicate effectively with peers (other department heads)	13	19	+6
Effectively resolve conflict between culinary workers and culinary supervisors	14	10	−4
Motivate culinary workers	15	7	−8
Counsel employees on job-related problems	16	8	−8
Enforce the use of standardized recipes	18	20	+2
Motivate supervisors	17	16	−1
Enforce positive sanitation practices of employees	19	11	−8
Handle employee grievances correctly when they occur	20	13	−7
Communicate effectively through the written word	21	18	−3
Enforce effective portion-control procedures	22	14	−8
Use different leadership styles when appropriate	23	22	−1
Counsel employees on non-job-related problems	24	23	−1
Conduct productive department/staff meetings	25	25	—

*Column 1 shows the general managers' ranking of the chefs' mastery of each skill (1 = a high degree of mastery, 25 = a low degree of mastery).
Column 2 shows the chefs' ranking of their mastery of each skill.
Column 3 shows the difference between the general managers' and the chefs' rankings.

EXHIBIT 8

Controlling skills: Executive chefs' current skill levels

As rated by:	Very Poor	Poor	Fair	Good	Very Good
General Managers	1.6%	6.5%	31.0%	42.8%	18.0%
Executive Chefs	.3%	.5%	11.7%	40.9%	46.6%

Rating of individual controlling skills*

	Ranking by General Manager	Ranking by Executive Chef	Difference
Control food cost	1	1	—
Reduce supervisory turnover	2	2	—
Appraise culinary-worker performance	3	3	—
Appraise supervisor performance	4	6	+2
Initiate operational and procedural changes effectively	5	4	−1
Reduce culinary-worker turnover	6	8	+2
Reduce employee absenteeism	7	7	—
Control labor costs	8	5	−3
Control and reduce utility expenses	9	9	—

*Column 1 shows the general managers' ranking of the chefs' mastery of each skill (1 = a high degree of mastery, 9 = a low degree of mastery).
Column 2 shows the chefs' ranking of their mastery of each skill.
Column 3 shows the difference between the general managers' and the chefs' rankings.

in the examination of the historical and organizational circumstances contributing to the disagreement. On the basis of such an examination, hoteliers and executive chefs may begin to consider what steps may be taken to develop more effective chefs and to foster a closer and more productive relationship between chefs and higher management.

HISTORICAL PERSPECTIVE

For many years, a large percentage of America's culinarians were recruited from Europe.[4] Many factors contributed to the prevalence of this practice. In the first half of this century, few American culinary training programs existed. In Europe, on the other hand, the culinary vocation was viewed as a respectable and important profession, and it attracted large numbers of young, committed trainees. Based on the painstaking development of basic skills and a rigid system of promotions, European culinary training programs produced chefs of great skill, who, attracted by the higher standard of living in the United States, often chose to settle there.

American hotel operators profited from these chefs' culinary expertise, but having failed to develop their own comprehensive culinary training programs and their own culinary manpower supply, were forced to accept the European role model for the chef. European culinary training has traditionally been based on the guild system, in which a kind of master-servant relationship exists between the head chef and his apprentices. Under this system, the young and impressionable apprentices are presented with an autocratic and authoritarian role model in the person of the head chef. As they rise through the system and attain the status of executive chef, the former apprentices internalize the authoritarian and autocratic characteristics displayed by their teachers. The apprentices acquire all the skills necessary to be fine culinarians, but, with this quirky and authoritarian role model, learn little about being competent managers. Over the years, this lopsided emphasis on culinary technique has become firmly entrenched within the organizational hierarchy of both European and American culinary departments, to the detriment of chefs' acquisition of modern managerial skills.

Even with the dramatic increase in the number of culinary-arts programs offered by secondary and post-secondary educational institutions in the United States in the last several years, upper management continues to contribute to the maintenance of this unfortunate role model through poorly conceived promotional policies and organizational designs.

ORGANIZATIONAL PERSPECTIVE

As shown in Exhibit 9, chefs typically attain their positions as a result of their performance as culinary craftsmen. This emphasis on technical skills to the exclusion of managerial skills in the promotion process creates a false perception among chefs concerning the skills required by their position.

In response to this emphasis, chefs often react by discounting the value of managerial development and subconsciously isolating themselves from exposure to contemporary management practices. This reaction exacerbates the negative effects of the promotion system, as the chefs attempt to avoid

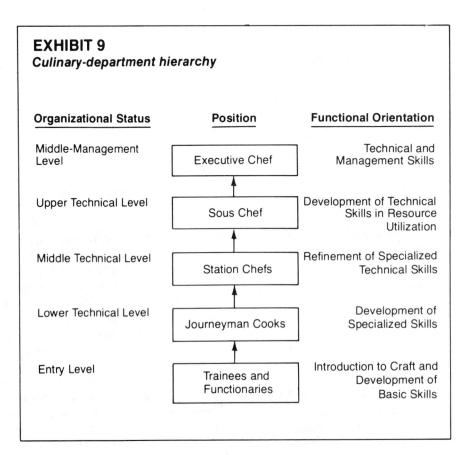

EXHIBIT 9
Culinary-department hierarchy

Organizational Status	Position	Functional Orientation
Middle-Management Level	Executive Chef	Technical and Management Skills
Upper Technical Level	Sous Chef	Development of Technical Skills in Resource Utilization
Middle Technical Level	Station Chefs	Refinement of Specialized Technical Skills
Lower Technical Level	Journeyman Cooks	Development of Specialized Skills
Entry Level	Trainees and Functionaries	Introduction to Craft and Development of Basic Skills

situations that would bring attention to their managerial deficiencies and gradually become more isolated from their departmental peers and superiors. Most destructively, the chefs often become generally frustrated with their work environment and alienated from upper management.

This vicious circle of conflicting perceptions and diminishing feedback is completed in upper management's response to chefs' managerial inadequacies. Rather than confronting the problem directly by discussing these difficulties with the chefs or establishing new promotion criteria within the organization, upper management often attempts to work around rather than with its chefs. Upper management relies increasingly on various quantitative measures such as food costs or labor costs to evaluate chefs' performance or simply becomes more and more frustrated with the managerially uninformed conduct of its chefs.

THE CURRENT SITUATION

Both chefs and general managers are clearly dissatisfied with the present situation. When asked whether their executive chefs possessed the managerial skills one would expect and desire at the chefs' salary level, 66 percent of the general managers said they did not. In addition, 71.8 percent of the general managers maintained that their culinary departments were plagued by more unresolved managerial and operational problems than any other department within their properties. Over 78 percent of the general managers noted that their chefs managed people ineffectively, and 98.6 percent of the general managers felt that their chefs' managerial skills needed improvement. In the view of the general managers, these problems will not soon be overcome. Over 87 percent of the general managers predicted that the industry would face serious shortages of chefs with adequate managerial skills five years hence, and 89.7 percent expected such shortages ten years in the future as well.

A corresponding degree of dissatisfaction, centering on their relationship with upper management,

was evident among executive chefs. In a series of interviews conducted with 121 executive chefs over the past year, the author asked the chefs what they most disliked about their positions. Three factors were cited by over 90 percent of the chefs: (1) poor communication with upper management; (2) the general manager's unawareness of the chef's problems; and (3) the lack of substantive appraisal of the chef's performance by upper management. Over 59 percent of these chefs had never been provided with job descriptions, and 80 percent had never been fully apprised of their responsibilities and authority by upper management.

It seems that both groups are aware of the difficulties surrounding the executive chef's role as manager. To date, however, the industry has done little to redress these difficulties, and what efforts it has initiated have been ill-conceived, undersupported, or undersubscribed.

Kitchen Managers

Several hospitality organizations have reorganized their culinary departments on the premise that chefs are, and will remain, poor managers and, therefore, must be considered expendable. The solution that follows from this premise involves the replacement of the executive chef with a kitchen manager, based on the idea that management of the kitchen need not be delegated to a highly skilled and expensive craftsman. If menus are cyclical or established at the corporate level, the kitchen manager needs only to schedule skilled and semiskilled station supervisors. Advocates of the kitchen-manager system maintain that it reduces labor costs while providing a consistent, standardized product. While innovative, this response to the executive chef's managerial problems can be faulted for a variety of reasons. Rather than developing managerial excellence, it limits both the managerial and the operational functions of the culinary department. Culinary employees will probably be frustrated by the elimination of opportunities for upward mobility and their performance will suffer as a result. In restricting individual creativity, this arrangement diminishes the opportunity for an adequate unit-level response to local market competition. In addition, the expansion of support staff and the probable increase in employee turnover resulting from this system could effectively cancel the reduction in labor costs obtained by eliminating the position of executive chef.

Training Sessions

A few corporations periodically bring their chefs together for group training sessions. Unfortunately, most of these sessions are devoted to company policies and procedures rather than to developing the chefs' managerial proficiency or a closer working relationship between chefs and upper management. Other organizations send their chefs to culinary training sessions. While valuable as a means of developing culinary technique, these sessions do little to promote chefs' managerial effectiveness or proficiency.

Recognizing the significance of these problems, the American Hotel and Motel Association has recently formed a culinary committee to investigate the issues surrounding the managerial difficulties of the executive chef and to determine how they can best be resolved. The hospitality industry would benefit if other national groups, representing the restaurant and club segments of the industry, were to follow the AH&MA's example and form their own culinary committees to deal with these problems.

The chefs themselves have also taken some preliminary steps toward clarifying and standardizing their responsibilities. The American Culinary Federation (ACF), an association of 10,000 culinarians, has recently initiated a certification program for cooks, working chefs, pastry chefs, sous chefs, and executive chefs. Although still in its infancy, the ACF's certification program is well conceived and, once fully established, will be helpful to both chefs and management. The program, however, is heavily geared toward the recognition of technical culinary skills rather than the development of managerial proficiency. Consequently, at this juncture, the ACF's certification program serves the industry primarily by providing a means of verifying chefs' technical proficiency and experience.

CONCLUSION

As the hospitality industry matures and grows more complex, there is an increasing need for organizational reexamination and role clarification. The position of executive chef is no exception to this rule; an effective executive chef now must possess both culinary and managerial skills. If the hospitality industry and its chefs are to maintain both the magic and the profitability of the culinary art in the coming years, new conceptions and policies regarding the role of the executive chef must be established.

A Table for 5,000? Right This Way!

Patti J. Shock
William E. Kent
Samad Karkouti

Catering executives or banquet managers must bring a wide variety of skills to their jobs. Catering executives plan wedding receptions, bar mitzvahs, elaborate state dinners, and annual banquets for Boy Scouts. They must have an impressive knowledge of food and beverages, and they must be able to guide a client through the intricacies of a major meal function, even when the client is not certain of what he or she wants.

The term "catering executive" has come into use only in recent years. The professional association, the National Association of Catering Executives (NACE), was formerly known as the "Banquet Manager's Guild." But "catering executive" is a better description of this person's function—half food and beverage manager, half salesperson, and all diplomat.

MAJOR HOTELS

Catering executives are far from the most numerous of hotel executives; NACE numbers just 1,000 members. They are employed mostly by larger hotels, although some work in large clubs, restaurants, or on cruiseships. Relatively few NACE members are off-premise or independent caterers.

WELTANSCHAUUNG

Because, as noted earlier, the "catering executive" is a fairly new breed of manager, the authors con-

ducted a survey of NACE members to compile a demographic and psychographic profile of these professionals. In addition to seeking demographic information, the survey included a job-satisfaction questionnaire to find out how these persons feel about their jobs. The authors received 197 responses to the survey, which was sent to all 1,000 NACE members (nearly a 20 percent response). While this sample may not be representative of the entire population of catering executives, or even of NACE members, it does afford the most comprehensive look to date at this important group of hotel executives.

YOUNG AND EDUCATED

Compared to the holders of other hotel-management positions, this group of catering executives is young and well educated (see Exhibit 1). The proportion of this group that is single (divorced or never married) is high, but no higher than that of other hotel managers. The fact that 60 percent of the respondents were female is not surprising, in view of the steady recent increase in the number of women hotel executives.

Hotel Majors

The large proportion of catering executives who majored in hotel administration in college is noteworthy. This proportion exceeds that found in a 1982 study of general managers, directors of sales, and directors of personnel (Kent 1982).

Because so many of the respondents reported majoring in hotel administration in college, the authors decided to test for any differences between

This article was originally published in the August 1986 issue of *The Cornell Hotel and Restaurant Administration Quarterly,* and is reprinted here with the permission of the Cornell University School of Hotel Administration. © 1986.

EXHIBIT 1
Demographic profile of respondents

College majors

• Hotel administration	29.7%
• Business	26.2
• Liberal arts	25.6
• Education	4.7
• Science	3.5
• Other	10.5

Income

• $0–$20,000	11.2%
• 20,001–25,000	18.8
• 25,001–30,000	23.0
• 30,001–35,000	12.8
• 35,001–40,000	8.7
• 40,001–45,000	6.6
• 45,001 +	18.8

Education

• Some high school	.5%
• High-school graduate	10.2
• Professional or technical school	5.6
• Some college	31.0
• College graduate	44.2
• Graduate work	8.6

Marital status

• Never married	35.7%
• Divorced	18.4
• First marriage	33.2
• Second (or more)	12.7

Age and gender

- Sixty percent of the respondents were under age 35
- Women outnumber men by a ratio of three to two

EXHIBIT 2
Analysis of respondents by college major

Respondents' indication of the helpfulness of their college degree in their career

Major	Percentage answering helpful or very helpful
Hotel administration	95%
Business	59
Liberal arts	57
Education	38
Science	50
Other	63

Median salaries of respondents by college major

Major	Salary
Hotel administration	$32,500
Business	27,500
Liberal arts	27,500
Education	30,000
Science	27,500
Other	27,500

this group and those who studied other collegiate fields. Respondents were asked to indicate on a five-point scale how helpful their education was to their career. As shown in Exhibit 2, hotel-administration majors were overwhelmingly positive about the helpfulness of their education—far more positive than any other group of respondents. Hotel-school graduates apparently perceive that their education gives them a real edge over those who majored in other fields. (Hotel educators, take heart!)

Pay Differentials

The survey indicated that hotel-administration graduates received a higher median salary than the other groups, but no firm conclusion is possible regarding this statistic. The differences in pay could be attributable to seniority, size of business, or age of respondents. Such an inconclusive result begs for further research into whether a hotel-management degree influences later earnings.

SATISFIED MAJORITY

Regardless of pay differentials, there were no statistically significant differences in job-satisfaction scores between the different college-major groups. One possible explanation for this finding is the principle of self-selection. The theory is that people tend to gravitate toward work that is suitable for them and that they enjoy. If this is true, time and self-selection would act as a "leveler" of job-satisfaction scores.

This study employed the Brayfield-Rothe Index of Job Satisfaction (BRI), which records job satisfaction on a five-point scale (Brayfield and Rothe 1951). This sample's BRI scores ranged from 40 to 89. Its mean BRI score was 71.0, a figure remarkably similar to scores of general managers, sales directors, and personnel directors. (These mean scores varied from 69.8 to 71.1. The BRI's maximum score is 90.) The authors considered the possibility that the BRI might not be a valid measure of job satisfaction for hotel executives, but supporting literature and statistical tests indicate its probable validity.

MAJOR DIFFERENCES

When the sample of catering executives was divided according to gender, the authors found a marked difference in average salary levels—a difference that has been reported in other studies (Kent, 1982). Male catering executives earned on average nearly twice the salary of their female counterparts. Not surprisingly, twice as many men as women reported being satisfied with their pay rates. Dissatisfaction has also been found in studies of pay levels among women in other hotel-executive positions (Kent and Shock 1983).

One other great difference between the sexes is that many more women than men in this group were not married.

Similarities

Equal percentages of men and women reported high levels of stress in their jobs, and the two sexes showed no difference in average job-satisfaction scores. The two groups reported a workweek av-

---

EXHIBIT 3
Similarities and differences between male and female respondents

Similarities
- Sixty percent of men and women reported high or very high levels of stress in their work
- Both men and women avarage a 58-hour workweek
- There were no differences in job-satisfaction scores of men and women

Differences
- Median salary for women: $22,500
- Median salary for men: $40,000

Percentage of men
- 60% satisfied with pay
- 43% single or divorced
- 59% college educated

Percentage of women
- 32% satisfied with pay
- 60% single or divorced
- 47% college educated

---

eraging 58 hours. These findings, too, match those of the 1982 study of other hotel positions.

MAJORDOMOS

The authors were surprised at the relatively large proportion of hotel-school graduates in the sample. It could be that these graduates are attracted to the "nuts and bolts" of banquet management, or perhaps general managers steer the hotel graduates to positions where they are most needed. In any event, a hotel-school education appears to have served these persons well; with a mean age of 29, they have an average salary of over $32,000. (It is true, however, that they are working nearly 60 hours a week to earn their money.)

It is worth noting again the considerable differences between average salaries for male and female catering executives. There is evidence of growing dissatisfaction with pay levels among women. This issue has important implications for the catering executives and the hotel industry as a whole, because of the growing number of women now working in and entering the industry. Being an exploratory profile, however, this study is not intended to address this issue. The authors recommend further research on the topic of apparent pay differentials between men and women in the hotel industry.

The similarity of average job-satisfaction scores reported by this sample of catering executives and by earlier samples of general managers, sales directors, and personnel directors is interesting, and may indicate that there is no "most-satisfying" position in a hotel. Still, catering executives seem a relatively satisfied group. Although the range of satisfaction scores in our study was wide, average job satisfaction was high.

Roomservice: No Longer a "Necessary Evil"

Denise Turk

"They've got 24-hour roomservice. Of course they're losing money on it, but it's a necessary evil."

That comment, uttered by an advertising executive while describing his client's (an Atlanta hotel) extensive guest services, echoes the feeling many hotel managers have toward roomservice. Rarely recognized as a potential profitmaker, roomservice is often branded as a "necessary evil." Necessary because some guests do prefer to eat in their rooms. Evil because of the high labor costs/low volume.

As a result of this thinking, roomservice departments are often notoriously undermanaged, and roomservice patrons, undeservedly underserved.

"It's ironic how we've taken roomservice for granted," says Steve Peeck, director of food and beverage for Sheraton's North American Division. "It is the one situation where we really do have a captive guest—the guest who wants to eat in his room. In our other foodservice outlets, we have to compete against the free-standing restaurants and lounges in the neighborhood. But roomservice is

something we can provide the guest that no one else can."

Peeck, who calls roomservice the "great untapped potential of hotel food and beverage operations," says that Sheraton has begun an aggressive program to boost its roomservice business. When *Hospitality* spoke with him, he had just emerged from an intensive two-day work session with Sheraton managers on roomservice. Their own experience with roomservice while traveling provided the managers with a checklist for correction.

"We tore the roomservice issue apart and put it back together again," Peeck said. "With regard to the profitability of it, we found that roomservice is not often merchandised effectively to the needs of the guest. We also found that we had not applied the same kind of industrial engineering perspective to our roomservice areas that we did to other parts of the kitchen, resulting in low productivity."

To increase productivity, Peeck is reviewing kitchen equipment, storage space, and the number of steps it takes employees to assemble an order. Improving kitchen efficiency, Peeck believes, will enable most Sheraton roomservice departments to handle more business without enlarging staff.

His biggest push, however, is on merchandising. "You have to figure out ways to make roomservice

Reprinted with permission from Turk, Denise. "Roomservice: No Longer a 'Necessary Evil.' " *Lodging Hospitality* (March 1979), pp. 26–28.

kind of a bonus that a guest can elect to treat himself to when on the road. That means that it has to have all of the ambience and quality you would expect from a good dining room."

From Sheraton's point of view, better merchandising means more elegant table settings, smartly uniformed roomservice personnel, and graphically interesting menus designed to sell roomservice to guests who want a nice light dinner while watching TV or working in their rooms. All these items are on Sheraton's checklist for improvement.

Breakfast time is busy enough, so Sheraton is concentrating on promoting lunch and dinner. One promotion Peeck is anxious to try is a tie-in of roomservice to in-room movies, a special feature of many Sheraton properties.

Another promotion would increase roomservice liquor sales on a drink-by-drink basis. "Roomservice," says Peeck, "often reflects the attitudes and trends taking place in our other foodservice outlets. A glass of wine or a cocktail with dinner is generally becoming popular, so I think we're going to see liquor and wine sales improve in our roomservice.

"However, simply listing all of the possible cocktails on the back of the roomservice menu is not my idea of strong merchandising. So, in some of these prototype programs, we're taking a look at some interesting new cocktails and promoting them with dinner and brunch. I think if we start merchandising liquor, we will see an increase of cocktail service in roomservice."

Peeck sees yet another trend in hotel roomservice. Demand for 24-hour roomservice, while not overwhelming, is growing. Part of the reason, he says, is that people nowadays have much more flexible lifestyles. "They're not dining at neatly prescribed times. There's more nightlife in virtually every city you go to. People come in late and want something to eat. That's affected our policies governing coffee shops as well."

Western International

Peter Blyth, VP of food and beverage for Western International Hotels, is well aware of the need for flexible dining hours within hotels. Because Western's primary source of business is the business traveler, its hotels must maintain quality foodservice around-the-clock to accommodate late arrivals. For that reason, 24-hour roomservice is standard policy for all Western hotels. According to Blyth, 24-hour roomservice is also a luxury that sets the chain apart from other hotel chains. He dubs it Western's "point of difference."

"Roomservice is a key area of performance for our food and beverage directors. They are provided with standards of performance and training materials, which enable them to provide at least the same quality of service that we provide in our restaurants."

Roomservice standards in Western hotels include such luxuries as specialty linens, fresh flowers, and silver hollowware; a separate roomservice kitchen that allows for speedy preparation and delivery of meals; and tough service standards.

"Many of our hotels will serve courses of roomservice dinners as they would in a restaurant," Blyth explains. "Instead of bringing all of the courses together, they may bring the salad and the appetizer, then come back with the entrée. That again adds a certain flair."

Blyth admits that roomservice is a highly intensive department and that labor costs are high. But he points out that hotels can make up the increase in labor costs by increasing roomservice volume.

"Providing timely roomservice requires a substantial number of employees on hand. But, if you provide prompt, quality roomservice, then your guests will use it. You get a reputation for it. Your revenue builds, you can carry the overhead, and you can start to make a profit."

In-Room Vending

While roomservice is still the mainstay of in-room dining service, many hotels are boosting foodservice revenues using such devices as honor bars and in-room vending machines.

Loews L'Enfant Plaza Hotel in Washington, DC, is reaping profits with mini-bars set up in each of the hotel's 372 guestrooms and 31 suites. The bars (an idea borrowed from Loews' European hotels) are stocked with 56 miniature bottles of vodka, scotch, gin, bourbon, rum, Dubonnet, and five different cordials. The bars are also stocked with Perrier water, soft drinks, and mixes, as well as snacks. Guests are charged $2.75 plus tax for the miniatures and 35 cents for snacks. Soft drinks are $1 unless used as a mix, in which case there is no charge.

A staff of five stewards checks the bars daily to restock and replenish the ice supply. Stewards also record the number of miniatures and other items missing.

George Bellis, food and beverage director for the hotel, says the system relies on mutual trust between hotel and guest. "If the guest comes down and disputes two drinks, we will not charge him for them," says Bellis, adding that thus far, guests have been very honest about what they've had to drink.

Bellis noted that although the hotel makes a profit on the mini-bars, L'Enfant adopted the program more for image than profit. "We're one of the best hotels in Washington, DC, and we felt it would be a nice service for the guest. He doesn't have to call roomservice at 2 a.m.; he can serve himself right there."

Having miniatures in the room is not only more convenient for guests, but Bellis says that guests who wouldn't normally order liquor through roomservice are now treating themselves to one or two drinks from the mini-bar.

Automatic Vending

L'Enfant's mini-bars have made a hit with guests, but the hotel still has to contend with high labor costs involved in restocking bars and manually recording the number of miniatures consumed by guests. Two companies serving the lodging industry, however, have found a way to reduce labor and still provide guests with the luxury of in-room vending of liquor.

M.R.E. Enterprises, Inc., of Miami Lakes, Florida, offers the Inn-Room Bar-Tender, an automatic

dispensing system that vends five different kinds of liquor. Guests are given a special key to operate the unit when they check in. With a turn of the key and push of a button, guests may select one of five brands, which are dispensed in one-ounce servings. A master computer at the front desk electronically records each drink, and the total is added to the room bill. M.R.E., which offers Bar-Tender units through lease, lease/purchase, or cash purchase, says the in-room vending units are tamper-proof and they can be programmed to comply with legal restrictions on hours of service using the front desk microprocessor, which turns the units off automatically at the state's legal closing time.

Another type of in-room vending system is offered by Bell Captain, Inc. Bell Captain vends bottled liquors, beer, wine, soft drinks, juices, and snacks. All items are kept in a refrigerated unit, which also contains space for ice trays. Like M.R.E., Bell Captain uses key/pushbutton operation and automatically records purchases at the front desk.

Dick Trifari, manager of the Clinton Motor Inn in Tenafly, New Jersey, installed Bell Captain units seven years ago in 25 of his guestrooms. Trifari says that he no longer promotes the in-room service because guests are aware of it and specifically request it when they check in. The hotel does a 65 percent repeat business.

"All of our guests find it to be innovative," Trifari said.

Trifari says that his biggest sellers on an item-per-item basis are juices and soft drinks, although liquor sales bring in more revenue. Beer is a fast mover, particularly in the summer months.

Because the hotel has Bell Captain units in only one-fifth of its guestrooms, the hotel did not have to hire an extra person to maintain and restock the units.

Complimentary Coffee

Saying good morning to a guest with a complimentary cup of coffee is one way hotels often create favorable impressions on guests. But, again, costs of delivering a single cup of coffee to each and every guest via the roomservice department often make that special luxury prohibitive. A solution to the problem is offered by Keefe Coffee Company, a firm that markets in-room coffee machines. The company provides all the necessary equipment at no charge, provided the hotel buys coffee supplies from Keefe.

"The most common misunderstanding about in-room coffee is that it will hurt roomservice or restaurant business," says Doug Albrecht of Keefe. "Actually it has no negative effect on either. Coffee is such a low-priced item that it's really a loser for roomservice. When roomservice is obligated to deliver coffee to a number of guests, it slows down service to guests ordering big breakfasts."

Keefe services hotels in every state and predicts that during 1979 it will serve 50 million cups of coffee to hotel and motel guests.

Room Service: Break-Even Convenience or Profit Center

Myrle Finn

With operating costs steadily rising, it's more important than ever that each department in a hotel or motel carry its own weight. And this includes room service, often considered the step-child of the food and beverage department.

It's true that room service is one of the most difficult areas of foodservice, but if it is a part of your operation, it should function as a profit center, not a loss leader.

Major lodging chains and corporations recognize this concept. They view room service as a guest convenience that can add profit dollars. To help managers and licensees realize room-service profits, many chains have devised extensive room service help programs that include feasibility studies, menu analysis, training, and promotion. For instance:

• Ramada Inns requires that all properties, whether company-owned or franchised, offer room service. The chain evaluates each property, determines the type of service and the minimum service hours necessary, and offers on-going assistance.

• More than two-thirds of Best Western's 1,800 independently owned properties have restaurant facilities, and many of the larger properties offer room service. At the request of members, the Best Western staff is preparing a restaurant training course that will cover the finer points of room service operation.

• Downtowner/Rowntowner/Passport Systems suggests that franchise holders who offer room service maintain reasonable prices to avoid penalizing the guest who prefers to eat in his room. The philosophy is that as operators of a service business, franchisees have an obligation to give as much good service as possible within profitable cost guidelines.

Breakfast is Biggest

With a few exceptions, breakfast is the busiest time for room service departments. The consensus among room service professionals is that big breakfasts are out and Continental breakfasts are in.

Many operations run successful "doorknob" pro-

Reprinted with permission from Finn, Myrle. "Room Service: Break-Even Convenience or Profit Center." *Lodging Hospitality* (December 1977), pp. 39–40.

grams in which guests check off breakfast items and the delivery time on a special card that is hung on the outside doorknob. The cards are usually collected at night for preparation and delivery in the morning.

Ninety percent of room service activity in the Drake Hotel in Chicago is at breakfast, and 70 percent of the guests order Continental breakfasts.

The Drake Hotel, which was built more than 50 years ago, has the almost unheard-of luxury of two room service elevators. This has allowed management to devise a system to get Continental breakfasts, which are served between 7:30 and 8:30 A.M., to guests in seven to ten minutes.

One of the elevators is converted into a Continental breakfast kitchen, and all necessary equipment is designed to fit into the elevator. A service counter, about two feet wide and six feet long, is wheeled into the elevator. It contains heating and refrigeration units plus space for bread, rolls, beverages, linens, and condiments.

The trays are set up the night before and put on racks that each hold 17 trays. Two of the racks are put into the elevator, with the rest stored in the kitchen close to the elevator. Continental breakfast orders are phoned directly to the elevator operator, who transports the waiters to the designated floors.

"What our system does," says Edwin L. Brashears, the Drake president, "is separate the fast boys from people who are not in a rush. It also permits the regular room service to operate more efficiently, because there is no conflict."

Utilizing Live Entertainment in Hotels, Restaurants, and Clubs

Geoffrey A. Parker
William E. Kent

The selection, hiring, and monitoring of live entertainment can be a perplexing task for the hospitality manager. Not only do matters of public taste and artistic style come into question, the manager is also confronted with the entertainment budget and a number of legal questions involving copyright laws. There is no substitute for a knowledgeable booking agent regarding choice of talent, nor is there a substitute for sound legal advice on matters of copyright. But every hotel, restaurant, or club manager dealing with live entertainment should become knowledgeable in the primary aspects of this activity.

Reprinted with permission of Pergamon Press from Parker, Geoffrey A., and William E. Kent. "Utilizing Live Entertainment in Hotels, Restaurants, and Clubs." *International Journal of Hospitality Management*, vol. 5, no. 1 (1986), pp. 13–22.

There has been relatively little written on the subject from the viewpoint of the hospitality manager. Hull and Kent (1977) pointed out certain aesthetic, financial, and legal aspects of hiring live entertainers. They concluded that customers generally expect and support live entertainment, that an act should be self-supporting, that guests' tastes in music should be reflected, and that there are performance license fees payable by the establishment. Lillo (1981) surveyed restaurants in the U.S.A. and concluded that live entertainment can assume many formats and can encompass a wide range of budgets. Wren (1981) pointed out that the restaurant business will become more closely affiliated with the entertainment industry because of an increase in patrons' leisure time and a corresponding demand for entertainment.

This article will provide the operator with detailed guidelines concerning the financial implications of hiring live acts and a look at the somewhat complex copyright and union-related issues associated with this type of entertainment. While some advice will be offered as to choosing talent, there is, of course, considerable subjectivity in this regard.

THE ENTERTAINMENT BUDGET

Expenditures for entertainment are usually expressed as a percentage of food and beverage revenues, since entertainment is normally provided in the same spaces where food and drinks are served. It is then logical to consider such an expense allocatable to food and beverage sales.

While there are no norms per se, there are available industry averages on a world-wide basis. Tables 1 through 4 indicate considerable variation in entertainment expenditure in the U.S.A., Europe, the Middle East, and the Caribbean. Some variations appear to reflect cultural differences, e.g., Saudi Arabia versus United Arab Emirates. Other variations are readily attributable to the nature of the area, e.g., the high expenditures in resort areas such as Bermuda.

Breakdowns by room rate and property size are also available. Generally, the larger and more expensive the property, the greater the percentage of food and beverage revenues committed to live entertainment. Expenditures among free-standing restaurants for music and entertainment vary considerably, but for full-menu table-service establishments in the U.S.A., the average in 1982 was 1 percent of food and beverage revenues.

Operators are encouraged to compare their own expenditures with these statistics, but it should be remembered that the figures represent averages and that every property is unique.

IS MY INVESTMENT BEING REPAID?

Another criterion by which to evaluate music and entertainment (M&E) expenditures is the ROI or return-on-investment criterion. In this instance, we consider money paid to entertainers as an investment that is expected to repay itself plus dividends. In order to calculate ROI on M&E expenditures, we employ a simple but highly useful formula known as the CVP formula (Coltman 1982).

The basic CVP formula is as follows:

$$\text{Total sales required} = \frac{\text{fixed costs} + \text{profit desired}}{100\% - \text{variable costs (as \% of revenue)}}$$

A modification of the formula is as follows:

$$\text{Total sales required} = \frac{\text{fixed costs} + \text{M\&E expenditure} + \text{profit desired}}{100\% - \text{variable costs}}$$

Expressed verbally, the formula is used to calculate the total sales required to produce the desired profit after having incurred certain fixed and variable costs. In the formula, M&E is considered a fixed cost, but is shown separately for illustration purposes.

TABLE 1
Music and entertainment expenditures in 325 U.S. transient hotels

	Northeast & Mid-Atlantic	North Central	South Atlantic	South Central	Mountain & Pacific
As % of food and beverage revenues	1.8	2.1	1.9	3.4	2.9

Source: Pannell, Kerr, Forster & Company (1983a).

TABLE 2
Music and entertainment expenditures in hotels in selected European countries

	France	Germany	Great Britain	Italy	Netherlands
As % of food and beverage revenues	1.5	1.2	1.0	1.2	1.0

Source: Pannell, Kerr, Forster & Company (1983b).

Example A

A lounge has *fixed costs* (rent, depreciation, licenses, insurance, certain salaries, etc.) of $30,000 per month. *Variable costs* (pouring costs, wages, etc.) total 75 percent of the revenue. Presume the operator spends $6,000 per month on *live entertainment* and desires a *profit* of $5,000. *Total sales required* may be calculated as follows:

$$\text{Total sales required} = \frac{\$30,000 + \$6,000 + \$5,000}{100\% - 75\%}$$

or

$$\frac{\$41,000}{0.25} = \$164,000$$

This may also be expressed in number of drinks, assuming an average price of $1.50 per drink:

$$\frac{\$164,000}{\$1.50} = 109,333 \text{ drinks}$$

Example B

A local talent booking agent approaches the lounge operator and says that by hiring a first-class band, he will increase his profits considerably. A first-class band, according to the agent, will cost $12,000 per month, or twice what the present band is costing. The operator states he won't consider the new band unless profits increase by 50 percent to $7,500 per month. While the operator knows there is no way to predict that such an outcome will occur, he can

TABLE 3
Music and entertainment expenditures in hotels in selected Middle East countries

	Israel	Saudi Arabia	United Arab Emirates
As % of food and beverage revenues	1.9	0.2	5.2

Source: Pannell, Kerr, Forster & Company (1983b).

TABLE 4
Music and entertainment expenditures in hotels in selected Caribbean locations

	Bahama Islands	Bermuda	Puerto Rico
As % of food and beverage revenues	5.0	7.4	2.7

Source: Pannell, Kerr, Forster & Company (1983b).

at least verify the *likelihood* of such an outcome. Again, using the CVP formula:

$$\text{Total sales required} = \frac{\$30,000 + \$12,000 + \$7,500}{100\% - 75\%}$$

or

$$\frac{\$49,500}{0.25} = \$198,000 \text{ or } \$132,000 \text{ drinks at } \$1.50$$

Compared to previous sales of 109,333 drinks, an increase of 20.7 percent to 132,000 seems unlikely to the operator. The lounge manager suggests raising bar prices to $1.75 to cover the increased entertainment costs. Revenue requirements remain the same at $198,000 but now only 113,143 drinks ($198,000)/($1.75) will be needed to meet all costs, pay for the band, and meet the new profit goals.

Example C

The agent, sensing the operator's interest, makes an additional offer. He will provide the new band at no fixed salary if the operator will agree to give the agent 6 percent of total sales. The operator once again employs the CVP formula, this time adjusting *variable costs*.

$$\text{Total sales required} = \frac{\$30,000 + \$0.00 \text{ (band)} + \$7,500}{100\% - 81\%}$$

or

$$\frac{\$37,500}{0.19} = \$197,368 \ (\$11,842 \text{ for the agent})$$

Computed in number of drinks, the operator would need to sell 131,578 drinks at $1.50 or 112,781 drinks at $1.75 to meet his profit goals. Of course, the operator will carefully consider the implications of the agent's becoming a "partner" in the business rather than a paid supplier.

There are many different scenarios the operator might consider, but the CVP formula may be used effectively in most as an aid to decision-making. Certain assumptions are implied when using the CVP formula, including: (a) costs associated with the present level of sales can be accurately broken down into their fixed and variable elements; (b) fixed costs will remain fixed over the period in question; and (c) variable costs vary in a linear fashion with sales.

WHERE DO I FIND THE TALENT?

After considering the fixed and variable costs associated with making a decision about the entertainment budget, the next step involves locating suitable entertainment for your establishment.

In the past, some hotel chains centralized their talent-purchasing functions. Ramada Inns had a national entertainment director who directed procurement activities for franchise operations, and they also established regional bureaus with marketing and entertainment representatives. Now the Ramada policy (as well as that for some Holiday Inn franchises) dictates that each location handle its own talent-buying. Sheraton corporate decision-makers never get involved in entertainment functions unless the location in question is a flagship site, club location within a property, or resort area. Even then they leave most of the decisions to the local general manager.

Most general managers, banquet, and food managers do not have the knowledge and/or time to be active talent scouts, but John Sansone, with Limelighters Agency in Nashville, Tennessee, suggests that one of the prerequisites for maintaining a profitable lounge is a market study. A thorough check of the competition in the area and demographic research regarding potential customers are necessary elements in any entertainment plan. This is where a booking agent can be helpful. Miles Bell, also of the Limelighters Agency, suggests finding an agent who represents the kinds of acts felt to be compatible with a particular location, and taking the time to go out and see what types of act the agent has to offer. This will give the buyer an opportunity to evaluate both the attractions and the agent himself. A good agent will also get involved with the venue's budgeting, marketing, and entertainment objectives so that there will be a clear-cut objective of providing the right entertainment mix.

Miles Bell feels that the potential buyer should evaluate the agent in much the same way as one would a lawyer or doctor, that is, by asking for a list of references and spending $10 and five minutes on the phone talking to the agent's clients. Some buyers are somewhat paranoid about their rooms, so Limelighters makes its own market study, visiting other rooms in the area, including neigh-

borhood bars, with hotel management, and attempts to find a concept that no other room is using.

There are no standard operating procedures for paying agents. Most are compensated by a percentage of from 10 to 15 percent of the gross fees paid the entertainers. In rare cases, some agents serve as entertainment consultants to the venue, becoming salaried employees. In this situation, the agent is hired by the operator to handle all entertainment tasks. However, according to David Snowden of Triangle Talent in Louisville, Kentucky, this is not common practice today. He states that when the disco franchises came around, the corporations saw little need for entertainment consultants. Also, with travel becoming more expensive, show bands and lounge acts do not travel across the country as often as they used to, and, as a result, agencies are becoming much more localized. If an agent is being used as a consultant, it is necessary to be aware of a potential conflict of interest known as "double commission," which occurs when the agent takes his usual commission from the band and also receives a salary from the venue. If locating a suitable agent in a particular area is a problem, the International Theatrical Agencies Association (telephone: 214-349-3025) provides a list of talent agents.

WHAT ARE MY LEGAL OBLIGATIONS?

Ten years ago it would have been presumptuous to assume that most buyers had an understanding of the legal responsibilities involved in hiring entertainers. Today, operators should, at least, have a working knowledge of performing-rights societies and their relationship to the copyright laws.

In 1909 Congress passed an amendment to the United States Constitution giving composers certain exclusive rights, among them the freedom to publicly perform their own songs and the right to license their copyrighted works for others to perform as long as the creators were duly compensated. The 1909 Act did not, however, provide for enforcement of the exclusive right of public performance, and in 1914 the American Society of Composers, Authors and Publishers (ASCAP) was formed to deal with this problem. In 1931, the Society of European Stage Authors and Composers (SESAC) came into being, followed shortly by Broadcast Music Incorporated (BMI) in 1939. These three organizations are performing-rights societies and their main function is to license the non-dramatic rights of public performance of a copyrighted song.

Let us consider a hypothetical situation. A general manager of a motel in a rural community is contemplating using a band to increase beverage and food sales during the slack season. Before the musicians start performing, the general manager would have to negotiate with the composer of each copyrighted tune that the band was intending to include in its repertoire. Not only would considerable time be spent gathering song lists (sometimes musicians do not prepare lists until half an hour before showtime), but the expense and research involved in successfully contracting with literally hundreds of composers would place an insurmountable burden on the financial resources of the establishment. Fortunately, such an effort by the motel management is not necessary.

Each performing-rights society issues a blanket license that allows the music user access to the songs in that society's repertoire. ASCAP and BMI license a majority of all copyrighted songs and since most establishments rely on popular music to please customers, a license with *both* societies is inevitable. SESAC, on the other hand, has the smallest catalog and it is possible to exclude any SESAC composition from being performed in your venue. *However,* someone would have to be responsible for checking each song's affiliation before every show. Some owners think their duty has been done when they pay the musicians, or that it is the responsibility of the musicians to obtain any license needed for their performance. This is not the law. The law is that without a license, the owner of the establishment using music is responsible for copyright infringement (ASCAP 1978).

HOW MUCH DO I PAY?

The license fee varies among the societies and different criteria are used depending on the type of music user. For example, hotels and motels, under an ASCAP license, pay an annual fee according to the total expenditure for all entertainment at the premises, and that fee escalates over a five-year period (the length of both the BMI and ASCAP hotel/motel agreements). If live music only is presented at a hotel or motel and the total entertainment budget is $100,000, the ASCAP license fee would amount to $1,725 in the first year of the contract and increase to $1,898 five years later. Using the same $100,000 entertainment budget, BMI's rates would be somewhat lower (approximately $975 during the first year, rising to around $1,045 five years later). SESAC employs a one-year contract and their fee would amount to $300. For example, the total license fees would, therefore, be $3,000 in 1984 and approximately $3,300 in 1988.

A separate rate schedule applies when a hotel/motel uses mechanical music only (tapes or records). ASCAP has five categories and the license fee depends on variables such as cover charges or admission charges, if dancing is allowed and if a show or act is used in tandem with the mechanical music. ASCAP calculates the basic rate by the number of rooms in the establishment and correlates the variables. For example, a hotel/motel with 210 rooms and no dancing, cover, or admission charge, and no show would pay $120 in 1984, whereas BMI would charge $75 for the same license. There are also rate schedules that apply when a location has both mechanical and live music. In the latest ASCAP agreement, video is considered as a new performance, so it is essential to include the ASCAP fee when calculating the entertainment budget for video screens, projectors, etc. BMI is using a different rate schedule to license video performances as from 1985.

There are other clauses in these license agreements that may affect the fee payable. Both ASCAP and BMI consider the value of accommodation or services (room and board) that are part of the entertainer's compensation to be included in the entertainment budget of the property. In addition, every location must submit a detailed accounting verifying all entertainment costs, and both societies have the right to examine the books and records of the licensee at *any* time during customary business hours. With respect to leasing space for industrial or trade shows, ASCAP's license does not authorize these performances. Legally, the hotel or the private organization could be held accountable for another license fee. However, according to Robin Dickson of Ray Bloch Productions, Atlanta, Georgia, most companies that specialize in providing entertainment for industry have not been contacted by any performing-rights society. The license is also limited strictly to the premises. ASCAP and BMI do not authorize the broadcasting, telecasting, or transmission by wire otherwise of such performances to persons outside the property unless the hotel has written permission. The contract further stipulates that any broadcast of a performance emanating from any point outside the premises or transmitted to the premises is also unauthorized (ASCAP 1984). If you are using a background music service as Muzak, cable, or pay television, make sure you have the necessary permits and licenses. (Appendix 1 illustrates the information that ASCAP requires of all licensees.)

The license fee for clubs, restaurants, lounges, discos, piano bars, and similar establishments is calculated differently from that for hotels and motels. This contract is one year in duration and takes into consideration the seating capacity of the venue. The variables (admission charge, etc.) remain the same but apply to the number of instrumentalists on stage at any given time. If a club has a seating capacity of 78 and a solo performer is presented four nights a week, the base rate would be $324 per year. If there is any change in policy, such as an entertainment charge, the license fee may climb to $770, depending upon the circumstances.

BMI, on the other hand, uses the hotel method and simply bases its fees on the total entertainment costs for the establishment. There are also seasonal rates for those venues in operation only during certain months of the year. The seasonal rate is one-half the annual rate for a period of up to four months. Each additional month is prorated at one-half the annual license fee. In the above example, the seasonal rate would be $162 for four months' operation and each additional month would cost the club $27 more for the ASCAP license.

ASCAP and BMI have reciprocal agreements with affiliated performing-rights societies in other countries (see Appendix 2). In Canada, the Performing Rights Organization of Canada Limited (BMI-affiliated) and Composers, Authors and Publishers Association of Canada Limited (ASCAP-affiliated) are the governing bodies for the collection of performance royalties.

The Performing Rights Organization of Canada Limited (PRO) collects a fee based on the total entertainment budget for a hotel lounge, restaurant, or tavern. If an establishment allocates more than $170,000 yearly for entertainment, the annual license fee would be $1,800 plus 0.5 percent of the excess. Composers, Authors and Publishers Association (CAPAC) issues a similar license based on the same criteria and the fee is almost identical but calling for a slightly higher percentage in excess of $100,000.

In England, the Performing Rights Society Limited (PRS) is the only performing-rights organization authorized to collect a tariff from hotels, restaurants, and cafes regularly employing or hiring musical performers where the annual entertainment expenditure is £3,500 or more. The license is calculated as follows: 2 percent on the first £35,000; 1.5 percent on any further amount. If the expenditure is less than £3,500 per annum, the license fee is £2.60 per 100 persons admitted to the function in question.

In Japan, the Japanese Society for Rights of Authors, Composers and Publishers (JASRAC) is the sole licensing society. The fee for the performances of musical works at cabarets, cafes, night clubs, or hotels is determined by calculating the size of the facility and the seating capacity, subject to a maximum of 50 percent of respective rates provided for performances of musical works at concerts or recitals. For example, an establishment with a seating capacity of less than 500 and an admission charge of less than 100 yen would be subject to an annual license fee of 20 yen.

CHANGES IN THE 1976 COPYRIGHT ACT, U.S.A.

The Copyright Law was amended in 1976 and there are several changes that affect the presentation of entertainment. The 1909 law excluded non-profit associations as fraternal organizations and private clubs from any license obligations but the 1976 amendment does away with that provision. In ASCAP's Private Club License Agreement, the rate is calculated according to the annual expenditure for all entertainment on the premises. If a sum less than $4,999 per year is allocated to musicians, the annual license fee would be $140. As with the other ASCAP contracts, mechanical music is rated differently. In a situation where a private club uses only tapes and records, then the fee is based on the number of members that belong to the club. For example, if a club has over 300 members, the annual mechanical music license fee is $70; fewer than 300 members constitutes a $50 rate.

Secondly, the infringement penalties have changed dramatically with the passage of the new law. Formerly offenders faced minimal penalties for copyright violations ($250 per infringement). The 1976 law gives the societies more flexibility when seeking damages, up to $50,000 per violation. ASCAP does not usually seek more than $1,000 per infringement, but calculation of the amount payable in damages is based on how long the operator has been avoiding paying the ASCAP fee, according to David Nelson, Southern Division Manager of ASCAP. A lawsuit varies according to the circumstances. An ASCAP representative attempts to visit the venue and discuss with the operator his/her legal obligations under the Copyright Act; a second attempt is made by the representative, and if the venue does not respond, the first written notice (Appendix 3) is forwarded to the establishment and

is followed by another visit. After a series of these maneuvers, ASCAP (BMI generally uses the same procedure) sends an inspection team (male and female) to the venue. This team writes down all the songs that are performed that particular evening, noting especially the time and date each song is performed. Additional information, such as the name of the group, physical description of the musicians, and design of the venue's interior, is compiled for the litigation and sometimes these teams are asked to testify in court. The Copyright Law indicates that if a copyrighted song, which is licensed by ASCAP, BMI, or SESAC, is performed publicly and the establishment does not possess the appropriate license, then this is in violation of the law and the incident is considered an infringement. If the performing-rights society seeks $1,000 per infringement plus all court costs, it seems prudent to secure the license, especially if the annual fee is minimal compared to what the court will award the plaintiff.

DO I HAVE TO HIRE UNION MUSICIANS?

The American Federation of Musicians was established in 1896 to benefit professional instrumentalists. It has approximately 335,000 members in more than 600 local unions throughout the United States and Canada. It is the largest and oldest entertainment union in the world.

There is considerable misinformation about the AFM, particularly with regard to the "right to work" states. Every local union affiliate negotiates minimum wage scales for its members for local jobs only. For example, the minimum compensation acceptable by a union musician in Rochester, New York, may be $100 per engagement, whereas in Chicago the wage scale could be 50 percent higher. AFM members cannot earn less than the amount specified but they can (and do) earn a great deal more in some instances. The larger hotels, for the most part, equal the minimum wage scales or pay more than the minimum in their locales, according to David Winston, President, New Orleans Federation of Musicians. There are several reasons why this occurs: Most large hotels in major cities have other union personnel besides musicians to consider and the last thing anyone wants is a wildcat strike (like the Las Vegas incident where hotels and casinos lost millions of dollars) where one union walks out in support of another union. Secondly, hotels generally pay more for entertainment than do other venues, with the exception of showcase clubs (Moonshadow, Atlanta; Bottom Line, New York). Lastly, most of the well-known groups do belong to the union.

The "right to work" stipulation dictates that the AFM cannot enter into any agreement with an employer to only use union musicians. A "right to work" state in the U.S.A. (there are almost 20 of them) prohibits contracts that require union membership as a condition of employment. The "right to work" is really a misnomer. It tends to prevent the union from organizing non-union musicians. In Mississippi, the Right to Work Law almost destroyed the locals, according to Mr. Winston. Basically, the law gives musicians the right to work wherever they choose for whatever wages they can negotiate. In a rural area, a small hotel/motel restaurant or club can virtually pay musicians whatever they feel is fair compensation. In Texas, the largest and most industrialized state to have the Right to Work Act, some Dallas and Houston operators pay little heed to union representatives. In Georgia (another "right to work" state), clubs and restaurants with $100,000 entertainment budgets are free to hire whom they want at whatever price the market will bear. But even in "right to work" states, some hotels service the union. Russ Byloff, Entertainment Director at Harrah's in Reno, Nevada, notes that since they always pay more than any local minimum anyway, Harrah's works with an AFM contract. It is essential to find out whether the particular state in question has a law that voids contracts requiring union membership as a prerequisite for employment. The AFM does frown upon their members working in a non-union establishment, or working with a non-union group, and sometimes fines them. So it is advisable to find out if union or non-union members are being hired and to refrain from mixing the two if possible. Even though it is a criminal offense for any union official to harass any non-union musician to join the union, it is better to avoid potential trouble at a venue, and work with either union or non-union musicians.

It can be readily seen that the selection and use of live entertainment in hotels, restaurants, and clubs is a complex matter. Styles and trends in music change and the operator, in addition to more traditional duties, must stay abreast (or pay someone else to stay abreast) of these changes. Industry averages for entertainment expenditures and the CVP formula can help the operator to answer some of the more pertinent financial questions arising from the use of live entertainment.

Some advice for finding the right agent has been offered and a detailed explanation has been given as to how performing-rights societies operate. (One last word on that subject: You need not call them—they'll call you.) Finally, the union question has been addressed.

As we pointed out earlier, live entertainment *is* special and a personal experience for your guests. It is an endeavor well worth pursuing, and, might we add, pursuing correctly.

Appendix 1

ASCAP hotels and motels statement

HOTELS AND MOTELS—STATEMENT

TO: AMERICAN SOCIETY OF COMPOSERS,
AUTHORS AND PUBLISHERS

DATE _____

HOTEL OR MOTEL _____

OPERATED BY _____

LOCATED AT _____

CITY _____ STATE _____ ZIP CODE _____

IF SEASONAL HOTEL OR MOTEL,* OPENING DATE _____ CLOSING DATE _____

This is to certify that the EXPENDITURE FOR ALL LIVE ENTERTAINMENT at the above premises during the period from _____ to _____ was as follows:

Payments made for all entertainment (see License Agreement, Paragraph "6") $ _____

Reasonable value of accommodations or services furnished to musicians and entertainers (see License Agreement, Paragraph "6")   _____

TOTAL $ _____

Applicable fee from Schedule I (see License Agreement) $ _____

MECHANICAL MUSIC (see License Agreement, Paragraph "6"):

	Yes	No
Was mechanical music furnished?	☐	☐
Was there dancing?	☐	☐
Was there any cover, minimum or admission charge?	☐	☐
Was there a show or acts?	☐	☐
Number of hotel or motel rooms	_____	

If mechanical music only was furnished, insert applicable fee from Schedule II (see License Agreement) $ _____

If both live entertainment and mechanical music were furnished, insert applicable additional fee from Schedule III (see License Agreement) $ _____

Fee payable (total of applicable amounts from Schedules I, II and III) $ _____

Subscribed and sworn to before me this _____ day of _____

_____
(Name of licensee)

_____, 19____

By _____

_____
(Notary Public)

_____
(Title)

*SEASONAL RATES

For seasonal licensees, the rates under Schedules II and III for periods up to four months of operation are one-half the annual rate; for each additional month the rate is one-twelfth the annual rate. The seasonal rate will in no case be more than the annual rate.

Appendix 2

ASCAP affiliated foreign societies

Sociedad Argentina de Autores y Compositores de Musica (SADAIC)
Buenos Aires, Argentina

Australasian Performing Right Association, Ltd. (APRA)
Sydney, Australia

Staatlich Genehmigte Gesellschaft der Autoren, Komponisten und Musikverleger (AKM)
Vienna, Austria

Societe Belge des Auteurs, Compositeurs et Editeurs (SABAM)
Brussels, Belgium

Sociedad Boliviana de Autores y Compositores de Musica (SOBODAYCOM)
La Paz, Bolivia

Sociedade Independente de Compositores e Autores Musicais (SICAM)
Sao Paulo, Brazil

União Brasileira de Compositores (UBC)
Rio de Janeiro, Brazil

Composers, Authors and Publishers Association of Canada, Ltd. (CAPAC)
Toronto, Canada

Departamento del Derecho de Autor (DAIC)
Santiago, Chile

Ochranny Svaz Autorsky (OSA)
Prague, Czechoslovakia

Slovensky Ochranny Zvaz Autorsky (SOZA)
Bratislava, Czechoslovakia

Selskabet til Forvaltning af Internationale Komponistrettigheder i Danmark (KODA)
Copenhagen, Denmark

The Performing Right Society Limited (PRS)
London, England

Saveltajain Tekijanoikeustoimisto (TEOSTO)
Helsinki, Finland

Societe des Auteurs, Compositeurs et Editeurs de Musique (SACEM)
Paris, France

Gesellschaft für Musikalische Aufführungs- und Mechanische Vervielfältigungsrechte (GEMA)
Berlin and Munich, Federal Republic of Germany

Anstalt zur Wahrung der Aufführungsrechte auf dem Gebiete der Musik (AWA)
Berlin, German Democratic Republic

Societe Hellenique pour la Protection de la Propriete Intellectuelle (AEPI)
Athens, Greece

Vereniging BUMA
Amsterdam, Holland

Composers and Authors Society of Hong Kong Ltd. (CASH)
Hong Kong

Bureau Hongrois pour la Protection des Droits d'Auteur (ARTISJUS)
Budapest, Hungary

Samband Tonskalda og Eigenda Flutningsrettar (STEF)
Reykjavik, Iceland

The Indian Performing Right Society Ltd. (IPRS)
Bombay, India

Societe d'Auteurs, Compositeurs et Editeurs de Musique en Israel, (ACUM)
Tel Aviv, Israel

Societa Italiana degli Autori ed Editori (SIAE)
Rome, Italy

Japanese Society for Rights of Authors, Composers and Publishers (JASRAC)
Tokyo, Japan

Sociedad de Autores y Compositores de Musica (SACM)
Mexico, D.F.

Norsk Komponistforenings Internasjonale Musikkbyra (TONO)
Oslo, Norway

Autores Paraguayos Asociados (APA)
Asuncion, Paraguay

Asociacion Peruana de Autores y Compositores (APDAYC)
Lima, Peru

Filipino Society of Composers, Authors and Publishers (FILSCAP)
Manila, Philippines

Stowarzyszenie Autorow (ZAIKS)
Warsaw, Poland

Sociedade Portuguesa de Autores (SPA)
Lisbon, Portugal

Sociedad Puertorriqueña de Autores, Compositores y Editores de Musica (SPACEM)
Santurce, Puerto Rico

South African Music Rights Organisation Limited (SAMRO)
Johannesburg, South Africa

Sociedad General de Autores de España (SGAE)
Madrid, Spain

Svenska Tonsattares Internationella Musikbyra (STIM)
Stockholm, Sweden

Societe Suisse pour les Droits des Auteurs d'Oeuvres Musicales (SUISA)
Zurich, Switzerland

Vsesojuznoje Agentstvo po Avtorskim Pravam (VAAP)
Moscow, U.S.S.R.

Asociacion General de Autores del Uruguay (AGADU)
Montevideo, Uruguay

Sociedad de Autores y Compositores de Venezuela (SACVEN)
Caracas, Venezuela

Savez Organizacija Kompozitora Jugoslavije (SOKOJ)
Belgrade, Yugoslavia

Appendix 3

ASCAP license fee letter

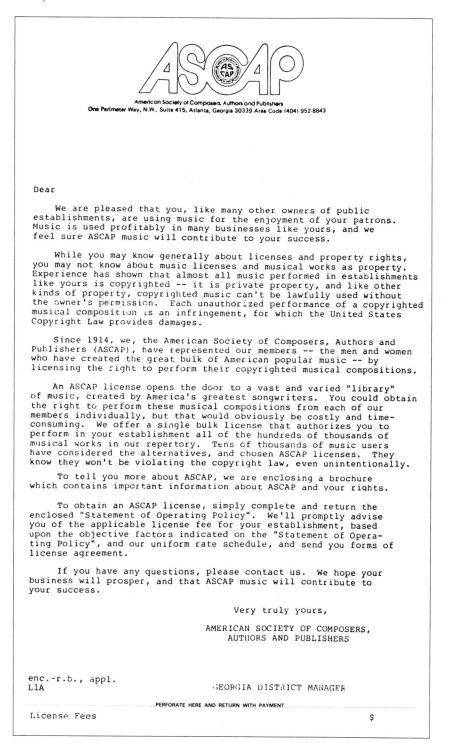

ASCAP

American Society of Composers, Authors and Publishers
One Perimeter Way, N.W., Suite 415, Atlanta, Georgia 30339 Area Code (404) 952-8843

Dear

    We are pleased that you, like many other owners of public
establishments, are using music for the enjoyment of your patrons.
Music is used profitably in many businesses like yours, and we
feel sure ASCAP music will contribute to your success.

    While you may know generally about licenses and property rights,
you may not know about music licenses and musical works as property.
Experience has shown that almost all music performed in establishments
like yours is copyrighted -- it is private property, and like other
kinds of property, copyrighted music can't be lawfully used without
the owner's permission. Each unauthorized performance of a copyrighted
musical composition is an infringement, for which the United States
Copyright Law provides damages.

    Since 1914, we, the American Society of Composers, Authors and
Publishers (ASCAP), have represented our members -- the men and women
who have created the great bulk of American popular music -- by
licensing the right to perform their copyrighted musical compositions.

    An ASCAP license opens the door to a vast and varied "library"
of music, created by America's greatest songwriters. You could obtain
the right to perform these musical compositions from each of our
members individually, but that would obviously be costly and time-
consuming. We offer a single bulk license that authorizes you to
perform in your establishment all of the hundreds of thousands of
musical works in our repertory. Tens of thousands of music users
have considered the alternatives, and chosen ASCAP licenses. They
know they won't be violating the copyright law, even unintentionally.

    To tell you more about ASCAP, we are enclosing a brochure
which contains important information about ASCAP and your rights.

    To obtain an ASCAP license, simply complete and return the
enclosed "Statement of Operating Policy". We'll promptly advise
you of the applicable license fee for your establishment, based
upon the objective factors indicated on the "Statement of Operating Policy", and our uniform rate schedule, and send you forms of
license agreement.

    If you have any questions, please contact us. We hope your
business will prosper, and that ASCAP music will contribute to
your success.

                    Very truly yours,

                    AMERICAN SOCIETY OF COMPOSERS,
                    AUTHORS AND PUBLISHERS

enc.-r.b., appl.
L1A   GEORGIA DISTRICT MANAGER

............................PERFORATE HERE AND RETURN WITH PAYMENT...........................

License Fees $

Bare Trap: The Legal Pitfall of Requiring Scanty Costumes

Jon P. McConnell

Almost all hotels, restaurants, and lounges require employees to wear specific uniforms or costumes. Most of these outfits are sedate and serviceable, but some (e.g., those worn by employees in some cocktail lounges) can be revealing. Although *many* employees may accept the outfits as a condition of employment, *others* might be uncomfortable when scantily clad. Generally speaking, it is women who are singled out to wear scanty costumes. This article discusses whether the practice of requiring such costumes is a violation of federal civil-rights laws. Unfortunately, the case law is about as skimpy as some of the costumes in question.

Among other provisions, Title VII of the Civil Rights Act of 1964 bans employers from discriminating against any individual—with regard to terms, conditions, or privileges of employment—because of the person's gender. The law also prohibits segregating or classifying employees because of their gender in any way that might adversely affect their status as employees.[5]

The civil-rights law is enforced by the federal Equal Employment Opportunity Commission (EEOC), which has written administrative rules addressing the question of sexual harassment.[6] (These rules are not legally binding, but are given substantial weight in court.) In part, the rules state that sexual harassment violates civil-rights law. The EEOC includes in its definition of harassment "unwelcome sexual advances, requests for sexual favors, and other verbal or physical conduct of a sexual nature," particularly when these actions create a hostile or offensive working environment. An

This article was originally published in the November 1985 issue of *The Cornell Hotel and Restaurant Administration Quarterly*, and is reprinted here with the permission of the Cornell University School of Hotel Administration. © 1985.

employer may be held responsible for harassment by nonemployees (e.g., patrons at a tavern) if the employer fails to take corrective action when an incident occurs.[7]

Under the law, an employer could be discriminating against or classifying employees based on sex by requiring women but not men to wear scanty costumes in a given situation. Furthermore, if a scanty costume leads to harassment that interferes with a female employee's work, the EEOC (under its rules) might consider this costume a violation of the law. This would be true whether the harassment stems from supervisors, fellow employees, or customers. Moreover, the costume need not invite direct overtures; merely creating a hostile or offensive working environment could constitute harassment.

THE UNHAPPY HOSTESS

In 1981, the EEOC favored the claim of a woman who had performed various clerical duties at a radio station. Her manager had made a number of sexual advances to her. On being rebuffed, he required her to wear a revealing outfit and act as a hostess to visiting VIPs. No other employees who entertained VIPs (male or female) were required to wear such a costume. She was consequently exposed to harassment from the parties being entertained, and she quit her job rather than continue as a hostess.

The EEOC found that both the initial sexual advances and the subsequent harassment had been made a condition of the woman's employment—clearly banned under the Civil Rights Act. Additionally, the commission found that the revealing costume unreasonably interfered with the woman's work. Looking at the fact that she was the only person required to wear a scanty costume, the commission also found this to be a case of sex discrimination based upon disparate treatment. Disparate treatment is often referred to as a "sex-plus" factor: one that may not be imposed on all females, but is not applied to males at all. Such an employment policy violates the civil-rights laws.

Although the EEOC's opinion did not specify the remedy, the woman probably received a lump-sum settlement of back pay from the time of resignation to her subsequent employment, less pay received (elsewhere) in the interim.

SIGNAL FLAG

A different case involving scanty costumes reached appellate court (one step beyond the EEOC) in 1981.[8] The plaintiff was a woman who was employed as an elevator starter by the defendant, Sage Realty. Throughout the course of her employment, she and the other elevator starters (all were women) were required to wear uniforms; there was no complaint about these. But as the U.S. bicentennial approached in 1976, new uniforms resembling the American flag were issued. The plaintiff found hers to be scanty, ill-fitting, and revealing. During the one day she wore it, she was the target of harassment and humiliation by men in the lobby, and on several occasions she tried to have the uniform altered so that it would be less revealing. Failing in this attempt, she refused to wear the uniform, came to work in her old outfit instead, and was fired.

When she brought a complaint, the EEOC found in her favor. The case then went on to U.S. district court in New York.

The district court first found that requiring the woman to wear the bicentennial uniform constituted a *prima facie* violation of the civil-rights law, because she would not have been required to wear it if she had not been a woman. The court also found that her failure to wear this uniform had been the motivating cause of her discharge. While granting the right of an employer to impose reasonable dress requirements on employees, the court found that in this instance the requirement was not reasonable,

because the employer knew that the costume exposed the woman to sexual harassment.

Where's the BFOQ?

Sage Realty raised an interesting point in rebuttal, citing the section of the civil-rights law that stipulates it shall not be unlawful to discriminate when gender is a bona fide occupational qualification (BFOQ). The plaintiff's costume, Sage argued, was a BFOQ. The courts have dealt strictly with the BFOQ exception, however, recognizing it only in extreme situations (e.g., permitting a requirement of same-sex nursing services for patients under intensive care). In this case, the court ruled that the requirement of wearing a revealing costume was not a BFOQ.

The plaintiff was awarded more than $33,000, plus attorneys' fees, an amount that covered the loss of pay during her period of unemployment, minus earnings and unemployment insurance received.

AVOIDING TRAPS

To date, the EEOC has not reported a case involving the mere requirement of wearing a scanty costume; some form of harassment or overt sex discrimination has always been part of the cases decided so far. (It is possible that complaints have been made and investigations conducted without becoming reported cases.) Scanty costumes are certainly evident in various clubs and stage shows, so it is clear that requiring scanty uniforms does not automatically result in action by the EEOC. It is likely that the EEOC waits for complaints to act on, rather than sending investigators to ferret out cases of discrimination. It is also possible that the EEOC does not consider the law applicable unless the offending costume is specifically required for the job but is not truly necessary to performing the job, *or* when the requirement to wear such an outfit is a sex-plus factor, *or* when the costume results in harassment.

Since the EEOC merely responds to complaints,

the employer would do well to deal with complaints of women who have been harassed when wearing scanty costumes. One could, for instance, transfer an aggrieved woman to a job that involves a different uniform (or no specific uniform).

With the uncertainty still extant in this area of law, it is difficult to recommend specific ways to avoid problems. Still, employers should consider the following guidelines to reduce the likelihood of legal difficulties:

1. Do not require employees to wear costumes that interfere with their work or expose the wearers to sexual harassment.
2. Avoid requiring scanty costumes when the requirement is immaterial to or detracts from the business involved. (If a cocktail lounge makes its employees' costumes part of an erotic environment, this might be acceptable; an airline that required its flight attendants to wear "peekaboo" outfits would probably find it difficult to justify this requirement.

3. Do not change rules in midstream. Making scanty costumes a condition of employment after employees have been hired—especially over the objections of the employees (as in the Sage Realty case)—is unwise.
4. If your firm has a longstanding tradition of requiring scanty costumes (e.g., Playboy clubs), make certain that those affected by the requirement are aware of it when they are hired.
5. Do not require men and women to wear markedly different costumes, particularly when the women's costumes are revealing. (To do so might invite charges of disparate treatment, or a sex-plus factor).
6. Remember the difference between providing entertainment and providing a service. (In the former, as in a theatrical production, costumes—or lack of them—are important; in the latter, a revealing costume may not be related to performance of the job.)

Beverage Servers: Management Challenge or Bar Room Side Show?

Leigh Tunney

"Short skirt" . . . "sex" . . . "false name" . . . "ratty hair" . . . "air-head" . . . "sleazy" . . . these are a sampling of words and phrases that came up when people were asked to respond to the phrase "cocktail waitress." Out of the thirty people questioned (most of them hotel restaurant employees), there was not a single positive response. Even the word "cocktail" itself, an American bastardization of the French word for mixed drink, sounds somewhat obscene. Adding to the problem of negative job image is the fact that the cocktail staff is often the most poorly trained in any hotel restaurant.

The bar area seems to be treated by most hotel restaurants as a separate entity, seldom acknowledged or even entered by the general manager, who usually is more concerned with how the housekeeping staff is performing or if the dining room is up to par. Bars often are left to run themselves under the sole supervision of the bar manager, who is generally a bartender with seniority and no actual management experience.

Where it is often enough to become bar manager after having simply outlasted all the bartending staff, it is also usually enough to have a winning smile and good legs to become a cocktail server. When a person is hired for a restaurant dining room position, some experience is required, as well as a

This reading is original to this book.

certain amount of knowledge pertaining to food, wine, and liquor. Unfortunately, most cocktail servers are only required to look good in a push-up bra; they are not required to know that Frangelico is a hazelnut liqueur and not an Italian director. Training for cocktail servers throughout the industry is fairly standardized: You are asked if you can smile and carry a tray at the same time and then told to do so. Product knowledge mostly comes through trial and error, resulting in many embarrassing moments. Though the cocktail server is the one who takes the rap for his or her ignorance, it is the management that is really at fault and ultimately responsible for the server's lack of training. Handouts containing information on food products, beer, wine, and all liquor sold given to new waitstaff, followed by a comprehensive test, would alleviate most of this problem and spare both the servers and the hotel restaurant they represent a lot of embarrassment.

Personal Perspective

Another problem that plagues cocktail servers is the issue of dress. For any employee dealing directly with the public, a clean, neat appearance is certainly in order, but "nice legs" are seldom a true job requirement. As a cocktail server, I have worn a low-cut miniskirt sailor outfit with red-and-white striped matching panties, a polyester wrap dress that had a tattered hem and short sleeves and looked as if someone had tried to tear it off, and a tank top and nylon running shorts required while I was employed by a hotel in Honolulu, Hawaii (the men in this last hotel wore long khaki shorts and polo shirts). The tank top was cut in such a manner that it was impossible to wear a bra and not have it show. I skirted the issue by donning a tube-top under my uniform and ordered a size extra large in the nylon shorts so they would not be too revealing. My huge baggy shorts soon became a source of hilarity for all except the management, which quickly moved me to the dining room, for they could see I was clearly not cocktail material. I often felt humiliated and degraded while wearing these outfits,

but could hardly expect someone who has imbibed three martinis to treat me with any respect when I was standing within arm's reach virtually unclothed.

Advice to Managers

You may be able to identify with these feelings and situations, or you may never have been put in the position of having to compromise your dignity in order to pay rent and cover your VISA payment. Regardless, the bottom line is that harassed or unhappy employees offend customers, whether intentionally or unintentionally. This fact seems to escape the attention of the average hotel restaurant manager.

Over the years I have come to the conclusion that people don't really care if their server is wearing high heels or a low-cut top. What customers care about is good service. They care whether the server knows which micro-brewery the beer is from and what it tastes like, or what beers are available on draft or in bottles. Guests care if the server knows what wines are served by the glass, and which are sweet and which are dry. They care if the server can suggest an aperitif they can sip on while waiting to be seated before dinner, or a good cognac or coffee drink that might be enjoyed after dinner. Most of all, guests would like all of this to be done with a genuine courteous smile, which is difficult to do if you've spent the last eight hours on a pair of high heels or if you feel like you've spent that same amount of time in a den full of hungry lions.

Self-respect and self-image are essential qualities of a good employee. If you feel valued as a person, not a commodity, you will take pride in what you do and that will reflect on your place of employment.

CASE STUDY—"Regional Cuisine"

The Corporate Food and Beverage Committee, through its executive director, has ordered each hotel in the chain (11 medium-sized, full-service hotels situated generally in the Southwest, West Coast, and Northwest) to submit a plan for one of its hotel restaurants to feature menus that emphasize local or regional cuisine. This menu is to utilize fresh ingredients—local meat, produce, and seafood—and should feature the ethnic and cultural diversity of each hotel's local market area. One thrust of this plan is to make the hotel restaurant appeal to local clientele in addition to its guests.

As food and beverage director, you have brought this plan to a meeting of your staff for purposes of general background discussion and ideas about how to implement it. Included in the meeting are the executive chef and the chief steward; the manager and the assistant manager of your (up to this point) formal French dining room; the wine steward and the director of purchasing.

After presentation of the corporate plan, you ask for ideas and comments. The chef, who is French, is absolutely devastated and seems to be treating the suggestion as a personal insult. He walks out in a huff, threatening to pack up his knives and recipes and go back to France. The restaurant manager is interested in the idea but says she has just spent five months hiring and training about one-half of her restaurant staff to learn tableside preparation and service of the French menu. She is worried that switching menus this fast may cause her operation to suffer, at least in the short term.

The wine steward considers this a challenge because, depending on what eventually is offered in the restaurant, he will have to choose a complementary wine list to enhance local foods when there is no significant wine industry in your locale. He does, however, think there are compromises that can be made and would like to talk with you further about it.

The director of purchasing is intrigued by the possibilities of exploring new local markets. He warns, however, that developing such a menu may have significant start-up costs, particularly relative to locally produced ingredients that may be very scarce.

Your job as director of food and beverage is to help each department head to come up with a plan that will satisfy their concerns while at the same time follow the dictates of corporate policy.

Endnotes

[1] All figures and percentages in this article are from statistics compiled by Laventhol & Horwath, principally *U.S. Lodging Industry* (Philadelphia: Laventhol & Horwath, 1983), and *Restaurant Industry Operations Report 1983* (Philadelphia: Laventhol & Horwath, 1983).

[2] Conducted under the auspices of the School of Hotel, Restaurant, and Tourism Administration at the University of New Orleans, the study was co-sponsored by the American Hotel and Motel Association and the American Culinary Federation.

[3] The sample for this survey was selected from hotel properties that (1) were located in the continental United States; (2) had 250 rooms or more; (3) had a single-room rate of $35 or more; (4) offered on-premises food services with gross food sales of $300,000 or more; and (5) employed an executive chef or working chef. The research committee of the American Hotel and Motel Association provided an initial listing of 620 properties, which was subsequently cross-referenced with a number of other sources to identify hotels meeting the above five criteria.

[4] In the absence of previous research on the position of executive chef, the remarks of this section are based on interviews conducted by the author with hotel personnel directors, general managers, executive chef recruitment firms, and executive chefs.

[5] Title VII, Civil Rights Act of 1964, 42 U.S.C.A. Section 2000e et seq., as amended in 1972, provides in part:

It shall be an unlawful employment practice for an employer:

(1) to fail or refuse to hire or to discharge any individual, or otherwise to discriminate against any individual with respect to his compensation, or terms, conditions, or privileges of employment, because of such individual's race, color, religion, sex, or national origin;

(2) to limit, segregate, or classify employees or applicants for employment in any way which would deprive or tend to deprive any individual of employment opportunities or otherwise adversely affect his status as an employee, because of such individual's race, color, religion, sex, or national origin.

[6]Administrative agencies may issue *"substantive* rules," which carry the force of law, or *"advisory* rules," which are not legally binding but represent the agency's understanding of what the law is. The rules cited in the text are of the latter type.

[7]EEOC Guidelines for Discrimination Because of Sex under Title VII of the Civil Rights Act of 1964: 29 C.F.R. Section 1604.11. The guidelines are lengthy, but the pertinent sections state:

(a) Harassment on the basis of sex is a violation of Section 703 of Title VII. Unwelcome sexual advances, requests for sexual favors, and other verbal or physical conduct of a sexual nature constitute sexual harassment when . . .

    (3) such conduct has the purpose or effect of unreasonably interfering with an individual's work performance or creating an intimidating, hostile, or offensive working environment.

(e) An employer may also be responsible for the acts of nonemployees, with respect to sexual harassment of employees in the workplace, where the employer (or its agents or supervisory employees) knows or should have known of the conduct and fails to take immediate and appropriate corrective action. In reviewing these cases, the commission will consider the extent of the employer's control and any other legal responsibility which the employer may have with respect to the conduct of such nonemployees.

[8]22 FEP Cases, 1160: 507 F. Sup. 599, 24 FEP Cases, 1521 (1981).

References

ASCAP. 1978. Music and the law. ASCAP Report, p. 2.

ASCAP. 1984. Memorandum of agreement, 7 January.

Blake, Anthony, and Quentin Crewe. 1978. *The great chefs of France.* New York: Harry N. Abrams.

Brayfield, A.H., and H.F. Rothe. 1951. An index of job satisfaction. *Journal of Applied Psychology* 35:307–11.

Coltman, M. 1982. *Hospitality management accounting.* Boston: CBI Publishing.

Hull, G.P., and W.E. Kent. 1977. Live entertainment: Considerations for hotels and restaurants. *Cornell Hotel and Restaurant Administration Quarterly* 18:13–16.

Kent, William E. 1982. Job satisfaction among hotel managers: Implications for hospitality educators. *Journal of Hospitality Education* 7:13–21.

Kent, William E., and Patti J. Shock. 1983. Women in hospitality management: Does quantity = equality? *HSMA Marketing Review* 1:16–21.

Lillo, S. 1981. Let us entertain you, operators say. *Nation's Restaurant News* 16:33–36.

Pannell, Kerr, Forster & Company. 1983a. *Trends in the hotel industry, U.S.A. edition.*

Pannell, Kerr, Forster & Company. 1983b. *Trends in the hotel industry, International edition.*

Wren, J.R. 1981. Restaurants and show biz: An individualized approach. *Food Service Marketing* 43:37–41.

Suggested Readings

Articles

Feltenstein, Tom. "New-Product Development in Food Service: A Structured Approach." *Cornell Hotel and Restaurant Administration Quarterly* 27(3), 1986:63–71.

Glickhouse, Michael. "The Seelbach: Ace Roomservice at an Old World Operation." *Lodging Hospitality* (May 1985):80–82.

Hackett, Carole. "The Woman Food and Beverage Manager." *Cornell Hotel and Restaurant Administration Quarterly* 22(3) (November 1981):79–85.

Lombardi, Dennis, and Richard Conti. "The Turnaround in Lodging Foodservice." *Lodging Hospitality* (May 1985):42–44, 46.

Price, Laurence. "A Case Study: The Big Turnaround in Hotel Food Rooms." *Lodging* 13/1 (September 1987):77–82.

Swinyard, William R., and Kenneth D. Struman. "Market Segmentation: Finding the Heart of Your Restaurant's Market." *Cornell Hotel and Restaurant Administration Quarterly* 27(1), 1986:89–96.

Marketing and Other Staff Departments

INTRODUCTION

Staff departments as defined earlier are those that typically have no regular day-to-day contact with a hotel's guests. The roles of these departments will vary in importance and intensity from company to company and in some cases within companies from hotel to hotel. What is important to understand at this stage is that in one form or another, each of these departments will exist either in fact or by implication in most hotel organizations. The people who perform staff functions and the specialization and intensity these people bring to their functions will vary, depending on the needs of the organization. In a "Mom and Pop" roadside motor inn with twelve units, the operators may find no need for data processing, let alone a separate staff department or person devoted to that activity. They will, however, in some way accumulate data about their business activities, store it in some fashion, and report it (most likely to themselves) on a somewhat regular basis to help them judge how successful their business venture may be.

As we also noted earlier, in any given organization, these activities or departments may find "organizational homes" in operating line divisions. On the other hand, the needs of other organizations will mandate a separate department staffed by one or more professional specialists who devote exclusive time to this activity on behalf of other departments in the entire hotel organization.

MARKETING

For most hotel companies, it has been only recently that the word "marketing" was anything more than a euphemism for sales. Indeed, in the competitive landscape of the not-too-distant past, most activities that related to putting guests in rooms could be accomplished by an aggressive and knowledgeable sales staff. In the competitive environment of the current time, this has become impossible. Hotel companies that design and market a sophisticated inventory of services need a concomitantly sophisticated scheme of letting their clientele know about their services.

For most hotel companies, true marketing has now evolved to reflect this sophistication. This also acknowledges increased sophistication on the part of guests and potential clientele. Business travelers, travel agents, and those who represent and book group business are well-educated and informed consumers. To serve this clientele, hotels have had to develop marketing efforts first to interest the market and second to allow people representing that market to make intelligent choices from among competitors.

"Marketing" is thus an umbrella term that covers a number of strategic and tactical activities designed to tell the clientele the "story" of the hotel's services and encourage that clientele to make choices based on how one hotel's marketing message compares to those of alternatives. In any given hotel or hotel company, marketing may include a range of sales activities; public relations; advertising in all media; design of symbols and images; and (increasingly) the departments of convention services and reservations.

It should also be noted that research plays a major role in designing marketing strategies and tactics. While no specific article on research is included in this section, the Suggested Readings both here and elsewhere include some that have to do with the systematic accumulation of data about a hotel's market. It is important that managers understand the range within which this data may be interpreted and applied. Successful managers and high-quality organizations will always be seeking information that allows them to make accurate decisions and design effective marketing and/or managerial efforts.

While many of the specific details or programs implied under the marketing umbrella may be farmed out to other agencies that specialize in advertising or public relations, the genesis of the hotel's strategic marketing plan has to be within the hotel organization itself.

The articles contributed to this section by Renaghan and Lewis both treat aspects of the strategic nature of marketing and attest to the new levels of sophistication that are becoming inherent in hotels' marketing activities. Plunkett and Berger, Whitney, and Troy each treat specific details attendant to the personnel structure of the modern sales staff.

The article by Jacques Cossé presents a traditionally oriented focus on the role of the public re-

lations professional in the generation of favorable publicity for his or her organization. A different but not contrary set of tactics is explored by Louis Richmond relative to the participation of the hotel organization as a conscientious corporate citizen of the community.

At the present time, advertising represents such a sophisticated and specialized range of activities that most companies rely on professional agencies to design and place in the various media a hotel's advertising message. In the Suggested Readings, the article by Glenn Withiam on hotel advertising in the 1980s provides an in-depth analysis and presentation of the range of possibilities available to a hotel company.

Convention services and reservations are both departments that represent relative newcomers to the space created under the marketing umbrella for hotels. As noted earlier, many hotel companies that recognize the importance of group business and the role that the sales staff plays booking hotel business have moved reservations from the front office to the marketing department. Another indication that group business plays an extremely important role in the hotel's marketing mix is the creation of convention services management departments within the marketing department. These departments are staffed by professionals who design their activities specifically to make sure that the efforts and promises of the sales department and marketing messages are delivered to the group while it is on the premises of the hotel. Holly Hughes's article on "a day in the life" of such a manager provides graphic evidence of the importance of this position, along with a detailed look at the responsibilities that are important for this professional to master in participating in the hosting of such an event.

Included in the Suggested Readings at the end of the section are a range of additional views and opinions on various aspects of the marketing umbrella.

A New Marketing Mix for the Hospitality Industry

Leo M. Renaghan

*Traditional marketing-mix concepts have little utility for **the** service industries, because they reflect strategies for selling products, rather than services.*

Most hospitality firms use the same methods to market services as other firms do to market products, even though such traits as the following substantially differentiate services from products:

1. *The intangible nature of services* makes choosing a service more difficult than choosing a product, because the consumer cannot taste, touch, feel, or try the service before selecting it.
2. *The simultaneity of production and consumption* makes location paramount and limits the consumer's choice of alternatives (the number of service outlets in a given area is likely to be limited).
3. *The perishability of services* increases a firm's financial risks and aggravates demand problems because service cannot be inventoried.
4. *The variability of output* makes services hard to predict and control, for several reasons: service is inherently intangible; the consumer is nearly always present at the point of production; and services are often affected by the whims, idiosyncrasies, and errors of the people who perform them.
5. *The ease of duplicating services* allows competitors to copy a service faster than they would a product, because there are few barriers to market entry.
6. *The risk that consumers perceive* in selecting services, in response to the foregoing factors, is considerably higher than the perceived risk in selecting products (Sasser, Olsen, and Wyckoff 1978).

To prosper in the decades ahead, hospitality firms must develop competitive strategies based on a marketing mix that reflects all of these characteristics, and that also satisfies the needs of the target market. The process of identifying and determining profit potential in target markets follows the same general principles for both products and services. The differences between services and products, however, become problematic as a firm begins to develop a marketing mix.

The business executive who blends policies and procedures, searching for the mixture that will produce optimum profits, is designing a "marketing mix," a concept pioneered by Borden in the early 1960s (Borden 1968). The marketing-mix concept has been refined continually as its acceptance has grown. The adaptation applied most frequently to the hospitality industry is known as McCarthy's "Four Ps":

- *Product:* A physical product or some combination of services that satisfies customer needs.
- *Place:* When, where, and by whom the goods and services are to be offered for sale.
- *Promotion:* Any method communicating information to the target market about the right product in the right place at the right time.
- *Price:* A price that makes the offering as attractive as possible (McCarthy 1975).

One problem with using this framework or similar product frameworks is that the traits that distinguish services from products have not been accounted for. Coffman (1970) mentions 12 "factors" in his

This article was originally published in the August 1981 issue of *The Cornell Hotel and Restaurant Administration Quarterly*, and is reprinted here with the permission of the Cornell University School of Hotel Administration. © 1981.

marketing mix, ranging from product planning through display and marketing research. Crissy, Boewadt, and Laudadio (1975) list the customer-service mix, the service mix, and the promotional mix. Eison (1980), on the other hand, offers no marketing mix at all. Because a marketing strategy should be built on the framework of a well-defined marketing mix, hospitality operators without a marketing-mix concept applicable to services may grow confused when attempting to develop a strategy.

For those attempting to develop a strategy that reflects the differences between products and services, the author proposes a new hospitality marketing mix based on a set of clearly delineated but interrelated elements.

The mix contains three major sub-mixes:

1. *The Product-Service Mix:* The combination of products and services, whether free or for sale, aimed at satisfying the needs of the target market.
2. *The Presentation Mix:* All elements used by the firm to increase the tangibility of the product-service mix in the perception of the target market at the right place and time.
3. *The Communications Mix:* All communications between the firm and the target market that increase the tangibility of the product-service mix, that establish or monitor consumer expectations, or that persuade consumers to purchase.

THE PRODUCT-SERVICE MIX

The term "product-service mix" has been chosen because it explicitly reflects the fact that hospitality firms offer a simultaneous blend of products and services. Generally, however, hospitality firms focus almost exclusively on selling products because most of the marketing-program mixes they employ are borrowed from product-strategy formulations, and because it is simpler to market products than to market services.

Products that can be seen and tasted can be described in concrete ways. Services can be described only in nebulous ways. Products can easily be test-

marketed; services cannot. Furthermore, services are difficult to define in terms of the target market, hard to offer, and harder still to control. Numerous hotels and restaurants advertise friendly service, for example, but even if operators and consumers agreed on what constituted friendliness, it would be difficult to determine what impact friendly service had on consumers' purchase decisions.

Consumers do not perceive the product and service elements of the mix separately; they perceive them instead as a unified whole. If the elements of the mix change, therefore, the consumer's perception of the entire mix changes, sometimes dramatically; thus, when a firm develops a marketing strategy, the service elements of the mix should be an important part of that strategy, even though they may be difficult to understand or develop. Firms must also decide which services to sell, and should be aware that consumers measure service by performance rather than by possession. Firms promising elegant, friendly, adventurous, unique, or exciting service sometimes misunderstand this idea when they attempt to promote these intangible qualities as if they were products. Companies that market services should make sure that their promises are not isolated sales-promotion ploys but part of the total product-service mix. In his novel *Mother Night,* Kurt Vonnegut put the idea succinctly: "We are," he said, "what we pretend to be and must therefore be careful what we pretend to be" (Vonnegut 1972).

Deciding what to be (or pretend to be) has been rendered easier in recent years by the development of sophisticated statistical techniques. With conjoint analysis, for example, the operator can pinpoint the elements in the product-service offering that are important to consumers—as well as clarify consumer purchase intentions and determine how they correspond to combinations of elements in the offering (Myers and Tauber 1977).

THE PRESENTATION MIX

The term "presentation mix" signifies an umbrella concept covering those elements under the firm's control that act in concert to make the total product-service offering more tangible to the consumer. The presentation mix is also the means by which the firm differentiates its product-service offering from competitive offerings.

Every restaurant sells food, of course, but not all restaurants are alike. Every hotel sells the use of a room with a collection of furnishings, but not all hotels are alike. In each instance, the customer perceives the whole offering: the restaurant, not just the food; the hotel, not just the room. Differences in the elements of the presentation mix allow the consumer to distinguish one establishment from another.

Major elements of the presentation mix are the physical plant, location, atmospherics (light, sound, space, smell, accoutrements), price, and employees. Some of these elements are routinely included in product-strategy formulation, but they should be viewed differently by a firm planning a service-marketing strategy.

Physical Plant

Both the exterior of the physical plant and the location of profit centers within the building are part of the presentation mix. If a physical plant has been designed successfully, the customer should be able to tell what is happening inside a building simply by viewing its exterior. The physical structure should reflect the intangible service elements that are part of the total offering. Trader Vic's, for example, looks like not only a restaurant, but also a *Polynesian* restaurant. A hotel designed by John Portman is not only a hotel, but also a specific type of environment.

"Profit-center proximities" is a term that describes the relationship between a property's profit centers and its customer traffic. Profit-center proximities are important elements of a service-strategy formulation for numerous reasons. First, because services are intangible, it is difficult to communicate to customers what is being sold in a way that will entice them to buy. Advertisements, especially those that appear in print, may

not fully describe the ambience of an "elegant" restaurant.

Second, because a service must be produced close to the point of consumption, a service outlet's proximity to the customer is important. Profit-center locations should correspond with a customer's normal movements through the property. An example of good profit-center proximity would be a layout that required hotel guests walking from the front desk to the elevator to pass and look into the cocktail lounge, the dining room, the game room, and the indoor pool. An example of poor profit-center proximity would be a cocktail lounge not visible from the hotel's lobby, and accessible only through the dining room.

Perceived risk is the third reason that profit-center proximities are an important element of service-strategy formulation. All purchase decision-making involves some element of risk. Warranties, guarantees against defects, and testimonials that assure consumers of a product's reliability are all elements of a product-marketing strategy intended to help consumers reduce perceived risk. These assurances are rarely available to someone buying services, and defects in services are not easily proven. For example, who advertises a money-back guarantee on a hotel room? How can a customer prove that a meal was unsatisfactory or the service unfriendly?

A recent study of consumer attitudes and behavior indicates that customers seek testimonials about service offerings. Consumers were asked which factors would influence their choice of a restaurant they had never patronized. Of the 13 factors mentioned, the two cited most frequently were friends' recommendations and the type of food offered. The appearance of a property and its location placed third and fourth. A favorable newspaper or magazine review was mentioned as the fifth most important factor.[1] In short, customers seek information that allows them to reduce the perceived risk of the purchase decision. If a customer is able to view the interior of a hotel before selecting it, or is given some clue as to the quality of a restaurant's food before electing to dine there, he reduces his risk because his choice is an informed one.

Location

Location is important for several reasons. Consumers are willing to travel a distance to locate the right offering if the cost of making the wrong decision is high enough. If the decision is less important, however, consumers will pick the most conveniently located offering. Fast-food restaurants are often clustered along one street, because consumers will not go far out of their way to find the right fast-food restaurant; the risk of making the wrong decision is slight. Location is therefore crucial to a fast-food operator. As one executive stated, "There's no such thing as a good secondary location in fast food."

Location can also act as a barrier to prevent competitors from entering a particular market. As part of its marketing strategy, every firm must consider how it can build and protect a strong competitive position. Product-oriented companies normally use capital and patents as barriers to their competition. For labor-intensive service businesses, multiple locations can serve as a barrier to entry (Thomas 1978).

Atmospherics

A firm promising elegance can support its promise through such atmospherics as furnishings, lighting, decor, music, and use of space. Atmospherics can act as cues to reinforce service offerings and make them more tangible to consumers. They can also affect purchase behavior by acting as attention-getting, message-creating, or emotion-creating media (Kotler 1973–74).

Price

In product marketing, prices are commonly established on the basis of costs. In service marketing, however, this approach simply doesn't work. (What does friendliness cost, for example?) The value consumers place on services, and its effect on their purchase behavior, might determine the cost. For example, low price may affect purchase intent adversely. When consumers with little information must purchase something new or unfamiliar, they often make inferences about quality on the basis of price.

Employees

A firm's employees are the final element of the presentation mix. Because of the intangibility of services and the consumer's presence at the point of production, a firm may find it difficult to establish service standards and even harder to ensure that the standards are met each time service is delivered. One way that service firms can solve this problem is through training programs designed to recognize employees as an important element of the service-marketing strategy. "For services," William George notes, "employees are perceived to be the product; they become the physical representation of the product. . . . The successful service company must first sell the job to its employees, before it can sell services to its customers" (George 1977). For this reason, fast-food outlets dress all employees in stylish uniforms, and theme parks hire young, attractive "actors," even though they incur higher costs as a result. Such companies have realized that, to a consumer, the employee is the product.

THE COMMUNICATIONS MIX

In a service-marketing strategy, a communications mix serves two major purposes. First, it persuades the consumer—that is, it re-creates the intangible qualities of a service and makes them more tangible to the consumer. An effective communications mix includes pictures that make the intangible more tangible. In some hotels, for example, slide shows and films that illustrate services can be viewed in guest rooms via closed-circuit television.

Second, a communications mix can both establish and monitor a consumer's expectations. Because of the intangibility of service and the variability of service output, operators may find it difficult to ensure that the meaning of "friendliness," for example, stays the same for the firm and the consumer, and that friendliness is delivered every time the consumer makes a purchase. Visual-communication techniques can help establish consumer expectations, but it is important to remember that communication is a two-way process, and that it involves more than the purchase persuasion we normally associate with advertising. Thus, the task of monitoring consumer expectations is also an essential part of a service-marketing strategy. Although many operators see this task as too difficult, new point-of-purchase computers that register guest attitudes and satisfaction levels will make it easier for firms

to develop monitoring programs (Cadotte 1980). Some monitoring programs have already been tested at hotels, with positive results (Cadotte 1979).

CONCLUSION

A new marketing mix, one that reflects the differences between products and services, should be part of every hospitality firm's total marketing strategy for improving performance and for competing successfully in the marketplace. Firms that strive to develop specific service-marketing strategies rather than follow traditional product-marketing strategies are those most likely to succeed.

Positioning Analysis for Hospitality Firms

Robert C. Lewis

The positioning of hospitality firms in the market-place is an essential component of effective marketing in today's highly competitive environment. Essential to optimal positioning is a knowledge of the importance and perceived deliverability of benefits to the consumer for both the firm and its competition. This paper describes a methodology for the determination and analysis of those benefits that can be utilized most effectively by a hospitality firm and that has practical implications for firms of any size.

Key words: Positioning; benefits; differentiation.

Marketing objectives need to be defined in terms of optimal market positioning. Today's highly competitive market-place in the hospitality industry gives overwhelming credence to this concept first introduced by Trout and Ries in 1972. Effective positioning in the minds of consumers sets a hotel or restaurant apart from the competition and becomes the *raison d'être* for "why should I go there?" The

Reprinted with permission of Pergamon Press and the author from Lewis, Robert C. "Positioning Analysis for Hospitality Firms." *International Journal of Hospitality Management,* vol. 1, no. 2 (1982), pp. 115–118.

difficult part occurs in the application. If the competition offers essentially the same features, how can positioning be used to set the property apart? This paper describes an analytical method to that end.

OPTIMAL POSITIONING

Optimal positioning includes three major elements (Lewis 1981):

1. It creates an image.
2. It promises to deliver certain benefits.
3. It differentiates from the competition.

The first step then is to define these elements within the resources, capabilities, and competence of the property in question. Management essentially asks, "What do we have to offer?" and develops a benefit matrix in terms of consumer needs and wants (Lewis 1981). This exercise is repeated for the competition so that differentiating factors, if any, can be highlighted. This provides the potential of positioning strengths against weaknesses.

Many property managements will stop at this point, but the most important work is yet to be done. Management only knows what it can do or is willing to do. This is an objective, rational, and necessary perspective but its efficaciousness resides in its correlation with the subjective, sometimes irrational, perspective of the consumer. The hard questions that have to be asked are:

- What is important to the target market?
- How does the target market perceive us?
- How does the target market perceive the competition?
- What should we differentiate on so as to best use our limited resources?

The reality of the matter is: If the target market doesn't perceive the image, it doesn't exist; if it doesn't believe that what you have to offer is a benefit, it isn't a benefit; if it doesn't believe you can deliver the benefit, your promises are meaningless; if the benefit isn't important to the target market, it isn't important; if your benefit is not perceived as different from that of the competition, you haven't differentiated. In short, images, benefits, and differentiation are solely the perception of the consumer, not management. The place to put market resources is where positioning does or can fulfill its criteria in the perception of the target market.

EFFECTIVELY POSITIONED BENEFITS

Effectively positioned benefits emphasize these vital elements: what the benefits do for the consumer, how important they are to the consumer, and how credible the promise to deliver them is to the consumer. These elements are especially pertinent to hospitality marketing because of the intangibility of the services offered and the simultaneous production and consumption of the offering which permits evaluation only after the purchase is a *fait accompli*. These factors underlie the need to use tangible surrogates to represent intangible service benefits in order to enhance the vital elements.

Research in the hospitality industry often fails to reveal the vital elements of benefits. Guest comment cards, for example, ask the customer if he or she liked certain features of the property or operation. They fail to reveal what those features do for the consumer or how important they are even if successfully accomplished (Lewis and Pizam 1981).

The architecture of a hotel, the decor of the lobby, the furnishings of a room are examples of hotel attributes that may be the reason behind a benefit, or tangible surrogates for intangible benefits, but they are not the benefit. The benefit is what they do for the consumer, e.g., give a sense of security, a sensation of grandeur, an aura of prestige, or a feeling of comfort. And the credibility of these benefits may diminish rapidly if an expectation is not fulfilled. Decor is soon forgotten if room service takes an hour. A sense of security may not be credible if slovenly characters are seen in the lobby or met on the elevator. It is this fulfillment of expectations, or lack of it, that creates the perception of deliverability for the consumer.

Finally, competing hotels may be seen as providing the same senses of security, grandeur, prestige, and comfort. The tangible surrogate attributes have lost their ability to differentiate and, at the same time, are no longer deterministic in the choice of a hotel.

Benefits, then, dwell in the perception of the consumer and are determinable only by asking the consumer. Optimal use of this information requires quantification of importance and perception aspects for proper positioning analysis.

POSITIONING ANALYSIS

The first step in positioning analysis is to identify those benefits that represent the range of possibilities for the target market in your type of property and that of your competitors. These can be culled from previous research, from focus groups, from personal interviews of your own customers, and from management.

The second step is to quantify these benefits in terms of their importance to the target market. This consists of asking consumers to rate the importance of each benefit on a five- or seven-point scale. The resulting data can be handled in one of two ways. One way is simple, convenient, and available to anyone. This consists of identifying as important only those benefits that have been rated by a majority of the respondents, preferably two-thirds or more, as being *very important*.

The second method is to use a multivariate analysis technique such as discriminant, factor, or regression analysis. These techniques require more sophistication and use of a computer but have the advantage of considering all benefit-importance ratings simultaneously and interactively rather than one at a time. They also give statistically significant measures. Because of the ready availability in many software packages, the explanation that follows was derived from the use of regression analysis. The number of variables was first reduced by factor analysis in order to simplify the explanation. This procedure collapses many variables or benefits into a few by statistically locating those with similar commonalities.

The second step in positioning analysis is to ask consumers in the target market group to rate your property and those of your competition on how well they provide each benefit. This is also done on a five- or seven-point scale, and the same analytical procedures discussed above can be utilized.

Two dimensions result from this research and analysis. One is the target market's attitude, or importance measurement, toward the benefits offered. The other is its perception of each of the properties on their ability to deliver the benefits. Plotting in benefit space is used to bring the two dimensions together in their marketing positions and to see how each property is positioned against the competition.

AN EXAMPLE

Guests of a 250-room motor inn (Hotel X) were queried in the method described above. Forty-one attributes were rated on their benefit importance when staying at a motor inn and on the respondents' perceptions of these attributes as being delivered by the motor inn and two competing properties (Hotels Y and Z). The data were factor-analyzed into ten categories, which were given general headings for demonstration purposes. The regression weights derived for Hotel X are shown in Table 1.

A matrix is then defined by the benefit ratings themselves by using the median of the importance and delivery ratings to divide the matrix into quadrants. The intercepts of the importance and delivery ratings are plotted on the matrix as shown in Figure 1 for Hotel X.

The quadrants in Figure 1 can be interpreted as follows: Quadrant I indicates a solid position for all benefits located here. These benefits are not only important to the target market but are also seen as being delivered by the property in question. In this case Hotel X is perceived as excelling in room and bath facilities and comfort (A) as well as in convenient location and availability to other attractions (D). Benefits in this quadrant are optimally positioned and can be used to differentiate and create an image in the product class to the extent that the competition is not in the same quadrant.

Quadrant II contains those benefits that are important but are not perceived as being delivered by the property. If the competition is positioned in Quadrant I on these benefits, the property in Quadrant II is at a disadvantage. If the competition is also in this quadrant, no differentiation occurs but there may be an opportunity to reposition, change consumer perception, and gain an advantage.

TABLE 1

Regression weights for Hotel X on importance and deliverability of benefits

Benefit	Importance rating	Deliverability perception rating
(A) Room and bath facilities and comfort	0.22	0.20
(B) Room service satisfaction	0.18	0.02
(C) Sports facilities availability	0.12	0.12
(D) Convenience of location and availability to other attractions	0.11	0.24
(E) Room and bath maintenance and cleanliness	0.10	0.06
(F) Professionalism and attitude of staff	0.09	0.10
(G) Restaurant availability and service	0.08	0.08
(H) Front desk service and attitude	0.05	0.13
(I) Prestige and aesthetics of property	0.04	0.19
(J) Prices—absolute and value	0.01	0.17

Note: Some of the importance ratings for Hotel X are counterintuitive. This appears to be due to the nature of the particular property. It demonstrates a contradiction between management's and consumer's ratings of importance benefits.

Quadrants III and IV represent benefits that are not all that important to the target market. Benefits in Quadrant III lack both importance and deliverability perception. There is no point, however, in attempting to increase favorable perception because these benefits are relatively unimportant. The benefits in Quadrant IV are perceived as being delivered but there is no real need to use them for positioning, again because of their relative unimportance. Resources should be concentrated, instead, on benefits in Quadrants I and II. In Figure 1 positioning potency is weak as there are only two prime positioning benefit candidates. Marketing needs to be made more efficient.

Figures 2 and 3 show the positions of the competition in Quadrants I and II. Hotel Y (Figure 2) has a positioning advantage in room and bath maintenance (E) but is perceived poorly in facilities and comfort (A). This creates both threats and opportunities for Hotel X. Housekeeping and maintenance departments need to be strengthened to at least nullify Hotel Y's position in this area. On the other hand, Hotel X has the opportunity to position strongly on benefit A. A real advantage could be gained by increasing favorable perception of sports facilities and room service. The latter, however, might be short-lived, as neither hotel in this example offered regular room service and Hotel Y could quickly follow if Hotel X instituted it.

Figure 3 adds emphasis to the fact that Hotel X

FIGURE 1

Positioning matrix for Hotel X

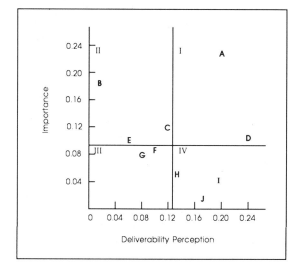

FIGURE 3

Quadrants 1 and 2 positioning for Hotel Z

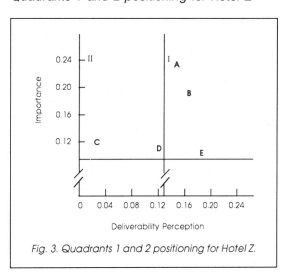

Fig. 3. Quadrants 1 and 2 positioning for Hotel Z.

FIGURE 2

Quadrants 1 and 2 positioning for Hotel Y

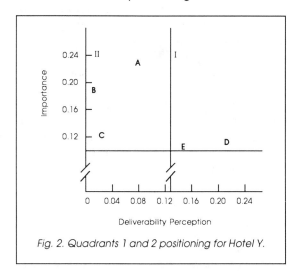

Fig. 2. Quadrants 1 and 2 positioning for Hotel Y.

had best make some strong improvements in room and bath maintenance. Hotel Z represents strong competition in its positioning potential against Hotel X. Again, however, an opportunity is available to Hotel X to differentiate on its sports facilities. Hotel X can also use its location to position against Hotel Z.

SUMMARY

The utility of positioning analysis is evident from the foregoing discussion. It quantitatively analyzes what is important to the target market, how the target market perceives a property and its competition, and on what benefits a property's resources can best be spent to position against the competition.

Perhaps equally important, positioning analysis pinpoints those areas that constitute threats and weaknesses. Some of these may be unavoidable, e.g., a location is not readily changeable. Others, however, provide a strong message to management about areas where it needs to take action and make positive improvements.

Optimal positioning is tantamount to marketing effectiveness. By the same token, a positioning ad-vantage should not be easily relinquished to the competition. Ideally, of course, management would like to see all important benefits located in Quadrant I. Conversely, if none are, or can be, located there, it may be time to define a different target market.

Unleashing the Hotel Sales Tigers

David A. Troy

The best hotel salespersons have drive, empathy, and ego strength. These factors are generally com-bined in just one out of every five persons on the typical hotel's sales staff—and the other four should be selling something else, or not selling at all. In this article, I will briefly describe the traits of a suc-cessful hotel salesperson, and then discuss how to put these to use in a strong marketing program.

Although we often hear that 80 percent of sales are made by 20 percent of salespersons, this rule of thumb has gained substance from a study by Personality Dynamics, which found that 20 percent of salespeople are making virtually all sales. In ad-dition to having drive, empathy, and ego strength, this group also has the ability to deal with complex sales concepts.

Drive

The number of successful women in sales has in-creased greatly in the last 20 years. I believe this is because it's socially more acceptable for women today to develop their ego drives. Women have been given the green light—eons later than they should have—to choose the fanatical pursuit of the satisfaction that comes with victory. Certainly Martina Navratilova or Mary Decker Slaney could sell if they chose to.

I once worked with a man named Bob Keilt, one of Sheraton's greatest one-on-one salesmen. He is the classic case—his delight is to take hopeless sales situations and turn them into victories. For example, a pharmaceutical firm once canceled its trade show at a Sheraton property. Instead of ac-cepting the promise of a *possible* future conference at another Sheraton, Keilt went after a three-year *contract* for future shows. In the pursuit of this goal, he and the managers of Sheraton properties in To-ronto and Washington wrote several letters to the drug firm. Sheraton offered specific packages in ad-vance, with guaranteed prices, firm commitments for complimentary meeting rooms, and a proposal for producing any of 26 theme parties during the show. In the process, Keilt showed the company that signing the contract would save nearly $200,000 over the cost of making individual annual bookings.

Another great example of ego drive is John Met-calfe, Fairmont's national sales director. John's slo-gan might be: "No is a negotiable word." When he was resting at home following open-heart surgery, he constantly pushed to have his company turn over its crisis files to him for resolution.

Empathy

The ability to see a situation through another's eyes is crucial to making sales. The empathetic sales-person senses how a prospect is reacting to a sales

This article was originally published in the November 1984 issue of *The Cornell Hotel and Restaurant Administration Quarterly,* and is reprinted here with the permission of the Cornell University School of Hotel Administration. © 1984.

presentation and alters it on the spot to fit the customer's reaction. If a group representative seems worried about meeting costs, for example, but is not concerned with the costs passed on to the group's members, an empathetic salesperson might bid rack room rates and "comp" a reception or function space. The empathetic salesperson lives by the rule, "Don't tell me what it does good; tell me what good it does me." Note that empathetic and sympathetic are not the same thing. A good boxer can be empathetic, but can hardly afford any sympathy.

My favorite story about salespeople who lack empathy is of a young insurance salesperson who wanted to practice his pitch on me. About halfway through his barrage of charts and graphs, I said, "Jack, that's the one for me; I'll buy that policy." His hardly empathetic response was, "No, not now. You'll mess me up. You're supposed to buy when I get to closing." Frankly, it's OK to stop when the customer says yes.

Ego Strength

Returning to tennis for a moment, consider why Billie Jean King would probably outsell some of her fellow tennis pros—because King still fights her way through singles at Wimbledon and makes it into the doubles finals every year, even though she is over 40, even though she has had six knee operations, even though she has felt public exposure that would have ruined other people. That's ego strength.

MANAGEMENT CHALLENGE

The challenge for managers is to point their sales tigers in the right direction. I received a great lesson in management about eight years ago when I was coaching my son's Little League "tee-ball" team. In tee-ball, a baseball is placed on a rubber tee about two feet high, and a young boy or girl hits the ball onto a baseball field filled with about 20 other kids who try to grab it. In this instance, my son hit the ball into the outfield, so he easily reached first base, where I was coaching. I told him, "Nice hit, Davey. Go to second base."

"No, Dad."

"What do you mean, no? Go on to second base."

"No, Dad."

"Why won't you go to second?" I screamed in desperation.

"I don't like second."

Simply put, I had failed to explain to the kids the point of the game. I thought they knew the rules and scoring, but they didn't. With this realization, I believe my coaching improved, and I know I became a better business manager.

This personal lesson has real business applications. Do we teach our salespeople about making profits, or do we just tell them to book business and get room-nights? We must communicate the team's goals and objectives to them, because otherwise they won't know what direction they're going.

If you don't set clear goals, you can run into real trouble. For several years, I ran a sales-incentive program. We attracted terrific talent, but we gave it up because we were wrecking the company. This great program had the wrong goals. The program was paying off in room-nights booked over quota, not in profit production. I liken it to a golf match in which the high score wins.

Today's salespeople want to know the rules for scoring. Pushing them out the door to make sales calls without a clear understanding of objectives is just like expecting those eight-year-old kids automatically to do the right thing on the tee-ball field. They want to please, but they don't know how.

LET LOOSE THE TIGERS

Giving your hotel's sales staff something to sell is just as important as setting clear sales objectives. Today's successful hotel companies are responding to the challenges of capitalizing on emerging buying publics. Special programs can be used to attract specific market segments that are important to your hotel. Holiday Inns, for example, courts businesspeople with its Priority One Club; Marriott ties in with airlines to reach frequent travelers; Days Inns aims for family business with its "stay and kids eat free" promotion. The reach of your sales staff can be greatly extended through airline personnel and travel agents. Discount programs will help win the business.

Property Sales

Property-driven marketing is the wave of the future, and property-driven sales must be a key component of this process. In short, property-driven marketing involves using each hotel to its best advantage. To do this, the chief operations officer in each division must be aware of the steps being taken at each property to overcome its local marketing difficulties.

Salespeople must be committed to generating new business where there was none before. They must give up evenings to participate in meetings of local buyers' groups, so they find out about changes in the marketplace firsthand. Most important, salespeople must be out of the building, visiting the customer, selling every day. Imagine the effect on a customer when the salesperson who has made no sale in four visits comes around the fifth time. By then a rapport has been established, and any possible bias the customer feels against the property begins to wilt in the face of such persistence.

General managers should sometimes go out on sales calls, accompanying the salesperson to the potential customer's place of business. The GM should review call reports, check weekly correspondence files, and comment on them. Furthermore, the GM should support the promotional efforts of salespeople—perhaps even by joining them at a trade show or exposition. In fact, the GM's job is to keep tabs on the sales operation, and structure the operation so that the sales function becomes a priority.

Twenty Ideas

A general manager who regularly applies the following 20 suggestions will improve the property's sales effort:

1. Train all people with customer contact to sell.
2. Make sure all printed material from brochures to menus to table tents is selling what you want sold.
3. Study the competition and its marketing efforts.
4. Integrate advertisements, public relations, and sales efforts.
5. Maintain and review a sales-marketing plan.
6. Spot-check sales correspondence to see that letters are going to the type of prospects you want to attract.
7. Review call reports to make sure the sales staff is reaching decision-makers.
8. Maintain an active and accurate trace system.
9. Maintain a lead-log system. Don't forget self-generated leads.
10. Monitor the sales department's coverage of key accounts.
11. Review the call frequency of transient prospects near the hotel.
12. Visit the sales office frequently to demonstrate your interest and support of the staff's activity.
13. Make certain the sales director is part of the operating committee.
14. Get to know and entertain marketing and operations managers of local car-rental, airline, and motorcoach companies.
15. Plan advertising to meet the needs of the hotel, focusing on those operations that have the greatest possibility of payback.
16. Make certain that the media chosen for advertising are appropriate to the target market.
17. Involve all interested parties in the advertising program.
18. Spend all possible time strengthening the hotel's community image, for no hotel can be successful without community acceptance.
19. Be involved in worthwhile community projects, and make sure your department heads do the same.

20. Get to know and entertain local newspaper, magazine, radio, and television reporters and executives.

This list is long, and it may seem superfluous for a hotel that is now making money, but the market is difficult and the competition is not standing still. Most hotels are diversifying their product lines—dividing operations into categories of elite, broad-appeal, and budget hotels. That means a company that essentially operates budget hotels may end up competing directly with a Westin or a Hyatt on an even-dollar basis. The only way to meet a challenge like this is with an aggressive sales staff that is prepared not only to go to bat, but to run around all the bases for a home run.

We had better know what we're doing, because the buyer is a smarter person today—well trained and generally a member of a buyer's organization (e.g., Meeting Planners International, the Society of Corporation Meeting Planners, Insurance Conference Planners). Hotels seeking the government market will probably deal with a member of the Society of Government Meeting Planners.

The qualities of successful salespeople have not changed in 20 years, but the customers have, the marketplace has, and so have the tools of the trade. There was no such thing as teleconferencing, press-tel, satellite linkage, timesharing, or condominiums 20 years ago. We had no bartering, no joint-coupon programs with airline and car-rental companies, no tie-in promotions with cosmetic or pharmaceutical companies. To meet this challenge, sales staffs must be ready to use their product-based data. They must know what marketing clues are contained in the monthly reports that come from central reservation systems. They must talk with their fellow employees who are serving the customers to see what is to be learned about the customers. They must cultivate repeat customers and agents who send them business.

The next few years are filled with promise. The recent increase in vacation travel is expected to continue; corporate travel should extend beyond previous levels. If you, at the property level, can be the market's most aggressive, marketing-minded, unified operations and sales team, your hotel's market position will be dramatically improved. Without coherent property-driven sales, your market share will erode, and your property will fall short of its potential.

Therefore, detest complacency; respect the intelligence of your customers and colleagues; work conscientiously and aggressively to provide the best possible product presented in the most creative way. Try always to be the first to attempt a new program or technique—once you're convinced that it has the potential to improve your profits. And, finally, remember that "no" is a negotiable word.

EXHIBIT 1
A profile of hotel salespeople

The following picture of today's hotel salespeople is drawn from *Patterns of Success* (Washington, DC: Hotel Sales Management Association International, 1983).

- They are young—70 percent are under 40; 31 percent are under 30.
- They are equally male and female. Significantly more of the young salespeople, however, are female.
- They are primarily salespeople—that is, not involved in most cases with other marketing functions.
- They are well-educated—57 percent are college grads; 90 percent have some college background.
- Half got into the business by accident, half on purpose. Only a very small minority went to hotel school.
- Most have been in the business between three and 10 years.
- Most have been with their current property fewer than two years.
- Of those who have worked at multiple properties, over 40 percent have stayed with one company—good companies *can* retain good salespeople.
- Over 89 percent believe they are moving upward. They are very much oriented toward upward mobility.

Sales Skills in the Hospitality Industry

Robert L. Plunkett
Florence Berger

Two surveys were conducted with the intention of increasing insight into the nature of sales in today's hospitality industry. One hundred U.S. hotel sales and marketing managers were surveyed about attitudes within the hotel sales community regarding training, salesmanship, qualities of effective salespeople, and related issues. Also, the training directors of fifteen hotel companies were interviewed concerning their training programs for entry-level salespeople. Presentation of the results of these surveys is preceded by commentary from the literature and from selected hotel sales executives regarding the unique nature of sales in the hospitality industry.

THE UNIQUE NATURE OF HOSPITALITY SALES

In order to understand the nature of sales in the hospitality industry, one must appreciate the distinctions between marketing in manufacturing industries versus marketing in service industries. The principal difference is that in a service industry the "product" sold usually is not a physical good that can be demonstrated or tested; this means the selling challenge for a service can be substantially harder. Similarly, there is considerable immediacy in the provision of a service. "The hamburgers have to be hot, the motel rooms exactly where the sleepy travelers need them, and the airline empty when the customers want to fly" (Sasser 1976).

Several characteristics contribute to the extent to which immediacy sets the selling of services apart. Sasser (1976) notes that services are:

1. Intangible; they cannot be stored on a shelf, touched, tasted, or tried on for size.
2. Direct; they cannot be inventoried. In the production of a service there is a high degree of producer-consumer interaction. Manufactured

goods are produced at one location to be used elsewhere. Production and consumption of a service usually occur in the same place, and often simultaneously.
3. Usually not transportable; consumers must be brought to services such as airlines, hotels, and restaurants rather than vice versa.

This differentiation underlines the importance of adopting unique marketing and selling strategies for service industries. G. Lynn Shostack (1977), a vice president and marketing director for Citibank, noted that "marketing seems to be overwhelmingly product-oriented. Many service-based companies are confused about the applicability of product marketing, and more than one attempt to adopt product marketing has failed."

Specific attributes of the hotel/hospitality industry deserve particular attention when seeking the best approach to direct sales in the hotel industry. Foremost is the group-oriented nature of selling hotel services. Hotels, unlike banks, for instance, tend to market their services to groups, thereby achieving economies of scale in selling accommodation and convention facilities. Moreover, hotels emphasize corporate rather than individual accounts; therefore it is important to assess adequately both the needs of the potential client's corporation and the desires of the client himself. The unique aspects such as intangibility, direct producer-consumer interaction,

Reprinted with permission of Pergamon Press from Plunkett, Robert L., and Florence Berger. "Sales Skills in the Hospitality Industry." *International Journal of Hospitality Management*, vol. 3, no. 3 (1984), pp. 113–121.

and nontransportability contribute to the challenge faced by hotel sales and marketing executives.

According to Maayan Lowenthal (1982), a director of sales and marketing for Canadian Pacific Hotels, the lack of a concrete product makes it harder for salespeople in the hotel industry than in the manufacturing sector. "The hotel salesperson sells expectations, intangibles," she says. "This adds to the difficulty of selling hotel services. Expectations differ, making communication between the buyer and seller more difficult." George Ramirez, director of worldwide sales for Hyatt International, agrees— and thinks the problem is particularly acute in the luxury market. "In the hotel industry you are selling a concept, you're selling the sizzle," says Ramirez (1982).[2] "In the luxury/upscale market there are even more intangibles, making sales in this market more challenging."

Hotel salespeople cannot rely, for instance, on "samples" or demonstration models to sell prospective clients on the value or utility of their goods. Menus and pictures of a property are available, but the buyer must still visualize what he or she will be getting. There is no physical product to test, and because the quality of service offered by any particular hotel can vary widely from one day or even hour to the next, the buyer—and the seller as well—cannot be sure that the same level of service he sees on one day will be delivered at check-in.

The fact that hotel services are direct, requiring a high degree of product-consumer interaction in their production, causes considerable problems for hotel managers as well as salespeople. In manufacturing industries, product defects can be corrected by returning the goods to the factory. The consumer is temporarily inconvenienced, but at least he or she can expect future satisfactory use of the product. In the hotel industry, however, the situation is vastly different. Production and consumption for all practical purposes occur simultaneously. Any failure in production—in other words, any failure in service—is essentially irreparable. A poorly serviced convention represents a permanent loss to the association booking the convention. "In hotel sales the service sold must work the first time," says Robert Gibb (1982), sales manager for the Royal Connaught Hotel in Canada. "This adds to the difficulty of hotel sales because the product, so to speak, cannot be brought back for repairs."

The fact that salespeople have very little influence over the quality of the service they sell is particularly vital in hotel sales because of the immediacy of service. According to Ramirez (1982), "failure can happen at any moment. Hotel salespeople promise to deliver but they depend on operations people to perform." Since so many people are involved in the "production" and "delivery" of the hotel services—from desk clerks and room attendants to restaurant chefs—the potential for a "defect" in quality is much higher than in most other industries.

The intangible nature of services has further implications for salespeople. Because the purchaser cannot taste, touch, or feel the service, attention is focused on the salesperson. Levitt (1981) cites the importance of a service's "packaging," and he sees salespeople as important to the final package:

> The product will be judged in part by who offers it, not just who the vendor corporation is but also who the corporation's representative is. . . . The less tangible the generic product, the more powerfully and persistently the judgment about it gets shaped by packaging—how it's represented . . . and who presents it.

Similarly, Johnson (1978) argues that because buyers of services are usually unable to judge quality and value prior to purchase, "the service company's reputation and the reputation of its salesmen are far more essential to services marketing than to goods marketing."

Apart from intangibility, the variability of services makes it more difficult for the service company to maintain a large amount of repeat business. Repeat customers generally require less effort than the effort put in to attract new accounts.

Hotel salespeople must work with people from

all other operating departments to ensure that a "good product" is delivered. Ramirez (1982) feels that the hotel salesperson's role goes beyond this, that it is the "responsibility of salespeople to instill excitement in operations personnel."

While there are special problems for the hotel salesperson owing to the intangibility and variability of hotel services, one factor makes his or her job somewhat easier, as Coffman (1975) notes: "Because a hotel is a meeting place with charm and luxury, its representatives are usually received on a fairly friendly basis."

SURVEY OF HOTEL MARKETING MANAGERS REGARDING HOTEL SALES SKILLS

The questionnaire in Appendix 1 was sent to 100 sales and marketing managers in hotels across the United States.

Of the 43 responding, 100 percent felt that communication skills and product knowledge were "very important in sales training programs"; nearly 10 percent felt that sales technique was (only) of average importance; a majority—62.8 percent—felt that corporate orientation is of either average importance or no importance at all; 60 percent of those surveyed concluded that market research is "very important" in sales training (see Figures 1 through 6).

The survey therefore emphasized the relative importance of communication skills and product knowledge in training programs, especially as compared to corporate orientation (37.2 percent) or market research (60.4 percent).

When asked what specific factors distinguish hotel from other sales sectors (Question 2), most respondents in the survey pointed to the "intangible" nature of the product. One respondent called it a "perishable" product, on the grounds that a room-night that isn't sold "remains forever unsold." Several of the sales executives polled said that the heavily group-oriented emphasis in hotel sales leads to the involvement in the execution of any sale of a wide range of decision-makers ranging from sec-

retaries to corporate meeting planners. Hotel sales are also highly seasonal, more so than in most industries.

The response to Question 3, training methodologies, is discussed in the next section in conjunction with the general treatment of training of hotel salespeople.

Sales executives look for a wide variety of qualities in college graduates applying for hotel sales jobs. Those mentioned most in response to Question 4 were good communication skills and personal appearance. As one respondent put it, "First impressions are important." The respondents also look for graduates with a high degree of self-motivation and organizational skills. Important, but not as high on the list, is knowledge of the hotel industry; apparently it is generally felt that the industry can be learned on the job after hiring.

Figures 7 through 12 show the results of Question 5, "How important are the following skills and personality traits to the performance of the hotel sales representative?"

TRAINING HOTEL SALESPEOPLE

Question 6, regarding the "personality and behavior of the most effective salesperson," either was left unanswered or was answered in a highly anecdotal vein. It seems that in hotel sales, as in all other walks of life, the exceptional people are indeed so exceptional that there is no clearcut means for neatly categorizing them.

The replies in Question 7 show that commissions are usually not paid in hotel sales positions, mainly because so many sales are made years in advance. Most of those executives surveyed said that, as a result, financial incentives in hotel sales are not very attractive. A few of those polled said hotels are conducting limited experiments with quarterly bonuses based on the number of room-nights booked and that preliminary indications support the opinion that similar programs should be introduced at other properties.

Salespeople no longer just sell. Today, most business organizations view "sales" as encompass-

FIGURE 1
Communication skills

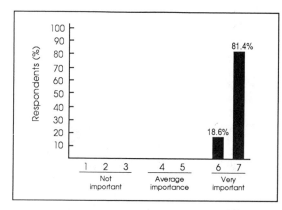

FIGURE 2
Product knowledge

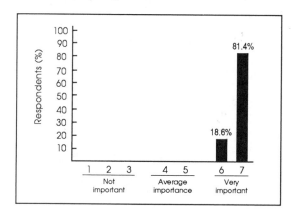

FIGURE 3
Sales techniques

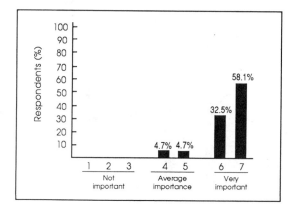

FIGURE 4
Corporate orientation

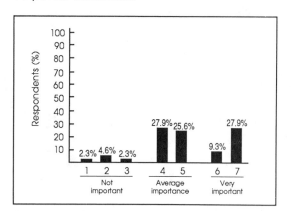

FIGURE 5
Market research

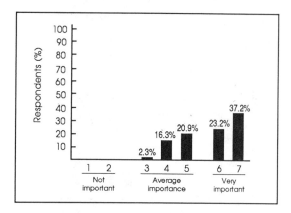

FIGURE 6
Summary table

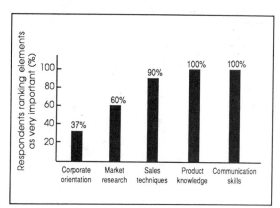

FIGURE 7

Importance of self-confidence to performance of hotel sales representatives

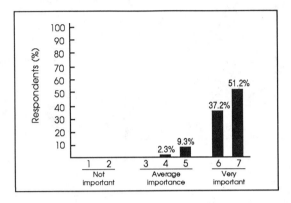

FIGURE 8

Importance of negotiating technique to performance of hotel sales representatives

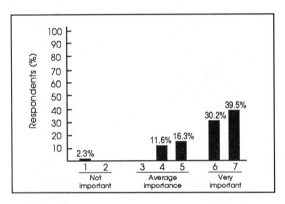

FIGURE 9

Importance of communication skills to performance of hotel sales representatives

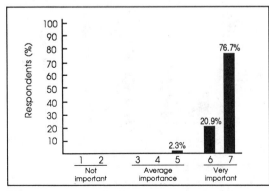

FIGURE 10

Importance of persuasive powers to performance of hotel sales representatives

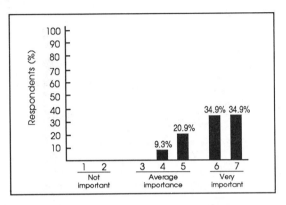

FIGURE 11

Importance of organization to performance of hotel sales representatives

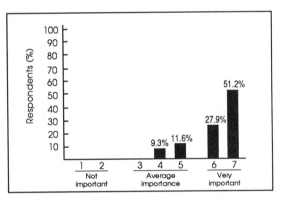

FIGURE 12

Relative importance of skills to performance of hotel sales representatives

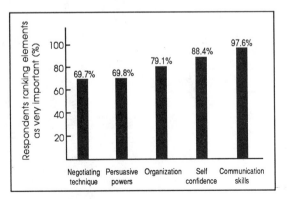

ing elements that go well beyond the obvious one of facilitating a sales transaction. This expanded view of the salesperson's function is based in part on a new emphasis on marketing. A "marketing approach," by contrast, focuses strictly on the promotion of a particular product or service.

Competition in the marketplace has therefore increased the need for sophisticated selling techniques and marketing know-how. More and more, companies are insisting that salespeople understand the concerns of management—primarily business profitability—rather than just the ways and means of boosting the volume of orders booked.

In short, modern business organizations require that salespeople act as "total representatives," not just "sales representatives" (Conference Board 1978). That transformation has enhanced the need for expanded training and development programs for entry-level sales positions.

In most industries, the typical formal sales training program includes: corporate orientation, product knowledge, market/industry knowledge, and techniques of salesmanship. In a survey of 156 major American corporations, the New York–based Conference Board discovered that, on average, 42 percent of training time for salespeople is spent developing product knowledge. In distant second place come "selling techniques," taking up only 24 percent of training time. The time it takes to develop a thorough familiarity with the product also appears to be the predominant factor in determining the length of training programs, which the Conference Board survey indicated varies widely from less than three months to a year or more. In general, the programs of consumer product manufacturers are shorter than for industrial goods makers or companies in the service sector (Conference Board 1978).

In large corporations, responsibility for sales training is:

1. Decentralized to the operating level (division or group);
2. Conducted at the corporate level; or
3. A mixture of the two approaches above. In this third version, recruits receive the elements of basic training from sales managers with field duties. They are then sent to corporate or group headquarters for classroom sessions on company orientation and other subjects.

In the hotel industry, training is done primarily on-site. The Sheraton Hotel chain operates a 12-week training program, one week being held at corporate offices and the rest shared among different departments at a hotel site. In most hospitality organizations, however, trainees in the hospitality industry are assigned to train under a designated sales manager at one hotel site.

Content of Training Program

According to the Conference Board survey (1978), corporations stress "need to know" elements in their training programs rather than "nice to know" ones. The consensus, the survey showed, is that knowledge that is not absolutely necessary is not fully absorbed.

There are three principal elements in general sales training programs:

1. *Product knowledge.* Salespeople must possess sufficient knowledge to deal effectively with customers. "The amount of product knowledge a salesperson requires ultimately depends on the diversity and technical complexity of the product mix" (Conference Board 1978). In the hotel industry, knowledge of the "product" is often achieved by putting the trainee through "mini" training programs in different parts of a hotel to better acquaint him or her with the overall service to be sold.
2. *Sales techniques.* Most training programs aim to enhance the natural selling abilities of salespeople. The content of such programs can run from teaching how to make an effective sales presentation to much wider attention to other verbal and written communication skills. Also, there is ample focus on the skills of negotiation and persuasion, including training to improve the salesperson's ability to overcome customer objections in the selling process.

3. *Corporate orientation.* Aside from product knowledge, there are substantial elements with which the salesperson must be familiar to sell effectively. Generally, these are policies or incentives unique to a particular company or site, and they include everything from credit and delivery terms to pricing, reporting requirements, and after-sale "service." The salesperson must also fully understand the administrative practices of the company as they bear upon expediting orders, securing adjustments, and generally making it easier for the customer to deal with the company (Conference Board 1978). The Marriott Hotel chain puts its trainees through a corporate orientation course, using it to explain the way the national sales force can be useful to sales representatives of the property level for convention-booking leads. Marriott also uses the sessions to inculcate in trainees various pricing systems that are important to effective negotiating with customers.

Approaches to Sales Training

There are basically two approaches to sales training: on the job, and in the classroom.

On-the-job training—also known as "coaching"—places the responsibility for training on the sales manager of the department to which the trainee is assigned. The notion is to get the trainee working side by side with more experienced salespeople and under the manager's guidance. The recruit is thereby exposed to the everyday work of the department. He or she starts out simply as an observer assisting experienced sales personnel on sales calls, etc. The trainee can also be given more responsible tasks at a pace to which he or she is most suited. Thus, the length of the training program can be shortened markedly if the trainee is a faster learner. This also circumvents the problem of the slowest learners slowing everyone down when many recruits are trained at once.

According to Harrison (1977), coaching works on four levels:

1. The trainer describes and demonstrates a specific sales task, and the trainee listens and observes; then,
2. The trainee tells his or her coach how to do the task while the trainer again demonstrates it correctly; after that
3. The trainee describes again how to do the task—and then does it alone; and finally,
4. The recruit learns to demonstrate the task correctly without any prompting or verbalization by the coach.

Classroom training is a very different experience for both trainer and trainee. Such training typically includes seminars, role-playing, and audio-visual taping. The objective of seminars is to provide the trainee with necessary information in an orderly fashion—and to do it in an environment that encourages participation. Unlike lectures, seminars can encourage active rather than passive participation on the part of the trainee.

Role-playing is equally important. Harrison (1977) maintains that role-playing is particularly well suited to sales training because it prepares the trainee for interpersonal contacts by:

1. Giving salespeople practice in selling before facing a similar situation in real life;
2. Calling for the best demonstration of the salesperson's ability;
3. Permitting the supervisor to judge the ability of the salesperson;
4. Showing which salespeople need further training and in which areas;
5. Allowing one person to learn by watching others perform;
6. Stimulating a flow of ideas that are more readily accepted when they are experienced or seen in action; and
7. Giving the salesperson a feeling of accomplishment and self-assurance in trying out sales techniques.

Audio-visual aids contribute to the role-playing approach. They provide instant feedback aimed at giving the sales trainee a frank portrayal of how he or she acted in a particular role. It "can be hard on the ego, but the camera is also an unprejudiced critic"—and therefore more effective than most teachers when it comes to criticizing the performance of a trainee (Conference Board 1978). The use of audio-visual aids should also make the trainer's role more constructive; the "instant replay" highlights mistakes, and the trainer then can demonstrate how those mistakes can be overcome. Finally, because of the medium, audio-visual aids help increase the trainee's interest and participation because his or her own self-image is on the line.

There is some controversy as to which is the more effective training method: on-the-job or classroom training. In his analysis of this issue, Rackham (1979) cites the importance of distinguishing between knowledge and skills. The thrust of his argument is that, while knowledge can be taught effectively and relatively inexpensively in the classroom, skills are best developed on the job.

Rackham (1979) notes two major disadvantages to developing skills in the classroom. One is that role-playing can appear artificial, especially to experienced or older trainees. The other is that there is insufficient time in the average program to allow the repeated practice that is necessary for acquiring skills. Because of the latter drawback, many large organizations are now moving their skills training out of the classroom and into the job.

Follow-up is highly important in developing skills, and the limited time frame of classroom instruction does not allow enough room for it. The Xerox Corporation, well known as a practitioner of sales training and as a marketer of learning systems, researched the importance of follow-up in skills training. The results of Xerox's study underscored that in the absence of follow-up coaching, 87 percent of the skills change brought about by the program was lost. The reason given is that performing a newly acquired skill does not feel natural at first and does not bring instant results. If the trainee continues, he or she feels more and more natural and performance improves. Moreover, it was concluded that skills are more subject to "learning overload" than

knowledge—especially when complex skills are involved (Rackham 1979).

The optimum approach clearly is to strike a proper balance. Use classroom education to impart basic information, product knowledge, and so on, and on-the-job training to develop selling and other skills.

The 43 hotel sales executives who responded to Question 3 of our survey noted overwhelmingly that various on-the-job programs take the largest share of training time. The Hilton Hotels chain places most of its emphasis on on-site training. Fully 75 percent of those responding to the survey underlined the importance of this type of training. Roughly 75 percent of the sales executives put emphasis on the need for various types of on-the-job training.

Classroom teaching does exist at some hotel chains. Some—like Americana—maintain training schools. Of the survey respondents, 20.9 percent noted that their entry-level sales representatives are put through some sort of orientation at corporate offices before being assigned to a site. As for the specific approaches developed in the classroom, 16 percent of those surveyed specifically mentioned using role-playing as a training method for sales trainees.

In short, most companies in the hotel industry develop skills and product knowledge among their recruits by means of on-the-job training sometimes supplemented by classroom and role-playing exercises. Here is a summary of the sales training programs of ten major hotel corporations.

Dunfey. All trainees partake in a one-year "Management Development Program." Trainees are exposed to all major hotel departments before concentrating in the sales and marketing area. A shortened program called "Fast Track," which lasts about three to six months, is available for experienced trainees. All sales training takes place on the job. The Director of Sales, or an experienced sales manager, acts as training advisor to the trainee.

Four Seasons. There is one management training program for all entry-level managers that, on average, lasts for two years. During this two-year period, approximately six weeks are spent in the sales and marketing department. Some Four Seasons properties, such as the Pierre in New York, do not have a separate sales department. Sales for these hotels are handled by regional offices. All training is done at the property level, except for an occasional sales conference at corporate offices in Toronto, Canada.

Holiday Inn. Trainees move directly into the sales department. For one year, trainees are considered "entry level." Trainees progress at their own pace; there is no set training schedule.

Howard Johnson's. No formal sales training program is used. Trainees are placed directly in the sales department. Trainees receive additional help from regional offices.

Hyatt. All trainees experience a year-long management training program that covers all major departments. The final two months are spent in the sales department. All training takes place at the hotel property. Trainees use Hyatt's training manuals known as the "Hyattrain" series. These manuals provide the trainee with information and self-examinations in all areas of hotel operations.

Loews. Only experienced hotel salespeople are hired. They are placed directly in the sales department, where they are trained on the job.

Marriott. After a week spent at corporate headquarters, where trainees attend an "Introduction to Management" workshop, they embark on a three-month "Individual Development" training program at a selected hotel property. The program requires completion of tasks in all major departments, particularly those most closely related to sales (i.e., front office, reservations, housekeeping, and catering). At the end of this three-month period, trainees are placed in the sales and marketing department of another Marriott hotel.

Radisson. The length of initial training at Radisson is approximately 16 weeks. All training is done at the property level. Trainees are assigned an advisor—the Director of Sales—at a particular property. The program for all management trainees, including salespeople, is called LCI, for Learner Controlled Instruction. Each trainee must plan, direct, and organize how he or she will proceed through the program. The program has been designed to help the trainee develop management skills in addition to knowledge of the operation.

Management trainees must complete 53 "contracts," as Radisson calls them. The trainee must contact and work with people in the various departments of the hotel. Both trainee advisor (Director of Sales) and department contact must agree that the trainee is ready to move on. These 53 contracts comprise what Radisson calls the "management core." In addition to LCI, a new program has been initiated at Radisson for sales trainees. Management finds that under LCI salespeople learn both good and bad habits of other salespeople. To help solve this problem, Radisson has designed a supplementary program for salespeople called "Managing for Sales at Radisson." This program emphasizes sales techniques. Role-playing and action exercises (a form of role-playing) are the primary training tools used. Implementation will be at the property level by the Director of Sales.

Sheraton. Sales trainees undertake a 12-week specialized sales training program. This program is distinct from their 12-month management or six-month food and beverage management training programs. For their sales training program Sheraton hires three trainees per class to work out of the Boston Sheraton. Training time is spent working with departments most closely related to sales—catering and front office. One week of the program is spent at corporate offices, where the trainee engages in role-playing while being video-taped. A second week is spent at a Sheraton property in another city on a sales blitz where the trainee makes sales calls. During the time spent at the Boston Sheraton, each of the three trainees is responsible for developing a market plan for a specific market segment.

Stouffer's. All trainees complete a one-year management training program called "The Generalist," before working full time in a sales department. Trainees must pass competency tests in each area before moving to another area. Once placed in a sales department, the sales representative learns by working closely with experienced salespeople.

CONCLUDING REMARKS

While certain recognized skills of selling are broadly applicable to all industries, sales and marketing executives must modify these skills to suit their particular product or service.

The survey of sales and marketing executives presented emphasizes the importance of communication skills to sales performance in the hotel industry. Communication between the salesperson and prospective client is made difficult by the in-

---

Appendix
Questionnaire

1. How important are the following in sales training programs in the hotel industry? (Circle one for each.)

	Not important		Average importance			Very important	
Sales technique	1	2	3	4	5	6	7
Corporate orientation	1	2	3	4	5	6	7
Communication skills	1	2	3	4	5	6	7
Product knowledge	1	2	3	4	5	6	7
Market research	1	2	3	4	5	6	7

2. What specific factors distinguished hotels sales from others?
3. What are the main methods used to train new sales people in your organization?
4. What are the qualities and characteristics you look for in hiring college graduates for hotel sales jobs?
5. How important are the following in sales training programs in the hotel industry? (Circle one for each.)

	Not important		Average importance			Very important	
Self-confidence	1	2	3	4	5	6	7
Negotiating techniques	1	2	3	4	5	6	7
Communication skills	1	2	3	4	5	6	7
Persuasive powers	1	2	3	4	5	6	7
Organization	1	2	3	4	5	6	7

6. Please describe the personality and behavior of the most effective salesperson you know in the hotel industry.
7. What financial or nonfinancial incentives does your company offer to successful sales people? Do you have suggestions for others?

tangibility and variability of hotel services. Hotel salespeople cannot rely on demonstrating or testing a physical good to convince meeting planners of the value of their hotels' services. Similarly, the variability of hotel services makes it harder for the salesperson to promise any given level of performance.

Despite the paramount importance of commu-

nication skills, most hotel sales training programs emphasize product knowledge; in many hotel companies, trainees spend close to a year in non-sales departments to expand their knowledge of operations. Given the findings of this study, it appears that hotel sales training programs should be focused at least as much on developing communication skills.

Attentional Styles and Stress Factors of Hotel Sales/Marketing Managers

David L. Whitney

Paying attention is critical to performance. However, individual attentional styles vary from broad to narrow focus, and from external environment to internal thoughts. Successful performance requires a proper match between attentional style and the performance demands of the situation. This study examines the attentional styles of hotel sales managers and how those styles may relate to key elements of the job.

Considerable research, both in the laboratory and in the field, has shown relationships between one's ability to concentrate (attend to task-relevant cues) and one's performance (Nideffer and Pratt 1982). Nideffer (1979) identified four different ways individuals concentrate on (or pay attention to) stimuli:

1. *Broad external:* Awareness of external environment needed in order to read and react to changing situations.
2. *Broad internal:* Used for long-range planning and integration. Anticipation of consequences, development of complex-flexible programs.
3. *Narrow external:* Focused nondistractable external attention, necessary for being able to perform a specific task (e.g., converse with one person, hit a ball, repair watches, perform delicate surgery).

4. *Narrow internal:* Necessary for intellectual tasks demanding focused concentration (e.g., computer programming, mathematical computations, meditation, and mental rehearsal). Optimal for working in a disciplined way on a problem over a long period in relative isolation.

These four types of attention are at the heart of the discussion of attentional style. Nideffer and Pratt (1982, 2) make a number of observations:

1. *It is impossible to demonstrate more than one type of attentional focus at a given time.* While one can learn to shift rapidly from one type of attention to another, one cannot, for example, attend to the broad external environment (a crowded hotel ballroom) concurrent with internal conceptualization (planning a sales blitz). Effective performance requires the ability to use the attentional style most appropriate to the situation at hand.
2. *Most individuals have a preferred attentional style; some from birth, others have learned it.* What is

Reprinted with permission of Pergamon Press from Whitney, David L. "Attentional Styles and Stress Factors in Hotel Sales/Marketing Managers." *International Journal of Hospitality Management,* vol. 5, no. 4 (1986), pp. 197–200.

more, every situation has its own best required attentional focus, whether it be broad external awareness of the environment or broad internal focus on analysis. The critical issue concerns the matching-up of an individual's preferred style and the demands of the immediate situation. As Nideffer and Pratt (1982, 2) express it, "Effective performance depends upon a good match between situational demands and attentional style—being in the right place mentally at the right time."

3. *Stress, whether based on fear, anger, frustration, or excitement, impairs one's ability to shift from one attentional style to another.* At first, individuals begin to fall back on their favorite attentional style, an area of greater comfort and strength. If that style happens to be inappropriate for the particular stress situation, the individual actually ends up increasing the stress, thus causing even greater narrowing on the favorite attentional style. Soon one loses the ability to effectively organize thoughts and a feeling of confusion and rush occurs. As stress further increases, there is increased physiological response—muscle tension, perspiration, and increased heart rate. Distraction is increased by negative thoughts and loss of self-confidence. The process is often called "choking."

4. *Under certain conditions, successful performance can be predicted.* Basically, this involves awareness of one's attentional strengths and weaknesses, knowledge of the performance demands of the situation, plus certain interpersonal and stress factors that may be involved.

Hotel Sales/Marketing Managers and Attentional Styles

A generally accepted trait-list of hotel sales and marketing managers seems based primarily on a lot of observation and a little research. Recent empirical research by Plunkett and Berger (1984) demonstrated that communication skills are thought by hospitality executives to be the most important element of sales success. However, in terms of at-

tentional style, a critical factor in performance, no research has involved hotel sales managers until now.

In this study, two questions were addressed: "What do hotel sales managers report as their attentional styles?" and "What, if any, relationship exists between those styles and stress factors of the job?"

Seventy members of the Seattle, Washington, Chapter of the Hotel Sales and Marketing Association (HSMA) were administered a short form of the Test of Attentional and Interpersonal Style (TAIS) plus a stress-identification questionnaire. In addition to measuring attentional styles, the TAIS identified tendencies of individuals to make certain types of attentional error due to various overloads which are identified and defined (Nideffer 1979, 34) as:

1. *Overloaded by External Stimuli (OET).* Individuals make mistakes because they become confused and overloaded with external stimuli.
2. *Overloaded by Internal Stimuli (OIT).* Individuals make mistakes by confusing themselves thinking about too many things at once.
3. *Reduced Attentional Focus (RED).* Individuals make mistakes because they narrow their focus too much.

Thus, each additional style has its corresponding overload factor. For example, when attending to the external environment (BET), one may become distracted or confused by too much external activity. That confusion is the overload factor, and in the case of external attention (BET), that overload is called OET, Overloaded by External Stimuli. Similarly, Broad Internal Thinking (BIT) and Narrow Focus (NAR) are subject to overload factors as described above, i.e., OIT and RED, respectively.

Results

As indicated in Table 1, the group's primary attentional style is Broad Internal Thinking (BIT). Not only is the mean BIT score higher than the others but the Internal Overload score (OIT) is lowest. This means that while attending to the broad internal realm of ideas and conceptual integration, these managers are rarely distracted or overloaded by too much information or too many ideas. This "distance" between attentional style and its corresponding overload is important. For example, the group was in the 87th percentile in Broad External Thinking (BET), and the 84th percentile in Narrow Focus (NAR). One might conclude, therefore, that BET is the stronger of the two styles.

But consider the corresponding overloads. BET's overload is in the 67th percentile, indicating that while the managers tested see themselves as high in external awareness, they are also high in external overload and highly distractable. The "distance" here between style and overload is only 20 points.

By comparison, the "distance" between Narrow Focus (NAR) and its corresponding overload (RED) is much greater, 48 points. This indicates that when narrowly focused, the managers are not prone to excessive narrowing of attention, which results in a reduced ability to switch to a more appropriate attentional style if called upon to do so. Therefore, Narrow Focus is probably the group's secondary attentional style.

Primarily, however, the group reported themselves to be Broad Internal Thinkers (BIT), indicating that the hotel sales managers tested see themselves as "able to integrate ideas and information from several different areas . . . analytical and philosophical" (Nideffer 1979). The strength of this attentional style is "the ability to organize and make long-range plans" (Pratt 1981). Conversely, Pratt (1981) warns that these individuals "can become overideational, have trouble sticking to one thing. May not react quickly enough."

Second, the managers see themselves as effective "with respect to being able to narrow their attention when they need to" (Nideffer 1979). This Narrow Focus attentional style (NAR) enables individuals to "concentrate on one thought or idea, [do] mental calculations, meditate" (Pratt 1981), but also leaves them susceptible to failure "to attend to and incorporate new information, [and insensitive] to what's going on around [them]" (Pratt 1981).

Contrary to popular notion, the managers tested see themselves as least effective when required to attend to a busy and stressful external environment. While their high BET score indicates they may not be particularly uncomfortable when doing so, the high External Overload (OET) suggests they may be very distractable, lose their concentration, and become error prone.

Sales Managers and Stress

The stress questionnaire listed 14 critical elements of the sales manager's job. Subjects were asked to rate each element in terms of the amount of stress it generates. Table 2 shows the results of the stress questionnaire. Items are numbered from "most stressful" to "least stressful."

Managers indicated that they found the imminent implementation of a sales blitz to be the most stressful and the advance planning of that blitz to be the least stressful. These findings seem appropriate for individuals with Broad Internal Thinking (BIT) as their primary attentional style. Long-range planning is their strength, whereas the intense,

TABLE 1

Hotel sales manager's mean TAIS scores (in percentiles)

(1)	Broad External Attention (BET)	87
	Overload by External Stimuli (OET)	67
(2)	Broad Internal Attention (BIT)	94
	Overload by Internal Stimuli (OIT)	35
(3)	Narrow Focus (NAR) (narrow internal and external attention)	84
	Reduced attentional focus (RED)	36

TABLE 2
Rank order of stress factors in sales managers' jobs

Rank order	Stress factors	Mean*
1.	Implementing a sales blitz beginning tomorrow	3.2
2.	Constant interruptions	2.9
3.	"Handholding" clients	2.8
4.	Trying to satisfy three clients at the same time	2.7
5.	Attending an active participation workshop	2.7
6.	Meeting sales quotas	2.6
7.	Anticipating next week's very busy work schedule	2.5
8.	Making cold calls in person	2.4
9.	Being given an annual performance review	2.3
10.	Making a formal presentation	2.3
11.	Defending ideas before the boss	2.2
12.	Attending (passively) an all-day computer lecture	2.1
13.	Making cold phone calls	2.1
14.	Planning a sales blitz for next year	1.9

*Mean on a 1–5 scale.

rapid activity of immediate implementation is apt to be most stressful. It may be noted that, in general, as the activities become less structured, less planned, and more extemporaneous and unpredictable, the stress level rises. If the managers had reported themselves to be Broad External Thinkers (BET), this increase in ad-lib activity would perhaps be less stressful, but as the group is strongest in Broad Internal Thinking (BIT), this reported increase in stress level is not surprising.

Conclusions and Implications for Managers

Hotel sales managers generally appear to be gregarious and extroverted, and they may well be. This study did not measure those qualities as such. However, in terms of attentional style the results have been reported, and while the outgoing "street-smart" Broad External awareness (BET) score is high so is the External Overload (OET), meaning that sales managers in hotels should benefit from being aware of possible mistakes in stressful external awareness situations. They may wish to limit the length of time they expose themselves to super-busy environments by planning quieter times for thought and mental "catching-up."

In so doing, they may also lessen the temptation to make snap decisions under stress. The high OET score indicates that the distraction of external activity may adversely affect the quality of those decisions.

A final suggestion to those who aspire to careers in hotel sales: It is wise to develop the critical ability to think in Broad Internal dimensions (BIT). An outgoing personality is important, but may not be enough. The career group tested reported themselves as able to analyze, conceptualize, and integrate ideas. That requires more than a winning smile and an outgoing personality.

Ink and Air Time: A Public-Relations Primer

Jacques C. Cossé

The individual charged with a hotel's public relations should not be viewed as a signpainter, or a listening post for the occasional disgruntled guest. Whatever the size of your hotel, someone on your staff should be assigned to the crucial task of presenting the property in the best light to the public.

The Public-Relations Function for hotels, like that for most business entities, is complex. The public-relations representative for a single hotel or a group of properties may have numerous audiences: the public at large, employees, the financial community, and specialized segments, such as the entertainment industry in my firm's case or the travel industry for resort hotels. In the present article I will outline the duties of a hotel representative addressing the public at large.

The general purpose of the public-relations representative's communications to this vast audience is to present your property in the best light. Regardless of how large or small your hotel is, *someone* should be assigned the task of managing this basic activity. In smaller properties, the person assigned the public-relations function is often the resident manager or the assistant to the general manager; in larger properties, one or more people may be assigned full-time. Regardless of how the staffing is handled, the representative should not be viewed as a signpainter and the listening post for the occasional disgruntled guest. Your public-relations representative is your contact with the outside world and should therefore be a person of responsibility and good judgment. The following paragraphs describe the basic elements of a professional public-relations program for a hotel of any size.

The Basics in Hand

One of the essential roles of a public-relations representative—whether at the individual property or at corporate headquarters—is to act as a source of reliable information. The basic tool of this function is the press kit, a simple compendium of facts that facilitates the public-relations representative's job, greatly assists his contacts in the media, and is generally the mark of a professional at work. Enumerated below are the essential elements of a press kit; your individual situation may call for other components or different emphasis on some areas, but the guidelines offered here are generally applicable and provide the basis for compiling a kit.

1. A *fact sheet* summarizes the essential information regarding your hotel and should include the following data:

   - The property's name, address, and telephone number, as well as its "800" number for reservations, if applicable
   - General manager's name
   - Number of rooms and suites
   - Number of restaurants
   - Number of bars and lounges
   - Special features and guest amenities—pools, health clubs, beaches, saunas, etc.
   - Names and capacities (including ceiling height) of ballrooms and meeting rooms
   - Parking information
   - Resident manager's name
   - Chef's name

2. A brief description of the hotel's location. Is it in a residential area? . . . the business district? . . . near the airport?
3. A brief commentary on special aspects of the hotel's ambience. Are there, for example, unusual suites in the hotel? Are facets of its architecture or decor worthy of note?
4. A detailed description of the hotel's restaurants and lounges, including mention of specialties available in these outlets.
5. Photographs of both the interior and exterior of the property, with special attention to features that may have come to characterize the hotel. (Especially when depicting food and beverage facilities, bear in mind that the photographs should include people, not merely scenes of the property. Nothing is more visually insipid than a picture of an empty restaurant or lounge.)
6. A brief biography of the hotel's general manager.

The assembled press kit is the public-relations professional's organizing tool and the first step in his overall task: the collection and dissemination of information. Before moving to a discussion of the mechanics of the process, a brief word on the nature of the information to be communicated is appropriate.

Your True Function: News versus Puffery

Among the numerous definitions we might advance to explain public relations is to say that its purpose is to generate sales for the hotel *indirectly*. Too often public-relations representatives define their purpose differently, failing to appreciate the importance of their indirect impact and concluding that any bit of puffery serving as a vehicle for mention of the hotel's name is worthy of ink or air time. Remember: The media are interested in *news*, not thinly disguised advertisements for your property. You may gauge for yourself the merit of information you release for public-relations purposes by asking yourself whether it is a story the public at large is interested in hearing. Never generate a press release or the idea for a television spot whose sole purpose is to publicize your property (with the exception of the media "event" designed to introduce a special promotion or service).

Media Mechanics

As a public-relations representative, you become part of the news-delivery system, and it therefore behooves you to have a reasonable knowledge of the system's mechanics and to become familiar with its personnel.

The print media. At your local newspapers, you should get to know the following staff members:

- City editor
- Food editor
- Travel editor
- Finance editor
- Women's-page editor
- Hotel-beat or visitor-industry reporter
- Feature columnists

The city editor is responsible for *hard news;* his counterparts manage the selection and development of features. Whatever you have to report—whether it is a national figure's stay or a food story—first approach the appropriate editor, who will then assign a reporter. Do not contact a reporter directly without first getting his editor's approval.

Editors and reporters are under constant pressure to meet deadlines, and you can considerably ease this burden by understanding their routine. On morning papers, reporters have the most time available after 1 p.m. To the extent possible, you should plan public-relations events with these times in mind. It is also desirable to vary the time of day at which you release important news items so that one paper does not consistently scoop its morning or afternoon counterpart.

The recent proliferation of city and regional magazines provides additional public-relations opportunities for hotels, especially in the placement of more in-depth articles than might be carried by local newspapers. Here again, you should become acquainted with the supervising editor as well as the individual feature editors and columnists.

If your property enjoys national recognition, the network of your media contacts should be wider, including local stringers or bureau representatives from such national magazines as *Newsweek* and *Time.* You should also have contacts with the financial and business press *(Wall Street Journal, Business Week, Dun's Review),* as well as the hotel and travel-trade press. Finally, you should not forget women's fashion magazines and the "shelter" magazines: These publications are constantly seeking new locations for modeling women's garments, and by serving as a set your hotel can gain much favorable exposure while helping to solve their practical problems.

Columnists. Newspaper and magazine columnists are frequent allies of hoteliers in their public-relations efforts. They can also be enemies, and it is important, therefore, to share your stories with them equitably (remember that, unlike hard news stories, the feature stories columnists use are—at least ideally—exclusive). Invite columnists individually for lunch or a cocktail, keeping them abreast of interesting people and developments at your property. As with hard news items, always keep in mind that you perform your public-relations function by helping the columnist do his job—and make sure the story ideas you pass to columnists contain genuine interest, not merely exposure for the hotel.

The broadcast media. A hotel's public-relations representative should become acquainted with the following people at local radio and television stations:

- Station manager
- News director
- News announcers
- Station "personalities"(e.g., talk-show hosts, entertainment critics, etc.)

Because of its frequent news spots and its very mobile equipment, radio represents a very flexible medium, and you should take advantage of every opportunity to use it, especially for the dissemination of hard news. Television is a medium with the potential for far more impact, but it requires more planning on your part. Because elaborate equipment and lights are required, television news coverage requires more lead time than newspapers or radio. In approaching both broadcast media, you should go through proper channels, dealing first with the news director—radio's and television's counterpart of the city editor—and rely on him to assign the reporter with whom you will work.

Many radio and television personalities, especially in smaller cities, prepare their own programs. It is acceptable, of course, to approach these journalists directly, and the enterprising public-relations representative will do well to become friendly with these personalities, who are perpetually on the lookout for interesting people and stories. During an election year, for example, even the smallest hotel in a remote location may play host to people of international repute. If you take the initiative to set up an interview between a local personality and a visiting dignitary, get the guest's, or his press representative's, permission *before* you invite the media.

GETTING THE NEWS OUT

The best two sources of news leads are the weekly staff meetings between the general manager and his department heads and the sales-department meeting. The public-relations representative should attend these meetings religiously, as they are a summary of all activity surfacing in the hotel in the near term.

Once you have identified a story of interest, you should proceed methodically, first getting the facts—all the facts, and at one time, if possible, because it's far easier to gather all the information than it is to go back and try to piece together a story. Be especially precise about names, initials, dates, ages, and corporate or organization names and titles. When a magazine or newspaper publishes your information, the editor takes full responsibility for the facts. Even a spelling error in a person's name reflects on the editor's professionalism, and you will in turn lose the editor's respect (and cooperation) for compromising his reliability—not to mention the reaction of the person whose name was misspelled.

News releases. A news release is perhaps the easiest document for a writer to prepare, yet it is frequently the most poorly composed, misdirected communication released. A professional news release requires only that you communicate the information—who, what, when, where, and why—as simply and precisely as you can. Avoid multi-syllabic and arcane words, as well as complicated constructions. No one using the news release is likely to be impressed by your scholarship, and the editor will lose valuable time rewriting your release to make it readable. As a rule of thumb, keep news releases to a maximum of two pages unless you are convinced the information is so compelling the editor wants—and will use—more. Some other pointers on news releases:

1. Design a suitable, informative news-release letterhead and use it consistently.
2. Always type and double-space the news release, leaving adequate margins and avoiding a crowded appearance.
3. Never fail to date the release and provide a name and telephone number (most often yours) to contact for further information.
4. Check your facts and get permission for any quotations used. Proofread the release carefully.
5. All releases should end with a signature ("###" and "30" are the most commonly used, and appear centered under the last line of the release).
6. Get the release to the media on time—hand-carry if necessary—and do not leave anyone out of the distribution process.

Pictures. Either the public-relations representative or someone on the hotel's staff should be capable of taking simple black-and-white photos. Most often these photos are used by newspapers and do not require a professional photographer. Timeliness, not training, is important: The best publicity photos are almost never the result of planning. Keep the camera ready at hand; have your eye out for opportunities; and shoot away, relying on more exposures to compensate for your lack of expertise.

Some additional tips on photographs:

1. Every hotel of a significant size (say, 250 rooms or more) should have a file of photographs available for use by the media, convention planners, travel agents, and wholesale tour bookers. These pictures—probably best taken by a professional photographer—should be standard 8″ × 10″ glossy prints. You should also maintain a file of 35mm color slides of various aspects of the property, as these are frequently requested. In addition to the shots contained in the basic press kit, you should probably have pictures of the following in your photo library:

   - Hotel exterior from many angles, including depictions of special features (e.g., fountains, sculptures)
   - An aerial view, showing the hotel's location in relation to nearby landmarks, if any
   - Special amenities or recreational facilities— i.e., pools, golf courses, tennis courts
   - Various types and classes of guest rooms and suites
   - Key personnel

2. It is a good idea to identify three or four locations in the hotel suitable for impromptu photo sessions. If you can subtly get the hotel's name into pictures taken at these locations, you should of course do so, but this additional opportunity should not be your overriding consideration. The locations chosen for these photo opportunities should be characteristic of the hotel and its lo-

cation—palm trees if your property is located in Florida, a toasty *après-ski* lounge if yours is a winter resort in Vermont.

3. Avoid shots of groups of people staring woodenly into the camera and groups of four or more people. Make sure those people depicted in your photos are *doing* something, even if it is only conversing.

4. All pictures should be captioned, with the partial overleaf bearing the caption directly attached to the photo. Be sure the information in the caption is correct: Who are the people depicted? Where are they from or whom do they represent? What are they doing in the photograph?

Attribution. When a reporter or columnist interviews a hotel's public-relations representative, he assumes your comments are on the record and therefore may be published or broadcast. If you are tempted to make remarks to the journalist off the record, you should resist, recalling that it's his business to gather and disseminate news. Although you might not be quoted directly or identified as the source, off-the-record news is considered the best by journalists because it is exclusive—and it therefore tends to spread.

Unless you are a recognized expert in the field or you are discussing the public-relations function, you are normally not quoted by the media. The general manager is the hotel's spokesman; quotations and statements are usually attributed to him.

The bad news. No hotel, regardless of its clientele or location, is without incidents of sensationalism, including suicides, fires, and crimes. With equal inevitability, the bad news makes its way to the media—so you should be prepared to respond appropriately when an unpleasant story surfaces.

You can perform an important service for both the hotel and the individuals involved in potentially tragic events if you get the facts, dismiss the rumors, and tell the truth. Once you have the story and its details in order, it is generally better to let the media contact you, although this is a matter of experience. Each incident of bad news must be handled on a case-by-case basis, reflecting the individual circumstances; use your judgment.

IN CONCLUSION: WHAT JOURNALISTS ASK OF YOU

Your effectiveness as a hotel's public-relations representative depends heavily on the rapport you establish with the media. A few general rules regarding your relationship with journalists will serve to guide many of your activities as a public-relations professional.

Always attempt to give journalists advance notice that an event is scheduled or an important guest expected. Facilitate this function by distributing a weekly schedule of the hotel's events to each newspaper, radio, and television station that is part of the media network in your area. List the organization, time and date of functions, names of speakers, and the number expected to attend. There will always be surprises, of course, but your orderliness will demonstrate that you are a professional and will gain you the respect and cooperation of journalists.

Play fair—release a story to all media at the same time. Finally, remember that all representatives of the media who make an inquiry should receive equal courtesy. Treat a young reporter for a small-town weekly in the same manner as you would the editor of *Time*. After all, even Dan Rather started somewhere.

Putting the Public in Public Relations

Louis B. Richmond

The powerful world of not-for-profit organizations can make or break a hotel. That seems like a very strong statement when you consider that the hotel may have potential revenues of $30 million a year in rooms, food, and beverage and employ more than 600 people. However, the fortune of large convention hotels usually rests on the approval of large associations, meeting planners, Mobil and AAA awards, and myriad corporate decisions. All of these organizations definitely have the potential to provide revenue for the hotel and their food and beverage outlets. Shouldn't this be the emphasis of the public relations department? The simple answer is "Yes"; but remember, the time you spend with the not-for-profit organizations can make public relations, in the long run, much more effective and can influence destination decisions, meeting planners, and major associations.

DONATIONS, DONATIONS

Every day our hotel, the Seattle Sheraton Hotel and Towers, receives three to four letters from local organizations soliciting donations of cash, rooms, and meals for their benefits, auctions, and raffles. This simple number works out to nearly 1,000 requests every year. All of these organizations have non-profit status and are doing valuable work in the community. They range from the symphony, opera, and ballet to large hospitals. The smallest of preschools and local grassroots citizen activist organizations are also regular solicitors. Each of these organizations has a mission and purpose, which if realized would make your community a better place to live. Each of these requests for

the most part is valid. How then does the hotel go about deciding which organizations to support? Each decision must be based on how it will benefit the hotel.

Let me give you an example of how working with the community has, indeed, benefited our hotel. One such request was a handwritten note from an elementary student requesting a complimentary room for their school raffle. We were promised in the letter that we would be mentioned in the raffle and that they would give us as much publicity as possible. This school was located 20 miles from the hotel in a small town that on the surface did not seem as though it would provide many return benefits to the hotel. It was decided that due to the sincerity of the request, we would donate a room package. About four months after the donation was made, the public relations department received a call from a gentleman who worked for a very large company in Seattle wanting to make room reservations. When he was informed that we would be happy to make the reservations, but it would be best to go through the reservation number, he informed me that he was making the reservations with us because of our donation to his child's school. We were the only hotel to donate a room and he felt that he owed it to the hotel to have his guests stay in our hotel. What it meant was that his company was moving from another hotel to ours because of a donation that cost the hotel about $14 in marginal cost. The potential revenue from his account was valued in the thousands of dollars and his company is a member of many trade associations that hold regional and national conventions. It is hoped that in the near future, Seattle will be selected as the host city for one of the conferences his company sponsors. All of this is due to our one small donation.

The other benefits linked to this donation were that the Sheraton's name was seen in print on more than 1,000 raffle tickets and that the people who attended the drawing were made aware of the Sheraton's contribution. The return on investment

This reading is original to this book.

from this one donation was enormous in direct revenue alone, but also generated an excellent amount of goodwill in the local community, which could be turned into even more future revenue.

ASSOCIATIONS, NATIONAL MEETINGS

When large associations decide that Seattle will be the host city for their national conferences, the individual hotels bid on being the host hotel. The host hotel is in a very favorable situation concerning room rate and food and beverage functions. A well-thought-out public relations program can play a very important role in having an association decide which hotel to use. Working with the sales staff, the public relations director can obtain as much information about the association as possible and decide how we can then influence the association to use the Sheraton. The following case explains how this can work.

A major Southwest association was deciding which hotel to use for its Seattle conference. By research we found that this organization supports two major national charities a year. One of the charities is also supported by the Seattle Sheraton Hotel and Towers. We immediately had the director of the local charity organization phone his counterpart in the southwestern city to describe how the Sheraton has helped the organization and to let them know that one of the charity's large corporate sponsors was deciding what hotel to use in Seattle. The executive director of the organization called up their contact in the corporation and informed them that if they were going to Seattle, the Sheraton was a very strong supporter of their non-profit organization and they felt it would be good business to support the Sheraton. The corporation decided to have their meeting at the Sheraton. Whether it was directly a result of this call or of a combination of other sales efforts, we feel that our support of the local non-profit organization helped us in securing a major piece of corporate business. We have found that the non-profit world is more than pleased to help corporations that provide support for their

work. They can then in turn go to other companies and use such examples as evidence of an additional benefit of working with non-profit organizations.

SOCIAL EVENTS AND FUND-RAISERS

The social catering business is fiercely competitive. Non-profit organizations are always seeking the lowest possible rates and prices, but at the same time, because of their standing in the community, they sponsor very important events at hotels. The more prestigious the organization the higher the ticket price and the greater the likelihood that the attendees may produce revenue for the hotel in the future by booking rooms and other events. Most members of the boards of directors of non-profit organizations are leaders in the community and business world. Their recommendations can go a long way toward securing a very favorable image for the hotel in the local market.

In dealing with the non-profit social catering business, we always inform the organization that we will be happy to work with them in making their event happen at the hotel, but that we are a "for profit" organization. We have to "strike a deal" that is good for the organization and good for the hotel. We inform the organization that only if the hotel is profitable, can we continue to support their organization. Therefore, by offering the organization special services rather than excessively lowering the price, we feel we can help the organization actually raise more money for their event. We have come up with many creative contributions to non-profit organizations that not only increase their potential for raising money, but favorably highlight the services of the hotel.

One of our most popular donations to non-profit organization auctions is a series of cooking classes for ten people that includes a kitchen tour and lunch. This enables couples to combine their financial resources to bid for this item. We usually set a minimum bid of $500 to $700 to ensure that the organization will realize a large percentage of the donation. This also enables the hotel not only to highlight one of its chefs, and its restaurant, but also to give people an illuminating back-of-the-house view of the kitchen. We have been able to track the success of these cooking classes and have found that almost every one of the participants has booked future reservations in the hotel restaurants. This means that what we give away, as a donation, comes back to us many times over in increased business, plus it enhances the concept of our goodwill to the community.

Another innovative donation has been tours of the corporate art collection given by our curator. The hotel is well known for its art collection and employs a professional curator. Most of the major social service organizations or non-profit organizations have always shown an interest in the arts, and this, again, makes our donation stand out from the overnight accommodations that are typically offered by other hotels.

We have also used our limousine as part of our donation program. The use of the limousine has always added an air of prestige to our gift and has been able to raise more money for the organization while costing the hotel a minimum labor cost.

We feel that by making a major donation to social catering fund-raisers that are booked in our hotel, we are helping ensure the event will be rebooked the following year, assuming that the food and service are of high quality. This saves in staff time and marketing and is a good business decision.

When major social catering events are held in other hotels, we have also made significant donations to show the group that we are interested in supporting their cause no matter where it is held; although of course, we remain interested in having the group book its event at the Sheraton next season. We always buy up some of the tables at events hosted in our hotel to show support for the organization, to have our staff see how the event is put together, and also to ensure quality control of service and food.

HOLIDAY CARD

One of the most significant community contributions we make is our annual holiday card. Each year we select a different organization to be the beneficiary of our holiday card program. We print our corporate holiday card and then provide the organization with an extra 10,000 cards for a fund-raising campaign. These cards are printed at no charge to the organization as long as they provide us with artwork. The organization chosen is always picked so that there is a return to the hotel. The 1987 organization had previously held a major event at another hotel. We informed them that if they switched to the Sheraton, they would be the beneficiary of the 1987 holiday card campaign.

CONTROL

The hotel has certain prerequisites in making donations to non-profit organizations.

1. The organization must be a 501(c)(3) organization as recognized by the Internal Revenue Service.
2. A request must be received in writing on the organization's stationery.
3. The organization must return to the hotel written notification of the donation through a raffle-advertisement, program book, or announcement.
4. The donation must be in a "live" and not a "silent" auction. All responses are filed and when a request for next year's gift arrives, we check to see if we received the recognition that we require.

Different levels of donations are awarded based on the event and the amount of recognition received. There have been times when gift certificates to our famous Dessert Buffet have been donated and in one or two other instances a dinner for 100 people has been donated.

Our commitment to the community is based on

the fact that each member of the community can act as a public relations spokesperson for the hotel. By helping out organizations, the people who belong to these organizations tend to become loyal to the giver. Our goal is to reach out to all areas of the community and to be an aggressive good corporate citizen. At the same time, we want the community to know that we need their business. The more business that they give to us, the more help that we can return to the community.

CLASSIFICATION OF ORGANIZATIONS

The not-for-profit world can be divided into six general areas, as set out below. For cash classification, some major examples of the many possible representative organizations are listed.

Cultural Organizations

Most of these organizations have large and prestigious boards of directors. There is a tremendous amount of potential room business and catering functions from the organizations and the board members.

- Symphony orchestras, opera companies, ballet companies, chamber music organizations, and presenting organizations, as well as campus cultural organizations
- Art museums, museums of history and industry, science museums, and craft and folk art museums
- Major theater companies, avant garde theaters, alternative theaters, and community theaters, as well as minor ballet and contemporary dance companies

Health Organizations

- Hospitals
- Medical schools
- Research centers

Educational Organizations

- Alumni associations
- University and college fund-raising drives
- High school and PTA organizations
- Preschool and private school fund-raisers

Religious Organizations

- Churches
- Synagogues
- Religious schools and camps
- Adult religious community organizations

Social Service Agencies

- United Way
- Community charity groups
- Neighborhood grassroots organizations
- Charities such as Easter Seals and March of Dimes
- Food banks

Social and Fraternal Organizations

- Rotary
- Kiwanis
- Elks
- Shriners

MARKETING APPROACHES

Before you approach an organization, you need to have a plan that puts you on the offensive rather than the defensive. Hotels often are put in the position of having to respond to people asking for money rather than approaching the organization first to tell them that they are there to help. The more creative and prepared you can be, the easier it is for the organization to work with you. Your plan should include the following items:

- Find out who is on the board of directors and with what companies they are affiliated.

- Explore the needs of the organization.
- Find out something about the organization's budget. This is easy if it is a tax-exempt organization.
- Research the organization's past catering functions, where they were held, prices, and number of covers.
- Find out if the organization has any housing needs and how you can help.
- Read newspapers about the organization and totally familiarize yourself with its goals. Make sure you meet with both a major staff member and a board member. To have a meeting with just a member of the staff or a member of the board simply means you will have another meeting to review what you discussed at the last meeting.

The most important overall consideration is to understand the non-profit organization's needs and to work together with their representatives for a "win-win" solution.

Work out before the event how the hotel will be credited and recognized. This is one of the most important aspects that is usually forgotten or left to chance. There are many ways that the hotel can be recognized. For example, if you are working with a cultural organization, a complimentary ad in a season's program will go a long way in justifying your investment but you should make sure that the program will reach an audience that is part of your marketing mix. Calculate what it would cost to advertise in the program book throughout the season and bargain with the organization to receive a complimentary ad that will justify the amount of donation that you are making.

Other possible returns for your donation include

- Having the organization give the hotel complimentary tickets that can be used by the staff for entertaining clients. This can be very effective if a certain concert or other event is sold out and your hotel is in possession of the only tickets.
- Asking the organization to give you access to its mailing list. This can be crucial in trying to publicize a new weekend program or the opening of a new food and beverage outlet.
- Requesting the organization to commit to a two-year contract. This not only makes it easier for the organization to plan ahead, but helps the hotel in projecting revenues.

You should also be willing to donate meeting rooms to the organization for seminars and retreats if food and beverage is ordered. Most organizations have to pay for meeting facilities.

One of the most important aspects of any donation is the follow-up. Make sure you are aware of the news that is created by the organization you are helping and make them feel that they are part of your organization. If major events take place, have the general manager send a congratulations letter. If someone is having a birthday, have your pastry chef send over a birthday cake. If you can help them in publicizing their events in your newsletter, work with them and inform them that you are giving them complimentary publicity. Work together all the time so that each organization receives something from the other.

CASE STUDY

We approached Symphony A in hopes that they would move a major luncheon to our hotel. We told them that we would be happy to host their conductor and his wife for the duration of the season if they could use their influence to help their women's organization decide that the Sheraton would be the best place to hold their luncheon. By hosting the conductor and his wife in the best available room, we not only built a good relationship with the conductor, but also showed the board of directors that we were very interested in supporting the symphony.

We met with the board of directors to inform them of our commitment to Symphony A, but at the same time, let them know that we could not continue this donation unless we received some support from the symphony in return. Although we were happy to support the symphony for cultural reasons, we also hoped that our donation would be a good business decision since most members who serve on boards of directors of large cultural organizations such as Symphony A are business leaders. They understood the wisdom of a sound decision, and, tried to offer their help to the Sheraton. The symphony moved the luncheon to the hotel and the luncheon has remained at the hotel for the last three years because we were able to satisfy the group's expectations and needs. We still have a very strong relationship with the conductor, and the symphony always approaches the Sheraton for all their room, food, and beverage business. This is a classic example of a "win-win" situation. The Symphony supporters, their board of directors, and their musicians act as public relations spokespeople for the Sheraton. In many ways, it is simply an extra several hundred people working on our behalf.

PRESS AND MEDIA

It must be remembered that the community is made up of many people who have opportunities to help the hotel in both the short- and long-term generation of income. The press and other media are also part of the community. Eventually these donations will come to the attention of many press and media people as they help local organizations, such as schools, hospitals, social service, and cultural organizations. It is also important to realize that the more events that are held in the hotel, the more press activity is created in the local newspapers. Organizations like to be involved in active and exciting hotels. If X number of events are in one hotel and twice that number are in another hotel, the more active hotel is bound to have more requests for events.

CO-SPONSORING

Another effective way to maximize public relations in the area of community involvement is to co-sponsor events with radio stations or newspapers that benefit charities. The exposure that can be provided not only places your property with other responsible companies, but helps spread the word of your company's involvement automatically through the media.

Take advantage of your local and regional radio stations to work up joint promotions. Work with the station's promotion director to find out how the hotel can help the station's favorite charity. Donate the ballroom or smaller meeting rooms for dances, parties, and so forth, with the guarantee of having a no-host bar available. The radio station acts as a free advertising service to draw people to the event. You should also have the non-profit organization receive an admission charge to the event so that it is up to the non-profit organization to also try to draw a large audience. By working with the radio station and the charity, the hotel can not only maximize their exposure, but also increase the potential for revenue.

REGIONAL ORGANIZATIONS

Identify major non-profit organizations in feeder markets and work with them in their major fundraising events. This will help increase weekend business and act as a reinforcer to advertising that is placed in those markets. The impact of these regional organizations can be just as strong as your local organizations. If your property has a strong regional weekend market, this program can be a very effective way to increase room business.

Identify corporations that have branches in feeder cities with ties to major non-profit organizations. Any time that your property can get its name across to the public in a major feeder market, you reinforce or actually save advertising dollars. Remember, the return on investment, if carefully monitored, can be very significant.

CONCLUSION

The goal of any program of local community involvement is to associate your property's name with the concept of a superior, successful, and involved hotel. The more times the property is written and heard about, the more people automatically identify your property with positive community activity. It becomes in their best interest to make sure you are successful because they know that you will probably help one of the organizations in which they are involved or at the very least, that you will benefit

the community as a whole. In order to work with the community, you must educate the community *to work for you.* The best recommendation is the recommendation made by the public, and only when public relations truly works with the public can the property benefit. By putting the public in public relations, the public speaks for you and your property.

A Day in the Life of a Convention Services Manager

Holly Hughes

Convention services managers are an important part of the team that produces your smooth-running meeting. But that's just the tip of the iceberg. While one meeting is in house, there are several others waiting in the wings—and a plethora of details to be juggled at the hotel.

7:25 A.M.

Tom Donohue screws open the blue plastic lid of his Thermos and pours the day's first cup of coffee, hot and black. His small, bare, windowless office is still quiet. On the 46 stories above, life is stirring at the Chicago Marriott Downtown Hotel—a hotel never sleeps—but down here in the staff's basement offices, no one else is around yet. "I'm a day person. I like to get in early—before the phones start." Tom rolls his eyes.

First things first. Call the front desk to check that a limo was sent to O'Hare airport early this morning to pick up a couple coming in on a red-eye flight from Hawaii. They're attending the National Business Education Association (NBEA) convention, the biggest meeting in house this week. Satisfied that the connection was made, Tom hangs up and swivels around to pull from a bookcase a black notebook, in which has been filed every scrap of paper referring to next week's National Association of Realtors (NAR) meeting. NAR people will

be coming in for a pre-convention meeting tomorrow, so Tom must list every detail that still needs to be resolved. He carefully fills out a complete rundown on NAR functions for his secretary, Valerie, to type today while he is busy racing around the hotel.

7:45

Leaving the NAR papers on Valerie's desk, Tom grabs the hotel's schedule of convention functions for today, April 18, and looks it over in the elevator. He gets out on the fifth floor (the first of Marriott's three convention floors), where NBEA is setting up for its 8:30 registration. Even though Tom helped store their materials nearby last night, there is the expected chaos this morning as files, forms, typewriters, and adding machines are hauled out and arranged on the counters of a converted cloakroom. NBEA's executive director, O.J. Byrnside, and the convention's coordinator, Arthur Rubin, have been working together for many years. O.J. has a slight southern drawl and Arthur, a light New York accent; together, they function almost like Bob and Ray, a comedy team with no straight man.

Luckily, they keep their sense of humor in the midst of this flurry of activity.

One of NBEA's committee chairmen slips sheepishly up to Tom. She forgot to order coffee and rolls for her committee meeting this morning. Tom grins, steps over to the house phone, and dials catering. No problem.

Then he slips behind the counter to help O.J. find another electrical outlet for the calculators. The space was, after all, built as a cloakroom; it's not loaded with outlets. Tom signals to a houseman, and extension cords quickly appear.

8:05

NBEA members are already milling around, aimlessly waiting for registration to start. Eyeing the crowd, Arthur Rubin mentions that they might need more ropes to form a line up to the desk. Tom whisks downstairs to the front desk. There isn't much action down there right now—could they spare a rope and a couple of stanchions?

8:10

In the Chicago Ballroom, across the lobby from registration, exhibits were set up yesterday by the Freeman Companies. Now Tom speeds around the room, casting one last glance over everything. Almost without thinking, he bends over to clear away a crushed cigarette pack tossed carelessly behind one booth. He picks up a phone and dials engineering. "The lights in the Chicago Ballroom are making things hot. The air conditioning should be turned up. . . . Oh, you did already? When? . . . So it should be cooling off soon. Great. Thanks."

8:15

Elevator up to the sixth floor, to the Big 10 Suites. Tom's calm, low-key manner can be deceptive; he travels through the hotel at a wicked

clip that betrays the pace he's really working at. First, he whips around to the committee meeting that ordered the last-minute continental breakfast. He peers discreetly through the door. Great—everybody's drinking coffee and munching croissants. On around to the other side of the floor, where two rooms have been set up for computer workshops. Conventioneers are already sitting in front of terminals, tapping keyboards. One woman looks up as Tom steps into the room. "I'm from the hotel," he explains himself, showing her his badge.

"Oh. The young woman who's running this workshop was just *looking* for someone from the hotel," the woman replies.

Tom perks up and swings down the hall. Two workshop leaders rush up to him, complaining about the heat. Tom reassures them that the air conditioning has already been turned up. They return, relieved, to their rooms, while Tom heads down the hall, automatically sweeping a messy pile of ashes off a hall table.

8:30

Up to seven, where the Grand Ballroom is set up for this afternoon's opening session. Tom prowls the dais, checks the placement of the lectern, eyes the row of flags decorating the platform. A houseman promises Tom they'll hang the NBEA banners around noon. Tom nods and heads back downstairs, now that he's got NBEA off and running.

8:45

Pink phone slips have accumulated at the corner of Tom's desk. He spreads them out like solitaire cards, so he can keep them all in sight. Otherwise, his desk is astonishingly clear. "If I didn't keep it neat, the whole system would fall apart," he admits. His out tray holds only a few pieces of paper; each one represents a detail to be cleared, a crisis to be averted. He shuffles through them, pulls out one sheet to deal with. Just as he reaches for the phone to make a call, it rings. He blinks, counts to three so he won't startle the caller by answering too quickly, then picks it up.

O.J.'s calling from upstairs. The couple from Hawaii has just arrived, but the room they're supposed to check into isn't cleaned yet. They're dead on their feet, and have nowhere to go. With a couple of quick calls, Tom arranges for a parlor on the concierge floor to be opened for them to take a nap.

9:10

Mark Toebbin, one of Tom's two assistants, brings in notes he has made for a meeting planner's guide to the property. "It has to be useful—it can't look like a sales brochure," Tom reminds Mark. "We want to put the kind of information planners really need in here." They bend their heads together over the typewritten pages.

9:30

In the sales department's basement conference room, Tom attends the weekly restaurant forecast. Chefs in white sit at one end of the table, front desk clerks at the other. Tom and his assistants, Mark Toebbin and Tom Kuk, report on who the hotel's guests will be, and how they will use the restaurants. This is more than a sales report. The restaurants need to know how to schedule staff to accommodate rush hours, especially when conventions break between sessions and have no food functions planned. The staff needs to predict which restaurants will attract a given group, according to its tastes and spending habits—will they gravitate to the gourmet restaurant, J.W.'s, or to the family-style restaurant, Allie's Bakery? Tom analyzes the incoming groups. The NAR, for instance, is mostly a local group, likely to know Chicago and go out of the hotel. Another group that will be in house is known for partying; the bar and lounge managers duly take note.

9:50

Back to the office, another litter of pink phone slips. One of Tom's three young floor managers, Tom Ernstein, sticks his head in to report on room setups for this afternoon; as he talks, the beeper clipped to his belt goes off. "Cool it!" he reacts, before he trots off to a phone to answer the call. Tom Donohue grins his impish Irish grin. "A pager is a man's best friend and his worst enemy. Know how you can tell a person in operations?" he asks. He opens his suit jacket. "The pager wears holes in your lining. Never buy an expensive suit when you wear a pager." Sure enough, there's a hole in his jacket lining, right at belt level.

10:00

Appointment with Bob Doeppel and Mark Fisher of Production Contractors, Inc. They worked with Tom on the program for Beatrice Foods' huge annual meeting here at the Marriott two weeks ago; now that they know the hotel's capabilities, they'd like to set up an arrangement whereby Tom can use them—or refer planners to them—for any production work that's needed. They describe lavish shows they've put on for parties and meetings in the past. Tom discusses the possibility of developing sets and props for theme parties, which the hotel can hold available for conventions. "If we help groups keep their production budgets down," he reasons, "then they'll have more leeway in spending on other parts of the meeting—like on food and beverage." The puckish grin again. In the meantime, he asks—since they're here—could Mark and Bob give him some suggestions on this meeting planner's guide?

10:35

The minute Production Contractors leaves, Tom and Mark Toebbin go over the guide again, incorporating the new suggestions.

10:45

Back on the phone, Tom fields questions about several upcoming meetings—next week's NAR, early May's Chemical Specialties Manufacturers Association (CSMA), the Consumer Electronics Show (CES) in the beginning of June, a Campbell Sales Company meeting in August. CES presents particular problems because it's city-wide, with several hotels hosting the crowds. CES organizers must approve each hotel's arrangements, yet individual CES exhibitors work directly with the hotels. Tom has to call Sue at CES to verify every request from exhibitors headquartered at the Marriott.

10:50

Head for the diary room, a small cubicle in the sales department, with counters full of ledgers and walls full of charts, where all room bookings are logged. Tom discovers that a room he needs for a group has already been booked by sales manager Mark Brooks (meetings under 100 people are handled by sales managers here). Tom catches Mark in a hallway and convinces him to swap rooms. A lot of his work is done this way, in transit—which means he has to keep carrying a lot of details in his head, waiting for a chance to work them out. Another sales manager, Francine Pepitone, corners Tom, offering him tickets to a play tonight. Tom shakes his head—he's playing basketball tonight, in a pick-up league with other hotel people, in a parochial school gym on the north side. Sorry.

11:00

Back in the office. Another stream of room changes for CES. After Tom has changed the appropriate forms in the thick black CES notebook, he zestfully crunches up that pink slip and lobs it high into the wastebasket in the corner. Valerie brings in more pink slips to replace the one he just cleared away.

11:15

Laura Missitzis, from NAR, drops off papers. Tom pulls out the NAR notebook (putting the CES one away first) and asks Laura for a capsule description of her group to add to the NAR resume, which Tom will send out to other hotel staffs. Laura explains that there will be few spouses, that the group will probably eat breakfast in but go out for lunch and dinner. She mentions that they'll have a lot of high-tech exhibits this year. Tom makes a mental note to call Illinois Bell and warn them about extra use of the phone lines for computers.

11:25

Back to the diary room to enter those room changes for CES. The dates for CES are marked with Day-Glo stickers on the ledgers; rooms for other groups will be released only after CES has firmed its plans, but CES can't monopolize the space much longer.

11:30

Representatives from the shipping company Flying Tigers are waiting in the office. Tom deftly switches them over to Darryl Hall, a senior member of the house crew, who's officially the shipping clerk.

11:40

A lunchtime cruise around the NBEA floors. Registration is past the crunch; Tom orders a crew to clean up the coffee cups and water glasses that inevitably accumulated. Up to Salon I, on the seventh floor, where Delta Pi Epsilon, the business educators' honorary organization, is holding a luncheon. Arthur Rubin is standing by the door with a broad grin plastered over his face. He's been hawking last-minute tickets at the door, and has a fistful of cash to turn over to the hotel. (He persuaded his house crew to set up an extra couple of tables at the back of the room to accommodate them.) He's glad to make the hotel some money, he points out, to pay them back for the breaks he got on rates (and NBEA is also bringing its convention back to the Chicago Marriott Downtown in five years—it never hurts to establish a good working relationship).

Tom leads Arthur next door to okay the Grand Ballroom for this afternoon's opening session. The NBEA banners—which turn out to be heavy hooked rugs—have just been hauled in. The engineers are shaking their heads. Cloth banners are one thing, but these—they'll need cranes to get them up. And you can't just hang them from the draperies covering the ballroom wall.

Rubin says that the banners have to be hung high in the center; what's more, the row of flags is all wrong, they should extend like two wings off to the sides. Tom scurries off to rustle up a house crew. He has to find risers, so they can get the crane up on the dais to hang the banners; then they have to move the flags all outward a few feet, and stair-step them at the sides of the platform. In ten minutes, the ballroom looks just the way Arthur wants it. He beams and returns to his sold-out luncheon.

12:10 P.M.

Stop by the front desk to check out how things worked out for that couple from Hawaii. The clerk reports that their regular room is clean, their luggage has been moved in, and they are sound asleep where they should be.

12:15

Down deeper into the bowels of the hotel, to the employees' cafeteria. It may seem funny to see white-hatted chefs sitting here, eating typical cafeteria glop, when they've been cooking better stuff upstairs all morning, but those are the rules. All employees eat down here unless they are meeting with clients in one of the restaurants. Tom eats a cheeseburger, fries, and a chocolate milk. Someone from the controller's office who's in the market for a VCR asks Tom about passes to CES—can he get comps?

12:45

Heading back to his office, Tom passes through the accounting department, where he squares figures on a rebate from a recent meeting. Mike Steigman, the hotel's acting general manager, snags Tom to talk about the condition of the loading dock after yesterday's exhibit move-in; Tom, in turn, asks Mike if he can be a breakfast speaker for a meeting next week. Mike flips open his pocket calendar—no, he'll be in Miami. Tom makes a mental note to find someone else.

12:50

Back in the office, more calls—one from a high school teacher who wants advice on going into meeting planning (she's sure it has to be easier than teaching). Another from Helen Sellman, of the NBEA staff, who needs to know where the vans bringing in musicians for this evening's reception should park. Tom makes calls to clear the loading dock for the van, and to assign a security officer to be there to show the band where to go.

1:10

Tom Ernstein and Mark Toebbin bring in a budget sheet to review. Crew wages must be scaled to catering and room revenues, so the whole budget has to be considered before they can assign extra workers to handle elaborate setups or quick room turn-arounds. The budget looks tight for next week; can they go over their ratio this time? Tom pores over the figures with them.

1:20

Greg Braun from Andrews Bartlett, the drayage company, drops off setup plans for a future meeting. After he's left, Tom studies room diagrams, trying to figure out how much space NAR's exhibits will take. If the booths only fill half the ballroom, can a dividing wall be put up so the rest of the space is freed for other functions? He remembers now to call Illinois Bell about those phone lines.

1:50

Up to the sixth floor to look over the room where this afternoon's monthly hotel staff meeting will be. Tom casts a careful eye over the arrangement; even when the meeting's internal, it's his department's responsibility. He nods, satisfied. Then he stops by the floor managers' office—operations central, a tiny cubicle up in the heart of the convention floors. The floor manager who's just come on duty is Karen Mack, a sharp, tough-minded young black woman. Tom and Karen go over the schedule for tomorrow, looking ahead to room setups that Karen can oversee tonight. Tom notes a funny arrangement for round-table discussions at an NBEA session—the usual round of chairs for each table will be doubled, with a second ring around the outside. Karen frowns and nods. Tom adds another last-minute session to the typed schedule, then Karen takes it to be photocopied and distributed among the crew.

2:10

As department manager, Tom can't possibly monitor every detail of the day's meetings. For this, he relies on his floor managers. Though they're young, they bear a lot of responsibility—they have to feel able to make decisions on the spot, to trouble-shoot effectively. They also work closely with the house crews, and are more involved with the physical setups than Tom is. Karen now heads back up to six, to go over the room for the hotel staff

meeting at 2:30. Whereas Tom's inspection was a once-over, Karen's is a critical examination. She flicks on the lights, checks the water pitchers, and looks at each length of skirting on the tables.

Then it's up to seven, for the final check on the ballroom before the NBEA opening session at 2:30. Karen's job is to find mistakes. She zooms in on the stool behind the lectern; she decides it isn't nice enough. She sends Tony, the foreman of the evening house crew, to find a better one. Then she coasts down to six to get a No Smoking sign to stand at the front of the room, by the section of chairs without ashtrays. Tom Ernstein, the floor manager who's going off duty, follows her, explaining that the sign has to be placed so that the Navy band (tuning up in a nearby room) won't be blocked from view.

2:40

In the floor managers' office, Tom Ernstein and Karen review the evening's events and what to watch for. There's a tricky turn-around in the ballroom between 4:45 and 5:30, when the opening session's theater-style seating has to be struck and replaced with a reception setup. Karen steels her nerves. Does the crew know about it, are they ready to go? Tom nods. Well, there's nothing they can do then until NBEA lets out at 4:45.

They go on to discuss which part-time workers to add to next week's shifts. Who's a good worker? Who is dependable? Tom Donohue has been pushing lately to improve appearances—focusing on neat haircuts and clean clothes, but especially regulation workboots. A sign on the bulletin board pointedly shows an ad for a sale on workboots at Sears. "But if the man is dependable, we can work on his appearance," Karen hard-headedly points out. They discuss a difficult bunch of guys clustered on one shift and how to break them up; Tom Ernstein mentions that one man's been needing money lately and wants overtime—but is he too tired to work more shifts? It's a lot of hard-core labor management for junior staff to take on, but both seem to rise to it. Perhaps it's a reflection of Tom Donohue's management policy—if you keep your expectations high and demand a lot, your staff will perform better.

3:05

Tom Ernstein's beeper goes off; someone has called to ask if Anthony has been around lately. No, Tom answers. As soon as he hangs up the phone, the beeper goes off again, and he picks up the phone again. It's Anthony calling, wanting work. "We tried to call you to work today," Tom explains, and his clean-cut young face grows tough. "We called but you weren't in. If you want work, you have to stay in touch. It's too bad, but the shifts are already full for this week."

Karen jingles the huge ring of keys she must carry around to unlock rooms, electrical cabinets, storage areas, air walls. She flips through a folder full of BEOs (Banquet Event Orders) for the next month; in free moments, floor managers should always be looking ahead, anticipating a need for extra linens, pencils, strange setups, etc. There's an order for 500 pads of paper for tomorrow. Karen looks over the schedule of events, trying to figure out which seems to fit. "Well, I guess we'll hang onto them until someone screams, 'Where are our pads?' Then we'll know."

3:15

Staff meeting over, Tom Donohue takes over again. His office downstairs seems calm after the frontline tension of the floor managers' office. Tom proofreads the resume of events for NAR next week; he scribbles changes on yellow slips of paper and sticks them onto the typed forms. Valerie, his secretary, is still new; Tom goes over each change carefully, so she'll understand the reasons behind them herself next time. "It's worth spending the extra time now so I won't have to double-check your work later," Tom explains. Valerie nods a lot and swivels on one high heel as she studies the complex forms, learning how the whole system grows out of the paper.

3:40

Doug Fiedler, from the catering department, pops in with a mischievous grin, waving in the air a memo sheet covered with tiny triangles of colored fabric. Following up a pre-convention meeting they held yesterday with Fletcher Layton, of Campbell Sales, Doug has prepared a sampler to show all the possible colors of tablecloths available for the August meeting's final banquet. (You never know what you'll be asked to do when you're catering a convention.) Doug has spent hours cutting out each triangle with zig-zag scissors, stapling them to the paper, writing the color names in tiny handwriting. It's a crazy break in the day, and both he and Tom giggle.

3:50

After a trip to the diary room, to enter room changes for CSMA in May, Tom is stopped by the hotel's new director of sales, Greg Deininger, who asks if a particular room is good for a function he's scheduling. Tom helps him visualize the room and how it can be set up; Greg nods, still busy learning the property. Tom has been here less than a year, but he knows the rooms by heart by now.

4:10

A CES exhibitor—Casio—calls to request a dinner during the week. Tom looks over the space that's left. There's a room free at dinner time, but it's booked through late afternoon; there wouldn't be time for it to be set up for dinner. Unless . . . could Casio hold the cocktail party beforehand out in the foyer, while the dinner tables are being set up? The Casio manager agrees.

As with all CES plans, Tom must then call Sue

at CES to confirm this new function. While he's got Sue on the phone, Tom reviews other requests they've received. "No, that room can't go much bigger than 100," he warns her. "If the session grows, we'll have to get it out of there. . . . That room isn't equipped for heavy audiovisual; a microphone and a slide projector are about all you can do in there." It's his business to anticipate problems and forewarn clients. He smiles ruefully. "You don't ever lie to a client. It's like trying to smoke in your bedroom—you'll always get caught; there's a scent about you that gives you away."

4:30

Back to the diary room to enter the CES changes confirmed with Sue.

4:42

In the copier room, Tom finally tracks down sales manager Mark Lauer, who's holding rooms for a group in August. Tom has a group that's wanting to expand, but all the hotel's space is booked. Can Mark release space?

4:45

Valerie has finished retyping the NAR resume. Tom looks it over one last time, then approves it to go out to all hotel staffs—setting the gears in motion for next week.

5:00

Weekly sales meeting in the basement conference room. The number of reservations for each group through the end of July is monitored so that other groups can be booked accordingly. The group business must also be judged against the patterns of transient business, so neither one impinges on the other. Jim Schultenover, director of marketing, runs the meeting. Tom and his assistants review the groups they'll be handling (both Mark Toebbin and Tom Kuk have their own groups, besides the ones Tom Donohue runs). Tom Donohue warns sales managers about CES affiliates, who should not be dealt with without CES approval. A sales manager points out that health club coupons can be used as a negotiation sweetener with groups—which would boost the club's business, too. Tom tells everyone about Production Contractors, who could be a useful resource to call upon. Someone else mentions that a Dr. Who convention may be booked in the near future (mixed reaction to that). A call goes out for volleyball players to join in a game against the American Medical Association. The meeting is a grab bag of announcements, partly just to keep communication open among staff members who are usually scattered and racing around.

5:50

Somehow, while Tom has been in this meeting, the frantic turn-around of the Grand Ballroom went off without a hitch. Upstairs now, the chairs are all gone, the ballroom darkened, refreshments laid out; a long receiving line snakes across the front of the room, and conventioneers are chatting in clumps. O.J. Byrnside is circulating, shaking hands, catching up with people he hasn't seen since last year's convention. He stops to touch base with Tom Donohue, to report that everything's going smooth as a dream. O.J.'s beaming—all his planning is over, and now comes the fun part, the meeting itself. Tom makes sure there's nothing he can do, then fades away, to let the meeting run its course. They know he's there if they need anything.

6:05

Tom stops off to check in with Karen, but the floor managers' office is empty. She's off already setting up rooms for tomorrow's workshops and seminars.

6:20

In the office, Tom takes one last run through the phone slips, trying to catch people he couldn't get before. Most are gone for the day, however. He pulls the last few papers from his out tray and tries to work them up, but, again, he needs information from people who don't answer their phones this late. Tom finally gets the message that the working day is over. His desk is as clear and clean as it was this morning—though the work, of course, is never done.

7:10

Tom Ernstein, who officially went off shift hours ago, stops by the quiet basement office to discuss a few details. He and Tom Donohue grab their coats and head out the door. After all, there's that basketball game tonight.

CASE STUDY—Reorganizing the Marketing "Umbrella"

You are the new executive assistant manager of Arze's Hotel. Arze's is the flagship hotel in a chain in the northeastern United States that has become a major player in its regional competitive marketplace. As you look over your hotel's organization, you notice that what is euphemistically called the marketing department is nothing more than a collection of salespeople, all of whom have carved out certain niches for themselves. They seldom, if ever, work as a group or a team on any single project.

The general manager has given you permission to dismantle and restructure the marketing department, and if need be, to move components from other operating or staff departments to the new marketing department in an effort to reflect modern realities more accurately.

Propose a model marketing department for this hotel that can be adapted easily to the rest of the chain. Include in your proposal what new components would be included in the marketing depart-

ment, where those components would come from, or whether they are to be created specifically to reflect this new mission. It may be useful to think of the marketing department as another "line" division in your restructuring, recognizing that a comprehensive marketing department will have significant interaction with a broader range of hotel clientele.

Endnotes

[1] *Consumer Attitudes and Behavior in the Foodservice Marketplace: A Report to the National Restaurant Association* (Chicago: Market Facts, 1974), 20.
[2] Reference not cited in original article.

References

Borden, Neil H. 1968. The concept of the marketing mix, in *Managerial marketing: Perspectives and viewpoints,* ed. Eugene J. Kelley and William Lazar (Homewood, IL: Richard D. Irwin).

Cadotte, Ernest R. 1979. The push–button questionnaire: A new tool for measuring customer satisfaction. *Cornell Hotel and Restaurant Administration Quarterly* 19(4).

Cadotte, Ernest R. 1980. Tellus computer lets retailers conduct in-store marketing research, *Marketing News* 12 December.

Coffman, C. DeWitt. 1970. *Marketing for a Full House* (Ithaca, NY: School of Hotel Administration, Cornell University).

Coffman, C. DeWitt. 1975. It's a breeze: In the hotel world, anyone can sell. *Hospitality,* April:16.

Conference Board. 1978. *Training the sales force: A Progress Report.* New York, p. 2.

Crissy, W.J.E., Robert J. Boewadt, and Dante M. Laudadio. 1975. *Marketing of hospitality services: Food, travel, lodging.* East Lansing, MI: Educational Institute of the American Hotel and Motel Association.

Eison, Irwin I. 1980. *Strategic marketing in food service: Planning for change.* New York: Chain Store Publishing.

George, William R. 1977. The retailing of services—A challenging future. *Journal of Retailing* 53 (3).

Gibb, R. 1982. Sales Manager, Royal Connaught Hotel, Montreal. Personal interview.

Harrison, J.F. 1977. *The sales manager as trainer.* Reading, MA: Addison-Wesley, p. 59.

Johnson, E. 1978. *Handbook of modern marketing.* New York: McGraw-Hill, p. 2.

Kotler, Philip. 1973–74. Atmospherics as a marketing tool. *Journal of Retailing* 49 (4).

Levitt, T. 1981. Marketing intangible products and product intangibles. *Harvard Business Review* (May–June): 97.

Lewis, R.C. 1981. The positioning statement for hotels. *Cornell Hotel and Restaurant Administration Quarterly.* (22):51–61.

Lewis, R.C., and A. Pizam. 1981. Guest surveys: a missed opportunity. *Cornell Hotel and Restaurant Administration Quarterly.* (22):51–61.

Lowenthal, M. 1982. Director of Sales and Marketing, Canadian Pacific Hotels, Jerusalem. Personal interview.

McCarthy, E. Jerome. 1975. *Basic marketing: A managerial approach* (Homewood, IL: Richard D. Irwin).

Myers, James H., and Edward Tauber. 1977. *Market structure analysis.* Chicago: American Marketing Association.

Nideffer, R.M. 1979. *Predicting human behaviors: A theory and test of attentional style and interpersonal style.* San Diego, CA: Enhanced Performance Associates.

Nideffer, R.M. 1981. *The ethics and practice of applied sports psychology.* Ann Arbor, MI: Movement Publications.

Nideffer, R.M., and R.W. Pratt. 1982. A review of the test of attentional and interpersonal style. *Enhanced Performance Associates Quarterly Report* 1:1–2.

Plunkett, R.L., and F. Berger. 1984. Sales skills in the hospitality industry. *International Journal of Hospitality Management* 3:113.

Pratt, R.W. 1981. *Taking care of business.* San Diego, CA: Enhanced Performance Associates.

Rackham, N. 1979. The coaching controversy. *Training and Development Journal* November:12–13.

Sasser, W. Earl. 1976. "Match supply and demand in service industries." *Harvard Business Review* November–December:133–140.

Sasser, W. Earl, R. Paul Olsen, and Daryl Wyckoff. 1978. *Management of service operations* (Boston: Allyn and Bacon).

Shostack, G. Lynn. 1977. Breaking free from product marketing. *Journal of Marketing* April:73.

Thomas, Dan R.E. 1978. Strategy is different in service business. *Harvard Business Review* July–August.

Trout, J., and A. Ries. 1972. The positioning era cometh. *Advertising Age* 24 April:35–38.

Vonnegut, Kurt, Jr. 1972. *Mother Night.* New York: Avon.

Suggested Readings

Articles

Bowen, John. "Computerized Guest History: A Valuable Marketing Tool." In *The Practice of Hospitality Management II,* edited by Robert C. Lewis, Thomas J. Beggs, Margaret Shaw, and Steven A. Croffoot, 193–201. Westport, CT: AVI, 1986.

Escalera, Karen Weiner. "A PR Primer for the Hotel Opening: The Case of Vista International." *Cornell Hotel and Restaurant Administration Quarterly* (May 1984): 70–81.

Haywood, Michael K. "Scouting the Competition for Survival and Success." *Cornell Hotel and Restaurant Administration Quarterly* 27 (3), 1986: 81–87.

Howey, Richard M. "An Individual Choice Model of Hotel/Motel Selection." Paper presented at Travel and Tourism Research Association Conference, June 10, 1987, Seattle, WA.

Jarvis, Lance P., and Edward J. Mayo. "Winning the Market-Share Game." *Cornell Hotel and Restaurant Administration Quarterly* 27 (3), 1986: 73–79.

Levitt, Theodore. "Marketing Intangible Products and Product Intangibles." *Cornell Hotel and Restaurant Administration Quarterly* (August 1981): 37–44.

Lewis, Robert C., and Abraham Pizam. "Guest Surveys: A Missed Opportunity." *Cornell Hotel and Restaurant Administration Quarterly* (November 1981): 37–44.

Makens, James C. "Don't Let Your Sales Blitz Go Bust." *Cornell Hotel and Restaurant Administration Quarterly* 27 (1), 1986: 65–71.

Warren, Peter, and Neil W. Ostergren. "Trade Advertising: A Crucial Element in Hotel Marketing." *Cornell Hotel and Restaurant Administration Quarterly* 27 (1), 1986: 56–62.

Witham, Glenn. "Hotel Advertising in the 1980's: Surveying the Field." *Cornell Hotel and Restaurant Administration Quarterly* (May 1986): 32–55.

Yesawich, Peter C. "Hospitality Marketing for the '90s: Effective Marketing Research." *Cornell Hotel and Restaurant Administration Quarterly* 28(1), 1987: 49–57.

Yesawich, Peter C. "Planning: The Second Step in Market Development." *Cornell Hotel and Restaurant Administration Quarterly* 28 (4), 1988: 71–81.

Human Resources and Personnel Management

INTRODUCTION

Among observers and participants in the hotel management scene are those who have compared human resources and personnel management to the weather, which everyone talks about but very few people have done anything about. This is a dilemma that faces a good many managements. If personnel departments (or, in their modern appellation, Human Resources Departments) are to be effective in dealing with the people-related issues of hiring, training, and retaining employees, they require a significant dedication of resources and a firm commitment to including human resources as part of the firm's strategic vision.

Historically, in operation after operation, those that effectively compete (even in the worst of times) are those that have made a solid and enduring commitment to recruiting, hiring, training, and retaining the highest quality of people to staff their operations. Unfortunately for short-sighted managements in times when occupancies take a dive or business is otherwise slow, it becomes too easy to adopt a "short" view and ignore strategic vision. Because of this, when trouble arises, it is all too easy to cut costs by cutting back on personnel/human resources activities such as recruiting and training. In many ways this creates cycles followed by cycles. A low point in the business or occupancy cycle will be followed within a few months by the effects of cutbacks in personnel, recruiting, and training. The most effectively managed firms will always be looking for ways to improve the quality of their staffs and in so doing, will be better able to weather the downturns in business cycles. They will also be better able to participate in recovery from those downturns. All this is simply by virtue of the strength of their human resources.

It has become very popular in the modern era to change the name of what we have traditionally called the Personnel Department to Human Resources Department or Human Resources Management Department. In some cases this is nothing more than a cosmetic change of designation. To be totally effective, a human resources department needs to pay attention to a vast range of activities and issues. In this section, readings have been chosen to highlight some of these activities and many of the issues. Several of the Suggested Readings provide additional insights and/or other views about the range of issues and management activities that face the modern hotel human resources manager.

Professor Umbreit addresses the spirit of the foregoing comments. He asks some tough questions about what is really happening in the field of human resources management in the hospitality business. Pickworth's article, profiling the hotel personnel manager, provides some insights into an inventory of demographic data and the potential range of activity over which hotel personnel managers can exert authority.

In their article on managing employee turnover, Wasmuth and Davis treat probably the most vexing issue facing hotel managers and human resources people alike in modern times. Their insightful comments about the issues related to turnover in the various hotel departments should be instructive for any potential operations manager or those involved in the management of human resources. It should be noted that this is the first of a series of three articles published on the same general topic. The other two are cited in the Suggested Readings, and in those the authors offer additional insights.

Helping department managers and general managers establish objective criteria for evaluating employees' performance is an operational and legal problem that has only recently come to light. In the not-too-distant past, operational and department managers were generally fairly free to evaluate subjectively an employee's performance based on the manager's definitions and criteria, which may not have been based on objective standards. The article by Umbreit, Eder, and McConnell explores one suggested way that human resources departments and operational managers can design measurable, behaviorally anchored management standards. Lothar Kreck's contribution to this section presents another side of the issues related to evaluation. Training and its effectiveness are discussed, and the author suggests a strong linkage between how well an employee is trained and how that employee may subsequently be evaluated.

In the Suggested Readings are included some recent writings that elaborate on topics selected for this section, but also some novel, "high-tech" ideas about the process of human resources management. It should be remembered, though, that there exists no "quick fix" or easy answer to the various issues implicit in the topic of human resources management. The answers lie in careful planning, attention to detail, and a managerial commitment to the personnel or human resources process.

When Will the Hospitality Industry Pay Attention to Effective Personnel Practices?

W. Terry Umbreit

According to Naisbitt and Aburdene (1985), three powerful trends are transforming the business environment and compelling companies to re-invent themselves. The three trends are:

1. The shift in strategic resource from financial capital in the industrial society to human capital in the information society.
2. The whittling away of middle management.
3. The labor shortages and coming seller's market of the booming 1980s and 1990s.

Traditionally, the concept of human resource management has been given obligatory lip service by the hospitality industry. If Naisbitt is correct, human resources will be the competitive edge in the hotels and restaurants of the future. Nowhere was the value of treating employees more evident in the success of organizations than in the stories told by Peters and Austin in their book entitled *A Passion for Excellence: The Leadership Difference* (1985). Each company they discussed placed a high value on employees. This in turn resulted in the customer's receiving better service and the organization's achieving a high level of profitability.

Executives from the hospitality industry have supported the importance of human relations in a number of research studies, but in practice do not value highly its significance in comparison to other business functional areas (Umbreit and Eder 1987). This paper will summarize these recent studies and discuss why the hospitality industry has not fully embraced the importance of effective human resource management. Furthermore, the conditions under which the hospitality industry might utilize human resource management techniques to a greater extent will be examined. Implications for hospitality educators will be outlined.

REVIEW OF PREVIOUS RESEARCH STUDIES

Hospitality industry executives participating in research studies have, in general, supported the importance of human resources management. For example, in Arnaldo's study (1981), hotel managers identified personnel as the most important topic of study for novice managers. Alumni from the University of Massachusetts in the hospitality industry indicated hospitality personnel management and general management were the most valuable subjects taken while in college (Brymer, 1979). Other studies have documented the importance of human resource management (Sapienza 1978; Lukowski, Budde, and Cournoyer 1974; and Gotsche 1970).

Studies that have empirically identified important aspects of hospitality managerial positions also support the valuable contributions of human resource management. Umbreit (1987) identified human resource management as one of the important job aspects of multi-unit, fast-food managers. Hales and Nightingale (1986) identified the common core elements of the role sets of unit managers in every sector of the industry, which included such human resource areas as training, motivating, recruiting, and disciplining staff. Mariampolski, Spears, and Vaden (1980) surveyed 89 restaurant managers in a study to determine what a restaurant manager needs to know in three general areas: technical information, human-relations information, and conceptual information. Human skills deemed essential by the managers surveyed included:

1. Selection, training, and orientation of personnel;
2. Effective communication with personnel;

Reprinted with permission from Umbreit, W. Terry. "When Will the Hospitality Industry Pay Attention to Effective Personnel Practices?" *Hospitality Education and Research Journal*, vol. 11, no. 2 (1987).

3. Employee motivation; and
4. Evaluation of employee performance.

Finally, several studies have actually revealed the need for hospitality managers to receive additional training and instruction in human resource management. Over 60 percent of the 73 food service executives participating in Umbreit's study (1987) identified the job aspect of human resource management as the one area unit managers experience the most difficulty with in the transition to multi-unit responsibility. The lack of human resource skills in the same study was mentioned as the principal contributor to high turnover among district managers. This finding was further confirmed by a study that revealed treatment by superiors as one of the primary reasons managers leave their job in quick-service restaurant chains (McFillen, Riegel, and Enz 1986).

A second research investigation conducted by Umbreit (1986) revealed that hotel managers were rated lowest on the dimensional categories of communicating with employees and handling personnel responsibilities. In summary, it has been documented that hospitality industry executives not only feel human resource management is important, but need further training in this increasingly critical area.

HOTEL INDUSTRY PERSPECTIVE

While the hospitality industry supports the importance of human resource management, what they actually do in practice differs, according to two recent research studies. Umbreit and Eder (1987) asked hotel managers from three separate companies to weight the importance of seven hotel manager performance dimensions. Hotel managers from all three companies attached the lowest value to the dimension dealing with handling personnel responsibilities. The greatest weight was given to such job aspects as monitoring operations and developing market strategy. Geller (1985b) found none of the hotel companies he surveyed had a sophisticated personnel information system. It is interesting to note that the critical success factor most frequently mentioned in the above research study was the cultivation of positive employee attitudes. Top management in the hotel industry, while expressing a high level of interest in human resources, still uses common indicators of success such as occupancy percentage, average room rate, gross operating profit, cash flow, and rooms-departmental profit. Essentially, the hotel industry recognizes the importance of human resources, but continues to focus its efforts on short-term profitability and market-related operational issues.

CONDITIONS FOR CHANGE

At what point in the future will the hospitality industry recognize and elevate the importance of effective human resource practices? The first factor is already upon us—labor force demographic shifts. The hospitality industry has relied on young people, whose numbers are rapidly declining as a percentage of the available workforce. Fast-food restaurants in suburban areas find themselves shuttling in teenage workers from the inner city to fill their needs. As competition within the industry increases and the labor supply of suitable employees shrinks, rising productivity costs will erode a firm's competitive position. Under-staffed, under-trained, under-motivated hospitality employees are a prescription for low productivity.

In the short run, these productivity costs include higher turnover, absenteeism, materials cost, worker safety violations, and lower quality of service provided. Managerial focus on effective recruitment, selection, training, and staff supervision can have direct effects on both employee job satisfaction and productivity—provided managers are held accountable for effective human resource practices. Corporate executives will need to be as concerned with the yearly human resource performance of their firms as they are with monthly or quarterly financial performance. Umbreit and Eder (1987) contend that tangible effects of successful managerial practice will take a minimum of three to six months to yield desired results. Continual emphasis on short-term business strategy will force unit managers to forego concern about workforce development as they worry about day-to-day sales volume. This is hardly a prescription for long-term corporate health and profitability.

In the long run, the hospitality industry will shift its focus toward effective human resource practices when the basic business strategy evolves from marketing service to customer centered service. Repeat business is crucial to the success of any hospitality operation. The quality of guest services provided by employees dictates greater management attention to human resource development. Hospitality firms that recognize the need to be more customer centered will place a higher premium on quality of worklife and staff development. Genuine enthusiasm and pride in one's work does not happen by accident; it must be nurtured.

The final factor to help the hospitality industry focus its collective attention on effective human resource practices will be the evolving nature of hospitality education. Initially, hospitality management was taught as a technical level with emphasis on finance and accounting practices. Today's college graduate is more likely to have additional training in marketing and management. Curriculum emphasis and current research on how human resource practices affect the corporate "bottom-line" will produce awareness among hospitality managers of the performance advantage they will have if they pay closer attention to workforce needs.

IMPLICATIONS FOR HOSPITALITY EDUCATORS

Hospitality educators can play an important part in helping industry improve human resource management practices. First, educators can place much greater emphasis in their curriculums on the development of student interpersonal management relations. Brymer (1979) proposed such a course that would encompass such topics as personal and career objectives, management strategies and styles, communication skills, managing opponents, and conflict resolution. Students must learn the techniques of how to motivate and discipline employees. In addition, students must be taught how to deal with diverse personalities and how to achieve results through people. Secondly, educators should offer a course in personnel and teach students how to utilize the techniques available in such areas as selection, hiring, orientation, training, and career development. Students must understand the value of human resource management and develop competencies sufficient to influence managerial practice.

A Profile of the Hotel Personnel Manager

James R. Pickworth

Although the effective use of human resources is crucial to the success of any business enterprise, it has been observed that the "personnel function has been misunderstood, undermanaged, or mismanaged in many enterprises" (Glueck 1978, 4).

This article was originally published in the May 1981 issue of *The Cornell Hotel and Restaurant Administration Quarterly,* and is reprinted with the permission of the Cornell University School of Hotel Administration. © 1981.

When a company reaches sufficient size to warrant a personnel department, the personnel function shifts from line managers in the company's various departments to a personnel manager. What are the specific functions of the hotel personnel manager at the unit level? Do they vary with the size of the operation? In what areas does a personnel manager have the most and least discretion? Which parts of his job does he find most satisfying? To answer these and related questions, the author undertook a study of persons working as personnel managers in hotels.

The results of the study should be useful to those in education and those in the industry. Educators designing personnel-administration courses should benefit from the study's insights into the content of the personnel manager's job. Executives in the industry should find the survey's results useful in making policy decisions relating to the personnel function.

METHODOLOGY

Of the 83 questionnaires mailed in 1979 to hotel personnel managers,[1] 48 were returned, for a response rate of approximately 58 percent.[2] The composition of the sample by hotel size is shown in Exhibit 1.

So that a profile of job functions could be derived, personnel managers were asked to indicate the extent of their responsibilities in certain major areas. A series of job activities that might typically be encountered by a hotel personnel manager were listed on the questionnaire. The respondents were asked to indicate the degree of discretion they were permitted in regard to each of these activities,[3] as follows:

- Able to take action without reference to others: The manager is able to act on his own and to set policy.

- Able to take action with minimal reference to others: The manager is able to act on his own within broad company guidelines.
- Able to take action within narrowly prescribed guidelines: The manager's actions are determined by company policy (e.g., as set forth in a policy manual).
- Able only to recommend action: The manager is not permitted to make decisions in this area.
- Unlikely to become involved in this activity: The activity specified is not part of the manager's job.

RESULTS

Because responsibilities varied with hotel size, respondents were placed in two categories—those working in hotels with up to 450 rooms, and those working in hotels with more than 450 rooms—for the purposes of analysis. A description of respondents and the properties at which they work appears in Exhibit 2.

Responsibilities

The four areas in which most personnel managers said they held considerable responsibility were recruitment advertising, selection interviewing, fringe-benefit administration, and orientation. Full responsibility for training new personnel was cited by only 17 percent of the managers employed in smaller hotels, as opposed to 41 percent of those in larger hotels. In a similar finding, orientation was described as a major responsibility by only 44 percent of the managers in smaller hotels, compared to 73 percent of those in larger properties.

Managers of both smaller and larger hotels enjoyed the most discretion is establishing the scope of personnel records (see Exhibit 3). Personnel managers in larger hotels had more discretion in many of the activities listed. For example, where decisions concerning wage scales and structures were involved, only 31 percent of those in smaller hotels were able to take any action whatsoever. The remainder could only recommend action, or

EXHIBIT 1
The study sample

Hotel Size	Questionnaires Sent	Responses
0–300 rooms	26	8 (31%)
301–450 rooms	25	18 (72%)
451–600 rooms	15	9 (60%)
601–750 rooms	8	5 (63%)
Over 750 rooms	9	8 (89%)
Total	83	48

EXHIBIT 2
Profile of the hotel personnel manager

	Smaller Hotels* n = 26	Larger Hotels n = 22
Typical Hotel Characteristics		
% of chain-managed hotels	81%	91%
% located downtown	65%	86%
Sales volume	$6–$7.5 mil.	Over $9.0 mil.
No. employees	251–500	500
% employing over 500 employees	4%	50%
% not unionized	31%	5%
Typical Personal Characteristics		
Age	30–39 yrs.	30–39 yrs.
% under 30 yrs. of age	35%	28%
% between 30–39 yrs.	42%	50%
% male	38%	36%
% female	62%	64%
% bilingual	54%	45%
% with bachelor's degree	27%	32%
Working week	46–50 hrs.	46–50 hrs.
Experience at this level in personnel	1–3 yrs.	4–5 yrs.
Salary, incl. bonuses†	$12,500–$14,999	$15,000–$17,499
% receiving bonus	21%	23%
% earning under $12,500	21%	5%
% earning under $15,000	75%	23%
% earning over $20,000	8%	23%
% very satisfied with their job	50%	68%

*Smaller hotels are those with 0 to 450 rooms; larger hotels are those with more than 450 rooms.

†Salary data as of October 1979 in Canadian dollars.

---

were not likely to be involved. In contrast, approximately 73 percent of those in larger hotels could take some form of action on wages.

Job Satisfaction

Of the personnel managers interviewed, 58 percent indicated they were very satisfied with their jobs, and 33 percent described themselves as quite satisfied, leaving only 9 percent expressing a lesser degree of job satisfaction.

Personnel managers were also asked to rate their degree of satisfaction with specific personnel activ-

ities (see Exhibit 4). Counseling employees was rated as the most satisfying activity, while those in larger hotels selected negotiating union agreements as very satisfying. Fringe-benefit administration also rated high with both groups.

COMPARISON WITH OTHER STUDIES

Although few similar studies have been undertaken to explore the role of unit personnel managers, some comparisons between the results of the author's study and other studies' findings can be drawn.

EXHIBIT 3
The personnel manager's activities

Level of Discretion	Smaller Hotels*		Larger Hotels	
Able to take action without reference to others	**Practices:**		**Practices:**	
	Scope of records	54%	Scope of records	68%
	Advertising budget	35%	Employing handicapped	55%
	Scope of medical benefits	32%	Advertising budget	45%
	Selection tests	29%	Selection tests	43%
			Newsletters	43%
	Procedures:		**Procedures:**	
	Notification of vacancies	47%	Notification of vacancies	60%
	Selection process	44%	Orientation process	57%
	Performance evaluation	35%	Selection process	48%
			Termination process	38%
Able to take action with minimal reference to others	**Practices:**		**Practices:**	
	Nature of staff parties	58%	Suggestion schemes	65%
	Scope of sports activities	43%	Nature of staff parties	63%
	Offers of employment	40%	House rules	59%
	Suggestion schemes	40%	Employment-management committee	57%
			Offers of employment	52%
	Procedures:		**Procedures:**	
	Termination process	32%	Training process	52%
	Orientation process	31%	Selection process	48%
	Performance process	31%	Performance evaluation process	48%
			Policies on Benefits:	
			Educational assistance	47%
Able to take action within narrowly prescribed guidelines	**Practices:**		**Practices:**	
	Apprenticeship	28%	Wage structure	44%
	Litigation	25%	Wage scales	41%
			Litigation	37%
	Procedures:		**Procedures:**	
	Selection process	20%	Disciplinary process	24%
	Policies on Benefits:		**Policies on Benefits:**	
	Educational assistance	33%	Relocation expenses	32%
			Educational assistance	32%
Able only to recommend	**Practices:**		**Practices:**	
	Wage scales	46%	Staffing levels	48%
	Wage structure	42%	Prices for employee meals	30%
	Staffing levels	39%		
	Procedures:		**Procedures:**	
	Training process	32%	—	
	Disciplinary process	32%		
	Termination process	32%		
	Policies on Benefits:		**Policies on Benefits:**	
	Vacations	79%	Vacations	82%
	Sick leave	78%	Insurance	76%
	Medical plans	74%	Medical plans	75%
	Insurance	68%	Sick leave	70%
Unlikely to get involved in this activity	**Practices:**		**Practices:**	
	Selection tests	39%	Scope of sports activity	28%
	Scope of sports activity	39%	Prices for employee meals	25%
	Prices for employee meals	36%	Litigation	21%
	Attitude surveys	32%		
	Procedures:		**Procedures:**	
	Training process	16%	—	
	Policies on Benefits:		**Policies on Benefits:**	
	Relocation expenses	35%	Relocation expenses	21%
	Pensions	20%	Pensions	18%

*To 450 rooms.

EXHIBIT 4
The personnel manager's satisfaction with specific activities

Personnel Activity	Degree of Satisfaction with Activity (1 = very satisfied; 5 = very dissatisfied)										Not involved in this activity	
	Most								Least			
	1		2		3		4		5			
	S*	L	S	L	S	L	S	L	S	L	S	L
Employment interviewing	37%	18%	42%	32%	17%	32%	0%	9%	4%	9%	0%	0%
Counseling employees	46%	54%	34%	32%	4%	14%	4%	0%	12%	0%	0%	0%
Negotiating union agreements	37%	54%	4%	9%	13%	14%	8%	9%	4%	0%	34%	14%
Paperwork & correspondence	12%	0%	38%	32%	31%	27%	7%	27%	12%	14%	0%	0%
Liaison with government agencies	20%	14%	42%	44%	17%	14%	8%	14%	0%	9%	13%	5%
Recruitment advertising	27%	9%	34%	18%	27%	41%	4%	27%	4%	5%	4%	0%
Training employees	19%	41%	27%	18%	16%	23%	0%	9%	0%	0%	38%	9%
Attending management meetings	42%	19%	24%	43%	27%	33%	0%	0%	0%	5%	7%	0%
Arranging employee functions	34%	23%	24%	44%	15%	14%	0%	5%	0%	0%	27%	14%
Employee newsletters	12%	5%	12%	32%	15%	14%	0%	18%	7%	5%	54%	26%
Tours for colleges	16%	5%	20%	28%	8%	28%	4%	5%	8%	5%	44%	29%
Payroll accounting	23%	9%	20%	18%	4%	14%	4%	9%	7%	5%	42%	45%
Fringe-benefit administration	34%	41%	27%	32%	12%	14%	12%	5%	0%	4%	15%	4%

*S = smaller hotels (up to 450 rooms); L = larger hotels (more than 450 rooms).

Job Satisfaction

A time-activity study showing that personnel managers spend 65 percent of their time conversing with others (Carroll 1960) may be relevant to the author's finding that the activity of counseling employees contributes to job satisfaction among personnel managers.

Staffing

The average ratio of personnel employees to total employees has been found to be approximately 1:239 nationally (Census of Canada 1971).[4] In the present study, it was found that the personnel manager worked alone in 45 percent of the hotels with fewer than 250 employees. In hotels with 500 to 750 employees, the average personnel department comprised three employees. The typical personnel manager worked approximately 46 to 50 hours per week, a workload in line with that of other industries.

Career Profile

The percentage of personnel managers who are women has risen over the past decade from 11 percent to 25 percent (Kumar 1975). In comparison, a full 63 percent of the hotel personnel managers represented in the author's survey were female. It appears that personnel management is one facet of hotel management in which women have established a definite career path (Census of Canada 1971; Fletcher and Pickworth 1978). Exhibit 5 shows a comparison of male and female respondents.

The present study's sample also differed from that of an earlier study in regard to age; the 1971 Canadian census revealed that a quarter of personnel managers were younger than 35 (Census of Canada 1971), while 77 percent of the hotel personnel managers surveyed by the author were under the age of 39. While many hotel personnel managers acquire responsibility at a young age—a

positive feature of a career in the industry—employers may sometimes find it necessary to provide additional training for less-experienced managers. Approximately 61 percent of all personnel managers surveyed had been employed in their present positions for a period shorter than four years, and 38 percent had been employed less than one year.[5]

It was expected that personnel managers in both smaller and larger hotels would receive extensive job training and would spend a substantial amount of time training others. Instead, the personnel managers surveyed by the author had attended an average of only 0.7 training courses. Moreover, 25 percent of the respondents indicated that they held *no* responsibility for training other employees, and only 10 percent had training officers in their departments. In contrast, a full 96 percent had some degree of responsibility for the related activity of orientation.

FURTHER OBSERVATIONS

Job Functions

It was not expected that personnel managers would be involved in payroll computation, but 15 percent

EXHIBIT 5
Comparison of male and female personnel managers

	Female (n = 30)	Male (n = 18)
% of respondents	63%	37%
Usual age range	30–39 yrs.	30–39 yrs.
No. years in this position and comparable personnel positions	1–3 yrs.	4–5 yrs.
% with college degrees	33%	33%
Salary range	$12,500–$15,000	$15,000–$17,500
% working in hotels with over 450 rooms	46%	44%

of the managers surveyed were fully responsible for computing payroll; a further 32 percent indicated they were partially responsible for this activity. One might question whether personnel managers' involvement in payroll detracts from their performance of other personnel functions, including training.

Hotel Size

How were personnel departments affected by the size of hotels they served? In most hotels with 200 to 250 rooms, department heads were responsible for the personnel function,[6] but in a considerable number of properties, personnel matters were handled by the accounting department. This may be relevant to the author's finding that personnel departments were often responsible for computing payroll.

There were some clear differences between the responsibilities of managers working in hotels with up to 450 rooms and those of managers in hotels with over 450 rooms. Personnel managers in larger hotels were often more responsible for such traditional personnel functions as training and orientation than those in smaller hotels. Also, the managers' involvement in computing payroll decreased as hotel size increased (see Exhibit 6).

The survey also showed that personnel managers in unionized hotels were responsible for more personnel functions than those in nonunionized properties. The author speculates that when a hotel unionizes, the scope of the personnel manager's responsibilities increases.

What was the status of the personnel function at the corporate level? Did the executive responsible for personnel at the hotels surveyed have the status of a vice-president?[7] Of the nine companies with separate corporate personnel departments, only

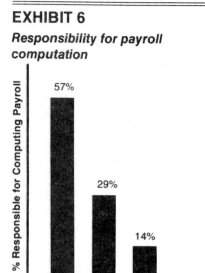

EXHIBIT 6
Responsibility for payroll computation

one-third were headed by an individual holding the title of vice-president.

CONCLUSIONS

The author's study indicates that most personnel managers receive little training and conduct less employee training than expected. Personnel managers in larger hotels spend considerably more time in activities that involve the orientation and training of employees than do their counterparts in smaller hotels. They also have more decision-making authority. Most of a personnel manager's duties in a hotel of virtually any size, however, are administrative. Finally, regardless of specific job responsibilities, hotel personnel managers seem to enjoy an extremely high level of job satisfaction.

Managing Employee Turnover

William J. Wasmuth
Stanley W. Davis

Employee turnover rates in the hospitality industry, it is generally agreed, are as high as or higher than in any other industry. It is also common knowledge that a significant reduction in employee turnover can lead to reduced labor costs. In view of the potential savings in this area, it is surprising that relatively little attention is being given to managing employee turnover, in spite of the fact that hospitality operations world-wide are struggling to maintain profit margins.

To explain this lack of attention and to answer other related problems, we undertook a one-year research study of turnover in the hospitality industry.[8] Data were collected through interviews with approximately 200 general, executive-assistant, and departmental managers in a sample of 20 large national and international hotels in North America and Europe.[9] Those interviewed were asked to respond to a questionnaire designed to identify the characteristics and turnover experiences of each hotel.

The interviews focused on the following four areas:

- The rates of employee turnover both for the organization as a whole and for major departments and key job categories;
- The cost of turnover;
- The causes of turnover; and
- Various strategies for managing turnover.

The initial goal of the study was to clarify the current level of turnover rates in the hospitality industry in relation to other industries, to analyze costs, and—most important—to develop a strategic

This article was originally published in the February 1983 issue of *The Cornell Hotel and Restaurant Administration Quarterly,* and is reprinted here with the permission of the Cornell University School of Hotel Administration. © 1983.

framework that could be used by hoteliers in managing turnover and thereby enhancing profits. Before proposing such a framework, however, we would like to present some background on employee turnover.

WHAT CAUSES TURNOVER?

Companies that experience excessive turnover are in a constant state of flux and turmoil. The formal and informal relationships that are established between worker and supervisor, and among fellow workers—as well as the way people do their jobs—all change when someone leaves an organization and a replacement enters. The way that the organization functions is weakened because of a lack of communication, and disrupted because routine tasks—especially those that require coordination between two or more individuals—are not being accomplished.

Many studies have demonstrated that turnover, which can be a measure of organizational productivity (Katz 1964), is the result of employee alienation, as well as "symptomatic of a variety of personnel problems" (Strauss and Sayles 1980, 323). Job satisfaction, for example, although it does not necessarily show a high correlation with productivity, is highly related to turnover (Brayfield and Crockett 1955). In 14 of 15 studies covering a range of workers in different types of organizations, turnover was found to be higher when overall job dissatisfaction was higher (Bass and Ryterband 1979, 73). Other studies show that turnover is related to the prevailing economic conditions in the labor market (Heneman et al. 1980, 165). As unemployment increases, employee resignations decrease; conversely, as unemployment decreases (i.e., as jobs become easier to find), employee resignations increase.

March and Simon (1958, Chapter 4) postulated that turnover is a function of the following two components: (1) the perceived desirability of leaving the organization; and (2) the perceived ease of movement from the organization. The March and Simon model, modified by Heneman et al. (1980), is shown in Exhibit 1. As demonstrated in this exhibit, some of the variables can be generalized and could affect workers in an entire company, industry, or group of industries. If poor economic conditions were widespread, for example, many industries would be affected simultaneously, thus reducing the average national turnover for a period of time. Some of the variables, however, might be specific to an organization, department, or individual. A change in the design or style of a restaurant in a hotel, for example, might create the potential for turnover (e.g., if advancement within the organization was limited, some individuals might desire to leave).

In regard to the satisfaction portion of the model, Ross and Zander—in a study of the relationship between need-satisfaction and turnover—have shown that there are two different types of reasons for leaving a job: (1) the job itself does not satisfy employee needs, and (2) the job prevents employees from receiving satisfaction from other sources (e.g., satisfaction from involvement with family and community) (Ross and Zander 1957). This second reason is particularly relevant to the hospitality industry, where long hours and unusual shift arrangements are commonplace.

The quality and nature of supervision have also been shown to affect turnover. For example, departments with punitive foremen are more likely to

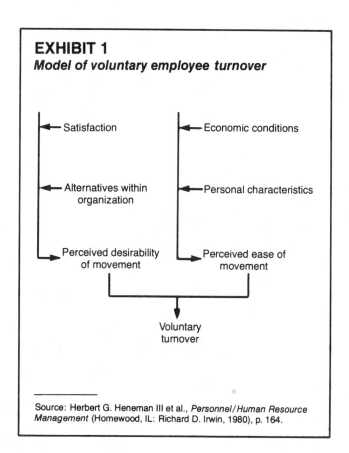

EXHIBIT 1
Model of voluntary employee turnover

Source: Herbert G. Heneman III et al., *Personnel/Human Resource Management* (Homewood, IL: Richard D. Irwin, 1980), p. 164.

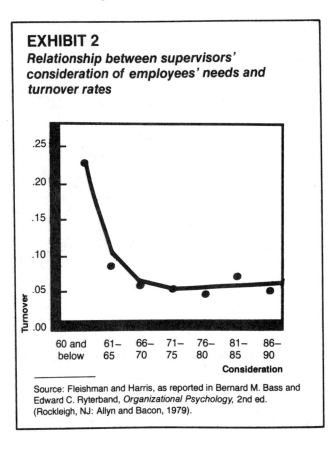

EXHIBIT 2
Relationship between supervisors'
consideration of employees' needs and
turnover rates

Source: Fleishman and Harris, as reported in Bernard M. Bass and
Edward C. Ryterband, *Organizational Psychology,* 2nd ed.
(Rockleigh, NJ: Allyn and Bacon, 1979).

have a low level of productivity and high rates of absenteeism and turnover (Bass and Ryterband 1979, 216). In studies performed by Fleishman and Harris (1979), turnover was found to be particularly high in those departments where supervisors were viewed as being inconsiderate of employees' needs (see Exhibit 2).

Turnover, it appears, is the end product of a complicated series of interactions between the individual and the organization. Because of this, there are no easy solutions to it. As Hawk has pointed out, there are potential difficulties associated with two commonly used strategies. "Absentee-control programs"—designed to punish employees with a high rate of absenteeism—"may be successful in the short run, but their success will probably be costly in terms of scrap rates, reduced productivity, or sabotage in the long run" (Hawk 1976). Another

common strategy to manage turnover is to try to get "better people" by raising entry-level qualifications. This, of course, means additional expense, and frequently results in "overhiring" (acquiring people who are over-qualified for their jobs). This, in turn, leads to higher rather than lower turnover.

HOW TO MANAGE TURNOVER

In assessing organizational strategies designed to manage turnover, there are two areas that should be defined: (1) the rate of turnover, which ranges from low to high; and (2) the degree of management control over turnover, which ranges from planned to unplanned. A typology of these two variables that we developed for our study is shown in Exhibit 3. The titles given to each of the four categories in this exhibit were coined to dramatize what we believe are the major consequences of each strategic option. For example, low turnover that is unplanned (category II) could easily lead to the retention of larger numbers of poor performers or deadwood; thus the caption "stagnant." In contrast, unplanned turnover at a high level (category IV) is the most "chaotic" option because it represents the potential loss of many good performers as well as a lack of understanding as to why they left or what management can do in the future to change this negative pattern.

Obviously, developing strategies for planned organizational control of turnover, whatever the level, is the best course of action.[10] This means operating within categories I and III rather than II and IV. Less obviously, there may be some situations for which category III (appropriately named "revolving door" to connote frequent movements in and out) would be preferable to category I (generally thought to be the most cost-efficient). For example, if a company were to realize overall net savings by replacing high-salaried employees with lower-salaried workers, then category III would be preferable. Questions to ask: Where in actual practice are mixed-retention strategies most appropriate? Do some departments or key-employee categories re-quire different planned approaches to turnover when labor-market conditions are unstable? To answer these questions, we began by collecting data on the levels, costs, and causes of employee turnover.

LEVEL OF TURNOVER

Obtaining data on turnover rates was not a problem during the study because monthly records were routinely prepared in almost all of the hotels surveyed. Somewhat of a surprise, however, was the discovery that the average turnover in these large luxury properties was approximately three times greater than the national average of turnover for all industries. (A recent study cited by Heneman estimated that the annual rate of turnover for all companies in the U.S. was 20 percent (Heneman et al. 1980); in comparison, the mean rate of turnover during the year 1981 for the 20 hotels in our study was 60 percent.[11])

COST OF TURNOVER

While soliciting information on rates of turnover was relatively easy, collecting data on turnover costs was quite a different matter. Disappointingly, no

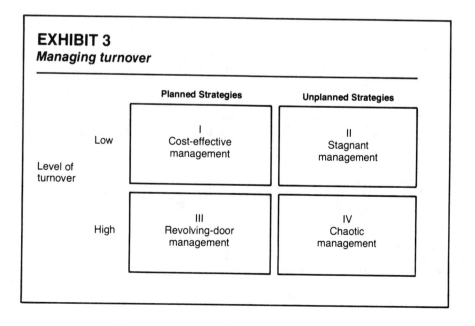

EXHIBIT 3
Managing turnover

		Planned Strategies	Unplanned Strategies
Level of turnover	Low	I Cost-effective management	II Stagnant management
	High	III Revolving-door management	IV Chaotic management

EXHIBIT 4
Framework for costing turnover

Turnover Cost Factors	Degree of Certainty of Cost Quantification			Comments
	High	Moderate	Low	
A. SEPARATION*				
Exit interview	X			Interviewers' *and* employees' time
Administrative functions		X		Payroll, benefits, personnel records, and so forth
Separation pay (if any)	X			
Unemployment tax (if applicable)	X			Turnover experience factor determines change in base rate
Staff party (if any)		X		
B. REPLACEMENT*				
Advertising	X			Less costly for low-skill jobs or where files of good candidates are maintained
Employment agency (if any)	X			
Pre-employment administrative functions		X		Requisitions, labor-market assessment, bidding, and so forth
Hiring interview	X			
Staff time regarding hiring decision		X		Includes testing, reference checks, selection alternatives, and so forth
Medical examinations	X			
Post-employment administrative functions		X		Acquisition and dissemination of information
Salary adjustments (if any)	X			
Payroll taxes (if applicable)	X			Based on larger payroll
Moving expenses (if any)	X			
Uniforms	X			

*Included in Cascio's analysis as well as the authors' framework.
†Included only in the authors' framework.

EXHIBIT 4 (*continued*)

Turnover Cost Factors	Degree of Certainty of Cost Quantification			Comments
	High	Moderate	Low	
B. REPLACEMENT (cont.)				
Workers' compensation and accident insurance (if applicable)	X			Incremental change based on workers' experience
Additional overtime	X			During new hires' learning periods
C. TRAINING*				
Informational literature	X			Including orientation
Formal training OR employee instruction by senior employee		X		Cost of instruction
D. COST OF LOST PRODUCTION†				
Time for new hire to learn the job		X		Assumes average rate of learning to reach job standards of performance, as shown in Exhibit 5
Loss from time employee decides to leave until actual separation occurs			X	
Higher spoilage or error rate	X			Likely during break-in period for many jobs
E. MORALE AND PUBLIC RELATIONS†				
Effect on other employees		X	X	Often has "ripple" effect— one leaves and others follow; especially in close-knit work groups
Effect on customers			X	Most detrimental to repeat customers who look for "familiar" faces and recognition
Effect on management and supervision			X	"Poor" attitudes of employees planning to leave (if they are dissatisfied)

systematic data of any kind were available on this subject, nor did any of the respondents know where such information could be obtained. But while all of the survey's respondents indicated that they did not calculate or know the cost of turnover, they also surmised that it was probably quite costly (their estimates ranged from $500 to $5,000 for each incidence of turnover, depending on the level of the position, and other variables). Interestingly, when asked whether data on turnover costs provided through the study would be of value to them, *every* respondent answered "yes." The value of costing turnover, it appears, was never questioned. Rather, how its cost would be determined seemed to be the problem.

Although most managers would agree with the survey's participants that turnover is indeed costly to an organization, few strategies to manage turnover are used in current manpower planning or personnel cost control. At most, the task of managing turnover is viewed as an indirect measure of managerial performance, particularly in situations where an increase in turnover is thought to have an adverse impact on service and profit objectives. It is our view that the low priority given to managing turnover is due primarily to the fact that, at present, hotel managers have no way to determine the impact of turnover on the bottom line. It follows, therefore, that if a reasonable framework for costing turnover could be provided, given the high level of turnover in the hospitality industry, more managers would develop viable retention strategies.

Modifying our findings to include those of Cascio and Hickey, we propose a framework for measuring turnover costs, outlined in Exhibit 4 (cf. Cascio 1982, 6; Hickey 1974).

Although measuring personnel costs of any kind is a difficult task, much progress has been made in recent years on costing human resources, and many of the results achieved in the personnel area can now be measured in dollars, as is done for sales, food and beverage, and other functional areas of the business.

In costing labor turnover, dollar figures, if available, should be attached to each factor. This method, which Cascio points out measures not the value of the individual but the dollar consequences of his or her behavior, provides an *expense* model for costing turnover (Cascio 1982, 6).

As noted in Exhibit 4, Cascio's research on costing turnover focuses on separation, replacement, and training costs, each of which is relatively easier to measure than lost production, morale, and public-relations costs—the additional factors that we propose in Exhibit 4. In regard to the first three categories, we agree with the Cascio approach to costing outlined below:

1. Cost elements for each factor must be identified and their separate dollar values computed either as *outlay costs* or *time costs*. For example, the time cost of an exit interview would be as shown below:

$$\left[\begin{array}{l} \text{time required of} \quad\quad \text{time} \\ \text{interviewer prior} + \text{required} \\ \quad \text{to interview} \quad\quad \text{for interview} \end{array} \right] \times \begin{array}{l} \text{interviewer's} \\ \text{pay rate} \end{array}$$

$$+ \left[\begin{array}{l} \text{time required for} \quad\quad \text{pay rate of} \\ \text{terminated employee's} \times \text{employee} \\ \quad\quad \text{interview} \end{array} \right]$$

2. The focus should be on *variable* or *incremental* costs—for example, determining the overtime cost resulting from the departure of employees in a department.

To arrive at a comprehensive total turnover figure, we estimated the costs of lost production as well as morale and public-relations costs. The cost of lost production for staff personnel is shown conceptually in Exhibit 5. Note that we assume the average staff person requires two months to reach acceptable (break-even) quantitative and qualitative standard levels of performance. Given our framework, note that *four months* of salary and effort constitute the total cost break-even point, and that two more months of production time are needed to overcome the initial two-month loss (i.e., area W = area Z). For hourly employees, we assume that standard performance levels can be reached and sustained after one month. For these individuals, *two months* of salary and effort equal the cost break-even point.

Estimating the cost of turnover on company morale and on public relations—while not an easy task—is essential because, as the study's findings revealed, most managers feel that these factors are the most costly in the long run and can affect an organization's ability to compete (and possibly even to survive). As cited earlier, there is also evidence that sustained job dissatisfaction has a negative effect on productivity and on the quality of customer service. If productivity drops because of low morale

and increased turnover, costs in terms of lost production will rise further. It is clear, then, that employee morale can have a significant impact on turnover and the cost of turnover.

Public relations influences customer satisfaction, according to the survey's participants, who, without exception, related their distress at the loss of skilled and effective employees in such key customer-contact areas as sales, reception, dining, cashier, and so forth. Many employees in these areas—because of their interpersonal skills, their knowledge of the hotel, and their ability to solve customer problems and extend courtesies—help retain customers. While a hotel can make adjustments for the loss of

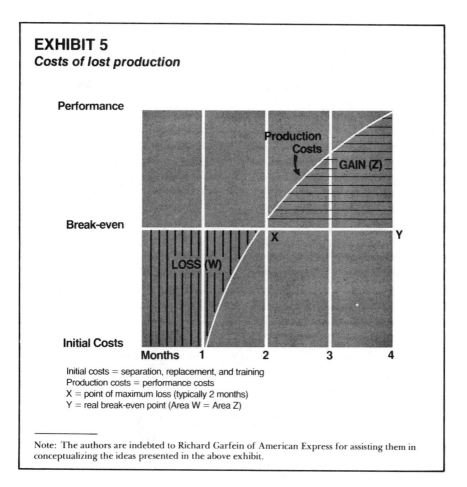

EXHIBIT 5
Costs of lost production

Initial costs = separation, replacement, and training
Production costs = performance costs
X = point of maximum loss (typically 2 months)
Y = real break-even point (Area W = Area Z)

Note: The authors are indebted to Richard Garfein of American Express for assisting them in conceptualizing the ideas presented in the above exhibit.

a few qualified employees, there is no doubt that each loss damages customer goodwill and eventually affects profits. It is also clear that, in sustaining such losses over a period of time, a hotel may jeopardize its ability to compete for the treasured resource—repeat customers. These factors make clear how high the cost of poor public relations can be.

SUMMARY OF COSTING TURNOVER

Using the framework described above, supported by cost estimates provided during the interviews, we have calculated several reasonable approximations of turnover costs.

First, using our modified Cascio and Hickey framework, we determined the cost of turnover, as shown in Exhibit 6.

Second, using our survey interview data (based solely on estimates that were "extracted" primarily from fiscal and personnel managers), we estimated the cost of turnover as ranging from $500 to $5,000; the mean for hourly employees was $1,500, and for

---

EXHIBIT 7
*Cost savings in reducing level of turnover**

	# Employees
Average size of full-time work force:	300
Current turnover per year, or 60%, = turnover of:	180
Goal-reduction to one half of current level, or 30%, = turnover of:	90

Cost savings in reducing turnover by 90 people @ $2,500 per person = **$225,000 per year.**

*The figures used in this assessment are hypothetical and are based on average turnover rates at a typical luxury hotel similar to those used in the authors' study. The savings shown are, we believe, a conservative estimate; many hotels have higher turnover rates and could therefore realize even greater savings.

EXHIBIT 6
A method for calculating the cost of turnover

	Hourly Employees	Staff Employees
Separation, replacement, and training costs *	$ 500	$ 750
Costs of lost production	$ 750 (assumes average of $750 per month—*one* month lost production)	$2,200 (assumes average salary of $1,100 per month—*two* months lost production)
Morale and public-relations costs	$ 850	$1,250
Totals:	**$2,100**	**$4,200**

Assuming that turnover is 80% hourly and 20% staff employees, costs = (2,100 × .80) + (4,200 × .20) = *$2,520* average cost per employee.

*It should be noted that Cascio calculated the cost of turnover for a 200-bed hospital employing 1,200 people with an annual turnover rate of 24 percent (288 employees). The total cost for *only* separation, replacement, and training factors in his example was $314,181, or $1,091 per employee. This figure includes $95,155 separation pay, or $331 per employee. Without separation pay, costs per employee were $760.

staff $3,000. The average overall cost estimate was $2,300 per turnover, surprisingly similar to the calculations shown in Exhibit 6.

Given these cost analyses, which are supported by reasonably comparable estimates from the field, the authors contend that an average cost per employee of $2,500 is a reasonable basis for determining the dollar implications of turnover on the bottom line.

IMPLICATIONS FOR THE BOTTOM LINE

As mentioned earlier, most of the managers interviewed felt that the levels of turnover at their operations were too high and could be reduced to one-half of current levels to achieve an optimum amount of basically noncontrollable turnover. Is it worth the effort to strive for controllable levels of turnover? The answer, we contend, is "yes," basing our response on the calculations in Exhibit 7, which show savings from reduced turnover to be close to a quarter of a million dollars.

Even more significant than the estimated savings, however, is the fact that such savings can be achieved with little or no new direct cost outlays. What *is* required is time to ascertain the causes of turnover and to develop various retention strategies that can be used for managing turnover.

Performance Appraisals: Making Them Fair and Making Them Work

W. Terry Umbreit
Robert W. Eder
Jon P. McConnell

The validity of performance appraisals is an important management issue. Because performance appraisals have several uses (e.g., personnel tool, management tool, legal documentation), establishing a valid performance-appraisal system for managers and employees is necessary for any business. Performance appraisals are used to stimulate the productivity of managers, supervisors, and staff. The ratings also are often the basis for decisions about promotions and transfers, pay increases, and terminations. In cases where an employee feels that one of these decisions was improper, the perfor-

mance appraisal may become part of the evidence in a legal case. As a result, performance appraisals have become more than just a yearly ritual for employees and supervisors.

Hospitality operators especially need a valid method of appraising staff performance, because their employees and management staff change jobs quickly and in large numbers. But an effective appraisal system can also afford property managers a way of improving the efficiency of a stable staff.

The major difficulty with most performance-appraisal systems is that the judgments involved are frequently subjective, relating primarily to personality traits or to observations that cannot be verified. In this article, the authors will review the minimum legal requirements for a performance-appraisal system, based on recent analyses of relevant court

This article was originally published in the February 1986 issue of *The Cornell Hotel and Restaurant Administration Quarterly,* and is reprinted here with the permission of the Cornell University School of Hotel Administration. © 1986.

cases, and discuss the issues involved in modifying existing-performance appraisal procedures. We hope to help you establish appraisal procedures that are fair to employees, legally sound, and useful to corporate staff and property managers. Our focus is primarily on the evaluation of management personnel, but minimal standards for legal defensibility apply to all job categories.

An Early Caveat

There exists no rating instrument, based on subjective judgment, that can guarantee a "true" reflection of a person's job performance. Furthermore, there are jobs in which the outcome is not solely the result of one employee's efforts, so rating specific accomplishments cannot paint a full picture of each person's work. It is also difficult to represent the full scope of a person's job in a single objective measure. Therefore, perfect objectivity is not the goal here. What you should seek to develop is a performance-appraisal procedure that withstands dispassionate scrutiny, is legally defensible, and meets the current state of the art in performance appraisal.

MINIMUM STANDARDS

Under the law, a "valid" appraisal rating is one that correlates highly with established, objective measures of performance or one that accurately predicts future job success (which itself must be measured in a valid way). For instance, if your managers are evaluated on communication skills, you must use an appropriate rating scale and be able to show that communication skills are essential to excellent job performance. Furthermore, if one group usually scores high on your appraisal scale and another scores low (say, men score high and women score low), and you have no objective data against which to compare these subjective ratings, you will be hard-pressed to demonstrate the validity of your appraisal system, no matter how sophisticated it is (Kleinman and Durham 1981).

Thus, recent legal decisions can help provide a basis for developing appraisal standards, but we believe it is unwise to make legal requirements the *sole* determinant for your evaluation systems. Certainly, your appraisals must be legally defensible, but a rating system that merely meets the minimum legal standards will hardly be useful for you as a management tool. Instead of simply reacting to the lessons of the legal precedents mentioned below, we recommend that you make these the foundation of your appraisal procedure, and build on that base to create a truly effective appraisal system. The evaluation format you select depends, for example, on how you intend to use the information generated and on the type and diversity of job categories in your company.

If your firm uses performance appraisals to make employment decisions, you are using what the courts consider a "test" of qualifications. This test must meet all federal legal standards, as stated in civil-rights legislation, equal-pay laws, and age-discrimination statutes.[12] This is a particularly important point if your female employees are paid on average less than male employees, for whatever reason (e.g., length of tenure, skill differentials, quantity of output). If an employee makes a complaint about your performance appraisals, the courts will examine your evaluation system to determine whether it is valid and whether it embodies a sex-, race-, or age-based bias. (The complaint will likely rest on allegations that your personnel policies have "adverse impact," as explained in the accompanying box, *Adverse Impact: Three Strikes and Out.*) Any kind of age limit for employees may also come under scrutiny. If you cannot induce employees who have grown incompetent to retire, for example, your performance-appraisal system will have to do the work for you, showing that the employees cannot do the work required of them (Schuster and Miller 1982).

Rarely does an organization inform an employee that he or she has lost a promotion or is being laid off because of race, gender, or age. This would be a blatant violation of federal laws. But if a female

Adverse Impact: Three Strikes and Out

Many hotel companies lack the documentation they would need to protect themselves if one of their employees filed a discrimination claim with the Equal Employment Opportunity Commission (EEOC). The EEOC is responsible for enforcing the federal laws that protect certain groups of individuals (e.g., women, members of ethnic groups, persons over 40) from employment discrimination.

The typical adverse-impact case might start when a 53-year-old hotel manager is passed over for promotion to the corporate offices of the fictitious Prestige Hotel Company. The Manager files an age-discrimination claim with the EEOC (which will refer the complaint to a state or local agency, if the state or municipal government has passed a fair-employment law). The EEOC deems the complaint worthy of investigation, and an EEOC investigator interviews the top management of Prestige Hotels. (If the EEOC refuses to pursue the case, the manager can still hire a lawyer to file a civil suit.)

Strike one. During the investigation, the EEOC asks Prestige to supply information on *applicant-flow data,* the proportion of under-40 and over-40 managers who applied for promotion during the past year. According to Prestige's records, 20 managers over age 40 and 30 younger managers applied for promotion. Of the 20 older managers, six (30 percent) were promoted, but 18 (60 percent) of the 30 younger managers were promoted. The federal government applies a so-called "80-percent rule" in this case, by multiplying the promotion frequency for the unprotected group (young white men) by 80 percent. Since the resulting figure (48 percent) is greater than the 30 percent of older managers who were promoted, the

EEOC makes a preliminary finding of adverse impact—that Prestige Hotels screens out a disproportionate number of older persons from consideration for promotion.

Strike two. But even if Prestige passed the test on applicant flow, it might fail other tests.* Say that the EEOC finds in favor of Prestige, based on it promotion record. The aggrieved manager then points out that Prestige has a reputation for promoting only young men to corporate ranks. This reputation would cause older managers to leave instead of hoping for promotion. To check this claim, the EEOC uses *population statistics,* comparing the percentage of protected persons employed at Prestige Hotels to the percentage of protected persons in the labor market. In this hypothetical case, the EEOC would compare the number of older hotel managers at Prestige Hotels to the number of managers over 40 working in the relevant labor market. The exact definition of the "relevant labor market" is still a topic of legal and academic debate, but it might include employed hotel managers, individuals seeking work, and hotel employees who are eligible for promotion to management.

Strike three. As explained in the accompanying article, the case is not over even if Prestige passes *both* the above tests. If the company's performance-appraisal system routinely yields lower ratings for older persons (or any other protected group) than for young white men, the EEOC or a court may still find adverse impact.

---

*L.S. Kleiman and R.L. Durham, "Performance Appraisal, Promotion, and the Courts: A Critical Review," *Personnel Psychology,* 34, No. 1 (Spring 1981), pp. 103–121.

manager is denied a promotion, for instance, and the position remains vacant or is filled by a male (especially one who is not any more qualified), she may charge that she was a victim of disparate treatment (e.g., *McDonnell-Douglas v. Green,* 411 U.S. 972 (1973)). Once again, the performance-appraisal system would be examined by the courts, because the woman's appraisal was presumably the basis of the decision not to promote. In such a case, the employer would be required to show that the appraisal was based on criteria specifically related to job performance.

TEN TESTS

Based on court cases and recent research, we suggest you meet the following minimal legal standards for any appraisal system.[13] Five of these standards relate to the *content* of the appraisal, because your appraisals must be restricted to job-related issues. The other five standards are related to *procedure*, because your appraisal system must ensure due process for each employee and contain checks and balances against capricious ratings.

Content Requirements

1. Performance standards must be based on an analysis of job requirements. In cases of adverse impact, courts frequently find in favor of the plaintiff when the employer is unable to demonstrate that the appraisal criteria used are connected with relevant job descriptions. A formal job analysis is not strictly necessary, but it is valuable. You should at least present a current job description to your employees for review and discussion before the performance appraisal (Bernardin and Beatty 1984). Check the description for "fuzzy" performance standards; vague criteria that appear unrelated to actual job outcomes would certainly be suspect.

2. Evaluation should be based on specific dimensions of job performance, and not on single "global" measures. A typical global measure is a bottom-line measure of profitability or occupancy. But this measure might obscure many other factors (e.g., the costs of achieving the goal in terms of product quality or employee turnover). Paired comparisons and forced distributions among managers within a single job category are also questionable, because there is no way to determine the weights accorded to various parts of the job and no way to know whether the same process of judgment is used to measure the effectiveness of all managers (*Albemarle Paper Company v. Moody*, 422 U.S. 405 (1975)). Again in these cases, a formal job analysis would provide the information necessary to ensure that all important dimensions are represented in a performance evaluation. The analysis would also reveal the various weights to be assigned to each dimension of the job, reflecting the relative importance, the consequences of error, or the amount of work time devoted to each activity.

3. Performance standards should be objective and observable. Personality traits are not valid yardsticks. Yet many rating instruments use a five- or seven-point scale to measure a handful of such broad attributes as quantity of work, quality of work, cooperativeness, dependability, or work attitude. The courts usually take a dim view of evaluations heavily weighted toward personality traits.

Evaluators should be able to give consistent ratings for a given managerial attribute. When the trait being measured is "dependability" or "cooperativeness," a consistent score is nearly impossible, because different evaluators will have different definitions of these attributes. Instead, performance standards should be based on what the manager *does* (behavior) or what that behavior *produces* (i.e., direct contribution to organizational goals). Both of these are measurable, so they provide a more solid foundation for appraisal. These standards also reduce the possibility of systematic bias that often results from considering personality traits that are only weakly linked to job performance.

4. Ratings should be documented. Your company should establish a uniform procedure for documenting the performance of each manager or employee *throughout* the appraisal period, and not as an *ex post facto* rationale or comment attached to the rating. Specific accomplishments, failures, or critical incidents should be part of the documentation of a manager's performance. Our recommendation for explicit documentation of all aspects of performance is a caution against a rater's paying attention only to the extremes of employee behavior (outstanding performances or mistakes), because this emphasis fosters a climate in which selective attention is given to the employees' successes or failures, rather than a balanced effort made to document all important aspects of performance.

5. The validity of individual raters' ratings should be assessed. The courts have occasionally asked for supporting evidence showing why some raters give lower ratings than others. Unfortunately, without objective measures against which to correlate ratings by different evaluators or multiple ratings by the same evaluator, there is no way to show that the evaluators are in fact giving valid or worthwhile ratings.

Process Requirements

1. Performance standards should be communicated to and understood by the employee. Employees often are not informed of performance expectations. Too many organizations have informal and decentralized procedures for evaluation, under which only a summary evaluation or ranking is routinely required and managers do not see the need to be explicit about performance standards. Furthermore, many managerial jobs may largely be evaluated on the solution of *nonroutine* and unexpected problems. In either of these cases, the evaluators cannot explain the job expectations or the rating criteria. At minimum, the employee should be shown a job description.

The only review criteria given to many managers are goals and objectives set at the beginning of a fiscal year. The problems with focusing on goal achievement are that managers do not always have control of the outcome, and managers are rarely given information on what behavior is appropriate to achieving the goal. Sometimes, in fact, evaluators may *deliberately* keep their managers in the dark, on the theory that the uncertainty will spur the manager to greater efforts. This attitude is typified by a comment heard by one of the authors at a stress-management workshop: "In my organization, we want them to sweat, and not to relax. A little fear and uncertainty can go a long way!"

2. Specific instructions for evaluators should be put in writing. There is no way to be certain yourself or to show anyone else that all your evaluators know how to conduct and document employee ratings unless they have been given explicit written instructions.

3. Use more than one evaluator whenever possible. It is unwise to give an employee's immediate supervisor the sole responsibility for rating that employee. The immediate supervisor may not have the opportunity to observe and document the entire range of an employee's performance, and any evaluation by a single rater may encompass personal bias. This is particularly true when the rating is used as the basis for promotion or salary increments, it is best to include peers and other supervisory staff. We should note, however, that combined ratings are not always superior to those from a single observer unless the individuals involved are trained evaluators and are familiar with the job-performance expectations.

4. The evaluator should review the appraisal results with the employee. The evaluator will be less likely to make capricious judgments when he or she must document the performance appraisal and explain it to the employee. The discussion may give valuable insights into the reasons for a given performance rating, and the evaluator may gain additional documentation. Failing to review the evaluation with the employee may be interpreted as a unilateral action against the employee.

5. The employee should have a formal appeal procedure. The existence of a formal appeal process should encourage the evaluator to be even more conscientious in establishing a fair performance rating.

APPRAISAL FORMATS

In choosing the performance-appraisal format that is best for your hotel, restaurant, or company, you should consider the above legal tests, because if you are faced with an employment discrimination suit, the characteristics of your appraisal system will probably have great influence on whether you win the case (Bernardin, Beatty, and Jensen 1980).

But you should also consider your own management needs and resources. In the remainder of this article, we will explain and compare four appraisal formats. Then we will discuss ways you can improve your company's rating procedures. Three of these formats—financial indices, trait ratings, and management by objectives—are commonly used. The fourth format, behaviorally anchored rating scales, is relatively new.

Financial Indices

Hospitality firms frequently evaluate managers on profit or financial indices (Geller 1985a). For example, hotel general managers are usually appraised on total income before fixed charges, revenue generation, income levels from operated departments, or control of undistributed operating expenses. One study found that hotel managers chose the following financial indices as the most appropriate criteria for evaluating their job performance: average annual room rate, ratio of payroll to room sales, and the ratio of payroll to food and beverage sales (Arnaldo 1981, 29–40).

Trait Ratings

Financial indices and other end-result measures are frequently supported by trait-oriented rating scales. In this rating format, the property manager is evaluated on traits that are considered important to successful job performance. The rating scale is usually a continuum ranging from excellent through average to unsatisfactory. Traits that typically are rated include attitude, communication skills, creativity, dependability, and initiative.

Management by Objectives

Like financial indices, management by objectives (MBO) is an outcome-oriented appraisal. MBO measures a manager's contribution to the organization's success and goal attainment. The typical MBO program has been described as follows:

. . . a managerial process whereby organizational purposes are diagnosed and met by joining superiors and subordinates in the pursuit of mutually agreed-upon goals and objectives that are specific, measurable, time-bounded, and joined to an action plan (McConkie 1979).

For the hotel GM, goals must include a particular market share, a favorable ratio of positive to negative guest comments, a small number of employee complaints, greater employee productivity, or an improved safety record. See Exhibit 1 for a sample MBO appraisal form.

Behaviorally Anchored Rating Scales

Instead of concentrating on outcomes or personality traits, behaviorally anchored rating scales (BARS) are designed to evaluate managers' *actions* (cf. Umbreit 1984; Bernardin and Smith 1981).[14] BARS scales are designed to overcome certain flaws in the methodology of conventional rating scales (Smith and Kendall 1963). The specific behaviors to be rated are those that are essential to successful management. BARS are used to evaluate what individuals actually do on their jobs, rather than the results or level of effectiveness.

The BARS format developed by one of the authors for hotel managers contains seven rating scales, one for each of the important aspects of job performance (Umbreit 1984). Each scale is divided into points ranging from excellent to poor, with brief descriptions of the behavior that fits each rating point. The statements are actually critical incidents illustrating effective and ineffective job performance. Exhibit 2 shows the BARS rating scale for communication. The other six rating scales are as follows:

1. Handling guest complaints and promoting guest relations;
2. Developing marketing strategies and monitoring sales programs;
3. Motivating and modifying employee behavior;

EXHIBIT 1
Sample MBO appraisal form

Hotel _____ Name of Manager _____

Review Period _____ Reviewer _____

Performance Goals	Measures of Results	Results
(1) Market share	Room-nights	Increased by 3 percent
(2) Guest service	Ratio of positive guest comments	Increased from 90 to 94 percent
(3) Rooms departmental profit	Rooms department income percentage	Increased by 1 percent
(4) Employee morale	Grievance rate	Decreased by 5 percent
(5) Employment development	Number of training completions	Increased by 10 percent
(6) Maintain health and safety conditions	Number of accidents	Decreased by 10
(7) Maintain hotel's external relations	Number of leadership positions	No change

4. Implementing policy, making decisions, and delegating responsibilities;
5. Monitoring operations and maintaining product quality; and
6. Handling personnel responsibilities.

The rater's job is simplified by the job statements, because he or she can compare the manager's performance to the critical-incident statements.

APPRAISAL FORMATS COMPARED

The characteristics of your appraisal system will be a factor in any legal action involving employment discrimination. Exhibit 3 shows a comparison of how the four rating systems meet legal standards.

At the beginning of this article, however, we stated that in addition to meeting legal standards, your appraisal system should withstand dispassionate scrutiny and match the state of the art in performance appraisal. We believe that the BARS scales most completely meet those criteria. They are consistent with legal-liability assessment, they are closely linked to job analysis, they are behaviorally specific (or based on work outcomes), and they encourage rater documentation. On the other hand, like an MBO program, BARS are more expensive to develop than systems using financial indices or trait scales. Your firm should therefore assess the costs as well as the benefits of a BARS format.

Content Standards

The measurements in your performance-appraisal system should relate directly to the job being performed. This lesson is clear in the legal cases involving performance appraisals. *Trait scales,* for instance, are widely used by many businesses, but they are not objective or specific measures and they cannot be documented effectively. If traits are defined in specific behavioral terms and documented

EXHIBIT 2
BARS scale for rating hotel managers' communication skills

Relevant behavior: Attending departmental staff meetings and involving subordinates in discussions; visiting with executive committee regularly on personal basis; using memos to communicate special instructions and policies to departments; disseminating financial and other operating information to subordinates; conducting periodic meetings with employees.

Rating		Sample Actions
Communicates effectively with staff members and attends meetings frequently.	7.00 —	
	6.00 —	This manager calls a "town hall" meeting to explain why the hotel will be cutting back staff. Employees are permitted to ask questions and discuss why certain positions in the hotel are being eliminated.
	5.00 —	During a busy expansion program, this manager increases the frequency of policy committee meetings to improve communications and coordination of the project.
Communicates satisfactorily with staff members and attends some meetings.	4.00 —	Once a week this manager invites several line employees into his or her office for an informal talk about hotel activities.
	3.00 —	This manager neglects to discuss with his front-office manager the problem of overstaffed bellmen during certain periods of the day, yet expresses concern to the resident manager.
Experiences difficulty in communicating with staff members and attends meetings infrequently.	2.00 —	This manager misses departmental meetings and fails to visit with subordinates individually, but leaves memos around the hotel with instructions on what should be done.
	1.00 —	During weekly executive committee meetings, this manager dismisses most subordinate comments as stupid.

EXHIBIT 3
Comparison of appraisal formats (extent of compliance with legal standards)

	Outcome measures		Behavioral measures	
	Financial indices	MBO	Trait scales	BARS
Content standards				
Appraisal content based on job analysis	Low	Moderate	Low	High
Evaluation on specific dimensions rather than global measures	Moderate	Moderately high	Moderately low	High
Objective and observable rating criteria	High	High	Low	High
Documented ratings	High	Moderate	Moderately low	Moderately high
Process standards				
Employee informed of rating criteria	Moderately high	Moderate	Moderately low	High
Explicit instructions for using rating format	Moderately low	Moderately high	High	Moderately high
Results reviewed with employee	Moderately low	Moderately high	Moderately low	Moderately high

with task-related information, it is possible that measurement of traits might survive legal scrutiny.

Financial indices are objective and well documented, but they may measure only a portion of a manager's job responsibilities. Financial indicators do not even hint at such matters as supervisory ability. Furthermore, an emphasis on overall profitability resembles a global measure of performance, one over which the manager often has little real control. Financial indices are excellent tools for determining departmental bonuses, but they do not readily translate into specific assessments of managerial job performance. A hotel manager's wide repertoire of skills cannot be captured in a few financial measures.

The *MBO* format is an excellent tool for developing managerial skills. But when MBOs are set separately for each manager, they cannot be used to compare the performances of different managers. Like financial indices, MBOs are quantifiable and objective—very specific goals that the employee is to achieve—but they may or may not be tied to job content. Also, they may or may not reflect all relevant aspects of the job.

Even if the goals were similar for all managers, it would be difficult to show that achieving the goals predicted future job success. In reality, few employees show a constant record of success. Some measure of managerial behavior is needed in addition to MBO.

A *behaviorally based rating format* (e.g., BARS) can meet the legal standards for relating ratings to job performance. BARS are derived from a job-analysis procedure in which critical incidents that relate to a manager's job are identified and compared to the manager's actual performance (refer again to Exhibit 2).

The BARS format involves specific evaluation of a number of dimensions of the manager's job and is particularly conducive to documentation of the manager's behavior. While BARS are not always explicitly valid and no format can entirely eliminate bias, BARS do rate all relevant job aspects. Still, if your firm started using BARS as the basis of promotion and salary decisions, you would have to show that favorable BARS ratings are indicators of job success.

Process Standards

Poor processing can render even the best rating systems useless. But the BARS format makes the evaluator's job easier by explicitly stating what is expected from the manager, which type of behavior is preferred, and how that behavior should be assessed. It is more difficult for evaluators to specify how financial indices or trait ratings are compiled and assessed or how achievement of goals is measured.

If your company chooses to use the MBO or BARS formats, evaluators must be trained in how to use them properly (i.e., trained in observation, documentation, etc.). On the other hand, trait scales and financial indices require relatively little instruction.

We said earlier that performance appraisals can be excellent management-development tools, but trait ratings and financial measures give little indication of how a person could improve his or her work. Most of the discussion in an employee review based on these ratings typically revolves around the definition of the measures, when the evaluator should more appropriately be concerned with how the employee can improve job performance. A discussion of performance is more likely with the MBO or BARS ratings, during which the evaluator and employee can review specific goals or actions that serve as a springboard for a discussion of achievements and shortcomings. Both MBO and BARS give the evaluator the information needed to make a performance review the beginning of a constructive dialogue that enhances employee relations.[15]

EVALUATING EVALUATIONS

You should consider many factors in reviewing your company's performance-appraisal methods, and not just the legally based issues raised here. (Some other issues are listed in Exhibit 4.) You may want to form a task force to research and analyze the

EXHIBIT 4
Issues to consider in designing a performance-appraisal system

Organizational factors and constraints

(1) How big a budget has top management created for appraisals?
(2) To what extent are managers accountable for employee development?
(3) What are the existing legal or contractual requirements?
(4) What are the primary objectives or purposes for conducting performance appraisals?
(5) What technical support is available?
(6) What is your organization's climate or managerial style?

Identification of performance standards

(1) How many job categories will require separate evaluation standards?
(2) Are performance standards achievable, understood, agreed upon, job-based, specific and measurable, time-oriented, written down, observable, discriminable, and valid predictors of job success?
(3) Are performance dimensions weighted according to job analysis by relative importance, consequence of error, or required percentage of work time?
(4) What comparative standards will be used—individual improvement over time, absolute standard of performance, or comparison among workers?
(5) Are the identified outcome measures attributable to employee performance?
(6) In addition to assessing individual performance, will you appraise group or departmental performance?

Observation, documentation, and evaluation

(1) What rating sources are available (in addition to immediate supervisor)?
(2) How adequate is the informal feedback and coaching currently given employees?
(3) Are evaluators trained in accurate observation and complete documentation, and can they conduct performance reviews that will decrease employee defensiveness during the review and increase commitment to improved performance?
(4) How adequate are your grievance and appeal procedures for employees who disagree with the evaluator's assessment?

information needed to diagnose your appraisal needs. The evaluation system that works well for one company will not automatically be the right one for another establishment. After your study has been completed, though, we expect your company will choose a variation of either MBO or BARS.

The choice between MBO and BARS depends largely on the nature of the jobs being evaluated. Housekeepers, for instance, should be evaluated on the results of their efforts. A room that is cleaned and made presentable in accordance with hotel standards, the number of rooms cleaned over time, and containing the cost of supplies are three ex-amples of objectives for housekeepers. For restaurant servers and front-desk employees, the evaluation standards involve behavior—in essence, their response to customer needs.

Given the critical and complex nature of their position, hotel managers should be evaluated on *both* critical-behavior scales (BARS) and the accomplishment of goals (MBO) associated with effective job performance. In short, one single type of evaluation is not enough. Given the number of distinct management categories, your firm should probably have multiple evaluation systems, each with valid performance measures, for management staff.

If comparisons are to be made across employees, BARS is more appropriate. BARS is an absolute scale in which behavioral standards are predetermined. On the other hand, MBO is an excellent employee-development format, because it allows employees to set the goals attendant upon improving their current level of performance. But employee comparisons are of questionable validity when employees have different types and levels of goal accomplishment.

THE REAL BOTTOM LINE

The performance review has become an annual ritual in many companies, but waiting until an appointed review time undermines the primary purpose of any evaluation system—improving employee performance. Both BARS and MBO can be used in frequent informal reviews.

Given the critical role of performance appraisals in the management of human resources, any change in your company's evaluation system should be carefully formulated, accepted by employees, and monitored for effectiveness. Current legal standards are just the starting point for a performance-appraisal system that works for your organization. A complete consideration of an appraisal system should allow your firm to develop an equitable rating system that brings out the best in your employees.

Evaluating Training Through Work Performance Standards

Lothar A. Kreck

Why should training be evaluated, and why and how are work performance standards used for training evaluation? In the following, an attempt will be made to connect work performance standards with training accomplishments.

Performance appraisal systems in general are central to effective management control. An appraisal has at least three functions: (1) to provide adequate and timely feedback to the employees, (2) to serve as a basis for modifying or changing the behavior of the employees toward more effective work habits, and (3) to provide data to managers with which they may judge future job assignments and compensations (Levinson 1976).

In the sphere of training, it can perhaps be said that training performance appraisal or evaluation is necessary (a) to provide goal-oriented feedback to the participants, in this case trainees and trainers; (b) to provide data to management, for decisions on future training efforts; and (c) to serve as the basis for modification of the various inputs into any training process. Brandenburg (1982) sees the major function of evaluation as one of internal support of the training process. There seems to be little doubt that the overriding reason for evaluating training is to see how effective that training has been. Expressed differently, the ultimate goal of training efforts is effective performance on the job (Burack and Smith 1977, 242) or, as Goldstein and Sorcher (1974, 59) expressed it, acquired learning "finds enduring expression in successful work performance."

It is fortunate that many trainers will agree on the need for critical training performance evaluation. When they agree, they seldom seem to agree on the best method of evaluation (Donaldson and Scannell 1978, 125), even though they recognize that reasonable and adequate standards of training

Reprinted with permission of Pergamon Press from Kreck, Lothar A. "Evaluating Training Through Work Performance." *International Journal of Hospitality Management*, vol. 4, no. 1 (1985), pp. 27–37.

performance would enable them to have proper progress measures that contribute to the goals of the organization.

Although there are several traditional training evaluation approaches, only three will be considered. The least complicated is probably the pre-test, post-test approach. The problem with this approach is that even if the training result was spelled out—e.g., not more than one wrong answer in the post-test—there is no guarantee that the new behavior will be job performance related. Another approach is to use two groups of randomly selected employees, half of which are placed in the experimental group and the other half in a control group. The experimental group, which receives the training, is supposed to show improved behavior over the control group. What is questionable with this approach? First, it is very unlikely that one hotel or restaurant will have a sufficient number of trainees of the same job category—e.g., front office clerks—assignable to the two groups to result in meaningful data, except perhaps during a hotel's pre-opening activities. Secondly, if used as a pre-opening activity, it is unlikely that a manager would be willing to gamble to find out which of the two approaches is more successful. It is more or less a laboratory method. Finally, mention should be made of quasi-experimental designs that often are used where "better designs are not feasible" (Campbell and Stanley 1963, 34). Since full experimental control is lacking, the question of validity in the interpretation of results becomes a crucial factor. In an industry that has little research sophistication, these types of design would overtax the ability of most chain operations, let alone single operations.

HOW IS TRAINING EVALUATED IN INDUSTRY?

In the following section, the results of two studies are described that examined how executives in ten European hotels and in ten U.S. hotels evaluated training. Because of the limited size of the sample, no attempt has been made to draw conclusions about the entire hotel industries of Europe and the U.S.

The ten hotels in Europe were located in Austria, Switzerland, West Germany, France, and Spain. Forty executives participated. The personal interviews were conducted by hotel students of Washington State University. In the U.S., ten executives were interviewed by telephone.

Of the 40 European executives in the hotels, six indicated they did not conduct any training. Of the remaining 34, 29 said they measure training progress, while five said they did not. In the U.S., all ten executives said that training was being conducted. Nine indicated that they measured training progress and one said that no measuring was done.

The central, most important, question here was, "How do you measure it?" (see Table 1). During the discussion of this question, additional information emerged that shed light on the selection and communication of standards to the employees (see Table 2).

TABLE 1
Methods of measuring training progress

	European	U.S.
1. Inspection, observation; personal checking; guest comment cards	17	3
2. Performance evaluations: discussion evaluation; written evaluation	7	2
3. Results on job; how fast, how clean; productivity and service level; solution of problems	2	2
4. Measuring success of employees; personal enthusiasm; staff satisfied; attendance of training sessions; management test written and oral, no numbers; government test	5	2
(Multiple answers given) Total	31	9

TABLE 2
Selecting and communicating standards

	European	U.S.
1. Quantitative standards are selected and communicated to employees	1	1
2. Verbal expectations	1	
3. A general feel	1	
4. Government plan	2	
5. Supervisor's own criteria, no numbers	1	
6. Based on job description, no numbers	1	

As shown above, only two of the executives interviewed used quantitative standards. However, it is not clear on what they based their quantitative standards.

When one examines Tables 1 and 2, a picture emerges that is only too well known: subjective standards, seldom communicated to the trainees, are often the basis for evaluation of training progress. Two points should be made with regard to European hotel operations and employees. There was a time when the job knowledge, the detailed expectations of work performance of the non-supervisory employees, simply did not need to be discussed—employees knew exactly what was expected of them.

The second point that merits discussing deals with the ratings "Government Test" and "Government Plan," which are related to the apprenticeship system. In West Germany (and other European countries), the government sets training standards, e.g., for apprentice cooks. In Appendix A, one page of the three-page "curriculum" is reproduced.[16] As one can see, the particular dishes a cook must be able to produce are specified within meal categories, although this is a long way from what experts such as Mager (1962) or Smith and Kendall (1963) proposed. However, some elements of quantitative measures are visible. For example, 20 sauces are spelled out, 14 vegetables, etc. (The "Z" indicates the dishes that are required for a mid-term examination.) The executive chef certifies the progress of the trainee after the first, second, and third years of apprenticeship.

At least one quantitative standard is available in this example to help the evaluation of the training process. Of the 20 sauces required for the final examination, if the trainee knows the preparation of 12, it means he/she still has eight to go. The progress test is in line with this author's proposal: to use quantitative work performance standards for feedback on training performance. Laird (1978, 84) writes:

> Several principles are important to successful feedback systems: The data in the feedback system should be quantitative. Many experts feel that if it can't be expressed in numbers, it shouldn't be done.

Although many trainers agree on some evaluation system, Dessler (n.d., 411) observed that most managers do not spend much time evaluating the effects of their program, even though they have to authorize the use of funds. Funds are diverted to training from other usages with the expectation of higher productivity, higher guest satisfaction, lower employee turnover, etc. It seems as if a myth shrouds training activities: As long as training is carried out, it must be effective. This can be a self-defeating attitude for management. What is needed instead is a deliberate effort to build an evaluative component into the training process.

Evaluation should start in the design phase—not after the program has ended (Laird 1978, 256). Forrest (1983, 33) described it similarly: "Evaluation should occur before the training begins so that behavior reference points can be established." Since trainers are generally not required to come up with standards, and since general managers often do not possess enough technical knowledge to establish standards themselves, training often does not produce results noticeable to those managers. Because training does not always produce immediately visible results, e.g., in job performance, the trainer should suggest training performance measures to the general managers, who can then accept, modify, or reject those measures. The training manager, or person in charge of a given training phase, should be interested in measurable outcomes of training, if for no other reason than that those results may support the request for funding for the next training project.

In the following, the questions of why and how work performance standards are used for training evaluation will be answered, and a device is introduced to help visualize the training process in an organization.

The Systems Approach

Many planned activities take place within a structural and functional context, including the change of behavior, ". . . to be effective, efficient, lasting and not disruptive to the environment within which the behavior occurs" (Morasky 1982, 8). This structural and functional context is provided by systems. Systems can be divided into behavioral and non-behavioral systems. Non-behavioral systems are those organizations, programs, groups, etc., that are not dependent upon the behavior of people within the system, whereas behavior systems ". . . depend on the behavior of people or . . . have a behavior component that is critical to system functioning," wrote Morasky, who further suggested that educational and training programs are primarily behavioral systems (Morasky 1982, 9).

The systems approach also helps to present a lucid picture of sometimes complicated processes. Katz and Kahn (1980, 162) feel that "People who attempt the difficult task of . . . organizational change should adopt a systems perspective." For that reason, the systems approach is used in the present study.

Beer (1964, 9) defines a system as "anything that consists of parts connected together." Any system consists of three parts: inputs, process, and output(s). The output is of special importance for this discussion.

How are systems established? A specific output is established first, and then consideration is given to what is necessary to achieve the output(s). The requisite ingredients are entered into the system as inputs. The process part converts the inputs into outputs. Only the system that is specifically designed for a stated output will come closest to reaching that output (Jenkins 1976).

What are some examples of outputs? A restaurant would probably want satisfied guests and profit as its output. Two other examples: The output of a hotel school should be students who do well in the industry; and the output for training should be that it be successful. One question should be asked, though, concerning the above outputs. Do they have measures or standards specific enough to be used for comparisons with the actual situation? The answer is "no." At a minimum, standards should be specific and measurable, practical and reliable, as well as relevant and observable.

Thorndike (1949), among others, has categorized some measures in the past. His four categories were used here as a base. They are:

1. *Objective-subjective.* Objective measures can be observed, and contain common criteria, such as time (i.e., one minute) or distance (i.e., three yards). Subjective measures depend on opinions and/or judgments, which can be biased. The ideal evaluation situation is to have only objective measures. However, this might not be practical in certain situations. Later, it will be shown how a certain measure of objectivity (or numbers) can be introduced into subjective ratings.

2. *Direct-indirect.* The trainee's behavior or its result can be measured directly, as opposed to a behavior that can only be measured by its influence on the actions of others. An example of direct behavior measure would be "The waitress will serve no fewer than 40 breakfasts during the breakfast shift." Now compare an indirect standard for a hostess in the same operation: "The hostess will manage the breakfast service in the coffee-shop in such a manner that satisfied guests will result (e.g., absence of complaints)." Obviously, the hostess cannot serve the breakfasts—she depends on the actions of the waitresses, whom she might or might not be able to influence. There is probably no single position

in a hotel that is not dependent on another position. The art seems to be to come as close to direct measures as possible without being overwhelmed by a bureaucratic maze.

3. *Immediate-ultimate.* Immediate measures are used to measure the short-range impact on an organization; and ultimate contributions measure the long-range impact. Often, organizations' training efforts will result in long-range benefits. But general managers may not accept long-range training goals when they are often pressured into immediate goals by the corporation. Maintenance is another example. Many corporations appear to have a "fix it when someone complains" attitude, and general managers have to play along. It seems that immediate standards prevail in the U.S. hospitality industry, which is contrary to the results for the ten European hotels, where a philosophy was often found that simply stated that if one takes care of the guests, profits will follow.

4. *Specific-summary.* If a specific job is measured, specific measures are called for. It is not difficult to determine measures for specific jobs, e.g., a management trainee should devise an improved registration system for checking in groups. If it previously took 2 minutes to register one person, the new standard might be 1 minute 30 seconds. A summary standard merely gives long-range organizational goals. For example, "The management trainee should come up with an improved registration system because guests are impatient and unhappy," makes clear what evaluation problems the second measure would present.

It might be appropriate to recall what brought this discussion on. It started with examples of outputs: among them, one dealing with training, which said that training "should be successful." In this example, the output is neither explicitly defined and observable nor easily obtainable (Donaldson and Scannell 1978) in its present form. Besides, it is not clear if the standards expressed in the output are realistic and within the trainee's ability (Plunkett 1979, 281). What, then, should the output of training

in industry be? Burack and Smith (1977) and, similarly, Goldstein and Sorcher (1974) advocated that effective performance on the job is the ultimate criterion of training. Expressed differently, it is the improvement of results on the job that training in industry is all about. Improvements should bring greater guest satisfaction and/or elimination of factors that would reduce profit (Donaldson and Scannell 1978).

The first step in the right direction has been taken, to state the output in general operational terms. The second step is to develop more specific standards. Remember, standards should be practical, reliable, relevant, observable, explicitly defined, and measurable, among other criteria. There is a very practical question involved: Can this be done in a hospitality operation with a reasonable amount of effort and accuracy? (After all, most hospitality operations are not professional training institutes.) It can if certain necessary operational tools are present. What are these tools? First, position descriptions, developed from job analysis, must be available for the different job categories; and, secondly, work performance standards must be developed from position descriptions. Work performance standards are the anchors against which performance will be measured (Smith and Kendall 1963). Expressed differently, Mager (1962, 53) calls for the identification of the desired terminal behavior, which again will be found in performance standards.

Many hospitality operations today have position descriptions for different job categories. There is no particular format in which they should be written. However, it is most helpful if they are already behavior- and result-oriented (Lawless 1972, 471). If they are behavior- and result-oriented, it will be easier to develop work performance standards from them. "Work the process from the position and the desired performance backward. If training is developed with a view toward *the learner in his or her position performing some task,* much ineffectiveness can be minimized" (Cicero 1976, 12-2).

However, besides position descriptions, work performance standards must take into account company policies, house division, and departmental rules, as well as any conditions imposed by union contracts.

Work Performance Standards

Work performance standards can be defined as quantitative and qualitative measures to appraise whether pre-selected job goals have been reached. These measures should be developed by department heads with specific supervisors (e.g., Food and Beverage managers with the coffee-shop manager), and with the aid of one or more outstanding employees, for example, a waitress, for the performance standards dealing with the waitress category. These employees will best be able to suggest criteria that are relevant, realistic, and fair. Another way is to determine the outstanding employee's average performance (e.g., serving 65 breakfasts during a shift) and then to determine from the top performance a variance, e.g., 0.75 or 0.5. That then would become one of the suggested standards.

Even when involving superior employees, perception of the relative merits of job criteria can vary to certain degrees. Employees and supervisors in the PBX department of a U.S. hotel were asked to rank certain criteria from 1 to 12, 1 being the most important (see Table 3).

Although there is agreement about the first two criteria between the two groups, from then on the ranking is different. Some agreement on work performance standards has to be reached in order for the evaluation to work.

In Appendix B are house rules—standards of dress and appearance (Illustration 1) as well as the position description for a waitress in the coffee shop (Illustration 2).[17] The appropriate sections of the work performance standards are indicated in Roman numerals at the left-hand side of the position description. Illustration 3, work performance standards, demonstrates how the information of Illustrations 1 and 2 has been utilized to come up with realistic job-related standards.

As can be observed, the work performance standards come from the position description. Different sections and subsections carry different weights. A "Calculations" sheet is attached for computation

TABLE 3

Supervisors' and employees' ratings of job criteria

Supervisor	Employee	Job criteria
1	1	Failure to report to work or notify supervisor in time
2	2	Lateness
3	7	Insubordination
4	5	Reliability
5	8	Work performance
6	9	Willful neglect of equipment, material, supplies
7	10	Carelessness with equipment, material, etc.
8	4	Improper conduct, e.g., disrespect for guests, supervisor
9	3	Selling
10	6	Appearance
11	12	Violating safety standards
12	11	Violating health standards

of points, which can total 1000. A minimum expected score is also indicated; in this case, 800 points. One determines standards but also sets a tolerance. That may sound like a negation of the standards, but it actually means dealing with reality.

In Appendix C is a second example, standards for the PBX operator. The house rules are the same as for the waitress and are not repeated here. The position description (Illustration 4) again has the appropriate work performance standards sections indicated in Roman numerals. The resulting work performance standards are shown in Illustration 5.

As can be expected, particular sections of work performance standards can be used in more than one job classification. Many will vary according to the job classification, as will the weight given to each section. For example, while appearance/grooming was assigned a 10 percent weight for a waitress, who works in front of the guests (on the stage, so to speak), only 5 percent was assigned to the PBX operator performance because of the operator's limited physical contact with guests.

A question now arises. Should the trainer be the one to establish work performance standards? It is suggested that the supervisor of the employees is ultimately responsible for the development of the standards. (This does not mean that employees' input should be disregarded. We demonstrated this point before with the case of service personnel.) Therefore, a trainer should only use the standards, not establish them. There can only be one training result, not one as assumed by the trainer and one as assumed by the supervisor: The trainer trains for the supervisor. The supervisor sets performance goals, because in turn, the supervisor is responsible for his/her actions to the next supervisor up the line.

Earlier it was said that standards should have certain characteristics; among others, they should be practical, reliable, relevant, observable, and explicitly defined. Looking at Section IV (Appendix B, Illustration 3) of the waitress standard "Ordering/ selling," the first standard specifies, "Takes order within 3 minutes [after the guest is ready]." This standard is explicit, reliable, relevant, and observable, and would conform to Mager's (1962) criterion, "describing the important conditions under which the behavior will be expected to occur." Other standards for the same job category are also very explicit: "Acknowledges guests within 30 seconds," "Sells dessert to at least 50 percent of the guests," "Serves soup or salad within 2 minutes," etc. The PBX operator's standards are, as well, explicitly defined: "Answers phone within 3 rings," "Handles an average of 200 calls per hour," "Gives names," "Uses prescribed language," "Thanks guests when leaving," etc. Although some of those standards do not appear as quantifiable as those containing numbers, "Gives names"[18] is a short form of "Always gives names" and "always" calls for a 100 percent performance. The same goes for "Uses prescribed language." "Always uses prescribed language," a 100 percent performance, is the ideal situation. Tolerances were discussed earlier.

The handling of the house rules—standards of

dress and appearance—still needs to be discussed. It was earlier pointed out how important the use of objective measures was. However, whether "Makeup" is too much or just right can easily be a matter of opinion, a subjective judgment; and the same goes for "Hands" and "Cleanliness of uniform." One way of overcoming subjectivity is, as presented in Section 1 of the work performance standards (Illustrations 3 and 5), to group items together and then introduce a numerical value to the whole section. A degree of objectivity is thereby introduced to subjective measures. This seems to be in line with what Jacobs et al. (1980) suggest in dealing with behaviorally anchored rating scales, or BARS. They say that ". . . any system of performance appraisal should be evaluated as to (1) utilization criteria, (2) qualitative criteria, and (3) quantitative criteria." They point out that the most important requirement of qualitative criteria is relevant to job performance.

It might be interesting to look at the four categories of measures or standards suggested earlier, and see how some of the above-mentioned standards can be classified. First, many seem to be objective (versus subjective), not based on opinion. Second, most are direct (versus indirect)—the behavior of the individual can be measured directly (in 30 seconds, within 2 minutes, 200 calls). Third, measures are immediate (versus ultimate); there is a possible immediate contribution to the organization (however, even if they make an immediate positive contribution, the chance for an ultimate contribution is also present). The same holds true for a negative contribution (or absence of a positive contribution). Finally, they are more on the specific side (versus summary). They measure a specific phase (or many specific phases) of the job, rather than the total job.

Considerable attention has been given so far to the establishment of work performance standards, despite the fact that this discussion primarily deals with training and training evaluation, partly to bring out the importance of objective measures. Another reason was to urge management to evaluate training with performance-related objective measures. In the survey mentioned earlier, only one hotel in Europe and the U.S. used quantitative measures and communicated them to its employees.

As previously explained, the system approach is an aid for thinking in progressions or in steps. The output was described as "satisfied guests, to be achieved at a profit." In its present form, "satisfied guests" is specific enough (100 percent performance, which might include, for example, a certain number of positive comments; or a specific percentage of return guests), while "achieved at a profit" needs additional specific standards; for example, a certain percentage of sales. Inputs include the following: land, labor, capital, professional knowledge, and information on market and supply. It is assumed that position descriptions and work performance standards are a part of professional knowledge, and will be available for the employees of the organization. Waitresses and other personnel will be hired (input: labor). In the process part, among many other activities, the training for waitresses will take place because, without an end to the training task, the output of the organization, "satisfied guests . . . ," cannot be reached. Therefore, the standards are attached to the training task.

To give an example, it has been established through her job application and employment interview that the new waitress already has certain skills relevant to the job. This point can be called point A, "Present behavior." With the help of the position description and the previously discussed work performance standards, the "new behavior," or point B, can easily be established. The distance between point A and point B is the training task.

Work performance standards will also help to facilitate decisions concerning the categories of training involved, e.g., skills or concepts; the type of training, e.g., on-the-job or classroom training; and specific methods suitable to the particular type of training (Kreck 1982). Work performance standards will further provide the necessary ingredient to measure the interim progress of training, by comparing actual performance on the job with standards.

Theoretically, the training task has been completed when all work performance standards for employees, as well as managerial standards involving time, required number of trainees, and budget[19]

have been reached. However, the true determinant of training effectiveness is the planned output of the organization; more specifically, that portion of the total organizational effort that depends on the performance of the employees, as defined by the work performance standards. The following point needs to be reemphasized: Actual performance can only be measured if standards are available, and what better job-related standards to use in job-related training than work performance standards?

CONCLUSION

Three questions were dealt with in this report. First, why should training be evaluated? The seemingly obvious answer was to find out whether or not the training effort was successful. The second question asked was "Why use work performance standards as the basis of training evaluation?" It was suggested that since job-related training is designed to move the behavior of trainees toward the requirements of a particular job, work performance standards are most effective because they spell out the requirements of the particular job in considerable detail. The third question addressed how work performance standards are used for training evaluation. The paper also described the results of two surveys that made an effort to ascertain how executives in ten European hotels and in ten U.S. hotels evaluated and measured training.

APPENDIX B
Illustration 1

House rules—standards of dress and appearance (corresponding work performance standard section: I in Illustration 3)

Hair
A. Male employees' hair is to be neatly trimmed, and the length of the hair is not to extend below the collar of the usual uniform when on duty. The hair may not cover the ears.
B. Female employees' styles should not be extreme, but appropriate for work. Scarves are not allowed for full head coverage. Short hair should be styled and combed neatly. Long hair (longer than shoulder length) should be tied together or pinned up securely.

Sideburns are to be neatly trimmed, not bushy, and the maximum length may not extend below the bottom of the ear. Sideburns must be trimmed straight—no 'mutton chops.'

Moustaches may be worn only with the individual approval of the department head. If approved, they should be neatly trimmed and not extend beyond the corners of the mouth.

Uniforms should be kept clean, and in good repair.

Shirts—If no uniform shirt is provided a white shirt is to be worn in conjunction with any type of the hotel uniform.

Skirts must be of sufficient length to cover the knees.

Makeup should be used so that it is complimentary but not obvious or overdone.

Shoes—Colors are to be recommended by department head to complement the uniform. Tennis shoes, sandals, and slippers are not permitted. The employees must have their shoes shined and in good repair at all times.

Stockings must be worn at all times and must be in good repair.

Jewelry—The only jewelry items permitted are small earrings, if ears are pierced, wedding bands, and a wrist watch.

Body odor as well as strong perfumes must be avoided under all circumstances.

Hands must be kept clean, nails properly maintained. The use of colored nail polish is not allowed.

For those employees not wearing a uniform, a dress standard will be set by the department head.

Illustration 2

Position description

Ms Greenthumb's waitress

Food & Beverage Department, Ms Greenthumb's Coffee Shop
(with corresponding work performance standard sections*)
Salary class: 50

Major duties: Takes customer orders, serves orders, services guests
Collateral duties: Busses tables, helps set tables
Work performed:

III; IV;*	a.	Takes guests' orders and services water and coffee
V; VII;*	b.	Serves orders
II; *	c.	Sets up and cleans station
II; *	d.	Helps bus and sets up tables when busy V,4;
*	e.	Handles credit cards and payment of tickets when requested to do so by the guest
	f.	Does other duties as assigned by coffee shop manager

Supervision:
a. Directly responsible to coffee shop manager
b. Indirectly responsible to executive chef

Responsibilities:
Employee relations: Works closely with other waitresses, cooks
Materials and products: Responsible for serving attractive and appetizing plates to guests and for garnishing properly
Money: Responsible for all monies collected
Business contacts: Frequent contact with guests

Minimum requirements:
Education: 8th grade or better
Experience: At least six months prior experience as a waitress
Skills: Waitress skills, communication skills
Knowledge: Good working knowledge of menu items and the overall functions of the coffee shop

Reviewed by Food & Beverage Director: _____ Date: ____
Approved by General Manager: _____Date: ____

Illustration 3

Work performance standards for Ms Greenthumb's waitress

I. Appearance, grooming (0–10 points)   Weight 10%
    a. Dress
    b. Hair
    c. Jewelry
    d. Body odor
    e. Makeup
    f. Hands
    g. Name tag
    h. Cleanliness and repair of uniform & shoes
                          Points: _____

II. Station setup (0–10 points)   Weight 10%
    a. Sets tickets
    b. Chairs, benches are clean
    c. Silver, china, glasses are clean
    d. Silver, china, glasses properly placed
    e. Table tent present and clean
    f. Salt, pepper, sugar filled and clean
    g. Is ready for business when dining room opens
    h. Helps bus and sets up tables
                          Points: _____

III. Greeting (0–10 points)   Weight 10%
    a. Acknowledges guests within 30 seconds
    b. Smiles while conversing
    c. Gives name
    d. Uses prescribed language
    e. Thanks guests when leaving
    f. Invites guests back
                          Points _____

IV. Ordering, selling (0–10 points)   Weight: 10%
    a.   Takes order within 3 minutes
    b.   Suggests alcoholic beverages (lunch, dinner)
    c.   Sells dessert to at least 50% of the guests (lunch, dinner)
    d.   Takes correct and complete orders (variance: once a week)
    e.   Takes ladies' orders on mixed tables first
    f.   Suggests a choice of dessert, e.g. '. . . pie or ice cream'
    g.   Uses proper abbreviations
    h.   Writes clearly
                            Points _____

V. Servicing   Weight: 30%
1. 20% Timing (0–10 points, _____ points × 0.2 = _____ points)
    (1) Serves soup or salad within 2 minutes
    (2) Picks up order from kitchen within 1½ minutes after being readied
    (3) Serves all orders at once
    (4) Serves wine with entree (not after)
    (5) Serves dessert 3 minutes after order is taken
    (6) Serves after-dinner alcoholic beverages 4 minutes after order is taken

2. 20% Quality control (0–10 points, _____ points × 0.2 = _____ points)
    (1) Checks if all is satisfactory 2 minutes after guest starts to eat
    (2) Serves only appealing food
    (3) Serves hot food hot (min 150°F)
    (4) Serves cold food cold (max 50°F)
    (5) Does not pick up wrong orders (variance: less than twice a month)

3. 40% Service etiquette (0–10 points, _____ points × 0.4 = _____ points)
    (1) Serves, removes from proper side if possible
    (2) Does not ask guest 'who gets what?'
    (3) Does not place plates into guest's hand
    (4) Serves all entrees at one time
    (5) Changes ashtray when serving food
    (6) Otherwise changes ashtray when not more than 2 butts in it
    (7) Serves main item on plate facing guest

4. 20% Guest checks (0–10 points, _____ points × 0.2 = _____ points)
    (1) Presents check right after clearing plate (breakfast)
    (2) Presents check after checking for desserts and/or after-dinner beverages (lunch, dinner)
    (3) Uses right prices
    (4) Makes right additions
    (5) Accounts for all checks
                            Points: _____

VI. Attitude, conduct (0–10 points)   Weight: 15%
    a.   Always helpful to guests and employees
    b.   Always smiles during guest contact
    c.   Uses subservient vocabulary
    d.   Is friendly
    e.   Helps in other stations if possible
    f.   Gets along with co-workers
    g.   Carries out orders of supervisor
    h.   Does not violate any company or department policies
    i.   Willingly supports procedures established by supervisor
    j.   Helps train others when asked
    k.   Is not late for work (less than 2 times per month)
    l.   Is not careless with equipment, material, and supplies
    m. Is dependable (showing up for work)
    n.   Does not eat, drink, smoke, or chew gum in front of guests
    o.   Does not call across room
    p.   Talks in a low voice
    q.   Does not carry on private conversations with employees
    r.   Does not discuss tips within earshot of guests
    s.   Does not give personal information to a guest
    t.   Does not date guests
                            Points: _____

VII. Work load (0–10 points)   Weight: 10%
    a.   Handles 25 covers/station
    b.   Serves 70 breakfasts/shift
    c.   Serves 60 lunches/shift
    d.   Serves 35 dinners/shift
    e.   Does assigned side work
                            Points: _____

VIII. Housekeeping, safety, accidents (0–10 points)   Weight: 10%
    a.   No litter on floor anywhere
    b.   No liquid on floor
    c.   Breakage less than $5.00/month
    d.   No spilling of food or beverage on guests more than once/year
    e.   Carrying safe amount of glasses, china
                            Points: _____

Calculations
1. Appearance, grooming
    Total points × 10 =   _____
2. Station setup
    Total points × 10 =   _____
3. Greeting
    Total points × 10 =   _____
4. Ordering, selling
    Total points × 10 =   _____

5. Servicing
   Total points × 30 =   _____
6. Attitude, conduct
   Total points × 15 =   _____
7. Work load
   Total points × 10 =   _____
8. Housekeeping, safety, accidents
   Total points × 5 =   _____
Grand total

_____

Expected minimum number of points   800

_____

APPENDIX C
Illustration 4

Position description
Telephone Department: PBX operator   Salary class:

Major duties: Keeps guest information up-to-date; completes guest calls
Collateral duties: Takes room reservations, assists at front desk
Work performed:
III, 1;   a. Handles equipment with care
II, VI;   b. Completes guests' calls
III, 2;   c. Enters and removes guests' information
III, 2;   d. Handles wake-up calls
III, 3;   e. Knows all emergency procedures
III, 4;   f. Provides information
IV   ;   g. Assists in selling the facilities of the hotel
IV   ;   h. Assists the front desk

Supervision:
a. Directly responsible to front office manager
b. Indirectly responsible to reservations manager

Responsibilities:
Employee relations: Works closely with other PBX operators, front office employees and reservation personnel
Equipment: Handles equipment with care
Business contacts: Frequent contacts on the phone or in person

Minimum requirements:
Education: 12th grade
Experience: At least 6 months prior experience
Skills: Speaks proper English, well enunciated
Knowledge: Good working knowledge of a switchboard, some knowledge of front desk operation

Reviewed by Front Office Manager: _____ Date:____
Approved by General Manager: _____ Date: ____

Illustration 5

Work performance standards for PBX operator

I.   Appearance, grooming (0–10 points)   Weight: 5%
     a. Dress
     b. Hair
     c. Jewelry
     d. Body odor
     e. Makeup
     f. Hands
     g. Name tag
     h. Cleanliness and repair of uniform and shoes
                              *Points:*_____

II. Verbal communication (0–10 points)   Weight: 15%
     a. Uses prescribed format
     b. Uses name of guest when known
     c. Talks in a cheerful voice
     d. Answers phone within 3 rings
                              *Points:*_____

III. Servicing guests   Weight: 30%
     1. 20% handling equipment (0–10 points; _____
         points × 0.2 = _____ points)
         Knows how to use all equipment without hesitation
         Handles equipment with great care
         Reports any malfunctioning equipment to supervisor immediately
         Does not let unauthorized persons operate equipment
                              *Points:*_____

     2. 25% entering information (0–10 points; _____
         points × 0.25 = _____ points)
         Enters all registrations within two minutes after received from front desk
         Makes no mistakes entering guest's name
         Files registration copies in prescribed way
         Never forgets to set any wake-up call (night shift)
         Checks wake-up calls (a.m. shift)
         Sends bell person after second wake-up call to room

     3. 30% emergencies (0–10 points; _____
         points × 0.3 = _____ points)
         Knows what to do in case of fire without hesitation
         Knows whom to call for other emergencies
         In all cases remains calm and helpful
         Does not admit liability
                              *Points:*_____

4. 25% miscellaneous (0–10 points; _____
points × 0.25 = _____ points)
Makes no mistake looking up guests' names on CRT
Follows company policy exactly in regard to divulging information about guests
Does not discuss one guest with another
Handles mail and messages in prescribed way
Adds the prescribed service charge to the amount of all guest long-distance charges
Completes all forms as prescribed
Knows daily events and their locations in the hotel
Knows major events in the community
Updates 'cash only' guest list at 3 p.m.

IV. Selling/reservations (0–10 points)   Weight 25%
Never assures potential guests of a particular room, floor or view when taking reservations
Checks room availability sheet first
Knows basic room terminology
Knows features, and location of all rooms
Knows proximity of elevators, ice machine and fire exit to rooms
*Points:*_____

V. Attitude, conduct (0–10 points)   Weight: 10%
Always helpful to guests and employees
Uses subservient vocabulary
Is friendly
Helps other PBX operators
Gets along with co-workers
Carries out orders of supervisor
Does not violate any company/department policy
Willingly supports procedures established by supervisor
Helps training others when asked
Is not late for work (variance twice per month)
Is not careless with equipment, material, supplies
Is dependable (e.g. shows up for work, carries assignments to the end)
Does not eat, drink, smoke, or chew gum in view of guests
Talks in a low voice
Does not carry on private conversation with employees while on the phone
*Points:*_____

VI. Work load (0–10 points)   Weight: 10%
Handles an average of 200 calls per hour
*Points:*_____

VII. Housekeeping, safety (0–10 points)   Weight: 5%
No litter or liquid on floor
Work area organized

No cups, glasses, etc., in work area
No more than two cigarette butts in ashtray
*Points:*_____

Calculations:
1. Appearance, grooming
   Total points × 5 =   _____
2. Verbal communication
   Total points × 15 =   _____
3. Servicing guests
   Total points × 30 =   _____
4. Selling/reservations
   Total points × 25 =   _____
5. Attitude/conduct
   Total points × 10 =   _____
6. Work load
   Total points × 10 =   _____
7. Housekeeping, safety
   Total points × 5 =   _____
Grand total
                            _____

Expected minimum number of points
required   800
                            _____

CASE STUDY—"The Disappearing Managers"

As the new vice-president for human resources of Colossal Hotels, Inc., you are confronted with the statistic that the rate at which department heads and assistant managers are discharged and disciplined exceeds that which is to be expected by approximately 150 percent. Additionally, records from the university recruiting function indicate that you have approximately a 60 percent falloff rate among recruited management trainees before their five-year anniversaries. As a consequence, among its mid- and junior-level managers the company is experiencing a turnover rate considered unacceptable by top management.

Telephone interviews you have conducted with some of the discharged or recently resigned managers and trainees have indicated deep-seated feelings of frustration on their part because of inconsistently applied and subjective performance reviews. These managers were never given clear indications of what their goals and objectives should be. Former members of the various management trainee classes indicate that what is promised in recruiting interviews is not always delivered during subsequent training and evaluation periods.

Your task, as directed by the Executive Vice-President for Operations, is to formulate a plan to research and gather accurate data about why this turnover is occurring and, based on those results, to propose a structured human resources-oriented plan that will reverse this trend.

Endnotes

[1] The mailing list for the questionnaire included all known hotel personnel managers in Canada. A telephone survey conducted by the author revealed that there are virtually no full-time personnel managers in properties with under 200 rooms.

[2] This figure increases to 79 percent when properties with under 300 rooms are excluded.

[3] A similar approach was described in James R. Pickworth and Edgerton L. Fletcher, "The Role of Today's Food-Service Manager," *Cornell Hotel and Restaurant Administration Quarterly* 21(3):68–72.

[4] 1971 Census of Canada (unpublished data). The U.S. national average, according to the Bureau of National Affairs, is 1:200.

[5] Most personnel managers with less than one year's experience in their present positions were employed by smaller hotels (hotels with fewer than 450 rooms).

[6] B.E. DeSpelder, *Ratios of Staff to Line Personnel*. (Columbus, OH: Bureau of Business Research, Ohio State University, 1962). This study showed that a formal personnel department was generally formed when a business grew to include 200 employees.

[7] Because several respondents to the survey worked for the same chain, the author conducted a company analysis to expand the findings of the initial research.

[8] The study, which took place in 1981–82, was conducted with the support of Cornell's School of Hotel Administration.

[9] Large hotels (minimum of 300 rooms) were chosen for the study because it was felt that these properties would be able to provide personnel data and records relevant to the research. The sample size was limited to 20 hotels due to time limitations and cost constraints. The countries in which these hotels were located included the

United States, Canada, France, West Germany, Austria, Switzerland, the Netherlands, and England.

[10] A planned turnover strategy would involve reducing controllable and dysfunctional turnover to a minimum, and would focus on retaining essential employees.

[11] Annual turnover in the organizations studied ranged from 30 percent to 112 percent; reasons for this wide variation as well as recommended methods for managing turnover will be discussed by the authors in a future *Quarterly* article.

[12] Courts assess the legality of personnel actions under various state and federal laws. The germane federal laws are the Equal Pay Act of 1963, the Civil Rights Act of 1964, the Age Discrimination in Employment Act of 1967, and the Equal Employment Opportunity Act of 1972.

A 1973 court decision, *Brito vs. Zia Company*, 478 F.2d 1200 (10th Cir. 1973), provides an example of an employment test. The plaintiffs in the suit alleged that Hispanic employees had been discriminated against in a wave of layoffs from the Zia Company in New Mexico. In fact, the Hispanic employees had been rated lower than other ethnic groups in a performance appraisal conducted by their immediate supervisor, and this group was laid off in proportionally greater numbers than other ethnic groups. Looking at the company's performance appraisal, the court ruled that the company had not presented adequate substantiation of the validity of the performance assessment, which was considered an employment test. The Zia Company lost the case.

[13] c.f. Cascio and Bernardin 1981; Feild and Holley 1982.

[14] Since their creation, specific BARS forms have been developed for such occupations as dietitian, manager of a retail store, and managerial employees.

[15] The 1978 Civil Services Reform Act (Chapter 43 of Title V, U.S. Code) is being used as a model by private industry, particularly with regard to employee participation in standard-setting and evaluator training.

[16] The original Appendix A was in German and therefore is omitted from this book [the editor].

[17] The author spent several weeks in a major U.S. lodging operation developing work performance standards and numerical evaluation devices from existing house rules and position descriptions.

[18] A different standard would have to be set up for a fine dining restaurant.

[19] Different standards have to be developed to measure the particular criteria.

References

Arnaldo, Mario J. 1981. Hotel general managers: A profile. *Cornell Hotel and Restaurant Administration Quarterly* 22:53–56.

Bass, Bernard M., and Edward C. Ryterband. 1979. *Organizational psychology*, 2d ed. Rockleigh, NJ: Allyn and Bacon.

Beer, S. 1964. *Cybernetics and management.* New York: John Wiley.

Bernardin, H. John, and Richard W. Beatty. 1984. *Performance appraisal: Assessing human behavior at work.* Boston: Kent Publishing.

Bernardin, H. John, Richard W. Beatty, and Walter Jensen, Jr. 1980. The new uniform guidelines on employee-selection procedures in the context of university personnel decisions. *Personnel Psychology* 33 (2):301–6.

Bernardin, H. John, and Patricia C. Smith. 1981. A clarification of some issues regarding the development and use of behaviorally anchored rating scales (BARS). *Journal of Applied Psychology* 66(4):458–63.

Brandenburg, D.C. 1982. Training evaluation: What's the current status? *Training and Development Journal* 17.

Brayfield, Arthur H., and Walter Crockett. 1955. Employee attitudes and employee performance. *Psychological Bulletin* 52:396–424.

Brymer, Robert A. 1979. Interpersonal management relations: A hospitality curriculum oversight. *Hospitality Education and Restaurant Journal* 4:1–13.

Burack, E.H., and R.D. Smith. 1977. *Personnel management—A human resource systems approach.* St. Paul: West Publishing.

Campbell, D.T., and J.C. Stanley. 1963. *Experimental and quasi-experimental designs for research.* Chicago: Rand McNally.

Carroll, S.J., Jr. 1960. Measuring the work of a personnel department. *Personnel* July–August:55.

Cascio, Wayne F. 1982. *Costing human resources: The financial impact of behavior in organizations.* Belmont, CA: Kent Publishing.

Cascio, Wayne F., and H. John Bernardin. 1981. Implications of performance-appraisal litigation for personnel decisions. *Personnel Psychology* 34 (2):211–25.

Census of Canada. 1971. Unpublished data.

Cicero, J.P. 1976. Instructional systems. *Training Development Handbook* 2:12–22. New York: McGraw-Hill.

Dessler, G. n.d. *Human behavior—Improving performance at work.* Reston, VA: Reston Publishing.

Donaldson, L., and E.E. Scannell. 1978. *Human resource development.* Reading, MA: Addison-Wesley.

Feild, Hubert S., and William H. Holley. 1982. The relationship of performance-appraisal system characteristics to verdicts in selected employment-discrimination cases. *Academy of Management Journal* 25 (2):392–406.

Fletcher, F.I., and J.R. Pickworth. 1978. *Managerial Salaries, benefits and responsibilities in the hotel sector of the hospitality industry.* Guelph, Ontario: University of Guelph.

Forrest, L.C., Jr. 1983. *Training for the hospitality industry.* East Lansing, MI: Educational Institute of the American Hotel and Motel Association.

Geller, A. Neal. 1985a. Tracking the critical success factors for hotel companies. *Cornell Hotel and Restaurant Administration Quarterly* 25(4):76–81.

Geller, A. Neal. 1985b. The current state of hotel information systems. *Cornell Hotel and Restaurant Administration Quarterly* 26:14–17.

Glueck, W.F. 1978. *Personnel: A diagnostic approach*, 2d ed. Dallas: Business Publications.

Goldstein, A.P., and M. Sorcher. 1974. *Changing supervisor behavior.* New York: Pergamon Press.

Gotsche, Anton W. 1970. A study of executive development programs in the American hotel/motel industry. Ph.D. dissertation, New York University.

Hales, Colin, and Michael Nightingale. 1986. What are unit managers supposed to do? A contingent methodology for investigating managerial role requirements. *International Journal of Hospitality Management* 5:3–11.

Hawk, Donald L. 1976. Absenteeism and turnover. *Personnel Journal* June:293.

Heneman, Herbert G., III, et al. 1980. *Personnel/human resource management.* Homewood, IL: Richard D. Irwin.

Hickey, James V. 1974. *Employee productivity: How to improve and measure your company's performance.* Stratford, CT: Institute for the Advancement of Scientific Management and Control.

Jacobs, R., D. Kafry, and S. Zedeck. 1980. Expectations of behaviorally anchored rating scales. *Resource Psychology* 33:595–640.

Jenkins, G.M. 1976. The systems approach. In *Systems behavior,* eds. J. Beishon and G. Peters. London: Open University Press, Harper & Row, pp. 78–104.

Katz, Daniel. 1964. The motivational basis of organizational behavior. *Behavioral Science* 9:131–46.

Katz, D., and R.L. Kahn. 1980. In *Organizational assessment,* eds. E.E. Lawler, D.A. Nadler, and C. Cammann. New York: John Wiley, p. 162.

Kleinman, L.S., and R.L. Durham. 1981. Performance appraisal, promotion, and the courts: A critical review. *Personnel Psychology* 34(1):103–21.

Kreck, L.A. 1982. Training with a system analysis approach. In *The practice of hospitality management,* eds. A. Pizam, R.C. Lewis, and P. Manning. Westport, CT: AVI, pp. 293–305.

Kumar, P. 1975. *Personnel management in Canada: A manpower profile.* Kingston, Ontario: Industrial Relations Center, Queens University.

Laird, D. 1978. *Approaches to training and development.* Reading, MA: Addison-Wesley.

Lawless, D.J. 1972. *Organizational behavior,* 2d ed. Englewood Cliffs, NJ: Prentice Hall.

Levinson, H. 1976. Appraisal of *what* performance? *Harvard Business Review* 160:30–46.

Lukowski, Robert F., Ray Budde, and Norman B. Cournoyer. 1974. Higher education for the hospitality industry. *Cornell Hotel and Restaurant Administration Quarterly* 15(55):14–21.

Mager, R.F. 1962. *Preparing instructional objectives.* Palo Alto, CA: Fearon.

March, James G., and Herbert A. Simon. 1958. *Organizations.* New York: John Wiley.

Mariampolski, Arnold, Marian C. Spears, and Allene G. Vaden. 1980. What the restaurant manager needs to know: The consensus. *Cornell Hotel and Restaurant Administration Quarterly* 21:77–81.

McConkie, M.L. 1979. A clarification of the goal-setting and appraisal processes in MBO. *Academy of Management Review* 4(1):29–40.

Morasky, R. 1982. *Behavioral systems.* New York: Praeger.

Naisbitt, John, and Patricia Aburdene. 1985. *Re-inventing the corporation.* New York: Warner Books.

Peters, Tom, and Nancy Austin. 1985. *A passion for excellence: The leadership difference.* New York: Warner Books.

Pizam, Abraham, and Robert Lewis. 1979. Predicting career success and satisfaction: A study of hospitality graduates. *Cornell Hotel and Restaurant Administration Quarterly* 20:12–16.

Plunkett, W.R. 1979. *Supervision—The direction of people at work,* 2d ed. Dubuque, IA: Wm. C. Brown.

Ross, Ian C., and Alvin Zander. 1957. Need satisfactions and employee turnover. *Personnel Psychology* 327–38.

Sapienza, D.L. 1978. What university hotel students ought to study: Opinions expressed by a selected group of Nevada executives. *Journal of Hospitality Education* 2:11–16.

Schuster, M.H., and C.S. Miller. 1982. Performance evaluations as evidence in ADEA cases. *Employee Relations Law Journal* 6:561–83.

Smith, Patricia C., and L.M. Kendall. 1963. Retranslation of expectations: An approach to the construction of unambiguous anchors for rating scales. *Journal of Applied Psychology* 47(2):149–55.

Strauss, George, and Leonard R. Sayles. 1980. *Personnel: The human problems of management,* 4th ed. Englewood Cliffs, NJ: Prentice Hall.

Thorndike, R.L. 1949. The estimation of test validity: Criteria of proficiency, in *Personnel selection.* New York: John Wiley, 119–59.

Umbreit, W. Terry. 1984. Development of behaviorally anchored rating scales for evaluating job performance of hotel managers. Doctoral dissertation, Washington State University.

Umbreit, W. Terry. 1986. Developing behaviorally anchored scales for evaluating job performance of hotel managers. *International Journal of Hospitality Management* 5:55–61.

Umbreit, W. Terry. 1987. What are the job responsibilities of multi-unit managers in the food service industry? *Restaurants USA.*

Umbreit, W. Terry, and Robert W. Eder. 1987. Linking hotel manager behaviors to outcome measures of effectiveness. *International Journal of Hospitality Management.*

Suggested Readings

Articles

Antil, Frederick H. "Career Planning in the Hospitality Industry." *Cornell Hotel and Restaurant Administration Quarterly* (May 1984):46–52.

Berger, Florence, Martin E. Evans, and Bonnie Farber. "Human Resources Management: Applying Managerial Profile Databases." *Cornell Hotel and Restaurant Administration Quarterly* (November 1986):44–50.

DeMicco, Fred J., and Jiri Giridharan. "Managing Employee Turnover in the Hospitality Industry." *F.I.U. Hospitality Review* (Fall 1987):26–32.

Ferguson, Dennis H., and Florence Berger. "Employees as Assets: A Fresh Approach to Human Resources Accounting." *Cornell Hotel and Restaurant Administration Quarterly* (February 1985):24–29.

Jones, Casey, and Thomas A. DeCotiis. "Video-Assisted Selection of Hospitality Employees." *Cornell Hotel and Restaurant Administration Quarterly* (August 1986):68–73.

Kent, William E. "Taking the Dread Out of Employee Evaluations." *Cornell Hotel and Restaurant Administration Quarterly* (May 1981):47–50.

Reid, Robert D., and Michael R. Evans. "The Career Plateau: What to Do When a Career Bogs Down." *Cornell Hotel and Restaurant Administration Quarterly* (August 1983):83–91.

Wasmuth, William J., and Stanley W. Davis. "Managing Employee Turnover: Why Employees Leave," *Cornell Hotel and Restaurant Administration Quarterly,* May 1983, pp. 11–18.

Wasmuth, William J., and Stanley W. Davis. "Strategies for Managing Employee Turnover," *Cornell Hotel and Restaurant Administration Quarterly* (August 1983): 65–75.

SECTION 10

Purchasing

INTRODUCTION

No discussion of staff activities in a hotel would be complete without some attention paid to the extremely important function of purchasing.

In the past, when the bulk of a hotel's purchasing revolved around food and beverage items, the executive chef, chief steward, and other department managers usually developed their own sources for the goods and services they needed to run their departments effectively and efficiently. In the modern context, with the vast and diversified needs of the various hotel operating and staff departments, this practice is no longer advisable. Most hotel companies have adopted a policy of establishing a professional purchasing function. If this is not a whole department, it is at least one highly experienced individual.

The purchasing director or manager will typically be a person who knows a great deal about departmental operations in every phase of the hotel. He or she will be able to discuss and analyze intelligently the needs of the various department managers. This individual will also be one who is an expert in the markets where hotels purchase goods and products essential to accomplishing their departments' and hotels' missions. The purchasing director will be familiar with variety, quality standards, style, and methods of packaging. Such arcane technical details as chemical composition, fabric and furnishing lifetimes, and other details too numerous to mention here will also be the responsibility of the purchasing manager.

Schnitzler's article on purchasing for a new hotel effectively establishes a model that can be utilized to understand the breadth and depth of importance of the modern purchasing manager's job. In the Suggested Readings, Tabacchi's article on fresh produce zeroes in on establishing standards and specifications for one narrow class of goods regularly purchased by hotel or other hospitality operations. Finally, listed among the Suggested Readings is Kotshevar's classic text on purchasing, which probably should be a part of any managerial library as one of the most well-recognized reference books of its type. It should also be required reading for purchasing directors.

It is unfortunate that more contemporary analysis and commentary do not exist on purchasing and other less-understood staff departments. It should be acknowledged, however, that each of these departments has a fundamental mission that is crucial to the overall success of the hotel enterprise. All well-trained and prepared managers will recognize the importance of all staff departments for the services they provide to each segment of the hotel organization.

Purchasing for a New Hotel

Hans J. Schnitzler

For the executive who makes the final choice about furnishings, fixtures, and equipment (FF&E) for a new hotel, every scrap of information about the products is extremely important. Careful selections at the beginning will reduce labor and replacement costs and allow the hotel to function more efficiently.

Because the task of purchasing FF&E is so specialized, it is generally assigned to a buyer (or, less frequently, to an interior or kitchen designer), who acts as a purchasing agent for the hotel corporation. The buyer then coordinates his efforts with the hotel's architect, interior designer, general contractor, developer, and food and beverage director.

This article focuses on the purchasing needs of a new hotel, and addresses the establishment of par-stock requirements, the preparation of budgets, controls, and the coordination both of warehouse deliveries to the job site and of direct deliveries by suppliers to the hotel. Although the example given is a hypothetical one, the principles illustrated here are applicable to most hotels.

THE MARKET AND THE BUYER

The market function can be divided into four basic categories: information, exchange, physical supply, and general business. A buyer who thoroughly understands these functions will be able to purchase goods effectively.

Information—what, when, how much, what quality, what price, and which trends to follow—is important to the buyer. This information can be obtained by consulting market reports in newspapers and professional journals as well as comprehensive buyers' guides sponsored by these journals. Pre-

vious experience with reliable buying sources is also helpful.

Exchange involves price setting, merchandising, buying, selling, and other factors required to move goods. Sellers must find buyers, offers must be evaluated and compared, and prices and services to be rendered must be negotiated. Buyers should develop their own buying guide by compiling a list of firms with which they have done business in the past. The list should be alphabetically cross-referenced and divided into three categories, as follows: (1) name of company, full address, and brief listing of goods sold; (2) contact person and brief listing of goods sold; and (3) listing of goods sold and name of company.

Physical supply involves transportation and storage. To choose sources wisely, the buyer must be familiar with shipping costs and delivery dates. Adequate storage is also an important factor. A minimum of 25 to 30 square feet per room should provide a new hotel with sufficient space to store goods and equipment. (New installations often suffer from lack of storage space, however, because high construction costs cause owners and developers to cut back on the amount of square footage allotted to storage.)

The *general-business* function revolves around finance. Proper financing can reduce costs. Buyers should keep in mind that theft, waste, carrying charges, and excess inventories that occupy space all cost money.

Most supplies can be obtained within days or weeks (the exceptions are custom-made items, such as chinaware, flatware, and table napery with logo imprints or engravings—which can take anywhere from 60 to 120 days to arrive). The task is to establish a par stock that is operational but that includes no excess inventory. (How to determine par-stock requirements is explained further on in this article.)

This article was originally published in the August 1982 issue of *The Cornell Hotel and Restaurant Administration Quarterly,* and is reprinted here with the permission of the Cornell University School of Hotel Administration. © 1982.

The type of market from which the buyer can choose depends upon the type of hotel company he represents. Chain operations prepared to buy in volume often realize savings by purchasing directly from manufacturers, while individually owned operations must acquire their goods through distributors at a higher cost. Because of the advantages of buying in volume, purchasing from chain operations should be centralized as much as possible. Basic goods that won't detract from the interior-design concept should be chosen wherever possible, using specifications adaptable to all units. For a hotel operation purchasing in volume, these items might include hotel bedding materials, some terry goods, hotel-room supplies and amenities, cleaning equipment and supplies, and general office equipment and supplies. For a food and beverage outlet buying in quantity, these items might include basic room-service equipment, basic restaurant-service equipment, kitchen utensils and kitchen-service equipment, banquet-service equipment and banquet furniture, basic bar-service equipment, uniforms for food production, printed forms (except guest checks and menus), paper goods and supplies, glassware, flatware, and table napery.

A competent buyer should know how to negotiate with vendors in a highly competitive market to obtain "the best for the least." He should be honest, patient, ethical, and open-minded, with a wealth of technical knowledge. In addition, to remain in the driver's seat in the dynamic field of purchasing, he should continually study new methods and products.

DEFINING PURCHASING NEEDS

Purchasing needs vary with hotels. Hotels with considerable room service—resort hotels, for example—need an expanded supply of hollowware, glasses, china, flatware, table napery, and tabletop accessories. Similarly, a convention hotel needs more banquet-service equipment than, for example, a corporate business hotel, to provide meals for large groups of people. Accordingly, the inventory for banquet tables and chairs for both meetings

---

EXHIBIT 1
Determining seating capacity for different functions

1. Meeting Functions

Theater style: 8 sq. ft. per seat
Classroom style: 10–12 sq. ft. per seat

2. Food and Beverage Functions

Reception: 7–8 sq. ft. per person
Meal service: 10–12 sq. ft. per person

The number of tables and chairs needed for various functions can be computed as follows:

Maximum seating, theatre style
14,000 sq. ft. ÷ 8 sq. ft. = 1,750 chairs

Maximum seating, classroom style
14,000 sq. ft. ÷ 12 sq. ft. = 1,167 seats
1,167 seats ÷ 3 (3 persons per table) = 389 tables
1,167 seats ÷ 4 = 292 tables (if 18″ × 96″ are used)

3. Meal Functions Without Head Table

14,000 sq. ft. ÷ 12 sq. ft. = 1,167 seats
1,167 seats ÷ 10 (10 persons per table) = 117 tables, or
1,167 seats ÷ 8 (8 persons per table) = 146 tables

Inventory for portable stage and other meeting props, including chalk boards, lecterns, flip charts, easels, U. S. and state flags, and so forth, should be based on the number of banquet rooms.

---

and meals should be based on the seating capacity for various functions (see Exhibit 1). Additionally, there is a list of basic requirements—ashtrays in every room, for example—that buyers can anticipate and, with a minimum of calculations, provide for.

PAR-STOCK REQUIREMENTS

To establish an adequate par stock for both F&B outlets and hotel operations, buyers should prepare a par-stock analysis, listing quantities needed under each category. To help determine par-stock needs, some manufacturers offer general ratio guidelines for specific operations. These should be adjusted, however, to meet the needs of individual operations. Par-stock ratios can easily be established for the glassware, chinaware, and flatware to be used in food outlets, and for bedding and terry goods in hotel operations (see Exhibits 2 and 3). Factors to consider when deciding how much glassware, chinaware, and flatware should be purchased include the type of outlet and speed of turnover, and the outlet's seating capacity, ordering time, and warewasher availability.

Type of F&B Outlet and Speed of Turnover

Par-stock requirements vary for different types of F&B outlets. For example, a coffee shop and restaurant might anticipate three "turns" at breakfast, two at lunch, and one and a half at dinner. A facility where demand varies will need to adjust par-stock requirements accordingly. Buyers should ensure that frequently used items (e.g., teacups, saucers, bread and butter plates, salad or pie plates, dinner plates) are in sufficient supply. The par-stock requirements for a freestanding restaurant should be larger than those for a hotel restaurant, which can draw from other areas in the facility when supplies run out during peak service hours.

Quantities

The amount of glassware, chinaware, and flatware to order can be established by multiplying the par-stock ratio by the seating capacity of each outlet.

Ordering Time

If custom-made chinaware is to be used, buyers should allow for a minimum of 90 to 120 days for delivery, and should aim for a par stock of at least 3.5 to 4 for those items most frequently used.

EXHIBIT 2
Par-stock ratio for chinaware for a 100-seat food outlet

Item	Par Stock Per Seat	Dz. Per Item (suggested)	Usage
B & B plate	3	25	Bread, rolls; beverage underliner
Pie-cake plate	2	18	Pies, cakes
Salad plate	4½	36	Salads, desserts; supreme underliner, grapefruit underliner
Dinner plate	3	25	Entrees, sandwiches
Bouillon	¾	6	Soups, packaged sugar
Grapefruit bowl	¾	6	Breakfast cereal, chili, salads, fruits, grapefruit
Deep soup plate	½	4	A la carte soups and salads
Vegetable dish	2	18	Vegetables, cobblers
Teacup	4	33	Coffee, tea, cocoa
Tea saucer	4	33	Cup or bouillon underliner
Platter	½	4	Prime rib, whole fish, fruit platter
Sauce boat	¼	2	Gravy, salad dressing
Celery tray	¼	2	Relishes
Platter	¼	4	Strip steaks, large whole fish

Source: Shenango China.

EXHIBIT 3
Sample par-stock ratios for glassware, chinaware, and flatware, per seat

Glassware	Specialty Dining Room	Coffee Shop Rest.	Dinner Cabaret	Grand Ballroom	Lobby Bar	Entrtnmt. Lounge
Juice	—	1	—	—	—	—
Highball	1	1	2	2	1.5	1.5
Old-fashioned	1	.5	2	2	1.5	1.5
Collins	—	1	1	.5	.5	1
Water goblet	1.5	1.5	1	1.5	—	—
Wine (special)	1.5	—	—	—	—	—
Rhine wine	.5	—	—	—	—	—
Tulip champagne	1	—	.5	—	.5	—
Wine, all-purpose	1.5	1	1	1	.5	.5

Chinaware						
Teacup	2.5	3	1.5	2		
Saucer	2.5	3	1.5	2		
Bouillon cup (unhandled)	—	2	1	1.5		
Bouillon cup (two–handled)	1.5	—	—	—		
Soup tureen	1	—	—	—		
B & B plate	2.5	3	2	2		
Salad dessert plate	2.5	2.5	1.5	2		
Dinner plate	2.5	3	1.5	2		
Dinner (fish) plate	2	—	—	—		
Soup plate (deep rim)	—	2	—	—		
Cereal bowl	—	1	—	—		

Flatware						
Knives						
Dinner (utility knife)	2.5	2	1.5	1.5		
Fish knife (special)	2.5	—	—	—		
Butter spreader	2.5	—	—	1.5		
Forks						
Dinner fork (utility)	3	4	3	3		

EXHIBIT 3 (continued)
Sample par-stock ratios for glassware, chinaware, and flatware, per seat

Glassware	Specialty Dining Room	Coffee Shop Rest.	Dinner Cabaret	Grand Ballroom	Lobby Bar	Entrtnmt. Lounge
Fish fork (salad fork)	2	—	—	—		
Oyster fork (cocktail)	1.5	1.5	—	1.5		
Spoons						
Teaspoon	5	4	3	3		
Bouillon spoon	2	1	1	1		
Tablespoon (serving spoon)	—	—	—	—		
Demitasse spoon	2	—	—	—		

Warewasher-Unit Availability

Those operations that depend on a single centralized warewasher unit should place one-third of their total chinaware inventory in reserve storage for emergency use in case of washer breakdown.

A par stock for other service equipment, such as tabletop accessories, can be set at 10 percent over the total requirement expected to be in use at any one time. The quantity of restaurant-service equipment needed for specialty dishes can be determined by estimating the amount of covers to be served.

Operators, conscious of limited storage facilities, excess inventories, and replacement costs, will select service equipment that can be used for more than one food or beverage presentation. For example, an attractive water goblet can be used to serve water, tea, milk, or soft drinks. Multiple functions can also be found for chinaware and flatware. Selecting one pattern for items that will be used in several F&B outlets will greatly reduce overall operating and inventory expenses, and cut down on replacement costs.

Table Napery

As a general rule of thumb, food-service outlets should operate with a par stock of 3 for all types of table napery. To further determine table-napery requirements for food outlets, buyers should consider the following: design concept and color coordination, tabletop size, seating capacity, turnover, maintenance requirements, and available laundry facilities. For example, damask table napery should be considered only if a heavy-duty mangle is available for ironing. A greater variety of interchangeable tablecloths is available to buyers if standard-sized tabletops (as shown in Exhibit 4) are selected.

A well-stocked restaurant should allow for at least 4 to 5 cloths per table and 9 to 12 napkins per seat, with a three-day supply for weekends if in-house laundry services are available only on weekdays.

Bedding and Terry Goods

Buyers can determine how much bedding and terry goods to purchase for hotels by counting rooms, beds, and bed sizes. (Most hotels should maintain

EXHIBIT 4
Standard tabletop sizes

Seating	Top Size	Cloth Size*
Table for 2	30" × 30"	54" × 54"
Table for 4	42" × 42"	54" × 54"
Table for 4	30" × 50"	54" × 72"
Table for 6	54" dia., rnd.	72" × 72"

*These sizes allow for a 6- to 12-inch tablecloth drop around the table.

a par-stock ratio of 3 sheets per bed, and 4 hand towels, bath towels, and washcloths each per room. A standard par-stock ratio for blankets and mattress pads should be set at 10 percent over the total amount expected to be in use at any one time.) The figures for other guest-room furnishings and amenities should correspond to the number of rooms. If a hotel offers a special service (e.g., using three sheets per bed to cover blankets from both sides, or providing guests with extra towels at the pool

or beach), this must be taken into consideration when par stocks are computed. Color selection for bedding, terry goods, and bedspreads should be made by interior designers to ensure continuity in color schemes.

Pre-Opening Budget Proposal

A budget proposal for hotel and restaurant operating and service equipment should be prepared in two stages: (1) a *preliminary budget proposal,* outlining purchasing needs and quantities according to established par-stock requirements and costs, and (2) a *final budget proposal,* presenting a summary of proposed expenditures for each purchasing category as well as supporting documents. Buyers preparing preliminary budget proposals should do so in the following manner:

1. Separating purchasing categories into two segments—one for F&B outlets and one for hotel operations, as shown in Exhibit 5—and analyzing expenditures in each segment.

EXHIBIT 5
Purchasing categories for hotel and restaurant operating equipment

F & B Operating Equipment	Hotel Operating Equipment
Glassware	Hotel Bedding and Terry Goods
Chinaware	Housekeeping and Supplies
Flatware	Cleaning Equipment
Table Napery, Buffet Skirts	Uniforms for Hotel Personnel (Front Office, Housekeeping, Maintenance)
Tabletop Accessories	
Restaurant-Service Equipment	Front-Office Equipment and Supplies
Bar-Service Equipment	General Office Equipment and Supplies
Kitchen-Service and Cleaning Equipment	Icemakers (Guest Floors)
	Engineering Tools and Service Equipment
Cafeteria-Service Equipment	
Banquet Props and Service Equipment	Garden Tools and Service Equipment
Uniforms (Food Production)	Recreation Equipment (Health Spa)
Uniforms (F & B Service)	Guest-Employee Lockers
Printed Forms	Mobile Carts
Supplies	

2. Preparing a list of items needed for each category, applying par-stock ratios where applicable.
3. Obtaining current prices for all items in each category.

Buyers who have recently furnished a similar installation may base part of their preliminary budget proposal on a per-seat and a per-room-and-bed analysis, using costs at the previous installation, provided that they will be comparable to those in the new operation. A total cost per seat at the previous installation can be determined by multiplying the cost of each F&B item by the quantities needed at each outlet, and dividing this figure by the number of seats. The totals can then be applied to the number of seats at the new installation. The estimated cost of kitchen-service equipment and uniforms can also be calculated in this manner.

A cost analysis for hotel rooms can be derived by dividing the cost of the room furnishings and amenities at the previous installation by the number of rooms and beds at the new installation. If the previous installation opened some time ago, an appropriate factor must be added to these estimates to reflect inflation. The greater the time between the two openings, of course, the less reliable the estimates derived in this manner will be.

An additional contingency fund of at least 5 percent should be set aside to cover overproduction of custom-made items, alternative (and more costly) selections, and items previously not included in the budget proposal.

The final budget proposal should summarize all cost factors established in the preliminary proposal, specify total requirements for each product category, and take the following form:

1. Hotel and restaurant operating and service equipment (by purchasing category);
2. Par-stock ratio and purchasing requirements for categories (where applicable);
3. Cost analysis on a per-seat basis for F&B outlets;
4. Cost analysis on a per-room and per-bed basis for hotel bedding, terry goods, hotel amenities, and supplies;
5. Addendum to budget proposal.

The addendum to the budget proposal should contain a brief listing of items to be purchased in each category,[1] with cost estimates based on firm bid quotations.

Master Budget

Once the budget for hotel and restaurant operating equipment has been approved, proposed expenditures should be combined with the FF&E budget proposal and added to the hotel's master budget. Unlike an operating budget, in which proposed figures serve as guidelines rather than as the final word handed down, the pre-opening master budget for a new installation must be controlled closely to avoid expenditure overruns.

To stay within budgetary limitations, a bimonthly or trimonthly review is essential. Such a review will show the exact status of each category and help prevent overruns. A budget review should list purchasing categories (by number), budget (and dates approved) for each category, total purchases to date, additional purchases committed, variances from the approved budget, and total proposed expenditures.

Purchase orders that are recorded by computer should be assigned two main numbers, one for F&B and one for hotel operations, with a subordinate number for subdivisions within each category. Say, for example, the F&B category were assigned the number 505. The number for glassware—a subdivision of F&B—might be 505-001, chinaware 505-002, and so forth.

Schedule of Payment

A schedule of payment arranged at the same time a purchase order is issued will make preparing monthly draws for construction, FF&E, landscaping, and other costs an easier task. To be effective, the form should group purchasing categories by vendors, list total amounts spent under each category, state approximate delivery dates, and post deposits and partial and final payments for each vendor.

Selection of Operating and Service Equipment

Buyers should select operating and service equipment after color schemes have been chosen for hotel rooms and public areas and the ambience set for restaurants and bars, allowing enough time for production and delivery of custom-made goods.

Quantities for goods needed in the F&B department can best be established either by seating capacity or estimated covers; quantities for goods needed in hotel operations, by numbers of rooms and beds; and quantities for hotel suppliers, by projected occupancy rates.

Quantities for other goods should be based either on past experience or estimates furnished by various departments. Buyers should meet new department heads as they join the operation to discuss their needs and inform them of orders placed thus far.

Invitations to Bid

Invitations to bid on operating and service equipment for a new installation should include the following information: complete address of hotel corporation, name of person issuing bid sheet, issuance date, expected return date, items and quantities to be purchased, specifications and unit packed, and completion date. In addition, a letter outlining any additional information or requirements should accompany the bid sheet. Method of payment and billing instructions should be stated, as well as the terms of reimbursement or credit for incorrect or damaged goods, shortages and overshipments, and discount offers.

Purchasing Procedures

Policies for purchasing procedures should be established and approved by management to reflect the following: adequacy of storage facilities for quantity purchasing; general market and economic conditions, such as availability of products and price fluctuations; production time for custom-made goods; and taxes, insurance, and other costs involved in financing purchases.

With the constantly rising cost of goods affecting everything from a simple syrup dispenser to a fancy flambé cart, buyers may prefer to ignore the cost of money and instead purchase the entire FF&E inventory immediately after construction contracts have been signed and purchasing selections made. Buyers who desire to do this have two purchasing options available: (1) "bill and hold," and (2) outright purchase and delivery. With the bill-and-hold option, merchandise is sold at current prices or at special rates, and is invoiced but held until the agreed-upon delivery date. Under this arrangement, buyers are obligated to pay promptly within normal terms. This method is advantageous for both the buyer and the seller: The buyer avails himself of a special price offer or the current market prices, and the seller receives immediate full payment for the merchandise sold even though it may be delivered at a later date.

The buyer who opts for outright purchase and delivery must provide full warehousing for the goods purchased—a costly commitment because of high insurance and storage rates. Buyers considering this option should compare the cost of warehousing and its related expenses with bill-and-hold costs to decide which option is best for their operation.

Assessing Vendors

Prices should be obtained for comparison from at least three vendors, using formal bid sheets (as described earlier in this article). Some vendors may promise higher-quality merchandise for a higher price, some may tout quality service, and some may offer low prices to get a foot in the door. Contracts should be awarded to the most reputable seller providing both quality merchandise and prompt delivery, and selection should be based on references provided both by the vendors and by hotels that have previously dealt with the firms being considered.

The final and most important step in the purchasing process is the writing of the purchase order. The order should be written in precise language and be presented in a format that is easy to read, to avoid misunderstandings. Copies should be color-coded and distributed to the receiving clerk, buyer, accounting office, hotel manager, and department head. Vendors should be asked to confirm the order in writing within 30 days from the date of purchase to assure the buyer that the order can be met.

A purchase order is a binding agreement between the buyer and the seller and should be treated as such. Cancellations or changes by either party should be put in writing well before the manufacturer has begun production or the shipments are en route. Buyers should allow enough time to make alternate purchases and sellers enough time to secure substitutes.

Schedule of Deliveries

If proper care is not taken in receiving, the entire purchasing function will be compromised, no matter how well the purchasing procedures were planned. Buyers should set up two major delivery schedules—one for warehouse deliveries and one for direct shipments to the hotel—to accommodate FF&E purchases.

Drop-shipments to the warehouse should be scheduled at least four to six weeks prior to the target opening date to ensure that goods will be available when needed. Items that should be included in drop-shipments are cleaning equipment, housekeeping supplies, hotel bedding, and service equipment. Custom-made goods should be requested much further in advance of the hotel opening because delivery dates for these items are often undependable.

Warehouse personnel receiving drop-shipments should report deliveries on a weekly basis (and, as the opening date approaches, on a daily basis). Receiving reports should include the following information: receiving date, item, quantity, vendor, purchase-order number, purchasing category, and condition of merchandise.

Any damaged packages, containers, or cartons should be checked and buyers notified immediately about defective goods so that reorders or alternate decisions can be made. Damaged goods should be refused without hesitation.

Buyers should keep accurate records of their receiving reports from the warehouse, maintaining spreadsheets, prepared much as purchase orders are. By checking receiving reports against these spreadsheets, buyers and receiving clerks will know at a glance which merchandise has been inventoried at the warehouse.

Goods not received within the specified time of delivery should be traced by the buyer, and sellers urged to expedite orders.

A physical count of all goods received at the warehouse should be made at the hotel site by receiving clerks or department heads, and quantities received recorded on purchase-order copies. An invoice approved for payment should accurately correspond with quantities and price quotations listed on the receiving order. Any discrepancies should be reported to the buyer before final payments are made.

Direct Deliveries

Direct deliveries (i.e., deliveries to the hotel site) should be coordinated with the completion schedule. For example, because rooms are usually finished before other areas of a hotel, housekeeping operating and service equipment should be delivered early, provided that linen rooms, laundry facilities, and shelving space have been completed to house and maintain such supplies.

Conclusion

Buyers, because they must be informed about the purchasing needs for each department, should take the time to review their purchasing list—separated into categories—with the various department heads at a new installation. The extra effort taken to prepare such a list and to verify selections will not only ensure that the right choices have been made but will also provide buyers and developers with a means of evaluating costs for similar installations in the future.

Endnote

[1] A complete listing of items to be purchased in each category—as well as other exhibits and forms to facilitate the purchasing function—is included in the reprint of this article, which can be ordered for $5.00 from *The Cornell Quarterly*, 327 Statler Hall, Ithaca, NY 14853.

Suggested Readings

Book

Kotshevar, Lendel H., and Charles Levinson. *Quantity Food Purchasing*, 3d ed. New York: Macmillan, 1988.

Article

Tabacchi, Mary H. "The Manager's Guide to Fresh Produce." *Cornell Hotel and Restaurant Administration Quarterly* (February 1982): 72–79.

Accounting

INTRODUCTION

As a department, accounting in a hotel is far more important to the success and management of that hotel than the few articles included here would suggest. In most major hotel firms the chief accountant or controller, as this manager is more often called, ranks among the top two or three decision-makers in the hotel's hierarchy. The importance of this job can be established by the observation that many traditional hotel departments have been reorganized so that major portions of their functions are now responsible to the controller's office. The prime example of this is in the front office, where in the past the front office manager supervised the activities of the night audit staff, cashiers, and other front desk clerks. Increasingly, hotel firms are transferring the responsibility for night audits and cashiers to the accounting office, with the ultimate responsibility for these information-gathering and controlling functions resting with the hotel controller.

It should also be noted that an increasingly important department in hotels is one that coordinates and supervises all of the electronic data processing (EDP) or management information systems (MIS). In many instances, EDP and MIS functions are now also the responsibility of the hotel controller. This recognizes the training and ability of hotel controllers to provide for the structured accumulation, storage, and reporting of data in forms that are most useful to the operating departments and executives of the hotel.

The article contributed by Geller and Schmidgall opens a previously obscure window on the hotel controller as a career path in management of the modern hotel corporation. In the past, students have been merely instructed in the process of accounting and auditing, and for the most part have been unaware of the sort of career that can result from a flair for both management and "number crunching."

For similar reasons, Richard Howey's essay on the "Evolution of the Night Audit" is included in this section. With the increasing availability of EDP and a similarly important emphasis on providing management information, the role of the night auditor has become more critical to overall management of the hotel than simply the preparation and balancing of guest accounts. Howey traces the development of the night audit from its earliest practical applications through to the modern era. Among the Suggested Readings are other articles and essays that deal with illustrations of more narrow technical applications of the accounting or controlling function.

The Hotel Controller: More Than a Bookkeeper

A. Neal Geller
Raymond S. Schmidgall

In most businesses, the top financial officer is a well-respected member of the management team. In contrast, the prevailing view of the hotel controller is that of a necessary evil—to be tolerated only because of rules, laws, or a mandate from the home office. Perceived largely as a bookkeeper, known as the "wearer of the green eyeshade," the stereotypical controller is locked away in a damp basement office, let out once per period to produce the dreaded financial statements (or, worse yet, a government report requiring cash).

Does this rather unflattering caricature accurately describe the hotel controller of today? Hoping to answer this question, the financial-management committee of the American Hotel and Motel Association requested that a study of hotel controllers be prepared to address such issues as controllers' compensation, financial responsibility, level of authority, education, and status. The authors accordingly conducted a scientific survey of a large sample of hotel controllers, providing the first projective profile of this group.

WHO ARE THEY?

The survey was based on a two-page questionnaire mailed to 1,000 members of the International Association of Hospitality Accountants (IAHA).[1] Three hundred sixty-six members responded (a 36.6 percent response rate), of whom 311 identified themselves as hotel or hotel-company (area or corporate) controllers. The findings presented in this article are drawn from this subset of responses.

This article was originally published in the August 1984 issue of *The Cornell Hotel and Restaurant Administration Quarterly,* and is reprinted here with the permission of the Cornell University School of Hotel Administration. © 1984.

The survey produced the following thumbnail sketch. The typical controller:

- holds a bachelor's degree in accounting;
- is required to know accounting principles, capital budgeting, cash management, statistics, auditing, internal control, personnel management, and, to a lesser degree, electronic data processing (EDP) and taxes;
- has the authority to sign checks, approve purchases, and extend credit;
- is responsible for general accounting, payroll, accounts receivable, accounts payable, auditing, and the cashier function;
- is a member of the executive committee of the hotel;
- receives a salary of more than $30,000; and
- receives a bonus of over 9 percent of base salary.

In the following pages, we will discuss these and other findings in detail, drawing a profile of a well-educated member of the hotel management team. We will conclude by discussing the implications of our findings as they relate to the future of hotel financial management.

Titles and Tenure

Most of the 311 respondents listed their job title as hotel controller (89 percent); the remainder worked as area or corporate controllers for hotel firms. The largest number worked for chains (24 percent), but almost as many worked at independent properties (20 percent) or franchise properties (also 20 percent). The geographical distribution of respondents and the size of the respondents' properties are summarized, along with information on the foregoing characteristics, in Exhibit 1.

EXHIBIT 1
Profile of surveyed hotel controllers and their properties (n = 311)

Job title:

Hotel controller	89%
Area or corporate controller	11

Property location:

Center city	44%
Resort	21
Suburban	13
Airport	7
Highway	7
2+ locations	7

Property affiliation:

Chain	24%
Independent	20
Franchise	20
2+ affiliations	15
Managed	10
Owned	9
Leased	2

Property size (# rooms):

<250	22%
250–500	49
501–1,000	21
>1,000	9

Annual room sales:

<$3 million	23%
$3–6 million	33
$6–9 million	16
$9–12 million	10
>$12 million	18

Note: Nonrespondents were eliminated from the percentage calculations. Due to rounding, columns do not always total 100 percent.

EXHIBIT 2
Educational level of controllers

High school	10%
College:	
Two-year	16%
Four-year	61
Master's	11
Other	2%

Education

In light of the perception that a controller is a mere bookkeeper, the fact that a 72 percent majority of the respondents had at least a bachelor's degree was among the most surprising findings of the study. As shown in Exhibit 2, only a handful of respondents lacked a college degree—and, as shown in Exhibit 3, those with only a high school education were more likely to work for a smaller property than a larger one. Similarly, the controllers with a master's degree were more likely to work at a medium-size or larger property than at a smaller one.

The most common major area of study (see Exhibit 4) was accounting (56 percent), followed by hotel and restaurant management (8 percent), business management (7.5 percent), and finance (7 percent). Nearly 22 percent held degrees in such other areas as economics, marketing, and psychology.

Like educational level, college major was strongly related to hotel size. Three-quarters of the controllers at the largest hotels had majored in accounting, while only 50 percent of those at smaller

EXHIBIT 3
Educational level by hotel size

	% at hotels with:		
Of controllers with:	< 250 rooms	250–500 rooms	500+ rooms
High-school education	**39.3%**	**39.3%**	**21.4%**
College:			
Two-year	29.2	45.8	25.0
Four-year	18.0	50.3	31.7
Master's	12.5	50.0	37.5

(Rows, not columns, total 100 percent.)

EXHIBIT 4
College majors

Accounting	56%
Finance	7
Hotel-rest. mgmt.	8
Business	7.5
Other	22

EXHIBIT 6
Extent of authority over specific functions

	% citing authority
Sign checks	87%
Extend credit	85
Approve purchases	83
Set or change prices	31
Borrow funds	19
Invest funds	2

properties held accounting degrees—suggesting, perhaps, a greater necessity for specialized accounting expertise as hotel size increases.

The controllers were also asked what, if any, professional certification they had received. A rather scant 13 percent were certified public accountants (CPAs), and 8 percent had been certified as hotel accounting executives (CHAEs).

Skills

Exhibit 5 shows the technical skills and knowledge the respondents said they needed to perform the job of controller. The areas of knowledge most frequently cited were auditing and internal control (cited by 95 percent of the sample), accounting principles (90 percent), and cash management (89 percent). Although cash management was seen as an important area by the respondents, Exhibit 6 shows that most of the controllers were not given

authority over two traditional cash management functions: borrowing funds and investing funds.

WHAT DO THEY DO?

Most of the controllers *did* have the authority to sign checks, approve purchases, and extend credit (see Exhibit 6), but those with the authority to set or change prices were in the minority (although, among controllers at properties with annual sales under $3 million, 42 percent of the respondents did exercise authority over prices).

Whether electronic data processing was part of a controller's responsibility depended on the size

EXHIBIT 5
Technical skills and knowledge required by controllers

Auditing and internal control	95%
Accounting principles/FASB	90
Cash management	89
Statistics	82
Capital budgeting	80
Personnel management	78
EDP	70
Taxes	60

EXHIBIT 7
Relationship between sales volume and controller EDP involvement

	Controller cites:	
Annual Room Sales	EDP Knowledge Required	Responsibility for EDP
< $3M	47%	23%
$3–6M	72	38
$6–9M	74	57
$9–12M	74	56
> $12M	**80**	**74**

EXHIBIT 8
Controllers' responsibilities

	% citing
Accounts receivable	95%
Accounts payable	93
General accounting	91
Payroll	89
Night auditors	83
Income auditors	79
Cashiers	63
Food controls	53
EDP	52
Purchasing	50
Receiving	50
Storage	34
Security	9

EXHIBIT 9
Controllers' involvement in committees

Committee	% belonging
Executive	82%
Compensation	23
Planning	41

of the hotel, as shown in Exhibit 7. It is clear that the greater the hotel's sales volume, the greater the controller's involvement with EDP.

Exhibit 8 depicts other general areas of controllers' responsibility. Most of the respondents indicated that their jobs included responsibility for accounts receivable, accounts payable, general accounting, and payroll. Of the areas listed, there were only two for which fewer than 50 percent of the respondents said they were responsible: storage and security.

To determine controllers' role on the management team (Exhibit 9), we asked those surveyed whether they were members of their properties' executive, compensation, or planning committees.[2] Fully 82 percent of the controllers said they be-

longed to the executive committee of their property; 41 percent belonged to the planning committee; and 23 percent said they were members of the compensation committee.

WHAT ARE THEY PAID?

One area of particular interest, and one with general implications for the industry, is compensation. We asked for information on controllers' salaries, bonuses, and fringe benefits, with the following results (see Exhibit 10).

With respect to salaries, we must admit to a heinous error in our questionnaire design. We ended our list of fixed alternatives for salary at $39,999, believing as academics that our "greater than $40,000" category referred to hypergalactic sums. This, however, turned out to be the largest single response category for both area and corporate controllers and hotel controllers, so we lack considerable information in regard to the highest salaries among the respondents.

EXHIBIT 10
Controllers' salaries

	Area-Corporate Controllers	Hotel Controllers	Total Sample
< $20,000	3%	5%	5%
$20,000–$24,999	6	9	9
$25,000–$29,999	3	20	18
$30,000–$34,999	24	23	23
$35,000–$39,999	15	16	16
> $40,000	**49**	**27**	**29**

EXHIBIT 11
Relationship between hotel size and controller salary

# Rooms	Annual Room Sales	Median Salary
0–249	< $3 mill.	$25,000–$29,999
250–500	$3–6 mill.	$30,000–$34,999
501–1,000	$6–12 mill.	$35,000–$39,999
>1,000	> $12 mill.	> $40,000

EXHIBIT 13
Overview of controllers' bonuses

- 62% of the controllers received a bonus of some sort.
- Bonus was most often based on salary (59%) or sales (29%), although it was sometimes linked to performance or GOP.
- As a percentage of salary, bonus was most often 9 to 12% of salary (cited by 29% of those receiving bonuses) or more than 12% (30%), although many controllers (23%) received a more modest bonus of 3 to 6% of salary.
- Average bonus as a percentage of salary increased as salary rose. Controllers citing a salary under $20,000 cited an average bonus of under 3%; those earning $20,000–24,999 claimed a bonus of 6 to 9%; in all other groups but one (the $35,000–39,999 category), the average bonus amounted to 9 to 12%.

Median salaries varied by location, averaging between $25,000 and $29,999 at highway and suburban properties and between $30,000 and $34,999 at resort and airport hotels. The best-paid controllers, at an average salary of $35,000 to $39,999, were those working at center-city properties.

Factors other than hotel location were related to salary. Average salary rose steadily with hotel size (see Exhibit 11) and with the controller's education level (see Exhibit 12). In addition, as one would expect, area and corporate controllers were better compensated than were hotel controllers, with almost half reporting salaries in excess of $40,000.

In addition to their salaries, more than half of the controllers received a bonus (see Exhibit 13). The controllers at larger properties were more likely to be on a bonus plan than were those at smaller properties; unlike salaries, however, bonuses did not seem to be related to property location. Only 10 of the 311 controllers received a bonus amounting to less than 3 percent of their salary; bonuses most often exceeded 9 percent of controllers' salaries. And, in general, the larger the salary, the larger the percentage bonus.

Information on the fringe benefits enjoyed by the controllers is provided in Exhibit 14. Almost all of the respondents received health insurance, vacations, life insurance, and dining privileges, while use of a company automobile was fairly rare.

Property size strongly affected the extent of

EXHIBIT 12
Relationship between education and salary

Controller's Education	Median	Mode
High school	$25,000–$29,999	$25,000–$29,999
College:		
Two-year	$30,000–$34,999	$30,000–$34,999
Four-year	$30,000–$34,999	> $40,000
Master's	$35,000–$39,999	> $40,000

EXHIBIT 14
Controllers' fringe benefits

Health insurance	99%
Vacation	95
Life insurance	89
Dining privileges	87
Dental insurance	78
Disability insurance	75
Retirement	50
Automobile	11

---

benefits. The most dramatic size-related difference was in retirement plans; among controllers at hotels with sales under $3 million, only 27 percent had retirement coverage, compared to 80 percent of those at properties with sales exceeding $12 million.

NOT THE UNIVERSE

This study represented the first known attempt at a scientific assessment of hotel controllers. Its results are indicative, but they should not be viewed as definitive. The implications drawn from this initial measure are largely the opinions of the authors. Because hotel controllers who are not members of IAHA were not included in the sample (and because we estimate that there are two or three times as many hotel accountants as there are IAHA members), the findings presented here cannot be generalized to the entire universe of hotel controllers. We hope to repeat the study in subsequent years, using the current study as a base to measure changes in the profession over time.

SUMMARY

The survey indicated that the modern hotel controller is very well educated, and must employ high levels of technical skill in such areas as financial accounting, taxation, finance, and controls. The controllers responding to the survey had considerable authority over the financial and general management of their hotels; most were solely responsible for the accounting and financial-management functions at their properties, and over 80 percent belonged to the hotel's executive committee.

Moreover, hotel controllers appeared to be well compensated in terms of both salaries and privileges; over 60 percent received more than $30,000 in base pay. This combination of authority and compensation shows that the hotel controller is emerging as a member of top management, a conclusion with some important implications for the hotel industry.

IMPLICATIONS

One of the study's findings was disturbing: the lack of professional certification among controllers. With the prevalence of college degrees and particularly of accounting majors, one would surely anticipate finding more CPAs among the respondents. We believe more controllers should also work toward the CHAE designation sponsored by the IAHA.

We expect that as the hotel controller grows increasingly more professional, hotels will have to place more emphasis on retaining their financial managers through the provision of opportunities for challenge and growth. Several other industries with a similar demand for well-trained financial professionals provide higher salaries. Additionally, hotel companies should provide more opportunities for their controllers' professional development through such means as encouraging continuing education and professional certifications.

In the opinion of the authors, the hotel controllers responding to this survey fared well in comparison to financial-management professionals in many other industries. If we assume that the average hotel controller's educational level and technical expertise have risen over time, the result may be better decision-making and the use of modern management tools heretofore not widely used in the hotel industry.

Evolution of the Night Audit

Richard M. Howey

Hotels have always needed methods for keeping guest accounts up to date and ready for submission to the guest when he or she checks out. Because check-outs occur early in the morning, it has fallen upon the front office night shift—those people working from 11:00 p.m. to 7:00 a.m.—to accumulate all charges and credits guests have accrued, and prepare the bill for presentation. Over the years, the procedure has become known as the night audit, and the individual who performs it as the night auditor.

As the size and complexity of hotels increased and the demands on the night auditor grew, the night audit procedure evolved from a relatively simple, handwritten process to the sophisticated, electronic systems that even small hotels use today. Nevertheless, the fundamental process has remained the same.

WHAT IS THE NIGHT AUDIT?

Part of the night audit procedure involves compiling the guest bill for presentation. These bills are the accounts receivable to the hotel, and must be readied daily, since guests might wish to look at their bill or to check out at any time.

There is, however, more to the night audit than just preparing guest bills. The main task, and the real "audit" portion of the process, is to reconcile all the accounts, ensuring that all charges are correctly posted (assigned) to the proper guest accounts. Records of each hotel department's charges are forwarded to the night auditor, who compares what has been posted to the guest accounts with what was actually charged in the department. This process culminates in the auditor's performing a trial balance of all of the different guest accounts, thus

ensuring that all accounting transactions relating to these accounts were handled correctly.

The reason that this has to be done nightly is simple. Since guest accounts must be kept current, a "normal" accounts receivable system that bills the individual at the end of a longer period (such as a month) would clearly be inadequate. Most hotel operations would never consider the latter billing procedure, because the guests would be spread over a large geographical area, making collection difficult. Additionally, even a small hotel would accumulate a large number of bills in a relatively short time. For example, a 250-room hotel that was 70 percent occupied during a month with only one person per room would generate 5,250 guest days of business ($250 \times 30 \times 0.7$). If each guest stayed for 3 days, that would mean there would be 1,750 different bills (5,250/3) to prepare at the end of the month! Clearly it would be better to collect when the guest checked out.

Evolution of the Night Audit

The purpose of the night audit procedure was to ensure that the bills presented to guests were accurate and up to date. The accounts needed to be reconciled before the guest departed. Since this was usually in the morning, and since the late night shift at a front desk was usually quiet, it was logical that the procedure would be done at this time. It also allowed someone to post all of the accounts that the guest accrued before he or she went to bed, including the charge for the room itself. By midnight, it could be assumed that everyone who was going to check into the hotel had. The accounting day would end with the closing of the last department, usually the lounge, and *all* charges for the day could be posted.

The history of the night audit procedure can be separated into three main categories: (1) the hand

This reading is original to this book.

transcript, (2) the machine audit, and (3) the electronic audit. Each of the categories evolved as a necessary response to the increased size and complexity of hotel operations, alongside the development of new technologies to aid the night auditor. While these three categories evolved in the order presented, it should be remembered that there are a number of hotels today that use a hand transcript or machine audit, and have for good reasons not completely adopted the latest technology.

The hand transcript. In the early days of hotels, the hand transcript evolved from the need for room clerks to account for the increasing number of guests hotels were accommodating. During the nineteenth century, hotels were growing rapidly in size, and it was no longer possible for a landlord or owner to perform all of the tasks required as host. Traditionally, the desk of the smaller hotel, if there even was one, would close at night. However, as hotels became larger, the need for desk clerks and other employees increased and the notion of a twenty-four-hour front desk operation arose. Similarly, there evolved a need to keep track of guest accounts, since more and more establishments were allowing patrons to charge for services instead of requiring cash up front. It was no longer practical for accounts to be prepared when guests asked for them. Additionally, hoteliers in general were discovering the increased need for control over the monies that were being generated. As a consequence, the concept of the night audit developed.

The original night audit was a handwritten, manually totaled list of guest accounts. On a large sheet of paper, or in a ledger book, individual guest accounts were arranged in rows, while the different departments that a guest could charge in were arranged in columns. After guest charges were accumulated and each individual bill was tabulated, the entries on the bills were transferred to the night audit transcript. Exhibit 1 provides an example of a typical hand transcript.

Both debit (charge) and credit (payment) entries were included. Row totals were calculated as *debits* minus *credits* equals *amount due*. Column totals were calculated and represented the total charges or credits for each department. In this fashion, the auditors would be able to verify each guest's bill by comparing it to the bill as originally created. More importantly, the auditors could then compare the departmental totals with another set of totals prepared in the individual department. Any discrepancies would have to be resolved. In essence, this was the true audit part of the night audit—to review the accounts as posted, and make sure they were all done correctly.

Unfortunately, several other tasks were asked of the auditors that limited their time and ability to actually audit the books. These will be discussed in the next section. What is important is that the basic function of the auditor, and the underlying methodology of how the audit works, has remained essentially unchanged as the audit process has evolved. The primary task of the night audit today is still to review the accounts, and isolate and remedy any mistakes. What has changed are the tools by which the audit is done.

The machine audit. As electric cash registers became more popular, specialized machines were developed for specialized purposes, one of which was a machine that would perform the mechanical aspects of the night audit. Perhaps the most famous of these were the series of posting machines built by the National Cash Register Company. Almost every front office manager or hotel manager who started a career from the 1930s to the present time has had experience on one or another of these machines.

The advantages of these machines were several. First, they would automatically total the charges or credits for each department, eliminating the need for hand calculations. Second, the folio that is the permanent guest record could be processed through the machine, providing to the guest (and to the front office personnel) complete information on charges and credits during the guest's stay, including the date of the transaction, the department involved, the amount of the transaction, and the room number the charge was posted to. This automated approach eliminated much of the drudgery involved in the bookkeeping aspect of the audit, and freed the aud-

EXHIBIT 1

Daily transcript of accounts receivable

1	2	3	4	5	6	7	8	9	10	11	12	13	14	15	16	17	18	19	20	21	22
								TELEPHONE													
Folio No.	Room No.	No. of Guests	Opening Balance DB (CR)	Room	Room Tax	Restaurant	Beverages	Local Calls	Long Distance	Laundry	Valet	Misc. Charge	Cash Disb.	Transfer Debits	Total Daily Charges	Cash Receipts	Allowances	Transfer to City Ledger	Transfer Credit	Total Credits	Closing Balance
	201																				
	202																				
	203																				
	204																				
	205																				
	206																				
	207																				

EXHIBIT 2
Night auditor's machine balance

D — NIGHT AUDITOR'S MACHINE BALANCE NO. _____

DATE _____

	DATE	TRANS SYMBOLS	NET TOTALS	CORRECTIONS	MACH. TOTALS	
ROOM						
RESTAURANT						
TELEPHONE						
LONG DISTANCE						
LAUN. & DRY CLEAN						
MISCELLANEOUS						
PAID OUT						
TOTAL DEBITS						
MISCELLANEOUS CR.						
PAID						
TOTAL CREDITS						
NET DIFFERENCE						
OPENING DR. BALANCE						
NET OUTSTANDING						
TOTAL MCH. DR. BALANCE						
LESS CR. BALANCE						
NET OUTSTANDING						

DETECTOR COUNTER READINGS:

AUDITOR'S CONTROL _____

MACH. NUMBER _____

NCR Systemedia Division 456421

❑ DATE CHANGED

❑ CONTROL TOTALS AT ZERO

❑ MASTER TAPE LOCKED

❑ AUDIT CONTROL LOCKED

AUDITOR

_____

(Courtesy of NCR Corporation)

itors to spend more time on the audit portion of the job—finding mistakes and correcting them. As a result, the number of individuals needed to complete the night audit could be reduced; one person could reasonably be expected to do the entire audit for a hotel with 300 rooms, assuming a 70 percent occupancy rate.

A third advantage of the machine was that each individual posting clerk could be controlled by having separate locks on the machine. Therefore, it was easier to monitor the activity at the front desk. This became especially important as hotels grew larger, and the posting clerks were made responsible for posting charges to the guest accounts as charges were accumulated during the day's operation. The goal was to require the night auditor to post as few charges as possible, thus freeing time to perform the actual audit.

A fourth advantage, and perhaps the most important from the standpoint of the night auditor, was the ability to print out a form referred to as the "D" card. The "D" card, as shown in Exhibit 2, was a special form that automatically totaled the entire day's activity. This gives departmental totals for all debit and credit transactions that were made on the posting machine. This particular form was printed out while the night auditor was clearing the machine, or "zeroing out" the totals on the posting of the machine, making it ready for the next day's transactions. Obviously this would only be done when all posting for the day had been completed. The "D" card naturally followed the "A," "B," and "C" cards, which were individual shift totals for the posting clerks during the three eight-hour shifts of each day (in fact, the night auditor could be the "C" shift posting clerk). This system allowed for three levels of control to be placed on the employees involved in posting charges. The department cashiers could validate the charges made by the individual clerks in the departments. The posting clerks could validate any charges coming from the various departments. The night auditor could validate the work of the posting clerks, and was the only person who could reset the machine. Note, however, that this system did not apply when the night auditor posted accounts as well as verifying them.

One other situation arose during the time that the posting/auditing machines developed. To this point all discussion has centered on the charges made by guests staying at the hotel, or the transient guests. These accounts were grouped together in what came to be known as the Transient Ledger. However, another entire category of guests existed: guests who were not currently staying in the hotel, but were nevertheless allowed charging privileges. Originally, these individuals would probably have lived in the city where the hotel was, and as a result came to be known as City Ledger guests. The City Ledger accounts were, and still are, very similar to the standard type of accounts found in any retail store, since the difficulty of billing them was not as great as billing the transient guests. Moreover, since the majority of transactions in the hotels remained Transient Ledger accounts, the night auditor's function was expanded to include these charges as well. This simplified the bookkeeping process, by having all charges funnel into one area.

In general terms, then, the job of the night auditor would include the following steps:

1. Post any remaining departmental charges to their proper accounts, whether City or Transient Ledger.
2. Post all room charges, including tax, to their proper accounts.
3. Perform a trial balance of accounts, to ensure all accounts are posted correctly. Make any adjusting entries necessary.
4. Finalize the audit by clearing the machine, and setting for the next day.
5. Prepare any reports that management has requested.

There were problems associated with the machine audits. First, the machines would post to whatever accounts the posting clerks asked of them. This meant the problems of posting to a wrong account, posting the wrong amount, and forgetting to post entirely were still problems. Additionally, since any posting made was now a part of the machine's accumulated total, making changes was not simply a matter of erasing the wrong number and replacing it with the correct one. As a consequence, a new series of accounts had to be created to allow for corrections in statements. This new situation, of course, created more paperwork.

The electronic audit. The final type of audit, and the type still very much in the development state, is the electronic audit. Essentially, this evolutionary trend is an offshoot of the computer revolution. While the machine audits were much more sophisticated and had better controls built in than the hand transcripts, they were no more than specialized adding machines. While any discussion of the sophistication of the electronic audit would by necessity be outdated the moment it is written, there are several advantages over the manual or machine audit that bear mentioning.

Even with the machine audit, the job of tracing errors and proving the trial balance still fell on the auditor. Today, however, computer systems have been designed that can "think" in the sense that they can be programmed to search for the posting errors within the system, thus eliminating another need for the auditor to waste time. For example, a computer can be programmed to perform validity checks on accounts, meaning it can verify the accuracy of the postings. Essentially, the number of controls that can be programmed into the computer are unlimited.

Another advantage of the electronic system is that information the auditor needs, as well as any number of reports management might want, can be arrayed in any fashion desired. Exhibit 3 is an example of a night audit report made to look very similar to the hand transcript, but there are virtually hundreds of different reports that could be generated out of the same data bank stored in the system.

These reports range from room status reports to food and beverage reports to housekeeping reports to any reports that management requires. In fact, this situation could be a problem if too much irrelevant paperwork is generated.

Perhaps the most important advantage of the electronic audit to the night auditor is that it allows him or her to spend more time on other activities. Most systems have commands that will allow the posting of room charges (room rate, room tax, and local telephone) to be done automatically. This in and of itself saves an enormous amount of time since the auditor does not have to post to every folio separately. There are many other ways in which these systems can save time. Perhaps the ultimate example is in the point-of-sale system, where the departmental charges are posted directly from the department cash register onto the guest folio, thus eliminating the need for the intermediary posting clerks. For example, there are point-of-sale systems in lounges and dining rooms that will transmit any charge made at the location to the central computer, which will automatically post the charge to the indicated account. What these sophisticated systems demand is a different kind of auditor, one who understands the computer process, and can perform the audit functions necessary in the electronic data processing age.

There are, of course, still problems associated with computer systems, including the one mentioned above concerning an overkill of reports generated. The problem also remains that accounts can be posted incorrectly. Many of the systems feature built-in safeguards that effectively minimize these human mistakes. One example is the point-of-sale register that has prices programmed into it, so no pricing errors can be made.

A third problem concerns the fact that electronic machinery does not necessarily produce physical copies of the hotel's records. Thus, if the system should break down and there were no hard copies made, there might be no way to reproduce guest accounts. Worse, they might all be lost. It is extremely important that the operating procedure of the system prevent this catastrophic occurrence. It has happened that front office employees have had to literally knock on guest doors, find out if anyone is staying in the room, and then ask the guest how much his bill should be!

There is one final caveat to all of those who are learning computer or even machine night audit sys-

EXHIBIT 3
Guest ledger balances report—SEP13—registered

Folio	Room	Name	Opening Balance	Room /Tax	Incidental	Food	Beverage	Payment	Closing Balance	Pay By	Over Limit
00004	104	HOWEY, M/M	99.75 +	.00	.00	.00	.00	.00	99.75 +	CA	99.75
00006	110	MCKNIGHT, PATTI	1068.25 +	.00	.00	.00	.00	.00	1068.25 +	MV	568.25
00007	108	MCKNIGHT, PATTI	.00	.00	.00	.00	.00	.00	.00	AX	
00011	202	ROACH, ROCKY	47.18 +	.00	.00	.00	.00	.00	47.18 +	CA	47.18
Total			1215.18 +	.00	.00	.00	.00	.00	1215.18 +		

tems. Machines break down, and people who are responsible for generating the folios for presentation to the guest will always need to know how to do the job manually, should the system go down. Even the most conscientious controller or front desk manager will inevitably face a crisis situation where the system cannot provide the information needed. It is for this reason all employees involved in the preparation of guest folios should know how to accumulate the required information necessary to keep the information flow between guest and hotel operating. While the computer systems currently available can work wonders, the job ultimately is the employee's, and a working knowledge of how to keep the front office system operating, by hand if necessary, will always be important.

Endnotes

[1]The IAHA has a total of 1,300 members; foreign members, club controllers, and individuals working in ac- counting firms were eliminated from the list before the mailing. The surveys were distributed in May 1983.

[2]Because we did not ask whether a respondent's property had committees of these three types, the results should be interpreted with caution. For example, the low percentage of controllers citing membership in compensation committees may simply indicate that such committees are not prevalent.

Suggested Readings

Book

Coltman, Michael M. *Hospitality Management Accounting,* 2d ed. Boston: CBI Publishing, 1982.

Article

Orlando, Michael J. "Controlling Rooms Revenue and Occupancy." *Lodging* (May 1981):33–35.

Data Processing and Information Services/Systems

INTRODUCTION

Few people would disagree in this day and age that the computer is a tool and a very useful one. Ten years ago this was not universally recognized within the hotel industry. The installation and application of computers in hotel companies was viewed with a certain amount of distrust, confusion, and even fear on the part of some hotel managements. A lot has happened in the ensuing years. If you refer back to the Alvarez, Ferguson, and Dunn article in Section 4 about the trials and tribulations of mistakenly automating a front office system, the commentary and analysis presented in this section will be all the more instructive.

Like all tools, computers can be used properly or improperly. The warning voiced by Richard Howey in Section 11 about night auditors' EDP systems being able to generate too many useless reports is a warning that should be heeded.

The two articles by Geller included here in many ways build on the front office experiences and Howey's warnings. The first takes a strategic view of what hotels want to accomplish in the way of goals, what the critical success factors are in achieving those goals, and how those goals are measured. In the second article, Geller analyzes the current state of hotel information systems and introduces some eye-opening facts about what should and should not be included in an executive's information system.

The success of many hotel firms in the future will depend on how well they manage, control, and utilize the information that is available to them. Not only is this true for their own operations, but managers also need to develop other sources of information in the business environment that affect their markets, their regulatory structure, and competition.

Tracking the Critical Success Factors for Hotel Companies

A. Neal Geller

Before a company can design an effective executive information *system,* it must first determine what its information needs are. One useful way of pinpointing these needs is through "CSF analysis"—identifying *critical success factors,* or the characteristics necessary to the success of a business (Rockart 1979). CSFs are the few key areas in which things *must* go right if a business's goals are to be achieved.

CSFs may vary from company to company within an industry (as discussed later), and among the managers in a given company. They are factors requiring the careful and constant attention of management, and are thus factors about which ongoing information is needed.

This article explains how CSF analysis is performed, and lists the top goals and CSFs cited by the hotel executives participating in the author's survey.

THE PROCESS

The task of identifying CSFs begins with a review of a company's strategic-planning process and the key *goals* it has established[1] (in fact, unless a company embraces a clearly defined set of goals, it cannot develop a reliable set of CSFs). The next step is to look at each goal and ask, "What must the company do right to meet this goal?" The answer is a *CSF.* The last step is to identify the *measures* that will enable the executive to monitor the CSF.

The relationship between goals and CSFs—as well as measures of performance—is outlined and illustrated in Exhibit 1.

This article was originally published in the February 1985 issue of *The Cornell Hotel and Restaurant Administration Quarterly,* and is reprinted here with the permission of the Cornell University School of Hotel Administration. © 1985.

Exhibit 2 depicts a portion of the CSF analysis of one executive participating in the study. This executive's hotel company is in the luxury segment, and his goals reflect the nature of his market and the steps he feels are critical to making his company a well-known brand within that segment. He cited effective staffing as a CSF, and said that measures of turnover and internal promotion were vital to determining the company's success in this area. Through the process of working from goals and CSFs to measures in this manner, his company can determine its needs for an executive information system.

COMPANY-SPECIFIC CSFs

Like goals, CSFs can vary throughout an organization and among companies, but certain CSFs will be common to most companies in a given industry. For example, some concerns are universal in the hotel business; it would be hard to imagine a hotel executive denying that good guest service and clean rooms are essential.

The critical areas unique to individual companies—reflecting industry position, age, competitive strategy, environmental factors, management style, financial strength, and so on—are referred to as company CSFs. A few examples of how CSFs differ among companies should help the reader understand the process of CSF analysis better.

Some company-specific CSFs are temporary, resulting from short-term or unusual circumstances. Examples would be operating losses, major building programs, divestiture programs, diversification programs, and adverse economic conditions. Hotel Company B, whose CSFs are shown in Exhibit 3, is currently suffering from major operating losses; accordingly, the company's current areas of concern include cutting costs, raising revenues, and di-

EXHIBIT 1
Goals, critical success factors (CSFs), and measures

GLOSSARY

Goals
  Broad, overall aims of the organization; the end points an organization hopes to reach.
Critical Success Factors
  The areas in which good performance is necessary to ensure attainment of the goals; the few key areas where *things must go right* for success (thus, performance in these areas should be continually measured).
Measures
  Indicators or pieces of information that help monitor performance in a key area; some measures are "hard" (objective), others are "soft" (subjective).

SOME EXAMPLES

Goals	Critical Success Factors (CSFs)	Measures
Market share	Good service	Ratio of repeat business
		Occupancy
		Informal feedback
	Employee morale and loyalty	Turnover
		Absenteeism
		Informal feedback
Financial stability	Image in financial markets	Price earnings ratio
		Share price
	Profitability	Earnings per share
		Gross operating profit
		Cost trends
		Cash flow
	Strength of management team	Turnover
		Divisional profit
		Rate of promotion
		Informal feedback
Owner satisfaction	Adequate cash flow	Occupancy, sales
		Gross operating profit
		Departmental profit

vesting unprofitable properties—emergency measures for a short-run turnaround. The company's longer-term priorities are evident at the bottom of the list.

One point implicit in Company B's CSF list is the need to perform CSF analysis on an ongoing basis—and especially frequently when a company is facing a difficult situation. At any given time, every company will have some CSFs that reflect temporary circumstances.

Another issue affecting the nature of a company's CSFs is its management style—the way areas of responsibility are managed, the nature of company policies, and so forth. Whether a company is centralized or decentralized, for example, will affect the nature and relative ranking of the factors it considers important.

Exhibit 4 demonstrates this point through a comparison between Company C, which is centralized, and Company D, which is decentralized. The two

EXHIBIT 2
Sample goal, CSFs, and measures from Hotel Company A

Goal	Critical Success Factors (CSFs)	Measures
Become a well-known "brand name" in the high-quality market	1. Provide well-planned and well-built physical plants	a. Rate of repeat business b. Recognition by industry awards (for example, Mobil 5-star) c. Occupancy rate d. Average room rate e. Citations in the press
	2. Provide effective staffing	a. Rate of promotion from within b. Low turnover c. High productivity d. Recognition programs
	3. Produce high-quality food and beverage service	a. Volume of food and beverage business b. Guest comment cards c. Local food and beverage market (for example, ratio of local F&B business to total) d. Volume of local banquets
	4. Provide strong marketing	a. Quality and volume of business booked b. Rate of repeat business c. Achievement of positive market share in each targeted segment

companies share many CSFs, but their emphasis differs. Most of Company C's CSFs deal directly with guest satisfaction and have little to do with human resources; as a centralized company, Company C aims to meet its guest-satisfaction goals by exerting fairly strong control over operations. Company D, on the other hand, is also concerned with guest satisfaction, but emphasizes its employees—their hiring, training, and motivation—as the means of achieving this satisfaction.

Another issue with a bearing on a company's CSFs is its stage in the product life cycle (i.e., introduction, growth, maturity, or decline), for this will affect what actions the company needs to take for successful performance (e.g., diversification, product differentiation).

As an example, Exhibit 5 compares the CSFs of Company E, a relatively young hotel company, and Company F, a mature company. Although both firms are concerned about providing a good product to guests, the younger company heavily emphasizes such development functions as site selection, product design, and financing; the mature company—which is still concerned with developing new properties—emphasizes marketing strategies to differentiate its product, as well as the inspection and elimination of existing properties.

EXHIBIT 3
Sample goals and CSFs at Hotel Company B, a company experiencing operating losses

Goals	Selected CSFs
To break even and eventually to remain profitable To maintain our position in the market	Increase sales volume Control costs Develop more competent middle management Train staff; boost morale Broaden permanent business Reinvest in properties

HOTEL-INDUSTRY CSFs

Given all of these possible influences on CSFs, one of the author's objectives in this survey was to identify the commonalities and differences among hotel companies' CSFs. The survey sample of 27 hotel companies was well-rounded in that it included both small and large companies, fledgling and older companies, and publicly and privately held companies, so the findings should be indicative of industry-wide CSFs.

All of the 74 executives interviewed were asked to state their companies' goals and CSFs, through the process outlined earlier, with some interesting results.

Goals

The ten goals most often cited are listed in Exhibit 6, ranked by frequency. It is hardly surprising that

EXHIBIT 4
Sample goals and CSFs from Hotel Company C, a centralized company, and Hotel Company D, a decentralized company

Hotel Company C

Goals	Selected CSFs
Build repeat-visitor loyalty Profitability matched with quality of service	Develop best accommodations Develop best service Reduce complaints Develop customer perception of price-value Good financial image Good investment policy

Hotel Company D

Goals	Selected CSFs
Highest return on investment Deepen management strength Expansion	Customer satisfaction Motivate employees Attract and hire people motivated to careers Develop human resources Develop policy manual Good product mix Accurate financial reporting

EXHIBIT 5

Sample CSFs from Hotel Company E, a young firm, and Hotel Company F, a mature company

Hotel Company E

Selected CSFs

Identify and purchase good sites
Develop pool of management talent
Ensure clean, well-maintained rooms
Ensure courteous service
Obtain sufficient financing
Have current design for hotel product
Develop cost controls

Hotel Company F

Selected CSFs

Provide favorable guest experience
Use market research effectively
Pricing policy that ensures a high guest perception of value
Continue to reinvest in properties
Tough inspection programs
Develop new properties
Weed out poor properties

EXHIBIT 6

Goals most frequently mentioned by respondents

Goal	Number of Responses	Rank
Profitability, return on investment	20	1
Growth	15	2
Best management (including image)	14	3
Greatest market share	12	4
Guest satisfaction	12	4
Shareholder wealth—value	9	5
Employee morale	9	5
Maximize cash flow	5	6
Brand loyalty	5	6
Financial stability	4	7

profitability and *growth* top the list of the hotel executives' corporate goals. These are common business goals one might find on a list of objectives for almost any kind of company, and they are reasonably easy to measure. The third most common goal—developing the *best management* (in fact as well as in image)—is somewhat more elusive, but by it the respondents generally seemed to imply the need to develop the best management people.

Next, tied for fourth place, came *market share* and *guest satisfaction*. Definitions of increased market share varied, but most respondents used it to mean outperforming the competition. Guest satisfaction, which needs no explanation, was one of the two goals that was also frequently mentioned as a critical success factor—the second being *employee morale,* which ranked fifth in number of responses.

Tied for fifth place with employee morale was *wealth*—maximizing shareholder wealth in the case of publicly held companies, creating general value for owners in the case of the privately held ones. Next on the goals list came maximization of cash flow (most often cited by management companies, for which cash flow to owners is an important objective) and brand loyalty (important to companies with special marketing programs). The last of the most frequently cited goals was *financial stability,* mentioned most often by companies not currently in the best financial condition.

Although this list of common goals contained few surprises, it provided the foundation for the next step of the analysis—the identification of CSFs— and confirmed the belief that hotel companies have much the same strategic outlook as most other modern businesses.

CSFs

The results of the CSF analysis were somewhat less predictable—both in terms of which items led the list and in their implications for the development of information systems. Exhibit 7 shows, in rank order, the most frequently cited *industry* CSFs— the "generic" success factors mentioned in all companies.

Leading the list is *employee attitude.* In other words, when asked what a company must do right to attain its goals, the number-one response among hotel executives was the cultivation of a proper employee attitude. It is not so surprising that employee attitude is on the list—the hotel industry has always viewed itself as "a people" business— but it *is* surprising that employee attitude leads the list, and by so large a margin. Remember that employee morale was on the list of the top ten goals, and that the third-ranked goal, having the best management, also has a "people" connotation. Taken together, these responses show an undeniably high level of interest by top management in human resources.

The next most frequently cited CSF was *guest satisfaction* (or guest service), encompassing such

EXHIBIT 7
CSFs most frequently mentioned by respondents

CSF	Number of Responses	Rank
Employee attitude	25	1
Guest satisfaction (service)	21	2
Superior product (physical plant)	19	3
Superior location	11	4
Maximize revenue	8	5
Cost control	8	5
Increase market share	6	6
Increase customer price-value perception	5	7
Achieve market segmentation	4	8

items as cleanliness, level of service, and courteousness. Two factors that might reasonably be linked to guest satisfaction—the attitude of employees (ranked first) and a *superior product,* meaning the condition of the physical plant itself, which ranked third—were specified separately as CSFs. Respondents were clearly concerned with guests' acceptance of the property, its style, appeal, and convenience. *Superior location,* the fourth CSF, seemed important in terms of its impact on occupancy (and sales) rather than as it related to guest acceptance; it was mentioned with much less frequency than the three more universal CSFs at the top of the list.

Tied for fifth were *revenue maximization* and *cost control.* Given the prominence of profitability as a goal, it was somewhat surprising that these two financially oriented factors were this far down the list of CSFs. We might infer from this a reasonable level of sophistication and maturity in the hotel industry. Although executives set profitability as a basic business goal, their view of how to achieve it goes far beyond financial functions. Most of the companies interviewed already had reasonably sophisticated cost-control systems in place and working well, and the author found evidence of a shift from a "bottom-line" orientation to "top-line" concern—the marketing mentality was prevailing over the cost-cutting mentality. The marketing orientation seems evident in the rest of the CSFs listed in Exhibit 7: increasing market share, enhancing customers' price-value perception, and achieving market segmentation.

The obvious importance attached to marketing and personnel by the hotel executives has important implications for executive information systems. As will be discussed further [in the next article in this book] current executive information systems are *weakest* in these two areas, and it is difficult to determine adequate, accurate measures of performance in these areas.

MEASURES

After listing their goals and CSFs, the respondents were asked what measures they found useful in monitoring their CSFs. Since measures are CSF-specific, and since numerous CSFs were mentioned by respondents during the course of the research, only a few illustrative measures can be listed here. The measures respondents currently use, listed in order of frequency, appear in Exhibit 8.

It is instructive that most of the top six measures deal with the two leading CSFs, employee attitude and guest satisfaction. Although occupancy percentage and average rate are not direct measures of these factors, there is at least an indirect link between guest satisfaction and these two widely tracked hotel statistics. Also interesting is the importance placed on guest comment cards—a fact noted throughout the interview process.

CONCLUSIONS AND IMPLICATIONS

Several recommendations can be drawn from the findings presented above. First, certain critical success factors were identified as fairly universal within the hotel industry, and a company planning to do CSF analysis might well use these as a starting point. Second, CSFs must be derived from estab-

EXHIBIT 8
Measures most commonly used by respondents to monitor CSFs

Measure	Number of Responses	Rank
• Occupancy percentage	30	1
• Guest comment cards	29	2
• Turnover (employee)	21	3
• Inspections	18	4
• Average rate	15	5
• Rate of promotion (internal hire)	15	5
• Rate of repeat business	14	6
• Rate of return (on investment)	12	7
• Sales ($)	10	8
• Profit (or cash flow)	9	9
• Scientific sampling (of guests)	9	9
• Complaint letters	8	10
• Gross operating profit	7	11
• Outside "shoppers"	6	12
• Employee opinion surveys	6	12

Other often-cited measures: Market share, market-research reports, nonunion operations, grievances, reservations backlog.

(Respondents were also asked to rate the usefulness of each measure; the results will be presented in the next article.)

lished goals and objectives set forth in a strategic plan. These goals form the basis for identifying and "prioritizing" a company's own set of CSFs, a process that should also be informed by such matters as the life cycle and other characteristics.

Although the CSF examples cited in this article should be helpful to readers, each company must develop its own specific CSFs on a trial-and-error basis. In fact, the process itself can be quite valuable in clarifying corporate goals, identifying redundancies, refining existing information systems, and determining which measures are truly important to monitor.

The next segment of this series will explore the latter issue: the measures currently used by executives to monitor their companies' performance, and the adequacy (or inadequacy) of those measures.

The Current State of Hotel Information Systems

A. Neal Geller

This article focuses on the performance indicators or measures hotel executives deemed most important. Although the executives acknowledged they were suffering from information overload, most could provide wish lists of additional indicators they would like to monitor.

WHAT'S THE USE?

A questionnaire was administered to each of the participating companies to ascertain the relative importance of 16 commonly used hotel indicators. The respondents were asked to rate the usefulness of each indicator on a scale of 1 (not useful) through 5 (critical). The results are shown in Exhibit 1.

The top seven indicators had average scores of over 4; 12 of the 16 average scores were over 3; none of the indicators had an average below 2. That the scores were skewed to the top was not especially surprising, because the measures listed on the questionnaire were prescreened and by definition commonly used; the scores suggest they all possess a fair degree of usefulness. Nonetheless, one can discern clear differences. The five top indicators—occupancy percentage, average room rate, gross operating profit, rooms-department sales, and rooms-department profit—had average scores far above the others.

The scores in Exhibit 1 provide a relative scale of the indicators' usefulness. Just because an indicator scored high, though, does not necessarily mean that it was the most important indicator to the respondent. Therefore, participants were also asked to rank what they saw as the five most important indicators, with these results (listed in descending order):

- Occupancy percentage
- Average room rate
- Gross operating profit
- Cash flow from operations
- Rooms-department profit

Except for the fourth indicator, this list is identical to the top five in Exhibit 1. It seems clear that these particular indicators were both very popular and very useful.

But let us take a closer look at occupancy and average rate, which emerged as important in other areas of the research and were discussed repeatedly in the informal portions of the interviews. It is possible that these two venerable hotel standbys are prominent on the list strictly out of habit. Consider the importance executives assigned to the areas of employee attitude and guest satisfaction; one cannot discern more than a weak, indirect link between these two success factors and such measures as occupancy and average rate. Hotel companies wishing to make the best use of their executive information systems need to identify and track the measures that are *direct* indicators of the areas most

This article was originally published in the May 1985 issue of *The Cornell Hotel and Restaurant Administration Quarterly,* and is reprinted here with the permission of the Cornell University School of Hotel Administration. © 1985.

EXHIBIT 1
Executives' ratings of common indicators' usefulness

Indicator	Average Response	Number of Responses
Occupancy percentage	4.96	26
Average room rate	4.92	26
Gross operating profit	4.60	25
Room sales	4.40	25
Rooms-department profit	4.31	26
Cash flow	4.15	26
Food and beverage department profit	4.08	26
Food and beverage sales	4.04	26
Net income	3.92	24
Management fees	3.72	25
Undistributed operating expenses	3.60	25
Fixed charges	3.50	26
Double-occupancy percentage	3.23	26
Beverage/food and beverage sales	2.73	26
Room sales/total sales	2.69	26
Food and beverage sales/total sales	2.54	26

(1 = not useful; 5 = critical.)

critical to top management. There is nothing wrong with continuing to report certain measures out of habit, or for "peace of mind," as long as these measures do not displace the measures directly linked to successful performance.

TOO LITTLE, TOO LATE

When the survey participants were asked whether their current executive information systems (EIS) supported their responsibilities adequately, opinions were mixed. Among 66 respondents, 26 said their systems *did* support their responsibilities, and 33 felt their EIS did *not;* seven had no answer.

This question elicited some interesting comments. Those feeling that their systems were adequate mentioned the thoroughness and high level of detail the systems produced—particularly in the hotel operations and financial areas. The negative comments focused on the systems' lack of marketing and competitive data. While most executives felt that their systems provided adequate budgeting and historical information, many faulted the systems for their lack of timeliness and for their failure to provide predictive data. A representative comment: "I get excellent analytical information, but when I get it, it's already history. It's too late to do anything about it. I need systems that will point out the problem, that will lay out courses of action, and that will tell me what lies ahead."

When the participants were asked to enumerate the specific pros and cons of their EIS, the results were similar. The advantages of the systems included the completeness of the operational and financial data they provided, and the accuracy and uniformity of the systems. The disadvantages cited were numerous: weak in the marketing area, antiquated in the personnel area, not timely enough, too much data, not selective enough, too much duplication, the need for more of a planning orientation. (The latter comment may reflect the lack of a clear planning process at some of the participating companies. It is difficult for an information system to support a planning process that does not exist!)

Wish List

Since the respondents had been asked to rate a given list of 16 indicators, they were also asked to provide an information "wish list"—what information would they want if they had a free hand and no constraints? The intent was to determine what other indicators the executives deemed important. The most common responses appear in alphabetical order in Exhibit 2.

This summary wish list is one of the bright spots of the research findings. That the list includes truly innovative information needs is indicative of the increasing sophistication of the hotel business. Let us briefly consider the two biggest emerging areas of concern: marketing and human resources.

EXHIBIT 2
Executives' "wish lists" (alphabetical)

Better ways to measure customer satisfaction
Cash-management information
Computerized complaint system
Daily sales information
Day-of-the-week sales and occupancy information, by day and type of hotel
Demand forecasts—general
Demand forecasts—local
Exception reporting
Exception reporting tied to forecasts
Filtered (summarized) information
Financial modeling
Guest-history information
Hotel properties "on-line"
Marketing information
Personnel system; tracking human resources
Productivity data
Qualitative information
Repeat-business information
Site analysis
Speedier data
Terminals for all executives; on-line data
Turndown, sales-backlog information
Weekly "flash" reports on marketing

MARKETING

The hotel companies are interested in moving forward quickly in the important area of marketing. Many of them are mature companies, and must implement more sophisticated marketing programs—based on better marketing information—to survive.

There are two kinds of data upon which marketing efforts will depend: information about current and past guests, and information about target groups of future guests. Obtaining the latter will require surveys of target populations. Because such surveys are usually conducted by professional marketing research firms, the main implication for designing a hotel company's information system is to include the capability to capture and use these data. The source of guest-history data, on the other hand, is at the hotel, in its data-processing and guest-accounting and reservations systems. Problems surface when these systems have not been designed to acquire marketing information.

It is important to note how easily marketing data can be captured at hotels, in comparison to other businesses. Hotels have a captive audience because guests must register. In contrast, packaged-goods manufacturers have no direct way of tracking their product from the store to the customer. The hotel guest is *in* the hotel, has made a reservation (or walked in), has registered, has provided credit evidence, is beginning to accrue charges, and will eventually settle the bill and check out. The idea is to use all of these processes to obtain the marketing data needed, and to do so in a way that creates the smallest amount of inconvenience to the guest. The high technology of today provides the mechanical tools necessary to do the job. It is simply a matter of forethought, redesign, and reeducation—redesign for the processing systems, forms, and reports, and reeducating for the employees.

The author was surprised to learn during the field interviews that, in the early part of this century, many of the larger hotels had extensive guest-history systems; the information was posted by hand. This method came into disfavor over the years because of inaccuracies and the high cost of postwar labor. Designing guest-history systems, then, is hardly revolutionary; we are simply talking about returning the hotel industry to the high level of hospitality and human contact it once provided.

HUMAN RESOURCES

Just as automated systems can capture marketing data, so too can "high tech" restore "high touch" in the personnel area. Employee attitude and morale can be measured and tracked; the availability of better information can lead to more frequent and more meaningful contact between supervisors and subordinates; key dates, events, and accomplishments can be flagged and dealt with in a timely fashion; positions can be filled more quickly and effectively from within if the hotel's databases are able to match the people with the jobs. All of these innovations should result in better service and improved morale, primary concerns of the hotel executives surveyed.

THE LITTLE YELLOW SHEET

The author suspected that most successful executives, regardless of the sophistication of their EIS, would track, by hand, certain key items for their peace of mind—and a majority of the respondents stated that they did indeed track a few favorite items in this manner. Often they must ferret out the data themselves, or extract them from the figures in the reports they receive. Exhibit 3 is an alphabetical list of the items most common on the executives' "little yellow sheets."

INFORMATION OVERLOAD

The fact that executives must extract information from the reports they receive leads to the question of information overload—receiving so much information that one stops looking at any of it. The executives were asked whether they received too much information and to estimate what percentage of the information they received was not useful.

EXHIBIT 3
Items executives track (the "little yellow sheet"—alphabetical)

Accidents and lawsuits
Acquisitions and new properties
Average number of employees
*Average room rate**
*Cash balances, daily cash positions
Cash distribution
*Cash flow
Construction costs
Contract negotiations
Cost per available room
Customer attitude
Customer counts
Customer-satisfaction index, major complaints
Food-department profit
Good and bad inspections
Growth rates
Losses of major pieces of business
*Occupancy**
Payable/receivables
Payroll
Performance versus budget
*Profit (bottom line)
*Profit margins (including GOP)
Problem or critical properties
Productivity
Return on equipment/return on inventory
Rooms available
Rooms-department profit
Rooms occupied
Sales/revenues
Turnover
Undistributed operating expenses

*Frequently cited.
**These two measures were the most frequently cited, appearing dozens of times.

Most acknowledged that they were in fact overloaded. A common answer was "I used to get too much, but I don't now because I stopped it." Among those able to estimate what percentage of the information they received was not useful, the average answer was 31.5 percent. In other words, nearly one-third of the information being received by these hotel executives was perceived to be of little or no value.

Endnote

[1]While the goals of a company and those of the company's top executives are often the same, they may also differ. The company and the chief executive, for example, may cite financial stability as a major goal, while the chief financial officer may cite more "functional" goals—e.g., ensuring adequate cash balances—that are related to (or derived from) the company's goals. Typically, as one looks down the company ladder, goals and success factors become increasingly more narrow. This research, however, focused on the needs of top managers—in other words, the broadest critical issues.

Reference

Rockart, John F. 1979. Chief executives define their own data needs. *Harvard Business Review* (March–April):81–93.

Suggested Readings

Articles

Cummings, Leslie E., and William J. Robinson. "Computer Confusion: Relief Is in Sight," *Cornell Hotel and Restaurant Administration Quarterly* (August 1986): 75–85.

Geller, A. Neal. *Executive Information Needs in Hotel Companies.* New York: Peat, Marwick, Mitchell, 1984. (Complete study on which Professor Geller's series in this section was based.)

(Kasavana, M.L. "Computer-Assisted Hospitality Information Systems." *International Journal of Hospitality Management* 1 (1982):91–94.

Moll, Steve V. "Front-of-the House Computer Systems: A User's Guide." *F.I.U. Hospitality Review* 2 (Fall 1984):37–42.

Smeltzer, Virgil L. "The Integrated Approach to Hospitality-Management Systems." *Cornell Hotel and Restaurant Administration Quarterly* (November 1987): 48–56.

SECTION 13

Future Issues

COMMENTARY, OVERVIEW, AND PREDICTIONS

Without access to a working crystal ball, it is sometimes dangerous or foolish to predict the future. We can, however, in this instance suggest that based on research currently and recently published; various empirical databases; personal observation; and a judicious amount of "Kentucky windage" speculation, the following topics will be among those that will be of increasing importance and concern to hotel and hospitality managers of the near future.

DEMOGRAPHICS OF AGING

Various census and demographic data strongly suggest that after the turn of the century a significant portion of the population of the United States will be over 55 years of age. Unlike this age cohort of the past, these people will be better educated, enjoy higher incomes, have fewer health problems, will be more active, and will probably travel more. As such, they represent a potent and potentially vital market for the hotelier of the future. Indeed, several hotel firms have recognized this reality and have created divisions that have as their central mission major components that cater to and understand this particular market. The some insights into the di

WOMEN

When I was an undergraduate, there two women in the hotel and restaurant tion program I attended. Now, as I look classes, in most instances, fully 50 percent of the class population are women.

As greater numbers of women enter the work force in managerial ranks, hotels, their organizations, and their operations are becoming affected in a number of different ways. First, there is the fairly well documented phenomenon of the female business traveler. Most hotels that host significant numbers of women among their guests have instituted physical and operational changes to attend to the needs of the female traveler. Most women, however, will tell you that what they appreciate more in a hotel is not so much special hangers, security locks, peepholes in the door, and other such amenities but the correct attitude on the part of the hotel and its staff. They want the hotel to demonstrate by actions and words that the hotel does not care what sex a traveler is but will do its best to deliver its services at the same high levels of quality to all travelers.

hat through the
ssional system,
vernmental en-
onstantly being
) manage their
) be aware of
most effective
is legislative
of your in-
ions. These
membership
and regu-
and active
ade asso-
academic
sion, and
gathering
all rec-
nal man-
y envi-

HER

par-
ions
ment.

designed to provide
their members in a number of different
ways, the one element that almost all share is an
annual national meeting. They also have many regional, local, and state meetings. The American
Society of Association Executives (ASAE) reports
membership of over 6,000 executives, who represent associations with a total membership of over
55 million. When these people meet in convention,
they all stay in hotel rooms; hence the importance
of associations, and their annual conventions and
meetings, to the hotel industry.

Increasingly, large conventions are being attracted to cities that have major, specifically designed convention facilities and a large number of
nearby first-class hotel rooms. It has been said that

Suggested Readings provide
ensions of this issue.

e were exactly
administra-
out at my
r more

port

he or she is playing

ules.

These laws, rules, and regulations manifest
themselves in a number of different ways. Their
impact, in effect, is greater or lesser on different
departments, but for the most part it can be generally said that in one form or another each departmental manager has some measure of responsibility to ensure that the hotel is in compliance with
these rules. Among them are equal employment
opportunity rules, affirmative action, various health
and safety regulations, employment laws, operational laws relative to guest safety, foodservice

form or another. It is also instructive to note that most of the major hotel companies are actively establishing resort divisions that feature full-service hotels in highly desirable vacation and recreational areas. These developments include significant investment in meeting facilities. This trend recognizes the desire of many groups to be able to combine work and meeting business with leisure and recreational activities that are highly desirable and attractive to members and their families. The resort environment allows them to do this in an exclusive fashion because many groups can take over an entire resort for their convention and make full use of the facilities of the resort hotel.

The conventions, meetings, and group-business market is a substantial one and will continue to play a significant role in the management and operation of hotel facilities. It is also a market that is evolving in a number of different ways. Many large groups are fragmenting their annual meetings to pay attention to regional concerns. Some groups and associations have policies and politics that dictate their choices of meeting sites. Other groups are only discovering the value of face-to-face meetings. Communications technology, travel modes and expense, changing leisure and recreational tastes, and the imagination of hotel marketers will all combine to influence the future of group business in the hotel industry.

Among the Suggested Readings in this section are descriptive and analytical articles that provide some useful insights into this exciting and interesting adjunct of the hospitality industry.

HEALTH ISSUES

If you had said the word "AIDS" to the average hotel manager ten years ago, he or she would probably have assumed that you were speaking about a diet candy, a United Nations organization, or some paraprofessionals who assist people in the health services. This is not to make light of the impact of Acquired Immune Deficiency Syndrome, but to point out that health issues can indeed become major considerations for hotel and hospitality managers. While we know that AIDS is not a con-

tagious problem in terms of casual contact, the great amount of ignorance about this disease and other similar diseases is such that it becomes a difficult process to manage an industry in which people interact and come in close contact. The point here is not to belabor the issue of AIDS, but to suggest that in the future other similarly threatening health issues are almost certain to affect your ability to manage your operations. It is important for managers to have a means to access high-quality, accurate information about the implications of these diseases and to work that information into the fabric of their managerial actions.

Since the dawn of recorded history, humans have found numerous ways through chemical substances to alter their feelings, usually in the pursuit of pleasure of some kind. The fact that we now refer to these as alcohol and drug problems does not diminish the fact that, in one form or another, these problems have always been with us. The way the issues are playing out now, it is a health-related phenomenon that on one hand is seen as a societal problem. On the other hand, it is seen as having an impact on the ability of the manager in the enterprise to do business.

For hotels and restaurants, the issues of dealing with employees and guests who use and abuse alcohol and drugs are complicated by the fact that alcohol, in its various consumable forms, is legal to sell and use in moderation. Alcohol products in one form or another make up a significant base of a hospitality operation's service mix. As such, there is an incumbent obligation upon hospitality managers to demonstrate responsibility in selling these products and give informed thought and attention to the implications of their sale.

It is equally important that managers realize that alcohol and drug abuse is generally considered by the health professions as a disease. The extent to which these diseases affect your employees and colleagues may have a significant effect on how your business is operated. Most forward-looking companies are now significantly and seriously involved in programs designed to salvage their personnel affected by these diseases. The Suggested Readings presented in this section take a collectively positive and progressive view of the impact of these issues on your ability to manage.

Fortunately, the handicapped and disabled citizens of the world are no longer considered useless burdens on society, as may have been the case in the past. As such, they are finding new ways to lead active and productive lives and to participate in leisure, recreational, and economic activities— generally by means only slightly different, if at all, from those used by their able-bodied fellow citizens. This is an important concept to understand. As both potential guests and employees, the disabled for the most part are only limited by specific aspects of their disability. If given an opportunity, the individuals can easily manage these disabilities, making them as eligible as anyone else to be a guest or an employee. Some of the Suggested Readings focus on the issue of handicapped guests and the hotel's need to be sensitive and receptive to the disabled.

RESEARCH

There is an anecdote among scientists that says that most great scientific discoveries are not accompanied by some scientist looking through a microscope and screaming, "Eureka!" In most circumstances, what is involved is a scientist or investigator looking over a very familiar field and spotting something out of the ordinary, then instead of screaming, "Eureka!" saying something on the order of "That's odd."

The suggestion here is that those people who are able to make the most beneficial discoveries and those who tend to be most sensitive to the way things are evolving are those managers who know intimately the details of their environment. When that environment is a hotel's market niche or the operations of a food and beverage facility, the better you do your research and the better you know your product, the more sensitive you will be to change, anomaly, or the need for change.

Research is not simply blowing the dust off of books in some dark corner of the library. Research is an active, inquisitive process that suggests the

systematic accumulation and storage of data and facts, their retrieval and their interpretation. The best managers in the future will be those who are best able to manage the "information explosion" in such a way that they can glean from these data the facts that allow them to make high-quality decisions and to recognize when something is "odd."

Among the Suggested Readings are those that can help the manager codify his or her bases of information. All of the future hotel managers will not need to be statisticians, but they certainly will need to be able to interpret data and facts.

CONCLUSION

The one thing we can say for sure about the future is that we don't know exactly what it is going to hold for us either as individuals or as members of the hospitality industry. Students can, however, through reading, learning, talking, and interviewing about their profession, better prepare themselves to be managers in the future. We hope that our efforts in producing this book and making these suggestions will have been of some value in this process.

Suggested Readings

Demographics of Aging

Browne, Colette V. "The Older Traveler: Challenge and Opportunities." *Cornell Hotel and Restaurant Administration Quarterly* (August 1984): 12–14.

DeVito, Richard. "The Senior Citizen Travel Market: Still in Its Growth Stage." In *The Practice of Hospitality Management II,* edited by Robert C. Lewis, Thomas J. Beggs, Margaret Shaw, and Steven A. Croffoot, 467–71. Westport, CT: AVI, 1986.

LaForge, Mary C. "Elderly Recreational Travelers: A Profile." *Cornell Hotel and Restaurant Administration Quarterly* (August 1984): 14–15.

Women

Christensen, Julia. "Women in Management: Advice to Recent Graduates." *Cornell Hotel and Restaurant Administration Quarterly* (August 1987): 48–49.

Hackett, Carole. "The Woman Food and Beverage Manager." *Cornell Hotel and Restaurant Administration Quarterly* (November 1981): 79–85.

Kent, William E., and Patti J. Shock. "Women in Hospitality Management: Does Quantity = Equality?" *HSMA Marketing Review* (Winter 1982–1983): 16–21.

Conventions and Meetings

Astroff, Milton T., and James R. Abbey. *Conventions Sales and Service,* Dubuque, IA: Wm. C. Brown, 1978.

Berman, Frank W., David C. Dorf, and Leonard R. Oakes. *Convention Management and Service,* East Lansing, MI: Educational Institute of the American Hotel and Motel Association, 1978.

Hosansky, M. "The $27.8 Billion Meetings Industry." *Meetings and Conventions* (December 1983).

The Handicapped

Brodsky-Porges, Edward. "Making Hospitality Operations Hospitable: The First Step in Accessibility for the Handicapped." *Cornell Hotel and Restaurant Administration Quarterly* 20 (August 1979): 8–9.

———."Welcoming the Handicapped Traveler." *Cornell Hotel and Restaurant Administration Quarterly* 19 (November 1978): 6–7.

Health Issues

Beeman, Don R. "Is the Social Drinker Killing Your Company?" *Business Horizons* (January–February 1985): 54–58.

Brown, Abby. "Employment Tests: Issues Without Clear Answers." *Personnel Administrator* (September 1985): 43–56.

Feinberg, Mortimer R. "The Cocaine Problem." *Restaurant Business* (1 November 1984): 96.

Flax, Steven. "The Executive Addict." *Fortune* (24 June 1985): 24–31.

Johnson, Theresa. "Law Prohibiting Employment Discrimination Against the Alcoholic and the Drug Addict." *Labor Law Journal* (September 1985): 702–6.

Liberson, Mark J. "AIDS: A Managerial Perspective." *Cornell Hotel and Restaurant Administration Quarterly* 28 (November 1987): 57–61.

Palmer, Robert Alan. "Employee Drug Use: Just Say No." *Cornell Hotel and Restaurant Administration Quarterly* 28 (May 1987): 20–22.

Susser, Peter A. "AIDS: Legal Considerations." *Cornell Hotel and Restaurant Administration Quarterly,* 28 (August 1987): 81–85.

Research

Lewis, Robert C. "The Measurement of Gaps in the Quality of Hotel Services." *International Journal of Hospitality Management* 6 (2), 1987: 83–88.

Sheldon, Pauline J., Juanita C. Liu, and Chuck Y. Gee. "The Status of Research in the Lodging Industry." *International Journal of Hospitality Management* 6 (2), 1987: 89–96.

Index

This book may be kept